Sweet Land of Liberty

The Spirit of Growing America

Heritage Studies 3

HOME TEACHER'S EDITION

Second Edition

BJU PRESS

Greenville, South Carolina

Advisory Committee
from the administration, faculty, and staff of Bob Jones University
Carl Abrams, Ph.D., *Professor, Department of History*
James W. Deuink, Ed. D., *Dean of the School Education*
Linda K. Hayner, Ph.D., *Chairman, Department of History*
Philip D. Smith, Ed.D., *Provost*
James R. Davis, M.A., *Director of Product Development, University Press*
Melva M. Heintz, M.A., *Principal Emerita, Elementary School*

Note:
The fact that materials produced by other publishers may be referred to in this volume does not constitute an endorsement of the content or theological position of materials produced by such publishers. Any refererences and ancillary materials are listed as an aid to the student or the teacher and in an attempt to maintain the accepted academic standards of the publishing industry.

Home Teacher's Edition for
HERITAGE STUDIES 3 Second Edition

Writers
Dorothy Buckley
Debra White

Contributing Writers
Eileen M. Berry
Peggy J. Davenport
Stephanie J. Ralston
Dawn L. Watkins
Gail H. Yost

Computer Formatting
Peggy Hargis

Project Editor
Carolyn Cooper

Graphics Coordinator
Mary Ann Lumm

Graphics
Johanna Berg
Paula Cheadle
Jim Hargis

Brian Johnson
Sam Laterza
Dick Mitchell
John Nolan
Kathy Pflug
John Roberts
Lynda Slattery

Photo Acquisition
Fonda Johnson
Terry Latini

ISBN 978-1-57924-243-5

15 14 13 12 11 10 9 8 7

CONTENTS

Heritage Studies 3 for Christian Schools
written especially for a home setting

1 Encourages Christian growth.

What a child learns in Heritage Studies can affect his spiritual growth and ministry. The child should learn discipline in his approach to and his performance of responsibilities. He should be prepared to evaluate and reject false philosophies. He should have a better testimony among unbelievers.

2 Develops good citizenship through the use of history, geography, economics, culture, and government skills.

The Heritage Studies program emphasizes Christian philosophy, character, and attitudes. It gives the child opportunities to use many skills such as making decisions, inferring relationships, and showing respect for his heritage. It also teaches him practical skills such as reading maps and charts, sequencing events, and working with time lines. Thus, the program promotes a balanced approach to social studies instruction.

3 Promotes historic and geographic literacy.

The goal of historic literacy is to emphasize God's plan for the individual, the family, and the nation. Although history is the study of man's actions, it is essentially the record of God's dealing with men. The Christian teacher must be able to distinguish God's leading in historical events and to impress upon the child the significance of the events. Learning history well helps the child more fully appreciate and comprehend his own times. This broad perspective, then, helps him make better decisions and become a responsible Christian citizen.

4 Presents events by incorporating a more traditional emphasis on skills.

The product of Heritage Studies is organized according to a scope and sequence. The scope is *what* knowledge will be covered in the program. There is disagreement among educators about the scope of knowledge that should be presented on the elementary level. Some still hold to the post-1920s experiment in "socializing" the study of history, organizing the material around the child and his environment. Recent research recommends, however, that true historic and geographic understanding rests on the more traditional emphasis on skills, such as working with maps and sequencing events.

5 Organizes knowledge in a spiral pattern and chronological order.

There are many ways to present Heritage Studies knowledge. For example, it can be organized around a unifying framework of themes. Another approach is a spiral pattern in which the same general topics are taken up periodically—every year, or two or three times in a program. Another option, supported by research and experience, is to study history chronologically, exploring eras in order, thereby helping the child see connections between events. This program combines the spiral pattern and the chronological approach.

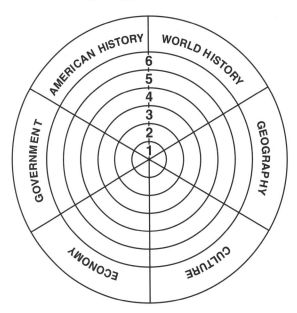

6 Promotes an understanding of and an ability to discern connections among events.

By viewing history in a chronological manner incorporating a time line, the child gains an understanding of and an ability to discern connections among events. He learns how events and people from other countries influenced his own American heritage and how they relate to each other in history.

7 Strengthens a knowledge of God.

Creation tells us about God (Ps. 19:1; Rom. 1:20). By studying the history of the world and the features of the earth, we can see illustrations of God's wisdom, omnipotence, sovereignty, and benevolence.

TEACHING HERITAGE STUDIES 3

How do I schedule the lessons?

You, the teacher, have a choice in scheduling the teaching of Heritage Studies. Some suggested methods follow.

- You may teach an entire lesson each day, completing the Heritage Studies program in a semester. Science would then be taught the other semester.
- You may teach an entire lesson of Heritage Studies two days a week for the whole year. Science would also be taught two days a week for the whole year.

Day 1

- You may use the scheduling plan provided by the Day symbols in each lesson. By following the numbered days throughout the lesson, you have logical starting and stopping points for discussions and activities. This plan will provide approximately 120 to 130 teaching days.

You will want to arrange the lessons to accommodate your schedule. Many lessons offer several procedures and activities. You may choose to use all of each lesson or only parts of a lesson. You may choose to adapt the material to your own methods. It is recommended that Heritage Studies be taught in twenty- to thirty-minute sessions. The Supplemental lessons are optional.

Where will the needed materials be listed?

You can find lists of the materials you need in order to teach the Heritage Studies program in the following sections of the manual:

Instructional Materials, a section in the introduction to this manual, lists all the essential curriculum items that need to be purchased to teach Heritage Studies 3.

Chapter Overview, at the beginning of each chapter, contains a list of materials that need to be prepared or purchased ahead of time.

Materials, in the Preview of each lesson, lists the materials needed to present that particular lesson.

Materials List, found in the Supplement of the manual, lists all materials needed to teach the entire program.

What pages do I need to copy?

All the pages that you will need to copy for teaching the lessons can be found in the Appendix. The pages in the Supplement may also be copied, though it is not essential. These pages may be viewed by your child directly from the teacher's manual. **Please note:** Although you are permitted to copy pages for your own use, copyright law prohibits the making of copies for any other purpose. Making copies and distributing them in whole or in part to other institutions or individuals is unlawful.

What is in the Student Text?

The student book presents for the child a summary of the more detailed study that the lessons will offer. It reinforces with grade-level text the concepts developed in the teaching time. Although it contains much information, it is only part of the complete package of learning provided by the combination of teacher's edition, Time-Line, Student Text, and Notebook.

The student book has twelve chapters, each emphasizing one of six categories: American history, world history, geography, government, culture, and economics. To determine the focus of the chapter, look at the color that highlights the chapter number. It corresponds to the color of one of the main category symbols.

In addition, some chapters have special sections. One such section is *Famous People,* which highlights influential people of nineteeth-century America. Another section is *Things People Do,* focusing on common trades, skills, or hobbies of the past and present. *How It Was* takes a detailed look at single moments in American history. *Echoes in History* sections study the connection of the present with past events. The *Learning How* sections provide hands-on activities that enliven the lesson and allow your child to experience some flavor of the times as well as learn map skills and develop thinking skills.

What is historic and geographic knowledge?

History and geography can be defined as a body of knowledge. History can also be defined as a way of thinking. The study of these topics, therefore, is a product (body of knowledge) and a process (way of investigating and thinking). The Bob Jones University Press Heritage Studies series continually interweaves the product *and* process of history and geography.

The products of history and geography are stated in several forms. For example, knowledge can be expressed as a fact. A *fact* is an event that has been observed and recorded by more than one person, the records showing no disagreement among the observers. (This does not mean that a fact cannot be in error.) Knowledge can also be expressed as a *concept,* a set of ideas derived from objects or events. Finally, knowledge can be expressed as a *principle,* a statement predicting interrelationships among concepts. The Bob Jones University Press Heritage Studies program uses the words *main idea* to include all three forms of knowledge. Note the following examples of each form of knowledge:

□ *Fact:* The Separatists founded Plymouth Plantation.

□ *Concept:* Religious freedom (The words *religious freedom* encompass the commitment to and struggles for worshiping as one believes proper.) To make a set of examples that accompany the label, think of people who have sacrificed for their beliefs.
William Tyndale—martyred for translating the Bible into English
John Bunyan—imprisoned for preaching
The Huguenots—persecuted in France for their beliefs, some fleeing to America

□ *Principle:* The Constitution of the United States guarantees religious freedom. (Notice the interrelationship between the concepts *Constitution* and *religious freedom.*)

How should I teach history and geography skills?

The child should be deriving knowledge through practical experiences that involve action—"hands-on" or "learning-by-doing" activities. Christians can use the inductive method in good conscience, provided they remember that historical recording is fallible and changeable and often disregards many biblical truths. It would be helpful to all Christian teachers to study the principles discussed in *The Christian Teaching of History,* available from Bob Jones University Press.

It is not necessary to follow a certain set of steps, but there are *process skills* employed in this method of teaching. A list of the process skills in the program follows.

□ Sequencing events
□ Summarizing data
□ Making predictions
□ Inferring relationships
□ Making decisions
□ Formulating opinions
□ Working with time lines
□ Identifying sources of information
□ Working with maps and globes
□ Using cardinal directions
□ Working with tables, graphs, charts, and diagrams
□ Identifying key documents

□ Valuing the rights of citizenship
□ Showing respect for heritage

What attitudes are being developed as I teach?

The dictionary defines *attitude* as "a state of mind or feeling with regard to some matter." Some of the attitudes that you will see develop as your child learns through the Bob Jones University Press Heritage Studies program fall into the following broad categories.

□ *Attitudes Toward Schoolwork*
• Cooperatively share responsibilities and tasks.
• Demonstrate proper care and handling of maps, globes, and other equipment.
• Stay with the task in search of comprehension and evaluation of ideas.

□ *Attitudes Toward Interests and Careers*
• Pursue history- or geography-related leisure-time activities.
• Voluntarily seek additional information about history and related studies.
• Seek information about careers in research, history, and geography.

□ *Attitudes Toward Personal Application of Heritage Studies Principles*
• Use an objective approach in problem solving.
• Display a willingness to consider other points of view.
• Demonstrate divergent thinking in problem solving.
• Demonstrate curiosity about history, geography, and related subjects.
• Show an appreciation for his heritage.
• Uphold foundational principles of his government.
• Counteract influences detrimental to the perpetuation of his heritage.
• Reflect a knowledge of history in everyday decision making.

□ *Attitudes Toward Oneself*
• Display confidence in his ability to use geographic skills successfully.
• Demonstrate a scriptural view of himself through the study of history.

□ *Attitudes Toward History and Society*
• Select cause-and-effect relationships to explain contemporary problems.
• Identify historical precedent as a way of solving some current problems.
• Describe historians as persons sensitive to normal human concerns.
• Demonstrate an awareness of the need for conservation, preservation, and the wise use of natural resources.
• Demonstrate patriotism.
• Explain how the study of history and geography can have positive (or, if unbalanced, negative) effects on one's personal life.

INSTRUCTIONAL MATERIALS

Student Materials

Text

HERITAGE STUDIES 3 for Christian Schools is a four-color text containing a variety of developmental subtopics built around six major topics: American history, world history, geography, culture, economics, and government.

Notebook

The *HERITAGE STUDIES 3 Student Notebook* is a consumable companion tool for the text. It is used primarily for evaluating your child's understanding of the material. The Notebook will also save the teacher time. The pages are designed to be used in a notebook binder.

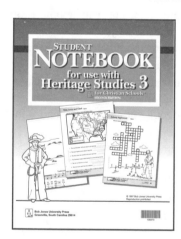

Miscellaneous school supplies

The child will need standard school supplies: crayons or felt-tip pens, pencils, scissors, glue, and so on.

Library trade books

No history program can provide enough information for enthusiastic young readers. A collection of trade books (library books) must be available to your child. Be careful of books that slant the history of certain events. For example, library books about Puritans are generally written by people who do not believe in the God of the Puritans. In these instances, try to find books that present a truthful and objective account of these people.

Teacher Materials

Teacher's edition

The home teacher's edition for *HERITAGE STUDIES 3 for Christian Schools* (this volume) is the foundation of the program from which all the activities originate. This volume contains the parts labeled below. Maps and More is a section of colored maps and visuals.

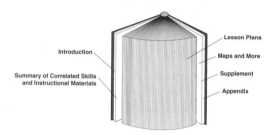

Optional Materials

TimeLine Snapshots

The *TimeLine Snapshots* is a visual working chart of the seventeenth through the twentieth centuries. It contains figures representing important events or people studied in grades 2-5, including pictures of all the presidents. It enhances the child's chronology skills. See Lesson 5 for additional details.

Heritage Studies Listening Cassette

The cassette tape contains songs and readings that will enhance the child's enjoyment of, understanding of, and participation in the study of history. Cassette A contains selections used in grades 1-3.

Heritage Studies supplies

Refer to the materials list in the Supplement of this book.

Tests

The test packet includes a test for each chapter.

LESSON PLAN FORMAT

━━ Preview ━━

Main Ideas are short statements of historic or geographic knowledge.

Objectives are statements describing the outcome of instruction in terms of the child's behavior.

Materials is a list of items to be obtained or prepared.

Notes is a section of helpful hints.

━━ Lesson ━━

Introducing the Lesson suggests a way to start the lesson.

LESSON 17
Successful Journey
Text, pages 59-62
Notebook, pages 18-19

━━ Preview ━━

Main Ideas
- Nations gain land in different ways.
- Native Americans lived in all areas of what is now the United States.

Objectives
- Construct a time line
- Make a journal of an "expedition"

Materials
- 2 sheets of white or tan construction paper

> Prepare the construction paper by making the sheets into a small journal. Fold each sheet into fourths. Place one folded sheet inside the other. Cut across the top folded edges to remove the folds. Staple together along the side folds.

Notes

The "expedition" in this lesson may be as simple or as extensive as you wish. Suitable material for the journal can be obtained in a journey through areas of your neighborhood or a local park with which your child is not familiar. If you have an older child, he could become a guide, similar to Sacajawea on the Lewis and Clark expedition. You may arrange for other family members to represent the Shoshone and provide gifts with which to barter.

Day 1

━━ Lesson ━━

Introducing the Lesson

Notebook Activity, page 18

> Where do you think the drawings on Notebook page 18 were originally made? They are from the journal of William Clark.
> Write Clark's name in the first blank on page 18 to complete the sentence.

66

Journal Drawings Name _____

William Clark made drawings like these in his journal.

Label the pictures.

1. Northwest Indian arrow
2. Rocky Mountain pheasant
3. Plains Indian battle gear
4. Pacific Coast canoe
5. trout
6. evergreen shrub

Place the number for each of the first four pictures on the map in the area where that item was found.

Heritage Studies 3 Student Notebook   Lesson 17 Successful Journey   18

> **What do you think each of the drawings represents?**

As I tell you how Clark labeled the drawings, I would like for you to write the labels under the pictures. *Read the labels as shown in the answer key above.*

Notice that the plains, the mountains, and the coast are represented by these drawings.

> Write the numbers 1-4 in the correct locations on the map.

Teaching the Lesson

An "Expedition"

> Get the "journal" and a pencil.

I will be leading you on an expedition. You are to record in your journal interesting and important things that you see, just as Lewis and Clark did. Often, Lewis and Clark wrote in their journals in camp, rather than as they were walking.

> **Why do you think the men might have done that?**

They may have done it to save time in traveling or to allow themselves time to write enough detail. Some of the drawings had to be sketched on the spot and filled in later. Some of the drawings were made in camp.

Heritage Studies 3 Home TE

Teaching the Lesson suggests a procedure for instruction.

Evaluating the Lesson gives ideas to evaluate the child's grasp of the material presented.

◆ FAMOUS PEOPLE ◆

Frank and Jesse James
1843-1915 and 1847-82

Young Jesse James

There is more than one way to become famous. The James brothers chose the wrong way. The two had been Confederate soldiers in the Civil War. When they went home to Missouri, Frank and Jesse were roused out at night by men with guns. The men wanted to arrest the brothers for what they had done during the war.

Soon after, the James brothers and some other men began robbing trains and banks. During the robberies, many people were shot and killed. Thousands and thousands of dollars were stolen. Always the gang of robbers got away—with three from the gang were killed and three more were captured in Minnesota.

Frank James when he was older

Frank and Jesse were never caught. Years later, Jesse was shot in the head by a man pretending to be his friend. Frank turned himself in to the law. He stood trial for robbery and murder. Surprisingly, there was universal sympathy for him because of the way Jesse was killed, and he was acquitted. He returned home and worked in a small Wild West show. He later died peacefully at home.

239

Text Discussion, page 239   *Day 3*

> Read page 239 to see what happened to another famous outlaw pair. *(Jesse was killed; Frank was arrested and tried but was acquitted, or found not guilty.)*
> Why do you think some people think the life of an outlaw is exciting and admirable?

They do not understand the truth about how the outlaws really lived and what they were really like; perhaps they do not see right from wrong clearly.

> God tells us in His Word what is right and what is wrong and that we are to follow His Word. (BAT: 6d Clear conscience)

The stories about things that happened, both good and bad, make up the history of a people. Think about your personal history, the stories about yourself.

> Is the history you are making showing forth Christ more and more? (BAT: 7b Exaltation of Christ)

Chapter 12: Lesson 67

Evaluating the Lesson

"Fast-Draw" Game

> Take out the holster and rectangles you prepared earlier.
> The yellow rectangle stands for "wrong" and the green rectangle stands for "right."
> Put the rectangles in the slots on the holster and lay the holster in front of you.
> I will read several actions. You are to draw a rectangle out of your holster and hold it up as soon as you decide whether the action is a right action or a wrong one.

- Robbing a bank *(yellow)*
- Picking up litter *(green)*
- Lying to a parent *(yellow)*
- Getting angry because you lose a game *(yellow)*
- Cleaning up the kitchen after dinner *(green)*
- Hiding when you have broken something *(yellow)*
- Being friendly to a new neighbor *(green)*
- Warning someone of danger *(green)*
- Giving up free time to help someone *(green)*
- Obeying the law and your parents *(green)*

━━ Going Beyond ━━

Enrichment

Make an enlargement of the holster and rectangles from Notebook page 93. Write on the rectangles different actions, both right and wrong. Your child can color the rectangles: green for right actions, yellow for wrong actions. He should put all right actions into one holster and all wrong actions into the other.

Additional Teacher Information

The Dalton Gang was named for the three brothers in it—Gratton, Bob, and Emmett. These men had turned to horse thievery and then went on to train robbery and murder. They had begun as lawmen, wearing badges and searching for the men who had killed their deputy marshal brother, Frank. The raid on Coffeyville was meant to upstage the exploits of the Younger Gang, whose primary members, Bob and Cole Younger, were second cousins of the Daltons. The Daltons thought the simultaneous robbing of two banks in daylight would be unbeatable—especially since Coffeyville was their hometown.

285

━━ Going Beyond ━━

Enrichment includes activities and games. Some of these activities may be done independently.

Additional Teacher Information provides the teacher with extra information to help him expand his knowledge of related topics. It is not necessary to understand or even to read the information in this section to teach the lesson.

BIBLE ACTION TRUTHS

The quality and consistency of a man's decisions reflect his character. Christian character begins with justification, but it grows throughout the lifelong process of sanctification. God's grace is sufficient for the task, and a major part of God's gracious provision is His Word. The Bible provides the very "words of life" that instruct us in salvation and Christian living. By obeying God's commands and making godly decisions based on His Word, Christians can strengthen their character.

Too often Christians live by only vague guidance—for instance, that we should "do good" to all men. While doing good is desirable, more specific guidance will lead to more consistent decisions.

Consistent decisions are made when man acts on Bible principles—or Bible Action Truths. The thirty-seven Bible Action Truths (listed under eight general principles) provide Christians with specific goals for their actions and attitudes. Study the Scriptures indicated for a fuller understanding of the principles in Bible Action Truths.

Thousands have found this format helpful in identifying and applying principles of behavior. Yet there is no "magic" in this formula. As you study the Word, you likely will find other truths that speak to you. The key is for you to study the Scriptures, look for Bible Action Truths, and be sensitive to the leading of the Holy Spirit.

1. **Salvation—Separation Principle**
    Salvation results from God's direct action. Although man is unable to work for this "gift of God," the Christian's reaction to salvation should be to separate himself from the world unto God.
    a. **Understanding Jesus Christ** (Matthew 3:17; 16:16; I Corinthians 15:3-4; Philippians 2:9-11) Jesus is the Son of God. He was sent to earth to die on the cross for our sins. He was buried but rose from the dead after three days.
    b. **Repentance and faith** (Isaiah 55:7; Luke 13:3; Acts 5:30-31; 16:31; Hebrews 11:6) If we believe that Jesus died for our sins, we can accept Him as our Savior. We must be sorry for our sins, turn from them, confess them to God, and believe that He will forgive us.
    c. **Separation from the world** (John 17:6, 11, 14, 18; Romans 16:17-18; II Corinthians 6:14-18; James 4:4; I John 2:15-16; II John 10-11) After we are saved, we should live a different life. We should try to be like Christ and not live like those who are unsaved.

2. **Sonship—Servant Principle**
    Only by an act of God the Father could sinful man become a son of God. As a son of God, however, the Christian must realize that he has been "bought with a price"; he is now Christ's servant.

    a. **Authority** (Matthew 22:21; Romans 13:1-7; I Thessalonians 5:12-13; I Timothy 6:1-5; Hebrews 13:17; I Peter 2:13-19) We should respect, honor, and obey those in authority over us.
    b. **Servanthood** (Ephesians 6:5-8; Philippians 2:7-8) Just as Christ was a humble servant while He was on earth, we should also be humble and obedient.
    c. **Faithfulness** (Matthew 25:23; Luke 9:62; I Corinthians 4:2) We should do our work so that God and others can depend on us.
    d. **Goal setting** (Proverbs 13:12, 19; I Corinthians 9:24; Philippians 3:13; Colossians 3:2) To be faithful servants, we must set goals for our work. We should look forward to finishing a job and going on to something more.
    e. **Work** (Ephesians 4:28; II Thessalonians 3:10-12) God never honors a lazy servant. He wants us to be busy and dependable workers.
    f. **Enthusiasm** (Romans 12:11; Colossians 3:23) We should do *all* tasks with energy and with a happy, willing spirit.

3. **Uniqueness—Unity Principle**
    No one is a mere person; God has created each individual a unique being. But because God has an overall plan for His creation, each unique member must contribute to the unity of the entire body.
    a. **Self-concept** (Psalm 8:3-8; 139; II Corinthians 5:17; Ephesians 2:10; 4:1-3, 11-13; II Peter 1:10) We are special creatures in God's plan. He has given each of us special abilities to use in our lives for Him.
    b. **Mind** (Proverbs 4:23; 23:7; Daniel 1:8; Luke 6:45; Romans 7:23, 25; II Corinthians 10:5; Philippians 2:5; 4:8; James 1:8) We should give our hearts and minds to God. What we do and say really begins in our minds. We should try to think of ourselves humbly as Christ did when He lived on earth.
    c. **Emotional control** (Proverbs 16:32; 25:28; Acts 20:24; Galatians 5:24; II Timothy 1:7) With the help of God and the power of the Holy Spirit, we should have control over our feelings. We must be careful not to act out of anger.
    d. **Body as a temple** (I Corinthians 3:16-17; 6:19-20) We should remember that our bodies are the dwelling place of God's Holy Spirit. We should keep ourselves pure, honest, and dedicated to God's will.
    e. **Unity of Christ and the Church** (John 17:21; Ephesians 2:19-22; 5:23-32; II Thessalonians 3:6, 14-15) Since we are saved, we are now part of God's family and should unite ourselves with others to worship and grow as Christians. Christ

is the head of His Church, which includes all believers. He wants us to work together as His Church in carrying out His plans, but He forbids us to work in fellowship with disobedient brethren.

4. **Holiness—Habit Principle**

Believers are declared holy as a result of Christ's finished action on the cross. Daily holiness of life, however, comes from forming godly habits. A Christian must consciously establish godly patterns of action; he must develop habits of holiness.

   a. **Sowing and reaping** (Hosea 8:7; Matthew 6:1-8; Galatians 6:7-8) We must remember that we will be rewarded according to the kind of work we have done. If we are faithful, we will be rewarded. If we are unfaithful, we will not be rewarded. We cannot fool God.

   b. **Purity** (I Thessalonians 4:1-7; I Peter 1:22) We should try to live lives that are free from sin. We should keep our minds, words, and deeds clean and pure.

   c. **Honesty** (Proverbs 16:8; Romans 12:17; II Corinthians 8:21; Ephesians 4:25) We should not lie. We should be honest in every way. Even if we could gain more by being dishonest, we should still be honest. God sees all things.

   d. **Victory** (John 16:33; Romans 8:37; I Corinthians 10:13; 15:57-58; I John 5:4) If we constantly try to be pure, honest, and Christlike, with God's help we will be able to overcome temptations.

5. **Love—Life Principle**

We love God because He first loved us. God's action of manifesting His love to us through His Son demonstrates the truth that love must be exercised. Since God acted in love toward us, believers must act likewise by showing godly love to others.

   a. **Love** (John 15:17; I Corinthians 13; Ephesians 5:2; I John 3:11, 16-18; 4:7-21) God's love to us was the greatest love possible. We should, in turn, show our love for others by our words and actions.

   b. **Giving** (Proverbs 3:9-10; Luke 6:38; II Corinthians 9:6-8) We should give cheerfully to God the first part of all we earn. We should also give to others unselfishly.

   c. **Evangelism and missions** (Psalm 126:5-6; Matthew 28:18-20; Romans 1:16-17; II Corinthians 5:11-21) We should be busy telling others about the love of God and His plan of salvation. We should share in the work of foreign missionaries by our giving and prayers.

   d. **Communication** (Isaiah 50:4; Ephesians 4:22-29; Colossians 4:6; James 3:2-13) We should have control of our tongues so that we will not say things displeasing to God. We should encourage others and be kind and helpful in what we say.

   e. **Friendliness** (Psalm 119:63; Proverbs 17:17; 18:24) We should be friendly to others, and we should be loyal to those who love and serve God.

6. **Communion—Consecration Principle**

Because sin separates man from God, any communion between man and God must be achieved by God's direct action of removing sin. Once communion is established, the believer's reaction should be to maintain a consciousness of this fellowship by living a consecrated life.

   a. **Bible study** (Psalm 119; II Timothy 2:15; I Peter 2:2-3) To grow as Christians, we must spend time with God daily by reading His Word.

   b. **Prayer** (I Chronicles 16:11; Psalm 145:18; John 15:7, 16; 16:24; Romans 8:26-27; I Thessalonians 5:17) We should bring all our requests to God, trusting Him to answer them in His own way.

   c. **Spirit-filled** (Romans 8:13-14; Galatians 5:16, 22-23; Ephesians 5:18-19; I John 1:7-9) We should let the Holy Spirit rule in our hearts and show us what to say and do. We should not say and do just what we want to do, for those things are often wrong and harmful to others.

   d. **Clear conscience** (Acts 24:16; I Timothy 1:19) To be good Christians, we cannot have wrong acts or thoughts or words bothering our consciences. We must confess them to God and to those people against whom we have sinned. We cannot live lives close to God if we have guilty consciences.

   e. **Forgiveness** (Matthew 18:15-17; Mark 11:25-26; Luke 17:3-4; Ephesians 4:30-32; Colossians 3:13) We must ask forgiveness of God when we have done wrong. Just as God forgives our sins freely, we should forgive others when they do wrong things to us.

7. **Grace—Gratitude Principle**

Grace is unmerited favor. Man does not deserve God's grace. However, after God bestows His grace, believers should react with an overflow of gratitude.

   a. **Grace** (I Corinthians 15:10; Ephesians 2:8-9) With out God's grace we would be sinners on our way to hell. He loved us when we did not deserve His love and provided for us a way to escape sin's punishment by the death of His Son on the cross.

   b. **Exaltation of Christ** (John 1:1-4, 14; 5:23; Galatians 6:14; Ephesians 1:17-23; Philippians 2:9-11; Colossians 1:12-21; Hebrews 1:2-3) We should realize and remember at all times the power, holiness, majesty, and perfection of Christ, and we should give Him the praise and glory for everything that is accomplished through us.

c. **Praise** (I Chronicles 16:23-36; 29:11-13; Psalm 107:8; Ephesians 1:6; Hebrews 13:15; I Peter 2:9) Remembering God's great love and goodness toward us, we should continually praise His name.

d. **Contentment** (Psalm 77:3; Proverbs 15:16; Philippians 4:11; I Timothy 6:6-8; Hebrews 13:5) Money, houses, cars, and all things on earth will last only for a little while. God has given us just what He meant for us to have. We should be happy and content with what we have, knowing that God will provide for us all that we need. We should also be happy wherever God places us.

e. **Humility** (Philippians 2:3-4; I Peter 5:5-6) We should not be proud and boastful but should be willing to be quiet and in the background. Our reward will come from God on Judgment Day, and men's praise to us here on earth will not matter at all. Christ was humble when He lived on earth, and we should be like Him.

8. **Power—Prevailing Principle**

Believers can prevail only as God gives the power. "I can do all things through Christ." God is the source of our power used in fighting the good fight of faith.

a. **Faith in God's promises** (Romans 4:16-21; 8:28; Philippians 4:6; I Thessalonians 5:18; Hebrews 3:18–4:11; I Peter 5:7; II Peter 1:4) God always remains true to His promises. Believing that He will keep all the promises in His Word, we should be determined fighters for Him.

b. **Faith in the power of the Word of God** (Jeremiah 23:29; Psalm 119; Hebrews 4:12; I Peter 1:23-25) God's Word is powerful and endures forever. All other things will pass away, but God's Word shall never pass away because it is written to us from God, and God is eternal.

c. **Fight** (Ephesians 6:11-17; I Timothy 6:12; II Timothy 4:7-8; I Peter 5:8-9) God does not have any use for lazy or cowardly fighters. We must work and fight against sin, using the Word of God as our weapon against the Devil. What we do for God now will determine how much He will reward us in heaven.

d. **Courage** (Joshua 1:9; I Chronicles 28:20; Acts 4:13, 31; Ephesians 3:11-12; Hebrews 13:6) God has promised us that He will not forsake us; therefore, we should not be afraid to speak out against sin. We should remember that we are armed with God's strength.

BIBLE PROMISES

A. **Liberty from Sin**—Born into God's spiritual kingdom, a Christian is enabled to live right and gain victory over sin through faith in Christ. (Romans 8:3-4—"For what the law could not do, in that it was weak through the flesh, God sending his own Son in the likeness of sinful flesh, and for sin, condemned sin in the flesh: that the righteousness of the law might be fulfilled in us, who walk not after the flesh, but after the Spirit.")

B. **Guiltless by the Blood**—Cleansed by the blood of Christ, the Christian is pardoned from the guilt of his sins. He does not have to brood or fret over his past because the Lord has declared him righteous. (Romans 8:33—"Who shall lay any thing to the charge of God's elect? It is God that justifieth." Isaiah 45:24—"Surely, shall one say, in the Lord have I righteousness and strength: even to him shall men come; and all that are incensed against him shall be ashamed.")

C. **Basis for Prayer**—Knowing that his righteousness comes entirely from Christ and not from himself, the Christian is free to plead the blood of Christ and to come before God in prayer at any time. (Romans 5:1-2— "Therefore being justified by faith, we have peace with God through our Lord Jesus Christ: by whom also we have access by faith into this grace wherein we stand, and rejoice in hope of the glory of God.")

D. **Identified in Christ**—The Christian has the assurance that God sees him as a son of God, perfectly united with Christ. He also knows that he has access to the strength and the grace of Christ in his daily living. (Galatians 2:20—"I am crucified with Christ: nevertheless, I live; yet not I, but Christ liveth in me: and the life which I now live in the flesh I live by the faith of the Son of God, who loved me, and gave himself for me." Ephesians 1:3—"Blessed be the God and Father of our Lord Jesus Christ, who hath blessed us with all spiritual blessings in heavenly places in Christ.")

E. **Christ as Sacrifice**—Christ was a willing sacrifice for the sins of the world. His blood covers every sin of the believer and pardons the Christian for eternity. The purpose of His death and resurrection was to redeem a people to Himself. (Isaiah 53:4-5— "Surely he hath borne our griefs, and carried our sorrows: yet we did esteem him stricken, smitten of God, and afflicted. But he was wounded for our transgressions, he was bruised for our iniquities: the chastisement of our peace was upon him; and with his stripes we are healed." John 10:27-28—"My sheep hear my voice, and I know them, and they follow me: and I give unto them eternal life; and they shall never perish, neither shall any man pluck them out of my hand.")

F. **Christ as Intercessor**—Having pardoned them through His blood, Christ performs the office of High Priest in praying for His people. (Hebrews 7:25—"Wherefore he is able also to save them to the uttermost that come unto God by him, seeing he ever liveth to make intercession for them." John 17:20—"Neither pray I for these alone, but for them also which shall believe on me through their word.")

G. **Christ as Friend**—In giving salvation to the believer, Christ enters a personal, loving relationship with the Christian that cannot be ended. This relationship is understood and enjoyed on the believer's part through fellowship with the Lord through Bible reading and prayer. (Isaiah 54:5—"For thy Maker is thine husband; the Lord of hosts is his name; and thy Redeemer the Holy One of Israel; the God of the whole earth shall he be called." Romans 8:38-39— "For I am persuaded, that neither death, nor life, nor angels, nor principalities, nor powers, nor things present, nor things to come, nor height, nor depth, nor any other creature, shall be able to separate us from the love of God, which is in Christ Jesus our Lord.")

H. **God as Father**—God has appointed Himself to be responsible for the well-being of the Christian. He both protects and nourishes the believer, and it was from Him that salvation originated. (Isaiah 54:17— "No weapon that is formed against thee shall prosper; and every tongue that shall rise against thee in judgment thou shalt condemn. This is the heritage of the servants of the Lord, and their righteousness is of me, saith the Lord." Psalm 103:13— "Like as a father pitieth his children, so the Lord pitieth them that fear him.")

I. **God as Master**—God is sovereign over all creation. He orders the lives of His people for His glory and their good. (Romans 8:28—"And we know that all things work together for good to them that love God, to them who are the called according to his purpose.")

SUMMARY OF CORRELATED SKILLS AND INSTRUCTIONAL MATERIALS

Chapters and Lessons	Suggested teaching days	Lesson pages	Text pages	Notebook pages
WE THE PEOPLE				
1 New Country, New Problems	2	2-6	2-5	1-2
2 The Constitutional Convention	1	7-10	6-8	3
3 A New Government	2	10-14	9-12	4-5
4 The Great Compromise	1	14-17	13-15	6
5 A Rising Sun	2	18-22	16-19, 272	7
6 The Bill of Rights	2	22-25	20-22, 247, 273	8
THE FIRES OF FREEDOM				
7 The Poor and the Powerful	2	28-33	24-29, 247	9
8 Storming the Bastille	2	33-36	31-33	
9 The Terror	2	36-41	30, 34-37, 282-83	10-11
10 Give Honor	2	41-44	38-40	12
11 After the Revolution	1	44-47	41-42, 248	13

Section number **1** labels the "WE THE PEOPLE" group; section number **2** labels the "THE FIRES OF FREEDOM" group.

Bible Action Truths; Bible Promises	Heritage Studies skills
BAT: 2c Faithfulness	inferring relationships, formulating opinions, working with maps, working with diagrams
BATs: 2a Authority, 2c Faithfulness, 4c Honesty	inferring relationships, formulating opinions, working with maps, identifying key documents, showing respect for heritage
BATs: 2c Faithfulness, 2d Goal setting	sequencing events, inferring relationships, formulating opinions, valuing the rights of citizenship, showing respect for heritage
BAT: 5d Communication	making predictions, inferring relationships, formulating opinions, identifying key documents
BAT: 2b Servanthood	inferring relationships, formulating opinions, working with time lines, identifying key documents
BATs: 2a Authority, 3c Emotional control, 5a Love, 5d Communication, 6c Spirit-filled	sequencing events, summarizing data, inferring relationships, making decisions, formulating opinions, identifying sources of information, working with charts and diagrams, identifying key documents, valuing the rights of citizenship, showing respect for heritage
BATs: 2a Authority, 7b Exaltation of Christ; Bible Promises: D. Identified in Christ, H. God as Father, I. God as Master	summarizing data, making predictions, inferring relationships, making decisions, formulating opinions, valuing the rights of citizenship
BATs: 2a Authority, 4b Purity, 4c Honesty	sequencing events, summarizing data, making predictions, inferring relationships, making decisions, formulating opinions, working with time lines
BATs: 1b Repentance and faith, 7a Grace; Bible Promise: A. Liberty from Sin	sequencing events, summarizing data, making predictions, inferring relationships, making decisions, formulating opinions, valuing the rights of citizenship, showing respect for heritage
BATs: 1a Understanding Jesus Christ, 1b Repentance and faith, 7b Exaltation of Christ, 7c Praise	formulating opinions, working with maps, using cardinal directions, working with charts, showing respect for heritage
BATs: 7a Grace, 7b Exaltation of Christ, 7c Praise; Bible Promises: H. God as Father, I. God as Master	sequencing events, summarizing data, making predictions, inferring relationships, making decisions, formulating opinions, working with time lines, working with maps

Bible Action Truths; Bible Promises	Heritage Studies skills
Bible Promise: I. God as Master	making predictions, making decisions, identifying sources of information, working with maps and globes
BATs: 2f Enthusiasm, 7c Praise, 7d Contentment	summarizing data, working with maps, using cardinal directions
Bible Promises: H. God as Father, I. God as Master	making predictions, inferring relationships, formulating opinions, working with maps
BAT: 1b Repentance and faith	inferring relationships, making decisions, working with maps and globes, using cardinal directions
BATs: 2b Servanthood, 5e Friendliness, 7e Humility	making predictions, working with time lines, identifying sources of information, working with maps
BATs: 2c Faithfulness, 7c Praise, 7d Contentment	sequencing events, summarizing data, making predictions, inferring relationships, working with time lines, identifying sources of information, working with maps
BATs: 4a Sowing and reaping, 4c Honesty, 6c Spirit-filled, 7c Praise	sequencing events, inferring relationships, making decisions, identifying sources of information, formulating opinions, working with maps, using cardinal directions, working with graphs
BATs: 2a Authority, 2c Faithfulness, 2d Goal setting, 2e Work, 2f Enthusiasm, 5e Friendliness, 6c Spirit-filled, 8a Faith in God's promises	sequencing events, summarizing data, making predictions, making decisions, formulating opinions, working with maps, using cardinal directions, valuing the rights of citizenship, showing respect for heritage
BAT: 5a Love	summarizing data, inferring relationships, working with time lines, identifying key documents, valuing the rights of citizenship, showing respect for heritage
BATs: 1a Understanding Jesus Christ, 1b Repentance and faith, 5b Giving, 5c Evangelism and missions, 7d Contentment, 8b Faith in the power of the Word of God	making predictions, making decisions, working with maps, using cardinal directions, working with graphs
BATs: 2c Faithfulness, 2e Work, 4c Honesty	sequencing events, summarizing data, making decisions, formulating opinions
BATs: 2c Faithfulness, 3a Self-concept, 4c Honesty, 5a Love, 5e Friendliness, 6c Spirit-filled, 6d Clear conscience	summarizing data, making predictions, working with maps, valuing the rights of citizenship
BATs: 1a Understanding Jesus Christ, 1b Repentance and faith, 4a Sowing and reaping, 5c Evangelism and missions, 8a Faith in God's promises, 8b Faith in the power of the Word of God, 8c Fight, 8d Courage	summarizing data, inferring relationships, formulating opinions, showing respect for heritage
BATs: 4c Honesty, 5a Love, 7d Contentment	sequencing events, summarizing data, making predictions, working with time lines, working with maps and globes, working with graphs and charts

Bible Action Truths; Bible Promises	Heritage Studies skills
BATs: 4a Sowing and reaping, 5a Love, 6a Bible study, 7d Contentment, 8a Faith in God's promises, 8b Faith in the power of the Word of God	summarizing data, making decisions, formulating opinions, identifying sources of information
BATs: 2c Faithfulness, 2d Goal setting, 2e Work, 3a Self-concept, 4a Sowing and reaping, 5a Love, 5e Friendliness, 6a Bible study, 6c Spirit-filled, 7b Exaltation of Christ, 7e Humility	sequencing events, summarizing data, making predictions, inferring relationships, making decisions, formulating opinions
BATs: 2c Faithfulness, 2d Goal setting, 2e Work, 3a Self-concept, 4a Sowing and reaping, 5a Love, 5e Friendliness, 6a Bible study, 6c Spirit-filled, 7b Exaltation of Christ, 7e Humility	sequencing events, summarizing data, making predictions, inferring relationships, making decisions, formulating opinions
BATs: 2b Servanthood, 2d Goal setting, 2e Work, 3a Self-concept, 5b Giving	sequencing events, inferring relationships, formulating opinions, showing respect for heritage
BATs: 2c Faithfulness, 2e Work	summarizing data, formulating opinions, working with time lines
	summarizing data, making predictions, inferring relationships, making decisions, formulating opinions
BATs: 2b Servanthood, 2c Faithfulness, 3d Body as a temple, 5a Love, 5d Communication	sequencing events, summarizing data, inferring relationships, making decisions, formulating opinions, working with maps, showing respect for heritage
BATs: 2c Faithfulness, 3a Self-concept, 7b Exaltation of Christ; Bible Promise: I. God as Master	sequencing events, summarizing data, inferring relationships, making decisions, formulating opinions, working with maps, showing respect for heritage
BATs: 2b Servanthood, 2c Faithfulness, 2d Goal setting, 2e Work, 2f Enthusiasm, 3a Self-concept, 5a Love, 7b Exaltation of Christ	sequencing events, summarizing data, making decisions, formulating opinions, working with maps, showing respect for heritage
BATs: 3c Emotional control, 5a Love, 5d Communication, 5e Friendliness	sequencing events, inferring relationships, making decisions, formulating opinions, working with maps, showing respect for heritage
BATs: 1a Understanding Jesus Christ, 3a Self-concept, 5a Love, 5c Evangelism and missions, 7b Exaltation of Christ, 7c Praise, 7d Contentment, 8d Courage; Bible Promise: H. God as Father	making predictions, inferring relationships, making decisions, formulating opinions, working with maps, showing respect for heritage

Bible Action Truths; Bible Promises	Heritage Studies skills
BATs: 1b Repentance and faith, 5a Love	summarizing data, inferring relationships, making decisions, formulating opinions, working with maps
BAT: 5b Giving	summarizing data, making decisions, formulating opinions, working with maps
BAT: 8d Courage	summarizing data, making decisions, formulating opinions, using cardinal directions, working with maps, working with time lines
BAT: 5c Evangelism and missions	summarizing data, inferring relationships, making decisions, formulating opinions, working with maps
BATs: 2a Authority, 2d Goal setting, 5a Love, 5b Giving, 8d Courage	summarizing data, making decisions, formulating opinions, identifying sources of information
BATs: 2b Servanthood, 4c Honesty	summarizing data, making decisions, formulating opinions, showing respect for heritage
BAT: 2b Servanthood	summarizing data, making decisions, formulating opinions, working with time lines, using cardinal directions, working with graphs
BATs: 3a Self-concept, 7b Exaltation of Christ; Bible Promise: I. God as Master	sequencing events, summarizing data, making predictions, inferring relationships, formulating opinions, working with time lines, working with graphs
BATs: 2d Goal setting, 2e Work, 3a Self-concept	summarizing data, making predictions, formulating opinions, working with maps
BATs: 3a Self-concept, 3b Mind, 3c Emotional control, 7b Exaltation of Christ, 7c Praise, 8a Faith in God's promises	formulating opinions
BATs: 1a Understanding Jesus Christ, 1b Repentance and faith, 6a Bible study, 6b Prayer, 7a Grace, 7b Exaltation of Christ, 7c Praise, 7d Contentment, 8a Faith in God's promises; Bible Promises: A. Liberty from Sin, B. Guiltless by the Blood, I. God as Master	summarizing data, making predictions, inferring relationships, formulating opinions, working with maps
BATs: 1a Understanding Jesus Christ, 1b Repentance and faith, 7b Exaltation of Christ, 7c Praise	sequencing events, summarizing data, making predictions, inferring relationships, formulating opinions, working with time lines, identifying sources of information, showing respect for heritage

Bible Action Truths; Bible Promises	Heritage Studies skills
BAT: 1b Repentance and faith; Bible Promise: A. Liberty from Sin	making predictions, inferring relationships, working with time lines, identifying sources of information, working with maps, working with charts
BATs: 5b Giving, 5c Evangelism and missions, 7b Exaltation of Christ, 7c Praise	sequencing events, inferring relationships, formulating opinions, working with maps
BAT: 7d Contentment	summarizing data, inferring relationships, formulating opinions, working with maps, working with diagrams
Bible Promises: A. Liberty from Sin, B. Guiltless by the Blood, E. Christ as Sacrifice	sequencing events, inferring relationships, working with time lines, identifying key documents
Bible Promise: E. Christ as Sacrifice	summarizing data, formulating opinions, working with time lines, working with maps and globes
BATs: 2b Servanthood, 6e Forgiveness, 7e Humility	summarizing data, making predictions, making decisions, formulating opinions, working with time lines, identifying key documents
BATs: 2a Authority, 2e Work	summarizing data, inferring relationships, making decisions, identifying sources of information, showing respect for heritage
BATs: 1a Understanding Jesus Christ, 1b Repentance and faith, 5a Love; Bible Promises: A. Liberty from Sin, B. Guiltless by the Blood, D. Identified in Christ, E. Christ as Sacrifice	sequencing events, summarizing data, inferring relationships, making decisions, formulating opinions, showing respect for heritage
BATs: 5a Love, 7c Praise	sequencing events, summarizing data, making decisions, formulating opinions, identifying key documents, valuing the rights of citizenship, showing respect for heritage
BATs: 2c Faithfulness, 2d Goal setting, 5a Love, 5e Friendliness, 7b Exaltation of Christ, 7c Praise	sequencing events, summarizing data, making decisions, formulating opinions, showing respect for heritage
BATs: 7b Exaltation of Christ, 7c Praise	sequencing events, inferring relationships, working with time lines, working with tables, showing respect for heritage

Bible Action Truths; Bible Promises	Heritage Studies skills
BATs: 1c Separation from the world, 3b Mind, 4b Purity	sequencing events, making predictions, formulating opinions
	sequencing events, summarizing data, inferring relationships, formulating opinions, showing respect for heritage
BATs: 2d Goal setting, 2e Work, 3a Self-concept	sequencing events, summarizing data, making predictions, making decisions, formulating opinions
BATs: 2c Faithfulness, 2e Work, 3a Self-concept	making predictions, making decisions, formulating opinions
BAT: 1b Repentance and faith	working with maps, using cardinal directions
BATs: 1a Understanding Jesus Christ, 1b Repentance and faith	sequencing events, summarizing data, making predictions, inferring relationships, making decisions, formulating opinions, working with time lines, working with maps, using cardinal directions
BATs: 2d Goal setting, 2e Work, 3a Self-concept, 6a Bible study, 6b Prayer	summarizing data, making predictions, making decisions, formulating opinions, working with maps and globes, using cardinal directions, showing respect for heritage
BATs: 2c Faithfulness, 2e Work, 5a Love, 5e Friendliness	summarizing data, making predictions, inferring relationships, making decisions, formulating opinions, valuing the rights of citizenship, showing respect for heritage
BATs: 2c Faithfulness, 2e Work, 4c Honesty, 6d Clear conscience	inferring relationships, making decisions, formulating opinions, identifying sources of information, working with maps
BATs: 2a Authority, 2b Servanthood, 3c Emotional control	sequencing events, summarizing data, making decisions, identifying sources of information, working with diagrams
BATs: 2a Authority, 6d Clear conscience, 7b Exaltation of Christ	making decisions, formulating opinions, working with maps, using cardinal directions, valuing the rights of citizenship
BAT: 4c Honesty	formulating opinions, working with time lines, identifying sources of information, working with maps, using cardinal directions, valuing the rights of citizenship
BAT: 1c Separation from the world	sequencing events, summarizing data, inferring relationships, working with time lines, working with maps

LESSON PLANS

We the People

At the heart of this chapter is the Constitution of the United States. Your child will learn about the Constitutional Convention and about the men who helped to write this great document. Chapter activities include reciting the Preamble to the Constitution; making a poster; and writing a journal entry, a letter, and a rule.

Materials

The following materials must be obtained or prepared before the presentation of the lesson. These items are labeled with an asterisk (*) in each lesson and in the Materials List in the Supplement. For further information see the individual lessons.

- *HERITAGE STUDIES 3 Student Textbook*
- *HERITAGE STUDIES 3 Student Notebook*
- Pictures of Mount Vernon (optional) (Lesson 1)
- Appendix, page A2 (Lesson 1)
- A box (Lesson 1)
- Colored paper or fabric (optional) (Lesson 1)
- Ribbon (optional) (Lesson 1)
- A copy of some of your rules (Lesson 2)
- A cassette player (Lesson 3)
- *HERITAGE STUDIES Listening Cassette A* (Lesson 3) (*NOTE*: The cassette will be used in many lessons throughout the curriculum.)
- Appendix, pages A3-A4 (Lesson 4)
- The TimeLine Snapshots (Lesson 5) (*NOTE*: The TimeLine Snapshots will be used in many lessons throughout the curriculum.)
- Appendix, pages A5-A6 (Lesson 5)

1

We the People

Maps, charts, games, and other black-and-white visuals can be found in two places in your teacher's manual—the Supplement and the Appendix. All the pages that need to be copied for use in the lessons can be found in the Appendix. Those found in the Supplement can be used directly from your manual and do not need to be copied, though they may be copied if you so desire. (*NOTE:* Maps and More, the group of color visuals that follows the lessons, is not a part of the Appendix or Supplement and may not be copied.)

LESSON 1
New Country, New Problems

Text, pages 2-5
Notebook, pages 1-2

━━━ Preview ━━━

Main Ideas
- When people are dissatisfied with their government, they respond in different ways.
- Americans value their freedoms.

Objectives
- Use a key to read a diagram
- Write a journal entry

Materials

> School supplies such as crayons, glue, scissors, pencils, and paper that you would have in your teaching area are not listed in the Materials list of each lesson.

- A box* (*NOTE:* The box needs to be large enough to put a fly swatter into it.)
- Red, white, and blue paper or fabric (optional)*
- A length of red or blue ribbon (optional)*
- A few silver coins
- Appendix, page A2: We the People time line*
- Maps and More 1 and 2, pages M1-M2

> Maps and More is a collection of colored maps, visuals, charts, and graphs. Display the charts from your teacher's manual as you teach the lessons. These visuals may not be copied.

- A *HERITAGE STUDIES 3 Student Textbook**
- A *HERITAGE STUDIES 3 Student Notebook**
- Pictures of Mount Vernon (optional)*

Notes

In each lesson of this chapter, you will use a "mystery box" to introduce the topic for that lesson. You may want to decorate the box with the paper or fabric, covering the box and the lid separately. For Lesson 1, put the coins into the prepared box and tie the ribbon around it.

September 17 is the anniversary of the United States Constitution. America has also set aside that day to honor its citizens and to welcome new citizens to the United States. In some states, the entire week of September 17 is designated as Constitution Week. If you will be studying this chapter at that time in September, you may want to establish your own celebration to cover all the days during which your child will be working on the chapter. Decorate the room with red, white, and blue streamers; make patriotic banners; and display copies of America's famous documents.

> You may choose to teach this lesson or other lessons in one day. If you would like to spread the lesson over more than one day, the suggested teaching days are marked for you.

━━━ Lesson ━━━
Day 1

> As you read the lesson, you will notice that there is a variety of types or styles of print. **Questions are in bold print.** Information to be given directly to your child is in regular print. *(Answers to questions are shown in italics within parentheses.) Instructions and information directed to you as the teacher are given in a different italicized print. (NOTEs give information to the teacher also.)* **Terms** *that you will want your child to become familiar with are in bold, italic print.*

Introducing the Lesson

Inferring Activity

➤ *Show your child the mystery box.*
➤ Guess what is in the box.
➤ **What could you do to get a clue? Could you shake the box?**
➤ Open the box.
➤ **What is in the box?** *(silver coins)*
➤ **What do people use coins for today?** *(Answers will vary but may include making small purchases, putting them into coin banks, and collecting them.)*
➤ **How do people pay for larger purchases such as a sofa or lawn mower today?** *(They use paper money, checks, or credit cards.)*

Modern coins are thought of as change or pocket money. The silver coins used in early America were different. Some coins were ***minted,*** or made, in other countries, such as France and Mexico. They were more valuable than much of the paper money of the day. They were difficult to get. People had to pay many of their debts in silver.

New Country, New Problems

The bells of Philadelphia rang as they never had before. The redcoats had given up. America was free of kings forever! People ran into the streets and cheered. They fired their guns. They thanked God for His help.

No one was happier that the war was over than General George Washington. He made sure that all his men were taken care of, and then he went to his home in Virginia.

For a moment it must have seemed as though all the problems were solved. But after the shouts and the gunfire died down, the citizens of the new United States found they did not always get along together.

2

The leaders in the thirteen states needed to get money. The new country owed money to England and to some American soldiers. The leaders made the people pay taxes. Farmers and shopkeepers and traders had just come home from war. They did not have the money to pay taxes.

The worst sign of trouble was in Massachusetts. The leaders there said that the taxes had to be paid in silver. Some men said, "No! We will not pay in silver! We will fight first!" And they picked up their guns again. But this time they meant to throw their American leaders out.

3

Teaching the Lesson

The Text Discussion is a guide to help as you read and discuss the text pages. When instructions say to read the text, your child should read silently for comprehension. He will be asked occasionally to read aloud for interpretation. You know your child best. Adjust the reading to meet his needs. Take time to help your child answer the questions found in the text.

Text Discussion, page 2

➤ **Read page 2 to find out why the people of Philadelphia were celebrating.** *(The redcoats had given up, and America was free of kings.)* The colonies had been fighting for their freedom from England. The war was over.

➤ **Who was happiest about the ending of the war?** *(George Washington)*

➤ **Why do you think General Washington would be so happy?**

When your child is asked to give his opinion (a "what-do-you-think" question), an answer may not be listed. Accept any reasonable answer and, if needed, guide your child by asking further questions to reach a better answer.

➤ **Did everyone's happiness last very long? Why?** *(No, the citizens did not get along together for very long.)*

Text Discussion, page 3

➤ **Read page 3 to find out what payment had to be made in silver.** *(taxes)*

➤ **Read aloud what the men said about paying the taxes.** *("No! We will not pay in silver! We will fight first!")*

➤ **Why do you think the men were so angry about having to pay in silver?** Silver coins were more valuable than paper money and were almost impossible to get.

➤ **Who were these men in Massachusetts going to fight?** *(their own leaders)*

Shays's Rebellion
Springfield, Massachusetts
January 25, 1787

Daniel Shays got a thousand men to go with him. They all carried muskets, and they all were angry about the taxes.

Daniel Shays said, "You cannot make us pay in silver!"

The governor of the state got a bigger army together. He sent his army to fight Shays's men.

Shays's men lost the fight. They made peace with their neighbors.

4

The states did not always get along either. Each had its own government. The states were like separate countries, not parts of one country. Something needed to be done. But first, the people wanted to rest from fighting a war.

George Washington wanted to rest too. He said, "I'm going to be a farmer for the rest of my days." But after Shays's Rebellion, his friends came to see him. They said, "You must go help start the new government. If you don't go, the work might not get done. And then all the states will have trouble just as Massachusetts did."

George Washington looked out at his fine fields and his good horses. He wanted to stay home. But if he did, the freedom he had fought for might be lost. The states might get into

fights with each other. Then other countries would try to get American land. He nodded. He had to go.

General and Mrs. Washington in front of Mount Vernon, the home they loved so well

5

Text Discussion, page 4

➤ **Read page 4 to find out what caused Shays's Rebellion.** *(The men rebelled because they were angry about taxes and about having to pay in silver.)*
➤ Look at the title. **In what state did the rebellion happen?** *(Massachusetts)*
➤ **What day did the rebellion begin?** *(January 25, 1787)*
➤ **Who won the fight?** *(The governor's army, or the state of Massachusetts, won.)*
➤ **What did Daniel Shays's men do when they lost?** *(They made peace with their neighbors.)*

Map Activity,
Maps and More 1

➤ Look at Maps and More 1.
➤ Point to the state where Shays's Rebellion took place.
➤ **How many states are named on the map?** *(thirteen)*
➤ **What is the group of states called?** *(the United States)*

Text Discussion, page 5

➤ **Read page 5 to find out what George Washington's friends asked him to do.** *(to leave his home and to help start a new government)*

➤ **Why did the United States need a new government?** *(The states were like separate countries, not part of one country.)*

Although the thirteen states together were called the United States, people felt more loyalty to their own states than to their country. The only thing that held the states together was a set of rules for a "firm league of friendship." But if the states did not feel like following the rules, they did not. The United States government could not force the states to obey its rules, and the states knew that.

➤ **Why do you think that people went to George Washington for help?**

People knew what kind of man Washington was: dependable, hardworking, true to his country. It is important to be dependable. (BAT: 2c Faithfulness)

➤ George Washington's home was called Mount Vernon. Look at the painting of George Washington at Mount Vernon on page 5. **Why did Washington want to stay at Mount Vernon?** *(He wanted to rest, to be a farmer, and to enjoy his fine fields and good horses.)*

➤ **Why did he decide to help start a new government?** *(He was afraid that the people's freedom might be lost and that other countries might take over the land.)*

Map Activity,
Maps and More 1 and 2

➤ Look at Maps and More 1. Find the state of Virginia where Mount Vernon is located.

> If you would like to pinpoint the area of Mount Vernon more specifically, you may want to look at the map on page 285 to find the location of Washington, D.C. Mount Vernon is about fifteen miles south of Washington, D.C.

➤ The meetings to start a new government took place in Philadelphia, Pennsylvania. Locate Philadelphia.

➤ **How do you think Washington traveled from his home in Virginia to Philadelphia?** He traveled by horse.

➤ **Do you think it was a long trip?**

Washington left Mount Vernon on May 9 and arrived in Philadelphia four days later. *Discuss the ways that travel is different now.*

➤ Look at Maps and More 2.

Today George Washington's estate covers about five hundred acres in Fairfax County, Virginia. It was even larger during Washington's time. Washington was a farmer until serving in the War for Independence.

When the war ended, Washington came back to Mount Vernon to retire. In 1789, he was elected as the first president of the United States. At the end of Washington's second term of office, he returned to Mount Vernon and lived quietly until his death two years later.

➤ Find the mansion on the map of Mount Vernon.

There are twenty rooms in the two-and-one-half-story house. George Washington's father built the main part of the house in the 1730s and called the country estate Little Hunting Creek Plantation. It was George Washington's elder half brother who inherited the estate in 1743. He renamed it Mount Vernon in honor of his former commander in the British navy, Admiral Edward Vernon. In 1761 George Washington inherited Mount Vernon. Washington added the piazza *(pē-ăz´ə),* a two-story porch facing the Potomac River.

➤ **Can you find the Potomac River on the map?**

➤ Locate the different gardens on the estate.

Almost everything that the family needed was either grown or made on the estate. Flower gardens, fruit trees, and shade trees surround the estate. George Washington himself planted many of the trees that still flourish.

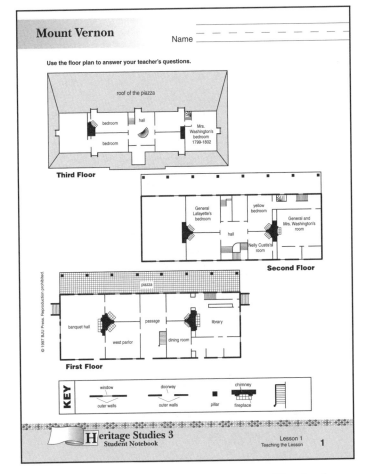

➤ Find the tomb in the upper right corner. The simple ivy-covered tomb is where George and Martha Washington are buried.

➤ Point to the kitchen.

This was separated from the main house as a precaution against possible fires caused by cooking over the open flames of the fireplaces.

Notebook Activity, page 1

➤ Study the key on Notebook page 1.

➤ Use the key to answer these questions.

- **How many fireplaces does the house have?** *(twelve)*
- **On which floor is there a chimney without a fireplace?** *(third)*
- **How many pillars hold up the roof of the piazza?** *(eight)*
- **What is a *piazza?* *(a porch)*
- Look at the piazza and then at the key. **With what might the piazza be confused and why?** *(The piazza might be confused with a fireplace because the symbols are similar.)*
- **Where is the kitchen?** *(There is no kitchen in the floor plans.)*

➤ *Show any pictures that you have of Mount Vernon.*

Pretend that you are George Washington. You must leave Mount Vernon and go to Philadelphia. Write about what you will miss.

July 2, 1787

© 1997 BJU Press. Reproduction prohibited.

Heritage Studies 3
Student Notebook

Lesson 1
Evaluating the Lesson 2

Evaluating the Lesson

Creative Writing Activity, Notebook page 2

➤ Read the directions on Notebook page 2.
➤ Perhaps you may want to write the letter to your wife, Martha, telling her what you will miss. Complete the journal entry.

Time Line Activity

➤ *Give your child the We the People time line.*
➤ Read the date on the bell. *(July 4, 1776)* This is the date that the colonies declared their independence from England.
➤ Read the next date. *(January 25, 1787)* This is about ten and a half years after independence was declared.
➤ **What happened on this date?** *(Shays's Rebellion)*
➤ **Why were Daniel Shays and his men rebelling?** *(They were angry about the taxes and having to pay in silver.)*
➤ Write *Shays's Rebellion* in the oval above the date on the time line.

This time line will be used in each lesson of the chapter. It will help your child to picture the events in the order that they happened.

Going Beyond

Additional Teacher Information

At the end of the Revolutionary War, money was in short supply, and farmers were feeling the shortage more acutely than others. When farmers in Massachusetts were taxed one-third of their income by a legislature that insisted on payment in silver, many lost their farms and equipment and were imprisoned. The farmers pleaded with the authorities to accept payment in farm products, to lower taxes, and to stop jailing debtors. Seeing that their pleas fell on deaf ears, a group of farmers rebelled.

Daniel Shays, a former Revolutionary War captain, led the rebels. The group marched outside courthouses in attempts to keep the courts from meeting and attacked an ammunitions storehouse. Soldiers paid by wealthy merchants broke up the storehouse attack, killed some of Shays's followers, and captured several leaders.

Although Shays's Rebellion failed in its original purpose, it did awaken American leaders to the need for a stronger central government.

Here are several suggestions for using prepared tests such as those in the *HERITAGE STUDIES Test Packet*. Teach the chapter as you normally would. Do not try to "teach to the test." Before giving your child the chapter test, preview the questions. If there is a question(s) covering material that you did not emphasize, you may mark through the question. You may also consider awarding bonus points for the question or replacing it with a question of your own.

LESSON 2
The Constitutional Convention

Text, pages 6-8
Notebook, page 3

━━━ Preview ━━━

Main Ideas
- Americans have fought for freedom in many wars.
- Rules help people live and work together.
- People follow rules for their own benefit and the benefit of others.
- Past events influence current events.
- Significant documents have influenced American history.

Objectives
- Write a rule
- Determine the rights and responsibilities that the rule involves

Materials
- A copy of some of your rules* (*NOTE*: These may be rules for your home or rules that are used in your teaching. For example, do not interrupt when someone is speaking, do not run in the house, and do not talk with your mouth full of food.)
- The mystery box used in Lesson 1
- Maps and More 1, page M1
- We the People time line from Lesson 1

Prepare the mystery box by placing the copy of your rules inside. Eight Pringles cans or paper tubes will be needed for Lesson 8. See the lesson for more information.

━━━ Lesson ━━━

Introducing the Lesson
Inferring Activity

➤ Open the mystery box.
➤ **What did you find?** *(some rules)*
➤ Read the rules. **Why do we need rules?** *(to keep order, etc.)*

Your child may better understand the discussion of the following question if you personalize it. Use a specific rule when asking the question. It may also help if you ask the question several times using a different rule each time.

➤ **How does a particular rule help to guarantee you certain rights?** *(Answers will vary. For example, the rule requiring a person not to talk while someone else is talking guarantees that the person talking will have an opportunity to finish his story.)*
➤ **What are rules for a state or a country called?** *(laws)*
➤ **Can you choose which rules or laws you want to obey?** *(no)*

Once a law or rule is in effect, we have a responsibility to obey it, whether or not we want to obey it. (BAT: 2a Authority)

Teaching the Lesson

In the back of the student text is a glossary. Encourage your child to look up in the glossary words that he is unfamiliar with.

Text Discussion, page 6

➤ **Read page 6 to find out why the men had gathered at the *Constitutional Convention*.** *(to start a new country, to write new laws)*
➤ **In what city did the Constitutional Convention meet?** *(Philadelphia)*
➤ **In what building was the convention?** *(the State House, now called **Independence Hall**)*
➤ **What is the date of the beginning of the Constitutional Convention?** *(May 25, 1787)*
➤ The text says, "They all knew what Americans had given for their freedom." **What had the Americans given for their freedom?** *(Answers will vary but may include that many had given their fathers, husbands, or sons; some had been injured or even lost their lives; some had lost their homes and their belong- ings; and many had been separated from their families during the fighting.)*

Inside Independence Hall

The Constitutional Convention

May 25, 1787

On a cool, rainy Friday morning a group of men took their seats in the State House in Philadelphia. Today we call the building *Independence Hall.* The men's chairs scraped on the wooden floor. Talking and a cough or two echoed in the room. It may not have looked so, but one of the most important meetings in American history was about to begin.

The men had come from twelve states to start a new country—the United States of America. They had come to write laws. They were lawyers and farmers and soldiers and statesmen. Many had been in the War for Independence; many were leaders in their states. They all knew what Americans had given for their freedom. Do you think the men took the meeting seriously?

During the war, the people had lived by laws called the *Articles of Confederation.* That title meant that the rules were to help keep the colonies together. Some of the men thought those laws could be changed a little. Others wanted completely new laws.

6

Benjamin Franklin was sick that day. But he sent Robert Morris to take his place. Ben Franklin wanted George Washington to be in charge of the meeting. Everyone agreed. Washington was the great hero of the war and a man they all trusted. Washington went and sat in a big chair at the front of the room. The chair had a sun carved on the top of the back.

Then the group chose three men to make a list of rules for holding the meetings. Why do you think they made rules for themselves first? Do you have rules to follow in different places? What happens when you do not follow the rules? What would happen if there were no rules?

This mural painted by Violet Oakley for the Pennsylvania capitol building in Harrisburg shows Washington's chair.

7

➤ **What were the *Articles of Confederation?*** *(rules to help keep the colonies together)*

➤ **When were the Articles of Confederation used?** *(during the war)*

➤ **Why do you think the men might have thought that those laws should be changed or rewritten?**

The states were acting like separate countries, not parts of one country. The Articles must not have been working as they were supposed to.

Map Activity, Maps and More 1

➤ **How many states were represented at the Constitutional Convention?** *(twelve)*

➤ **How many states were there in America at that time?** *(thirteen)*

➤ Look at Maps and More 1. By reading the key and looking at the way the states are colored, you can find out which state did not attend the convention.

➤ **Which state did not attend the convention?** *(Rhode Island)*

➤ *Briefly review the names and locations of the other states.*

Text Discussion, page 7

➤ **Read page 7 to find out why George Washington was chosen to be in charge of the Constitutional Convention.** *(He was a hero of the war, and everyone trusted him.)*

We please God when we are the type of person that others can trust. (BATs: 2c Faithfulness, 4c Honesty)

➤ *Discuss with your child the different rules that he must obey in the schoolroom and in the home.*

➤ **What are the penalties for not following those rules?**

➤ **What would happen if there were no rules?**

ECHOES IN HISTORY

The Mayflower Compact

One hundred sixty-seven years earlier, some other people made rules to live by in a new place. They were the Separatists who came to the New World from England. Do you remember what we call the rules they made for themselves? The rules were the *Mayflower Compact.*

The Separatists brought clothes and food and the Bible. They also brought the idea that they needed the freedom to worship God as they wanted. They also wanted their new settlement to succeed.

The men on the *Mayflower* believed that rules were important. They believed people needed rules to live by. These beliefs "echoed" in the State House of Philadelphia in 1787.

8

Rule Writing

Name _____

Write a rule for your classroom. Think about the rights and responsibilities that go with your rule.

This rule would make our classroom a better place.

_____

These rights go with my rule.

_____

These responsibilities go with my rule.

_____

Heritage Studies 3
Student Notebook

Lesson 2
Evaluating the Lesson

3

Text Discussion, page 8

You will direct attention to an *Echoes in History* for the first time this year. These sections deal with the connection of present events to past events.

➤ **Read page 8 to find out what idea the Separatists brought to the New World.** *(They brought the idea that they needed to worship God as they believed.)*

➤ **What was the *Mayflower Compact*?** *(rules the Separatists made in the New World)*

➤ **What is an echo?** *(repetition of a sound slightly after the original sound)*

We can echo or imitate another person's dress, ideas, and opinions. In history, we can see echoes or imitations of people's beliefs and actions.

➤ **What beliefs did the Separatists have concerning rules?** *(They believed that rules were important and that people needed rules to live by.)*

➤ **How were these beliefs echoed years later in the State House in Philadelphia?** *(The men at the State House felt rules were important also and that the country needed rules to live by.)*

Evaluating the Lesson

Rule-Writing Activity, Notebook page 3

➤ Look again at the rules that were in the mystery box. **Are there any other rules that you think should be added?**

➤ Read the instructions on Notebook page 3. You may want to write a rule for your home instead of a rule for your schoolroom.

➤ Complete the page. *Your child may need guidance with the rights and responsibilities that go with his rule.*

Time Line Activity

➤ *Give your child the We the People time line. Review what happened on January 25, 1787.*

➤ Read the next date. *(May 25, 1787)*

➤ **What did we study about today that began on May 25, 1787?** *(Constitutional Convention)*

➤ **Why did the leaders meet at the Constitutional Convention?** *(to start a new country; to write laws)*

➤ Write *Constitutional Convention* in the oval above the May 25 date.

Going Beyond

Enrichment

To make "parchment," give your child a square of white construction paper, a large cake pan half-filled with brewed tea, a metal cooling rack, and paper towels or old rags for wiping up drips. He should put the construction paper into the tea, let the paper soak for about an hour, and then set it on the cooling rack until it has completely dried. The dried parchment paper may be used for writing his rule or any other important documents.

Additional Teacher Information

The Mayflower Compact (1620) was the first legal document in America. A simple agreement, the compact was drawn up by the leaders and was not subject to revision by the masses. It provided the Pilgrims a way to force the non-Pilgrim adventurers to stay with the colony. No man went ashore until he had signed, including the bondmen.

The Articles of Confederation, under which the colonies were governed from 1776 to 1788, had a number of serious problems. The Articles did not give Congress the power to collect taxes or to control trade among the states. Although Congress had the power to pass laws, no provision was given to carry out those laws or to bring lawbreakers to justice. The Articles did not protect personal freedom for travelers from state to state, nor did they deal with threats from foreign nations.

Not everyone recognized the problems of the Articles of Confederation, though. Even George Washington thought that the deficiencies could be handled by a broad interpretation of the Articles. Prior to the Constitutional Convention, James Madison read hundreds of books and prepared a study of the defects in the Articles.

LESSON 3
A New Government

Text, pages 9-12
Notebook, pages 4-5

Preview

Main Ideas
- All societies have some kind of government.
- The kind of government a nation has can change.
- The United States is a republic.
- The United States government is divided into legislative, executive, and judicial branches.

Objective
- Write a letter as though from a member of the Constitutional Convention to his daughter

Materials
- A cassette player*
- *HERITAGE STUDIES Listening Cassette A**
- Maps and More 1, page M1
- We the People time line from Lesson 2
- The mystery box used in Lesson 2
- A fly swatter

> Prepare the mystery box by placing the fly swatter in it.

Notes
HERITAGE STUDIES Listening Cassette A includes songs and readings for grades 1, 2, and 3. This is the first time the cassette is used in grade 3.

Day 1

Lesson

Introducing the Lesson

Inferring Activity

➤ **What was in the mystery box in Lessons 1 and 2?** *(coins, rules)*
➤ Shake the box. **What do you think is in the box today?**
➤ Open the box.
➤ **What do you think the fly swatter might have to do with this lesson?**

Week after week the men met in the State House. Some days it was hot and big flies buzzed around. The flies bit the men on their legs and necks. Still the men came every day except Sunday to talk about how to run a country. They had many different ideas. If you had been there, what would you have said?

Finally James Madison said, "The Articles will not work any more. We must write a whole new set of laws. We must write a Constitution." The other men sighed. But they knew it was true. They would be away from home many more weeks. They stayed to do the work. They loved their country more than they loved themselves.

Charles Wilson Peale painted this miniature of James Madison in 1783.

June 15

One man said, "I think each state should have one vote in the government." Another man said, "That's not fair! Some states are big. Yours is small. Why should a small state have as much say as a big state?" The first man said, "Why shouldn't it? Shouldn't we all be treated the same?"

9

Loud voices boomed through Independence Hall. Some men called for a chance to speak. Others argued with those beside them. One man said, "States with more people need more votes. What are you small states afraid of?" Another answered, "Of you greedy big states!" Gunning Bedford of Delaware said, "The big states say they will not hurt the small states. I do not, gentlemen, trust you!"

James Madison listened to the men arguing. He hoped that his ideas for a new government would not be lost. He looked over at George Washington. If you had been in Washington's chair, what would you have done then? Washington frowned a little. The men lowered their voices. But the matter was not settled.

10

Teaching the Lesson

Text Discussion, page 9

➤ **Read the first two paragraphs on page 9 to find out why a fly swatter might have come in handy at the Constitutional Convention.** *(Big flies buzzed around and bit the men on their legs and necks.)*

To make things worse, the leaders had decided to nail shut all the windows of the meeting room and lock all the doors.

➤ **Why do you think the men would do that?**

They wanted to keep everything secret. The delegates were forbidden to talk about anything that went on during the meetings.

➤ **Read aloud what James Madison said.** *("The Articles will not work any more. We must write a whole new set of laws. We must write a Constitution.")*

➤ **Why did the men sigh after hearing what Mr. Madison said?** *(They knew that doing what he had said would take a long time.)*

➤ **Why did the men decide to stay and do the work?** *(They loved their country more than they loved themselves.)*

The men at the convention exercised the character traits of faithfulness and determination to finish the job. These are the traits God wants us to exercise also. (BATs: 2c Faithfulness, 2d Goal setting)

George Washington and James Madison were both delegates from Virginia. Madison had come to the convention well prepared. He had read hundreds of books and had written a paper about the faults of the Articles of Confederation. Madison must really have liked to write because every day he sat near Washington at the front of the meeting room and wrote down everything that anyone did, said, or read.

➤ **Why was it important to the history of the United States that Madison was writing down all that happened at the convention?** *(We would have no way of knowing what happened at the secret meetings if Madison had not recorded everything.)*

Text Discussion, pages 9-10 and Maps and More 1

➤ **Read the last paragraph on page 9 and all of page 10 to find out what the men were arguing about on June 15.** *(how many votes each state should have)*

July 2

This day was bright and hot. Some men who came into the hall did not smile. Some of the other men sat in their seats without talking. They had all agreed that the new government should have three *branches*, or parts. One branch would make laws; one branch would see that the laws were followed; one branch would deal with those who did not obey the laws.

The branch that would make the laws had two groups. One was called the *House of Representatives*. The other was called the *Senate*. But the big states and the small states still could not agree about how many votes each state should get in lawmaking. Time seemed to be running out.

* Suggests legislation
* Calls special sessions
* Vetoes bills
* Impeaches and removes officials, including the president
* Approves or rejects treaties and presidential appointees
* Overrides vetoes

President

* Rules on constitutionality of executive actions
* Appoints judges
* Grants pardons
* Interprets treaties

Supreme Court

* Determines constitutionality of laws
* Interprets laws and treaties
* Regulates types of appeals
* Impeaches judges
* Determines the number of Supreme Court judges

Congress

* Establishes lower federal courts

11

The House of Burgesses

Having two houses in the part of the government that makes laws was not a new idea. In 1619, one year before the Mayflower Compact, Jamestown in the Virginia colony had just such a plan.

The first legislature formed in the New World was in Jamestown.

Jamestown had eleven *boroughs*, or areas. Each borough had two men in the government. The men were called burgesses. The government was called the House of Burgesses. The House of Burgesses had two parts.

Voters elected burgesses to make laws. Who do you think could vote? Only men over sixteen could vote. Can you tell what "echoes" from Jamestown reached Philadelphia in 1787?

12

➤ Gunning Bedford was a delegate from Delaware. **Do you think Delaware was a small state or a large state?**

➤ Look at Maps and More 1 to see if you were right. Find Delaware, the small state that Mr. Bedford represented.

Day 2

Text Discussion, page 11

➤ **Read page 11 to find out why the delegates were not smiling or talking on July 2, 1787.** *(They still could not agree on the number of votes each state should have in lawmaking.)*

➤ **What had the delegates agreed on?** *(that the new government should have three parts)*

➤ Look at the diagram on the bottom of the page.

The three parts of the government are called **branches.** The **legislative branch** makes the laws. The legislative branch is represented by Congress. The part that sees that the laws are followed is the **executive branch.** The president is the executive branch of our government. The third part is the **judicial branch** or the Supreme Court. It deals with those who do not obey laws.

➤ **Which branch was causing all the disagreement among the delegates?** *(the legislative branch or the branch that would make the laws)*

➤ The delegates had agreed that the legislative branch, or Congress, would have two groups. **What were the two groups called?** *(the **House of Representatives** and the **Senate**)*

Text Discussion, page 12

➤ **Read page 12 to find out what the government was called in Jamestown. *(House of Burgesses)***

➤ **What were the different areas in Jamestown called? *(boroughs)***

➤ **Which part of the American government plan echoed or was like Jamestown's House of Burgesses?** *(the legislative branch, because both had two houses)*

Singing Activity, Notebook page 4

 Some of the words to "America the Beautiful" are discussed in this activity. Your child may experience difficulty with other terms or concepts as well. Give help as needed.

➤ Follow the words to "America the Beautiful" on Notebook page 4 as you listen to the song on the cassette.

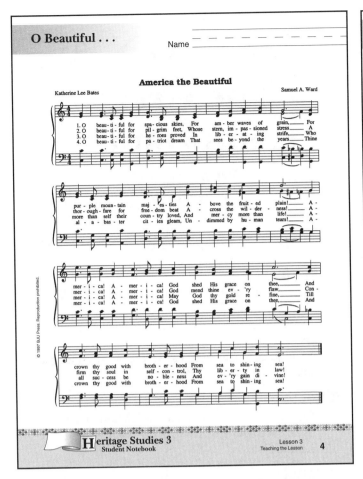

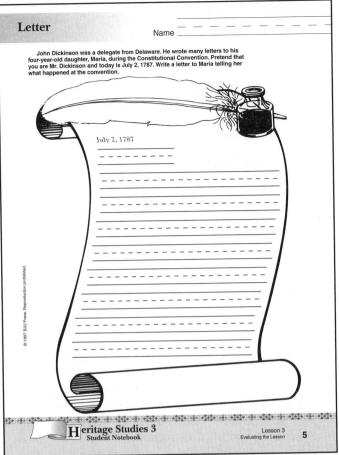

Letter   Name

John Dickinson was a delegate from Delaware. He wrote many letters to his four-year-old daughter, Maria, during the Constitutional Convention. Pretend that you are Mr. Dickinson and today is July 2, 1787. Write a letter to Maria telling her what happened at the convention.

July 2, 1787

➤ **Read the first two lines in stanza 3.**

Liberating strife means "a conflict or fight that makes people free."

➤ **Do you think that the phrase "Who more than self their country loved" could apply to the men at the Constitutional Convention?**

A person does not always need to risk his life in battle to be a hero. Being a hero sometimes means doing the right thing, even at personal loss.

➤ **Read the first two lines of stanza 4.**

Alabaster cities are cities whose buildings are made of light, smooth stone.

➤ Katherine Bates was the poet who wrote the words to this song. **What does she want God to do for America?** *(Answers will vary but may include shed His grace on the country, mend the flaws of the country, and make it a good land with people that love each other.)*

➤ **Which stanza or verse might help you to draw a picture of America?** *(stanza 1)*

The poet describes America's wide skies; light brownish yellow fields of grain; tall, purple mountains; plains where crops are growing; and a bright sea on each side of the country.

➤ Let's sing the song with the recording.

Evaluating the Lesson

Creative-Writing Activity, Notebook page 5

➤ Read the directions.
➤ Complete the letter.

Time Line Activity

➤ *Give your child the We the People time line. Review the January 25 and May 25 dates.*
➤ Read the next date. *(July 2, 1787)*
➤ **What agreement about the new government did the delegates reach on July 2, 1787?** *(There would be three branches.)*
➤ **What were the three branches called?** *(legislative, executive, and judicial)*
➤ Write *Three Branches in Government* in the oval above the July 2 date.

Going Beyond

Enrichment

Make other patriotic songs available for your child. (*NOTE: HERITAGE STUDIES Listening Cassette A* includes several patriotic songs. If you wish, you may order the cassettes *Songs of Our Heritage* and *For God and Country* from Bob Jones University Press.)

Additional Teacher Information

To guarantee secrecy during the Constitutional Convention, delegates took an oath not to speak, publish, or print anything spoken during the meetings. As a further measure, the windows of the State House were nailed shut, and guards stood at the doors. Talkative Benjamin Franklin was assigned delegates to prevent him from revealing anything that he had observed. James Madison asserted later that the Constitution would never have been framed had the convention not held its sessions in private. What we know today about the happenings inside the State House is due largely to Madison's diary, in which he wrote every day and polished every night.

Gunning Bedford, a champion of the small states at the Constitutional Convention, followed Delaware's instructions to insist on one vote for each state in the national legislature. Frustrated by the arguments of the large states, Bedford even suggested that the small states call on a European king to unite America by force.

The eventual compromise to give all states an equal vote in the Senate was due in part to Bedford's presence on the committee that drafted it. He subsequently signed the Constitution and supported it in Delaware, making the state the first to ratify it.

LESSON 4
The Great Compromise

Text, pages 13-15
Notebook, page 6

Preview

Main Ideas
- A compromise involves both sides giving up things that they want.
- Disagreements can sometimes be settled by compromise.
- Significant documents have influenced American history.

Objective
- Complete a crossword puzzle by defining terms associated with the writing of the Constitution of the United States

Materials
- A Bible
- 2 envelopes, one marked with a *1* and the other with a *2*
- We the People time line from Lesson 3
- Maps and More 1, page M1
- The mystery box used in Lesson 3
- Appendix, pages A3-A4: cards with state maps*

 Some reproducible pages in the Appendix have gray shaded areas, such as the states labeled on these cards. These areas do not always copy. Shade these areas an appropriate color, using a crayon or colored pencil. Cut apart the cards. Put the state cards from each page into separate envelopes. Place the envelopes in the mystery box.

Day 1

Lesson

Introducing the Lesson

Inferring Activity

➤ Open the mystery box.
➤ **What do you think are in the envelopes?**

July 5

Men from the big states glared at the men from the small states. Then a man got up and offered a *compromise*. A *compromise* is an agreement that is not exactly what either side wants but is good enough for both sides to like. What do you think he suggested?

The man said that in the House of Representatives votes would be given according to how many people lived in each state. Would this idea please the small states or the big states? Then he said that each state should have an equal number of votes in the Senate. Which states would this please?

Have you ever had to work out an agreement with a friend? If you have, you probably made a compromise. Compromises are sometimes good. They are bad only if something in the agreement goes against what you know to be right. Would you say the compromise about the votes was good or bad?

These girls compromised to make the big sign they will use for their bake sale.

13

July 16

The *Great Compromise* was up for a vote. One man asked how anyone would know how many people lived in a state. Why would that be important? Another said that every ten years the government would count the people, or *take a census*. Has your family ever filled out a census form? It asks how many people live in your house.

Nine states were ready to vote. Five states said yes. Four states said no. The compromise passed by one vote. The men could now write the laws.

The laws are called the *Constitution*. We call the meetings of 1787 the *Constitutional Convention*. What might have happened if the vote had gone the other way?

A copy of the Constitution

14

➤ Open one of the envelopes and arrange the contents in a group on the table. Open the second envelope and put the contents in a different group on the table. Read the names of the shaded states in each group.

➤ **How are the two groups of shaded states alike and how are they different?** *(Answers will vary.)*

Lead your child to conclude that the states in both groups were included in the thirteen original states and that all these states were represented at the Constitutional Convention. He should also notice that one group has four states and that the other has five. It may be helpful to allow your child to compare the two groups of states to Maps and More 1.

Teaching the Lesson

Text Discussion, page 13

➤ **Read page 13 to find out what the people came up with when they could not agree.** *(a compromise)*

➤ **What is a *compromise*?** *(an agreement that is not exactly what either side wants but is good enough for both sides to accept)*

In a compromise each side has to give up something. Sometimes a compromise lets everyone do what he wants but for a shorter time than he originally wanted to do it. Sometimes each side gives up less important points in order to gain larger goals each has in common.

➤ **Describe the compromise that the delegates reached.** *(In the House of Representatives, states would receive votes according to the number of people who lived in that state; and in the Senate, each state would get an equal number of votes—two.)*

➤ **Which states were pleased about the number of votes that states would have in the House of Representatives under the compromise?** *(the large states)*

➤ **Which states were pleased by the two votes that each state would have in the Senate?** *(the small states)*

➤ **Do you think the compromise about the number of votes per state was good or bad?** It did not go against anything known to be right.

➤ Give an example of a time that you made a compromise to work out an agreement.

Text Discussion, page 14

➤ **Read page 14 to find out what happened on July 16.** *(The delegates voted to accept the compromise.)*

➤ **What was the *Great Compromise*?** *(In the House of Representatives, each state would receive the number of votes according to how many people lived* *in the state [population]. In the Senate each state would receive the same number of votes.)*

➤ **What is a *census*?** *(a counting of the people)*

➤ *Write the word* **enumerator.** *An* **enumerator** *is the name given to a person who counts people.*

➤ **Why would counting the people be important?** *(to help the government know how many people live in each state; to find out how many votes each state would get in the House of Representatives)*

Each state would get one vote in the House of Representatives for every forty thousand people who lived in that state.

➤ Look at the two groups of states that were in the mystery box. **What do you think these states represent?**

One group is the states that voted for the compromise; the other is the states that voted against it.

➤ **Which group of states voted yes?** *(the group of five states)*

➤ **Do you notice anything about the size of the states that voted no?** *(They are all big states.)*

➤ **What would have happened if North Carolina had voted with the other large states?** *(The compromise would not have passed.)*

➤ *Write the word* majority.

This word means "the greater number or part of something." The five states that voted yes were the *majority* because five is the greater part of the total number of states voting: nine.

➤ After the Great Compromise passed, the delegates could begin writing the laws. **What do we call the laws they wrote?** *(the **Constitution**)*

Map Activity, Maps and More 1

➤ Use the key on Maps and More 1 to find the states that attended the convention.

➤ Compare the two groups of states that voted on the Great Compromise to these states.

➤ **Which states were present at the convention but did not vote on the compromise?** *(New York, New Hampshire, Massachusetts)*

Roger Sherman
1721-93

The man who thought up the Great Compromise was Roger Sherman. He was known for being fair and serious. Thomas Jefferson said that Sherman "never said a foolish thing in his life."

Sherman helped write the Declaration of Independence, the Articles of Confederation, and the Constitution. These are three of the most important papers in American history, and he signed them all.

"The words of a wise man's mouth are gracious."
Ecclesiastes 10:12

15

Text Discussion, page 15

➤ **Read page 15 to find out who thought of the Great Compromise.** *(Roger Sherman)*

➤ **What three papers did Roger Sherman help write and sign?** *(the Declaration of Independence, the Articles of Confederation, and the Constitution)*

➤ **What did Thomas Jefferson say about Roger Sherman?** *(He "never said a foolish thing in his life.")*

Roger Sherman was known for being fair and serious. Read Ecclesiastes 10:12-14. Ask your child why, according to these verses, a man such as Roger Sherman was so respected. *(Answers will vary.)* Lead him to see that a person who is always talking, always speaking foolishly, is not often considered wise. His opinion is not valued, and few think he is able to be a good leader. (BAT: 5d Communication)

Heritage Studies 3 Home TE

Crossword

Name _ _ _ _ _ _ _ _ _

The laws written at the Constitutional Convention are called the CONSTITUTION.
Much work went into that important paper. Some problems were solved by
COMPROMISE. Use the clues below to complete the puzzle.

ACROSS

4. Five states voted _____ on the Great Compromise.
6. The author of the Great Compromise was Roger _____.
8. the greatest number of votes
9. Four states voted _____ on the compromise.
10. Counting people is called taking a _____.

DOWN

1. The first important paper in American history is the _____ of Independence.
2. the number of states that voted on the Great Compromise
3. Another important paper in American history is the _____ of Confederation.
5. worker who counts people
6. In the _____, all states have the same number of votes.
7. States have different numbers of votes in the _____ of Representatives.

© 1997 BJU Press. Reproduction prohibited.

D	N	A	Y	E	S	
E	I	R		N		C
C	O	N	S	T	I	T	U	T	I	O	N
L	E	I		M		M
A		C		E		P
R		L		R		R
A	S	H	E	R	M	A	N		O
T	E	S		T		M	A	J	O	R	I	T	Y
I	N		N	O		I		U
O	A			R		S		S
N	T					E	C	E	N	S	U	S
	E								

Heritage Studies 3
Student Notebook

Lesson 4
Evaluating the Lesson

6

Evaluating the Lesson

Crossword Activity,
Notebook page 6

➤ The two keywords from today's lesson, *Constitution* and *compromise,* are already written in the puzzle.

➤ Read the directions and complete the puzzle.

> You may want to write the puzzle answers in random order in the white space on the Notebook page or allow your child to use his textbook as he works the puzzle.

Time Line Activity

➤ *Give your child the We the People time line. Review the January 25, May 25, and July 2 dates.*

➤ Read the next date. *(July 16, 1787)*

➤ **What happened on July 16, 1787?** *(The Great Compromise passed.)*

➤ **What did the delegates begin writing after the Great Compromise passed?** *(the laws or the Constitution)*

➤ Write *Great Compromise* in the oval above the July 16 date.

━━ **Going Beyond** ━━

Additional Teacher Information

The taking of the first United States census began in August 1790 and lasted about eighteen months. Because the fewer than four million people were so widely scattered, the enumerators had to ride on horseback to count much of the population. This first census counted the number of free persons, slaves, and free white males. It also documented the sex and color of free persons and the names and addresses of heads of families. The results of the census were published in a fifty-six-page volume.

Since 1960, self-enumeration procedures have been added to the work of the enumerators. People who participate in self-enumeration are asked to fill in small circles on special question forms. The basic population questions (age, sex, and family relationship) are asked of everyone, but a certain percentage of responders are asked additional questions about their education, income, and occupation. The information on the forms is compiled on computers, which then produce graphs and tables of statistics. With the increased population and the additional information, published census reports have grown in bulk. The results of the 1990 census, for example, filled about five hundred thousand pages.

LESSON 5
A Rising Sun

Text, pages 16-19, 272
Notebook, page 7

═══ Preview ═══

Main Ideas
- The United States government rests on the Constitution.
- The beliefs for which the American colonists fought are the basis for the freedoms protected by the Constitution.

Objective
- Recite the Preamble to the Constitution

Materials
- We the People time line from Lesson 4
- A Bible
- The mystery box used in Lesson 4
- The TimeLine Snapshots*
- The figure of the signing of the Constitution (1787) from the TimeLine Snapshots*
- Appendix, page A5: property tag*
- Appendix, page A6: the viewer*

> Place the property tag from the Appendix in the mystery box.

Notes
If you have purchased the TimeLine Snapshots, you will refer to it for the first time in this lesson. A time line is a simple way to organize the important events in history. It can easily be used to establish a sequence of events and illustrate relationships between the events pictured.

You will want to post the TimeLine before beginning this lesson. If you are teaching only third grade, post the TimeLine sections from 1775 to 1900. If you are teaching other grade levels also, be sure to include the years studied on those levels. If you do not have enough space to hang the TimeLine along your schoolroom wall, consider hanging it in the hallway or garage. You may want to hang it in levels, leaving room between the levels for the pictures. The figures will be added throughout the year. You may also choose to add pictures of your own to the TimeLine as opportunities arise.

August 25

The men had worked the whole month of August on the Constitution. They argued over how the president should be elected. They argued over how much members of the House and Senate should be paid. At last they thought the Constitution was ready. Most of the men had been in Philadelphia since May. They wanted to go home.

One man said, "What about the slaves? How can we talk of our freedom and not of theirs?" Another man said, "Slaves are property. They are not important here." The men yelled at each other. Some hated slavery; others did not see anything wrong with it.

George Mason said, "Slavery brings the judgment of heaven on a country." His voice got louder. "God will punish the United States for this sin." Many others agreed with him. But they did not want to talk about it. Why do you think that was? What do you think of Mr. Mason's words?

> *"For God shall bring every work into judgment."*
> Ecclesiastes 12:14

16

Day 1

═══ Lesson ═══

Introducing the Lesson

Inductive Activity

➤ Open the mystery box and remove the contents.
➤ **What do you think such a tag is used for?**
➤ Write your name on the tag and put it on something in the room or house that belongs to you.
➤ *Using questions such as the following, discuss with your child the relationship between a piece of property and its owner.*

- **Is there anything special you do to take care of this piece of property?**
- **Has anything ever happened to it as a result of your neglecting or forgetting about it?**
- **May you sell it to anyone you choose?**
- **If you did sell it, are there any ways you could prevent the new owner from neglecting it?**

Teaching the Lesson

Text Discussion, page 16

➤ **Read page 16 to find out what "property" the men were arguing about.** *(slaves)*

➤ **Read aloud the quotation in which slaves are called property.** *("Slaves are property. They are not important here.")*

➤ Pretend you are a slave owner. *Pose some of the questions that you have already discussed about objects as property in the Introducing the Lesson section of this lesson.*

A slave was a person who was actually owned by another person. The slave had no rights or privileges other than what his owner gave him. Even a servant (one who agreed to work for a master for a period of time without pay in return for food, clothing, and a place to live) had the promise of an end to his service.

➤ **Can you see why some of the men at the convention hated slavery so much?**

➤ **Who said, "Slavery brings the judgment of heaven on a country"?** *(George Mason)*

➤ **What did George Mason think would happen to the United States because of slavery?** *(God would punish the United States.)*

> Read Ecclesiastes 12:13-14. Point out that a Christian's main responsibility in life is to fear God and to keep His commandments. When a person does that, he will not be afraid of his works being judged by God. Discuss the Sonship-Servant Principle: As a son of God, the Christian has been "bought with a price" and is Christ's servant. (BAT: 2b Servanthood)

Text Discussion, page 17

➤ **Read the first two paragraphs on page 17 to find out what was done about the question of slavery.** *(A compromise was made.)*

➤ **What was the compromise?** *(that slaves could be brought to America for twenty more years)*

➤ **How was this compromise different from the Great Compromise?** *(Answers will vary.)*

Neither side of the Great Compromise was right or wrong, but many people considered slavery wrong.

➤ **Read the rest of page 17 to find out what happened on September 17.** *(the signing of the Constitution)*

➤ **What did three men refuse to do at the convention?** *(sign the Constitution)*

The three men—George Mason, Elbridge Gerry, and Edmund Randolph—disagreed with parts of the Constitution. Their main objection was to the lack of power that the Constitution gave the federal government.

The men made another compromise. Slaves could be brought to America for twenty more years. Some men who hated slavery voted for the compromise. Why do you think they did that?

If slavery had been stopped, some states would not have signed the new Constitution. Then the country would have had no government at all. What do you think of this compromise? How is it different from the Great Compromise?

September 17

At last the Constitution was finished. One man read it to the others in Independence Hall. Benjamin Franklin asked all  the men to sign it. Most of the men did. Mr. Mason and two others did not. Ben Franklin looked at the sun on Washington's chair. He said, "That is a rising, and not a setting sun." What did he mean?

17

➤ **What do you think Benjamin Franklin meant when he said, "That is a rising, and not a setting sun"?** He meant that the United States is a growing, not a dying, nation.

TimeLine Snapshots Activity

➤ Place the TimeLine figure, the signing of the Constitution, on the TimeLine at the year 1787.

➤ Although three men did not sign the Constitution, the *majority* of the men did sign it. The signing did not put the laws immediately into effect. The Constitution would have to be voted on by the states before it would actually go into effect.

The Constitution had a *Preamble* and seven *Articles*. A *preamble* means "words that go before." The Preamble tells why the Constitution was made. The Articles are the main laws that the nation follows.

One law says that the president of the United States must be born in the United States. How old do you think he has to be? He has to be thirty-five. Do you know someone thirty-five? Why do you think the leader is called a president? America is a *republic*, not a country ruled by a king. A *republic* is a government with a constitution.

Another law says that no state may coin money. Why do you think the Constitution says this? What would happen if every state had its own money? It would be confusing.

18

The Constitution of the United States
Preamble

We the people of the United States, in order to form a more perfect union, establish justice, insure domestic tranquility, provide for the common defense, promote the general welfare, and secure the blessings of liberty to ourselves and our posterity, do ordain and establish this Constitution for the United States of America.

Articles of the Constitution

Articles are the parts of the Constitution that describe the workings of the federal and state governments. The seven articles set forth a general plan that tells how the United States government should be organized.

Articles I through III discuss the three parts of the federal government: the legislative, the executive, and the judicial branches. Article IV outlines the relationships of the states with each other and with the federal government. Articles V and VII describe the processes of amending and ratifying the Constitution. Article VI discusses the handling of the national debt that existed prior to the writing of the Constitution. These seven articles precede the Bill of Rights.

272

Text Discussion, page 18

➤ *Write the word* preamble *and pronounce it for your child.*

➤ **Read the first paragraph on page 18 to find out what the word means.** *("words that go before")*

➤ **What does the *Preamble* to the Constitution tell?** *(why the Constitution was made)*

➤ **What are the *Articles*?** *(the nation's laws)*

➤ **Read the rest of the page to find out about two of the laws that the Constitution contains.** *(The president must be born in the United States and must be at least thirty-five years old. No state may coin money.)*

The title *president* means "the one who presides." The president presides or has the authority over the United States.

➤ **What is a *republic*?** *(a government with a constitution)*

➤ **Do you know what it means to "coin money"?** It means to make money from metal.

Text Discussion, page 272

➤ Turn to page 272. Listen as I read the Preamble of the Constitution. We will discuss the meaning of the Preamble in a moment.

➤ **Read the rest of page 272 to find out about the Articles of the Constitution.**

➤ **How many articles are there in the Constitution?** *(seven)*

You will direct attention to a Learning How activity for the first time this year. One of your purposes in teaching these sections will be to teach your child to follow the directions for gathering materials, doing the activity, and considering the results of the activity.

Learning How Activity, page 19 and Notebook page 7

➤ **Read the three steps on page 19.**

➤ *Give your child the copy of the viewer.*

➤ Cut out the viewer along the outside lines. Cut out the two rectangles on the viewer.

➤ Fold the viewer along the dotted line. Tape the viewer together along the edge opposite the fold.

To Recite the Preamble

1. Take out Notebook page 7.

2. Talk about it as your teacher leads you. Read it with your teacher. Learn the words.

3. Be ready to recite the words for your teacher.

We the People...

19

Preamble

Name _____

Follow your teacher's instructions.

We the People of the United States, in order to ...	
form a more perfect union,	build the best nation possible,
establish justice,	set up fair treatment under the law,
insure domestic tranquility,	make sure of calmness and peace for our homes and our country,
provide for the common defense,	be ready to protect our people from attack,
promote the general welfare,	encourage well-being for everyone,
and secure the blessings of liberty to ourselves and our posterity,	and guard liberty for ourselves and others,
... do ordain and establish this Constitution for the United States of America.	

Heritage Studies 3
Student Notebook

Lesson 5
Teaching the Lesson **7**

➤ Cut along the cutting lines on the Notebook page, fold the paper on the fold line, and tape the strip along the long cut edge.

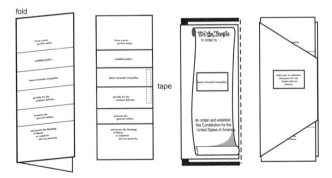

➤ *Show your child how to slide the Preamble strip that he has just made into the viewer. Point out that both sides of the strip are visible, one phrase at a time. Direct your child's attention to the Preamble as it is printed, phrase by phrase, on the front of the viewer. As you read each phrase, discuss the paraphrase or meaning in the rectangle on the back of the viewer.*

Evaluating the Lesson

Time Line Activity

➤ *Give your child the We the People time line. Review the January 25, May 25, July 2, and July 16 dates.*

➤ Read the next date. *(September 17, 1787)*

➤ **What happened on September 17, 1787?** *(signing of the Constitution)*

➤ **Did all the men sign the Constitution?** *(no, but the majority did)*

➤ **Did the signing of the Constitution automatically put the laws into effect?** *(no)*

➤ Write *Signing of Constitution* in the oval above the September 17 date.

Memorized Recitation Activity

➤ Use your Preamble viewer or text page 272 and memorize the Preamble of the Constitution.

➤ Recite the Preamble.

Going Beyond

Enrichment

If a museum or the library in your area has historical documents on display, plan a field trip for your child to view these documents.

Additional Teacher Information

The original Constitution of the United States can be seen at the National Archives building in Washington, D.C. The document is protected and preserved in a helium-filled storage case, which is lowered into a vault in the floor of the building each night and then raised for viewing in the morning. Each year, more than a million people visit the National Archives to see this important document of American history.

LESSON 6
The Bill of Rights

Text, pages 20-22, 247, 273
Notebook, page 8

Preview

Main Ideas

- The Constitution protects the rights of all citizens.
- Americans have unique freedoms.

Objectives

- Make a list of ways your child's life might be different without the Bill of Rights
- Make a poster depicting the right for which he is most thankful

Materials

- A local newspaper in the mystery box used in Lesson 5
- The presidential strip which includes the figure of George Washington (1) from the TimeLine Snapshots
- Art paper
- We the People time line from Lesson 5
- The figure of the Bill of Rights (1791) from the TimeLine Snapshots

Notes

This is the first use of the presidential figures from the TimeLine Snapshots. TimeLine figures for events should be placed above the dates; strips of presidential figures should go below the TimeLine at the specified places.

Day 1

Lesson

Introducing the Lesson

Guessing Activity

➤ **After the Constitution was written and the men at the convention had signed it, do you think the citizens of the country would need to know about the Constitution?**

➤ **How would we spread such news?** *(by radio, television, satellite, fax, letter, electronic mail, newspaper, word of mouth, etc.)*

Heritage Studies 3 Home TE

After the Convention

October 30

Newspapers printed the words of the Constitution. The men who had helped write it made speeches about it. Why do you think they did that? The people of the United States had to know what the Constitution said. They had to decide what they thought of its ideas.

Shopkeepers talked it over with customers. Trappers talked about it to farmers. People talked about it after Sunday church and on busy streets. Soon everyone in the United States had an opinion.

Some people worried. The freedom to have ideas and tell them to others was not mentioned in the Constitution. They thought it should be. James Madison and Alexander Hamilton wrote essays to help people understand that Americans' rights would be safe.

20

Votes on Ratification of the Constitution

Year	Day	State	Votes For	Votes Against
1787	Dec. 7	Delaware	Unanimous	-
	Dec. 12	Pennsylvania	46	23
	Dec. 18	New Jersey	Unanimous	-
1788	Jan. 2	Georgia	Unanimous	-
	Jan. 9	Connecticut	128	40
	Feb. 6	Massachusetts	187	168
	Apr. 26	Maryland	63	11
	May 23	South Carolina	149	73
	June 21	New Hampshire	57	47
	June 25	Virginia	89	79
	July 26	New York	30	27
1789	Nov. 21	North Carolina	195	77
1790	May 29	Rhode Island	34	32

People said there had to be a *Bill of Rights*, a list of freedoms. They said the list should be added to the Constitution. The leaders said they would add the list after the Constitution was voted on.

Nine states had to *ratify* the Constitution for it to become "the law of the land." What do you think ratify means? It means "to approve of or agree to." What state do you think ratified the Constitution first? It was Delaware.

New Hampshire was the ninth state. What was the second state? What was the last? What day and year did Rhode Island ratify the Constitution?

21

➤ Inside the mystery box is an item representing the main way the news about the Constitution was spread. **What do you think is in there?**

➤ Open the mystery box and remove the contents.

Teaching the Lesson

Text Discussion, page 20

➤ **Read page 20 to find out what the newspapers printed.** *(the words of the Constitution)*

➤ **How did the people of the United States react to the Constitution?** *(People talked about it and had opinions about it.)*

➤ **What did some of the people worry about?** *(that the freedom to have ideas and to tell them to others was not mentioned in the Constitution)*

Text Discussion, page 21

➤ **Read page 21 to find out what had to happen before the Constitution could become the law of the land.** *(Nine states had to ratify it.)*

➤ **What does *ratify* mean?** *(to approve of or agree to)*

➤ **When would the list of freedoms or *Bill of Rights* be added to the Constitution?** *(after the Constitution was voted on)*

Chart Reading Activity, page 21

➤ Look at the chart on page 21.

If your child has not already answered the questions in the text concerning the chart, have him do so before continuing with this activity.

➤ Examine the chart carefully to answer these next questions.

• **In which year did the most states ratify?** *(1788)*

• **How many more states ratified in that year than in 1787?** *(five more)*

• **How long after North Carolina did Rhode Island ratify?** *(6 months, 8 days)*

 Figuring the elapsed time to the year and/or month is sufficient. The days have also been included for those who want to be more specific.

• **How much time went by between the first state's ratification and the last state's ratification?** *(2 years, 5 months, 22 days)*

• **Do you remember which state did not send representatives to the Constitutional Convention?** *(Rhode Island)*

• **Were you surprised that Rhode Island was the last state to ratify the Constitution?**

April 30, 1789

No one doubted who would be the first president. George Washington was the best choice. He was elected and took the oath of office. He repeated the words that the Constitution says each president must say. He said, "I will protect the Constitution."

December 15, 1791

James Madison worked to add a *Bill of Rights* to the Constitution. It says that Americans have rights that cannot be taken away. Do you know what these rights are? Americans are free to worship, speak, gather in groups, and print what they want. They have the right to a fair trial. Nowhere else in the world do people have all the freedoms that Americans have. Why is it good to have these freedoms?

Because he worked on the Constitution and the Bill of Rights more than anyone else, James Madison is called the Father of the Constitution. He helped write the laws Americans live by today. We must be good citizens too. We should learn about our government and help to keep it strong.

22

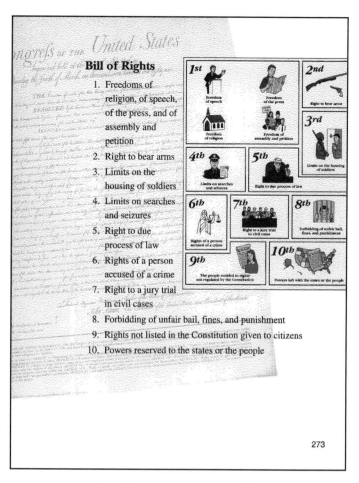

Bill of Rights

1. Freedoms of religion, of speech, of the press, and of assembly and petition
2. Right to bear arms
3. Limits on the housing of soldiers
4. Limits on searches and seizures
5. Right to due process of law
6. Rights of a person accused of a crime
7. Right to a jury trial in civil cases
8. Forbidding of unfair bail, fines, and punishment
9. Rights not listed in the Constitution given to citizens
10. Powers reserved to the states or the people

273

- **Why do you think it took so long to ratify the Constitution?** Many of the states wanted a list of rights before they agreed to the Constitution.

Day 2

Text Discussion, page 22

➤ **Read the first paragraph on page 22 to find out what happened on April 30, 1789.** *(George Washington became the first president.)*
➤ **Read aloud the words that George Washington said as he took the office of president.** *("I will protect the Constitution.")*
➤ **Why do you think every president must say those words?**

The Constitution gives the rules for the United States government. The president must "protect" the rules or be sure that the government follows those rules.

➤ **Read the last two paragraphs on page 22 to find out who worked on the Bill of Rights more than anyone else.** *(James Madison)*
➤ **What is James Madison called because of all his work?** *(the Father of the Constitution)*
➤ **Read aloud the sentences that tell what some of the rights are.** *(paragraph 2, sentences 4 and 5)*

Text Discussion, page 273

Anything added to the Constitution is called an ***amendment.*** All of the first ten amendments, which make up the Bill of Rights, were ratified in 1791.

➤ **Read the first ten amendments, or the Bill of Rights, on page 273.**
➤ Look at the First Amendment in the pictorial version of the Bill of Rights on the page. **What are the four freedoms?** *(speech, press, religion, and assembly and petition)*

The freedoms guaranteed in the First Amendment are often called ***basic freedoms.*** The First Amendment says that the government cannot pass laws that do the following: stop people from worshiping as they want, stop people from saying what they think or writing what they want, stop people from meeting in groups, or stop them from discussing problems that they have with the government.

➤ **What are some ways our lives might be different if we did not have the rights that are guaranteed in the Bill of Rights?**

You may want to mention the differences listed below. (NOTE: The parenthetical statements suggest a Christian's attitude in exercising his rights.)

Poster　　　　Name _____

Make a rough draft of a poster telling about the right you are most thankful for.

Heritage Studies 3
Student Notebook

Lesson 6
Evaluating the Lesson　　**8**

- A person might not have a choice about where his family goes to church. (A Christian should be kind to people who choose another church. [BAT: 5a Love])
- A person might not be able to say that he disagrees with something that the president does. (A Christian should be respectful of the president's position as the elected leader of the United States. [BAT: 2a Authority])
- A person might not be able to write a letter to the editor of his newspaper to say that a law is unfair. (A Christian should explain why he thinks the law is unfair and consider the opinions of others. [BATs: 5d Communication, 6c Spirit-filled])
- A person might have to let someone into his house to search for something that a family member has been accused of taking. (A Christian should be gracious in refusing. [BAT: 3c Emotional control])

TimeLine Snapshots Activity,
page 247

➤ Add the presidential strip with the figure of George Washington below the TimeLine at the year 1789.
➤ **Read the information about George Washington on page 247.**
➤ Add the Bill of Rights figure to the TimeLine at the year 1791.

Evaluating the Lesson
Poster-Making Activity,
Notebook page 8

➤ **Which of the rights in the Bill of Rights are you most thankful for?**
➤ Read the directions on Notebook page 8.
➤ Make a final draft of your poster on art paper.

Time Line Activity

➤ *Give your child the We the People time line. Review the January 25, May 25, July 2, July 16, and September 17 dates.*
➤ Read the next date. *(April 30, 1789)*
➤ **What happened on April 30, 1789?** *(George Washington became president.)*
➤ **What words did George Washington repeat that the Constitution says each president must say?** *("I will protect the Constitution.")*
➤ Write *George Washington Became President* in the oval above the April 30 date.

▬▬ Going Beyond ▬▬

Additional Teacher Information

The Second Amendment protected the members of the state militias from having their guns taken away by the federal government. The Third Amendment protects homeowners from being forced to let soldiers stay in their homes. The Fourth Amendment protects people's privacy and their belongings in their homes. The government cannot search a home or take anything from it without a written order from a court. The order must state who and what is to be searched and tell why.

The Fifth through Eighth Amendments give rights for people accused of crimes. The fifth gives an accused person the right to a fair trial, says that no one can be tried twice for the same crime, and protects a person from having to testify against himself. The sixth gives an accused person the right to a quick and fair trial and guarantees that the government will provide a lawyer for any accused person who cannot afford to hire his own lawyer. The seventh guarantees that when one person sues another person, the trial will be held in front of a jury. The eighth says that courts must treat accused people fairly.

The Ninth Amendment gives to the people any right that is not listed in the Constitution, and the Tenth Amendment gives to the states and to the people any rights that the Constitution does not give to the federal government.

The Fires of Freedom

This chapter helps to give your child a greater understanding of world history during the late 1700s. America's constitutional government is contrasted with the weak French government and the upheaval that eventually led to revolution. Your child will learn about such key figures as Marie Antoinette, Louis XVI, Lafayette, and Napoleon.

Materials

The following materials must be obtained or prepared before the presentation of the lesson. These items are labeled with an asterisk (*) in each lesson and in the Materials List in the Supplement. For further information see the individual lessons.

- Play money (Lesson 7)
- A paper crown (Lesson 7)
- A loaf of French bread (Lesson 7)
- A globe (Lesson 7)
- Appendix, pages A7-A8 (Lesson 7)
- A cardboard box (Lesson 8)
- 8 Pringles cans or paper tubes (Lesson 8)
- Brown paper (Lesson 8)
- A wall map of the United States (optional) (Lesson 9)
- A red hat or scarf (Lesson 10)
- Red ribbon (Lesson 10)
- A set of encyclopedias or an atlas (Lesson 10)
- A wall map of Europe or an atlas (Lesson 11)

LESSON 7
The Poor and the Powerful

Text, pages 24-29, 247
Notebook, page 9

Preview

Main Ideas
- All societies have some kind of government.
- When people are dissatisfied with their government, they respond in different ways.
- The king and queen of France lived in luxury while the common people were poor and hungry.

Objective
- Identify true statements about France in the 1700s

Materials
- Play money*
- A paper crown*
- A loaf of French bread*
- A Bible
- A globe*
- Maps and More 4 and 5, page M3
- Appendix, page A7: map of France*
- Appendix, page A8: peasant*

Notes
You may want to place the map of France on the wall beneath the date 1789. Collect pictures that illustrate the time period and display them as a collage around and on the map of France. You may look for pictures which include King Louis XVI, Marie Antoinette, French perfume, the Eiffel Tower, the Arc de Triomphe, Napoleon, the Bastille, French songs, or French books.

> Student text page 26 is used in the Introducing the Lesson section for reference to the picture only. It will be read later in the lesson.

Lesson

Introducing the Lesson

Contrast Marie Antoinette and a Peasant, page 26

➤ Study the picture of Marie Antoinette on page 26.
➤ *Give your child the peasant picture. Study the picture of the **peasant**. This is what poor people were called in France in 1789.*

> *The following questions will help your child compare and contrast the pictures of the two people.*

➤ **Do you think these people lived in the same country?** *(Answers will vary. The correct answer is yes. Both are from France.)*
➤ **Which person looks rich?** *(the one pictured in the textbook)*
➤ **What makes this person look rich?** *(fancy dress, elegant hairstyle, etc.)*
➤ **Where do you think the rich person lived?** She lived in a palace.
➤ **Do you think that the rich person is happy?**
➤ **What do you think the rich person wants most?** *(Possible answers include power, fame, a new dress, a bigger house, or enjoyment.)*
➤ **What makes the other person look poor?** *(ragged, simple clothing)*
➤ **Where do you think the peasant lived?**
➤ **Do you think that the peasant is happy?**
➤ **What do you think the peasant wants most?** *(Answers will vary; probably something to eat)*

What the peasant wanted most was bread. Many peasants lived in France at that time. The peasants needed bread in order to survive. It was difficult for the peasants to get bread. They did not have enough money to buy bread or the ingredients to make bread.

➤ **Do you think the rich lady had trouble getting bread?**

The rich lady, Marie Antoinette, was queen of France at that time. She did not have trouble getting bread or anything else she wanted.

> The following activity is designed for involvement with several family members or a small group. If you are working with just one child, you will want to adapt this section. You may choose just to discuss the plight of the poor in France.

Buy-the-Bread Activity

Assign roles and provide the props for the various characters. You will need a baker with a loaf of French bread. You will need a king or queen wearing a crown. Designate an amount of money, such as twenty dollars, to represent a full day's wages. Choose one or more citizens (common workers) and give them a small amount of money. Be certain that no one receives a full day's wages. Choose one or two peasants who have no money at all.

➤ **How much do you think a loaf of bread cost in France in 1789?** One loaf of bread cost as much as a full day's wages.

➤ If you have money, count your money.

➤ **Who has enough money to buy the bread?** *(Nobody does.)*

➤ *Ask the "peasants" how they might get the bread. (Possible answers are trading something for the bread, working to earn the bread, or stealing.)*

➤ **Since everyone must eat, is there a way that one of the citizens can purchase the loaf of bread?** *Tell the citizens to talk among themselves and find a way to solve the problem. (Answers will vary but should include some form of bargaining or trading to put their funds together.)* When a solution has been found, the citizen should take his money to the baker to buy the loaf of bread.

As this is going on, explain to the king what he is to do. Just as the citizen goes to buy the bread, the king should stride up, take the bread, and proclaim loudly, "I am the king. I want the bread, so it shall be mine."

➤ *Conduct a brief discussion of what was just depicted and what their opinions are about the situation.* This lesson gives more information about these kinds of events in France in 1789.

Read I Timothy 6:10 aloud, reminding your child that it is the love of money that makes people selfish. Point out that many wealthy people are kind and generous.

➤ *Slice the loaf of bread and give your child a piece to eat.*

Day 2

Teaching the Lesson

Text Discussion, pages 24 and 247

➤ **What famous American is shown in the picture on page 24?** *(George Washington)*

➤ **Read the first paragraph to find out how the Americans felt about their first president.** *(They were happy with him.)*

➤ **Did they seem to think their new government was a good and fair one?** *(yes)*

George Washington stood on the balcony of a building in New York City. The people in the streets cheered their new president. He waved back to them. The bells rang out, and guns on ships burst forth with a salute. Americans felt happy. They had a good Constitution. They had a good president. They had a good future.

Across the ocean in France, things were different. It was night in the capital city, Paris. A farmer stumbled through the gates. He was starving and barefoot. "Bread?" he said to a man passing by. "Ha!" said the man. "Where would I get any bread? Only the rich can eat." The farmer dropped to his knees and cried.

24

➤ Look at the box with the picture of George Washington on page 247.

The number in the green square tells which president he was. George Washington is best known for being the first president of the United States.

➤ **Read the dates below the square to find the year that George Washington became president of the United States.** *(1789)*

In 1789, at the time of Washington's inauguration, the people of France were having many problems with their government. We will learn about some of their troubles in our lesson today.

➤ Look at the map of France on the wall. Notice the shape of this country.

➤ **Can you find France on the globe?** It is located in Europe, across the ocean from New York where George Washington was greeting the people.

➤ **Read the rest of page 24 to find out what one big problem in France was.** *(People were starving and begging for food.)*

➤ **What city is the capital of France?** *(Paris)*

➤ Point to Paris on our map of France.

A shopkeeper sat up late in his house. "You can't get married," he said to his daughter. "I have no money to pay the marriage tax. I can't even pay the tax on this salt." He shoved a small dish away. Suddenly he stood up and his stool fell back on the floor. His face got red. "The king has taxed away all the money I ever had!"

The king was Louis XVI. His grandfather, Louis XV, had been the last king. Louis XV spent more money than he had. How do you think he got more money? He made new taxes for the working people to pay. What do you think he did with the money? He bought things for himself and sent soldiers to fight for land in the New World. How do you think the French people felt?

Louis XVI knew the people had not liked his grandfather. Do you think he tried to be a better king? Someone told him, "The people are unhappy." Louis XVI said, "I'm sorry. Really. Bring me my horse in the morning. I want to go hunting."

Louis XVI

25

Marie Antoinette

Queen Marie Antoinette looked at herself in a long mirror. Her dress had gold threads in it. It shimmered in the light. She wanted always to live in the beautiful palace and wear pretty clothes. "You are still beautiful," her maid told her. Marie Antoinette smiled.

In the streets of Paris a baby cried. The mother had no food and no money to buy any. Nearby a group of men talked about the Americans. "They have their own government. They do not pay taxes to a king! We should do as they did." "Shush!" said another. "We'll be thrown in jail!"

The men glanced toward the jail. It was called the *Bastille*. Everyone had heard of the terrible things that happened to people in there. Anyone who spoke against the king might be put in a dungeon with rats and spiders—or worse.

26

Text Discussion, page 25

➤ **Read page 25 to find the name of the rich ruler in France.** *(King Louis XVI)*

➤ **Read aloud the sentences on page 25 that tell what King Louis XVI's grandfather, Louis XV, did with his riches.** *("Louis XV spent more money than he had." "He bought things for himself and sent soldiers to fight for land in the New World.")*

➤ **Do you think that King Louis XVI spent his riches more wisely and was a better king?**

➤ **What did King Louis XVI do when he was told that the people of France were unhappy?** *(He said he was sorry, but he went hunting.)*

The king's reaction shows us something about King Louis XVI. He did not know what to do about the problems of France, or else he did not want to deal with these situations.

➤ **Do you think Louis XVI was a good ruler?**

During the reign of Louis XVI, France suffered from severe storms and blights that damaged crops for many years (1770, 1774, 1778, 1782, 1784, 1786). The population of France continued to increase steadily, but the years of crop damage left little for the people to eat. King Louis XVI was not a bad ruler, but he was not a strong, effective ruler

either. However, it is doubtful that any ruler could have solved the problems of France at this time.

God is the best authority for people's lives. As the ruler of a Christian's life, God guides and provides for the Christian wisely, fairly, and honestly. (BATs: 2a Authority, 7b Exaltation of Christ; Bible Promises: D. Identified in Christ, H. God as Father, I. God as Master)

Text Discussion, page 26 and Maps and More 4

➤ **Read the first paragraph to find out what was important to Marie Antoinette.** *(looking beautiful and living in the palace)*

➤ **Does this queen of France seem concerned about the poor, hungry, unhappy people?** *(probably not)*

Marie Antoinette was the queen of France because she was married to King Louis XVI. She loved being queen because it brought her riches and importance. She did not think about how she might use her position to help others in need.

➤ *Write the name **Bastille** on a sheet of paper and pronounce it.* **Read the rest of page 26 to find out what the Bastille was.** *(the jail or prison)*

In another town, workers stormed into a factory. They were angry that they did not make enough money. They broke down the doors and tore down walls. Then they burned the factory. Do you think that any of these actions helped them?

The king's soldiers rushed to the town. The people ran into the houses. They threw stones and flowerpots at the soldiers. They tore tiles off roofs and threw those. The soldiers fired their guns. Many people died. At last the fighting stopped.

A week after George Washington had become president of the United States, the French king made a decision. Louis XVI said, "I will meet with the leaders of the French government." What do you think he wanted to talk about?

27

There were three parts to the French government. There were the church leaders, the rich people, and the people who had to work, like shopkeepers, farmers, and servants. Which group do you think wanted the taxes to be lower? Which group do you think wanted bread to be cheaper?

The leaders of the three parts of the government went to see the king. The king came out of the palace to talk. The churchmen wanted the taxes to stay high. Why do you think that was? Churchmen did not pay taxes. Some of the money from taxes went to the Roman Catholic Church.

The rich people wanted the taxes to stay high. The rich people also got some of the tax money paid by the townspeople. The rich used the money to buy more things for themselves.

What do you think the common people wanted to do about taxes? What do you think King Louis wanted to do? The meeting went on for weeks. Why do you think it took so long? The shopkeepers and the cloth makers and others said, "We speak for more people than the other two groups. We should have more votes in the government. And the king should not have so much power."

28

➤ **Why did the men talking in the street think they might be thrown into jail?** *(for talking against their government)*

➤ Look at Maps and More 4. Describe what the Bastille was like or what you imagine prisoners might suffer there.

➤ **Do you think the French people were afraid of the Bastille?**

Text Discussion, page 27

➤ **Read page 27 to find out some ways that the French citizens showed their anger at the government.** *(They destroyed things, burned buildings, fought with the soldiers, and refused to obey the laws.)*

➤ **Were these methods the right way to let the king know they wanted change?** *(no)*

➤ **What did King Louis XVI decide he would do?** *(meet with the government leaders)*

Text Discussion, pages 28-29 and Maps and More 5

➤ **Read page 28 to find the three parts of the French government.** *(There were the church leaders, the rich people, and the common workers.)*

➤ Look at Maps and More 5 to determine which part of the French government each of these symbols represents. *(the cross—the church leaders;*

the jewels [necklace]—the rich people; the hoe—the common people)

The peasants were in a group below all of these and were not part of the government at all. Their greatest physical need was bread to eat.

➤ Identify the symbol or group that represents the correct part of the French government for each of the following questions.

- **Which group wanted the taxes to be lower?** *(the common people [hoe])*

- **Which group wanted bread to be cheaper?** *(the common people [hoe])*

- **Which group did not pay taxes?** *(the church leaders [cross])*

- **Which groups wanted the taxes to stay high?** *(the church leaders and the rich people [cross and jewels])*

- **Which groups got some of the tax money for themselves?** *(the church leaders and the rich people [cross and jewels])*

- **Which group bought more things for themselves with the tax money?** *(the rich people [jewels])*

King Louis listened to all the groups for many weeks. Finally he made his decision.

Then the king said, "I will not change things the way the workers want. I am the king. Go away and come back tomorrow." The rich people left. The churchmen left. The townspeople did not move. The soldiers in the back held up guns with bayonets on them. But the shopkeepers and farmers and others did not leave.

The leader of the townspeople said, "We take no orders." Someone told the king, "The poor people are not leaving as you told them to." "Well," said Louis, "then they can stay." What do you think of the king's answer? What do you think the people thought of it? They thought that now they were more powerful than the king.

29

Read the following statements. Color brown each loaf of bread that has a true statement.

1. Anyone who spoke against the king could be put in the Bastille.

2. When Louis XVI ruled France, George Washington was president of the United States.

3. The French peasants cried out for bread to eat.

4. The French workers fought for changes in the government.

5. King Louis XVI was a strong, wise ruler.

6. All French people had to pay taxes.

7. The French government included the church leaders, rich people, and the workers.

8. The Bastille was a French jail.

9. Marie Antoinette was queen of France.

10. Louis XV was the father of King Louis XVI.

11. All of the tax money went to the king.

12. George Washington gave King Louis XVI advice.

13. Marie Antoinette helped the peasants get bread.

14. Paris is the capital of France.

15. The Catholic Church leaders did not pay taxes.

© 1997 BJU Press. Reproduction prohibited.

Heritage Studies 3
Student Notebook

Lesson 7
Evaluating the Lesson   9

➤ **Read page 29 to find out about the king's decision and his order.** *(He would not change anything; everyone was to go home.)*
➤ **Which group did not leave when the king gave the order?** *(the common people [hoe])*
➤ **Which group thought that it had become more powerful than the king?** *(the common people [hoe])*

Evaluating the Lesson

Notebook Activity, page 9

➤ Read the directions on Notebook page 9.
➤ Complete the page.

——— Going Beyond ———

Enrichment

Encourage your child to make a map of France. Have available an outline map of France for your child to trace. Direct him to trace the outline on another sheet of paper. Tell him to place a star on his map to show the location of Paris. Tell him to write the name *Paris* at this point and to label at least one other city on the map.

Additional Teacher Information

The name *Louis* was the name of many French kings. *Louis* means "famous warrior," a characteristic of many early French kings but not of Louis XVI. Louis-Auguste was born in 1754, surviving both his father and his uncle to become next in line to rule France. Louis XVI succeeded his grandfather, Louis XV, who had become king of France at five years old and ruled France for fifty-nine years (1715-74).

Louis XVI came to the throne at age twenty. During his reign, the common people and the members of the middle class as well as the nobility were discontent, all for different reasons. The French government was bankrupt, and Louis XVI was too weak as a ruler to remedy the situation. Louis XVI seemed more interested in hunting than in public affairs. He often relied on his wife's advice. Tried for treason, Louis XVI died by guillotine on January 21, 1793.

Marie Antonia was born November 2, 1755, to Emperor Joseph and Empress Maria Theresa of Austria. When Marie Antonia was just a child, her mother began the work to unite her young daughter with the young dauphin, soon to become Louis XVI. At age fifteen, Marie Antonia renounced all claims to the Austrian throne, changed her name to Marie Antoinette, and was married to the French dauphin. Just four years after the marriage, the old king of France died, making Louis XVI and Marie Antoinette the new king and queen of France. Marie Antoinette was known for her excesses, frivolity, and love of parties. The people of France grew angry and resentful of her and her extravagances; they were in want of food to eat while she was discarding a new ball gown to gain an even grander gown. Suspicious of her, the people called her "the Austrian." (*NOTE:* Marie Antoinette was also from the Hapsburg family, who were ancient enemies of France.) She came to be blamed for all the troubles of France and gained the name "Madame Deficit." At age thirty-seven, Marie Antoinette was beheaded.

LESSON 8
Storming the Bastille

Text, pages 31-33

━━━ Preview ━━━

Main Ideas
- People everywhere want freedom.
- The people of Paris wanted to destroy the Bastille, a symbol of the king's power over them.
- When people are dissatisfied with their government, they respond in different ways.

Objectives
- Assist in building a model of the Bastille
- Answer questions about storming the Bastille

Materials
- A medium-sized cardboard box*
- 8 Pringles cans*
- Enough brown paper to cover the box and each can*
- Masking tape
- Maps and More 4, page M3

The box and Pringles cans will be used to build a model of the Bastille. You may prefer to substitute paper tubes from toilet tissue or paper towels for the Pringles cans. You will want to adjust the size of the box accordingly.

Day 1

━━━ Lesson ━━━

Introducing the Lesson

Model-Building Activity, Maps and More 4

➤ We are going to build a model of the famous French fortress shown on Maps and More 4. **Do you remember the name of the building?** (*the Bastille*)
➤ **What was it used for?** (*a prison*)
➤ Gather the cardboard box, Pringles cans, brown paper, and tape.
➤ Cut the brown paper to cover the box and each of the Pringles cans.
➤ Tape the towers to the two opposite sides of the box.

In some towns, poor people were hungry. Sometimes they robbed the bakers and the millers. If the people thought someone was storing food or grain in his house, they would break in to get it. What do you think of these actions? It is wrong to steal, no matter how good the reasons may seem.

The streets of Paris were always full of people. If a cart turned over, hungry people rushed to grab up any food that fell out. Men whispered together in shops. "The Americans do not live like this. I fought in their war. Now they are free." Another man said, "Be careful. Do you want to live in the Bastille?"

The people of Paris did not like the Bastille. It stood for the power that the king had over them. Big cannons loomed out from it. Soldiers guarded it. The people thought that anybody who could not pay taxes was held there.

31

A man got up on some steps. He said, "Why should we fear the Bastille? Let's go there and make the governor take the cannons down!" The crowd cheered. "Let's go!" they said. And they went, hundreds and hundreds of people.

"Take down the cannons!" they said. "Give us guns!" The governor peeked out at the mob. He ordered his men to take down the cannons and to board up the openings. Still the people were not happy. "Let us in!" they said. "Give us guns!" "No," said the governor.

What do you think the people did then? Do you think they went home? They smashed their way into the Bastille. They wanted to free all the prisoners. How many prisoners do you think there were? There were only seven. Then the mob killed the governor.

Unknown 18th-century French artist, Taking of the Bastille, July 14, 1789, Arrest of the Governor, Monsieur de Launay, ©PHOTO Réunion des Musées Nationaux

32

➤ Place your model of the Bastille where you can view it throughout this chapter. In this lesson you will learn more about this building and its importance in French history.

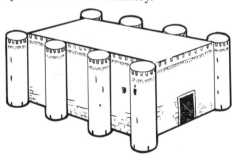

Student text page 30 will be read and discussed at the end of Lesson 9.

Teaching the Lesson

Text Discussion, page 31

➤ **Read page 31 to find out what the people thought of the Bastille.** (*They did not like it. It stood for the power that the king had over them. It held the people who could not pay their taxes.*)

➤ **Read aloud the second paragraph.**

➤ **Why do you think the man said "Be careful. Do you want to live in the Bastille?"**

The people were saying things that showed how unhappy they were with their lives. They actually criticized their own government. They could be put into the Bastille for that.

We are to respect and honor those in authority over us. We are to obey the laws of the land. (BAT: 2a Authority)

➤ **What did some poor, hungry people do to get food?** (*They stole it.*) **Was this right?** (*No, stealing is sin.*)

➤ **Could these people have been put into the Bastille for stealing food?** (*yes*)

The people were desperate and starving, so they did whatever was necessary to get food. No matter what the reasons or circumstances, it is never right to do wrong. (BATs: 4b Purity, 4c Honesty)

Day 2

Text Discussion, page 32

We have read about the meeting that the king had with the people. The king did not want to change anything, so he sent the people home. The rich people and the church leaders went home. The angry common people did not leave. Since the king did not make them go, they thought that they had gained power.

➤ **Read page 32 to find out what the crowds of angry people did**. *(They smashed into the Bastille, freed the prisoners, and killed the governor.)*

➤ **How many prisoners were freed from the Bastille?** *(seven)*

The mob's destruction of the prison is referred to as the "storming of the Bastille."

➤ **Read aloud this page, using expression to show how the people really felt.**

> If you are teaching several children, you can involve all of them in this reading. Assign parts for a narrator, spokesman, governor, prisoners, and crowd. You may even encourage them to act out their parts.

➤ **How do you think the people in the crowd might have felt?** *(Possible answers are excited, angry, and determined.)*

➤ **How do you think the prisoners would have felt?** *(Possible answers are relieved or maybe confused about what was happening.)*

➤ **Read the information beside the picture on page 32.**

The angry mob stormed the Bastille on July 14, 1789. They were not satisfied to free the prisoners and to smash their way into the Bastille. On the next day, the people started to tear down the Bastille, stone by stone. The people hated the Bastille and the power of the king that it represented so much that they wanted the building destroyed.

This event was an important statement by the French people to the government that they wanted and needed many improvements. Every year from that time until now, the French people celebrate July 14 as a national holiday called Bastille Day. It is at this time that the French people celebrate the spirit of freedom that they all desire.

➤ **On what day do people in the United States celebrate freedom?** *(July 4)*

Text Discussion, page 33

➤ **Read page 33 to find out what King Louis XVI did when he found out what had happened at the Bastille.** *(He sent his soldiers to Paris to fight against the people.)*

➤ **What did the soldiers do?** *(They joined the people.)*

➤ **What do you think happened next in France?** We will read about what the king did in our next lesson.

King Louis XVI came in from hunting. He had not gotten any deer. He went to bed. He did not know what had happened at the Bastille that day. What do you think happened when he found out?

The king ordered his soldiers to march to Paris. The soldiers went. But a surprising thing happened. The soldiers did not fire their guns at the people. The soldiers joined the people. Now the king did not have soldiers he could trust. If you had been King Louis, what would you have done?

33

Evaluating the Lesson
Oral Review Game

Draw a stone tower composed of twelve stones on a piece of paper or the chalkboard. Explain that you will ask questions to review what has been learned in this lesson. For each correct answer, a stone will be removed (crossed out or erased) from the tower.

> If you have several children, you may choose to build two towers and divide the group into teams. When all the questions have been answered, the team whose tower is the most torn down wins the game.

➤ The goal of this game is to try to knock the tower down to the ground.
Use the following questions or create your own.

- **Who was the king of France in 1789?** *(Louis XVI)*
- **Who was the queen of France?** *(Marie Antoinette)*
- **What did the poor people sometimes do to get food?** *(steal)*
- **What was the Bastille?** *(a prison)*
- **In what city was the Bastille located?** *(Paris)*

- **What did the people of France think about the Bastille?** *(They hated it.)*
- **What did the Bastille symbolize to the French people?** *(the king's power over them)*
- **What kind of weapon did the Bastille have?** *(cannons)*
- **How many prisoners were freed when the people stormed the Bastille?** *(seven)*
- **Who was killed?** *(the governor)*
- **When is Bastille Day in France?** *(July 14)*

Going Beyond

Enrichment

Display a color picture of the French flag. Provide three sheets of construction paper: one red, one white, and one blue; transparent tape; and a straw. Direct your child to cut the construction paper into strips approximately 4"×12" or 6"×18". Tell him to use the supplies to make his own French flag.

Additional Teacher Information

The word *bastille,* or *bastilde,* in medieval times meant "a fortress." Charles V had the Bastille built in 1370 to guard the entrance to Paris. The Bastille was a rectangular building with eight towers that were joined by hundred-foot high walls. A single-carriage gateway with a wicket gate for pedestrians was the only entrance to the Bastille. The gate was protected by two draw-bridges over a deep, wide moat that surrounded most of the fortress. For a long time, the Bastille was used as a military citadel and a refuge for important visitors. Eventually, the Bastille became the state prison and a much-hated symbol of unjust government power.

The taking of the Bastille on July 14, 1789, included the release of seven prisoners—four accused counterfeiters, one wayward nobleman, and two lunatics. One hundred twenty soldiers tried to protect the Bastille from the mob of approximately one thousand angry townspeople.

For years before the storming of the Bastille, the military had talked of tearing down the fortress since it was too expensive to keep up and served no useful purpose. So, after July 14, 1789, the demolition of the Bastille seemed to relieve some of the economic pressure as well as much of the emotional turmoil of the French people. The contractor of the demolition was Palloy, who, instead of heaping up the rubble, bought the stones and irons to sell as souvenirs of the Bastille.

LESSON 9
The Terror

Text, pages 30, 34-37, 282-83
Notebook, pages 10-11

Preview

Main Ideas

- Communities, states, and nations have people who make laws.
- All societies have some kind of government.
- Ideas spread from one part of the world to another.
- Marquis de Lafayette helped shape the history of France.
- The dissatisfaction of the French people with their government led to a time of great terror.

Objectives

- Memorize a section of the Declaration of Independence
- Solve word puzzles relating to the French Revolution

Materials

- A dictionary (optional)
- Maps and More 6, page M4
- A wall map of the United States (optional)*
- The figure of the Declaration of Independence (1776) from the TimeLine Snapshots

Day 1

Lesson

Introducing the Lesson

Declaration of Independence Discussion, pages 282-83 and Maps and More 6

➤ **Read with me the date and title from the document shown on Maps and More 6.** *("In Congress, July 4, 1776. The unanimous Declaration of the thirteen united States of America.")*

➤ **What is the name given to this important document in America's history?** *(the Declaration of Independence)*

➤ Let's calculate how many years ago the Declaration of Independence was written. *Guide your child as he subtracts to find the answer.*

➤ **What does the word *unanimous* mean?** *(all people agreeing completely)* If your child does not know, ask him to look up the word in a dictionary.

➤ **Was the state you live in one of those thirteen states agreeing with the Declaration of Independence?** If you are not sure, check the listing of the first thirteen states given on page 21 in the text. (*NOTE:* Although the chart on this page gives information about the ratification of the Constitution, it is referred to here because it lists the names of the original thirteen states.)

➤ Locate the thirteen original states on the map shown on pages 282-83 or on your wall map.

➤ **What do you notice about the location of the thirteen original states?** (*They are all close to each other and along the East Coast or Atlantic Ocean.*)

➤ **Do you remember why the Declaration of Independence was written?** It stated the colonies' independence from England and the birth of a new nation, the United States.

Notebook Activity, page 10

➤ Read the section of the Declaration of Independence printed on Notebook page 10 and then we will discuss what it means.

➤ **What do you think the word *self-evident* means?**

The word *self-evident* refers to a truth that does not need any proof or explanation. For example, we could say: It is self-evident that I am a man (woman). It is self-evident that we live in a house.

➤ Read the passage again to identify the two self-evident truths mentioned in this section of the Declaration of Independence. (*All men are created equal. All men are endowed by their Creator with certain unalienable rights.*)

The word *endowed* means "to be provided."

➤ **Who is the Creator who provided for all men?** (*God*)

The word *unalienable* means "not to be separated." Each citizen of the United States is guaranteed each of these rights. Three guaranteed rights are listed here which may not be separated from each other.

➤ **Let's read aloud together the *certain unalienable rights* as given in the Declaration of Independence.** (*life, liberty, and the pursuit of happiness*)

Declaration of Independence

Name _____

Follow your teacher's instructions.

We hold these truths to be self-evident,
that all men are created equal,
that they are endowed by their Creator
with certain unalienable Rights,
that among these are Life, Liberty,
and the pursuit of Happiness.

© 1997 BJU Press. Reproduction prohibited.

Heritage Studies 3
Student Notebook

Lesson 9
Introducing the Lesson **10**

➤ Let's read aloud the entire passage together.

➤ Try memorizing this section of the Declaration of Independence to recite in a few days. *Recite the passage with your child in a variety of ways to help him memorize it.*

TimeLine Snapshots Activity

➤ What year was the Declaration of Independence signed? (*1776*)

➤ Add the figure of the Declaration of Independence to the TimeLine.

People all over the world heard about and read the famous Declaration of Independence in the time following 1776. Many people wanted their governments to grant them the freedoms that the United States government granted its citizens.

The greatest freedom of all is freedom from sin that is available to anyone who accepts Jesus Christ as Savior. (BATs: 1b Repentance and faith, 7a Grace; Bible Promise: A. Liberty from Sin)

Declarations of Independence

The French common people put themselves in charge of the government. They called their government the *National Assembly*. "Now," they said, "*we* will make the rules for France."

The National Assembly wrote a paper to tell the people what the new government believed. The paper was called the *Declaration of the Rights of Man and of the Citizen*. It said that everyone should have the same rights. It said that the king should not have all the power.

Do you remember an American paper that said such things? The Declaration of Independence did. The United States Constitution also did. Ben Franklin had the Constitution written out in French. The French people read the Constitution. Some ideas from the American war "echoed" in the French Revolution.

34

The National Assembly offered to let King Louis stay as king. "You will have to give up some power," the leaders told him, "but you can live in your palace and be called the king." Do you think Louis should have taken the offer?

The royal palace of Versailles

Queen Marie Antoinette said, "Don't listen to the people. I don't want to give up power. Tell them you are still the king." Louis told the people what the queen wanted him to.

The people were angry. "Things will not go back to the way they were. We want change! If the king won't hear us, we'll throw him out."

> *"Better is a poor and a wise child than an old and foolish king."*
> Ecclesiastes 4:13

35

Teaching the Lesson

Text Discussion, page 34

➤ **Read page 34 to find out what the French people called their document telling what the new government believed.** *(the Declaration of the Rights of Man and of the Citizen)*

➤ **What is a *citizen*?** *(a person who lives in a place and who is supposed to obey the laws of that place)*

➤ **What did the French Declaration say about the rights of the citizens?** *(Everyone should have the same rights.)*

➤ **Did all the French people have the same rights?** *(no)*

➤ **What are the three rights mentioned in the Declaration of Independence?** *(life, liberty, and the pursuit of happiness)*

➤ **Do you think all the people of the United States in 1776 had the same rights?** Slaves and women did not have the same rights as white men.

➤ **Do all American people today have these rights?** *(yes)*

➤ **Read the last sentence on page 34 aloud and explain what you think it means.**

Text Discussion, page 35

➤ Look at the picture of the palace at Versailles *(vər-sī´)*, where the king and queen of France lived.

➤ **Read page 35 to find out what kind of agreement the French people tried to make with the king and queen.** *(King Louis could still live in the palace and still be called the king, but he would not have as much power.)*

➤ **Do you think that King Louis XVI should have accepted the terms of the National Assembly?**

➤ **Read aloud page 35, using the appropriate expression.**

➤ **Read aloud the verse at the bottom of the page.**

➤ **Do you think that King Louis XVI was an old and foolish king?** King Louis XVI was only thirty-eight years old but was considered to be a weak ruler.

➤ **What do you think the people meant when they said that they would throw the king out?**

Paris, France
January 21, 1793

King Louis XVI was put on trial. He was found guilty of being against the revolution.

"Off with his head!" the people cried.

He was taken to the *guillotine*, a machine that lets a heavy blade drop from high up.

A few months later, Marie Antoinette was also taken there.

36

Kings and queens in other countries were shocked at what had happened to Louis XVI and Marie Antoinette. They said, "That might happen to us. Our people might get bad ideas from the French." Some kings and queens sent armies to France. Some wanted to stop the French Revolution. Others wanted to take over France.

The French people began to fight among themselves. Some thought that the king should not have been killed. Leaders of the revolution arrested people who were not on their side. Many of those people went to the guillotine.

"No one is safe," said a baker. "Keep your voice down," said his wife. "Tell me," said the baker, "haven't we only traded one terror for another?" The whole next year was called *the Terror.* How was the revolution in France different from the American War for Independence?

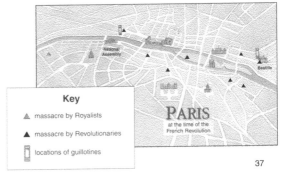

Key

▲ massacre by Royalists

▲ massacre by Revolutionaries

🎴 locations of guillotines

PARIS
at the time of the
French Revolution

37

Day 2

Text Discussion, page 36

*Write the word **guillotine** on a piece of paper. Pronounce it for your child. Explain that he will learn what this word means in his reading.*

➤ **Read page 36 to find out what happened to King Louis XVI and Queen Marie Antoinette.** *(They were put on trial, found guilty of being against the Revolution, and beheaded.)*

In the picture on page 36, King Louis is standing on the scaffold which held the guillotine, the French machine of death. The heavy blade fell from above and cut off his head. This terrible, gruesome way to be punished was an accepted method of punishment by death during this time in France. (*NOTE:* Beheading had been the privilege of the nobility. The guillotine extended it to the masses. Dr. Guillotin believed it to be the most humane way of death— better than the far more gruesome, brutal methods used during earlier days in France.)

Text Discussion, page 37

➤ **Read page 37 to find out if others were beheaded.** *(yes, many more people)*

➤ **What did the governments in other countries think about this revolution?** *(They were shocked. They were afraid that it might happen where they lived.)*

➤ **Why did some other countries send armies to France?** *(They tried to stop the Revolution. They wanted to take over France.)*

This period in the history of France is called **the Terror.** A *terror* is a horribly frightening event that puts intense fear into everyone.

➤ **Do you think things ever got better in France?** Yes, of course they did, but not for a while.

Historical Map Reading, page 37

➤ **Read the key to the map of Paris on page 37 to find out what the three symbols represent.** *(Royalist massacres, Revolutionary massacres, and locations of guillotines)*

A *massacre* is the killing of a large group of people. Notice especially the symbols shown at the location of the Bastille.

Marquis de Lafayette
1757-1834

Not all the rich people tried to keep the common people from having more votes in the French government. One of the most important nobles who liked the common people was the Marquis de Lafayette.

Lafayette had fought with General Washington in the War for Independence. He was a general. He commanded American soldiers. General Washington thought of Lafayette as his son. Lafayette brought many French soldiers and much French money to America. He helped the Americans win the war.

Lafayette told King Louis XVI that the common people should have a part in the government. He said, "The government used to listen to the people." Later Lafayette changed his mind about what the common people were doing.

30

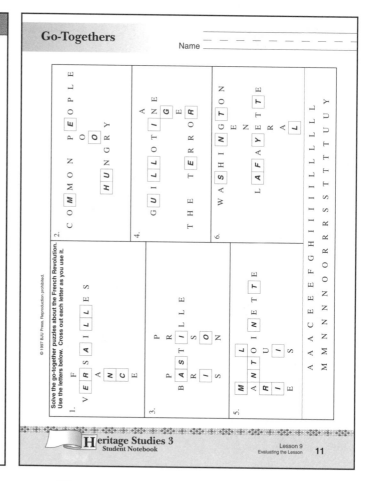

Solve the go-together puzzles about the French Revolution. Use the letters below. Cross out each letter as you use it.

© 1997 BJU Press. Reproduction prohibited.

Heritage Studies 3
Student Notebook

Lesson 9
Evaluating the Lesson **11**

➤ **What two symbols are near the Bastille?** *(Revolutionary massacre and a guillotine)*
➤ **Are the places of massacres and the guillotines only near the Bastille?** *(No, they are scattered around Paris.)*
➤ **How do you think the city of Paris was affected during this terrible time of war and revolution?**
➤ **Do you think Paris has changed much since that time?**

Text Discussion, page 30

➤ **Read page 30 to find out about a famous Frenchman who tried to help make things better in France.** *(Lafayette)*
➤ Lafayette is sometimes called "the Friend of America." **How do you think he got this nickname?**
➤ **Read aloud paragraph 2 on page 30 to give a more complete answer.**
➤ **Did Lafayette try to bring ideas of freedom and government from America to France?** *(yes)*

Reports to the French of what was happening in America were not totally dependent on Lafayette. By 1789, more than 35 percent of Frenchmen were literate or able to read. They read the news of the American Revolution and especially of Benjamin Franklin, who had become a folk hero in France.

Direct reports came from the more than nine thousand Frenchmen who fought in the American Revolution.

➤ **What did Lafayette tell King Louis XVI?** *(that the common people should have a part in the government)*

Lafayette defined the "common people" as the wealthy, literate members of the Third Estate, not peasants.

➤ Find a sentence that tells whether Lafayette continued to believe this. *(Later Lafayette changed his mind about what the common people were doing.)*

Evaluating the Lesson
Notebook Activity, page 11

➤ Read the instructions given on Notebook page 11.
➤ Complete the page.

Going Beyond

Enrichment

Provide glue, a sheet of construction paper, and a half sheet of handwriting paper. Instruct your child to glue the handwriting paper onto the construction paper. Encourage him to draw a picture and write a paragraph entitled *I Am Thankful for My Country Because. . . .*

Additional Teacher Information

A decapitating machine was invented in Italy in the twelfth century. The guillotine that was used during the Terror was originally designed by Dr. Louis, who worked with the Academy of Surgery in Paris. It was Dr. Joseph Ignace Guillotin, though, who altered the design slightly, for whom the machine was named. Dr. Guillotin claimed that his machine made for an easier death and was more humane than methods of torture being used in France at that time.

The trial of Marie Antoinette was the first of many trials after the Terror began. She was found guilty on all counts and was taken in a work cart to the guillotine on October 16, 1793. It is recorded that some applauded, some cheered, some shouted "Long live the Republic!" while others stayed silent, but all seemed satisfied. Marie Antoinette was no more.

Gilbert Lafayette was from one of the richest families in all of France. At age fourteen he entered the military academy at Versailles and joined the regiment of the Black Musketeers who served as bodyguards for King Louis XV. At age nineteen, Lafayette bought a ship, the *Victory,* and sailed to America to help in the cause for freedom. He was given a commission by the U.S. Congress to serve as a major general in the Continental army, fighting against the Redcoats. Lafayette respected and honored his great friendship with George Washington so much that Lafayette named his son after Washington. The friendship of Lafayette with America's leaders, as well as with her people, continued for life.

Upon his return to France, Lafayette tried to persuade the French government to adopt some of the ways of the American government. During the French Revolution, Lafayette was promoted from a member of the Assembly of Notables to commander of the National Guard. Eventually, the French people turned against this rich nobleman, calling him a traitor. He fled with his family to Belgium but was caught and imprisoned for five years. When the turmoil of the Revolution ended, Lafayette again became a popular figure with both the French and the Americans.

LESSON 10
Give Honor

Text, pages 38-40
Notebook, page 12

Preview

Main Ideas

- When people are dissatisfied with their government, they respond in different ways.
- The French revolutionists wore red caps, red scarves, and red ribbons to symbolize their ideas.

Objectives

- Use encyclopedias to find facts
- Answer questions about the French Revolution

Materials

- A red hat or scarf*
- Two red ribbons approximately 18" long*
- A set of encyclopedias or an atlas*
- *HERITAGE STUDIES Listening Cassette A*
- Map of France from Lesson 7

Day 1

Lesson

Introducing the Lesson

Guessing Activity

➤ Place the red hat or red scarf on your head. Carefully tie the red ribbon around your neck. (*NOTE:* Make sure the teacher also wears a red ribbon.)

There was a time in France when many of the people wore red caps or scarves on their heads or red ribbons around their necks.

➤ **Why do you think the French people wore these?**
➤ **What do you think the red caps, scarves, and ribbons represented?**

Teaching the Lesson

Text Discussion, page 38

➤ **Read the first paragraph on page 38 to find out why the red caps, red scarves, and red ribbons were worn.** (*People wore red caps and red scarves to show that they were revolutionists. People wore red ribbons to show that they knew someone who had died on the guillotine.*)

People wore red caps and scarves to show they were *revolutionists*. Why do you think they did that? They wanted the leaders to see they were on the right side. Some people who were not revolutionists wore red ribbons around their necks. What do you think the ribbons showed? They showed that the person knew someone who had died on the guillotine.

The leaders of the revolution got an army together. This army fought the armies of the other countries that came against France. The army also fought the French people who did not like the revolution.

The soldiers in the new army did not have much training. But they wanted to fight. That made them able to win many battles, even when the enemy had soldiers who had been in many wars.

38

Making Up National Songs

A man in the new French army liked to write songs. He wrote a song for the soldiers. He thought it would cheer them up and help them march better.

The mayor of a small town sang the song first. The soldiers and the people liked it. Soon everyone was singing it. It was called "The War Song of the Army." It said, "The day of glory now is here. Let us march! Let us march!"

Later the song was named for a town the soldiers marched from and became the *national anthem*. What is a national anthem?

39

The red represented the bloodshed of those who had met death at the guillotine. Although this period of history reminds us of injustice and the terrifying deaths that occurred many years ago, the Lord Jesus Christ endured the most painful death ever.

> The blood that Christ shed is the most precious blood of all. Jesus Christ was perfect. He was not being punished for anything He had done. He died on the cross willingly to pay the price for our sins and to make available the gift of eternal life. If time permits, sing a familiar song such as "Nothing but the Blood," "Jesus Paid It All," or "The Wordless Book Song." (BATs: 1a Understanding Jesus Christ, 1b Repentance and faith)

➤ *Write the following words:* revolutionist, revolution, *and* revolt. *Point out that the two larger words come from the base word* revolt, *which means "to fight against."*

➤ **Why did the French people revolt?** *(They were fighting against the power of the king over them.)*

➤ **Read the rest of page 38 to find out what the revolutionists did to try to change the government.** *(They formed armies and fought for their rights.)*

➤ **How could the untrained armies defeat the trained soldiers?** *(Answers will vary but may include that they were determined and believed in the cause they were fighting for.)*

Text Discussion, page 39

➤ Listen as I play a recording of a famous song, "La Marseillaise" *(mär sā yehz).*

➤ **Read page 39 to find out what this famous song is.** *(the French national anthem)*

This song was used first as a marching song for soldiers from Marseille *(mär sā′).* The song became popular and was adopted as the French national anthem in 1795 at the end of the French Revolution.

A country's national song, its **national anthem**, gives honor to the country and stirs up national pride, respect, and love in the hearts of the citizens for their country.

> Christians should enjoy singing about Christ and their heavenly home. In this way Christians show love and respect for the Savior. (BATs: 7b Exaltation of Christ, 7c Praise)

➤ Look at the map of France. Find Marseille and Paris on the map.

To Find and Chart Facts

1. Get a pencil and Notebook page 12. You will also need a set of encyclopedias.

2. Find the names of the national anthems of the countries listed. Find the date that the French national anthem was adopted.

3. Write the names of the anthems in the blanks.

40

National Anthems

Name _____

Write the name of America's national anthem. Then use encyclopedias to find the national anthems for at least five other countries. Write the national anthem next to its country.

United States	1.	*"The Star-Spangled Banner"*
France	2.	*"La Marseillaise"*
Switzerland	3.	*"Swiss Psalm"*
Germany	4.	*"Deutschland Uber Alles" ("Germany over All")*
Austria	5.	*"Land der Berge, Land am Strome" ("Land of Mountains, Land of the River")*
England	6.	*"God Save the Queen"*
Spain	7.	*"Himno Nacional" ("National Hymn")*
Portugal	8.	*"A Portuguesa" ("The Portuguese")*
Poland	9.	*"Jeszcze Polska nie Zginela" ("Poland Has Not Yet Perished")*
Norway	10.	*"Ja, vi elsker dette landet" ("Yes, We Love This Land")*
Netherlands	11.	*"Wilhemus van Nassouwe" ("William of Nassau")*
Sweden	12.	*"Du gamla, du Fria" ("Thou Ancient, Thou Free-Born")*

Heritage Studies 3
Student Notebook

Lesson 10
Teaching the Lesson **12**

➤ **In what direction did the soldiers march to get from Marseille to Paris?** *(north)*

➤ Calculate the distance from Paris to Marseille, using an encyclopedia or atlas. *(375 miles)*

Day 2

Learning How Activity, page 40 and Notebook page 12

➤ **Do you think that all countries have national anthems?**

Most countries today have a national song, composed as either a march, a hymn, or an anthem.

➤ **Read the instructions given on page 40.**

➤ Complete the activity on Notebook page 12. *Give help as needed. You may allow your child to use the computer if he has access to a program with similar information.*

If you are teaching more than one child, they may work together as partners. The actual name of each national anthem or its English translation is acceptable as an answer on the Notebook page.

Evaluating the Lesson

"March to Paris" Activity

➤ Pretend you are the leader of a French army unit. Your assignment is to "march to Paris." If you arrive safely, then you may try to return to Marseille.

➤ *Explain the army march to your child.*

I will read aloud questions related to things you have learned about France. You are to write the answer on a sheet of paper. You may use your book to look up any unknown answers. You will have a time limit of two minutes to write each answer. For each correct answer, your army will advance 75 miles. Remember that from Marseille to Paris is 375 miles.

If you are teaching more than one child, you may make this a game by assigning two armies. The first army to "march to Paris" wins the game. You may want to continue with the questions until each army marches back to Marseille.

• **Which French people wore red caps and red scarves?** *(revolutionists)*

- Why did some people wear red ribbons around their necks? *(to show that they knew someone who had died on the guillotine)*
- What is the capital of France? *(Paris)*
- What did "The War Song of the Army" become? *(the French national anthem or "La Marseillaise")*
- When did France adopt its national anthem? *(in 1795 or at the end of the French Revolution)*
- Name another national anthem and its country. *(Answers will vary.)*
- What is the name of the grand palace in France? *(Versailles)*
- Who was the king of France at the beginning of the French Revolution? *(Louis XVI)*
- Who was queen of France at the beginning of the French Revolution? *(Marie Antoinette)*
- What was the name of the instrument of death used in France during the Revolution? *(guillotine)*

Going Beyond

Enrichment

Instruct your child to read the words to "The Star-Spangled Banner" found on Supplement, page S2. Encourage him to listen to the anthem on *HERITAGE STUDIES Listening Cassette A,* following along silently with the written words of the song. (*NOTE:* If you live in another country, have available the printed words or a recording of your country's national anthem.) Encourage him to memorize the national anthem. Sing it together periodically throughout the school year.

Additional Teacher Information

Marseille, the oldest city in France, is the largest seaport of the country. It is located on the southeast coast of France on the Mediterranean Sea.

The national anthem of France, "La Marseillaise," is said to have been composed entirely by a young captain, Claude Joseph Rouget de Lisle, during the French Revolution. Some historians say that he applied war slogans to the tune of an old Protestant hymn. Others say that he composed the song while attending a banquet for army volunteers. The song was first heard in Paris when the battalion from Marseille marched to storm the Tuileries.

LESSON 11
After the Revolution

Text, pages 41-42, 248
Notebook, page 13

▬ Preview ▬

Main Ideas
- Ideas spread from one part of the world to another.
- Early Americans decided not to participate in the French Revolution.
- Napoleon Bonaparte became the leader of the French government.
- Every nation has a unique history.

Objective
- Differentiate between statements about America and those about France

Materials
- The crown from Lesson 7
- The presidential strip with the figure of John Adams (2) from the TimeLine Snapshots
- A wall map of Europe or an atlas*

Day 1

▬ Lesson ▬

Introducing the Lesson

Comparing Activity

➤ Place the crown on your head.
➤ **What are some adjectives that might describe a ruler who wears a crown?** *(rich, powerful, wise)*

Christ is the King of kings, the greatest ruler of all. He is loving, selfless, wise, and all-powerful. (BATs: 7a Grace, 7b Exaltation of Christ, 7c Praise; Bible Promises: H. God as Father, I. God as Master)

➤ **Who was the first president of the United States?** *(George Washington)*
➤ Point to the figure of George Washington on the TimeLine.

Remember that many early colonists wanted to make George Washington the ruler or king of the new nation because they remembered his strong leadership during the War for Independence.

➤ **Why do you think George Washington refused to be crowned king?**

➤ **What are some adjectives that describe George Washington?** *(compassionate, fair, hard-working) Write these adjectives on the chalkboard under the name of Washington.*

TimeLine Snapshots Discussion, page 248

➤ Look at George Washington on the TimeLine. Read the dates in which he served as president of our country. *(1789-97)*

➤ Read the name of the man who became the second president of the United States shortly after the French Revolution ended. *(John Adams)*

➤ Read the information given on page 248 about our second president, John Adams.

Listening Activity

The French government was very different from the government in America. France was ruled by kings. (*NOTE:* Queens were never sovereign but were always influential.) The French Revolution occurred during 1789-95. After Louis XVI and Marie Antoinette were arrested and put to death, attempts were made in France to set up a new government based on a constitution. These attempts for constitutional government failed, allowing an army corporal to take charge in 1804 as the leader of France.

➤ Listen as I read aloud the following excerpt that describes this change in government leadership.

> I stand here and before me waits the Pope, father of the Church who hurried from Rome at my invitation. We stand facing each other, the Pope and I. We are both in gorgeous robes, as befits a Coronation. He steps forward with the crown, but I will not allow . . .

➤ **Do you think that the person telling about the situation refuses the crown?** Listen to the rest of the story to find out.

> . . . but I will not allow another man to give me my title or my position. I earned it, I shall take it. I grasp the crown and place it firmly on my head. There. It is only right. I am the Emperor of France.

➤ **What are some adjectives that would describe this man who had just crowned himself the emperor of France?** *(determined, powerful, competent, proud) Write these adjectives on the chalkboard under the name Napoleon Bonaparte.*

➤ Compare the characteristics of George Washington and Napoleon Bonaparte. **Which one do you think made a better leader?**

Some Americans wanted to help the French people fight their enemies. They said, "The French helped us. We should help them." But others said, "We have just started our country. We should make America strong before we fight for France."

If you had been George Washington, what would you have said? Washington thought of Lafayette. Then he thought about the new United States of America. America had just come out of a war. He said, "I think we should not get into another war."

"You're wrong," said Thomas Jefferson. Washington said, "It is wrong to risk our new freedom. France was a strong, old country during our war. And the French were enemies of the English. We are just beginning a nation. And France's enemies are not our enemies." America stayed out of the French Revolution.

41

➤ **Do you think Napoleon gave the French people the freedoms that they desired and made the country strong again?**

This new emperor of France, Napoleon Bonaparte, ruled France as emperor for ten years. Napoleon fought many countries in his attempt to gain power and control in Europe. Although Napoleon was often criticized for his seeming arrogance, he was an able leader for France. His superb organizational skills, efficiency, and leadership abilities helped to produce a stronger France than had ever existed before. Some of Napoleon's accomplishments include the building of a strong army, the development of the Bank of France, the establishment of civil laws (Code Napoleon), the building and repairing of more than fifty thousand miles of roads, and the organization of the Imperial University. Many of Napoleon's reforms are still in place today.

Teaching the Lesson

Text Discussion, page 41

➤ **Read page 41 to find out whether the Americans helped France fight her enemies.** *(no)*

France had assisted America in her fight for freedom, giving money and "loaning out" men like Lafayette.

The French soldiers won many battles. The generals became famous and important. One general won a big battle against the English. He became a French hero. His name was Napoleon Bonaparte.

Napoleon, painted by Jacques Louis David

Napoleon won more battles. The revolution ended in 1795. A group of leaders tried to run the French government together. Then in 1804, Napoleon took his soldiers to Paris. "Make me head of the government," he said. "Or I will have the soldiers fire on the city." The people made Napoleon the head of the government.

Napoleon said, "You people do not know how to run a country. I will put things right for you." And he did make many good changes. But Napoleon made hard rules for the people. Some people began to wish France still had a king.

Napoleon in His Study, 1810-11, painted by Jacques Louis David

42

American or French? ___ Name ___

Read each statement. Write *A* on the blank if the statement refers to America. Write *F* if the statement refers to France. (NOTE: Three statements should be marked both *A* and *F*.)

__F__ 1. Napoleon crowned himself as ruler.

__A, F__ 2. The soldiers fought and won many battles.

__A__ 3. This was a new nation.

__A__ 4. George Washington was the leader.

__A, F__ 5. Lafayette lived here.

__F__ 6. They considered Napoleon Bonaparte a hero.

__A__ 7. The people valued their freedoms.

__A__ 8. They were not part of the French Revolution.

__F__ 9. They fought many countries of Europe.

__F__ 10. This was a strong, old country.

__A, F__ 11. They were enemies of the English.

__F__ 12. The people had to obey hard rules made by Napoleon.

➤ **Read aloud from paragraph three George Washington's explanation to Mr. Jefferson about how America would have been risking its freedom if it had gotten involved in the French Revolution.**

➤ **What countries do you think the French soldiers fought?**

France was fighting most of Europe, specifically Spain, Prussia, Austria, and England. (*NOTE:* Point out these countries on the map.) Because Napoleon was at the head of the armies and government, these wars are usually called the Napoleonic Wars.

Text Discussion, page 42

➤ Look at the pictures of Napoleon on page 42.

King Louis XVI's family members had either been killed or put into prison. Napoleon was not the next in line to rule France after King Louis XVI.

➤ **Read page 42 to find out how Napoleon became the country's leader.** *(He took his army to Paris and demanded that the people make him the ruler.)*

Remember that Napoleon actually took the crown from the Pope and crowned himself emperor of France. The French people honored him as a hero of the Revolution and allowed him to be the leader of the government.

➤ **Read the sentence on page 42 that tells that the French people were still unhappy with their government.** *("Some people began to wish France still had a king.")*

Napoleon ruled France for ten years. After the French defeat at the Battle of Waterloo, Napoleon was forced to abdicate (leave) the throne and was sent to St. Helena, a barren island in the South Atlantic Ocean, to live out the rest of his days. After Napoleon left, France once again was ruled by kings and queens.

Evaluating the Lesson

Notebook Activity, page 13

➤ Read the instructions on Notebook page 13.

➤ Complete the page.

═══ Going Beyond ═══

Enrichment

Provide art supplies such as construction paper, drawing paper, pencils, felt-tip pens, crayons, scissors, and glue. Direct your child to make a ribbon honoring someone that he considers a hero. He may glue a photograph or draw a picture of his hero at the top. Encourage him to write phrases on the ribbon describing the hero.

Additional Teacher Information

After the French Revolution, people in Paris planted trees as symbols of a change in government and their new freedoms.

During the aftermath of the French Revolution, a new calendar was written which renamed the months and introduced a ten-day week with no traditional Sunday. The belief in Christianity was so strong, however, that the old religion and the old calendar were both reinstated.

Napoleon Bonaparte was born into a noble Italian family on August 15, 1769, on the island of Corsica in the Mediterranean Sea. Napoleon's father, a lawyer, obtained an appointment to a French military school for his son's training. Napoleon rose through the ranks in the army and at age 24 had earned the title brigadier general. Although small in stature (5' 2"), Napoleon, nicknamed "the little corporal," was outspoken, energetic, and powerful. One of his officers said of Napoleon, "His presence on the field was worth forty thousand men." Under Napoleon's leadership, France once again became strong. Napoleon's military skill made him a national hero, and by 1800 he was in charge of the country. After conquering much of Europe, Napoleon crowned himself emperor in 1804. He held that position until he was forced to abdicate in 1814. He escaped from the island of Elba in the Mediterranean and led France into war. But at the Battle of Waterloo, he was defeated and exiled again. He spent his last days under the strict care of a British governor and died of cancer in 1821. Napoleon was buried on the island of St. Helena, but in 1840 the French government had his body moved to Paris and laid to rest beneath the dome of the Hotel des Invalides, a hospital for sick and aged soldiers.

From Sea to Shining Sea

In this chapter your child will learn about physical maps and the major geographical features of the United States. Lessons 16 and 17 follow the travels of Lewis and Clark, the men sent by President Jefferson to explore the Louisiana Purchase and the Far West.

Materials

The following materials must be obtained or prepared before the presentation of the lesson. These items are labeled with an asterisk (*) in each lesson and in the Materials List in the Supplement. For further information see the individual lessons.

- An atlas (Lessons 12-14)
- A globe (Lessons 12 and 15)
- Pictures of animals and plants characteristic of eastern woodlands and the prairie (Lesson 13)
- Appendix, pages A9-A10 (Lesson 13)
- Yarn or string (optional) (Lesson 13)
- An almanac (Lesson 14)
- Pictures of animals and plants characteristic of mountains and the desert (Lesson 14)
- Pictures of coastal plants and animals (Lesson 15)
- Books about transportation (optional) (Lesson 15)

 If you have not already purchased an easy-to-read atlas for your child to use, we recommend you do so for this chapter. The *Rand McNally Classroom Atlas*, available through the BJU Press, is appropriate for elementary usage.

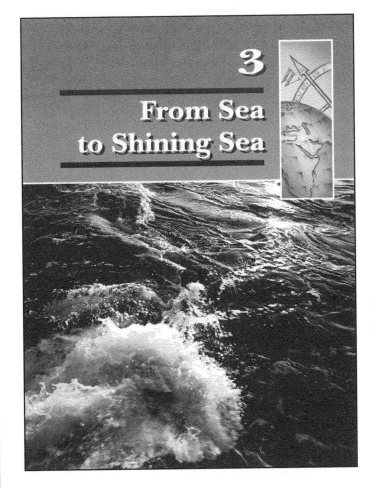

3

From Sea to Shining Sea

LESSON 12
Physical Maps

Text, pages 44-47, 284-85
Notebook, page 14

═══ Preview ═══

Main Ideas
- Maps and globes represent actual places.
- Land is divided into cities, states, countries, and other sections.

Objective
- Answer questions using a map

Materials
- An atlas with a physical map of North America*
- A globe*

Day 1

═══ Lesson ═══

Introducing the Lesson

Travel Adventure, page 44

➤ **Read the first paragraph on page 44, answering the questions.**

We will be using maps to take an imaginary journey to the place you have named. Think about what we would need for a journey to that special place.

➤ **What types of clothes do you think we will need in the place you have chosen to visit?**
➤ **Do you think the place is far from or near to the place we live?**
➤ **What do you think the map will tell us about that place?**
➤ **Read the rest of page 44 to find out some things that maps show.** *(streets and buildings, towns, boundaries for countries, roads, and cities)*

What if you could travel anywhere that you wanted? Where would you choose to go? What things might you see there? Of course, we cannot all go anywhere in the world. But we can learn about the places we would like to see. Maps can tell us some things about those places.

What kinds of things do maps show? Some maps show streets and buildings. Some maps show towns. Others show where one country ends and another country begins. Are these the only things maps show us?

Maps show us man-made things like roads and cities. And maps show us things man did not make. The things man did not make are called *physical features*. Who made these physical features?

"The sea is his, and he made it: and his hands formed the dry land."
Psalm 95:5

44

➤ **What do we call the features that God made?** *(physical features)*

There are many kinds of maps. Some maps show how high or low land is; some show what climate places have; some show cities and roads; almost all show distances.

➤ **Read aloud the verse at the bottom of page 44.**
➤ Name other things that God made. (Bible Promise: I. God as Master)

Teaching the Lesson

Map Activity, page 45

➤ **Read page 45 and answer the questions.**

The map shows oceans, continents, and countries. The oceans are the Pacific, Atlantic, Indian, and Arctic. The continents are North America, South America, Europe, Asia, Afric, Australia, and Antarctica. The seven continents are different in climate, size, and shape. The countries are not named.

Here is a map of the world. What things does this map show? It shows water. Water is blue on a map. The earth has four large bodies of water. What are these bodies of water called? They are *oceans*. Can you find all four oceans?

Most maps show land too. Big areas of land are called *continents*. How many continents do you see? There are seven. Each one has high land and low land. But all the continents are different too. Can you think of some ways in which they are different?

This map of the world also shows how the continents are divided. It does not emphasize land features such as rivers, lakes, and mountains.

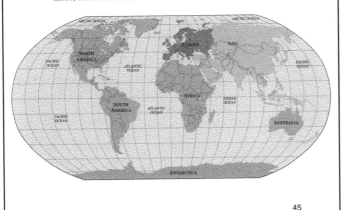

45

This map is a special kind of map. How is it different from the map you just looked at? It shows some of the physical features of our world. Maps like this one are called *physical* maps.

This physical map shows some of the rivers and lakes on six continents. Which continent does not have rivers and lakes? Other physical maps show different physical features. What other features might a map show?

Can you find the continent called North America on this map? America is part of this continent. How many rivers and lakes do you see? Do you think this map shows all the rivers and lakes?

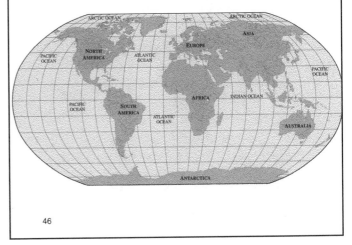

46

➤ **Do you think that the lines showing where countries begin and end actually appear on the land?**

Sometimes there are fences or signs to designate countries, but no lines are actually on the ground.

➤ **Are the lines designating separate countries called physical features?** *(No, only things that God made are physical features.)*

➤ Name the continent on which your chosen place to visit is located.

Map Activity, page 46

➤ Study the map on page 46 and compare it to the one on page 45.

➤ **Read page 46 to find out how this map differs from the previous map.** *(It shows rivers and lakes, but it does not show countries.)* Point out the blue lines representing rivers and the blue areas showing lakes, such as the Great Lakes in North America.

Antarctica is the continent with no lakes or rivers. North America is the continent on which the United States, Mexico, and Canada are located. A map this small cannot show all the rivers and lakes. Only the largest are shown.

➤ **What is this kind of map called?** *(This is a physical map because it shows physical features.)*

➤ **What features other than rivers and lakes might a map show?** *(mountains, vegetation, etc.)*

➤ Locate your chosen destination on the physical map. **Are there any rivers or lakes nearby?**

➤ Look at the globe. Compare it to the map on page 46. *(The globe models the shape of the earth, but a map is flat; both show continents and oceans; the globe does not have to distort land size; other answers may be given.)*

➤ Locate your destination on the globe. Locate several mountains, lakes, oceans, and rivers on the globe.

Evaluating the Lesson

Learning How Activity, pages 47 and 284-85 and Notebook page 14

> Use a map of the United States from your atlas in place of the "large map" named on text page 47 and Notebook page 14. The most useful maps may not be labeled as physical maps. The most appropriate map in the *Rand McNally Classroom Atlas* is labeled as a "merged relief" map.

➤ **Read page 47, following the instructions given.**
➤ Read the instructions on Notebook page 14.
➤ Complete the page using the map on pages 284-85 and your atlas.

━━ Going Beyond ━━

Enrichment

Give your child a physical map, a globe, paper, and pencils. Instruct him to choose one or more places on the map or globe and to write travel advice for the places, gleaning information about the places from only the map and the globe.

Provide paper and colored pencils. Allow your child to make a physical map of his state, using the map on pages 284-85 and the large map as guides.

Additional Teacher Information

The first known map of the coastline of what is now America was prepared by Juan de la Cosa, a mapmaker who traveled with Columbus on his second voyage. The coastline appears on this map as the eastern edge of China, which was still thought to be a huge landmass. This belief was founded on the maps prepared by Ptolemy, an ancient Greek who gathered information from seafarers of his day.

LESSON 13
Forests and Plains

Text, pages 48-51, 286-87
Notebook, page 15

━━━ Preview ━━━

Main Ideas
- Places change over time.
- People use directions to find their way.

Objectives
- Locate the American plains on a map
- Indicate the extent of the forest that once covered the eastern United States

Materials
- *HERITAGE STUDIES Listening Cassette A*
- Pictures of animals and plants characteristic of eastern woodlands and the prairie *
- Supplement, page S3: Home on the Range
- Appendix, page A9: Areas of the United States map*
- An atlas*
- Appendix, page A10: Indian Nations of Long Ago
- Yarn or string (optional)*

Day 1

━━━ Lesson ━━━

Introducing the Lesson

Text Discussion, page 48

➤ **Read the first paragraph on page 48.** *Discuss any landscapes and sights you have seen if your family has traveled to other parts of the country.*

One of the benefits of travel and of study is to see that things are not the same in every place. Land, people, climate, and animals are different in different places.

➤ **Do you think a person visiting from another country would find America different from his own land?**

The United States is a big country. If you traveled across the country, what things would you see? Would the land look the same in each place you went?

The Big Forest

Long ago, the land between the Atlantic Ocean and the Mississippi River was a huge *forest*. A forest is a place where many trees grow. Can you find the land that the forest covered on the map on page 49?

Not many people lived in the forest. But it was full of many kinds of animals. Look at the pictures of animals from the forest. Can you name them? What other animals might have lived in the big forest long ago?

48

Teaching the Lesson

Map Activity, pages 48-49

➤ **Read the second paragraph on page 48 to find out what used to cover the eastern part of the United States.** *(a huge forest)*

➤ Locate the Mississippi River and the Atlantic Ocean on the map on page 49.

The forestland stretched from the Atlantic Ocean to the Mississippi River when the settlers first came to America. Many referred to it as the Great Forest.

➤ **What do you think happened to the huge forest between the Atlantic Ocean and the Mississippi River?**

Settlers cut most of the forest down to build towns, cities, farms, and roads. Those forests which remain are referred to as the Eastern Woodlands.

How did the people who first came to America travel from place to place? Some people said that the forest was so thick that a squirrel could go from the Atlantic Ocean to the Mississippi River without ever touching the ground. It was hard to travel through such a thick forest.

Most of the time, the people traveled on *rivers*. A river is a large stream of water that flows across the land. Can you find any rivers on the map? Rivers are shown as thin blue lines.

Today some of this same land is still covered with forests. But most of the land is not. What other things would you see instead? Farms, small towns, and even big cities cover the land. Which of these places would you like to visit?

49

➤ **Read the last paragraph on page 48 and answer the questions.**

The animals pictured are a hawk, red fox, and white-tailed deer. Not all forests have the same kinds of animals. Rain forests have birds and animals that could not live in the cooler, drier forests of North America. Some animals that live in the North American forest are white-tailed deer, foxes, squirrels, turkeys, owls, mice, opossums, raccoons, bats, rattlesnakes, black bears, beetles, woodpeckers, and salamanders. *Show the pictures of woodland plants and animals.*

Map Activity, pages 286-87

The Indian Nations of Long Ago map found in the Appendix will help as you identify specific Native American groups. You may want to use this map as a reference any time you refer to the map on text pages 286-87.

➤ Find the area on this map that was the forestland. *Your child may wish to refer to the United States map in the atlas or on text pages 284-85 for comparison.*

➤ Determine which Native American groups lived in the forestland before the settlers came. (*Fox, Algonquin, Iroquois, Blackfoot, Pedee, Natchez, Choctaw, Seminole, Shawnee, Potawatomi*)

Text Discussion, page 49

➤ **Read page 49 to find out how most early Americans traveled.** (*by river*)
➤ **What was it like in the Great Forest?** (*very thick—dark, quiet, perhaps damp*)
➤ **Read the names of the rivers on the map.**
➤ **Can you find these rivers on the United States map in the atlas?** *Give help as needed.*

Song and Map Activity

➤ Listen as I play the recording of "Home on the Range."
➤ Sing along as I play the recording again, using the words from the song page.
➤ **What animals are named in the song?** (*buffalo, deer, antelope*) *Show the pictures of prairie animals.*
➤ **What do you think "the range" refers to?**

The range is the open grassland that existed between the forests in the East and the Rocky Mountains in the West.

➤ Find the Rocky Mountains on the United States map in the atlas. *You may choose to use the map on pages 284-85.*
➤ Point to the range on the map in the atlas. Find the same area on the map on page 49.
➤ **What do you think the meaning of this phrase is: "where seldom is heard a discouraging word"?** It means there is not much complaining or sadness.

When we are content with what we have and where we live, we can be cheerful and happy. (BATs: 2f Enthusiasm, 7c Praise, 7d Contentment)

Day 2

Text Discussion, page 50

➤ **Read the title on page 50 to find another word used to refer to the range.** (*prairie*)
➤ **Read page 50, imagining that you are a pioneer who has just traveled through the great forest and is entering the prairie on the way west.**
➤ Describe the prairie as though you have just passed through it. (*Answers should include details about the grass, the animals, and perhaps how far the people could see.*)

The Wide Open Prairie

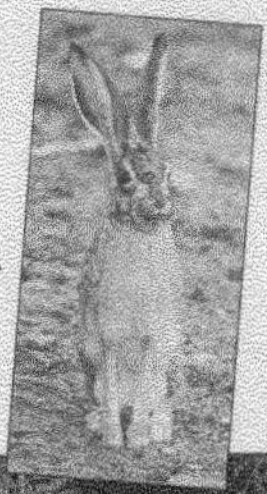

Beyond the wide and muddy Mississippi River, the land is different. It is flatter. Few trees grow there. Some people liked this flatter land, or *prairie*, better than they liked the forest land. Once they passed the trees along the riverbank, they could see for miles.

What things do you think the people saw on the prairie? First they saw grass. Some of the grass was as tall as a person. When they looked closer, the people saw other things too. They saw little animals, like prairie dogs and badgers, that lived on the prairie. Do you think these small animals saw the people? They did. And they ran to their underground homes to hide.

The people saw another kind of animal on the prairie. It was not like any animal they had seen before. The *bison* was the biggest animal on the prairie. One person told about a very big *herd*, or group, of bison. It took three days for that herd to pass. What kind of noise do you think such a big herd of bison made?

50

At one time, people thought that nothing but grass would grow on the prairie. They called the prairie the *Great American Desert*. Were these people right? Later they found out that the prairie soil was very rich. Farm crops grew well there.

This picture shows part of the same land today. How has the land changed? What do you think caused the change? More and more people came to live on the prairie land. They planted crops and trees. Today it is hard to believe that people once called this land a desert.

51

➤ **What was the largest animal on the prairie called?** *(bison)*

Many people call these animals buffalo. True buffaloes live in Europe and Africa. A water buffalo is a true buffalo. The American bison is similar to but larger than a buffalo. (*NOTE*: In this teacher's edition, the terms will be used interchangeably.)

Text Discussion, page 51

➤ **Read page 51 to find out what the settlers called the prairie and why**. *(Settlers called it the Great American Desert because they believed that nothing but grass could grow there.)*

➤ **How has it changed since then?** *(Now many different crops and trees grow there.)*

➤ **Do you think there are still bison and other animals living on the prairie?**

Wild animals still live in these areas but in much smaller numbers. *Show the pictures of plants and animals from the prairie.*

➤ **Why do you think trees grow well in the eastern part of the United States and prairie grass grows well in the central part?**

Rain and temperature determine what kinds of plants grow in a place. In turn, the kinds of plants determine what animals can live in a place.

Map Activity, pages 286-87

➤ Find the area of the United States which is known as the prairie.

➤ **What Indian nations first lived on the prairie?** *(Pawnee, Sioux, Kiowa, Caddo, Crow, Comanche)*

As more settlers came, there were fights about who owned the land. In order to settle the fights, sometimes *treaties,* written agreements, were made.

➤ **Do you think the treaties were always honored?** They were not.

➤ **What do you think happened then?** There was more fighting.

➤ Label the forest and prairie areas on your copy of the Areas of the United States map.

➤ Sort the pictures of plants and animals according to the area in which they would be found.

 You may choose to hang the map on the wall or paste it onto a poster board. Your child could then place the pictures around the map. He might also draw lines or stretch yarn or string from the appropriate areas on the map to the pictures. The display will be used again in Lessons 14 and 15.

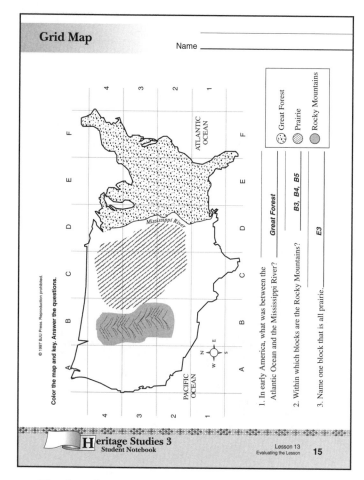

Grid Map   Name _____

Color the map and key. Answer the questions.

© 1987 BJU Press. Reproduction prohibited.

Great Forest

1. In early America, what was between the Atlantic Ocean and the Mississippi River?

Great Forest

2. Within which blocks are the Rocky Mountains?

_B3, B4, B5_

3. Name one block that is all prairie.

_E3_

	Great Forest
	Prairie
	Rocky Mountains

Evaluating the Lesson

Grid Map Activity, Notebook page 15

➤ Color the map and key on Notebook page 15. You may use your book. *Give help as needed.*

➤ Answer the questions on the page after you have colored the map.

> The shaded area for the prairie shown on the Notebook page is an approximation. It will not be incorrect for your child to color the entire area between the Great Forest and the Rocky Mountains. The answers to question 2 will be affected by the amount of territory which is shaded.

Going Beyond

Enrichment

Provide books about Native Americans so that your child can read about the people who lived in the eastern woodlands and on the plains.

Additional Teacher Information

The Great Plains stretch from Mexico to Canada along the eastern side of the Rocky Mountains. Although they appear level, they actually slant gradually upward from east to west. On the eastern edge where the Great Plains meet the Central Plains, the land is about a thousand feet above sea level. Where the mountains begin to rise on the western edge of the plains, the altitude can be five or six thousand feet. A few areas on the Great Plains do have some hills, but most of the four-hundred-mile-wide space is flat, inclined land.

The Great Plains receive less than twenty inches of rainfall per year—too little to support the growth of forests. Trees grow naturally in this region only beside streams and rivers. Even tall grasses do not grow well here, since the summer sun bakes larger plants. The prairie grass, with its long, tenacious roots, holds the top layer of soil—the sod—together.

This land, plowed and planted for years, became a giant "dust bowl" in the 1930s. The winds that swept over the plains picked up dust and carried it for hundreds of miles. Farmers have learned better methods for raising crops on dry lands. Irrigation helps produce large harvests in smaller areas. Instead of raising cotton, which weakens the soil, farmers grow wheat. Some of the dust bowl fields have been returned to grassland where beef cattle now graze.

LESSON 14
Mountains and Deserts

Text, pages 52-53, 286-87

——— Preview ———

Main Ideas
- Mountains have a unique climate.
- Deserts have special ecosystems.

Objective
- Name characteristics of mountain and desert animals and plants

Materials
- An almanac (optional)*
- An atlas
- Pictures of animals and plants characteristic of North American deserts and mountains, particularly a saguaro cactus*
- Map display from Lesson 13

Notes
Prepare the almanac by marking the page that tells the highest air temperature ever recorded in the United States. This information will be found in the meteorology section. Since almanacs may vary, you may need to adapt the instructions given.

Most almanacs contain some false information about evolution and the history of man. You may want to emphasize that almanacs are useful for finding factual information about dates, temperatures, geographical features, and so on, but untrustworthy in matters of philosophy and prehistory.

——— Lesson ———

Introducing the Lesson
Fact Find

➤ **What do you think was the hottest temperature ever recorded in the United States?**
➤ **Where can you find information about temperatures?** *(the weather service; an encyclopedia; a book of records)*

The almanac is the best source of significant data such as this. An *almanac* has many kinds of information in it. The information about highest temperatures is found in the section containing meteorological data. *Show your child where the information is recorded in the almanac.*

➤ **Read the information about the highest temperature given in the almanac.**

The highest temperature in the United States was recorded in Death Valley in 1913. Death Valley is a dry, hot region in California.

➤ *Give your child instructions for finding other information in the almanac.*

Look in the index of the almanac and find the listing for United States Facts. Turn to the corresponding pages. In the section containing U.S. Statistics, find the category for lowest point. Notice that the hottest place, Death Valley, is also the lowest point in the United States.

➤ In the same section of the almanac, U.S. Facts, find the highest mountain in the United States. *(Mount McKinley, Alaska)*
➤ **How do you think the temperatures at the top of Mount McKinley will compare to those of Death Valley?**

Temperatures at the top of the mountains are much cooler than in the low places. The coldest temperature recorded in the United States was from the mountainous regions of Alaska.

Snowcapped Mountains

Those people who crossed the wide prairie saw hills steeper and taller than any they had ever seen. Land that is much taller than the land around it is called a *mountain*. The Indians called these the "Shining Mountains." Why do you think they gave them that name?

Today we call these mountains the *Rocky Mountains*. Settlers had crossed much lower mountains in the East. Can you find these mountains on a map? The eastern mountains were not so steep and rocky. They were not covered with snow all year round either.

High in the mountains, the air is colder than it is on the prairie. It is too cold for most plants to grow. Do you think any animals can live there? A few can. Look at this animal. What would you call it? It is a bighorn sheep. Bighorn sheep live high in the Rocky Mountains.

52

Desert

Hot, dry, dusty, and brown. These words make many people think of just one thing—a *desert*. A desert is a place that gets only a little bit of rain each year—less than ten inches. Some deserts are scorching hot too. But other deserts are cold. Antarctica could be called a desert. Lack of water makes living in the desert hard.

Even though deserts are very dry, the land is not bare. What kinds of plants can you see in a desert? Do you think any animals can live there? God gave the plants and animals that live in the desert special ways of staying alive. Plants like the cactus have long roots that draw water into special storage places in the plant. Some cactuses can hold more than one hundred gallons of water. Animals get water when they eat these water-holding plants.

53

Teaching the Lesson

Text Discussion, page 52

High and low places usually have quite different landscapes as well as different plant and animal life.

➤ **Read page 52 to find out about life in the mountains.**

➤ **What is a *mountain*?** *(land that is taller than the land all around it)*

➤ **Why did the Native Americans call the Rocky Mountains the "Shining Mountains"?** *(Answers will vary; perhaps because of the snow on them; perhaps because of their size.)*

➤ **Do you know of any animals besides the bighorn sheep that live in the mountains?**

Animals such as mountain lions, eagles, marmots, mountain goats, and hares also live in the mountains.

At a certain height on the mountainside, trees stop growing. Only tough grasses and low plants grow there. The winds and cold destroy other plants. The roots of these grasses and low plants spread out far and wide just under the surface. The roots help the plants hold firm in the ground during high winds, and they gather water that falls onto the surface.

Map Activity, pages 286-87

➤ Find the area in which the Rocky Mountains are located. Compare to the physical map if necessary.
➤ Determine what group of Native Americans lived in the Shining Mountains before the settlers came. *(Shoshone)*

Day 2

Text Discussion, page 53

➤ **Read page 53 to find out how much rain a desert usually gets each year.** *(less than ten inches)*
➤ **What deserts have you heard of?**

Death Valley is a desert in the western part of the United States.

➤ **What plants and animals do you think might be found in a desert?**

Deserts are anything but barren. Cacti and sagebrush are plants commonly found there. Many kinds of animals also flourish there—even toads, which are generally associated with places having more water. One animal, the kangaroo rat, drinks no water at all. It gets enough from the food it eats. Other animals include rattlesnakes, iguanas, scorpions, gophers, mice, spiders, foxes, bees, roadrunners, and rabbits. God has provided all living things with the ability to live in their own environments.

➤ **How do you think the mountain goat compares to the desert fox?**

The goat is made for climbing steep places and for cold winter weather; the fox has special-sized ears for cooling off and can run incredibly fast. The goat's special abilities would not serve it well in the flat, hot desert. Nor would the fox's sprinting ability help much in the steep mountains, and its large ears would freeze in cold weather. God has carefully prepared every living thing for where it will live. (Bible Promises: H. God as Father, I. God as Master)

➤ Some deserts are hot in the day and cold at night. **How do you think the animals survive the changes?**

Many animals live in burrows underground, where temperatures remain more constant. Plants in the desert have long roots that reach deep into the ground for water. The saguaro *(sə·gwär′ō)* cactus, which can grow fifty feet high, has a long root. *Show the picture of the cactus.*

➤ **How do the roots of the cactus compare with roots of plants high in the mountains where no trees grow?** *(Those roots are shallow, spreading outward and creating a dense mass along the ground. In the mountains, such roots are necessary for getting the surface water and for stability.)*

The saguaro can hold several tons of water after a rainstorm. It can weigh as much as ten tons—more than an elephant—and live more than one hundred years. It has many spines.

➤ **What do you think the spines are for?**

Although the spines may keep some animals away, the saguaro is home to many birds and small animals. The spines cast shadows on the cactus, making shade for a quarter of the plant at all times. The spines also slow the wind before it hits the plant and takes moisture from it.

Map Activity, pages 286-87 and Atlas

➤ *Point out the desert areas of the southwestern United States on the physical map in the atlas.*
➤ Find the desert area on the map on pages 286-87.
➤ Determine what groups of Native Americans lived in the desert lands before the settlers came. *(Yuma, Navajo, Hopi)*

Evaluating the Lesson
Picture Activity

➤ *Give your child the pictures of the mountain and desert plants and animals.*
➤ Decide which animals and plants live in the mountains and which live in the deserts, giving your reasons for saying so. *Direct your child to add the pictures to the display you have chosen. Allow him to draw lines or stretch yarn or string from the appropriate places on the map to the pictures.*

━━━ Going Beyond ━━━

Enrichment

Give your child the almanac and a list of questions with it to encourage him to use it as a reference. The questions may include the following:

- What was the highest temperature ever recorded in the United States?
- What is the largest lake in the world?
- What is the population in your state?
- What was the lowest temperature recorded in the United States?
- What is the deepest place in the Pacific Ocean?

Additional Teacher Information

The grasshopper mouse is an unusual desert animal, so named for its preference for grasshoppers, scorpions, and lizards. It is no bigger than an ordinary field mouse, but there the similarity ends. It makes a high-pitched howl, a scream nearly beyond a man's capacity to hear. It is a voracious and aggressive hunter, and coyotes prey upon it.

Large mountain predators, such as the wolf and the puma, spend the summers hunting in the higher regions and then go down to the valleys for shelter in the winter. The smaller animals, such as hares and marmots, store up fat and hibernate through the coldest part of the winter.

LESSON 15
Down to the Sea

Text, pages 54-55, 286-87
Notebook, page 16

━━━ Preview ━━━

Main Ideas

- People use different methods to get from place to place.
- Methods of transportation have changed over time.

Objectives

- Name various modes of transportation
- Make a map showing his position in relation to familiar places
- Identify kinds of ocean shores

Materials

- Pictures of ocean shorelines and plants and animals that live on the West Coast*
- Map display from Lesson 14
- A globe*
- Books about transportation (optional)*
- A sheet of drawing paper

Day 1

━━━ Lesson ━━━

Introducing the Lesson

Transportation Search

➤ Using the resource books about transportation, list as many different kinds of transportation as you can in five minutes.

➤ Number the items on the list in order from the slowest to the fastest modes.

➤ **Which methods would the settlers going west have used?** *(walking, using wagons, riding horses; later, riding trains and stagecoaches)*

Notice that the methods are arranged not only from slowest to fastest but also roughly from oldest to newest.

◆ THINGS PEOPLE DO ◆

Traveling Across a Continent

North America is 2,807 miles wide from ocean to ocean. Have you ever traveled that many miles? Why did you make the trip? Some people travel that many miles every week. They make trips across the continent for different reasons.

Sometimes people want to see all the special places in their country. They might take weeks or even months to travel. People on a business trip zip across the continent in just a few hours. And some people even walk or ride a bike across their continent. Would you like to do that? How long would it take to ride a bike two thousand miles?

Today we have many ways to travel across a continent. But that was not true many years ago. In those days, a person could travel by boat on rivers. He could ride on a horse or in a wagon pulled by horses or oxen. Or he could walk. Which way would you have chosen to travel?

walking
733 hrs.

San Francisco

New York City

horseback
587 hrs.

bike
250 hrs.

steam engine
147 hrs.

car
49 hrs.

55

Teaching the Lesson

Text Discussion, page 55

> The student text pages are taught out of order in this lesson.

➤ **How many miles do you think it is from one side of North America to the other?**

➤ **Read the first paragraph on page 55 to find out how many miles there actually are.** *(2,807 miles)*

➤ **What is the distance if you round to the nearest thousand?** *(3,000 miles)*

Remember that, as far as that distance is, the Lord is able to remove our sins from us even further, as far as the east is from the west. (BAT: 1b Repentance and faith)

➤ **Read the rest of page 55 to see how transportation has changed.** *(It is much faster now.)*

➤ **How long would it take to ride a bicycle three thousand miles?** *(250 hours)*

➤ **How long would it take to walk from coast to coast?** *(at least 733 hours)*

Use the graph to complete the questions.

Travel:
(The distance traveled is the same in each case.)

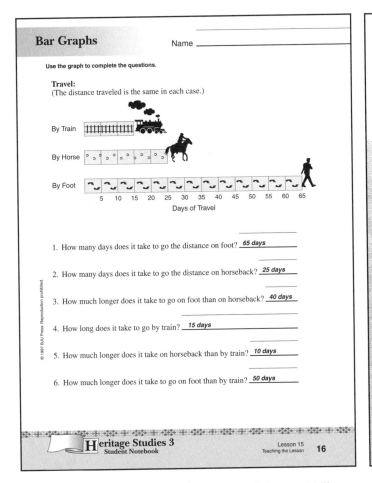

By Train

By Horse

By Foot

5 10 15 20 25 30 35 40 45 50 55 60 65

Days of Travel

1. How many days does it take to go the distance on foot? __65 days__

2. How many days does it take to go the distance on horseback? __25 days__

3. How much longer does it take to go on foot than on horseback? __40 days__

4. How long does it take to go by train? __15 days__

5. How much longer does it take on horseback than by train? __10 days__

6. How much longer does it take to go on foot than by train? __50 days__

Heritage Studies 3
Student Notebook

Lesson 15
Teaching the Lesson   **16**

By the Beautiful Sea

The mountains and the deserts stopped some people from moving farther west. Do you think that it was impossible to cross the deserts and mountains? It was not easy, but many people found a way.

Look at the map. Can you tell what these settlers found to the west of the mountains and deserts? They reached a thin strip of forest land. And beyond the forests, they found the *coast*.

The coast is the land at the edge of an ocean. We also call this land the *shore*. There are many different kinds of coasts. Some coasts are wide, sandy beaches. The ocean water rolls gently over these beaches. Other beaches are not so wide. Those beaches are filled with pebbles and shells. A third kind of coast is very steep and rocky. There the ocean water roars and crashes against the steep shore. Have you ever seen one of these kinds of coasts?

54

A long time ago, two men and those traveling with them walked and canoed from the Mississippi River to the West Coast and back in two years. The men became famous. We will learn about them in the next lessons.

➤ **How quickly can people get from coast to coast now?** *(in a few hours by plane)*

Graph Activity, Notebook page 16

➤ Study the graph on transportation.
➤ **What can you tell about the distance traveled by each form of transportation?** *(The distance is the same.)*
➤ **What does each segment in the bar represent?** *(five days of travel)*
➤ Complete the page. *Give guidance as needed.*

Text Discussion, page 54

➤ **Read page 54 to find out what people saw when they crossed the Rocky Mountains.** *(a thin strip of forest land, then the coast)*
➤ **Describe the different kinds of coasts.** *(sandy beaches, beaches with pebbles and shells, rocky and steep coasts)*

➤ **What definition is found in the first sentence of the last paragraph?** *(definition of* coast: *"The coast is the land at the edge of an ocean.")*
➤ **What is another word for *coast*?** *(shore)*
➤ **What plants and animals do you think live on shores?**

The plants and animals found depend on what kind of shore it is and how cool or warm the air tends to be. Much of the West Coast is steep cliffs where sea birds, such as the California gull, nest.

The northern part of our western shore borders the thin strip of forests. The cool, damp air helps firs and pines grow large. In northern California grow the famous giant redwoods. Animals such as bears, wolves, deer, and elk live in these forests near the coasts.

Picture Activity

➤ Examine the pictures of the coastal plants and animals, identifying as many as possible.
➤ Decide how these animals and plants differ from those in mountains, deserts, plains, and forests.
➤ Add the pictures to your map display. Draw a line or stretch yarn or string from the appropriate place on the map to the pictures.

Map Activity, pages 286-87

➤ Look at the map and find the coastal areas along the Pacific Ocean.
➤ **What people lived along the Pacific before the settlers came?** *(Tolowa, Lillouet)*

Day 2

Globe Activity

➤ Find the United States on the globe.

The United States is in North America—a continent. *Point out the North American continent, extending from Canada down through Mexico.*

➤ **Do you know what a *hemisphere* is?**

When people are talking about a globe, they call half of it a *hemisphere.* The word means "half a ball." *Point out the **Northern Hemisphere,** moving from the equator northward.*

➤ *Point out the equator.*

The *equator* is an imaginary line around the biggest part of the earth. It is represented on globes with a thick line.

➤ **Where do you think the *Southern Hemisphere* is located?**

It stretches from the equator southward. The hemispheres can also divide the globe into east and west. *Show the **Eastern** and **Western Hemispheres.***

➤ Locate your state or region on the globe. Name the hemispheres (Northern or Southern and Eastern or Western) it lies in.
➤ **Is your state above or below the equator?**
➤ **Why do you think that your town is not indicated on the globe?** Only the largest features can be shown on a globe.

Evaluating the Lesson

Mapmaking Activity

➤ Make a map of part of your neighborhood on a sheet of drawing paper. Choose an area which includes your home.
➤ Add a title and labels to your map as needed. *Provide assistance as your child draws his map.*

Going Beyond

Additional Teacher Information

California has an 840-mile coastline along the Pacific Ocean. If the state could be placed along the East Coast of the United States, it would reach from New York City to Savannah, Georgia. It would cover an area greater than the size of New Jersey, Delaware, Maryland, Virginia, North Carolina, and South Carolina combined.

LESSON 16
Setting Out

Text, pages 56-58, 248
Notebook, page 17

Preview

Main Ideas

• Nations gain land in different ways.
• Native Americans settled in all areas of what is now the United States.

Objectives

• Name members of the Lewis and Clark expedition
• Indicate the Louisiana Purchase on a map

Materials

• The figure of Lewis and Clark (1804) from the TimeLine Snapshots
• The presidential figure of Thomas Jefferson (3) from the TimeLine Snapshots

Day 1

Lesson

Introducing the Lesson

TimeLine Snapshots Activity, page 248

➤ Add the figure of Thomas Jefferson to the TimeLine at the year 1801.
➤ Read the information about Jefferson on page 248.

Teaching the Lesson

Text Discussion, page 56

➤ **Read page 56 to find out what land President Jefferson bought from Napoleon, the leader of France.** *(the Louisiana Territory)*

The land that was called Louisiana covered an area as big as the United States at the time. The purchase of the land, referred to as the Louisiana Purchase, took place in 1803.

➤ Trace with your finger the outline of the Louisiana Territory on the map on page 56.
➤ Find the city of New Orleans and the Mississippi River.

The United States had asked to buy only this river city, but Napoleon wanted to sell more land.

Exploring America

Thomas Jefferson held the letter in his hand. It was from his messenger to France, James Monroe. What would the letter say? Did Napoleon, the ruler of France, want to sell the city on the Mississippi River?

President Jefferson could not believe what the letter said! Napoleon had agreed to sell New Orleans. But that was not all. He wanted to sell all of Louisiana. James Monroe bought all the land for the United States. Now his little country was twice as big as it had been.

What was the Louisiana *Territory*, or area of land, like? No one really knew. But the president wanted to find out. He wanted, too, to make friends with the Indians in the territory. President Jefferson had already picked someone to lead a group of explorers. He asked his good friend Meriwether Lewis.

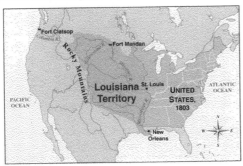

56

Meriwether Lewis planned carefully for the trip. His friend and assistant, William Clark, helped him. Together the men bought food and boats for the trip. They bought goods to give to the Indians as gifts of peace. And they chose thirty-one men to go with them.

The men left St. Louis on May 14, 1804. That summer they pushed and pulled their loaded flatboats and canoes up the Missouri River. It was hard work. Along the way they met many different groups of Indians. The men gave each chief a silver medal with President Jefferson's picture on it. They gave the other Indian people bracelets, cloth, and tools. The Indians promised to be the white men's friends.

Some of the Indians that they met had never seen white men before. They had only heard of them. But none had seen or heard of anyone like York, Clark's strong black servant. York would just laugh when the people tried to rub the "black paint" off his arms.

57

➤ **Why do you think that Napoleon, first consul or ruler of France, wanted to sell that much land?**

Napoleon wanted to keep England from having the land, and he wanted to raise money for a war that he was fighting somewhere else. Monroe was greatly surprised when Napoleon offered to sell almost a million square miles of land to the United States for approximately three cents per acre.

➤ **Do you think it was a big responsibility for James Monroe to decide whether to buy the land?**

Monroe had been given the power to make the decision by Thomas Jefferson, president of the United States.

When we have big responsibilities, we should not be distracted by our own importance but should focus on doing the job well, as Monroe did. (BATs: 2b Servanthood, 7e Humility)

➤ **Whom did Jefferson choose to explore the new lands?** (*Meriwether Lewis*)

Text Discussion, page 57

➤ **What do you think Lewis did to prepare for the trip?**

Lewis ordered supplies and learned how to take good notes. He and the others who went with him had some of the greatest adventures explorers have ever had.

➤ **Read the first paragraph on page 57 to find out who became Lewis's assistant.** (*William Clark*)
➤ **Read the rest of the page to find out who else accompanied the men on their long journey.** (*thirty-one men, including a man named York*)
➤ **What date did Lewis and Clark leave St. Louis to begin their great adventure?** (*May 14, 1804*)
➤ **Why were the Indians so interested in York?** (*They had never seen or even heard of black men.*)

York was tall and strong. His great strength often impressed the people he met.

➤ **How do we know that York was a friendly person?** (*because he would only laugh when someone tried to rub the "black paint" off his arms*) (BAT: 5e Friendliness)
➤ Listen to the following excerpt from the journals of Lewis and Clark.

Friday, August 16th, 1805: Some of the party had also told the Indians that we had a man with us who was black and had short curling hair; this had excited their curiosity very much and they were quite . . . anxious to see [him].

➤ **What did Lewis and Clark give to the people they met on the way?** *(silver medals to chiefs; bracelets, cloth, and tools to others)*

There were other gifts as well, such as salt, beads, mirrors, and gunpowder. Native Americans lived throughout the new lands.

➤ **Why did the men give gifts to the people they met?** *(to show they were friendly; to encourage the Native Americans to be kind to them)*

➤ **How do you think we know what happened on this trip?**

Lewis and his helpers kept careful records in a journal. Much of what we know of days long ago comes from letters and journals of people who lived then. This long adventuresome journey is often referred to as the "Lewis and Clark expedition."

➤ **What do you think your writing would tell someone about the times we live in?**

Encourage your child to keep a journal for a week or two. Later ask him to list all the modern items he has referred to in his writing.

Day 2

TimeLine Snapshots Activity

➤ Add the figure of Lewis and Clark to the TimeLine at 1804.

➤ Listen as I read an excerpt from the journals of Lewis and Clark.

Monday, May 14th, 1804: Rained the fore part of the day. I [Clark] determined to go as far as St. Charles . . . up the Missourie, and wait at that place untill Capt. Lewis could finish the business in which he was obliged to attend to in St. Louis and join me by land from that place 24 miles. . . . A heavy rain this after-noon.

Map Activity, page 56

➤ Find St. Louis on the map on page 56.

➤ **How do you think the men felt as they left St. Louis with Lewis and Clark on the great trip?**

Remember that as Lewis and Clark prepared for their trip, they knew they would have no inns or restaurants or even towns to go to. They had to take guns and knives in order to get food for themselves where they could find it. They had to take tents and blankets and every necessity with them.

Text Discussion, page 58

➤ **Read page 58 to find out who else joined the Lewis and Clark expedition.** *(a white man and his Native American wife and child)*

Lewis, Clark, and the men spent the winter near the Mandan Indian village. They built a fort and named it for the Mandans. "My wife and I can help you find your way," a man who came to visit Fort Mandan told Lewis and Clark. "I have traveled farther on this river than any other white man. And my wife is an Indian. Her people live in the Shining Mountains."

Lewis and Clark were not sure that they wanted to take a woman with them. She might make them travel more slowly. But they needed someone with them who could speak the language of the Indians in the Shining Mountains. The two men agreed to let the little family come along.

Soon the ice in the river began to melt. The group left Fort Mandan in canoes carved from trees. The Missouri River was not very wide, and the water flowed swiftly. They left behind the big flatboat and some of their supplies.

58

➤ **Where did the man say that his wife's people lived?** *(the Shining Mountains)*

This was the Indian name for the Rocky Mountains.

➤ **When did the group leave Fort Mandan?** *(when the ice began to melt)*

Lewis hired the man in order to have his wife go along as a translator. *Point to the name **Sacajawea** (Sac ə jə wē′ ə) on page 59.* The woman was a Shoshone named Sacajawea. We will read more about some things that Sacajawea did in our next lesson.

Map-Reading Activity, page 56

➤ Place your finger on the map on page 56 where the Lewis and Clark expedition officially began. *(St. Louis)*

➤ **Do you remember the river Clark mentioned in the journal entry of the first day?** He talked about traveling up the Missouri River.

➤ **Where did Lewis and Clark spend the first winter?** *(near a Mandan village; Fort Mandan)*

➤ Using your finger, trace a route along the Missouri River to Fort Mandan.

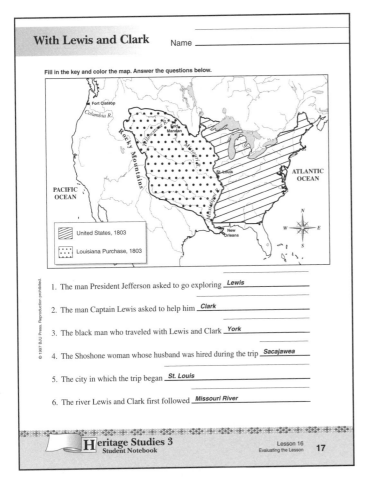

With Lewis and Clark

Name _____

Fill in the key and color the map. Answer the questions below.

United States, 1803

Louisiana Purchase, 1803

1. The man President Jefferson asked to go exploring _Lewis_____

2. The man Captain Lewis asked to help him _Clark_____

3. The black man who traveled with Lewis and Clark _York_____

4. The Shoshone woman whose husband was hired during the trip _Sacajawea_____

5. The city in which the trip began _St. Louis_____

6. The river Lewis and Clark first followed _Missouri River_____

© 1997 BJU Press. Reproduction prohibited.

Heritage Studies 3
Student Notebook

Lesson 16
Evaluating the Lesson   **17**

Evaluating the Lesson

Notebook Activity, page 17

➤ Color the map and key on Notebook page 17.

➤ Answer the questions at the bottom of the page.

➤ Trace the trip from St. Louis to Fort Mandan along the Missouri River and draw a small fort at Mandan. (*NOTE:* You may wish to encourage your child to compare his map with the one on text page 60.)

━━━ Going Beyond ━━━

Enrichment

Provide a copy of the reproducible of Lewis and Clark meeting the Mandans on Appendix page A11, notebook paper, and a cassette recorder with a blank tape. Explain that the people pictured are the Mandans, those with whom Lewis and Clark and the others spent the first winter. During this time, Sacajawea and her husband joined the expedition. Instruct your child to write a report of the meeting as though he were a newspaper reporter and to record his story on the tape.

Your child may prefer to write a play about the historic meeting instead of a report. After the play is written, the author may want to enlist the help of other family members to record the different characters' parts.

Additional Teacher Information

Lewis and Clark reached the Mandan villages in early November 1804. The Mandans lived in organized and permanent circular houses made of wood and covered with earth, the floors below ground level. Lewis ordered a small fort built, and by the first heavy snow (thirteen inches on November 29), the explorers were as ready for winter as they could be. They celebrated the coming of the New Year by firing their guns and visiting the Mandan villages. York surprised and pleased the Mandans with his agile dancing: they assumed his great size would keep him from quick physical moves.

Lewis and Clark and a few others joined the Mandans on a buffalo hunt. The river was frozen and the snow deep, so the group used sled dogs and sleds to bring the meat back to the village and fort. On the trip back, the temperature dipped to twenty below zero; several men suffered frostbite. Lewis had to amputate the toes of one Mandan boy.

In early February, food began to run out. Clark took eighteen men and went hunting. They were gone a week and came back with three buffalo, sixteen elk, and forty deer. But being exhausted, they were not able to bring the meat into camp by themselves. Lewis sent a small group to get it. This group was attacked by a Sioux raiding party. The Sioux stole some horses but were unable to find the cache of meat. Lewis ordered a larger company out; they brought in the meat and also some other deer they had shot on the way. This haul fed the company through the winter.

LESSON 17
Successful Journey

Text, pages 59-62
Notebook, pages 18-19

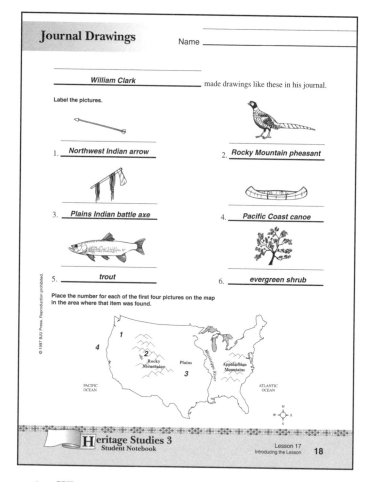

━━ Preview ━━

Main Ideas

- Nations gain land in different ways.
- Native Americans lived in all areas of what is now the United States.

Objectives

- Construct a time line
- Make a journal of an "expedition"

Materials

- 2 sheets of white or tan construction paper

 Prepare the construction paper by making the sheets into a small journal. Fold each sheet into fourths. Place one folded sheet inside the other. Cut across the top folded edges to remove the folds. Staple together along the side folds.

Notes

The "expedition" in this lesson may be as simple or as extensive as you wish. Suitable material for the journal can be obtained in a journey through areas of your neighborhood or a local park with which your child is not familiar. If you have an older child, he could become a guide, similar to Sacajawea on the Lewis and Clark expedition. You may arrange for other family members to represent the Shoshone and provide gifts with which to barter.

Day 1

━━ Lesson ━━

Introducing the Lesson

Notebook Activity, page 18

➤ **Where do you think the drawings on Notebook page 18 were originally made?** They are from the journal of William Clark.

➤ Write Clark's name in the first blank on page 18 to complete the sentence.

➤ **What do you think each of the drawings represents?**

As I tell you how Clark labeled the drawings, I would like for you to write the labels under the pictures. *Read the labels as shown in the answer key above.*

Notice that the plains, the mountains, and the coast are represented by these drawings.

➤ Write the numbers 1-4 in the correct locations on the map.

Teaching the Lesson

An "Expedition"

➤ Get the "journal" and a pencil.

I will be leading you on an expedition. You are to record in your journal interesting and important things that you see, just as Lewis and Clark did. Often, Lewis and Clark wrote in their journals in camp, rather than as they were walking.

➤ **Why do you think the men might have done that?**

They may have done it to save time in traveling or to allow themselves time to write enough detail. Some of the drawings had to be sketched on the spot and filled in later. Some of the drawings were made in camp.

Sacajawea

A baby girl was born into the family of Eagle Chief. The chief named her *Sacajawea*, "Bird Girl" in the Shoshone language.

Each fall Sacajawea's people left their mountain home. They traveled many miles to the edge of the prairie to hunt bison, or buffalo. Why do you think they hunted this animal? One year the herds of buffalo were small and hard to find. The Shoshone went far onto the prairie to hunt.

Then the Shoshone's enemies attacked! The enemy braves captured Sacajawea and made her a slave. She worked hard for her new master. But she missed her people in the mountains. She hoped that someday she would go home.

Years later Sacajawea, her husband, and her baby son joined Lewis and Clark at Fort Mandan. Sacajawea was a great help to the white men. She knew which herbs to use for medicine. She knew which plants and animals were good to eat. And she helped Lewis and Clark buy horses from her people, the Shoshone.

59

As the men came closer to the Shining Mountains, traveling was harder. The river got smaller and faster. Sometimes it was so fast that they could not float on it. Then they carried the boats and supplies.

Soon the group needed horses. They could not cross the mountains in a canoe. And if they tried to walk across the mountains, they would get caught in the winter snowstorms. Lewis set out to find Sacajawea's people.

Lewis left gifts for the Shoshone to find. When he met the Shoshone, he used the signs and Indian words Sacajawea had taught him. The Shoshone chief sold horses to Lewis and let an old Indian go with him to lead the men across the mountains.

Beyond the mountains, the traveling was easier. They built new canoes and floated quickly down another river. Then one foggy day they heard a steady crashing sound. As the fog

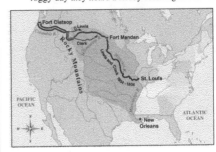

cleared, the men knew they had reached their goal. They had reached the Pacific Ocean!

60

➤ **What might have made the difference in how the drawings were completed?**

Some objects could be taken into camp and drawn, such as leaves and axes; others were too big or too dangerous, such as trees and bears.

➤ As you travel, you should make quick sketches and take a few notes, both to be completed later.

Journal-Keeping Activity

➤ Pretend that it is now nighttime. Complete the notes and sketches you made on your travels during the day.
➤ Complete your work in your journal.

Day 2

Text Discussion, page 59

➤ **Read page 59 to find out more about Sacajawea and what happened to her on a hunting expedition.** *(She was captured by enemies on the prairie and made a slave.)*
➤ **What did Sacajawea's name mean in her language?** *("Bird Girl")*
➤ **What do you think her name told about her?**

It may have meant that she was cheerful, quick, graceful, or small. Sacajawea once jumped into a

raging river to save the journal of Meriwether Lewis. It had fallen out when the canoe tipped over.

➤ **If she had not saved the book, how would that have changed what we know about the trip?** *(Much of what we know of the Lewis and Clark expedition might have been lost.)*
➤ **What are some of the ways Sacajawea helped the expedition?** *(She taught the men Shoshone words and signs, knew how to make medicine from herbs, knew which plants and animals were good to eat, and helped to buy horses.)*

Text Discussion, page 60

➤ **Read page 60 to learn more about the trip across the mountains.**
➤ **What were travel conditions like as the travelers reached the mountains?** *(Traveling was harder. Sometimes they had to carry the boats and supplies.)*
➤ **What did the Shoshone chief do to help Lewis and Clark get across the mountains?** *(He sold them horses and gave them a guide.)*

After many long years, Sacajawea had finally returned to her beloved mountains. The Shoshone chief was Sacajawea's brother, whom she had not seen in years. The whole village celebrated Sacajawea's return.

St. Louis
September 23, 1806

This day was a day for celebrating. Meriwether Lewis, William Clark, and their men had come back to St. Louis.

The men had been gone two years, four months, and twelve days. Most people thought that they all had died in the wilderness.

But Lewis and Clark had had good guides. They traveled all the way to the Pacific Ocean and back. Their journey took them more than eight thousand miles.

Imagine the things these men had seen! They would have many exciting stories to tell for years to come.

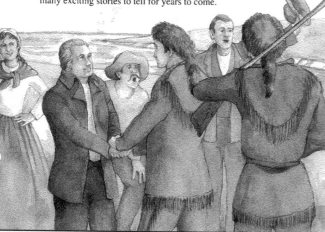

Today North America stretches from ocean to ocean. It covers all of the land that Lewis and Clark saw on their adventure and much more. It is a beautiful land of snow-covered mountains and grassy hills, deep, dark forests and sandy coasts. What parts of America do you like best?

"Thou art worthy, O Lord, to receive glory and honour and power: for thou hast created all things, and for thy pleasure they are and were created."
Revelation 4:11

62

➤ **What exciting view awaited the explorers on the other side of the mountains?** *(the Pacific Ocean)*
➤ Locate the Pacific Ocean on the map on page 60.
➤ **How would you feel if you saw an ocean that few people had seen before?**
➤ **How could you record your findings today?** *(photographs, videotape, film, writing, computers)*
➤ Imagine yourself with Lewis and Clark on the shore of the Pacific Ocean. **What might you have recorded in your journal?**
➤ Using your finger, trace on the map on page 60 the path that Lewis and Clark took to reach the Pacific Ocean as well as the path by which they returned.

Notice that during a portion of the return trip, Lewis and Clark took separate paths. However, they were reunited to complete the trip together.

Text Discussion, page 61

➤ **Read the headings on page 61 to find out what date the men returned to St. Louis.** *(Sept. 23, 1806)*
➤ **Read the page to find out how far the men had traveled on their journey.** *(more than eight thousand miles)*

➤ **How do you think Lewis and Clark felt when they returned to St. Louis?**

They may have been excited, happy, and proud. The people of St. Louis crowded along the river to cheer for Lewis and Clark and for all the members of the expedition. The people were glad to see them alive, and President Jefferson was thrilled to hear the reports about the new land. Lewis and Clark had done their jobs well. (BAT: 2c Faithfulness)

Text Discussion, page 62

➤ **Read page 62 and answer the closing question.**
➤ **Read with me the verse at the bottom of the page.**

Remember that no matter where we live, we can find much to be thankful for in the beauty God has created. (BATs: 7c Praise, 7d Contentment)

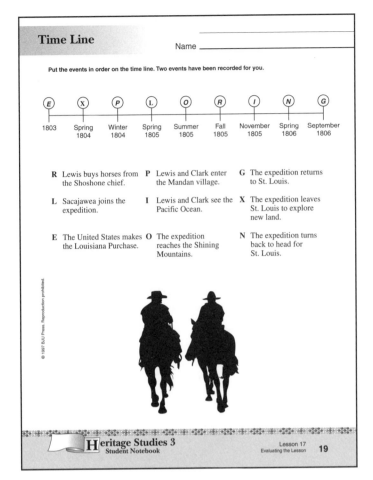

Time Line

Name _____

Put the events in order on the time line. Two events have been recorded for you.

(E) —— (X) —— (P) —— (L) —— (O) —— (R) —— (I) —— (N) —— (G)

1803 | Spring 1804 | Winter 1804 | Spring 1805 | Summer 1805 | Fall 1805 | November 1805 | Spring 1806 | September 1806

R Lewis buys horses from the Shoshone chief.

L Sacajawea joins the expedition.

E The United States makes the Louisiana Purchase.

P Lewis and Clark enter the Mandan village.

I Lewis and Clark see the Pacific Ocean.

O The expedition reaches the Shining Mountains.

G The expedition returns to St. Louis.

X The expedition leaves St. Louis to explore new land.

N The expedition turns back to head for St. Louis.

© 1997 BJU Press. Reproduction prohibited.

Heritage Studies 3
Student Notebook

Lesson 17
Evaluating the Lesson **19**

Evaluating the Lesson

Time Line Activity, Notebook page 19

➤ Read the events about the Lewis and Clark expedition listed beside each letter in the middle of the Notebook page.

➤ Arrange the events on the time line in the order that they occurred.

The letters in the circles will spell out the task that Lewis and Clark were involved in. Two events have already been placed on the line to help you get started. Do not be too concerned with the dates under the line at first; just arrange the events in order. (*NOTE:* Your child may refer to his text, if necessary.)

══ **Going Beyond** ══

Enrichment

Make available a baby name book or a dictionary that gives meanings of common names. Encourage your child to look up the meanings of his first and middle names. Instruct him to compose a Native American name that means the same thing as his name. For example, *Kimberly,* which means "from the royal meadow," could become *Royal Meadow* or *Princess Meadow.*

Additional Teacher Information

When Lewis and Clark returned to St. Louis, the people of the city gave them, as Clark records, "a harty welcom." Both men set immediately to writing reports and to compiling their journals into readable books. And both men were rewarded by their country for their arduous and dangerous service on its behalf. Clark was made a general in the militia and Agent General of Indian Affairs for Louisiana. This appointment was wise, for many Native American peoples had come to know and trust him. Lewis was appointed governor of the whole Louisiana Territory and was given sixteen hundred acres of land west of the Mississippi. But only three years after his glorious return, he was shot with his own gun and died. Some say that it was a suicide; others believe he was murdered for some boxes he carried with him, which contained the diaries of the expedition.

York was granted freedom from servitude and became a well-known figure in St. Louis. Sacajawea left the white settlements after her husband died. She married a Comanche and never again set foot in a white community. She is believed to have lived more than ninety years, making her the last member of the expedition to die, possibly on April 9, 1884.

The American Frontier

The lessons in this chapter cover much ground, geographically and chronologically. The exploration of the newly purchased Louisiana Territory and the first trips over the Oregon Trail will take your child thousands of miles. The chapter also presents the first settlers in the Kentucky wilderness, the Cherokee removal along the Trail of Tears, and the California gold rush. Not forgotten are those who had reasons for going west besides gold or land, particularly missionaries, who were often the first non-Native Americans in territories.

Materials

The following materials must be obtained or prepared before the presentation of the lesson. These items are labeled with an asterisk (*) in each lesson and in the Materials List in the Supplement. For further information see the individual lessons.

- Appendix, pages A12-A13 (Lesson 18)
- A set of toy building logs or alternative materials listed in the Notes section (Lesson 19)
- An ear of corn still in the husk (optional) (Lesson 19)
- Play props (optional) (Lesson 20)
- Appendix, pages A15-A17 (Lesson 21)
- Appendix, pages A18-A19 (Supplemental Lesson)
- Supplies for making a wagon (Supplemental Lesson)
- Appendix, page A13 (Lesson 22)
- Appendix, page A13 (Lesson 23)
- Appendix, page A20 (Lesson 24)
- Materials for Panning Activity (Lesson 24)

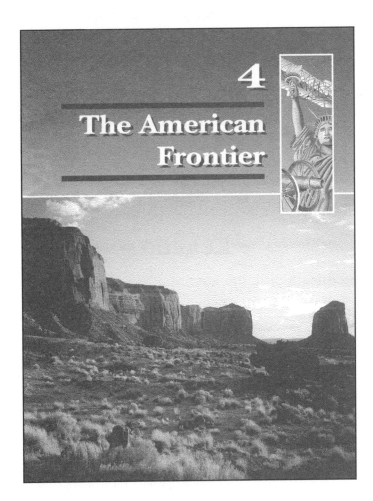

4

The American Frontier

LESSON 18
The Long Hunters

Text, pages 64-67, 286-87
Notebook, pages 20-21

―――――― **Preview** ――――――

Main Ideas

- Long hunters brought reports of the West to the East.
- James Beckwourth was a famous trapper and explorer.
- Disputes over land occurred as settlers moved west.

Objectives

- Trace James Beckwourth's path on a map
- Graph the number of rivers Beckwourth crossed or traveled alongside

Materials

- Appendix, page A12: The American Frontier map*
- Appendix, page A13: ovals*

Day 1

―――――― **Lesson** ――――――

Introducing the Lesson

Map Activity

➤ *Give your child The American Frontier map and the ovals.*

During this chapter you will be learning when and how the country gained possession of the land that is now the United States.

➤ Read the key. As you study, you will fill in the key and color the map.

➤ Locate the area labeled *The First Thirteen States.*

You can leave this area white. These states were part of the United States as of 1791.

➤ Cut out the oval with the 1791 date and glue it in *The First Thirteen States'* area.

➤ Find the area that is now Florida on your map. *Give your child help as needed.*

The United States received this land from Spain in 1819. This is all we will learn about this area of the United States in this chapter.

➤ Look at the key. Color the oval next to the words *Received from Spain.*

➤ Color the land received from Spain the same color.

➤ Cut out the oval with the 1819 date and glue it to the map over the land received from Spain.

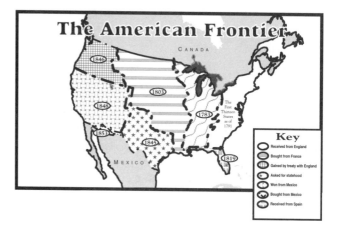

Game of Imagination

➤ Let's pretend that I have been somewhere that you have never been. Let me tell you what I saw there.

In the place I visited there was no water. The ground was covered with thick gray dust. There were high mountains and deep valleys but no animals or trees, and it was always daylight.

➤ **Do you believe such a place exists?**
➤ **Where do you think I was?**

Perhaps you thought it was a desert or the moon. Such a report would have sounded unbelievable fifty years ago because no one had ever been to the moon.

Heritage Studies 3 Home TE

Starting to Go West

Daniel Boone had tramped through deep woods and crossed many streams in his day. He had seen flocks of pigeons so thick that they blocked out the sun. He had heard the screams of bobcats; he had listened to the strange animal noises coming from the swamps. But not even Boone dreamed what was beyond the Appalachian Mountains.

Few settlers believed the tales the Indians told of huge trees and giant bears in the West. Few people believed Lewis and Clark, who reported millions of bison on the plains. They did not believe John Colter, who said there were great spouts of water in the Rockies and a lake so deep that it seemed bottomless. Today we know all about grizzly bears and redwoods and geysers. But try to imagine how wild all the stories must have sounded to someone in Franklin's Philadelphia.

Philadelphia had wide streets paved with stones. It had shops and brick houses. It had street lamps and a fire company. Sometimes pigs and cows wandered down the sidewalks. And now and then someone threw garbage out his front door. But most people thought Philadelphia was the best city in the world. What do you think the other big cities were like?

Giant redwoods

Castle Geyser, Yellowstone National Park, Wyoming

64

City life was not for everyone. Many people wanted to get to the open space of the West. At first, only the brave and strong went. They lived on what food they could find along the way, slept on the ground, and made clothes from the skins of animals.

Sometimes a man went out on a trip and did not come back for years. Such men were called *long hunters*. Why do you think they were called that? What do you think they were hunting for? Some were looking for land to farm. Some were looking for furs to sell. Some were just looking to see what was out there.

fur cap: the result of his marksmanship

homespun shirt: big square pockets to hold dried meat

handmade buckskin jacket: coat for protection against rain, cold, snow, and thorns

shot pouch: holds ammunition and occasionally other items such as new laces for boots

leather pouch: holds a compass, a tool made of bone, and perhaps a needle for repairing clothes

rifle: weapon for protecting himself and getting food

homemade boots or moccasins: sturdy protection for the journey of hundreds of miles

65

Text Discussion, page 64

➤ **Read page 64 to find out about some people who found reports from travelers hard to believe.**

➤ Put yourself in the place of the people who heard Daniel Boone's stories and the tales of Lewis and Clark. **Do you think you would have believed the reports?**

➤ **What was Philadelphia like?** *(description found in the last paragraph on page 64)*

Teaching the Lesson

Text Discussion, page 65

➤ **Why do you think that men like Boone, Lewis, and Clark went on exploring trips?**

➤ **Read page 65 to find some reasons that people left the cities to travel alone.** *(getting into the open space, finding land to settle, searching for furs, wanting to know what was there)*

➤ **What was the name the travelers were sometimes called?** *(long hunters)*

➤ **Do you think the name *long hunter* is a good one?**

The name was appropriate because the men hunted for long periods of time and traveled long distances.

➤ Study the picture on page 65 to see how some of the long hunters dressed.

Map Activity

➤ Look at your American Frontier map again.

➤ In the last chapter you learned about the Louisiana Territory, land that was purchased from France. Find the Louisiana Territory on your map. (*NOTE:* Your child may need to refer to text page 56 for help.)

➤ Find the oval *Bought from France* and color it and the Louisiana Territory the same color.

➤ Cut out and add the 1803 oval to the map.

➤ **Who were the men who explored the land for President Jefferson?** *(Lewis and Clark)*

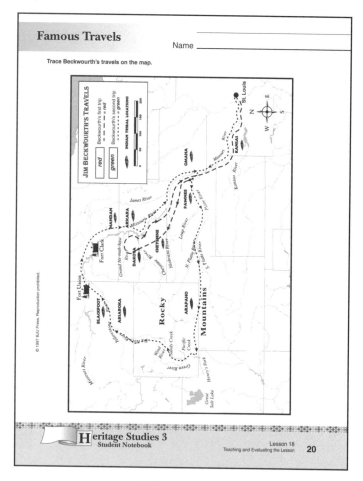

Famous Travels

Name _____

Trace Beckwourth's travels on the map.

Read the story slowly enough to allow your child to mark his map without missing the important details of the story. Pause when you see him marking on his map and then continue when he has completed. Allow your child to use a pencil to mark the route. After discussing his route, your child may mark over the pencil with a red crayon.

➤ Listen and mark the route as I read the story.

When James Beckwourth was a boy, he was apprenticed to a blacksmith. Although he liked the work, he did not like the blacksmith. The man was mean to him and wanted to make a slave of him. James decided that he would never be a slave, so he left.

One evening he was listening to some men talking in St. Louis. No one wanted to travel with the mountain man and scout "Black" Harris. The man traveled too fast and would not stop to help his companions. But James thought to himself, "Here's a way for me to make a name for myself." So he volunteered.

The next day James Beckwourth and Black Harris set off from St. Louis. They traveled along the Missouri River until they passed the Platte *(rhymes with flat)* River. When they found that the Pawnee had moved to winter quarters somewhere else, the two men decided to set out for the Grand Ne-mah-haw River. They walked for days. Beckwourth killed an elk. But it was thin, and the meat was barely edible. The men ate what they could and left the rest for wolves. They trudged on. They crossed four rivers. Their food was running low, and they were both getting tired.

After five days with no food at all, they finally made it to the Grand Ne-mah-haw River. They traveled down that river toward the Missouri River. Once on the Missouri again, Black Harris said that he was too tired to go on. James Beckwourth left him with a good fire and went on by himself. He had gone only half a mile when he met two Kansa Indians.

The Kansa Indians saw that Beckwourth was nearly starved to death. They took him and Harris to their village and fed them a thin mixture of cornmeal and water. When the men did not get sick, they fed them stew and meat. James Beckwourth and Harris were grateful to the Indians for helping them. The next spring the two men went back to St. Louis along the Missouri River. They later returned to the Kansa Indians and gave many presents to the people who had helped them.

Map Activity, Notebook page 20

➤ The travels and adventures of James Beckwourth are recorded in a book that he dictated to another man. **Do you think that a book written that way is a good source of information?**

The source is as reliable or as dependable as the man who tells the story. Some men tell the truth, and some men do not. Some people think that James Beckwourth made his adventures somewhat more exciting than they really were. Others believe that he was telling the truth.

➤ Look at the key on the map on Notebook page 20. Color red the rectangle next to *Beckwourth's first trip*.

I will be reading about some of the travels of a famous black explorer and trader, James Beckwourth. As you hear about his first trip, mark his route on your map.

➤ *Review the cardinal directions with your child using the compass on the map.*

➤ Beckwourth's trip starts in St. Louis. Find St. Louis on your map.

Your child's map route may vary in many ways from the way your map has been marked. For example, he may have Beckwourth arriving farther west on the Ne-mah-haw or traveling deeper into Pawnee country. As long as his map shows the route going along the Missouri, then swinging north toward the Ne-mah-haw and winding back along the Missouri, it is accurate enough. Look at your child's map, commending his effort and suggesting any changes. Notebook page 20 will be completed later in the lesson.

Ask your child whether he thinks the men did the right thing in rewarding the people for being kind to them. *(yes)* Remind him that God expects us to show gratitude to Him for His favors and to others when they help us. (BATs: 4a Sowing and reaping, 7c Praise)

After his ordeal, Beckwourth understood why Black Harris sometimes had to leave a companion.

➤ **What do you think would have happened if Beckwourth had not left Black Harris with a fire and gone on?** Probably both men would have died.
➤ **What did the Indians feed the men?** *(first a thin mixture of cornmeal and water, then stew and meat)*
➤ **Why do you think the Indians gave them only water and thin cornmeal at first?**

Feeding the men in this way would keep them from becoming sick by eating too much after they had gone so long without eating.

Map Activity, pages 286-87

➤ Look at the Indian Nations of Long Ago map on pages 286-87.

Native Americans already lived in every section of the country that the explorers had gone. James Beckwourth and Black Harris met two Indian tribes on their trip, the Pawnee and the Kansa Indians.

➤ Find the location of the Pawnee Indians on the map.
➤ Find the location of the Sioux. The Kansa Indians were a southwestern Sioux tribe, living in the area now known as Kansas.

◆ FAMOUS PEOPLE ◆

James Beckwourth
1798-1866

The young man wiped the sweat from his face and then pumped the blacksmith's bellows again. But all the while he thought of the wide prairies and the Indians that the traders had told about. A few months later he set off with some traders into the wilderness.

James Beckwourth soon became a good shot with a rifle and a friend of many Indians he met. He learned to track animals and to find food anywhere. Still he nearly starved to death one winter in the mountains. Just in time, a band of Kansas Indians found him and took him in. He was chased by bears; he was shot once; he nearly drowned in a flooded river.

Beckwourth made many trips west. He became a scout for the army. Then he built a trading post near the gold mines in California. He went out looking for gold himself—and found something more important. He found a *pass,* an easier way over the Rocky Mountains. Why was the pass a good find? It saved many from starving in the mountains. Today that pass, a mountain, a valley, and a town in Nevada are all named for the black pioneer Beckwourth.

66

Day 2

Text Discussion, page 66

➤ **Read page 66 to find out some of the other jobs that James Beckwourth had.** *(scout for the army, trader)*
➤ **For what is Beckwourth probably best remembered?** *(finding a pass through the mountains)*

A *pass* is an easy place to travel between mountains. Beckwourth Pass helped many people who might otherwise have died trying to get over the mountains.

After the long hunters came back with stories and advice, other people started moving west. They followed the trails the long hunters had followed. How do you think the stories of the long hunters helped them? The long hunters told where to find water, where Indians lived, where the trails were dangerous.

Still the going was not easy. Some Indian tribes did not want the white man to cross their land. Some shot arrows at settlers and burned the wagons. The travelers fought back. They thought the land did not belong to anyone. Why do you think they thought that?

Most Indians did not build permanent cities. They moved from place to place during different times of the year. They took only what they needed from a place. They did not "wear out" the land by staying too long. Settlers did not think about that. They said, "There are no houses here. No barns. This land is free for the taking." What do you think of that idea?

67

Text Discussion, page 67

➤ **Read the first paragraph on page 67, looking for ways the long hunters helped others who came behind them.** *(gave advice on where to find water, showed where Indians lived, pointed out the dangerous trails)*

We call the people who came to settle the land *pioneers* or *settlers.* As more people went west, problems arose for the pioneers.

➤ **Read the rest of the page to find out what some of the problems were.** *(Indian tribes did not want so many people crossing the land; settlers refused to believe that the land belonged to anyone because there were no permanent buildings on it.)*

➤ **Do you think that the settlers were right or wrong to say that the land did not belong to anyone?**

Many times the white settlers believed themselves to have the right answers, without considering the rights and ways of Native Americans. A Christian should never cheat anyone or cause God's name to be misrepresented. (BATs: 4c Honesty, 6c Spirit-filled)

Evaluating the Lesson
Map Activity,
Notebook page 20

➤ Look again at the key on Notebook page 20. Color green the rectangle next to *Beckwourth's second trip.*

I will read about another trip James Beckwourth took. Trace the route on Notebook page 20 in pencil as I read. Later you will trace it with your green crayon.

James Beckwourth tells how he and the men of the Rocky Mountain Fur Company left St. Louis in early May of 1824. They traveled up the Missouri River to Council Bluffs. Then they turned west and went along the Platte River. Along this river Beckwourth killed a buffalo, but he did not know what it was until someone told him. Since all the men were hungry, they were delighted with his hunting skills.

The men went west on the Platte to where it branched. Then they took the South Platte River. At the end of that river, some of their horses were stolen. But they went on to the Green River, just above Henry's Fork. They followed the Green River to Sandy Creek. Then they followed Sandy Creek to the Bighorn River. When the Bighorn River flowed into the Yellowstone River, they followed the Yellowstone to the Missouri. Then they went by the Missouri all the way back to St. Louis.

➤ **Which Beckwourth trip went farther north?** *(the second one)*
➤ **In what city did both of his trips begin?** *(St. Louis)*
➤ **Along what river did Beckwourth travel to begin both trips?** *(Missouri River)*

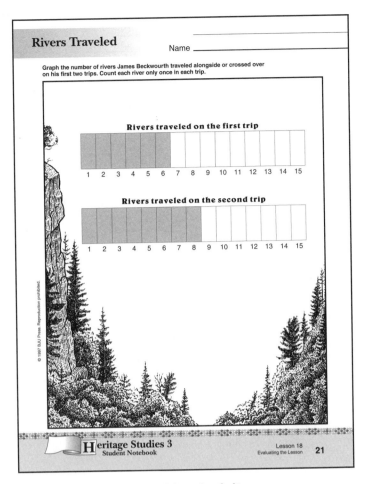

Rivers Traveled

Name _____

Graph the number of rivers James Beckwourth traveled alongside or crossed over on his first two trips. Count each river only once in each trip.

Rivers traveled on the first trip

1 2 3 4 5 6 7 8 9 10 11 12 13 14 15

Rivers traveled on the second trip

1 2 3 4 5 6 7 8 9 10 11 12 13 14 15

© 1997 BJU Press. Reproduction prohibited.

Heritage Studies 3
Student Notebook

Lesson 18
Evaluating the Lesson   **21**

Graphing Activity,
Notebook pages 20-21

➤ Read the directions on Notebook page 21.
➤ Use the map on Notebook page 20 to fill out the graph on Notebook page 21.

The count may vary by one or two, depending on whether your child thinks that Beckwourth did or did not cross a river to get to another. For example, he may count the Kansas River on the second trip since he may have traveled along it briefly before heading north. Accept any number within a reasonable range for which your child can demonstrate proof from his map.

━━ Going Beyond ━━

Enrichment

Give your child a copy of the map from the Appendix, page A14, and some colored pencils, felt-tip pens, or crayons. Tell him to decide how he would have traveled in the West if he had been an explorer and trapper. Tell him to mark two trip routes for himself, indicating them in the key with different colors.

Additional Teacher Information

James Beckwourth was the son of a slave and a Virginia planter. When he was seven years old, James moved with his family to St. Louis, where he went to school and was later apprenticed to a blacksmith. Some accounts say that James became angry and struck the blacksmith such a blow that he fell to the ground. After that, he had little choice about leaving.

Beckwourth attached himself to General Ashley, commander of the Rocky Mountain Fur Company. The general was given to bursts of rage, and in one of these rages, he blamed Beckwourth for something he had not done. Beckwourth quit the company and made ready to return alone to St. Louis. The general, recognizing that Beckwourth was the best hunter and scout he had, sent a French boy to apologize. Beckwourth relented, but afterward he spoke to the general only when circumstances demanded it.

On two occasions after that, however, James Beckwourth risked his own life to save Ashley. The general commented to another that he found the black scout a puzzle, for although Beckwourth would not pass the time of day with him, he would put himself in danger in his defense. Later, Beckwourth struck out on his own, and for some time he lived with the Crow people in their homeland, Absaroka. (*NOTE:* See the map on Notebook page 20.)

When Beckwourth was sixty-three, the United States government sent him and Jim Bridger, another famous mountain man, to keep the peace with the Crow nation. The Crow, who had kept track of their old friend, invited him to stay with them. They held a great feast in his honor. During the last day of the feast, Beckwourth became sick and died almost instantly. Some believe the Crow poisoned him in order to keep him with them. Others believe that he died of natural causes.

LESSON 19
Settling In

Text, pages 68-71
Notebook, page 22

━━━ Preview ━━━

Main Ideas
- Some settlers built log cabins for homes.
- Settlers often helped each other.

Objectives
- Build a model log cabin
- Recount the story of Daniel Drake's travels to Kentucky

Materials
- A set of toy building logs or alternative materials listed in the Notes section*
- The American Frontier map and ovals from Lesson 18
- Maps and More 7, page M5
- An ear of corn still in the husk (optional)*

Notes
If you cannot get toy building logs or a similar building set, you may use at least eighteen craft sticks, glue, brown or tan construction paper, a half-pint milk carton, and felt-tip pens. In the Evaluating the Lesson section, the *Learning How* Activity is listed twice, giving you the steps for both choices of cabin making—log building set or milk carton.

Day 1

━━━ Lesson ━━━

Introducing the Lesson

**Map Activity,
Notebook page 22**

➤ I will be reading about the Drake family, who moved from the East and went west. Follow the Drakes' move, marking the route in pencil on the map on Notebook page 22 as I read.
➤ Find Philadelphia, Pennsylvania, on your map.

> Your child may not be familiar with the cities mentioned in the story. Be sure to give him adequate time to locate each city and provide any help that he needs.

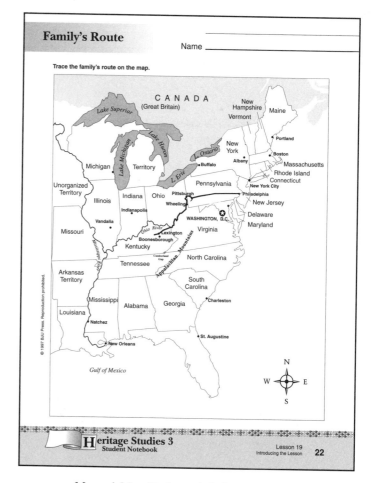

Family's Route   Name _____

Trace the family's route on the map.

CANADA (Great Britain)

Lake Superior · Lake Michigan · Lake Huron · Ontario · L. Erie

New Hampshire · Maine · Vermont · New York · Portland · Boston · Albany · Massachusetts · Rhode Island · Connecticut · New York City · Pennsylvania · Buffalo

Michigan Territory · Unorganized Territory · Illinois · Indiana · Ohio · Pittsburgh · Wheeling · Philadelphia · New Jersey · Delaware · Maryland · WASHINGTON, D.C.

Indianapolis · Vandalia · Missouri · Ohio River · Lexington · Boonesborough · Cumberland Gap · Virginia · Kentucky · Appalachian Mountains

Arkansas Territory · Tennessee · North Carolina · South Carolina

Mississippi · Alabama · Georgia · Charleston · Louisiana · Natchez · New Orleans · St. Augustine

Gulf of Mexico

N W E S

© 1997 BJU Press. Reproduction prohibited.

Heritage Studies 3
Student Notebook

Lesson 19
Introducing the Lesson **22**

Mr. and Mrs. Drake and their son Daniel left Philadelphia, Pennsylvania, on a rainy morning in 1810. They went west by horse and wagon to Pittsburgh. There Mr. Drake bought a flatboat. The Drakes put all they owned on that boat, including the two horses and the wagon. Then they floated down the Ohio River to Kentucky. Once they landed in Kentucky, they went by wagon to Lexington. The people there told the Drakes that good land was open farther west. They also said there were many rivers and streams with good water. Several other families had just arrived and wanted to go with them. So the Drake family and the others traveled a little west of Lexington and built a place to live.

> Check your child's map to see that he has approximated the route given in the guide. Accept any reasonable landing point on the Kentucky border.

➤ Look at your map to answer some questions.
- **What state is south of Kentucky?** *(Tennessee)*
- **Which direction would Daniel Drake travel to go to the Gulf of Mexico from his Kentucky home?** *(south)*
- **What direction did the Drakes travel across Pennsylvania?** *(west)*
- **What river does the Ohio join?** *(Mississippi)*

Daniel Drake was just a little boy when his father and mother went west to Kentucky. Do you think they had a place to live when they got there? They lived in a sheep pen until Mr. Drake could build a cabin of logs. Have you ever seen a log cabin?

Daniel's father laid the logs together as tightly as he could. He cut a notch in the ends of the logs so that the logs would fit snugly. Daniel could still see light between the logs. What do you think Daniel's father did about the cracks? He may have filled them with mud or clay or moss or all three.

The roof was made of boards and wooden slabs called *shakes*. Inside the cabin, the floor was dirt packed down hard. There was only one door with a heavy bar across it. The Drakes kept a rifle on the wall and an axe under the bed. They wanted to be ready for anything.

68

Food around the Drakes' cabin was easy to find in summer. Turkeys perched in trees and deer filled the woods. Daniel's mother picked berries and wild plums. The first winter the Drakes ate mostly meat, so much meat that Daniel cried for some bread.

The next summer Daniel's mother planted pumpkins, turnips, beans, and—most important—Indian corn. She made a sweet syrup from some of the pumpkins and dried the rest. The turnips and beans went into the cellar. Putting up the corn for the winter was more fun.

In places where neighbors lived fairly near, harvesting the corn became a *frolic*. Everyone came to help husk the corn. After all the work was done, they sat down to a dinner and joked and told stories until late at night.

70

- **What lake touches both Ohio and Pennsylvania?** *(Erie)*
- **What city in Kentucky is south of Lexington?** *(Boonesborough)*

Day 2

Teaching the Lesson

Text Discussion, page 68

➤ **Read the first two paragraphs to find out where Daniel's family lived first and what his father did to improve their living conditions.** *(They lived in a sheep pen until Mr. Drake could build a cabin.)*

➤ **Read aloud the sentence that tells what Daniel's father probably did to make the cabin tight against wind and weather.** *("He may have filled them with mud or clay or moss or all three.")*

➤ Describe the cabin in the picture on the page.

➤ Look carefully at the roof in the picture. **How do you think the roof was made?**

➤ **Read aloud the first sentence of the last paragraph.**

Shakes were like wide shingles. They were flat, almost square pieces of wood.

➤ **Read the rest of the last paragraph to see what the Drakes did to keep their new home safe.** *(They kept a rifle and an axe handy and barred the door.)*

➤ **Against what do you think Mr. Drake might have to defend his family?** *(Answers may include wild animals, thieves, and unfriendly Indians.)*

➤ **Do you think a dirt floor was warm or cold?** It was cold. It was cool even in the summer.

Picture Reading, Maps and More 7

➤ Look at Maps and More 7. **What do you think the man in the picture is doing?** He is making shakes for the roof of his cabin.

➤ **How do you think the tools work?** He will use the mallet or clublike tool to pound the adze through the wood, slicing a shake off. The adze is the axlike tool in the man's left hand.

Text Discussion, page 70

➤ **Read page 70 to see what the Drakes ate.** *(turkey, deer, berries, plums, pumpkins, turnips, beans, Indian corn)* The term we use for deer meat is **venison.**

➤ Name the event at which pioneers helped neighbors husk corn. *(frolic)*

The word *frolic* means "party" or "game." It is an event at which there is fun and merriment.

What kind of people do you think settlers were? Do you think they were scared and weak? Do you think they did whatever anyone said to do? Pioneers worked hard. They made rules to live by. They knew how to do things for themselves. Do you think Americans are still like the pioneers in any way?

Another War

England and France were fighting a war. England wanted to take Napoleon out of power. English sailors who did not want to fight the French sneaked onto American ships. They hid on the ships. England found out what the sailors were doing. What do you think the English did then?

English captains stopped American ships and searched them. English sailors on American ships had to go back to their own ships. How do you think Americans felt about having their ships stopped and searched? They were angry!

71

➤ **Why would the work of husking corn be made into a game?** *(Answers may vary. Work made into a game makes the work more pleasant and gets it done faster.)*

Having the right attitude makes tasks more enjoyable and less troublesome. (BATs: 2c Faithfulness, 2d Goal setting, 2e Work, 2f Enthusiasm)

Husking the corn—taking the husks off—lets the corn dry. The drying preserves the corn and keeps it usable through the winter. The drying also allows more corn to be stored in a small place. *If you have an unhusked ear of corn, show your child how to husk it.*

Text Discussion, page 71

➤ **Read aloud the first question on page 71.** *Allow your child to discuss his opinions about the pioneers.*
➤ **Read aloud the next question.** *Let your child voice his ideas about the courage of the pioneers.*

To help illustrate traveling to an unknown place, challenge your child to imagine that he has been told to leave his home and friends and to go by spaceship to another planet. He will not be able to return. He will have to leave some of his favorite possessions behind. To the pioneers, a trip of five hundred miles was as

frightening as a trip to the moon might be to us. Ask how he would feel as he left on this journey.

➤ **Read aloud the third question.**

Although it is wise to ask advice, it is not wise to do everything anyone tells you to do. (BATs: 2a Authority, 6c Spirit-filled) Most pioneers were independent. They made their own decisions and looked out for themselves. However, most were usually willing to help others. (BAT: 5e Friendliness)

➤ **Finish reading aloud the first paragraph.** *Discuss whether you do or do not believe that modern Americans are like pioneers.*

The American form of government was built on the idea that people should make decisions for themselves. We should respect the pioneer spirit of independence and courage but not forget that Christians depend upon the Lord for wisdom and life. (BAT: 8a Faith in God's promises)

The rest of page 71 will be discussed in the next lesson.

Day 3

Map Activity

➤ Find the section of land to the west of the thirteen colonies on your American Frontier map. This section of the United States was gained from Great Britain after the War for Independence in 1783.
➤ Use the same color to fill in this section on your map and the rectangle next to *Received from England* in your key.
➤ Glue the 1783 oval on the map.

Evaluating the Lesson

Choose one of the following activities according to the materials you will be using to make the cabin—building set or milk carton.

Learning How Activity, page 69
Using Building Set

➤ **Read the steps on page 69.**
➤ Construct a model log cabin from the log building set.
➤ Tell about the parts of the cabin.

Learning How Activity, page 69
Using Milk Carton

➤ **Read the steps on page 69.**
➤ Cover the carton with construction paper.
➤ Glue three craft sticks each on opposite sides of the carton and two craft sticks each on the other opposite sides.
➤ You may want to cut some craft sticks in half to use as rafters.
➤ Fashion *shakes* from the construction paper and glue them on to form a roof.
➤ Tell about the parts of the cabin.

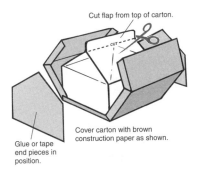

Cut flap from top of carton.

CUT

Glue or tape end pieces in position.

Cover carton with brown construction paper as shown.

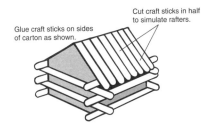

Glue craft sticks on sides of carton as shown.

Cut craft sticks in half to simulate rafters.

Cut small squares and rectangles from brown construction paper to represent shakes. Outline each shake with brown felt-tip pen or crayon. Glue the shakes closely together, with some overlapping.

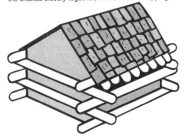

◆ LEARNING HOW ◆

To Build a Model Log Cabin

1. Get some toy building logs or some craft sticks. If you are using sticks, you will also need a felt-tip pen, scissors, an empty milk carton, construction paper, and some glue.

2. If you are using the logs, build a small cabin. Make sure the notches fit together. If you are using the sticks, use the pen to mark notches at the ends. Glue construction paper onto the sides of the carton first. Then build your cabin.

3. Make a roof with the pieces from the log set or in the way your teacher shows you. Do you think log cabins were comfortable to live in?

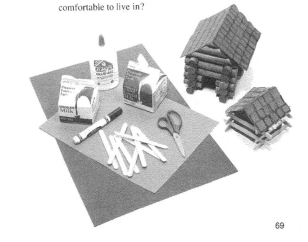

69

Going Beyond

Enrichment

Provide a basket with unhusked corn and an empty basket. Hold an old-fashioned husking bee with your child and family, letting everyone participate at once.

Additional Teacher Information

Frolics were not the only occasions for neighbors to help others with work. Cabin raisings were not uncommon. After a family had spent weeks felling trees and hand-hewing most of the logs and shakes, neighbors would come to help finish the cabin in a day. As the walls rose, long poles that slanted from the ground to the wall top allowed the men to drag the next log up by ropes. When the cabin was finished, it was the custom for the owners to invite the helpers in for a meal cooked over the first fire in the hearth. This custom gives us the term *housewarming.*

LESSON 20
Oh! Say, Can You See?

Text, pages 71-77, 249
Notebook, pages 23-26

Preview

Main Ideas
- America has had to defend her freedom in many wars.
- National anthems express national pride.

Objectives
- Sing the first verse of the national anthem of the United States of America
- Describe the circumstances under which the national anthem of the United States was written

Materials
- The figure of Francis Scott Key (1812) from the TimeLine Snapshots
- The presidential strip with the figure of James Madison (4) from the TimeLine Snapshots
- Play props such as flashlights, drums, rope, and toy rifles (optional)*

> If you have the time and can gather additional people as characters, you may want to provide some props and costumes for the play. Props may be simple, such as sticks for rifles and flashlights and drums for stage effects.

- *HERITAGE STUDIES Listening Cassette A*
- Supplement, page S4: words of "The Star-Spangled Banner"

Day 1

Lesson

Introducing the Lesson

Text Discussion, pages 71-72

➤ **Read the "Another War" section on pages 71-72 to find out why the Americans were fighting the British again.** *(British ships were stopping American ships and searching them.)*

➤ **What solution did President Jefferson try?** *(He ordered American ships to stay home.)*

What kind of people do you think settlers were? Do you think they were scared and weak? Do you think they did whatever anyone said to do? Pioneers worked hard. They made rules to live by. They knew how to do things for themselves. Do you think Americans are still like the pioneers in any way?

Another War

England and France were fighting a war. England wanted to take Napoleon out of power. English sailors who did not want to fight the French sneaked onto American ships. They hid on the ships. England found out what the sailors were doing. What do you think the English did then?

English captains stopped American ships and searched them. English sailors on American ships had to go back to their own ships. How do you think Americans felt about having their ships stopped and searched? They were angry!

71

President Thomas Jefferson made all American ships stay home for a year. Many Americans thought that rule would solve the problem. If no ships were sailing, no ships would get stopped. Others thought that President Jefferson was afraid of fighting.

Henry Clay did not like the plan. He said, "We should tell the English to stay off our ships!" He told the other members of the government what he thought. "We should fight England!"

James Madison became president after Jefferson. What do you remember about Madison? He agreed with Henry Clay. About twenty years after the War for Independence, the United States went to war again. English ships sailed up the Potomac River to Washington, D.C. The English soldiers set fire to the president's house and the new Capitol.

72

Washington, D.C.
August 24, 1814

President Madison sent word to his wife. "Leave the Capitol! The British are coming!"

Dolley Madison looked around. "Well, they won't get my china! Nor these papers and books!"

She packed up trunks with important letters, silver, and other things. Then she hurried out. She passed by a picture of George Washington. In a flash, she cut the picture out of the frame and took it with her.

Today we have many treasures from the early days because Mrs. Madison thought fast and acted quickly.

73

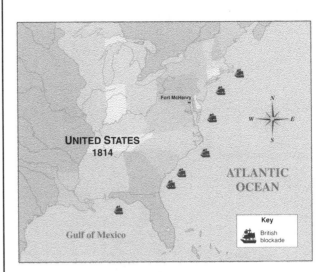

English ships kept American ships from sailing. Sometimes the English ships fired cannons at towns and forts on the coast. They fired on Fort McHenry. The cannons of the fort fired back. All night the guns roared. The blasts lit up the sky like lightning. People in the fort did not know what would happen.

If the English won, they would take down the United States flag and put up their own. Every time a cannon blast lit up the night, Americans tried to see which flag was flying over the fort. What do you think they saw?

74

➤ **Did that solution work?** *(As long as ships did not sail, they did not get stopped.)*

➤ **Why do you think Henry Clay did not like the plan?**

He did not want to let the British make the Americans stay home. He wanted to make the British leave American ships alone.

➤ **Which president agreed with Henry Clay?** *(James Madison)*

TimeLine Snapshots Activity, page 249

➤ **What important convention was James Madison a member of?** *(Constitutional Convention)*

➤ Add the presidential strip with the figure of James Madison to the TimeLine.

➤ **What year did James Madison become president?** *(1809)*

➤ **Read the information about Madison on page 249.**

Text Discussion, page 73

➤ **Read page 73 silently to find out what happened when the British set fire to the Capitol.** *(Mrs. Madison rescued many national treasures.)*

➤ **Why did Mrs. Madison risk her life to save the pictures and letters and other things?** *(She did not want them to be destroyed or taken.)*

People like to have reminders of past events. Although people should not worship pictures or flags, they can use them to help remember the bravery and sacrifice of the people who came before. Mrs. Madison knew that it was important for the country to have reminders of the War for Independence and of the people who fought in that war.

Text Discussion, page 74

➤ **Read page 74 to find out what happened at Fort McHenry.** *(The English fired cannons at the fort. The cannons of the fort fired back.)*

➤ **What would happen to the United States flag if the English won?** *(The English would take it down and put up their own flag.)*

Can You Still See the Flag?

Name _____

Can You Still See the Flag?

Name _____

Cast of Characters

Dr. Beanes
Five British soldiers
Jailer
British admiral
Mr. Jansen
Mrs. Jansen

Mrs. Lander
Mr. Francis Scott Key
President James Madison
Mrs. Skinner
Colonel Skinner

Scene One

(The scene takes place at night, near the home of Dr. Beanes. The stage is quiet and dimly lit. From offstage, three soldiers are heard singing. They enter, singing and making noise. Dr. Beanes can be seen sleeping upstage.)

Soldiers

(singing) With a hey-ho, hey-nonny-ho! *(break off with laughing)*

Dr. Beanes

(waking up) What? What's the racket? *(getting up and calling out the window)* Hey! How about some quiet out there?

Soldier 1

(loudly) Quiet? You want quiet? Not us! *(beginning to bang around and yell)* Give the man some quiet, boys! *(The soldiers make all the noise they can.)*

Dr. Beanes

Please, men, be quiet! I have to get some sleep. *(A jailer enters, swinging keys and whistling.)* I say, jailer! Can you make these men be quiet?

Soldier 2

No, he can't. We're British soldiers!

Soldier 3

Let him try! I say he can't!

Jailer

I certainly can. Stand still, you three. Drop your guns and come with me! Do as I say, or I'll shoot!

(The soldiers do as they are told. They file off, followed by the guard. Dr. Beanes falls asleep again.)

Teaching the Lesson

Play Activity,
Notebook pages 23-26a

➤ Look at Notebook page 23. This is the title page for a play. **What is the title of the play?** *("Can You Still See the Flag?")*

➤ **What do you think that the title refers to?** You will find the answer to the question in this historical play.

➤ **Read the list of characters on Notebook page 24.**

You will notice that each character's name appears in the center of the page in dark print before he begins speaking. The print that is in parentheses tells how the character should speak his lines and gives stage directions.

➤ **Read the play.**

➤ **How long do you think the war continued?**

The war was long and difficult. Many Americans were wounded, captured, or killed. The new country was glad to know that it could defend itself.

➤ **Was Mr. Key brave?** *(yes)* **How do we know?** *(He risked his freedom and his life for a friend.)* (BAT: 5a Love)

Scene Two

(The same night. Dr. Beanes is sleeping soundly. Two British soldiers enter.)

Soldier 4

Here's the house. *(loudly)* Dr. Beanes! Dr. Beanes! Get up! You are under arrest!

Dr. Beanes

What? Now what! Who's there?

Soldier 5

The soldiers of his majesty, King George III. Come down and go with us!

Dr. Beanes

What's the charge? What have I been accused of?

Soldier 4

You were mean to some soldiers earlier tonight. Our admiral wants to see you. Come down, or we'll come get you.

Dr. Beanes

Oh, very well. This is ridiculous.

(Dr. Beanes comes to the soldiers, and they march him off.)

Scene Three

(It is early morning. Friends of the doctor are on the street: Mr. and Mrs. Jansen, Mrs. Lander, Colonel and Mrs. Skinner, and Mr. Francis Scott Key.)

Mr. Jansen

They took him right from his bed—no time to dress! They rode him off on a mule. Now he's onboard the British ship.

Mrs. Jansen

Poor Dr. Beanes! He is always so kind and good to everyone! Why would they take him?

Colonel Skinner

No matter about that now. The thing to do is get him back!

Mrs. Lander

But how? The British ships have cannons and guns and so many soldiers. We can't get him back!

24a

Mrs. Skinner

Maybe not with guns—but we have a better weapon.

Colonel Skinner

And what is that?

Mrs. Skinner

Words! And who is better with words than Mr. Key?

Mr. Key

Me? You think I can get Dr. Beanes back?

Colonel Skinner

My wife is right! You're the best speechmaker I ever heard. You can go talk to the admiral. He'll listen to you!

Mr. Key

I am willing to do anything to help Dr. Beanes. If you think I can do some good, I'll certainly try. I must ask the president first, though.

Scene Four

(Mr. Key and President Madison are talking as they look over the harbor toward the British ships.)

President Madison

It is the best way, Mr. Key. I appreciate your bravery.

Mr. Key

I am always glad to help a friend.

President Madison

I've asked Colonel Skinner to go with you.

Mr. Key

There's no need for that, Mr. President. I'm sure it'll be—

President Madison

No, Mr. Key. Colonel Skinner will go. God bless you both.

Scene Five

(Onboard the British ship the next day. Dr. Beanes is sitting in a chair with his hands tied. He does not look angry, just a little tired. Mr. Key, Colonel Skinner, and the admiral are talking together downstage. Two soldiers stand guard.)

Heritage Studies 3
Student Notebook

Lesson 20
Teaching the Lesson **25**

Admiral

No, I will not hear any more. My men escaped from your jail and reported that this Dr. Beane had them thrown in jail for nothing. I've heard enough!

Mr. Key

But what of Dr. Beanes's side of it? Has the British Empire given up its great tradition of fairness in the courts? Has its long history of law broken down?

Admiral

None of your fancy speeches, Mr. Key. The answer is no.

Mr. Key

(looking at the Colonel) What can we say?

Colonel Skinner

(stepping up to Mr. Key) Show him these letters. They are from British soldiers Dr. Beanes helped care for.

Mr. Key

Admiral, with your permission—I would like to show you some letters. If you will not believe me on the matter of Dr. Beanes's good character, perhaps you will believe your own men. *(He hands over the letters.)*

Admiral

(opening a letter and reading from it) "And in that time I found I owed my life to an American doctor, Dr. Beanes." Harumph. *(He opens another letter and reads.)* "But I was treated kindly by one American, a Dr. Beanes. He came many times to see whether I had all I needed—" Well, it seems I may have been wrong. Untie the doctor.

(A soldier unties Dr. Beanes. The doctor stands up, rubbing his wrists.)

Mr. Key

Thank you, Admiral. We'll be going.

Admiral

Not so fast. The doctor is free of charges, but you are not free to go. There is a battle beginning here, and I cannot have you going to your friends and giving out any secrets. No, you will wait aboard my ship until I say otherwise. *(He turns and strides off.)*

25a

Mr. Key

I say! A battle! And we are to remain here?

Colonel

I shouldn't worry, my good fellow. See the flag flying over Fort McHenry? I dare say we shall see it there tomorrow as well!

Mr. Key

I pray that you are right, Colonel.

Scene Six

(The deck of a British ship. Mr. Key is pacing back and forth.)

Dr. Beanes

Come, Mr. Key. Please, come sit down and rest. You'll wear yourself out with all that pacing. And me with it, I fear.

Colonel

Yes, Key. We can do nothing but wait for morning.

Mr. Key

Oh! Did you see? In that bomb blast? The flag! Did you see it?

Dr. Beanes

I can't see anything. The smoke and mist are so thick.

Mr. Key

The American flag must not come down. Our defenses at Fort McHenry are strong enough, don't you think, Colonel?

Colonel

The fort is well defended. But these British guns are harder to hold out against than I thought.

Dr. Beanes

What will be will be, my boy. Sit down, now, and wait. The sun will soon be coming up, and then we will see.

Mr. Key

There's another bomb bursting. Look! Can you see if the flag is still there?

Colonel

Can't see a thing. Wait. There it is. I saw it for a moment—truly I did.

Heritage Studies 3
Student Notebook

Lesson 20
Teaching the Lesson **26**

Dr. Beanes

Praise be. Let us pray it is still there at sunrise.

Scene Seven

(Dr. Beanes is sleeping in a chair. The colonel is leaning against the rails of the ship. Mr. Key is straining to see the flag.)

Mr. Key

The sun is up enough, but I can't see the flag.

Colonel

If a breeze would stir, perhaps we could see it then.

Mr. Key

There it is! There it is! Praise be, the flag still flies! Wake up the doctor! The American flag is waving still!

(The admiral and two soldiers enter swiftly.)

Admiral

Put these Americans ashore! Then put to sea! Move!

(The admiral leaves on the opposite side of the stage as he entered. The soldiers stay and pantomime putting down a small boat into the water. The three Americans slap each other's backs and shake hands, saying together "hurrah." Mr. Key pulls out an envelope and writes on it.)

Dr. Beanes

What an adventure to tell my grandchildren!

Colonel

And what a story for the newspapers. Key, what are you doing?

Mr. Key

I'm putting this wondrous sight into a poem. "Oh, say, can you see by the dawn's early light. . . ."

26a

◆ THINGS PEOPLE DO ◆

Writing an Anthem

One man near Fort McHenry watched the United States flag at every bomb blast. When the sun started to come up, he strained to make out the stars and stripes on the fluttering cloth. "Please," he thought, "let it still be the American flag."

He took out a pencil and began to write a poem. It was a poem that asked the important question, *O, say, does that star-spangled banner yet wave?* When the sun was up, he had his answer. The United States flag was still there.

Francis Scott Key finished his poem the next day and put it in his pocket. Do you think it stayed there? No, it later became the words of our national anthem. We call it "The Star-Spangled Banner." What other national anthem do you know about?

75

The war was called the *War of 1812.* But the war lasted more than one year. At first England won most of the battles. Then America began to win. America hoped to take Canada from the English. Why do you think America wanted Canada?

For one thing, Canada had lots of beavers and foxes and otters. Hunting was good there. Americans also wanted to get the English off their borders. Americans still remembered the War for Independence. And they did not want the English to rule them again.

The War of 1812 ended with a treaty. The people of the United States were proud. They had proved that their country would defend its rights. Did the United States take Canada? No, Canada still belonged to England.

Modern political boundaries of the United States and Canada

77

Text Discussion, page 75

➤ **Read page 75 to find out what happened to the poem Mr. Key wrote.** *(It became the national anthem of the United States.)*
➤ **What do we call it?** *("The Star-Spangled Banner")*

The song became popular immediately. It did not become the official national anthem until 1931.

Day 2

The text pages will be taught out of order in this lesson.

Text Discussion, page 77

➤ **Read page 77 to see what this war with England was called.** *(War of 1812)*
➤ **What did the *War of 1812* end with?** *(It ended with a treaty.)*
➤ **Do you know what a treaty is?** A *treaty* is an agreement of peace between two or more states or countries.
➤ **What country did America hope to take?** *(Canada)*
➤ **Why did the United States want Canada?** *(Hunting was good there, and Americans wanted to get the English off their borders.)*

➤ **Read aloud the sentence that tells why the United States was proud of the treaty.** *("They had proved that their country would defend its rights.")*

TimeLine Snapshots Activity

➤ **What year marked the beginning of the war in which Mr. Key wrote the national anthem?** *(1812)*
➤ Add the figure of Francis Scott Key to the TimeLine at 1812.

Evaluating the Lesson

Learning How Activity, page 76

➤ **Read the steps on page 76.**
➤ Look at the words of "The Star-Spangled Banner" as I read them.
➤ Put the first few lines into your own words. *(Can you still see the flag that was there last evening?)*
➤ Describe what was happening when the song was written. *(The British were using cannons to bomb Fort McHenry. Mr. Key was being held on a British ship. All night he kept looking for the American flag by the light of the explosions. In the morning the American flag still waved. The British had not won.)*
➤ *Continue with the reading, letting your child put the lines into his own words.*
➤ Let's stand and sing the anthem along with the recording.

◆ LEARNING HOW ◆

To Sing "The Star-Spangled Banner"

1. Listen as your teacher reads the words of "The Star-Spangled Banner." In your own words, tell what these lines mean.

2. Sing the anthem along with the recording. Try to imagine that you are watching for the American flag at Fort McHenry with Francis Scott Key as you sing.

3. Learn the words to the first verse of the anthem as your teacher helps you.

76

Going Beyond

Additional Teacher Information

When "The Star-Spangled Banner" was being written, Thomas Jefferson was seventy-two years old, living at his beloved Monticello. In the backwoods of Kentucky, the Lincolns were contending with a frisky five year old named Abraham. The United States itself was only thirty-eight years old.

The song, although immensely popular within two weeks, did not become the official national anthem of the United States until 1931. It had been the official anthem for all the armed forces since Woodrow Wilson proclaimed it so in 1916. It is set to the tune of "Anacreon in Heav'n," a well-known English drinking song. The flag that flew over Fort McHenry that famous night hangs today in the Smithsonian Institution.

LESSON 21
More Settlers

Text, pages 78-81, 249-50, 284-85
Notebook, pages 27-30

Preview

Main Ideas
- People went west for many reasons.
- People settle where they think their needs can be met.

Objectives
- Explain what a landmark is
- Use landmarks to give and follow directions

Materials
- The presidential strip with figures of James Monroe (5) and John Quincy Adams (6) from the TimeLine Snapshots
- Appendix, page A15: a copy of Notebook page 28*
- Appendix, page A16: a copy of Notebook page 29*
- Appendix, page A17: a copy of Notebook page 30*
- A Bible
- A sheet of paper with a simple star drawn on it and hung on a wall of the schoolroom

Day 1

Lesson

Introducing the Lesson

Map Activity, pages 284-85

➤ Look at the map on pages 284-85. Find the Appalachian Mountains.

Before 1780, most new settlers lived east of those mountains. When we say that the pioneers or settlers "went west," we mean that they crossed the Appalachian Mountains and went west beyond these mountains.

➤ **What people lived both east and west of these mountains?** *(Native Americans)*

➤ **Why do you think that the new settlers did not go beyond the mountains for a long time?**

Traveling was too hard. There was enough land to share in the East.

➤ **What do we call the land between the Appalachian Mountains and the Rocky Mountains?** *(plains)*

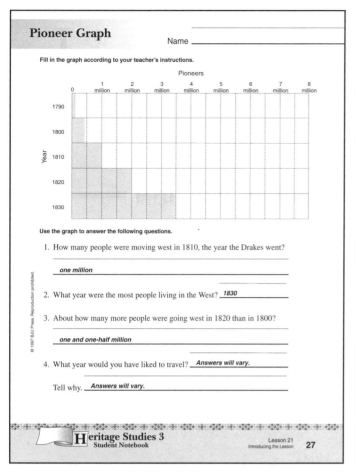

Pioneer Graph

Name _____

Fill in the graph according to your teacher's instructions.

Pioneers

Use the graph to answer the following questions.

1. How many people were moving west in 1810, the year the Drakes went?

   one million

2. What year were the most people living in the West? _1830_

3. About how many more people were going west in 1820 than in 1800?

   one and one-half million

4. What year would you have liked to travel? _Answers will vary._

   Tell why. _Answers will vary._

More People Go West

The first people to cross the Appalachian Mountains got a big surprise. They were used to deep woods and hills and rough roads. Suddenly the land flattened out in every direction. It looked like an ocean of short bluegrass. The prairie seemed like a whole new country. In the beginning the travelers thought, "This will be much better for travel."

The land was flat, but water was not always easy to find. And there were no *landmarks*—easily seen objects like mountains and trees—to go by. How do you think the people kept going in the right direction? Every night they turned their wagons toward the North Star. In the morning, then, they could figure out which way west was.

Sometimes the oxen or horses got too weak to pull the heavy wagons. Then the settlers had to lighten the load. They left behind organs, trunks, cupboards, and beds. Sometimes children had to leave their toys. How would you feel about that?

78

➤ **Do you think the number of people going west got larger or smaller?** *(larger)*

TimeLine Snapshots Activity, pages 249-50

➤ James Monroe and John Quincy Adams served as presidents of the United States during much of this westward movement. Find the figure of James Monroe on the TimeLine at the year 1817 and the figure of John Quincy Adams at the year 1825.

➤ **Read about James Monroe and John Quincy Adams on pages 249-50.**

Graph Activity, Notebook page 27

➤ Use a colored pencil or a crayon to fill in the graph on Notebook page 27 as I read some statements.

- After 1780 people began to live more and more in the lands beyond the Appalachian Mountains. *(no graph work)*
- By 1790 just a few thousand settlers had gone west. *(Color the 1790 band close to the zero mark.)*
- By 1800 almost half a million settlers had come. *(Color the 1800 band nearly to the half million mark.)*

- There were one million settlers pouring into the mountains and beyond in 1810. *(Color the 1810 band to the one million mark.)*
- In 1820 there were two million settlers there. *(Color the 1820 band to the two million mark.)*
- In 1830 about three and a half million settlers were living beyond the Appalachians. *(Color the 1830 band to the three and a half million mark.)*

➤ Answer the questions under the graph.

➤ The flow of people increased rapidly after 1810. **Why do you think the flow increased?**

Travel became easier. The number of people coming from Europe increased.

Day 2

Teaching the Lesson

Text Activity, page 78

➤ **Read page 78 to find out what surprised people who went over the mountains into the plains for the first time.** *(the flat land)*

➤ **What is a *landmark*?** *(an easily seen object)*

➤ **Why would early travelers use landmarks?** *(There were no maps; people who gave directions referred to the landmarks.)*

➤ Use a landmark to give directions to a well-known place such as your church or your father's work.

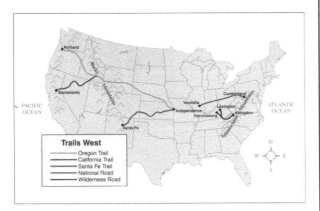

Most settlers followed the same trails. The trails had names like the *Oregon Trail*, the *National Road*, and the *Wilderness Road*. Can you find these trails on the map? What do the names tell you about the trails?

For a few years the people going west were like a small stream. Then the people and wagons became like a river. Why do you think people went west? Some wanted more land. Some wanted to get away from problems where they were. Some wanted to be left alone to live as they pleased.

79

The Mormons

One group that wanted to get away from other people was the *Mormons*. The Mormons believed that their leader, Joseph Smith, had been visited by an angel. Smith said that the angel had given him some teachings to add to the Bible. Wherever the Mormons went, the "extra teachings" made other people angry.

The Mormons were forced out of all the towns. People in one town burned the Mormon houses and killed Joseph Smith. Another man took over. He said, "We'll go west. We'll stay on land no one else will want."

Joseph Smith, the first Mormon leader

80

➤ **Tell how the pioneers traveled without land-marks.** *(At nighttime they pointed their wagons toward the North Star so they would know which way was west.)*
➤ Face the star on the schoolroom wall. **Which way would west be if that star were the North Star?** *(to the left)*

In the mornings, the leader among the travelers would look west and fix his gaze on a point on the horizon. He would lead the people all day in that direction. If the night were too cloudy for stars, the people would keep their wagons pointed in the direction they had been going. The next clear night they would use the star again.

➤ Discuss the last paragraph. **What are your feelings about leaving objects behind?**

The pioneers had to be careful about the weight of their wagons. Too much weight would cause the oxen or horses to become weak long before they reached their destination. Almost all the pioneers' diaries that record someone leaving something behind tell the story without any complaining. One woman, wife of a missionary to the Cowlitz people, had to leave behind her trunk of clothes. It held her wedding dress as well. She wrote, "Poor little trunk, I am sorry to leave thee, [but] thou must abide here."

Although we are to take care of the things God allows us to have, we should not become so fond of them that we cannot let them go for the good of another cause. (BATS: 5b Giving, 7d Contentment) Direct your child to think of something he owns that he would not like to part with. Ask what would prompt him to give up the possession. *(Answers will vary.)*

Map Activity, page 79

➤ **Read the first paragraph on page 79, answering the questions.**
➤ **Read the last paragraph to find some of the reasons people went west.** *(to get land, to get away from problems, to live alone)*
➤ **Which trail would you have taken?**

Day 3

Text Discussion, page 80

Read Proverbs 30:5-6. Ask your child what the verse means when it says "add thou not unto his words." *(We should not change what God has said by adding anything to it.)* Then read Revelation 22:18-19. Explain that the verses warn us not to change what God has said. (BAT: 8b Faith in the power of the Word of God)

Modern Salt Lake City, Utah

The Mormons crossed the prairies. They came to a dry, ugly place. The lake was salty. "This," said the new leader, "is the place." He told the settlers to dig ditches to bring water from the mountains to the flat land. He told them to build houses and plant trees. In a few years the Mormons made a green farmland out of a desert.

The place they settled in is now Utah. For a long time, Utah could not become a state. The Mormons had to agree to give up some of their ideas. They still believe that they can get to heaven by belonging to their church and doing good works. They believe that everyone is good. What do you think about these ideas?

81

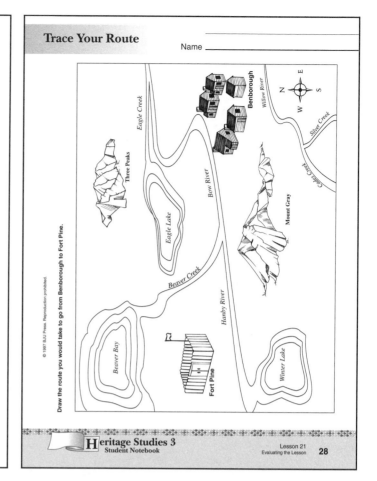

Draw the route you would take to go from Benborough to Fort Pine.

© 1997 BJU Press. Reproduction prohibited.

Three Peaks · Eagle Creek · Benborough · Willow River · Silver Creek · Cedar Creek · Eagle Lake · Bow River · Mount Gray · Beaver Creek · Hanby River · Beaver Bay · Fort Pine · Winter Lake

Heritage Studies 3
Student Notebook

Lesson 21
Evaluating the Lesson **28**

➤ **Read page 80 to find the name of a group of people forced out of all towns.** *(Mormons)*

➤ **Who was the first leader of the Mormons?** *(Joseph Smith)*

➤ **What did Joseph Smith base the new religion on?** *(changes in God's Word that he said an angel had given him)*

Joseph Smith and the next Mormon leader taught the people to work hard, to obey laws, and to do other good things. However, no number of good works can save a person. (BATs: 1a Understanding Jesus Christ, 1b Repentance and faith)

Text Discussion, page 81

➤ **Read page 81 to see where the Mormons went.** *(a dry, ugly place; it is now the state of Utah.)*

➤ **Were the Mormons good farmers?** *(Yes, they made a green farmland out of a desert.)*

➤ **Why did Utah not become a state for a long time?** *(The Mormons had to give up some of their ideas.)*

➤ **What do the Mormons believe is the way to get to heaven?** *(by belonging to their church and doing good works)*

Ask your child if the Mormon way to get to heaven is the same way that the Bible tells us to get to heaven. *(no)* Read Ephesians 2:8-9.

Today about 70 percent of Utah's people are Mormons. The influence of the Mormon Church is strong in the state. Irrigation systems built by the Mormons continue to bring water to Utah's dry land. The Mormon people need another kind of water— the living water of salvation. Some missionaries in Utah are witnessing to Mormons and starting churches that teach the truth of God's Word. More missionaries are needed to help reach these people with the gospel of Christ. (BAT: 5c Evangelism and missions)

Evaluating the Lesson

Landmark Activity, Notebook pages 28-30

These Notebook pages have been included in the Appendix for you to complete and exchange with your child. This will enable your child to use landmarks both to write directions and to follow them. You may want to ask another sibling near to your child's age to complete the pages.

➤ Read the directions on Notebook page 28. You may choose a name for the trail.

Give Directions

Name _____

Write out directions for your route.

To go from Benborough to Fort Pine, you should _____

_____
_____
_____
_____
_____
_____
_____
_____
_____
_____
_____
_____
_____
_____
_____
_____
_____
_____
_____
_____
_____
_____

Heritage Studies 3
Student Notebook

Lesson 21
Evaluating the Lesson **29**

Follow Directions

Name _____

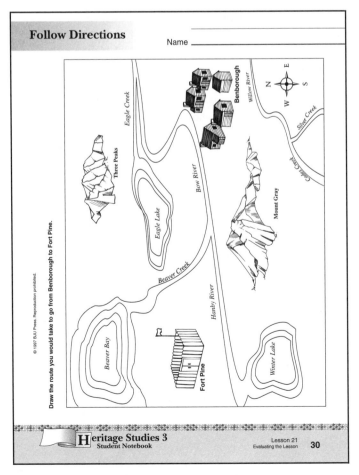

Draw the route you would take to go from Benborough to Fort Pine.

Heritage Studies 3
Student Notebook

Lesson 21
Evaluating the Lesson **30**

➤ Write out directions for your trail on Notebook page 29, using only directions—north, east, south, and west—and landmarks. For example, you might say, "Go north to Bow River."

➤ When you have finished, put away the map on Notebook page 28 with the trail drawn on it.

➤ Exchange your written directions with me. Use these directions to trace the trail on Notebook page 30.

➤ Compare the maps with the original maps.

━━ Going Beyond ━━

Enrichment

Give your child a copy of *Carolina's Courage* by Newbery Award winner Elizabeth Yates to read. This book tells of a family moving west and of a girl's courage along the way. *Carolina's Courage* is available from Bob Jones University Press.

Give your child the necessary supplies to make a map using landmarks to a well-known place in your area.

Additional Teacher Information

Salt Lake City, Utah's capital, is the world headquarters for the Church of Jesus Christ of Latter-day Saints. Members of the church are referred to as Mormons, but they call themselves "saints," taking the appellation from the church title.

Mormons live in many places besides Utah. Large numbers live in Colorado, Wyoming, Idaho, and Nevada. Other Mormons are scattered around the United States and in many foreign countries. Devout Mormons look to their church leaders in Salt Lake City for religious instruction.

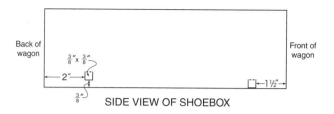

SIDE VIEW OF SHOEBOX

SUPPLEMENTAL LESSON
The Conestoga Wagon

━━ Preview ━━

Main Ideas

- People used wagons to travel and carry goods.
- The Conestoga wagon was the forerunner of the covered wagons of the westward movement.

Objectives

- Identify a Conestoga wagon and a covered wagon
- Name the parts of a wagon
- Make a model of a Conestoga wagon

Materials

- A shoebox*
- Two $8\frac{1}{2}$" $\times$ 11" pieces of cardboard or poster board for the wagon wheels and tongue*
- 2 unsharpened pencils, at least $\frac{1}{4}$" longer than the shoebox is wide*
- Brown water-based paint*
- A sheet of white poster board, approximately 12" $\times$ 20" for the cover of the wagon*
- Gray water-based paint*
- Glue
- Enough newspapers to cover the painting area
- A small paintbrush*
- 4 pushpins*
- An old shirt to wear while painting
- Some paper towels, clean rags, or sponges
- The American Frontier map and ovals from Lesson 19
- Supplement, page S5: the covered wagon and the Conestoga wagon
- Appendix, page A18: the patterns for the wagon tongue and front wheels*
- Appendix, page A19: the patterns for the back wheels*

Notes

The shoebox will need to be prepared before beginning the lesson. Cut on the back of the "wagon" two $\frac{3}{8}$" holes, one on each long side, about 2" from the back corners and $\frac{3}{8}$" from the bottom of the box. On the front of the wagon, cut two $\frac{3}{8}$" holes, one on each long side, about $1\frac{1}{2}$" from the front corners and flush with the bottom of the box. (See the illustrations.)

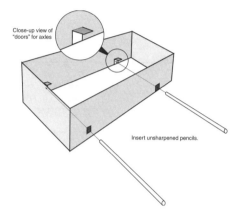

Close-up view of "doors" for axles

Insert unsharpened pencils.

━━ Lesson ━━

Introducing the Lesson

Story

➤ **How do you think the people going west traveled?**
➤ Listen as I read a story.

Jacob ran the length of the street in Lancaster, Pennsylvania. His father, the wagon maker, had probably not heard the news! A general was looking for all the wagons he could find. Benjamin Franklin himself had asked the farmers and wagon makers to lend their wagons.

Jacob skidded to a stop at the door of his father's shop. He had just opened his mouth to tell the news when he saw two men already giving his father the details.

"The general needs wagons to get the guns and supplies to battle. The king is willing to pay."

Jacob's father said, "How much?"

"Mr. Franklin says the army will pay fifteen shillings a day for a wagon with four good horses and a driver," said one man.

The other said, "I'm going. With what I make, I can buy enough seed to plant all the land I can plow this spring."

Jacob's father studied a bow that curved up gracefully on the wagon he was making. "Well," he said at last, "what if the general loses the battle? Do we still get our money?"

Jacob smiled to himself. His father always thought of everything.

The first man held out a paper. "Indeed. See here what it says. 'You will be paid in silver and gold of the king's money.' This is a letter from Benjamin Franklin himself. Mr. Franklin's word is good enough for me."

Jacob's father ran his hand down the bow and turned to the men. "This wagon can be ready in two days."

Story Discussion

➤ **Did this story take place before or after the War for Independence?** *(before)*

➤ **What clues did you base your answer on?** *(the mention of Benjamin Franklin and the king's silver and gold)*

The year was 1755. Most of the wagons that were borrowed for this war were *Conestoga* wagons. *Show the picture of the wagon in the Supplement, covering the covered wagon.*

➤ **Why do you think Jacob's father was not quick to say he would rent his wagon?**

Jacob's father was a good steward of his possessions, and he was not foolish in using them. He wanted to know all he could about the circumstances before he made a decision. (BATs: 2c Faithfulness, 2e Work, 4c Honesty)

➤ **Study the picture of the Conestoga wagon. Read the parts labeled:** *tongue, wagon bed, cover,* **and** *footrest.*

The Conestoga wagon beds were often painted blue, and their wheels were red. With their white covers they were colorful indeed, especially when they traveled in long lines along the roads of Pennsylvania and other places.

Teaching the Lesson

Map Activity

➤ Look at the American Frontier map. **How do you think the United States got the land to the south and west of the Louisiana Purchase?**

Settlers in that area wanted to belong to the United States, but the land was owned by Mexico. The settlers fought a war with Mexico and made their own country, Texas. Then Texas asked to become part of the United States in 1845.

➤ Use the same color to fill in the section on the map and the rectangle next to *Asked for statehood* in the key.

➤ Glue the 1845 oval on the map.

Comparison Activity

➤ *Show your child the pictures of both wagons in the Supplement.*

➤ **Tell what differences you see between the wagons.** *(Answers will vary.)*

The lower picture shows a later wagon, simply called a covered wagon. It was the wagon that most often went west. Wagons were usually used only to carry goods. The people walked beside the wagon.

➤ **Why do you think that was?** It made it easier for the horses or oxen to pull the wagon.

In some places people built buildings for others to stay in as they traveled. These places were sometimes called **inns.** Travelers could get food there and talk to other people going west. The inns had names such as "The Green Tree" and "The Scarlet Cloak."

➤ Find the part labeled *wagon bed* on the wagon pictures.

The beds of the wagons going west were not as deep or curved as the Conestoga wagon beds. As many more people started going west, the wagon makers had to find ways to build wagons faster and cheaper. They stopped making Conestoga wagons altogether.

The later covered wagons were not usually painted as brightly as the Conestoga wagons. Probably the main reason was that the wagons were built as quickly and cheaply as possible to meet the demand. The travelers had more important things to buy than paint for a wagon they did not intend to keep.

Wagon-Making Activity

➤ Today you are going to make a model Conestoga wagon. Help me cover the table with newspapers. Put on your paint shirt.

➤ Attach the wagon-tongue pattern to the cardboard. Cut it out.

➤ Attach the wheel patterns to the cardboard and cut them out. It is not necessary to cut out the area between the spokes of the wheels.

➤ Attach the wide part of the tongue under the shoebox. (*NOTE:* Liquid glue will hold the tongue in place better than a glue stick.)

➤ Paint your wagon bed and wagon tongue brown.

➤ Paint the outside rims and spokes of the wheels gray.

➤ While the paint dries, draw three or four straight lines across the length of the white poster board. These lines will represent the supports for the cover of the wagon.

➤ When the paint is dry, put the unsharpened pencils through the axle holes in the shoebox or wagon. Align the wheels to the axles and secure them with pushpins.

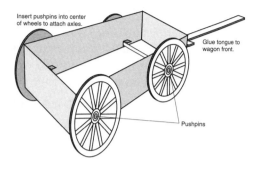

Insert pushpins into center of wheels to attach axles.
Glue tongue to wagon front.
Pushpins

➤ Curve the white poster board over the wagon bed. Use glue to attach the cover about 1" down inside the wagon bed. (*NOTE: Liquid glue will hold the cover in place better than a glue stick.*)

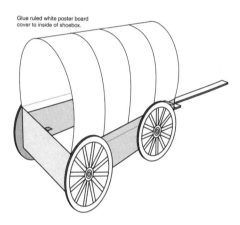

Glue ruled white poster board cover to inside of shoebox.

Evaluating the Lesson

Naming and Narrative Activity

➤ Name as many parts of your wagon as you can. (*the tongue, the bed, the wheels, the axles, the cover*)
➤ Tell about one event that might have happened on a trip in the wagon.

You may need to prompt your child with questions, such as "Where did you stop for the night?"

■ Going Beyond ■

Additional Teacher Information

The name for Conestoga wagons came from Conestoga Valley, Pennsylvania, where they were first built in the 1700s. Sometimes these wagons were called the "camels of the prairies" because they carried most of the people and freight that moved westward during the eighteenth and early nineteenth centuries. Conestoga wagons were often pulled by teams of four or six horses. The wheels of the Conestoga wagon could be removed so that the wagon could be used as a boat if necessary.

LESSON 22
Trail of Tears

Text, pages 82, 250-51
Notebook, pages 31-32

■ Preview ■

Main Ideas
• Nations gain lands in different ways.
• Early civilizations left their mark on the world.

Objective
• Recount events leading to the Trail of Tears

Materials
• Maps and More 8, page M6
• The presidential strip with the figures of Andrew Jackson (7) and Martin Van Buren (8) from the TimeLine Snapshots
• Appendix, page A13: Trail of Tears*
• A Bible

Day 1

■ Lesson ■

Introducing the Lesson

Discussion

➤ **Define the word *honesty*.** (*Although answers may vary, your child will probably say "telling the truth."*) Telling the truth is being honest, but there are other ways of being honest or dishonest.

Read Proverbs 20:23. Explain that the word *divers* means "different" or "uneven." The word *abomination* means "something to be hated." In the verse it means something God hates. Read the verse again, using the definitions. Ask your child why using uneven weights would be something God hates. (*It would be wrong; it would be unfair.*) Explain that a false balance is a scale that has been fixed to weigh things so that the person who owns it gets the better deal. Ask why that is wrong. (*It is cheating.*)

Imagine that you have bought a toy that you have been wanting. After you pay for it, you find out that the person who sold it has charged more than he should have.

➤ **What would you think?**

Other sins people commit in cheating someone are lying, greed, and perhaps jealousy. We are to be honest in all our dealings. Cheating always has consequences; sometimes the consequences may come years later. (BATs: 4c Honesty, 6d Clear conscience)

➤ You are going to read about a time in history when people did not keep their word and cheated others. **Why is it important to keep a promise?** *(People depend on us to do what we say we will.)* (BAT: 2c Faithfulness)

Teaching the Lesson

Review

➤ **Name some reasons that people went west.** *(to get land, to find gold, to worship in their own way, to have adventure, to see things no one had seen before, to hunt, etc.)*
➤ **Do you think anyone was ever forced to go west?**

Text Discussion, page 82

➤ **Read the first two paragraphs on page 82 to find out what people were given a promise.** *(the Cherokee and other Native Americans from the South)*
➤ **Who broke the promise to them?** *(the United States government)*

Almost fifty years earlier the United States government had made a treaty with the Cherokee that said the land would always be theirs. The government did not keep its agreement.

➤ **Name some reasons that the government wanted the Cherokee and others to leave their homeland.** *(so that white settlers could have the land; because gold was found on the land)*
➤ **Do you think any of the Cherokee people fought back?**

Some fought, and some hid in places that white men could not reach easily. Many of the Native Americans realized that there was no way to win against the government. They decided that they should agree to move.

Story and Discussion

The Cherokee had tried many ways to stay in their homeland. One man thought that it would help if the Cherokee had their own written language. If the Cherokee had a written language, then they could have a newspaper in which to read about what was happening. They could form a government to protect their rights.

➤ Listen as I read about Sequoya *(sĭ kwoi ´ ə).*

Sequoya, a Cherokee, could not read English, but he wanted his people to have the white man's secret of the "talking leaves." He decided to invent an alphabet. His plan was to draw a simple picture for each Cherokee word. He worked and worked for years, making thousands of drawings. But then his wife, who was angry with him for not doing more around the house and in the garden, burned all his pictures. Sequoya had to start over.

This time he decided to make symbols for the sounds in all the Cherokee words. He made eighty-six symbols. The Cherokee soon learned to read and write in their own language. They called Sequoya a genius. Many books and a newspaper were printed in the Cherokee language. Sequoya had done a great deed.

➤ **Do you remember the name *Sequoya* from another lesson?** The big sequoia trees in the West are named for the man Sequoya about whom you have just heard.
➤ **How would you have felt to see years of work burned up?**

Sequoya may have been discouraged. When he went back to work on his dream, he found an even better way to make the alphabet. What sometimes looks like failure or disaster may, in fact, be the chance to start over and do the work better.

➤ **Why is it better to have eighty-six symbols rather than thousands of picture words?**

Having fewer symbols makes learning easier. Writing letters is faster than drawing pictures. Alphabets allow ideas to be represented that are hard to picture, such as "time" and "memory."

➤ **Which did you learn to use—an alphabet or pictures?** *(alphabet)*

➤ **How many letters are in the English alphabet?** *(twenty-six)*

➤ **How many more letters are in the Cherokee alphabet?** *(sixty)*

Picture-Reading Activity, Maps and More 8

➤ Look at Maps and More 8, the front page of the Cherokee newspaper from Wednesday, June 4, 1828.

Because many sounds of the Cherokee language are different from the sounds of the English language, there is no way to match Cherokee symbols to English letters. For example, there is no symbol in Cherokee that stands for the English *z* sound.

➤ Find the Cherokee word for *Cherokee* and the Cherokee word for *Phoenix* in the title of the newspaper. *Phoenix* was a common title for newspapers.

➤ **Can you find any symbols that Sequoya used that he may have patterned after any of the English letters?** *(possibly the* A, J, W, Y, U, *and* O*)*

➤ **Read the English word in the center of the banner.** *(Protection)*

➤ **Why do you think the word appeared on the Cherokee newspaper?** Possibly to show why they printed the paper—to protect their rights.

Other Cherokee people decided to try to be like the white man in order to stay where they were. They built houses and became farmers. They sent their children to church and to school. They bought land and ran stores and mills. But even with their own written language and legally bought land, the Cherokee were hated by some of the other settlers.

➤ **Why do you think that was?**

Sometimes one group of people thinks it is better than another group. These people feel that they have more rights. Such an attitude is called *prejudice.* Prejudice is wrong. (BATs: 3a Self-concept, 5a Love, 5e Friendliness, 6c Spirit-filled)

Some Americans, such as Davy Crockett, a famous frontiersman, wanted to help the Cherokee keep their land. These people tried to get laws passed to protect the Cherokee and others. But there were more people, including President Andrew Jackson, who were less sympathetic. To them, the land was more important than the people who had lived on it for generations. The next president, Martin Van Buren, sent soldiers to push the Cherokee off the land and make them move to the West.

Day 2

Text Discussion, page 82 (cont.)

➤ Write a list of the attempts the Cherokee made to keep their land. *(invented a written Cherokee language, built houses, bought land, ran stores and mills, sent their children to school and church, fought back, got help from other Americans)*

In the end, all attempts failed, and the Native Americans had to move farther west. Although the United States government did not keep its promises, the Native Americans believed in honoring their promises. They kept their promise to move, traveling even when the hardships were great.

➤ **Read the last paragraph on page 82 to find out what some of the hardships were.** *(not enough food, no blankets, cold weather, walking, rough land, sickness, sorrow over having to leave home)*

➤ **What was the path that the Cherokee took called?** *(Trail of Tears)*

➤ **Why was the path the Cherokee and other Native Americans from the South took called the *Trail of Tears*?** *(because so many got sick and died, because the people had to leave their homes and go to a much different kind of place to live, because the people did not want to go)*

The wiser leaders of the Cherokee knew that many would die for nothing if they fought back. They told their people to move to the reservation.

➤ **What is a *reservation*?** *(land set aside for Native Americans)*

The climate on the reservation was much different from what the people were used to. The people had to learn a new way of living. For example, they had to learn to hunt buffalo. When they did hunt, they made enemies of other Native Americans who already lived in the area and depended on the buffalo for their food.

Trail of Tears

Name _____

Look at the map to answer the questions.

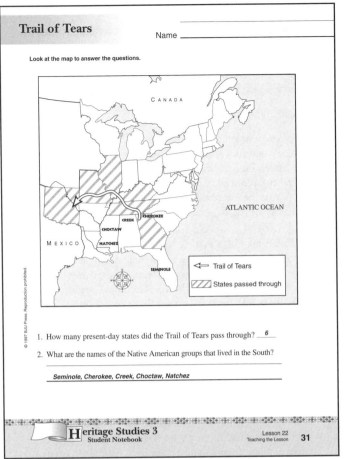

1. How many present-day states did the Trail of Tears pass through? __6__

2. What are the names of the Native American groups that lived in the South?

   Seminole, Cherokee, Creek, Choctaw, Natchez

A Lawyer's View

Name _____

Pretend you are a lawyer. Fill in what you would say in each case.

1. You are speaking for the Cherokee people. Tell the reasons they should

   be allowed to stay. *Possible answers: Cherokee were there first; Cherokee owned*

   land and stores; Cherokee children went to school; other Americans wanted

   the people to stay; it was unfair to trade Cherokee land for reservation land.

2. You are speaking for the white settlers. Tell the reasons they should have

   the land. *Answers may include the following: They knew how to farm it; they*

   needed more room; there was gold on it; they paid for it.

3. Speak for yourself. Say which side you would rather speak for and why.

   Answers will vary.

Day 3

Map Activity, Notebook page 31

➤ Read the directions on Notebook page 31.
➤ Color the map and the key.
➤ Complete the page.

TimeLine Snapshots Activity pages 250-51

➤ Find the figure of Andrew Jackson on the TimeLine at the year 1829 and the figure of Martin Van Buren at the year 1837.
➤ Read the information about Andrew Jackson and Martin Van Buren on pages 250-51.
➤ Place the picture of the Trail of Tears on the TimeLine at 1838.

Evaluating the Lesson

Notebook Activity, page 32

➤ Read the directions on Notebook page 32.
➤ Complete the page.

Going Beyond

Enrichment

Contact a local Indian Center or the Bureau of Indian Affairs, 1951 Constitution Avenue NW, Washington, D.C. 20242, for information on the current locations of Native American reservations. For a list of the available brochures, pamphlets, and other printed information about Native Americans, write to the Superintendent of Documents, U.S. Government Printing Office, Washington, D.C. 20402.

Additional Teacher Information

Most Indians believed that the land belonged to everyone. They did not, for the most part, use money, want to become rich, or want to own land. The changing seasons governed their lifestyles. They were determined to defend their hunting grounds and burial places. The European settlers, on the other hand, believed that the land should be held by those best able to make use of it—that is, to develop it. To them, the Indian ways were primitive and therefore inferior. The clash of these philosophies led to much bloodshed and swindling on both sides.

LESSON 23
Other Reasons to Go West

Text, pages 83-85
Notebook, pages 33-34

═══ Preview ═══

Main Ideas
- Beliefs about God underlie actions.
- Values and characteristics of early colonists and pioneers still shape the American way of life.

Objective
- Provide captions for a camp meeting scene

Materials
- *HERITAGE STUDIES Listening Cassette A*
- The American Frontier map and ovals from the Supplemental Lesson
- Supplement, page S6: "Brethren, We Have Met to Worship"
- Appendix, page A13: the picture of the Whitmans*

Notes
If you have a computer, you may wish to purchase *The Oregon Trail,* an award-winning program that gives children a deeper understanding of the dangers and difficulties of the Oregon Trail. As it teaches history and geography, the program develops problem-solving skills, persistence, and the value of planning ahead. It also provides opportunities for discussions on fairness, honesty, compassion, and other values. Encourage your child to keep a "journal" of his travels and to later compare the outcomes of different traveling styles. You may also want him to make a graph or chart, comparing where parties were on certain dates or how much ammunition each party had left. *The Oregon Trail* is available from Bob Jones University Press.

═══ Lesson ═══

Introducing the Lesson
Story and Discussion

➤ Listen as I read a story to you.

As people moved west, they often were in such a hurry that they did not take time for God. One man, Stephen Paxson, wanted to change that. Although he had trouble walking and could not speak clearly, he became the greatest Sunday school missionary in the history of the West.

Mr. Paxson rode a horse everywhere he went. He named his horse Robert Raikes, after the man who had started the first Sunday school in England. Together they traveled more than one hundred thousand miles over twenty-five years. The horse became so familiar with his rider's ways that every time he saw a child, he stopped. And he automatically turned in at every church and school. Children called the faithful horse "Dear Old Bob."

Mr. Paxson was just as popular. He taught himself to speak clearly, and he trained himself to walk without showing how much it hurt. He would ride into a settlement and find out whether the people there were studying the Bible and teaching their children to read. If they were not, Mr. Paxson scouted out a place to meet and began to teach the children and anyone else who would come about Jesus. Then he would find one or two people who could teach the Bible and would train them to take his place. When he got five dollars in donations, he would buy one hundred books for the new Sunday school and ride on to start another Sunday school somewhere else.

Paxson started thirteen hundred Sunday schools. His son joined him later and started seven hundred Sunday schools himself. Perhaps no one else did more than the Paxson family to spread the gospel in the West during those early days.

➤ **Why did Mr. Paxson work so hard to start Sunday schools in the West?** *(People were not taking time for God. He wanted everyone to hear the gospel.)* (BATs: 1a Understanding Jesus Christ, 5c Evangelism and missions, 8b Faith in the power of the Word of God, 8c Fight, 8d Courage)

Mr. Paxson made many sacrifices to do his work. He had to be away from his family much of the time. He had to suffer from his painful leg wherever he rode or walked. He often had to sleep in the open and find what food he could along the way.

> Remind your child that doing the Lord's work is often hard, but there is great joy in serving a kind, wise Master. Mr. Paxson looked back with great happiness on a life well spent. (BAT: 4a Sowing and reaping)

Mountain Men

Some people traveled by themselves. Fur trappers and hunters lived alone in the Rocky Mountains. Sometimes they would not see another person for months or years. They were a tough breed. One man, Peg Leg Smith, once hurt his leg badly. To keep from dying, he cut off his own leg. He was famous ever after.

When the mountain men wanted to trade their furs, they met at a *rendezvous*. At the planned time, dozens of them came out of the mountains to the Great Salt Lake. Indians came. Owners of fur companies came. The trading went on for weeks. The fur companies gave guns, gunpowder, food, and traps for the furs.

Missionaries and Preachers

Missionaries often were the first white people in a new place. The Whitmans and the Spaldings traveled across the prairies alone. They climbed the Rockies. Fur trappers helped them find their way to Oregon. Narcissa Whitman and Eliza Spalding were the first white women to see the Pacific Ocean.

83

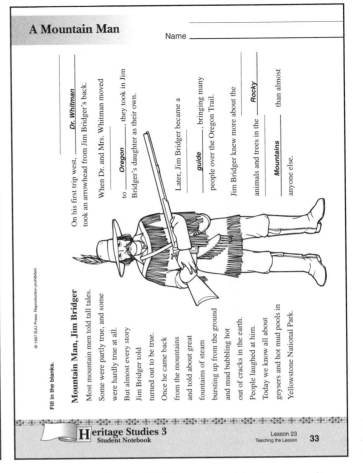

Fill in the blanks.

Mountain Man, Jim Bridger

Most mountain men told tall tales. Some were partly true, and some were hardly true at all. But almost every story Jim Bridger told turned out to be true. Once he came back from the mountains and told about great fountains of steam bursting up from the ground and mud bubbling hot out of cracks in the earth. People laughed at him. Today we know all about geysers and hot mud pools in Yellowstone National Park.

On his first trip west, __Dr. Whitman__ took an arrowhead from Jim Bridger's back. When Dr. and Mrs. Whitman moved to __Oregon__, they took in Jim Bridger's daughter as their own.

Later, Jim Bridger became a __guide__, bringing many people over the Oregon Trail.

Jim Bridger knew more about the __Rocky__ __Mountains__ animals and trees in the than almost anyone else.

© 1997 BJU Press. Reproduction prohibited.

Heritage Studies 3
Student Notebook

Lesson 23
Teaching the Lesson   **33**

Teaching the Lesson
Text Discussion, page 83

*Point to the word **rendezvous** in the second paragraph on the page. Explain that this comes from a French word, pronounced rän′dā·vōō′, which means "a meeting at a prearranged time and place."*

➤ **Read the first two paragraphs on the page to see who met at the rendezvous.** *(mountain men, Indians, traders)*
➤ **Why do you think the mountain men were known as "tough"?** *(Your child may recount the story of Peg Leg Smith; he may talk about the life these men led, living outdoors and mostly alone.)*

Not all white people tried to cheat the Indians, but the ones who did left a bad memory. The trappers had helped the missionaries get to Oregon. Some trappers were good friends with the Indians.

History Activity,
Notebook page 33

➤ One of the most famous mountain men was Jim Bridger. Read the sentences about Jim Bridger on the left side of Notebook page 33.
➤ Listen as I read more information about him.

Dr. Whitman went west first with Jim Bridger. During this trip, Bridger was shot in the back with an arrow, but Dr. Whitman was able to remove it. When Dr. Whitman went west to Oregon the next time, he took his wife and Jim Bridger's daughter with him.

There was no one alive who knew more about hunting in the Rocky Mountains than Jim Bridger. When he gave up trapping and hunting, he became a guide, helping people go west on the Oregon Trail.

➤ Fill in the blanks on the right side of the page.

Day 2

Text Discussion, page 83 (cont.)

➤ **Read the last paragraph on page 83 to find out about missionaries to the West.**
➤ **Who were the first missionaries to Oregon?** *(the Whitmans and the Spaldings)*
➤ Locate the Oregon Trail on the map on page 79.

Not only were Mrs. Whitman and Mrs. Spalding the first white women to see the Pacific Ocean, but they were also the first white women to travel the Oregon Trail. They proved that women could make the four-thousand-mile, six-month trip from the East.

➤ **Why do you think the Whitmans and the Spaldings went to Oregon?**

The missionaries went west to tell Indians about the love of Christ. When more settlers came, the missionaries sometimes became leaders of churches too. Why do you think most people wanted to travel in groups? Why do you think missionaries did not always wait for wagon trains?

Most new towns did not have a preacher. So one man would be the preacher for several towns. He would ride from one town to the next on a planned route called a *circuit*. Have you heard of circuit-riding preachers? In summer several preachers held *camp meetings* together. Lots of people came to hear preaching, to sing, and to visit with neighbors.

A circuit-riding preacher as shown in the film Sheffey (Unusual Films)

"How then shall they call on him in whom they have not believed? and how shall they believe in him of whom they have not heard? and how shall they hear without a preacher?"

Romans 10:14

84

A camp meeting scene from the film Sheffey (Unusual Films)

Camp meetings of long ago were a little like evangelistic services of today—and quite a lot different. As in today's services, the goal was to get people to turn from sin to the Lord. And many of the songs we sing in evangelistic meetings now were sung then. Perhaps you know "On Jordan's Stormy Banks" or "Brethren, We Have Met to Worship."

But the camp meetings were not just in the evenings. They began with prayers at five o'clock in the morning. After breakfast there was singing and preaching until noon. After lunch there was more singing and preaching. At night the services were mainly singing and a different kind of preaching called *exhorting. Exhorters* talked to the people. They begged them to come forward and be saved.

The camp meetings went on for several days. Many families lived in tents or wagons for the week. Often at the end, people cried when they had to leave. They were fond of the place where they had been saved. And they had become good friends with each other.

85

Three men of the Nez Perce and one man from the Flathead people had come almost three thousand miles in canoes, from the West to St. Louis. They had heard of Christianity and wanted to hear more. They went to Captain William Clark. Clark was the man who had traveled with Captain Lewis and whom the Nez Perce trusted. They asked Captain Clark to send teachers to their homes. Captain Clark had their request published in church magazines. The Whitmans were the first to say they would go.

TimeLine Snapshots Activity

➤ **To what area were Mr. and Mrs. Whitman missionaries?** *(Oregon)* Often, missionaries and preachers were the first people to enter new territories.
➤ *Give your child the copy of the picture of the Whitmans.*
➤ The Whitmans were missionaries from about 1836 to 1847. Place the picture at the appropriate time along the TimeLine.

Text Discussion, page 84

➤ **Read page 84 to see what kind of preacher most towns in the West had.** *(circuit-riding)*
➤ **What was a *circuit-riding preacher*?** *(a preacher who would travel from town to town to preach to people)*

➤ **Why was it important for missionaries and preachers to go west?** *(because many people were going west and needed the gospel)*

Read Romans 10:14 from the textbook page. Ask your child whether he thinks some of the missionaries to the West might have claimed this verse as their life verse.

➤ **Do you think life was easy for the missionaries and preachers?** The missionaries went because they loved God and cared about others. (BATs: 1b Repentance and faith, 8a Faith in God's promises)
➤ **What kind of meetings did preachers hold in the summer?** *(camp meetings)*

Text Discussion, page 85

➤ **Read page 85 to learn how long the camp meetings lasted.** *(all day long for several days)*
➤ Name some of the similarities and differences between modern church services and camp meetings. *(Answers will vary but differences may include the following: camp meetings were held outside, they lasted all day for several days, and usually several preachers and lay preachers conducted the services. Similarities may include singing, preaching of the gospel, and calls for people to be saved.)*

There were many sounds at a camp meeting. There were animals there: horses and dogs. Babies cried. Often, people talked together about the sermon as it was being preached. Sometimes two or three preachers preached at the same time to different parts of the crowd.

The *exhorters* were people who went among the crowd, trying to get listeners to respond. Children your age were expected to listen to the sermons, but they were allowed to play sometimes.

➤ Many of our modern church services had their beginnings in these earlier services. **Can you name some things in your church that may have begun in the camp meetings?**

Song Activity

The songs that were sung in the camp meetings were an important part of the service. The songs made the people ready to hear the preaching.

➤ **Read the words to the hymn "Brethren, We Have Met to Worship" as I play the recording.**

➤ Let's sing the song.

Map Activity, page 79

If you chose not to teach the Supplemental Lesson, you will want to teach the Map Activity using the American Frontier map from that lesson here. This will enable your child to complete his map.

➤ Look at the map on page 79. Find the area where the Oregon Trail ends.

England claimed the Oregon Territory. However, the people in the territory wanted it to belong to the United States. The United States and England signed a treaty that gave the territory to the United States.

➤ Find the Oregon Territory on your American Frontier map.

➤ Color the section of the map and the rectangle next to *Gained by treaty with England* in the key the same color.

➤ Add the oval for 1846.

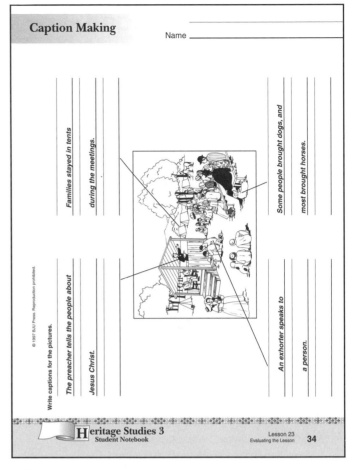

Caption Making   Name _____

Write captions for the pictures.

The preacher tells the people about

Jesus Christ.

Families stayed in tents

during the meetings.

Some people brought dogs, and

most brought horses.

An exhorter speaks to

a person.

© 1997 BJU Press. Reproduction prohibited.

Heritage Studies 3
Student Notebook

Lesson 23
Evaluating the Lesson   **34**

Evaluating the Lesson

Caption-Making Activity, Notebook page 34

➤ Read the directions.

➤ Write phrases on the lines, telling what part of the camp meeting is being pointed out.

The answers on the page are meant only as a guide for your review of your child's work, not as exact answers.

Going Beyond

Enrichment

Show the film *Sheffey*. This film depicts the life of the circuit rider Robert Sheffey and is available on videocassette from Bob Jones University Press.

Additional Teacher Information

Stephen Paxson lived in Illinois with his family before he became a missionary to the West. Once, at the request of his daughter, he joined her for a Sunday school class. Because he knew so little about the Bible, he returned week after week to learn more. After four years, he was saved. He was a missionary for forty years, from the Great Lakes to the Gulf of Mexico and from the Allegheny Mountains to the Rockies.

The Whitmans and the Spaldings built two missions along the Columbia River, about four miles apart. As more white settlers arrived, the Cayuse realized that their hunting grounds and homes were in jeopardy. When a measles epidemic spread, killing almost half the Cayuse population in the area, the distrust grew into hatred. Although Whitman, a doctor, treated many of the sick, most of his patients died. Some Cayuse believed that he poisoned them. A chief and several others arrived at the Whitman home one afternoon, and while the chief talked to Whitman, another man struck Whitman in the head with an axe. Mrs. Whitman came running to kneel by her husband and was struck by a bullet that came through a window. Meanwhile, other Cayuse warriors were killing other workers at the mission. The attack continued sporadically for a few days, resulting in the deaths of twelve men and two women.

LESSON 24
California Gold

Text, pages 86-88
Notebook, pages 35-36

■■■ Preview ■■■

Main Ideas

- People everywhere have needs and wants.
- Values and characteristics of pioneers still shape the American way of life.

Objective

- Give reasons for the increase of prices and population in California in 1849

Materials

- The figure of the prospector (1849) from the Time-Line Snapshots
- A globe
- Several small pebbles painted gold*
- A bucket of dirt

 You will need to mix the gold pebbles into the dirt for the Panning Activity.

- A small foil plate*
- A large dishpan or tub*
- A large pitcher of water*
- The American Frontier map and ovals from Lesson 23
- Appendix, page A20: the Comparing Prices chart*

 Add current prices to the "Prices now" column of the prices chart. The following are suggested prices: An egg, $0.09; a loaf of bread, $1.20; a two-pound bag of flour, $0.95; a potato, $0.49; a watermelon, $5.00; a pint of vinegar, $0.95.

California Bound

In 1846 America fought another war. This time it was with Mexico, the country to the south. America won the war. Can you find on the map the land America got from Mexico after the war?

John Sutter built a fort in the newly won land. He gave food and shelter to weary travelers coming west. He built his own mill and shops and put up houses for all the people who worked in the fort. In 1848 something happened that made Sutter's Fort famous around the world. What do you think that was?

UNITED STATES
IN 1846

Sutter's Fort

Land won
from Mexico

MEXICO

Gulf of Mexico

ATLANTIC OCEAN

PACIFIC OCEAN

86

◆ HOW IT WAS ◆

A Mill at Coloma, California
Spring, 1848

John Marshall was hired to build a mill for John Sutter. Marshall began his work on the American River. One morning he went walking along the river.

He said later, "My eye was caught by a glimpse of something shining in the bottom of the ditch." That "something" turned out to be gold! Sutter's Fort would never be the same. What do you think happened next?

Sutter wanted to keep the gold a secret. But word got out. In a year, thousands of men came to find gold in California.

Sutter's Mill

Advice to Gold Seekers

"Never Travel on the Sabbath; we will guarantee that if you lay by on the Sabbath, and rest your teams, that you will get to California 20 days sooner than those who travel seven days a week."
—from *The Emigrants' Guide to California,* a pamphlet for gold seekers traveling to California in 1849

87

Day 1

━━━━ Lesson ━━━━

Introducing the Lesson

Text Discussion, page 86

➤ **Read the first paragraph on page 86 to find out with whom the United States went to war in 1846.** *(Mexico)*
➤ **Who won the war?** *(the United States)*

Map Activity

➤ America went to war with Mexico in 1846. Point out the size of America in that year on your American Frontier map. *(all but the last two western sections included)*
➤ Find the large Southwestern section on the map that you have not filled in yet. This land was won from Mexico in the war.
➤ Color this section and the rectangle next to *Won from Mexico* in the key the same color.
➤ Place the 1848 oval on this section of the map.
➤ The last small section was bought from Mexico.
➤ Color the last section and the rectangle next to *Bought from Mexico* in the key the same color.
➤ Place the 1853 oval on this section of the map.

Text Discussion, page 86 (cont.)

➤ **Read the last paragraph on page 86 to learn what fort became famous.** *(Sutter's Fort)*
➤ **What is your prediction to the last question on the page?**

Teaching the Lesson

Text Discussion, page 87

➤ **Read page 87 to find out whether your prediction was correct.**
➤ **Why do you think that Sutter wanted to keep the gold a secret?**

Sutter was not trying to keep all the gold for himself. However, he did not want to see hundreds of people coming there looking for gold, either.

People came from the East and from many foreign countries to look for gold in California. *Point out on the globe the countries of Turkey, China, France, Australia, England, and Canada.* People came from all these places.

Panning for Gold

Name _____

Number the steps in order.

3

2

1

4. When the gold was gone from the rivers,

prospectors ___dug tunnels into___

___the hills___ _____

_____

© 1997 BJU Press. Reproduction prohibited.

Heritage Studies 3
Student Notebook

Lesson 24
Teaching the Lesson | **35**

Sequencing Activity, Notebook page 35

➤ **How do you think the men got the gold?**
➤ **Read the directions on Notebook page 35.**
➤ Number the pictures as I read a paragraph to you.

An easy way to look for gold in dirt was to let water run over it. At first, those looking for gold *panned.* The least expensive tool that a gold seeker could use was a shallow pan. He would fill the pan with dirt and gravel from the riverbed and wash it over with water. Gold was heavy enough to sink to the bottom of the pan and stay there. Other seekers, often called *prospectors,* took more time and money to build a shoot, or *sluice,* for water. Then they had only to shovel dirt and gravel into the end of the shoot and let the water wash away the mud and sticks, leaving the gold, if there was any. After a while, some prospectors banded together to build water wheels and bigger shoots for water. They agreed to split the gold evenly. When the gold from the rivers was gone, some prospectors turned to mining, digging tunnels into the hills.

➤ Finish the sentence on the page.
➤ **Do you think splitting the gold evenly always worked out?** *(no)* **Why do you think it did not work?** *(Not everyone was honest; greed sometimes made men do bad things.)* (BATs: 4c Honesty; 7d Contentment)

Panning Activity

➤ I have painted some pebbles gold so that we can "pan for gold." Fill your tin half full of dirt from the bucket. Hold it over the dishpan.
➤ I will slowly pour some water into the tin. Stir the dirt and pick out any "nuggets" you find.

When prospectors found a place to look for gold, they "staked a claim." That means that they put stakes at the edges of the property they intended to work.

➤ **What do you think the phrase "to pull up stakes" means?**

It used to mean that the person removed the stakes from the property and moved to another place. Now it has come to mean pulling out of an agreement or moving to a new place.

Many people named their claims and camps. Some named places for themselves, some for their hopes of getting rich, and some for rivers or animals nearby. Some names of camps were Rich Bar, Red Dog, Kelsey's Diggings, and Ford's Bar. The camp of Rich Bar was a good place to find gold. Each prospector there made about two thousand dollars a day.

Often, towns grew up around a camp. When the miners left, sometimes the town still grew. A town grew up at Sutter's Mill. It took the name of the nearby river, Sacramento. It is now the capital of California.

Chart Activity

➤ Look at the Comparing Prices chart. **How do you think storekeepers and others prospered or made money during the gold rush?**

Since no laws said that storekeepers had to charge certain prices, many storekeepers charged high prices for goods. Some storekeepers charged higher prices for people who had found the most gold. Some storekeepers made more money than the prospectors and with less trouble. We are always to be fair and honest with others. (BATs: 4c Honesty, 5a Love)

➤ Usually prices increase through the years. Compare the prices on the chart. **Have prices increased or decreased since 1849?**

Other people came to open inns and banks. Some were honest, but some wanted only to make as much money as they could.

The *gold rush* of 1849 brought gold miners from back east. It also brought them from England, France, Germany, and Ireland. They came by the pioneer trails. They came by ship. They called themselves *forty-niners*. They came and came and came. San Francisco went from two thousand people to twenty thousand people in one year.

Men set up tents and shacks and went right to the river to pan gold. They worked all day, day after day. Many who came were thieves; many were wicked men who would kill for money. Even among good men, fights started over gold dust. A few men got very rich. Many made some money. A lot more went home with nothing or died crossing the desert on the way.

Lots of people stayed in the West. They built farms and started families. California became more famous for vegetable farms and fruit orchards than it had been for gold.

88

Not everyone got "gold fever." A man who had lived in California for many years before the gold rush wanted to go on living as he had. His name was Luis Peralta. He told his sons that they should be thankful for the good land that God had given them. He said, "My sons, God has given this gold to the Americans. Had He wanted us to have it, He would have given it to us before now. Do not go after it, but let the others go. Plant your lands; . . . these be the best gold fields." And he was right. The people who had come to look for gold needed to eat. The Peralta family became successful ranchers, earning their living by working hard and honorably.

Text Discussion, page 88

➤ **Read page 88 to find out what happened to the prospectors.** *(Some made money; most did not.)*
➤ **What did the people during the gold rush of 1849 call themselves?** *(forty-niners)*
➤ **Do you know what California is known for today?** It is known for growing fruits and vegetables.

California Population Growth   Name _____

Population Growth in California 1848-52

(bar graph showing Number of people vs. Year 1848–1852)

Study the graph and answer the questions.

1. What was the population the year James Marshall discovered gold at Sutter's Mill? ___about 20,000___

2. What was the population the next year? ___100,000___

3. Give some reasons that people moved into California so quickly and that the state kept growing. ___Some people came to look for gold; others came to set up stores, banks, hotels, and other businesses. Some people stayed and built homes and raised families. Farmers and ranchers were successful. Towns grew up where mining camps had been.___

Heritage Studies 3
Student Notebook   Lesson 24
                        Evaluating the Lesson   **36**

TimeLine Snapshots Activity

➤ **Where do you think the nickname *forty-niners* for the prospectors of the gold rush came from?**

It came from the year 1849 in which they came to search for gold.

➤ Place the figure of the prospector on the TimeLine at 1849.

Evaluating the Lesson

Graph-Interpretation Activity, Notebook page 36

➤ Read the directions on the page.
➤ Complete the page. Use the information you have learned to support your answers.

The answers given in the teacher's edition are suggestions. The number in the first question, for example, may range from twenty thousand to twenty-five thousand. The reasons for the growth of population may vary. Your child should not be expected to name all the reasons given; two or three are sufficient.

Going Beyond

Enrichment

Provide brown construction paper, black felt-tip pens, scissors, and glue. Instruct your child to put his nuggets on display with a sign, giving the name of the "mine" or "claim" from which the gold came.

Explain that many phrases in our language come from the gold rush. *Pay dirt,* which means a profit, comes from the term miners used for dirt containing gold. *Strike it rich,* meaning to become suddenly wealthy, is a miner's phrase for discovering gold. *Clean up,* meaning to make a great deal of money, comes from the process of clearing out the sluice boxes and retrieving the gold in them. *Bonanza* is a Spanish word for "prosperity."

Additional Teacher Information

John Sutter, the miller on whose property the first gold was found, did not want word of the find to get out. He foresaw the terrible flood of get-rich-quick gold seekers. He was not wrong. When the gold rush was at its peak in 1852, Sutter's land was overrun and his sawmill was destroyed. Sutter lost all his investment in the mill and the store, and he died in poverty.

James Marshall, the man who discovered the gold at Sutter's Mill, could not compete with the more aggressive miners and lost all his holdings. He felt that everyone owed him a fee because he had found the gold first, but others did not agree. To make money and to air what he considered gross injustice, he went on a lecture tour. What little money he made there he soon lost, and he died in poverty. He was buried near the spot where he had made his history-changing find.

Stories from Long Ago

These lessons illustrate the contribution that literature made in early America. With the discussion and vivid examples of fables, legends, and folktales, your child will be entertained as well as enlightened. The supplemental lesson provides a play that will help him learn more about Johnny Appleseed and the legends surrounding him.

Materials

The following materials must be obtained or prepared before the presentation of the lesson. These items are labeled with an asterisk (*) in each lesson and in the Materials List in the Supplement. For further information see the individual lessons.

- Appendix, pages A21-A22 (Lesson 25)
- *Egermeier's Bible Story Book* (optional) (Lesson 25)
- An apple (Lesson 27)
- A 12-inch length of string (Lesson 27)
- A large, round apple for each team (Supplemental Lesson)
- A box of round wooden toothpicks (Supplemental Lesson)
- Appendix, pages A23-A33 (Supplemental Lesson)
- Appendix, page A34 (Lesson 28)
- Several different versions of the stories "Goldilocks and the Three Bears" or "Little Red Riding Hood" (optional) (Lesson 28)

LESSON 25
Tell Me a Story

Text, pages 90-91

━━━ Preview ━━━

Main Ideas

- Storytelling is an ancient art.
- Many different people and groups have contributed to American culture through their stories.
- Parables teach a lesson through things that people do.
- Fables teach a lesson through things that animals do.

Objectives

- Contribute to the writing of a surprise story
- Identify a story as either a parable or a fable

Materials

- Appendix, pages A21-A22 story papers (*NOTE:* Trim along the black-line border.)*
- *Egermeier's Bible Story Book* (optional)*

Notes

Egermeier's Bible Story Book, published by The Warner Press, gives a complete listing of the parables with their Scripture references and the principal point of each parable. (See pages 62-64 of the Supplement.) This book can be purchased from Bob Jones University Press.

Day 1

━━━ Lesson ━━━

Introducing the Lesson

Writing Activity

> To give the following story activity greater variety, have other family members contribute to the process. Consider handling this section as a family the night before the lesson.

➤ *Give your child the story papers.* We are going to write a surprise silly story. You will write a sentence and then fold the paper so that I cannot see your sentence. I will write the next sentence.

➤ Let's read together the story starter sentence (first sentence).

➤ Fold the paper along the first fold line.

➤ Read the first sentence and fill in the blanks.

➤ Fold the paper along the second fold line.

Once upon a time, people liked to tell stories around campfires or at tables after dinner was over and after the chores were done. Of course, people still like to tell stories today, and many stories they tell are the same stories people told long ago. Do you have a favorite story that you like to tell or hear? Maybe it was loved by people hundreds of years ago too.

We can learn about the people who lived long ago by listening to the stories they told. Some stories tell us what the people believed about the world around them. Other stories show us things that the people were afraid of or things that they wished for. Still others teach us about the ways people got along together.

90

➤ Pass the paper to me. I will write the second sentence, fold the paper, and pass it back to you.

> Repeat the directions, such as "write," "fold the paper," and "pass it to me," until both pages are completed.

➤ Unfold the story papers and read the silly surprise story.

For years people have made up stories and have told them to their children, who later told the same stories to their children. This storytelling process has continued for many years since there always are willing storytellers and eager listeners.

Teaching the Lesson

Text Activity, page 90

➤ **Read page 90 to find out what kinds of things stories can teach us about people long ago.** (*what the people believed about the world around them; what they were afraid of; what they wished for; how they got along*)

➤ **Can you think of a story that is repeatedly told in our family?**

➤ Look at the illustration on page 90. **Would you like to listen to stories sitting on someone's knee?**

Parables

> *"I will incline mine ear to a parable."*
> Psalm 49:4

Sometimes a story taught a lesson. We can read in the Bible some of these kinds of stories. Do you know what they are called? They are *parables*. Parables are usually about people.

Parable of the Lost Coin

Either what woman having ten pieces of silver, if she lose one piece, doth not light a candle, and sweep the house, and seek diligently till she find it? And when she hath found it, she calleth her friends and her neighbours together, saying, Rejoice with me; for I have found the piece which I had lost. Likewise, I say unto you, there is joy in the presence of the angels of God over one sinner that repenteth. (Luke 15:8-10)

Fables

Often storytellers would tell a lesson-story about animals instead. The animals in these stories acted like people, and each animal always acted a certain way. For instance, Fox was always tricky and Owl was always wise. How do you think a bear would act? Stories that teach a lesson through the things animals do are called *fables*. The Cherokee told this fable. Do you think the lesson it teaches is important today?

91

Text Discussion, page 91

➤ Write the words parable *and* fable. *Invite your child to tell the differences between these types of stories.*

➤ **Read page 91 to see whether your answers were correct.** *(A **parable** is a simple story, usually about people, that teaches a lesson. A **fable** is a story that teaches a lesson through the things animals do.)*

➤ **Which type of story is found in the Bible?** *(parable)*

➤ **Tell the parable on page 91.** *(A woman searches diligently for a coin she has lost and then greatly rejoices when it is found.)*

➤ **What lesson do you think is taught in this parable?**

> The Lord searches diligently for the sinner. When the sinner repents, there is great rejoicing. (BATs: 1a Understanding Jesus Christ, 1b Repentance and faith; Bible Promises: A. Liberty from Sin, B. Guiltless by the Blood, D. Identified in Christ)

➤ **Who are the main characters in a fable?** *(animals)*

➤ **What character quality was always given to Fox?** *(tricky)*

➤ **What characteristic was always given to Owl?** *(wise)*

➤ **What characteristic would probably be given to Bear?** *(Answers will vary but will probably include that he is strong.)*

Day 2

Evaluating the Lesson

Listening Activity

➤ I am going to read some short stories. Each story is either a parable or a fable.

➤ After each story I want you to tell me if it is a parable or a fable.

1. Suppose a shepherd has a hundred sheep to care for out on the hillside. If one little lamb strays away from the group, doesn't the kind shepherd, after making sure the ninety and nine are safe, go out on the mountains in search of the lost lamb? Yes, the good shepherd searches far and wide, whatever the weather, until he finds the little lamb. The shepherd cuddles the wayward lamb in his soft coat and takes it back to the warm fold where he gently treats the lamb's wounds, feeds it, and comforts its fears. The loving shepherd is concerned about each lamb. *(parable)*

2. A large rabbit (really a hare) was in a mood to show off one day. So the hare looked around 'til he found a slow-moving turtle—a tortoise, that is.

   The hare called to the tortoise and challenged, "Hey, buddy, how 'bout racin' with me? Everything will be fair and square—just me and you runnin' our little legs off to see who's the fastest."

   The tortoise slowly nodded his head and shuffled his feet 'til he got to the starting line. As the hare shouted "ready, get set, go," the tortoise bent his knee to take one step. The hare zoomed away in a cloud of dust, his legs moving so fast that they looked like turning wheels. As soon as he reached the first tree, the hare stopped, huffing and puffing. He'd rest a little while here and see where the tortoise was in the race. A gigantic smile spread across the hare's face. Why, that ol' tortoise was just a-creepin' along! There's no way the tortoise would ever win this race! So the hare decided that he'd send out for a bit of lunch, maybe do a little fishin' too, before jumping back into the race just in time to cross the finish line. The hare played around and dashed to and fro, not paying attention to the tortoise or the race at all. Meanwhile, the tortoise was seriously doing his best, steadily lifting one heavy leg after the other to plod along the path. He didn't look to the left or to the right; he kept right on course, heading straight ahead. Pretty soon, the tortoise crossed the finish line and patiently stood there waiting for his prize when a ball of dust wrapped in fur and long ears came whizzing by. The hare had crossed the finish line—but it was too late. The race had already been won by the one who remembered this lesson: Slow but steady wins the race. *(fable)*

3. One day as Fox was walking along, he looked up into the sky and saw something that made his mouth start to water. Crow was flying by with a piece of cheese in her beak. Oh, how Fox wanted that cheese!

Being quick-thinking and sly—as we suppose all foxes to be—Fox called up to Crow, "Good morning, Mistress Crow! How fine you are looking today! How shiny are your feathers! How bright are your eyes!"

Crow puffed out just a little bit more 'cause she was so pleased with the compliments. Crow loved to be flattered!

As Fox saw Crow's pride growing, he continued with his plan. He cried, "I'm sure your voice is even more beautiful than your feathers. Won't you sing for me, O Queen of Birds?"

Crow could hardly contain her pleasure at hearing such glowing words. She smoothed her feathers, lifted her head, closed her eyes, and opened her beak to sing. With that, the cheese fell to the ground and landed right in front of Fox.

With a little sneer, Fox called up to the now unhappy Crow, "Thank you, Mistress Crow, but here's some advice for you. Never trust a flatterer." And with those parting words, Fox picked up the precious cheese and ate every last bite. *(fable)*

━━ **Going Beyond** ━━

Enrichment

Give your child several other fables to read. Also have available some drawing paper and crayons. Encourage him to select a fable to illustrate, writing the title of the fable at the top of his paper and the moral or lesson to be learned at the bottom of his paper.

Additional Teacher Information

The terms *traditional literature* and *folk literature* imply that the story had an ordinary person as the storyteller and that the story originally existed only orally until a collector found, recorded, and published it. Since folk literature was passed from person to person over a period of years, parts of the stories were often embellished or changed in some fashion. Therefore, there is no final or "absolutely correct" version of a story of folk literature. Types of folk literature include folktales, fables, myths and legends, and folk epics.

Folktales rely on simple, easily recognized characters, usually some good ones as well as some bad ones. The plot of the folktale moves right along, with the climax coming at the very end, often closing simply with "And they lived happily ever after." Quick, lively action is the key element of the folktale. Sometimes folktales are subdivided into tales of magic, romance, religion, sillies, talking beasts, tall tales, and realistic situations. Folktales usually have themes but do not contain moral lessons.

The fable is a short story, usually with animal characters, that teaches a lesson or gives a warning. With each character having only a single trait, the story is told in a simple, straightforward fashion. The moral is usually given at the end of the story and is the sole purpose of a fable. Probably the most famous fables are those by Aesop, who is said to have lived in Greece between 620 and 560 B.C.

Myths and legends originate in the folk beliefs of people of other lands and often include situations involving supernatural forces. Legends usually have more historical truth and fewer supernatural elements than myths do.

Folk epics are long, narrative poems about an outstanding or royal character in a series of adventures. This character is the hero who undertakes every deed in a grand fashion. The story is a dignified one that often brings with it the message of great courage and moral strength.

LESSON 26
Play Ball!

Text, pages 91-95

━━━ Preview ━━━

Main Ideas
- Many different people and groups have contributed to American culture.
- A fable teaches a lesson or gives a warning.

Objectives
- Play an Indian game
- Answer questions about the fable *The Game*

Materials
- 4 moccasins, slippers, or shoes
- A small, round stone
- A Bible

━━━ Lesson ━━━

Day 1

Introducing the Lesson

Indian Game

We are going to play the moccasin game similar to one that the Indians played long ago. You will be the Indian scout. You will go outside the room while I hide the stone in one of the four moccasins.

➤ The Indian scout looking for the hidden stone will say a rhyme while he looks for the stone. Listen as I repeat the Indian rhyme for you.

> Moccasin you,
> Moccasin me,
> Oh, moccasin, moccasin—
> Where can that stone be?

➤ Let's practice saying the rhyme together a few times.

> If you are playing the game with several children, you can hide each moccasin behind a child. Allow the Indian scout to guess which child has the moccasin with the stone. If he successfully finds the moccasin with the stone, the Indian scout takes the seat of that child. The child then becomes the Indian scout.

➤ You will have two guesses to find the stone. Let's play the game. *You may want to play several times, changing places with your child.*

The Game

The Animals wanted to challenge their friends the Birds to a contest. But what kind of contest could they have? All the Animals thought and thought. "We can have a ball game," said Deer, who could run faster than any other Animal.

The Birds accepted the challenge, and when the chosen day came, they met on a grassy meadow near the river. The Animals chose Bear to be their chief because he was the biggest and strongest. The Birds chose Eagle as their chief, for he was the bravest.

The goal poles were in place and a good ball was ready. But before the game began, the players practiced together. Turtle beat the drum, and all the Animals practiced in the meadow. They bragged, too, about how they would surely win the ball game. Each reminded the others that they were faster and stronger than the Birds.

92

Not only did the Indians give us games to play and songs to sing, but they have also passed down through the ages wonderful stories for us to enjoy. This lesson offers us a fable from the Cherokee.

Teaching the Lesson

Text Discussion, pages 91-92

➤ **To review the meaning of a fable and introduce our story today, read again the last paragraph on page 91.**
➤ **Read page 92 to find out who was playing in the ball game and who the leaders of the teams were.** *(The Animals, with Bear as leader, played against the Birds, whose chief was Eagle.)*
➤ **Describe Bear and Eagle.** *(Bear was the biggest and the strongest of the Animals; Eagle was the bravest of the Birds.)*
➤ **What are some characteristics of a good leader?** *(Answers will vary but may include intelligent, confident, wise, hard working, organized, and brave.)* (BATs: 2d Goal setting, 2e Work)

> Not all Christians make good leaders, but all Christians need to seek the guidance of God in all decision making. (BATs: 3a Self-concept, 6a Bible study, 6c Spirit-filled, 7b Exaltation of Christ)

The Birds, practicing in the treetops, did not brag like the Animals. Eagle Chief told the other Birds, "We may not be as big and strong as the Animals, but we will play hard. We must do our best."

Just as the practice time was over, a tiny creature came to Bear Chief. "I am an Animal," he said. "I have four legs like all the other Animals. And I would like to play ball on the Animals' team."

Bear Chief laughed and laughed. "You are too little to play on our team. We are big and strong, and we do not need help from creatures like you."

The creature was very sad, but he did not give up. He went to Eagle Chief. "I want to play ball. Will you let me play on your team?"

93

When Eagle Chief heard this story, he felt sorry for the tiny animal. He called all the Birds together. "This creature would like to play ball on our team, but he cannot fly. What can we do?"

Now the small creature was very, very sad. "Don't be sad, for we can help you," said Hawk and Falcon. "Look here what you have on your sides." And they took hold of the skin on his sides and pulled. They said, "You have wings of a sort!" He said, "I am Flying Squirrel!"

It was time for the game to begin. The ball flew high in the air, and Hawk caught it. He passed it to Falcon. Falcon flew toward the poles. But then he dropped the ball!

94

➤ **Which team was more confident of winning the game and why?** *(The Animals were more confident of winning because they were the fastest and the strongest.)*

➤ **How many legs did each of the members on the Animals team have?** *(four legs)*

➤ **What did the Animals do to show their confidence?** *(beat the drum and bragged)*

The Bible calls bragging pride. Read Proverbs 16:18, explaining that boasting and bragging often bring destruction and failure. (BATs: 4a Sowing and reaping, 7b Exaltation of Christ, 7e Humility)

Text Discussion, pages 93-95

➤ **Read the rest of the story, pages 93-95, to find out what happened to the tiny creature who wanted to play and which team won the game.** *(Eagle Chief let Flying Squirrel play on the Birds' team, and they won.)*

➤ **How did the Birds' willingness to include the tiny creature in the game help them to win?** *(Flying Squirrel was an important player on the Birds' team. He helped win the game for the Birds because he did what the other Birds could not do.)*

➤ **Do you know a boy or girl who is different in some way?**

Some people are different because of their handicaps, language, or customs, but they are exactly as God intended them to be. They have everything that they need to serve the Lord. We need to talk with and try to include in our games and activities people who are different from us. (BATs: 3a Self-concept, 5a Love, 5e Friendliness)

➤ **Look back at page 93 to find the statement that gives the motto, or goal, of the Birds' team.** *("We must do our best.")*

➤ **Why is this a good goal for Christians to have too?** *(The Lord is honored when Christians do their best for Him.)* (BATs: 2c Faithfulness, 4a Sowing and reaping, 7b Exaltation of Christ)

➤ **Do you think that the lesson the fable teaches is important for today? Why?**

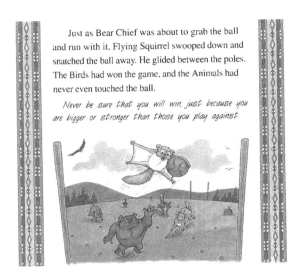

Just as Bear Chief was about to grab the ball and run with it, Flying Squirrel swooped down and snatched the ball away. He glided between the poles. The Birds had won the game, and the Animals had never even touched the ball.

Never be sure that you will win, just because you are bigger or stronger than those you play against.

Legends

Sometimes a favorite story might be about things that happened to a real person. But each time the teller told the story again, he told it a little differently. After many years, no one could be sure how much of the story was true. Stories like these are called *legends*. Read this legend of John Chapman. Do you know of other real people whose life stories became legends?

95

Day 2

Evaluating the Lesson

If you are teaching more than one child, you may want to handle the Evaluating the Lesson section as a fable game. Divide the children into two teams such as the Birds and Animals.

Question and Answer Time

➤ *Ask your child questions such as the following.*

- **Who was chosen as chief for the Birds?** *(Eagle)*
- **Whose idea was it to have a game?** *(the Animals')*
- **Who could run faster than any other animal?** *(Deer)*
- **Where was the game played?** *(on a grassy meadow near the river)* (*NOTE:* Accept any part of this answer.)
- **Why was Bear chosen as chief for the Animals?** *(He was the biggest and the strongest.)*
- **Why was Eagle chosen as chief for the Birds?** *(He was the bravest.)*
- **Where did the Birds practice for the game?** *(in the treetops)*
- **Who played the drum?** *(Turtle)*

- **Whose team did the tiny creature want to play on first?** *(the Animals' team)*
- **How many legs did the tiny creature have?** *(four)*
- **What did Bear Chief do when the tiny creature asked to play?** *(He laughed.)*
- **Why did Bear Chief not let the tiny creature play on his team?** *(He was too little.)*
- **What did the tiny creature need in order to play on the Birds' team?** *(wings or to be able to fly)*
- **Which Birds pointed out the creature's wings?** *(Hawk and Falcon)*
- **What name did the tiny creature have?** *(Flying Squirrel)*
- **When the game started, who caught the first ball?** *(Hawk)*
- **Who won the game?** *(the Birds)*
- **What lesson is being taught in this fable?** *(Never be so sure that you will win just because you are bigger or stronger than those you play against.)* (*NOTE:* Answer does not need to match exactly. Accept any answer that explains the moral.)

━━ Going Beyond ━━

Enrichment

Write each of the morals and simple paraphrases below on a separate index card. Encourage your child to match the index card that has the paraphrase, or meaning, to the index card that has the moral of the story.

- *Slow but steady wins the race.* If you keep working consistently, you may accomplish more than those who work quickly.
- *Little by little does the trick.* Big jobs can be done by doing a little bit at a time.
- *Look before you leap.* Think about the results of an action before you do it.
- *A strong voice often reveals a weak mind.* A person who talks a lot or talks loudly does not necessarily have the right answer.
- *He who has many friends has no friends.* If you have too many people as friends, you may end up with no close friends.
- *Misfortune tests the sincerity of friendship.* It is easy to be a friend when everything is going well; it is harder to be a friend when hard times come.

Additional Teacher Information

The Cherokee was one of the largest Native American groups in the southeastern part of North America. The Cherokee were divided into towns of about five hundred people each. Their houses were made of poles, woven in and out with the stems of cane plants and covered with wet clay which dried hard like plaster. The roofs of the houses were covered with bark. Often a smaller house was also built, partly underground, with a fire pit in the center and beds all around the edge. In the center of each town was built a seven-sided temple. The Cherokee were good farmers, fishermen, and hunters.

The Cherokee men enjoyed playing a game that they called "little brother of war." This rough game had from seventy-five to one hundred players on each team. Each player had two sticks with nets on the ends that he used to bat around a small ball. Much like the modern game of *lacrosse,* the object of the game was to get the ball to the team's goal at the end of the playing field. The first team to make twelve goals was the winner. Not only was the ball batted around with the sticks, but the players were often hit, kicked, or tackled as well.

The hidden-ball game was one of the most common of Indian guessing games and was an early variation of "Button, button, who's got the button?" It is said that early settlers adopted the hidden-ball game, changing its name to the bullet game. So many white settlers became addicted to the game, gambling and wasting their time, that at one time the Indian Territory passed a law forbidding the playing of the bullet game.

LESSON 27
Johnny Appleseed

Text, pages 95-99, 278
Notebook, pages 37-39

━━ Preview ━━

Main Ideas
- A legend is an unverified popular story about a real person.
- Many individuals and groups have shaped America's heritage.
- John Chapman became known as Johnny Appleseed.

Objectives
- Answer questions about Proverbs 25:11
- Prepare apples for drying
- Complete a crossword puzzle about Johnny Appleseed

Materials
- A Bible
- An apple, washed and cored*

> When coring the apple, try to keep the center hole as small as possible. This will make hanging the apple slices easier.

- A 12-inch length of string*
- An atlas

Day 1

━━ Lesson ━━

Introducing the Lesson

Notebook Activity, page 37

➤ Use your Bible to complete Notebook page 37.
➤ Write the verse on the lines following the reference.

> In Proverbs 25:11 the Lord tells us that a good, kind word is just as beautiful as a beautiful picture. We need to please the Lord with kind words every day. (BATs: 4b Purity, 5a Love, 5d Communication, 6d Clear conscience)

➤ Write inside the apple outline at least one kind thing you could say to another person.

Apples of Gold

Name _____

Follow your teacher's instructions.

Proverbs 25:11 *"A word fitly spoken is like apples of gold in pictures of silver."*

_____

_____

1. What fruit is mentioned in this verse? _____ *apples*

2. What kinds of words are "fitly spoken"? *Answers may vary but should*

   include good, kind words appropriate for the occasion.

3. How does Proverbs 25:11 describe words that are fitly spoken?

   "Like apples of gold in pictures of silver." They are beautiful.

Answers will vary.

Heritage Studies 3
Student Notebook

Lesson 27
Introducing the Lesson
37

George Washington's Cherry Tree

One of the most famous stories about George Washington is just that—a story. There is no proof that George Washington chopped down his father's cherry tree and owned up to doing it. A man named Mason Weems made up that tale. But it has been told for so many years and it seems so much like what honest George would have done, that many people think the story is true.

278

Apple-Drying Activity

This lesson is about apples and a famous man who had an important job long ago in America.

➤ Slice the apple into rings approximately $\frac{1}{4}$" thick.
➤ Place the apple rings on the string.
➤ Hang your string of apple rings to dry.

You can observe the apple rings every day to see the changes that take place. The drying process probably will be complete in two weeks. At that time you will be able to enjoy eating the dried apple rings.

The apple rings need to stay spaced apart for drying. If you are having difficulty keeping the apples apart, place macaroni, donut-shaped cereal, or clothespins between the apple slices. Try attaching the string with clothespins to a clothes hanger for drying.

Day 2

Teaching the Lesson

Text Activity, pages 95 and 278

➤ **Read the last paragraph on page 95 to find the name given to an exaggerated story about a real person.** *(a legend)*
➤ **Can you think of any legends you have heard about real people?**
➤ **Read on page 278 the story about George Washington.**
➤ **Do you think that this story is a legend?**

Map Activity

➤ Turn to the United States map in your atlas. Find the state of Massachusetts.
➤ Find the state of Pennsylvania. These two states are mentioned in the legend we will read today.
➤ Now find the city of Pittsburgh, Pennsylvania. This was as far west as most people traveled back then.
➤ **Is Pittsburgh in the West?** *(no)*

Johnny Appleseed

John Chapman was born on a farm in Massachusetts about the year 1775. Johnny was a good boy who loved his parents and the rest of his family. He always thought he'd stay right where he was, helping his father on the farm. He would have too if he hadn't seen all those people headed west.

Hundreds and hundreds of people, in wagons and on horseback, passed by his father's little farm. Why were they going west? One day Johnny decided it was time for him to find out for himself what was so great about the West. So he packed his belongings, said good-bye to his mother and father, and headed for Pittsburgh, which was about as far west as most people went back then.

96

Johnny didn't have much trouble deciding what to do when he got to Pittsburgh. He bought himself a piece of land, and he planted the thing he loved to tend to best: apple trees. His trees were strong and sturdy, and his apples made the best-tasting apple cider, apple pies, and apple dumplings around.

Soon Johnny saw that not every wagon stopped in Pittsburgh. Some people traveled even farther west. When he thought of all those people, living in the wilderness with no apples to be found anywhere, he felt he would cry. How could a person live without apples?

Johnny knew what he should do. He carefully saved and dried each seed from the apples he grew. He made little bags from deerskin and filled each bag with apple seeds, and he gave a bag to every wagon that passed his farm. Soon everyone was talking about that kind man, "Johnny Appleseed," who gave apple seeds away.

97

Text Discussion, pages 96-97

➤ **Read page 96 and the first two paragraphs on page 97 to find out what Johnny did when he got to Pittsburgh.** *(He bought land and planted apple trees.)*

When apple trees are planted side by side, they are called an ***orchard.***

Apple dumplings are made by baking cored apples that are filled with cinnamon, sugar, and raisins and wrapped in pastry.

➤ **What made Johnny want to cry?** *(Not all the people were stopping in Pittsburgh; many were going farther west and did not have any apple seeds to plant.)*

➤ **What does the question at the end of the second paragraph tell you about Johnny's feelings about apples?** *(He thought that the apple was the best food. He thought that nobody could survive without apples.)*

➤ **Read the rest of page 97 to find out what Johnny did to help the people who were traveling farther west.** *(He dried and saved apple seeds and gave away bags of seeds to every wagon that passed his farm.)*

➤ **What nickname did people give to Johnny?** *(Johnny Appleseed)*

➤ Johnny Appleseed could have sold his apple seeds to make some money. **Why do you think he did not sell the seeds?**

Still Johnny worried. Not everyone knew how to care for apple trees like he did. They might plant the seeds and never bother to care for the little trees, or worse yet, they might not ever plant the seeds at all. He hated to think that his good apple seeds were wasted that way. So he thought of a new plan.

Johnny sold his farm. He sold almost everything he owned. Then he loaded his apple seeds into a canoe and paddled down the Ohio River and into the wilderness. He would plant apple trees for the settlers in the West, and he would tend to them too.

People thought Johnny Appleseed was crazy, and you might have thought so too if you had seen him. The longer he stayed in the wilderness, the funnier Johnny looked. When his shirt wore out, he cut holes in a potato sack for his arms and his head and wore it instead. He lost his hat to a bear one night, and after that he took to wearing his cooking pot on his head.

Although the people laughed at Johnny at first, the laughing didn't last long. Soon Johnny was the favorite visitor in every camp and settlement in the West. He knew more about living in the wilderness, curing sicknesses, and, of course, raising and eating apples than anyone else. And he always had a good story to tell. The best stories of all were the ones he called "the good news from heaven," which he read from the big black Bible he carried everywhere.

Johnny spent the rest of his days in the wilderness planting apple trees. Forty years after he left Pittsburgh, he died in a little apple orchard in Indiana, his Bible lying open by his side.

Text Activity, pages 98-99

➤ **Read pages 98-99 to find out what Johnny Appleseed worried about and what he did about it.** *(He worried that people would not know how to take care of the apple trees. He sold his farm and went farther west to plant and care for apple trees.)*

➤ **Was Johnny Appleseed a favorite visitor in the camps and settlements?** *(yes)* He also made friends with the Indians.

➤ **Why did some people think Johnny Appleseed was crazy?** *(He looked funny with his potato sack shirt and a cooking pot for a hat.)*

➤ **What did Johnny Appleseed call the stories he read from the Bible?** *(good news from heaven)*

Name some of the "good news from heaven" that the Bible gives us. *(Answers will vary but should include salvation through Christ, the promise of a heavenly home with the Lord, forgiveness of sin, and provision for our every need.)* Challenge your child to read his Bible every day, reminding him that through the Bible the Lord speaks to Christians and teaches them how to live for Him. (BATs: 6a Bible study, 7a Grace, 8a Faith in God's promises, 8b Faith in the power of the Word of God; Bible Promises: A. Liberty from Sin, D. Identified in Christ, H. God as Father)

Use the clues below to complete the crossword puzzle on page 39.

ACROSS

1. All the wagons passing Johnny Appleseed's farm seemed to be going in this direction.
4. Johnny's real name was John _____.
7. Johnny Appleseed wore this on his head.
9. a large, unsettled area of land
10. small, black ovals in the center of apples
12. God is building mansions for Christians here.
13. Some are red; some are yellow; some are green. They are juicy and delicious.

DOWN

2. This was used to hold potatoes, but Johnny Appleseed wore it as a shirt.
3. a small boat carved from a tree
5. This town in Pennsylvania was as far west as most settlers went during Johnny Appleseed's day.
6. Johnny was friends with this group of people.
8. Many apple trees planted side-by-side make _____.
11. Most people grew corn and beans, but Johnny Appleseed grew apple trees on his _____.
14. An exaggerated story about a real person is called a _____.

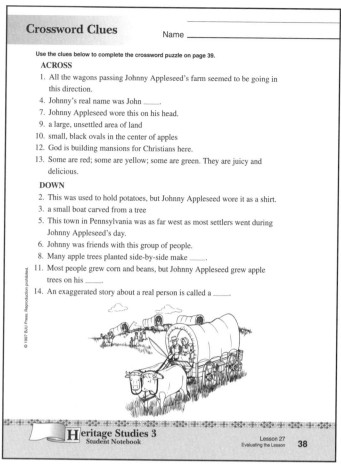

Arrange the circled letters to find out what wild animal became a constant companion for Johnny Appleseed as he roamed through the wilderness.

Write your answer here. _____ *wolf* _____

Evaluating the Lesson

Crossword-Puzzle Activity, Notebook pages 38-39

> You may want to write all the answers to the crossword puzzle in the white space on Notebook page 39. Your child will then have the correct spellings.

➤ Read the directions on Notebook page 38.
➤ Complete the crossword puzzle.
➤ Complete the last section below the crossword puzzle on Notebook page 39.

━━ Going Beyond ━━

Enrichment

Help your child make applesauce, using a blender and the following recipe.

Applesauce

4 apples, peeled and cut into small pieces

$\frac{1}{4}$ cup of light corn syrup

$1\frac{1}{2}$ teaspoons of lemon juice

2 tablespoons of sugar

A dash of salt

Place half of the apple pieces into the blender. Add all the other ingredients. Blend approximately one minute. Add the remaining apple pieces. Mix until all pieces are chopped and all the ingredients are well blended. Enjoy eating your homemade applesauce.

Additional Teacher Information

It is said that around 1628 John Endecott, one of the first governors of the Massachusetts Bay Colony, brought the first apple trees from England to America. To get an apple tree in early America, people planted apple seeds and waited for the apple trees to grow. Often, though, these apple trees grown from seeds did not always produce fruit of the same quality or variety as the apple that the seed was taken from. Today, apple trees are grown by grafting a bud or twig of an established variety onto a young apple tree grown from seed. Apple trees in orchards are usually planted in rows, allowing twenty to thirty feet on all sides between trees. This space allows room for the trees to be sprayed, cultivated, and harvested. Apple trees that are properly cared for will bear good fruit for thirty years or more.

There are approximately seventy-five hundred varieties of apples grown in the world. More than twenty-five hundred of these varieties grow in the United States. The leading apple-growing states are Washington, Oregon, and Idaho. Other important apple-growing states include Michigan, New York, Pennsylvania, Virginia, West Virginia, and California.

SUPPLEMENTAL
LESSON
Seeds of Hope

Text, page 276

━━━ Preview ━━━

Main Ideas

- People everywhere have needs and wants.
- People depend on each other to help them meet their needs.
- Individuals have unique attributes and skills.
- Johnny Appleseed gave away apple seeds and planted apple trees in many parts of early America.

Objectives

- Participate in a play about Johnny Appleseed
- Identify characteristics of Johnny Appleseed

Materials

- The date your state celebrates Arbor Day (*NOTE:* You may obtain this information from encyclopedias, your local chamber of commerce, or the National Forestry Association.)
- A large, round apple for each team*
- A box of round wooden toothpicks*
- Strips of masking tape (*NOTE:* Position the strips on the floor to mark the starting line and finish line.)
- Appendix, pages A23-A31: Seeds of Hope*
- Appendix, page A32: labeled apples*
- Appendix, page A33: apple tree outline*

> This lesson is a play and designed to be taught to a group of children. There are eight different characters in the play. You will need to make as many copies of the Appendix pages as you have children or family members participating. If you choose just to read the play with your child, you may use the play directly from your teacher's edition.

Notes

Seeds of Hope includes some factual information as well as some legendary information about John Chapman (Johnny Appleseed). To represent more authenticity, the play can be conducted outdoors under some trees—apple trees, if possible.

If you prefer to perform the play indoors, you can make trees, using one of the following methods.

Draw and paint large trees on refrigerator boxes. Cut around the leaf part of the "tree" and leave the "bark" (base of the box) to make the tree stand up.

To make trees from newspaper, roll two sheets of newspaper and tape them. Make six-inch cuts all around the top, untaped end of the newspaper roll. Carefully reach inside the cut newspaper roll and gently pull the insides up and out.

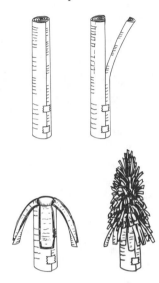

The following props would further enhance the play:

a hoe	a pitcher
a straw hat	several apples
a bale of hay	a rocking chair
an Indian headband	2 mugs
a doll (to represent an infant)	

━━━ Lesson ━━━

Introducing the Lesson

Game Activity

Divide the children into teams. Place one apple in front of the first child on each team. Have available enough toothpicks for each child to have one when his turn comes.

➤ Get down on your hands and knees and form a straight line.
➤ At the signal *Go*, the first member of each team will place a toothpick tightly between his lips. He will then use the toothpick to push the apple to the finish line and back again to the starting line.
➤ Each team member in turn pushes the apple with his toothpick upon the return of the child who is in line in front of him.
➤ The team to complete the relay first is the winner.

Special Days

Arbor Day

Every year, some states make one day a tree-planting day. The day is called *Arbor Day* because *arbor* means "tree."

The first Arbor Day was April 10, 1872, in Nebraska. Soon other states began to hold Arbor Days. Does your state?

276

Text Activity, page 276

➤ **Read the entry about Arbor Day on page 276.** *Tell your child what day your state celebrates Arbor Day.*
➤ **What does the word *arbor* mean?** *(tree)*

Teaching the Lesson

Reading and Acting of *Seeds of Hope*

Assign parts and distribute any necessary costumes or props. Encourage the children to notice the characteristics of Johnny Appleseed as illustrated in the play.

Evaluating the Lesson

Evaluation and Discussion

➤ Think about the characteristics of Johnny Appleseed that you saw illustrated in the play.

Give each child a copy of the labeled apples page and the apple tree outline.

➤ **Read the descriptive words on each apple.**

➤ Color and cut out the apples that have words that describe Johnny Appleseed. *(humble, generous, brave, kind, religious, hard working, adventurous)*

 Encourage your child to look up in a dictionary or thesaurus any of the descriptive words that he does not understand.

➤ Glue these apples on your apple tree.

Allow some time to discuss these characteristics, telling why they are honoring to God and are good qualities to develop. (BATs: 2b Servanthood, 2d Goal setting, 2e Work, 3a Self-concept, 5b Giving)

── Going Beyond ──

Additional Teacher Information

John Chapman was born in 1774 in Massachusetts. It is said that John's mother, who was part Native American, used to walk in the woods with him, acquainting him with the plants and animals. Before his second birthday, John's mother and his new baby brother died. By the time John was six, though, his father remarried and moved to another town in Massachusetts, where ten more children were born. As soon as John Chapman was old enough to leave home, he set out to explore the wilderness that led to the West.

John Chapman went to Harvard College, where he was an outstanding student with a deep religious faith. For a time, he worked as a minister with Abraham Buckles along the Potomac River. Desiring to journey west, John traveled with his half brother Nathaniel for a time. Wherever he went, John cleared plots of land and planted apple seeds from the pouch that he always carried with him. John Chapman gave away apple seeds and tiny seedlings, thus acquiring the nicknames *Appleseed Man, Appleseed John,* and the more familiar *Johnny Appleseed.* This "apple missionary" scattered apple trees over western New York, western Pennsylvania, Ohio, Indiana, southern Michigan, and other points west and south.

In March of 1845, while trudging through a snowstorm near Fort Wayne, Indiana, Johnny Appleseed became ill for the first time in his life. He sought shelter in a nearby settler's cabin and died there a few days later.

LESSON 28
Folks and Folktales

Text, pages 100-104
Notebook, page 40

―――――― **Preview** ――――――

Main Ideas
- Many different people and groups have contributed to American culture.
- Stories were preserved when people began to write them down.
- Authors are people who write stories.
- Folktales are often based on specific places or historical events.

Objective
- Answer questions about folktales

Materials
- Appendix, page A34: Evaluation Game*
- 8 pieces of construction paper
- Several different versions of the stories "Goldilocks and the Three Bears" or "Little Red Riding Hood" (optional)*

Notes
Jakob Grimm's name is sometimes spelled *Jacob*.

Day 1

―――――― **Lesson** ――――――

Introducing the Lesson

**Puppet Activity,
Notebook page 40**

The characters needed for "Goldilocks and the Three Bears" are Goldilocks, Papa Bear, Mama Bear, and Baby Bear. The characters needed for "Little Red Riding Hood" are Red Riding Hood, Grandmother, the woodsman, and the wolf. You may choose to have your child make all four puppets, help him make some of the puppets, or have a sibling participate in the activity.

➤ Choose to tell either the story "Goldilocks and the Three Bears" or "Little Red Riding Hood."
➤ Cut out the puppet pattern from Notebook page 40.

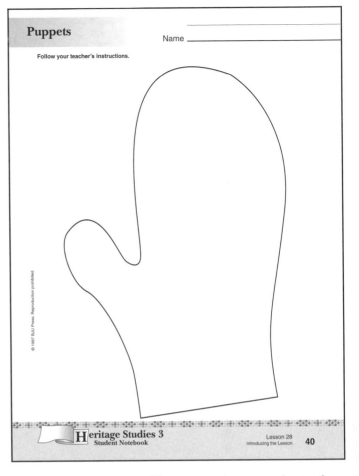

Puppets

Name _____

Follow your teacher's instructions.

© 1997 BJU Press. Reproduction prohibited.

Heritage Studies 3
Student Notebook

Lesson 28
Introducing the Lesson **40**

➤ Trace the pattern of the puppet mitt on two sheets of construction paper. Cut them out.
➤ Design a puppet for a character in the story that you have chosen.
➤ Draw and color that character on the front of your puppet mitt.
➤ Staple together the front and back of the puppet mitt.

Retelling a Story

➤ Discuss and decide upon the version of the story that you wish to tell.

Your child may have heard different versions of the story. If you have available several different printed versions, allow your child to look at these.

➤ Using the puppets, tell the story.

Chapter 5: Lesson 28

121

Writing Stories Down

For many hundreds of years, parents and grandparents remembered and told stories like "The Game." Few people could read or write, so the stories did not need to be written down. As more and more people learned to read, they realized that it would be good to have a written copy of some of these old stories.

Two of the first people to think of collecting stories in books were brothers named Jakob and Wilhelm Grimm. They listened to stories told by the people near their home in Germany. Then they wrote

the stories down and put together their first book in 1812. You have probably heard or read some things they wrote down. "The Elves and the Shoemaker," "Hansel and Gretel," and "Snow White and the Seven Dwarfs" are just a few of their stories.

Later, people in other countries began to write down their old stories. Missionaries in the West helped the Indians write their fables and myths. People still write down many different kinds of stories. Some of them are stories they have heard from other people, and some are stories they made up by themselves. We call people who write stories *authors.* Do you know any authors?

100

Folktales

Folktales are another kind of story told long ago. Many different kinds of stories can be called folktales. A folktale might tell about a lovely princess or a kind prince. It might tell about a brave hero who slays giants and monsters. Most people wished that they could be a princess or a hero like their favorite story character. Some folktales told funny stories about everyday happenings or about animals. Funny stories like these helped the people to forget the hard things in their lives. "The Gingerbread Man," "Sleeping Beauty," and "Little Red Riding Hood" are folktales. Can you think of any others?

The Alligator and the Deer

Long, long ago, tweren't nothin' around here but birds and animals and Indian men. Some animals, they get along. Some animals don't. Deer and Alligator not be getting along. Alligator want to kill Deer first chance him gets.

101

Teaching the Lesson

Day 2

Text Activity, page 100

➤ **Read page 100 to find out the names of two of the first people to collect stories in books.** *(Jakob and Wilhelm Grimm)*

➤ **Why was it a good idea for the Grimm brothers to write these tales in books?** *(Answers will vary but will probably include that this is how the stories could be saved and passed down from generation to generation.)*

➤ **Do you think that the Grimms wrote all of the stories in their books?**

No, they collected old tales from other people. Sometimes they changed the stories somewhat before writing them in their books.

Text Discussion, page 101

➤ **Read the first sentence on page 101 to find out what a *folktale* is.** *(a story from long ago)*

➤ **Read the rest of the first paragraph.**

Text Activity, pages 101-4

During the remainder of the lesson, you will hear an African American folktale entitled "The Alligator and the Deer." Some of the words used in the story will sound unusual because they are written

'Fore long, the new man comes to live here. He the white owner. He bring along he hounds to hunt Deer. Those hounds so fast when they chase Deer. He just as 'fraid of them hounds as he is of Alligator.

White owner's hounds are onto Deer. Him only chance to get away is to run in that water. But he know who in the water waiting for him. He sees Alligator's eyes. Deer is stuck. Those hounds is hungry. Alligator is very hungry. What Deer to do?

Just in time, Deer turn to the side. He run down the riverbank away from them hounds and Alligator. But the hounds don't know what he did. They don't see Alligator, either. Three of them run right into the water, and they land smack in front of Alligator.

102

"What this?" Alligator think to himself. "I not seen these things before, but they look good to eat." And he had heself two of them hounds for dinner. Then he takes a little rest.

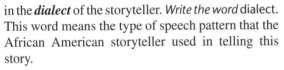

Soon Deer comes to the water. He needs a drink after he hard run. "Hey, Deer," Alligator calls. "Them things they call hounds is very good to eat. They easy to catch and they got no horn to scratch my throat when I swallow. I want to eat them all times. Let's us make a 'greement."

"What kind of 'greement you thinkin' of?"

"Just this," answered Alligator, "When them hounds be chasin' you, just run for the water. Then I'll eat the hounds which's after you."

103

So Deer 'greed. And when hounds take to chasin' Deer, he heads for the water. Alligator leave he alone and gets them hounds. But when Deer come to the water without the hounds be chasin' him, he have to take he chances.

Tall Tales

People told fables, legends, and folktales in many countries all over the world. But one kind of story was heard only in America. People who told *tall tales* stretched the truth. In fact, tall tales are full of outright lies. The bigger and more impossible the lies, the better the story is.

Almost every worker in America knew about a tall-tale character who did the same kind of work as he did. Cowboys, lumberjacks, sailors, and riverboat men all had their favorite tall-tale hero. This tall tale is about an unusual steel worker.

104

in the ***dialect*** of the storyteller. *Write the word* dialect. This word means the type of speech pattern that the African American storyteller used in telling this story.

➤ Listen carefully as I read the story on pages 101-4.
➤ **Why do Alligator and Deer not get along?** *(Alligator wants to kill Deer because he is very hungry.)*
➤ **Where could the story have taken place with "nothin' around . . . but birds and animals and Indian men"?** *(probably in America long ago)*
➤ **Who was the "new man" who came?** *(the white owner)*
➤ **What does history usually call this type of person?** *(a settler, colonist, or pioneer)*
➤ **Read aloud the last sentence of the story.**
➤ **What is meant by "he have to take he chances"?** *(With no hounds to eat, Alligator might eat Deer.)*

The rest of text page 104 will be read in the next lesson.

Evaluating the Lesson

Evaluation Game

➤ **Read the words in the squares on the Evaluation Game sheet.**
➤ I will read questions about folktales. If the answer to the question is on the game sheet, make an *X* in the square. Try to get four marks in a row.

If your child knows all the answers, he will have four in a row before all the questions are asked. If you are playing the Evaluation Game with more than one child, you may want to make another game sheet with the answers in a different order. You may also want to play more than one round.

• **Which brothers were among the first people to collect stories in books?** *(Grimm brothers)*
• **How many brothers from this family were writers?** *(two)*
• **In what country did they live?** *(Germany)*
• **What do we call people who write stories?** *(authors)*
• **What name is given to stories of princesses or everyday happenings or animals?** *(folktales)*

- **What kind of folktale is given in our lesson?** *(African American)*
- **According to the folktale, what kind of man was here long, long ago?** *(Indian)*
- **Which new man came to the land?** *(white man)*
- **What did the white owner bring with him?** *(hounds)*
- **Whom did the hounds chase?** *(Deer)*
- **Where did Deer go to get away from the hounds?** *(the water)*
- **Who ate the hounds for dinner?** *(Alligator)*
- **How many hounds ran into the water and landed smack in front of Alligator?** *(three)*
- **What did Alligator do after he ate?** *(rested)*
- **What did Alligator and Deer decide to make?** *(an agreement)*

══ Going Beyond ══

Enrichment

Make available some names and addresses of authors to whom your child can write. Generally, letters to authors can be sent in care of a book's publisher. Encourage your child to write a letter to an author whose book he has read.

Additional Teacher Information

The Grimm family lived in a small town in Germany. Jakob Ludwig Karl Grimm was born on January 4, 1785, and Wilhelm Karl Grimm was born on February 24, 1786. They were the oldest of six children, and because they were so close in age, they did everything together. Though both brothers studied law, they did not choose law as a career; instead, they wanted work that would give them time to research old German literature. They both were hired as librarians for the royal library and spent their free time collecting German folksongs and old tales from family members and friends. Many of the tales, such as "Snow White," "Little Red Riding Hood," and "Sleeping Beauty," came from Marie Muller, the nanny for the children of the only drugstore owner in the town in which the Grimms lived.

In December 1812 the first volume of *Grimms' Fairy Tales* was published. Their second volume of fairy tales was published in 1814 and contained many tales that had been told to the Grimms by Frau Katharina Dorothea Viehmann, a lady who delivered eggs and butter in the village. The most famous of Frau Viehmann's stories was "Cinderella," which had come from a French tale called "The Little Fur Slipper." Since the ancient French word for fur, *vair,* sounds just like the French word for glass, *verre,* the fur slipper became the glass slipper in the Grimms' second volume of fairy tales. The Grimms also gained fame in their publication of *German Folk Tales.* One tale, "The Pied Piper of Hamelin," is believed to be based on the Children's Crusade of 1212, when armies of children from Germany and France began a march to the Holy Land and were never seen again. (*NOTE:* This Children's Crusade ended at Marseilles, where most of the children were snatched and sold into slavery.)

Wilhelm Grimm died in 1859 and Jakob died in 1863, leaving behind writings that filled sixty-two volumes. They also contributed four books to the thirty-two-volume German dictionary that was not completed until 1962. It is said that the Brothers Grimm came to be much like the characters in their books, folk heroes themselves.

Most African American folktales originated with people who were brought to America long ago against their will. As slaves, they were subjected to hard labor, unfair treatment, and much suffering. In spite of this harsh lifestyle, the African Americans retained their imagination and added their songs, riddles, and stories to enhance the American heritage. The animals in their stories took on the characteristics of the people in their new homeland. The rabbit was a favorite of the slave storytellers. Though small and helpless compared to the other animals, Rabbit was always presented as a clever creature who won over the larger, stronger animals. It was Rabbit that the slaves always identified with. They used Rabbit to present their point of view and to tell of their experiences and dreams.

LESSON 29
Telling Tall Tales

Text, pages 104-8
Notebook, page 41

━━━━ Preview ━━━━

Main Ideas
- Many different people and groups have contributed to American culture.
- Tall tales are stories with highly exaggerated characters and events.

Objectives
- Write a tall tale
- Identify statements relating to the tall tale of Joe Magarac as true or false

Materials
- Maps and More 9, page M5
- Supplement, S7: Story Starters
- A sheet of $8\frac{1}{2}$" × 11" notebook paper

Day 1

━━━━ Lesson ━━━━

Introducing the Lesson

Listening Activity

➤ Listen as I read a story about a special man's breakfast preparations. Listen for clues to decide whether this story could really happen or not.

It was on the banks of the Red River of the North that Paul Bunyan set up his logging camp with the greatest crew of loggers that has ever existed. He had so many men in his camp that in one of his bunkhouses the bunk beds rose in the air thirty-seven beds high. Each night the men reached their beds with the help of balloons, and each morning they came down with parachutes. No alarm clocks were needed in Paul Bunyan's camp. You see, Paul knew lumberjacks pretty well, so he just had a big pipe with a blower stretched from the cook's kitchen to the bunkhouses. Each morning when breakfast was being prepared, the blower was turned on, and the smell of breakfast was blown right into the bunkhouses.

Paul found out that feeding these hard-working men was a big job! All the men were fond of flapjacks, just like Paul was, so a monster of a griddle was found to make all the flapjacks that his men wanted. The great griddle was perfectly round in shape, its edges as thick as a wagon road and its

weight greater than many mountains. Paul's method of getting the griddle to camp is a tale in itself, so let's leave that to another time and just be satisfied to say that the mighty Paul Bunyan figured it out and got the griddle in place. He then built a high fence around the griddle, and right beside it he put a couple of big buildings, like modern-day grain elevators, to hold his pancake flour. Paul also invented a machine, like the modern-day cement mixer, for mixing the hot cake batter. Ole, the blacksmith, made eight or ten of these fine mixing machines, and Paul had them placed into position beside the great griddle.

"There now," said Paul to Sourdough Sam, the head baker of the camp, who also had charge of all the flapjack making, "there is a griddle to be proud of—a griddle that should be a pleasure to work with."

It was truly a sight to see every day as Sourdough Sam and his kitchen crew got busy with the job of flapjack making. Along in the afternoon, every day, a gang of three hundred flapjack cooks would start getting down the flour and fixin's from the elevators, start the mixers going, and stir up the batter under the careful supervision of the boss baker. Meanwhile, as the batter was being mixed, the cook boys would have to grease the griddle. This they did by strapping whole hams or sides of bacon on their feet and skating around over the hot surface. When the batter was all ready and the greasing done, someone on the edge of the griddle would blow a whistle, and so big was the griddle that it took four minutes for the sound to get across. At this signal, all the cook boys would skate to the edge and climb high on the fence that had been fixed for that purpose. A cook would then trip the chute from the mixers, and out would roll a wave of flapjack batter ten feet high. To flip over the gigantic flapjack, Paul hit on the idea of using dynamite. Whenever one side of the flapjack was done, he would explode a ton or so of dynamite under it, and away up in the air the big cake would sail until it was almost out of sight. By putting a few more sticks of dynamite under one side than the other, Paul figured that the flapjack would turn over while in the air and would land exactly on the griddle with the brown side uppermost. Now Paul Bunyan's logging crew had the tastiest flapjacks around, cooked on both sides too. After this, Paul's men never had any cause for kicking about the flapjacks in the Red River Camp.

Story Discussion, Maps and More 9

➤ **Do you think this story could really happen? Why?**
➤ Look at the picture of Paul Bunyan on Maps and More 9. **Do you know anything else about this character?**

Paul Bunyan is a *tall tale* character, not because he is tall but because he does things that are unbelievable and highly exaggerated.

So Deer 'greed. And when hounds take to chasin' Deer, he heads for the water. Alligator leave he alone and gets them hounds. But when Deer come to the water without the hounds be chasin' him, he have to take he chances.

Tall Tales

People told fables, legends, and folktales in many countries all over the world. But one kind of story was heard only in America. People who told *tall tales* stretched the truth. In fact, tall tales are full of outright lies. The bigger and more impossible the lies, the better the story is.

Almost every worker in America knew about a tall-tale character who did the same kind of work as he did. Cowboys, lumberjacks, sailors, and riverboat men all had their favorite tall-tale hero. This tall tale is about an unusual steel worker.

104

The Best Steel Man

Steve Mestrovich's daughter was the prettiest girl in all the world, and even in all the Monongahela Valley. So of course, Steve knew that she must have the best husband around. To Steve, who was a hard working steel man, the best man meant the strongest man.

"I will hold a contest," Steve told Mary. "The strongest man will be your husband."

The day of the contest arrived. The young men came from town and all over the Monongahela Valley. One by one they tried to lift the heavy steel bars as Steve and Mary watched. "I hope that Pete Pussick wins," thought Mary. "He is the one I want to marry." It looked like Pete would win too. But that changed when Joe Magarac showed up.

105

Teaching the Lesson

Text Activity, page 104

➤ **Read the last two paragraphs on page 104 to find out what a *tall tale* is.** (*a story that stretches the truth, including outright lies, making an outrageous and impossible tale*)

➤ **Name some examples of people who told tall tales.** (*cowboys, lumberjacks, sailors, riverboat men, etc.*)

Text Activity, pages 105-7 and Maps and More 9

➤ Look at the picture of Joe Magarac on Maps and More 9.

You are going to read a tall tale about a steel man named Joe Magarac. The tale takes place in the Monongahela (*mə nŏn'gə hē'lə*) Valley, which is in Pennsylvania. *Point to the word on page 105 and give your child the proper pronunciation again before he reads the story. You may also need to help him with the pronunciation of Mestrovich (měz' trō vĭk), Magarac (măg' ă rāk), and Pussick (pŭs' ĭk).*

➤ **Read pages 105-7 to find out why Joe was called a steel man.** (*Joe was made of steel and was stronger than steel.*)

➤ **What was the contest all about?** (*The contest was to find the strongest man in the valley to marry Mary.*)

➤ **Why is this story a tall tale?** (*It contains so much outrageous exaggeration that there is no way it could be true.*)

➤ **What do you think the most unbelievable part of the story is?**

Day 2

Learning How Activity, page 108

➤ **Read Step 1 on page 108.**

➤ Fold a piece of notebook paper in half vertically to form a tall tale character writing sheet. *Demonstrate the steps to make the writing sheet for your child.*

➤ Cut the paper on the fold and glue the parts together to make one long sheet.

Never before had anyone in all the Monongahela Valley seen Joe Magarac. He was something to see. He stood taller than the trees in Steve Mestrovich's yard. His legs and arms were as big around as oak trees. His hands were big as shovels. And he was so strong that he picked up all the steel bars and Pete too!

"You are the strongest man in the world, and even in all the Monongahela Valley," declared Steve. "You will make the best husband for my Mary. Who are you?"

"I am Joe Magarac. Ho, ho, ho! Mary, you are the prettiest girl I ever seen. But I don't need a wife. What I need is a job. I'm the only real steel man in the world, or the Monongahela Valley even. See!" And with that he rolled up his shirt sleeve a bit, and everyone saw that his arms were made of shiny steel.

106

Steve Mestrovich gave Joe a job right there, and the next day he started work at the steel mill. It usually took eight men to run one of the huge furnaces, but Joe Magarac could do all the work by himself. When the steel was ready to be made into rails, he picked it up in his hands and squeezed it out between his fingers, eight rails at a time. He was the best steel man in the whole world, . . . but Mary married Pete anyway.

The stories that people told long ago in America came from many countries. They tell us about many different kinds of people. The stories tell us about the hopes and dreams, fears and humor of the "normal" people. They remind us that even though not everyone was a hero, everyone wanted to be.

107

➤ **Read Step 2.** *Briefly discuss your child's responses to the questions in Step 2, offering ideas for his tale.*

➤ *Show your child the Story Starters in the Supplement. Read the sentence starters for the first paragraph to him.*

➤ **Read Step 3.**

➤ Choose one of these sentences as an opening sentence for the first paragraph of your tall tale or make up an opening sentence of your own. In this paragraph describe the character in your tall tale more fully. Tell about some of the character's unusual experiences.

➤ **Read the possible opening sentences for the second paragraph from the Story Starters page.**

➤ Select one of these sentences or use one of your own. Write at least four more sentences to tell more about what the character in your tall tale did.

➤ Draw a picture of your tall tale character on your paper.

Choose one or more ways to "publish" your child's writing. Allow him to read it to you and the family. Display the tale tale in the schoolroom or on the refrigerator. Consider sending a copy to a grandparent or other relative.

◆ LEARNING HOW ◆

To Write a Tall Tale

1. Get your notebook paper and a pencil. Prepare the paper as your teacher tells you how to form a long, narrow writing sheet.

2. Read and select a story starter that your teacher suggests or think about something you would like to do. It might be a job or a sport you like to play. What would help you do that thing better? What if you were taller or shorter? What if you were made of iron, seashells, or rubber? Remember, the more impossible a tall tale is, the better the story.

3. Write a tall tale using one of the story starters or telling about a person who can do the job or play the sport you chose. Tell about the funny and impossible things that happen to this person. Share your tall tale with your friends. Why do you think people like tall tales so much?

108

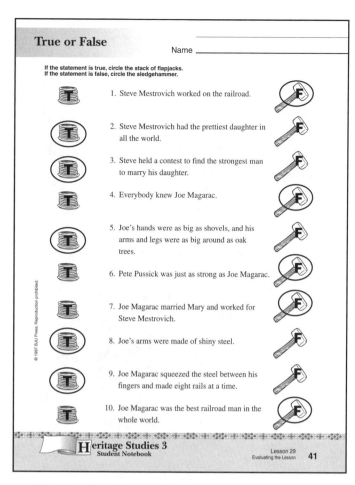

True or False

Name _____

If the statement is true, circle the stack of flapjacks.
If the statement is false, circle the sledgehammer.

1. Steve Mestrovich worked on the railroad.

2. Steve Mestrovich had the prettiest daughter in all the world.

3. Steve held a contest to find the strongest man to marry his daughter.

4. Everybody knew Joe Magarac.

5. Joe's hands were as big as shovels, and his arms and legs were as big around as oak trees.

6. Pete Pussick was just as strong as Joe Magarac.

7. Joe Magarac married Mary and worked for Steve Mestrovich.

8. Joe's arms were made of shiny steel.

9. Joe Magarac squeezed the steel between his fingers and made eight rails at a time.

10. Joe Magarac was the best railroad man in the whole world.

© 1997 BJU Press. Reproduction prohibited.

Heritage Studies 3
Student Notebook

Lesson 29
Evaluating the Lesson   **41**

Evaluating the Lesson

Notebook Activity, page 41

➤ Read the instructions on Notebook page 41.
➤ Complete the page.

▬ Going Beyond ▬

Enrichment

Encourage your child to draw a picture and write some sentences, telling what would have happened if Joe Magarac had married Mary Mestrovich.

Additional Teacher Information

Listed below are three other well-known tall tale characters.

1. Mike Fink, a keelboat man on the Ohio River, was well known for his skill with his rifle, Bang-All. He was always full of mischief and trickery; one time he dressed in an alligator hide to try to scare Mrs. Davy Crockett.

2. John Henry, so the story goes, was a steel-drivin' man, as big as an oak, as strong as a bull, and as black as a skillet. In just minutes, he laid hundreds of yards of railroad track simply by swinging the steel track around his head and slinging it straight out, spitting out the spikes and hammering them into place. With his powerful hammer, John Henry could drive the steel deeper and work faster than four men.

3. Pecos Bill was a cowboy who, according to the stories, talked the language of the animals and invented the lasso, branding, the roundup, and the rodeo. The exploits of Pecos Bill often include the colorful characters Widow-Maker (Bill's horse) and Slue-Foot Sue (Bill's bride).

The United States

To learn about the regions of the United States, your child will make a Travel Journal Passbook, complete with a U.S. map to color and a travel journal for each region. He will learn not only which states make up a region but also something about the history of those states, their state flags, nicknames, crops, cultural influences, famous landmarks, and tourist attractions.

Materials

The following materials must be obtained or prepared before the presentation of the lesson. These items are labeled with an asterisk (*) in each lesson and in the Materials List in the Supplement. For further information see the individual lessons.

- A road map or map of your state (Lesson 30)
- Appendix: pages A35-A36 (Lesson 30)
- Baby name book (Lesson 30)
- Pocket folder (purchased or made) (Lesson 30)
- *About Our States* (optional) (Lesson 30)
- A real cotton boll (optional) (Lesson 31)
- Post cards, brochures, or items from the different regions of the United States (Lessons 32-34)
- Hispanic-related items or pictures (Lesson 33)
- A recording of Spanish music (Lesson 33)
- Spanish food (optional) (Lesson 33)
- Spanish clothing (optional) (Lesson 33)
- A brochure from a local museum (Lesson 34)

 To enrich your child's learning in this chapter, you will want to collect post cards, brochures, books, and memorabilia relating to each region of the United States.

LESSON 30
The Northeast

Text, pages 110-13
Notebook, pages 42-42a

━━ Preview ━━

Main Ideas

- The United States can be divided into regions based on the closeness of states and common geographic features.
- The regions of the United States are Northeast, Southeast, Middle West, Southwest, Rocky Mountain, and Pacific.
- The Northeast region of the United States has a unique history of exploration, settlement, and growth.
- Names originate from words with special meanings.

Objectives

- Locate his hometown and state on a map
- Name the six regions of the United States
- Read maps to answer questions
- Complete a travel journal about the Northeast

Materials

- A road map or other large map of your state*
- *About Our States*, published by BJU Press (optional)*
- Maps and More 10, page M7
- A baby name book*
- Appendix, page A35: labeled map of the United States*
- Appendix, page A36: Travel Journal Passbook*
- A passbook folder*

The passbook folder may be a purchased pocket folder or a pocket folder of your own creation. You may use construction paper, tagboard, or file folders. To form the pocket on the inside, tape a half sheet of the material across the bottom and the two sides.

 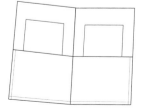

Regions of the United States

Choose a state and look at the map. Which section of the country is the state in? Why do you think it is in that group? What is one way that states are put into groups?

The United States can be divided into six groups of states. Find the Northeast, Southeast, Middle West, Southwest, Rocky Mountain, and Pacific regions on the map. Do the names of the groups give you a clue about how the groups are divided?

110

Day 1

━━ Lesson ━━

Introducing the Lesson

Map Discussion

> If you do not live in the United States, choose a state to study.

➤ Look at the map of your state. Trace the shape of the state with your finger.
➤ **What do you think the shape of your state resembles?** (*NOTE:* Point out that Colorado is an almost perfect rectangle; Michigan is in two parts, with the lower part looking like a mitten; Oklahoma looks like a cooking pot with a long, straight handle.)
➤ **Do you think your state is large or small in comparison to most other states?**
➤ **Do you know the name of your state capital?**
➤ **What symbol does a map use to identify the state capital?** (*usually a star or a red dot*)
➤ Locate the capital on this map.
➤ **Why is the state capital important to the state?** (*Answers will vary but should include something about the state government and the making and enforcing of the laws.*)

Heritage Studies 3 Home TE

The Northeast

What do you remember about how this area was settled? Who were the first comers? They were the Separatists from England. Where did they settle? What groups settled Pennsylvania? German

Reconstructed Separatist settlement

farmers and people called Quakers were some of the first settlers. Can you name some important events that happened in this region in America's early history?

What states are in this region now? Can you find the capital cities of the states? How are they shown on the map? Look at the map of the Indian nations on the next page. Before the white man came, who had lived in the northeastern section of this land?

111

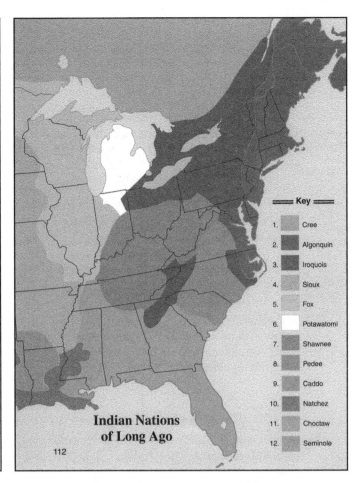

Indian Nations of Long Ago

112

=== Key ===
1. Cree
2. Algonquin
3. Iroquois
4. Sioux
5. Fox
6. Potawatomi
7. Shawnee
8. Pedee
9. Caddo
10. Natchez
11. Choctaw
12. Seminole

➤ If you have visited the state capital, tell about something interesting that you saw.
➤ Locate your city or town on the map.
➤ Tell something you think is interesting about your town or state.

Teaching the Lesson

Text Discussion, page 110

➤ **Read the first paragraph on page 110, answering the questions given.**

The different colors on the map represent different sections, or *regions,* of the United States.

➤ **Read the second paragraph to learn the names of these regions.** *(Northeast, Southeast, Middle West, Southwest, Rocky Mountain, Pacific)*
➤ Find our state on the map on page 110 and on the labeled map of the United States.
➤ **Which region is our state in?** Locate the other regions labeled on the map.
➤ **How do the names of the regions give a clue about how the groups are divided?** *(Location of each state is the most important factor in dividing the states into regions.)*
➤ **What other characteristics might the states within a region share?** *(Answers will vary but may include climate, history, dialect, favorite foods, or architecture.)*

Text Discussion, page 111

➤ Name the region shown on the map on page 111. *(Northeast region)*
➤ **Read and answer the questions in the first paragraph on page 111.** *(This region was settled by people searching for religious freedom, riches, and adventure. The first comers were Separatists from England who settled in Massachusetts. German farmers and Quakers settled in Pennsylvania. Some early historical events of the Northeast include the arrival of the Pilgrims on the Mayflower, the Boston Tea Party, the Revolutionary War, and the development of the colonies.)*
➤ **Read the second paragraph.**
➤ **What does the star in each state represent?** *(the capital)*
➤ Point to each Northeast state, naming the state and its capital. If you have visited any of these states, tell something interesting that you saw.

Map Activity, page 112

➤ Study the map on page 112 to determine which groups of Native Americans lived in the Northeast region before the white man came. *(Algonquin, Iroquois, and Shawnee)*

The Algonquin lived in bands of one hundred to three hundred members. These members were placed in smaller hunting groups of twenty-five members. A lodge of bent saplings and birch bark housed a husband and wife with their small children and any older unmarried daughters as well as married sons and their wives and children.

The Iroquois were sometimes called the *Five Nations* group. The Five Nations included the Mohawk, the Oneida, the Onondaga, the Cayuga, and the Seneca. (*NOTE:* Around 1722 the Tuscarora joined the federation, making it the Six Nations.)

➤ **Do you know what kind of house many Iroquois families lived in?** They lived in a *longhouse* made of wooden poles and bark.

For further information and pictures of longhouses, refer to the student text for *HERITAGE STUDIES 1.*

Some families today still have extended families living together under one roof. Often this type of living arrangement helps everyone. Family members can share in expenses and household responsibilities. They can also be companions and caregivers for each other. (BAT: 5a Love)

➤ **How do you think the lives of the early colonists were influenced by the Indians living in the Northeast?**

Many names of places, types of foods, and ways of doing things learned from the Indians still exist today among the people living in the Northeast.

Day 2

Text Discussion, page 113

➤ Look up your name or your nickname in the name book. **What is the meaning of your name?**
➤ Look up the meaning of a friend's name or nickname.

The name **Christian** means "like Christ"; therefore, the actions, words, and thoughts of Christians should honor Christ, the Lord. (BATs: 2b Servanthood, 2c Faithfulness, 3d Body as a temple, 5d Communication)

➤ States' names often have special meanings and nicknames. **Read page 113 to find the meaning of** *Vermont* **and the nickname of Massachusetts.** (Vermont *means "green mountain"; Massachusetts' nickname is "the Bay State."*)

Vermont gets its name from the two French words *vert* and *mont.* The words mean "green mountain." What does the name tell you about the state? Can you guess Vermont's nickname? It is "the Green Mountain State."

One nickname for Massachusetts is "the Bay State." A *bay* is a body of water that is nearly circled by land but has a wide opening to the sea. Look at the map on page 111. Can you tell why Massachusetts has the nickname it does?

The Northeast has many good *harbors,* safe places for ships to dock. The better the harbor, the bigger the town grows beside it. Which cities seem to be on the best harbors? The Northeast settlers built fine ships. Today many of the harbors are still busy.

New York Harbor

113

➤ **Do you think Vermont really has green mountains?** It does.
➤ **Read aloud from page 113 the definition of** *bay.* (*a body of water that is nearly circled by land but has a wide opening to the sea*)
➤ Look at the map on page 111 to find the bay that gives Massachusetts its nickname.
➤ **What large body of water does the bay flow into?** (*the Atlantic Ocean*)
➤ **What is a** *harbor?* (*a safe place for ships to dock*)
➤ **Why is a harbor important to a town?** (*A good harbor helps a town grow bigger because of the goods that are transported in and out.*)

The buying and selling of goods from the harbors in the Northeast to European countries helped make this region prosperous and strong in the early years. Notice the picture of New York Harbor on page 113. This is one of the world's busiest ports.

Name _____

Follow your teacher's instructions.

Northeast States	⭐ Capitals
Maine	Augusta
New Hampshire	Concord
Vermont	Montpelier
Massachusetts	Boston
Connecticut	Hartford
Rhode Island	Providence
New York	Albany
New Jersey	Trenton
Pennsylvania	Harrisburg
Delaware	Dover
Maryland	Annapolis

© 1997 BJU Press. Reproduction prohibited.

Heritage Studies 3
Student Notebook

Lesson 30
Evaluating the Lesson **42**

Fill in the blanks.

● Who were the first people to come to the Northeast region? to Pennsylvania?

    Separatists; Quakers

● Who lived in the Northeast region before these people came?

    Native Americans

● What large body of water lies next to the Northeast region?

    Atlantic Ocean

Select one state from the Northeast region and answer the following questions.

● State name: _____

● What is the state's nickname? _____

● What is the state bird? _____

● What is the state tree? _____

● What is the state flower? _____

● What is the name of one river in the state? _____

42a

Evaluating the Lesson

Travel Journal Activity, Notebook pages 42-42a

If you have purchased the book *About Our States,* your child may use it as a resource for completing the Notebook pages in this chapter. You may wish to allow an extra day for him to complete these pages. Please give as much help as needed as he begins this introductory phase to research.

➤ Color the Northeast region purple on your Travel Journal Passbook page.

➤ Glue the page to the front of the folder to form a cover for your passbook.

    This passbook will be used throughout the chapter as we discover information about each region of the United States.

➤ Complete Notebook page 42 by writing on the chart the name of each Northeastern state and its capital. You may use Maps and More 10, the student text, or other reference books if you need help.

➤ Complete Notebook page 42a using your resource materials.

➤ Place Notebook pages 42-42a in the Travel Journal Passbook.

━━━ Going Beyond ━━━

Enrichment

    Encourage your child to add a pictorial section about the Northeast region to his Travel Journal Passbook. Pictures of places from the region may be drawn or cut from magazines. He may also use photographs or post cards mounted on construction paper.

    Encourage your child to collect souvenirs from around the United States. Group and display the souvenirs according to the regions from which they came.

    Give your child a coin to add to his display. Tell him to find this motto on the coin: *E Pluribus Unum* —"Out of Many, One." Explain that the United States is one country made from many states and from many different kinds of people.

Additional Teacher Information

The names of twenty-six states in the United States are derived from Native American words.

Alabama means "clearers of the thicket" (Alibamu).

Alaska means "great land" (Aleut).

Arizona means "place of little springs" (Papago).

Arkansas means "the people who live downstream" (Sioux).

Connecticut means "at the long tidal river" (Pequot).

Idaho means "the sun is coming up" (Shoshone).

Illinois means "superior men" (Illinois).

Iowa means "sleepy ones" (Sioux).

Kansas means "people of the south wind" (Kansas).

Kentucky means "meadowland" (Cherokee).

Massachusetts means "people near the great hill" (Algonquian).

Michigan means "big lake" (Algonquian).

Minnesota means "sky-tinted water" (Sioux).

Mississippi means "big river" (Ojibwa).

Missouri means "people with the dugout canoes" (Sioux).

Nebraska means "flat water" (Oto).

New Mexico means "followers of the war god, Mexitli" (Aztec).

North Dakota and *South Dakota* mean "friends" (Sioux).

Ohio means "beautiful river" (Wyandot).

Oklahoma means "red people" (Choctaw).

Tennessee means "area of traveling waters" (Cherokee).

Texas means "ally," a word for the Teja Indians (Caddo).

Utah means "land of the sun" (Ute).

Wisconsin means "gathering of the waters" (Ojibwa).

Wyoming means "upon the great plain" (Algonquian).

LESSON 31
The Southeast

Text, pages 114-15
Notebook, pages 43-44a

═══ Preview ═══

Main Ideas

- The United States can be divided into regions based on the closeness of states and common geographic features.
- The Southeast region of the United States has a unique history of exploration, settlement, and growth.
- In early America many landowners in the Southeast used slaves in the production of cotton.

Objectives

- Sing a song about the states in the Southeast region
- Color the Southeast region of the United States on a map
- Read maps to answer questions
- Complete a travel journal about the Southeast

Materials

- An atlas
- Supplement, page S8: cotton boll
- A real cotton boll (optional)*

Day 1

═══ Lesson ═══

Introducing the Lesson

**Singing Activity,
Notebook page 43**

➤ Read the title shown on Notebook page 43. The region of the United States that we will "visit" today is called the ***Southeast.***

➤ Read silently and listen as I sing "Away Down South" for you. (*NOTE:* The song is sung to the tune of "Old MacDonald.")

➤ Sing the song with me.

➤ Color the Southeast region orange on your Travel Journal Passbook.

Away Down South

Name _____

Follow along as your teacher sings this song; then sing the song together.

Away Down South
(Tune: "Old MacDonald")

Gonna take a trip away down South—
Y'all come along with me!
There's Arkansas and Louisi-ann',
Virginia, and Tennessee—

With the sunshine here,
And the sunshine there,
Here the sun; there the sun;
Everywhere the sunny sun.
Gonna take a trip away down South—
Y'all come along with me!

Add Georgia, and West Virgin-i-a,
Alabama, and Mississipp-i—
To the Carolinas and Florida,
Then home to ol' Kentucky.

With the sunshine here,
And the sunshine there,
Here the sun; there the sun;
Everywhere the sunny sun.
Gonna take a trip away down South—
Y'all come along with me!

Heritage Studies 3
Student Notebook

Lesson 31
Introducing the Lesson **43**

The Southeast

Reconstruction of a home in early Charleston

Look at the map on this page. How many states are in the Southeast? What are their capital cities? Does the Southeast have good harbors? Charleston, South Carolina was an important harbor. Can you find it on a map?

Do you remember which state had the first English settlement that lasted? It was Virginia. What was the name of the town? It was called Jamestown, after the English king James I. The people who came to Jamestown were hoping to find gold. What they found instead was a place to grow tobacco. Soon they began to grow tobacco to send to England.

Now look at the map on page 112 to find the names of the people who lived in the Southeast before the Jamestown settlers arrived. Which group also lived in the Northeast?

114

Teaching the Lesson

Text Discussion, page 114

➤ Name each state located in the Southeast region of the United States, using the map on page 114.

➤ **Read and answer the first two questions on the page**. *(There are twelve states in the Southeast region. The states and their capital cities are Montgomery, Alabama; Little Rock, Arkansas; Tallahassee, Florida; Atlanta, Georgia; Frankfort, Kentucky; Baton Rouge, Louisiana; Jackson, Mississippi; Raleigh, North Carolina; Columbia, South Carolina; Nashville, Tennessee; Richmond, Virginia; and Charleston, West Virginia.)*

➤ **Turn back to page 113 and read aloud the definition of *harbor*.** *(a safe place for ships to dock)*

➤ **Read the rest of the first paragraph on page 114.** Locate Charleston, South Carolina, on a United States map in your atlas.

➤ Locate on the map in your atlas some other good harbors in the Southeast. *(Savannah, Georgia; Norfolk, Virginia; and Tampa Bay, Florida)*

➤ **Read the rest of page 114 to find out where the first permanent English settlement was established.** *(Jamestown, Virginia)*

The Native Americans who lived in the Southeast region before the white man came were the Sioux, Caddo, Fox, Natchez, Seminole, Iroquois, Pedee, Choctaw, Shawnee, and Algonquin.

➤ **Which of these tribes were also found in the Northeast?** *(Algonquin, Iroquois, and Shawnee)*

Many places in the Southeast grew cotton. Growing cotton was hard work. Workers had to hoe the ground between the cotton plants. Hoeing kept the weeds down. Then the cotton had to be picked. Some landowners made *slaves* work in the cotton fields and in their big houses. A slave is a person who must work for someone without getting paid.

Can you remember the problem that came up in the Constitutional Convention about slaves? Some members of the convention wanted to let slavery go on. Some wanted to stop it. Do you remember what happened? People were allowed to bring slaves to the United States until 1807. Do you think slavery stopped after that? No, it did not.

A slave family on a plantation in the South

115

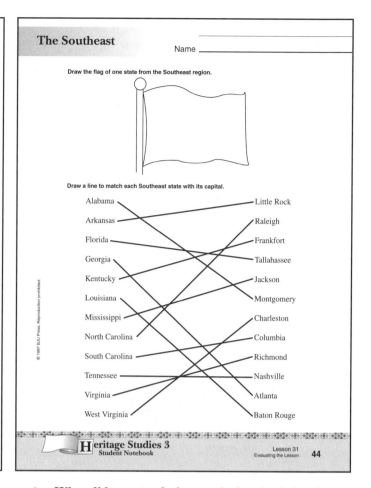

Text Discussion, page 115

➤ **Read page 115 to find out an important crop in the Southeast.** *(cotton) Show the picture of a cotton boll or a real cotton boll.*

In a few weeks, the seed grows to be a flowering plant from two to five feet tall. After the petals of the flowers fall, the *seedpod* develops into a boll that contains seeds from which *fibers* and *linters* grow. The seedpod matures and, in a few weeks, dries and splits open to reveal the cotton fibers and seeds, ready for harvest.

God, the Creator of all, made the cotton seed and controls its growth. God also made us and guides our lives. Christians should be willing to seek God's will for their lives and to do everything for His glory. (BATs: 2c Faithfulness, 3a Self-concept, 7b Exaltation of Christ; Bible Promise: I. God as Master)

➤ **Who did most of the work involved in the growing and harvesting of the cotton crop?** *(slaves)*

➤ **Read aloud the definition of** *slave* **from page 115.** *(A slave is a person who must work for someone without getting paid.)*

➤ Explain the problem that came up in the Constitutional Convention regarding slaves. *(Some people wanted slavery to continue; others wanted slavery to stop.)*

The law of 1807 forbidding more slaves from being brought into the United States did not work.

Evaluating the Lesson

Travel Journal Activity, Notebook pages 44-44a

➤ Complete Notebook pages 44-44a, using the textbook, atlas, or other reference books.

➤ Place the completed pages in your Travel Journal Passbook.

Fill in the blanks.

● A harbor is a _____ **safe** _____ place for _____ **ships** _____ to dock.

● The Charleston harbor is in the state of _____ **South** _____ **Carolina** _____

● The first English settlement that lasted in the New World was _____ **Jamestown** _____

   in the state of _____ **Virginia** _____ .

● Name three tribes that lived in the Southeast before the white man came.

   _____
   Possible answers include Seminole, Choctaw, Chickasaw, Cherokee,

   _____
   Creek, Natchez, and Calusa.

● Long ago _____ **slaves** _____ worked in the cotton fields in the Southeast. List

   six things that are made of cotton.

   _____
   Answers will vary.

   _____

   _____

   _____

44a

Going Beyond

Enrichment

Direct your child to look through newspapers to find articles about current events in the United States. Direct him to cut out the articles and mount each one on a plain sheet of paper or on construction paper. Encourage him to find a newspaper article about a current event from each region of the United States. Tell him to add these current events articles to his Travel Journal Passbook.

Additional Teacher Information

Each state flag depicts much about the state's heritage. Note the following descriptions.

Alabama's state flag bears the cross of St. Andrew, a large diagonal red cross, on a white field.

The state flag of Arkansas boasts a large blue diamond shape edged with white stars on a field of red. This represents Arkansas as a major diamond-producing state.

Florida's flag bears a red cross on a white field. In the center of the cross is the state seal, telling of Florida's beginning. On the seal is pictured a native Florida Indian maiden, a steamboat, and a sabal palm tree.

On the left side of Georgia's flag is the state seal on a field of blue. The seal depicts a man with a sword defending the Constitution. The remainder of the flag shows a Confederate battle flag.

Kentucky's flag bears its seal on a field of violet-blue. The seal shows a frontiersman embracing a statesman.

In the center of the blue flag of Louisiana are the words *Union, Justice & Confidence*. Above the words is the illustration of a mother pelican in a nest with three young pelicans, a graphic promise that Louisiana will protect its people and its resources.

Mississippi's flag has in its upper left corner the Confederate flag but shows its ties to the United States with its stripes of red, white, and blue.

The flag of North Carolina bears a red, white, and blue field with the state's initials.

South Carolina's flag bears a palmetto tree and a crescent on a field of blue. The crescent is an emblem that the state's soldiers wore on their caps in the Revolutionary War.

The red field on Tennessee's flag highlights a circle containing three stars representing east, middle, and western Tennessee.

The seal in the center of Virginia's blue flag shows Virtue, dressed as an Amazon, being triumphant over tyranny; the design goes back to 1776.

West Virginia's state flag bears the seal with a picture of a miner, a farmer, and the date of statehood, 1863.

L E S S O N 3 2
The Middle West

Text, pages 116-18
Notebook, pages 45-45a

═══ Preview ═══

Main Ideas
- The United States can be divided into regions based on the closeness of states and common geographic features.
- The Middle West region of the United States has a unique history of exploration, settlement, and growth.
- Land divisions include countries, states, and cities.
- A surveyor measures land and helps decide where the borders should be.

Objectives
- Identify the states in the Middle West region of the United States
- Read maps to answer questions
- Complete a travel journal for the Middle West region of the United States

Materials
- Post cards or brochures from the states of the Middle West region of the United States*
- Poster or picture with a border
- Labeled map of the United States from Lesson 30
- 12 small buttons or beans

═══ Lesson ═══
Day 1

Introducing the Lesson

Identification Activity

➤ *Give your child the assortment of post cards and brochures from the Midwest, the labeled map of the United States, and the buttons or beans.*

These post cards and brochures represent the states located in the next region that we will "visit." It is called the **Middle West,** or sometimes simply the **Midwest.**

➤ Find the Middle West region on the map of the United States.
➤ Look at each post card or brochure. Determine which state it represents. Place a button or bean on the state shown on the labeled United States map.

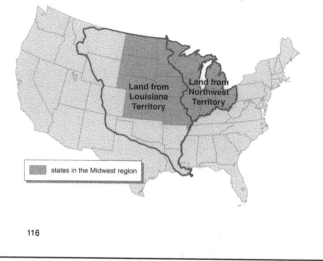

The Middle West

Some people from the East felt crowded in their cities. They wanted to move west. Soon after the American War for Independence, settlers swarmed into what is now Ohio. At that time it was part of the Northwest Territory.

The explorers Lewis and Clark went to look over the Louisiana Territory. Who asked them to go? They were among the first white men to see much of the land we now call the Middle West, or Midwest. How can you find out what people lived in the region when Lewis and Clark passed through?

Land from Louisiana Territory

Land from Northwest Territory

states in the Midwest region

116

➤ **What states have been identified from the Middle West region?**
➤ **Are there any Middle West states for which we did not have any materials?**

Teaching the Lesson

Text Discussion, page 116

➤ **Read page 116 to find out why settlers wanted to move farther west in the early days of America's history.** *(They felt crowded.)*
➤ **What state did many of the first settlers go to?** *(Ohio)*

At this time the land near Ohio was the farthest west that the settlers had ventured. They called the land the Northwest Territory. Notice on the map on page 116 the land known then as the Northwest Territory. It included Wisconsin, Michigan, Illinois, Indiana, Ohio, and part of Minnesota.

➤ **What kinds of transportation did many settlers use in their journeys westward?** *(Conestoga wagon and covered wagon)*
➤ **At what year is the figure of Lewis and Clark located on the TimeLine?** *(1804)*
➤ Review the events that came before and after this time period.

➤ **What are Meriwether Lewis and William Clark famous for?** *(They were explorers sent to the Louisiana Territory.)*
➤ **Who asked Lewis and Clark to make this expedition?** *(President Thomas Jefferson)*
➤ **Do you remember who Sacajawea was and how she helped in the journey?**

Remember that Sacajawea was a brave Shoshone woman who helped Lewis and Clark to survive their long journey by being a guide, helping them find food, making medicines from herbs, and dealing with other Shoshone tribesmen. Sacajawea had many abilities that she was willing to use to help Lewis and Clark.

God has given Christians special abilities to use for His glory. Christians should be willing to show their love for God and others by unselfishly putting God's will and the needs of others before their own desires. That is how they show that they are truly Christians—"like Christ." (BATs: 2b Servanthood, 2c Faithfulness, 2f Enthusiasm, 3a Self-concept, 5a Love)

➤ Use the map on page 116 and the labeled United States map to name the states located in the area called the Louisiana Territory. *(Arkansas, Colorado, Iowa, Kansas, Louisiana, Minnesota, Missouri, Montana, Nebraska, New Mexico, North Dakota, Oklahoma, South Dakota, Texas, and Wyoming)*
➤ **Which of these states are a part of what we call the Middle West region?** *(Iowa, Kansas, Minnesota, Missouri, Nebraska, North Dakota, South Dakota)*

Day 2

Text Discussion, page 117

➤ *Show your child the poster or picture with a border.* Describe the border of the picture.
➤ **What are the purposes of this border?** *(It is decorative, and it separates the picture from the outside edge.)*

Tell the students that a **border** is usually said to be a boundary, showing the outside edges of an area. Lands have borders too.

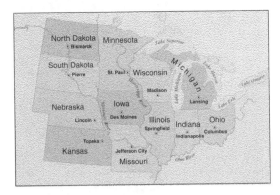

Which Midwest state borders the most other Midwest states? How many others does it share a border with? By looking at the map on this page, can you tell how some state borders are decided? What rivers make borders?

Other state borders are decided differently. Do you notice how many of the midwestern states have straight borders? Could these borders have been made along rivers? How do you think they were made?

Sometimes people agree that a line should divide land into states or counties or farms. Since the line is not actually drawn on the ground, the people hire a *surveyor* to decide where the border is.

"Thou hast set all the borders of the earth."
Psalm 74:17

117

➤ Look at the map on page 117 to find out something God made (natural boundary) that forms the border of some states. *(rivers)*
➤ **Read page 117 and answer the questions on the page.** *(Iowa shares a border with six other states—Illinois, Missouri, Nebraska, South Dakota, Minnesota, and Wisconsin. The Mississippi River, the Missouri River, and the Ohio River serve as natural boundaries for some states.)*
➤ Look again at the borders of the states.

Each of the Midwest states has at least one border that is a straight line. Probably someone **surveyed**, or measured, the land to establish where the borders should be "drawn."

◆ THINGS PEOPLE DO ◆

Surveying

A *surveyor* is someone who measures land and helps decide where borders are. He uses special tools to make the measurements.

The most important tool is called a *transit*. It is a small telescope. It sits on a three-legged stand. A line with a weight hangs down from the transit. It marks the very middle of where the transit sits.

If the surveyor knows that the border needs to go north, he aims his transit north. Then a helper can measure from the weight on the line to the point that the surveyor tells him.

George Washington was a surveyor in Virginia. He used a special chain to measure with. Today surveyors use calculators, computers, and photographs taken from airplanes in their work.

118

The Middle West

Name _____

Complete the names of the states of the Middle West region.

© 1997 BJU Press. Reproduction prohibited.

Il _linois_ _____ Mis _souri_ _____

In _diana_ _____ Ne _braska_ _____

Io _wa_ _____ No _rth Dakota_ _____

K _ansas_ _____ O _hio_ _____

Mic _higan_ _____ S _outh Dakota_ _____

Min _nesota_ _____ W _isconsin_ _____

● Another name for the Middle West region is the ___ *Midwest* ___ .

Heritage Studies 3
Student Notebook

Lesson 32
Evaluating the Lesson **45**

Text Discussion, page 118

➤ **Read page 118 to find out what a person who measures the land is called.** *(a surveyor)*

➤ **What tool is important for a surveyor?** *(a transit)*

➤ Describe the transit. *(It is a small telescope that sits on a three-legged stand. A line with a weight hangs down to mark the middle of where the transit sits.)*

➤ **What famous president was also a surveyor?** *(George Washington)*

➤ **What did Washington use to measure instead of a transit?** *(a special chain)*

➤ **What other kinds of tools are used by surveyors today?** *(calculators, computers, and photographs taken from airplanes and satellites)*

God gives Christians special abilities to use for His glory. (BATs: 2c Faithfulness, 2d Goal setting, 2e Work, 3a Self-concept, 7b Exaltation of Christ)

Evaluating the Lesson

Travel Journal Activity, Notebook pages 45-45a

➤ Color the Middle West region green on the front of your Passbook.

➤ Complete Notebook pages 45-45a, using the textbook, maps, or other reference books.

➤ Place these pages in your Travel Journal Passbook.

Worksheet (45a)

Unscramble the letters to spell out the names of the people who explored the Louisiana Territory.

WETIMERHER — Meriwether

SILWE — Lewis

LAMWILI — William

KARLC — Clark

Fill in the blanks.

● Which river forms a natural boundary between Iowa and Nebraska?

Missouri River

● Which river forms a western border for Wisconsin and Illinois?

Mississippi River

● Name the five Great Lakes.

Superior   Erie

Ontario   Huron

Michigan

● Which state is the nation's leading milk producer?

Wisconsin

45a

Going Beyond

Enrichment

Direct your child to make a post card of his own. Provide an unlined 4" × 6" index card, crayons, colored pencils, pens, felt-tip pens, a ruler, and sample post cards. Encourage him to make his own post card of something interesting in his state or of something interesting that he recently learned about in one of the other regions. Instruct him to draw a picture of the site on the front of the card. Tell him to draw a vertical center line on the back of the card to divide the space in half. Encourage him to write a message to a friend or relative in the space on the left and the name and address of this person in the space on the right. Provide a stamp for him to mail the card.

Additional Teacher Information

Some interesting places to visit in the Middle West region include the following:

Illinois—Abraham Lincoln's home is in Springfield, and Ulysses S. Grant's home is in Galena. The Cahokia Mounds, near Cahokia, include Monk's Mound, the largest known Indian mound in the United States.

Indiana—The town of Santa Claus, established in 1852, has the only U.S. post office with the name *Santa Claus*.

Iowa—The shortest and steepest U.S. railroad (today called the Fenelon Place Elevator) is in Dubuque. The track is 296 feet long and rises at an incline of 60°.

Kansas—The boyhood home and gravesite of Dwight D. Eisenhower along with a museum and memorial library are located in Abilene, Kansas.

Michigan—The Upper and Lower sections of the state are connected by the Mackinac *(măk'ə nô)* Bridge. Battle Creek is called the *Cereal Bowl of America* because most of the breakfast cereal in the world is produced there.

Missouri—The tallest monument constructed in the United States is the Gateway Arch in St. Louis. The arch rises 630 feet and commemorates the city's role in the settlement of the West.

Nebraska—The Nebraska National Forest is the largest planted forest in the United States—22,000 acres.

Ohio—The Pro Football Hall of Fame in Canton, the Rutherford B. Hayes Library and Museum in Fremont, and Zoar Village near New Philadelphia always attract many visitors.

LESSON 33
The Southwest

Text, pages 119-21, 286-87
Notebook, pages 46-46a

━━━ Preview ━━━

Main Ideas

- The Southwest region of the United States has a unique history of exploration, settlement, and growth.
- All states in the United States have capital cities.
- People use the earth's resources to meet their needs.
- The system of irrigation brings water from the rivers and lakes to the fields.
- The influence of the Spanish explorers of long ago is still evident in the Southwest region today.

Objectives

- Identify Spanish names, items, and foods
- Read maps to answer questions
- Complete a travel journal about the Southwest

Materials

- A variety of items or pictures from the Southwest region of the United States, including five Hispanic-related items* (*NOTE:* See suggestions in the Introducing the Lesson section.)
- Labeled map of the United States from Lesson 32
- A recording of Spanish music*
- Spanish foods to sample (optional)*
- Spanish attire for yourself (optional)*
- An atlas

Begin collecting metal tabs from soft-drink cans for use in making spurs. See Lesson 43 for details.

Notes

The term *Spanish* refers to anyone or anything originating from Spain. The term *Hispanic* has a broader definition relating to Spain as well as Spanish-speaking Latin America.

━━━ Lesson ━━━

Introducing the Lesson

Hispanic Heritage Appreciation Activity

Play some Spanish music and dress in Spanish clothing or in bright colors. Display items or pictures of items, with at least five items related to Hispanic heritage. For instance, display cans or boxes of foods such as chili, popcorn, taco mix, tuna, and refried beans. Set up a variety of hats, among them a sombrero, and other types of items that you may have available.

➤ Select the foods that are from Spanish heritage. *(chili, taco mix, refried beans)*
➤ Identify the Spanish style hat and any other items that reflect Spanish culture.

Teaching the Lesson

Text Discussion, pages 119 and 286-87

➤ **Read the names of the states in the *Southwest* region from your labeled map of the United States.** *(Arizona, New Mexico, Oklahoma, and Texas)*
➤ Look at pages 286-87 to find out which Native American groups lived in this region long ago. *(Yuma, Shoshone, Navajo, Hopi, Natchez, Caddo, Sioux, Kiowa, and Comanche)*

The Pueblo people referred to on page 119 are not shown on the map on pages 286-87. They comprise several small groups, the largest being the Hopi tribe. Direct your child to locate the Hopi on the map as representative of the Pueblo people.

➤ **Read page 119 to find the name of the Spanish explorer who came to the Southwest.** *(Coronado)*

Notice in the picture that the explorers wore iron helmets and rode horses.

➤ **What was Coronado looking for?** *(the Seven Cities of Gold)* (*NOTE:* Often these cities are called the Seven Cities of Cíbola [sē ´ bə lə].)
➤ **What did Coronado do to the Pueblo when he did not find gold?** *(He punished them.)*

God expects us to treat others as we would like to be treated: lovingly, kindly, and respectfully. (BATs: 3c Emotional control, 5a Love, 5d Communication, 5e Friendliness)

The Southwest

Almost at the same time that Columbus was landing in San Salvador, other explorers were marching into the Southwest. These explorers wore iron helmets and rode horses.

Coronado was a Spanish explorer who was looking for the Seven Cities of Gold. He had heard stories about rich lands to the north of Mexico. He searched and searched. When he did  not find gold, he punished the Pueblo people he did find. What do you think of his actions? Look at the map on pages 286-87 to find where the Pueblo people lived for hundreds of years before the men with the iron helmets came.

A reenactment of the Coronado expedition

119

What four states make up the Southwest? What are their capitals? Santa Fe is the oldest capital city in the nation. It was founded in 1610. Had the Pilgrims arrived in the Northeast yet? No, they would not come for another ten years.

Irrigation is bringing water from a river or lake to the fields. Since much of the Southwest gets little rain, farming depends on irrigation. The Hohokam people had used irrigation hundreds of years before the white man came. In the 1860s a white settler studied the old Indian town and built ditches like those he saw there. Soon many farmers nearby used the irrigation plan.

A town called Phoenix grew where these well-watered farms prospered. Look at the map on this page. What crops grow in the Southwest today? What do you think the map would look like if no one used irrigation?

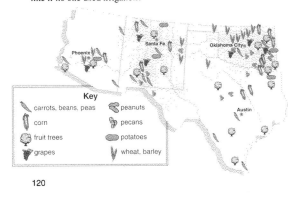

Key

carrots, beans, peas	peanuts
corn	pecans
fruit trees	potatoes
grapes	wheat, barley

120

Text Discussion, page 120

➤ **Read the first paragraph on page 120 and answer the questions.**
➤ **What is the name of the oldest capital city in the United States?** *(Santa Fe)*
➤ **How many years before the arrival of the Pilgrims on the *Mayflower* was the city of Santa Fe established?** *(10 years)* (*NOTE:* You may wish to refer to the TimeLine Snapshots to reinforce this point.)
➤ **Read the rest of the page to find out how crops are grown in the Southwest.**

➤ **Is the climate in the Southwest usually dry or wet?** *(dry)*
➤ **How do the farmers of this region get water for their crops since they get little rain?** *(by irrigation)*
➤ **What is *irrigation*? *(bringing water from a river or lake to the fields)*
➤ Find the city of Phoenix, Arizona, on the agricultural map of the Southwest at the bottom of page 20.
➤ **What crops grow in this area because of the system of irrigation used on the farms?** *(wheat, barley, potatoes, carrots, beans, peas, corn, fruit trees, and grapes)*
➤ **What other crops grow well in the Southwest because of the use of the irrigation system?** *(pecans and peanuts)*

ECHOES IN HISTORY

Spanish Flavors

The Spanish explorers changed the Southwest forever. They brought horses. They brought their own kind of food. They brought a new language. They brought the Roman Catholic religion. They built cities where once there had been open land.

A house showing Spanish influence

There are many "echoes" of the Spanish settlers in the Southwest today. Many buildings in Southwest cities have a Spanish look. Popular foods like chili con carne came from Spanish cooks. The cattle ranches, so famous for cowboys and roundups, came to be because the early Spanish had let their longhorn cattle run wild. The ranchers rounded up the longhorns and started herds.

The word *ranch* itself comes from the Spanish word *rancho*. When the cattle run wildly in a herd, they *stampede*. That word comes from a Spanish word meaning "crash or uproar." Can you find towns on a map of the Southwest that seem to have Spanish names?

121

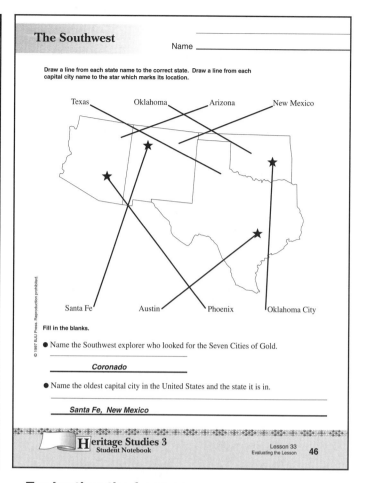

The Southwest

Name _____

Draw a line from each state name to the correct state. Draw a line from each capital city name to the star which marks its location.

Texas   Oklahoma   Arizona   New Mexico

Santa Fe   Austin   Phoenix   Oklahoma City

Fill in the blanks.

● Name the Southwest explorer who looked for the Seven Cities of Gold.

    Coronado

● Name the oldest capital city in the United States and the state it is in.

    Santa Fe, New Mexico

© 1997 BJU Press. Reproduction prohibited.

Heritage Studies 3
Student Notebook

Lesson 33
Evaluating the Lesson **46**

Text Discussion, page 121

➤ **Read page 121 to find some Spanish influences on the culture of the Southwest.** *(language, food, religion, buildings)*

The words *San* and *Santa* mean "saint" in Spanish and had their beginnings in the Roman Catholic religion of the Hispanic people.

➤ Find a map of the Southwest in your atlas. **Can you find towns that probably have Spanish influence in their names?**

> You may wish to enrich this lesson by teaching your child some Spanish words or a Spanish song. You may want to serve some typical Spanish foods, such as tamales, tacos, enchiladas, or burritos.

Evaluating the Lesson

Travel Journal Activity, Notebook pages 46-46a

➤ Color the Southwest region red on the front of your Passbook.
➤ Complete Notebook pages 46-46a with the information requested, using the textbook, maps, or other reference books.
➤ Place the pages in your Travel Journal Passbook.

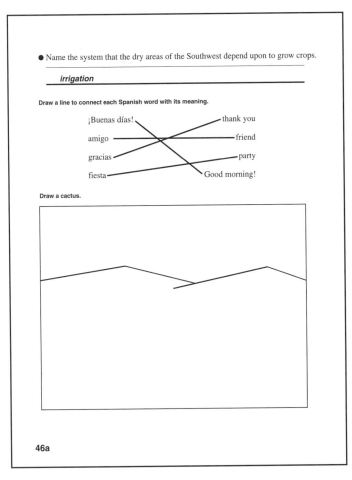

● Name the system that the dry areas of the Southwest depend upon to grow crops.

irrigation

Draw a line to connect each Spanish word with its meaning.

¡Buenas días! — Good morning!
amigo — friend
gracias — thank you
fiesta — party

Draw a cactus.

46a

Going Beyond

Enrichment

Provide materials to make a mobile of the major products grown in the Southwest region. Have available scissors, glue, yarn, old magazines and seed catalogs to cut, and one wire coat hanger. Tell your child to refer to the agricultural map on page 120 to find out which crops to include on the mobile.

Additional Teacher Information

Francisco Vásques de Coronado (1510-54) was a Spanish explorer who led an expedition of three hundred soldiers and a large number of Indian troops into the Southwest (1540-42). Coronado was commissioned by Mendoza, the viceroy of Mexico, to find the legendary Seven Cities of Cíbola and to claim the wealth for Spain. Coronado's army journeyed into what is now New Mexico and Arizona, finding groups of Native American people but no gold. In 1546, Coronado was accused of committing cruel acts against the Indians in his army, but he was found innocent of the charges.

You can stand in Utah, Colorado, New Mexico, and Arizona all at once in a place called "Four Corners." This is the only place where the corners of four states touch.

LESSON 34
The West

Text, pages 122-26, 286-87
Notebook, pages 47-49

━━ Preview ━━

Main Ideas

- The Americas offered settlers vast and diverse resources.
- The West is made up of the Rocky Mountain region and the Pacific region.
- The West has a unique history of exploration, settlement, and growth.
- A grid map is a useful tool in locating places on a map.
- By seeing and studying items from the past, people learn about history and appreciate their heritage.

Objectives

- Read maps to answer questions
- Locate places on a grid map
- Complete a travel journal about the Rocky Mountain region
- Complete a travel journal about the Pacific region

Materials

- Maps and More 13, page M8
- Items or pictures from the Rocky Mountain and Pacific regions*
- A brochure from a local museum*

You may wish to plan a trip to a local museum before teaching this lesson.

Day 1

━━ Lesson ━━

Introducing the Lesson

Museum Discussion

➤ Examine the items and pictures which are representative of the Rocky Mountain and Pacific regions of our country. Discuss the use and importance of the items.

➤ Look at the brochure of the museum. *Explain what a museum is and which of the items you have shown might be displayed in a museum.*

◆ THINGS PEOPLE DO ◆

Keeping Important Objects

Have you ever visited a museum? What was in it? Why do you think people keep things from the past? Sometimes they want to remember a person who owned the objects. Sometimes they want to help people who are born later to know about earlier times. Does your family have special items saved from the past?

John Quincy Adams, the sixth president of the United States, wanted to make a place to keep important things from all over the United States and from all times in our history. And he did. It is called the Smithsonian Institution. It is in Washington, D.C.

The Smithsonian is many museums and study centers together. The National Museum of American History houses the flag that flew over Fort McHenry and inspired the national anthem. It also displays the desk at which Thomas Jefferson sat to write the Declaration of Independence. It even has the first gold nugget found at Sutter's Fort.

This building is the original Smithsonian Institution Building. It is now called "the Castle."

126

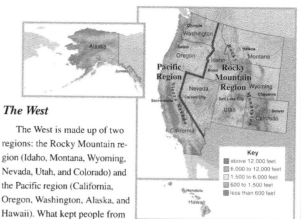

The West

The West is made up of two regions: the Rocky Mountain region (Idaho, Montana, Wyoming, Nevada, Utah, and Colorado) and the Pacific region (California, Oregon, Washington, Alaska, and Hawaii). What kept people from settling in the West for many years? The Rocky Mountains were like a giant wall, holding out the growing tide of settlers.

What people lived in the West first? How do you think the white settlers changed the way they lived? They took lands that the Indians had lived on for hundreds of years. They dug it up looking for silver. They built towns and railroads on it. In the end, the Indians lost all their hunting and fishing places.

Many of the states in this region were settled by people in a hurry to find gold and silver. Sutter's Creek was only one of the "rushes" west. What state is Sutter's Creek in? Gold and silver were discovered in Colorado too. Why do you think more people came to Colorado than to California? It was closer to the East.

122

The text pages will be taught out of order in this lesson.

Text Discussion, page 126

➤ **Read page 126 to find the name of a famous group of museums in Washington, D.C.** *(the Smithsonian Institution)*

➤ **Which president of the United States requested that such a museum be established?** *(the sixth president, John Quincy Adams)*

➤ Point to the figure of John Quincy Adams on the TimeLine.

➤ If you have visited the Smithsonian Institution, discuss some of the interesting things that you saw.

The items on display at the museum tell us about America's past, showing us how things were done and how people lived and worked. Many of the items are treasures that could never be replaced. They are treasures of the nation.

➤ **Do we have any family treasures, or *heirlooms*?** *Talk about your family heirlooms and how they remind you of your family's history.*

This lesson is about the West—its history, its people, and its treasures.

Teaching the Lesson

Text Discussion, pages 122, 286-87 and Maps and More 13

➤ Find the *Rocky Mountain* region on Maps and More 13.

➤ **Which states make up this region?** *(Idaho, Montana, Wyoming, Nevada, Utah, and Colorado)*

➤ **Which states make up the *Pacific* region?** *(California, Oregon, Washington, Alaska, and Hawaii)*

➤ Notice the colors and the key on this map.

This is a special type of map that shows how high or low the land is. This type of map is called an *elevation* map.

➤ Find the Rocky Mountains on the map.

➤ **Read the first paragraph on page 122 to find out what prevented people from settling in the West for many years.** *(the Rocky Mountains)*

The highest place in the West is in the Sierra Nevada mountain range. The gold rush caused some adventurous people to cross these mountains into California.

◆ LEARNING HOW ◆

To Use a Grid Map

1. Get a pencil, a ruler, your textbook, and Notebook page 47.

2. Look at the map of Colorado on your Notebook page. The straight lines down and across the map are helpful for finding places. What do you see on the left and right sides of the grid map? What do you see on the top and bottom edges of the grid map? Use the numbers and letters to find the cities your teacher names.

3. Grid maps come in all sizes. A globe can have a grid drawn on it. Can you find other grid maps in your textbook?

123

Grid Map

Name _____

Look at the grid map of Colorado. Use the map to answer the questions below.

1. What do you see on the right and left side of the grid map?   letters (numbers)
   (Circle one.)

2. What do you see on the top and bottom of the grid map?   (letters) numbers
   (Circle one.)

3. To find the capital of Colorado, first find column G. Then find row 6. Move your finger up column G until you come to row 6. The capital of Colorado is ___Denver___. It is located on the grid map at G6.

4. Find and name the cities located at these places on the grid map.

   G4 ___Colorado Springs___   D3 ___Powderhorn___

   B7 ___Elk Springs___   G7 ___Fort Collins___

5. Now write the grid location of these cities:
   Durango ___C1___   Hiawatha ___A8___
   Pueblo ___H3___   Grand Junction ___B4___

Heritage Studies 3
Student Notebook

Lesson 34
Teaching the Lesson   **47**

➤ **Read the rest of the page to find out why people came to the West.** *(to get land, silver, and gold)*

Sutter's Creek is in California. When gold was discovered in California, many men rushed to "strike it rich" there. Some of these men found gold, but most did not.

> Christians should be content with what they have. God provides for all their needs. He even grants many of their wants. (BAT: 7d Contentment)

➤ Using the map on pages 286-87, identify the Native Americans who lived in the West before the white man arrived. *(Tolowa, Shoshone, Lillouet, Nez Perce, Blackfoot, Sioux, Crow, Hare, Eskimo, and Aleut)*

➤ **How did the white settlers change the land of the West and the way that the Indians lived?** *(They took the land, dug it up, and built towns and railroads, so the Indians no longer had their hunting grounds.)*

➤ **Was this a fair and honest way to treat the Indians?** *(no)*

> God made each of us unique with special abilities to use for Him. God loves and cares for all. It is the responsibility of all Christians to care for others, telling them about Christ and the way of salvation. (BATs: 1a Understanding Jesus Christ, 3a Self-concept, 5a Love, 5c Evangelism and missions)

Day²

Learning How Activity, page 123 and Notebook page 47

➤ **Read the steps in the *Learning How* section on page 123 and answer the questions.**

➤ Complete Notebook page 47 by using the grid map of Colorado that is given. Use the ruler to line up the columns and rows on the grid map.

> Greely is also a correct answer for the city located at G7.

A lot of silver was found in Nevada. Then gold mines brought prospectors, people looking for riches, to Idaho and Oregon. Do you remember who settled Utah and why? Later gold was found in Alaska, and another rush was on.

When the United States bought the territory that is now Alaska, many people thought it was a bad idea. The land seemed too cold and too far away. Today no one thinks that. Alaska, the largest state, has far more than gold. It has many natural resources and vast areas of beautiful wilderness.

Summer beauty in Alaska

Hawaii, the fiftieth state, was not seen by a white man until 1778. Then Captain James Cook sailed into the islands and the Hawaiians greeted him and his crew with food and friendliness. Thirty years later missionaries from New England came to preach the gospel and to build schools and churches.

124

◆ HOW IT WAS ◆

Island of Hawaii
Summer of 1823

Queen Kapiolani went to the volcano Kilauea, one of the biggest in the world. Many people believed the goddess Pele lived in the volcano and would kill Queen Kapiolani for walking there.

Queen Kapiolani threw stones into the boiling pit of lava. She said, "Jehovah is God. God kindled these fires. I fear not Pele. You must fear and serve God alone."

Those with her sang a hymn and kneeled to pray. The queen's courage helped her people see that her God was the true God.

Text Discussion, pages 124-25

➤ **Read page 124 to find out where, in addition to Colorado and California, the settlers found silver and gold.** *(Nevada, Idaho, Oregon, and Alaska)*

➤ **Why did many people think that the purchase of the Alaskan territory was a bad idea?** *(It was too cold and too far away.)*

Alaska is the largest state and is rich in gold, petroleum, paper, and wood products. The people of Alaska are employed in various jobs, using these natural resources that God placed in the land. (BATs: 7b Exaltation of Christ, 7c Praise)

➤ **Who was the first white man to see Hawaii?** *(Captain James Cook)*

➤ **How do you think the teaching of the gospel and the building of schools and churches helped the people and nation of Hawaii?**

➤ **Read the account of one Christian, Queen Kapiolani** *(kăp ē ō län′ē),* **given on page 125.**

➤ **How did Queen Kapiolani's words and actions show that she was a Christian?** *(She prayed before the people and sang a hymn. She told the people not to be afraid but to serve God alone.)* (BATs: 5c Evangelism and missions, 7c Praise, 8d Courage; Bible Promise: H. God as Father)

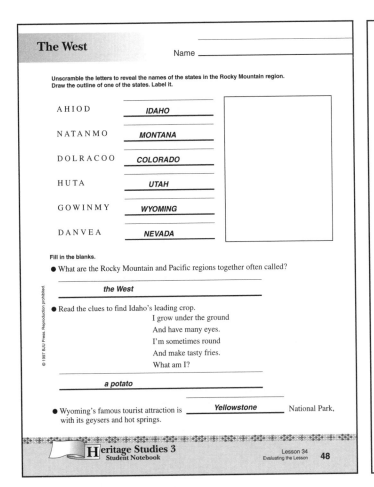

The West

Name _____

Unscramble the letters to reveal the names of the states in the Rocky Mountain region.
Draw the outline of one of the states. Label it.

AHIOD   *IDAHO*

NATANMO   *MONTANA*

DOLRACOO   *COLORADO*

HUTA   *UTAH*

GOWINMY   *WYOMING*

DANVEA   *NEVADA*

Fill in the blanks.

● What are the Rocky Mountain and Pacific regions together often called?

the West

● Read the clues to find Idaho's leading crop.
> I grow under the ground
> And have many eyes.
> I'm sometimes round
> And make tasty fries.
> What am I?

a potato

● Wyoming's famous tourist attraction is _____ *Yellowstone* _____ National Park, with its geysers and hot springs.

Heritage Studies 3
Student Notebook

Lesson 34
Evaluating the Lesson   **48**

© 1997 BJU Press. Reproduction prohibited.

● The most famous geyser is called Old _____ *Faithful* _____ .

Draw pictures of the following.

● a geyser "blowing off steam"

● the mountains and canyons you might see in Colorado (The Spanish word *Colorado* means "colored red." The Colorado River runs through canyons of red stone.)

48a

Evaluating the Lesson

Travel Journal Activity, Notebook pages 48-49a

➤ Color the Rocky Mountain region blue on the front of your Passbook.
➤ Color the states of the Pacific region pink.
➤ Read the instructions on Notebook pages 48-49.

Though this large section of the United States is often called the West, it is made up of two separate regions. You have a separate travel journal page for each of these regions.

➤ Complete the travel journals for the Rocky Mountain region and for the Pacific region, using the textbook, maps, or other reference books.
➤ Place these travel journals with the other information in your Travel Journal Passbook.

■■■ Going Beyond ■■■

Additional Teacher Information

Hawaii is made up of a chain of 132 islands in the Pacific Ocean. The eight main islands are Hawaii, Kahoolawe, Maui, Lanai, Molokai, Oahu, Kauai, and Niihau. Most of the population lives in Honolulu, which makes up most of Oahu. The people of Hawaii are of many cultures with different languages, traditions, and religions. Only about 15 percent are true Hawaiians, descendants of the Polynesians who first settled in the Hawaiian Islands. These true Hawaiians have bronze-colored skin, large dark eyes, and dark brown or black hair. About 35 percent of the people are of European ancestry. Another 25 percent are of Japanese background. Other nationalities include Chinese, Filipino, Korean, Samoan, and Southeast Asian. Many people are of mixed heritage. The blend of these different cultures makes Hawaii a unique state.

James Smithson was a wealthy British scientist for whom the mineral *smithsonite* (zinc carbonate) was named. As specified in his will, over five hundred thousand dollars was given to the United States to establish a place for the "increase and diffusion of knowledge among men." Congress accepted the gift and in 1846 created the Smithsonian Institution. Today many museums make up the Smithsonian Institution. All are available *without charge* for the people of the world to see. Famous paintings,

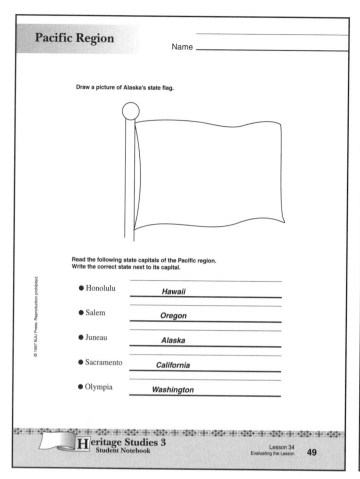

Pacific Region

Name _____

Draw a picture of Alaska's state flag.

Read the following state capitals of the Pacific region.
Write the correct state next to its capital.

- Honolulu   *Hawaii*
- Salem   *Oregon*
- Juneau   *Alaska*
- Sacramento   *California*
- Olympia   *Washington*

© 1997 BJU Press. Reproduction prohibited.

Heritage Studies 3
Student Notebook

Lesson 34
Evaluating the Lesson   **49**

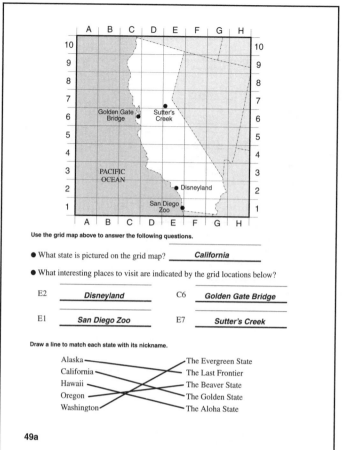

Use the grid map above to answer the following questions.

- What state is pictured on the grid map?   *California*

- What interesting places to visit are indicated by the grid locations below?

E2   *Disneyland*   C6   *Golden Gate Bridge*

E1   *San Diego Zoo*   E7   *Sutter's Creek*

Draw a line to match each state with its nickname.

Alaska   The Evergreen State
California   The Last Frontier
Hawaii   The Beaver State
Oregon   The Golden State
Washington   The Aloha State

49a

sculptures, and works of design are displayed in the National Museum of American Art, the National Portrait Gallery, the National Museum of African Art, the National Museum of Design, and several other national galleries of the Smithsonian. The National Museum of Natural History has exhibits pertaining to biology, human cultures, and mineral sciences, as well as plants and animals. The National Museum of American History houses collections from America's history—war relics, period clothing, furniture, important documents, and so forth. The National Air and Space Museum traces America's fascination with flying, from early balloons and gliders to the Wright brothers' plane, to rockets, astronauts, and trips to the moon. The National Postal Museum houses the largest stamp collection in the world. The National Museum of the American Indian displays a collection of Native American artifacts. In addition to the numerous museums, the Smithsonian Institution operates the National Zoological Park with over two thousand birds, mammals, and reptiles. A visit to the capital of the United States is incomplete without a visit to the Smithsonian Institution.

War Coming!

This chapter deals with the turbulent years before the American Civil War, from Eli Whitney's invention of the cotton gin to the firing of the first cannon at Fort Sumter. Your child will learn of the courage of the Texans at the Alamo, the fierce determination of the abolitionists, and the honesty and sincerity of Abraham Lincoln. He will see how people wrestled with the question of slavery and watched the struggle between the North and the South grow until all attempts at compromise failed. Special activities include learning how to read a circle graph and making a paper replica of Lincoln's stovepipe hat.

Materials

The following materials must be obtained or prepared before the presentation of the lesson. These items are labeled with an asterisk (*) in each lesson and in the Materials List in the Supplement. For further information see the individual lessons.

- A pint-sized basket (Lesson 35)
- Cotton balls (Lesson 35)
- Appendix, page A37 (Lesson 36)
- Appendix, page A38 (Lesson 37)
- Black construction paper (Lesson 40)
- Jump rope or other sturdy rope (Lesson 41)
- Examples of circle graphs (Lesson 41)

LESSON 35
An Invention for the South

Text, pages 128-31
Notebook, page 50

━━━━ Preview ━━━━

Main Ideas

- People have needs, feelings, interests, and preferences.
- People from different locations have different interests and opinions.
- The physical environment makes a difference in the way people live and work.

Objective

- Match quotations with the people most likely to have said them

Materials

- A Bible
- Supplement, page S8: cotton boll
- A pint-sized basket (perhaps an empty strawberry carton)*
- Enough cotton balls to fill the basket*

Day 1

━━━━ Lesson ━━━━

Introducing the Lesson

Imagination Activity

➤ Close your eyes and imagine sights and sounds as I read this story aloud.

Imagine that you are a slave. Your great-grandfather came to America from Africa. He lived and died on Master Brown's cotton plantation. Your grandfather, your mother, and you were born on the same plantation. Your father was sold to another farm shortly after you were born; you have no memory of him. Every morning you get up at dawn, eat a simple breakfast, and go out to the cotton fields to pick cotton. You are not allowed to play. You must always work, even when you are tired or sick.

Your brothers and sisters all work with you, and often you sing songs about people in the Bible. Your favorite song is about Moses leading the children of Israel to freedom in the Promised Land. Toward the middle of the morning, the sun grows hot on your

back, but you must keep bending, keep stretching, keep working. Mosquitoes drone around your head, but you are afraid to slap them away. There is an overseer watching you with a keen look in his eyes and his whip poised in his hand. You have felt that whip once before when you stopped to lie down in some tall grass because you were too tired to go on. You remember how the whip cut and stung, and you do not want to risk having to feel it again.

Somewhere in the sky a bird flies, high and brave and free. It calls to you, and you wish you could fly away to a place where there are no whips, where you can learn to read books and newspapers, where you can run and play.

Your master tells you, your mother, and your brothers and sisters that you should be thankful to be here. You have a home, food, and clothes to wear. He tells you that you are better off here than you would be if you had stayed in the jungles of Africa.

Would you like to be a slave on such a plantation?

➤ In this lesson you will learn how people from different parts of America in the early 1800s felt about slavery.

Teaching the Lesson

Text Discussion, page 128

➤ **Read aloud the first paragraph on page 128.**
➤ Study the map to find out what had changed. *(America had grown larger in land area.)*
➤ **Read the rest of page 128 to find out what had not changed.** *(People still owned slaves and made them work hard.)*
➤ **Do you think the slaves were happy working on the plantations?**

Probably many were not happy, although some masters were kind to their slaves. Slaves were bought and sold and traded at auctions just as cows or horses were. Most slaves were not allowed to learn to read or write. Families were often split up when fathers and mothers and children were sold to different farms.

Read aloud Ephesians 6:9 and Colossians 4:1. Discuss what these verses are saying about how masters should treat their slaves. (BAT: 5a Love)

➤ **Were all the slave owners obeying these verses in the way they treated their slaves?** *(no)*

The United States grew a lot in the thirty years after George Washington became the first president. Can you tell from the map something that had changed?

land owned by the U.S. in 1790

land gained by the U.S. between 1790 and 1820

Some other things stayed the same. Many Americans still owned slaves and made them work hard. Some masters treated their slaves well, but many did not. And even a well-treated slave was still a slave. He was not paid or thanked for his work.

Some Americans wanted to stop slavery. Many others did not. "Who will work in our fields?" they asked. Can you remember when Americans first argued about slavery?

The Slavery Question

What almost kept some states from signing the new Constitution? It was slavery. Some states wanted it to go on. Others wanted it stopped. Roger Sherman came up with a plan. It was not exactly what either side wanted. What do you think the men did?

They decided to compromise. They agreed that slave states could bring slaves in for twenty more years. That compromise pleased most of the voters. They signed the Constitution. But the compromise did not solve the problem of slavery.

Some people said that the compromise was "a deal with the devil." Others said that the Constitution gave each state the right to decide about slavery for itself. Years later in the 1820s, the debate over slaves was about to "echo" in another place.

Africans being brought in a ship to the United States to be sold as slaves

129

Read aloud I Corinthians 7:21-23. According to these verses, the slaves should not have thought too much about their slavery but rather focused on the freedom from sin they had if they knew Christ. There is a difference between being a slave to another human and being a slave to sin. Even today people are slaves to sin if they have not accepted Christ's payment for sin and become His servant. (BAT: 1b Repentance and Faith)

Eventually many Southern families had slaves. In some areas in the South, the African American population outnumbered the white population. The slave owners feared what would happen if slaves were allowed to go to school, learn about politics, and vote for their own leaders. They were afraid the slaves would rebel against them and one day govern them. But some people from the North wanted the slaves to be freed. Many Northerners felt that it was wrong for a person to own another human being.

➤ **Do you remember when this argument came up before?** It was one of the issues at the Constitutional Convention.

Text Discussion, page 129

➤ **Read page 129 to find out what agreement had been reached about slavery.** *(States could bring in slaves for twenty more years.)*

➤ **In what way was the compromise good?** *(Everyone was pleased enough with the compromise to sign the Constitution.)*

➤ **In what way was it bad?** *(It did not solve the disagreement about whether people should be allowed to have slaves.)*

You will see this disagreement becoming more and more of a problem between the North and the South as this chapter progresses.

When the men who wrote the Constitution made the slavery compromise, they thought they were doing a good thing. They felt sure that slavery would soon end by itself. And it might have, if it had not been for an invention called the *cotton gin.*

Cotton grew well in the warm South. It could be woven into cloth that made comfortable clothing. But the fluffy cotton *bolls* held sticky seeds. Slaves had to remove each seed by hand. Would you like to have that job?

It took too much time and too many slaves to pull the seeds from the cotton. Few people wanted to grow the cotton plants. Then Eli Whitney thought of a way to make removing the seeds easier. His machine could remove the seeds from as much cotton in one day as fifty slaves could by hand.

130

A typical Southern plantation

The cotton gin made preparing cotton much easier. Many plantation owners wanted to grow cotton now. They could make money from selling the cotton. They bought more farmland and more slaves to tend the cotton plants and run the cotton gin. Cotton soon became the most important crop in the Southern states. People in new territories even began to grow cotton.

Slavery: Yes or No?

Do you remember what a *territory* is? A territory is an area of land that belongs to a country, like the United States. As the United States gained more land in the West, people went to live in these new territories.

People who lived in a territory could not vote for president. They could not choose their own laws. So as soon as they could, people in each territory asked the government to make their territory a state.

131

Day 2

Text Discussion, page 130

➤ Look at the picture of the cotton boll.
➤ **Read the first two paragraphs on page 130 to find out what made cotton a popular crop in the South.** (*It could be used to make comfortable clothing; it grew well in the South's warm climate.*)

    Cotton could also be sold for a profit to cotton mills in England.

➤ **What was the one disadvantage of cotton?** (*It had many sticky seeds that were hard to remove.*)

    Each cotton boll is about the size of a tennis ball and contains 20 to 40 seeds.

➤ Look carefully at the basket filled with cotton balls. Pretend that these are freshly picked cotton bolls that need the seeds removed.
➤ **How long do you think it might take to pull all the seeds out of this much cotton?**

    It would probably take at least an hour. Each slave picked much more cotton than this on a normal working day. It often took up to ten hours to pick the seeds out of just one pound of cotton.

➤ **Would you like to have the job of removing seeds from cotton?**

➤ **Read the last paragraph on page 130 to learn who had a successful idea for cleaning cotton faster.** (*Eli Whitney*)
➤ Look at the picture of the cotton gin on page 130.

    Eli Whitney's cotton gin had wire teeth that worked much like a comb. As the cotton fiber moved through these teeth, the seeds were combed out and dropped into a separate compartment.

➤ **How do you think slaves felt about the cotton gin?**

    The slaves might have been glad that they no longer had to clean seeds from cotton by hand, but many were probably afraid that they would now have to pick cotton even faster to keep up with the machine.

Text Discussion, page 131

➤ **Read the first paragraph on page 131 to find out how the plantation owners felt about the cotton gin.** (*glad to have it, eager to grow more cotton*)
➤ **What did plantation owners do when they found out about the cotton gin?** (*They bought more farmland and more slaves to help harvest the cotton.*)

Quotations

Name _____

Match each quotation with the person most likely to have said it.
Fill in each blank with the letter of the correct choice.

A. Eli Whitney   C. a Northern factory worker
B. a Southern plantation owner   D. a slave

B   1. "See all those people at work in my field?
This year my cotton should have a great yield!"

D   2. "To bed after dark and then up with the sun.
Will all of my master's work ever be done?"

C   3. "I might work like a slave, but my wages I earn.
And my children go to school, read books, and learn."

A   4. "There must be a way to make cotton seed-free.
Perhaps a new powered machine is the key."

B   5. "It doesn't bother me to buy and to sell;
I'll trade cows and horses, men and women as well."

A   6. "With my new invention, the South will be set.
More cotton they'll plant, and more money they'll get."

D   7. "The master has bought a machine, swift and new.
But for me that just means even more work to do."

B   8. "Some men think I'm awful for owning these slaves.
But left to themselves, they would go to their graves."

C   9. "I will cast my vote to set all the slaves free.
Africans should have the same rights as me."

D 10. "I hear in the North there is freedom for all,
And perhaps one day soon I will follow its call."

Heritage Studies 3
Student Notebook

Lesson 35
Evaluating the Lesson   **50**

➤ **What kinds of things do we use cotton for today?**
(making clothing; lining jackets, blankets, and quilts; stuffing dolls and toy animals; packaging materials; applying medicine; creating art projects)

The rest of page 131 will be read and discussed in the next lesson.

Evaluating the Lesson
Notebook Activity, page 50

➤ Read the directions on Notebook page 50.
➤ Complete the page.

▬ Going Beyond ▬

Additional Teacher Information

Although most slaves in the South worked as field hands, some held other types of jobs. House slaves lived in their owners' homes and worked as servants. Women slaves often served as personal attendants, cooks, or maids. Some slaves were trained to do certain trades, such as blacksmithing, bricklaying, carpentry, or tailoring. Others did construction work on canals and railroads or industrial labor at docks or lumberyards.

After the invention of Eli Whitney's cotton gin in 1793, the slave population in the South grew rapidly. By 1800 approximately nine hundred thousand slaves were at work in the South, and by 1840 this figure had increased to two million five hundred thousand.

Although the Bible gives certain commands regulating the actions of masters and slaves, it also condemns racism, upon which the slavery of the African Americans was based. Racism is the notion that one's own ethnic stock is superior to another. Most of the justification of America's slavery system lay in the belief that the blacks were an inferior race. Several Scripture references clearly state that God is not a respecter of persons and does not place ethnic groups on any sort of scale of worth. See Acts 10:28, Acts 17:26, I Corinthians 12:13, Galatians 3:28, and Colossians 3:10-11. These verses indicate that God extends the same grace and favor toward all races and includes all in His plan of salvation.

LESSON 36
The Missouri Compromise

Text, pages 131-33
Notebook, page 51

━━ Preview ━━

Main Ideas

- People from different locations have different interests and opinions.
- Disagreements can sometimes be settled by compromise.

Objectives

- Participate in a vote to solve a problem
- Use clues from the lesson to solve a word puzzle

Materials

- Appendix, page A37: opinion cards*

━━ Lesson ━━ *Day 1*

Introducing the Lesson

Problem-Solving Activity

> If you are teaching more than one child, you may form two groups. Give each group one of the cards, asking it to represent that opinion in the decision-making process.

➤ Let's pretend that we must make a decision concerning whether or not to have gerbils in our schoolroom. Read each of the cards and select the one which best states your opinion.

➤ Read aloud your opinion about the gerbils.

➤ Pretend that I am another child in your school. Listen as I give my opinion about the gerbils. *Read aloud the second card.*

If we both think very strongly that the solution should fit our opinion, we have a problem. Perhaps we will each need to give up part of our expectations so that we can reach a compromise.

➤ Try to think of a way to solve the problem so that each of us can have something to be happy about.

A typical Southern plantation

The cotton gin made preparing cotton much easier. Many plantation owners wanted to grow cotton now. They could make money from selling the cotton. They bought more farmland and more slaves to tend the cotton plants and run the cotton gin. Cotton soon became the most important crop in the Southern states. People in new territories even began to grow cotton.

Slavery: Yes or No?

Do you remember what a *territory* is? A territory is an area of land that belongs to a country, like the United States. As the United States gained more land in the West, people went to live in these new territories.

People who lived in a territory could not vote for president. They could not choose their own laws. So as soon as they could, people in each territory asked the government to make their territory a state.

131

> If your child has trouble thinking of a compromise, suggest ideas such as the following: Could we arrange the seating so that the children with allergy problems would not be bothered by the gerbils? Could we put the gerbil cage in a place where it would not be a distraction? Is there another type of small pet that would still be entertaining and educational but would not cause allergy problems?

Many times it is hard to settle an argument when both sides feel very strongly about their opinions. Often, both sides have to give up something they want in order to reach a peaceful solution. (BAT: 5b Giving) In this lesson we will learn about a very important argument in Congress and about how it was settled.

Teaching the Lesson

Text Discussion, page 131

➤ **Read the last two paragraphs on page 131 to find out what a *territory* is.** (*an area of land that belongs to a country*)

➤ **What were the disadvantages of living in territories?** (*People in territories could not vote for a president or choose their own laws.*)

Every new state had to answer a very important question: Will this be a free state or a slave state? *Free* meant that slavery would not be allowed there. Look at the map on this page. How many states were free in 1819? How many were slave? The territory of Missouri wanted to be a state. Why do you think Missouri was so important to everyone?

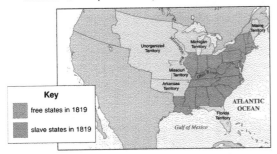

Key
free states in 1819
slave states in 1819

If Missouri became a free state, how many more free states than slave states would there be? People in the North called for Missouri to be a free state. People in the South said it must become a slave state. Everyone argued about it.

Men in Congress yelled at each other. A Southern man said, "If Missouri is not allowed to decide on her own, there are some who would leave the Union." Many states were ready to leave the United States and form their own country.

132

Henry Clay listened to the yelling. He did not want to see the United States broken up. He came up with the Missouri Compromise. This compromise said that Missouri would be a slave state. But the next state, Maine, would be free.

Congress said that the compromise was good. Maine became a free state in 1820. Missouri became a slave state in 1821. Many people were glad. They hoped that the argument over slavery had been solved.

Thomas Jefferson said that the problem was solved for the moment. "But," he said, "this is not the final sentence." What do you think he meant? Do you think he was right?

133

➤ **What do you think were some advantages of living in a territory?**

People in territories could be pioneers, explore and claim new land, and build their own towns and cities.

➤ **Would you rather live in a territory or in a state?**

Text Discussion, page 132

➤ **Read page 132 and answer the questions.**

Both the North and the South had eleven states.

➤ **Were states in the North free or slave states?** *(free)*
➤ **Were states in the South free or slave states?** *(slave)*
➤ **Why was the Missouri Territory so important?** *(It would upset the even balance of slave and free states if added to the United States.)*
➤ Locate the Ohio River and the Mississippi River on the map on page 132.

Until this time the Ohio River had been the dividing line between the free states and the slave states. The Ohio River does not continue west of the Mississippi River, where Missouri is. Both the free states and the slave states wanted to claim Missouri for their side.

➤ **What advice would you have given the men in Congress about how to resolve the argument?**

Text Discussion, pages 133 and 292

➤ **Read page 133 to learn the name of the man who settled the dispute.** *(Henry Clay)*
➤ **What was the name of his plan?** *(the Missouri Compromise)*
➤ **What is a *compromise*?** You may read the definition from the glossary on page 292. *("an idea that is not exactly what either side wants but is good enough for both sides to like")*
➤ **Do you remember another famous compromise that occurred earlier in America's history?**

The Great Compromise was reached at the time the Constitution was being written. The Great Compromise said that in the House of Representatives each state would get votes by the number of people living in that state. In the Senate each state would get two votes. This compromise made both the large states and the small states happy.

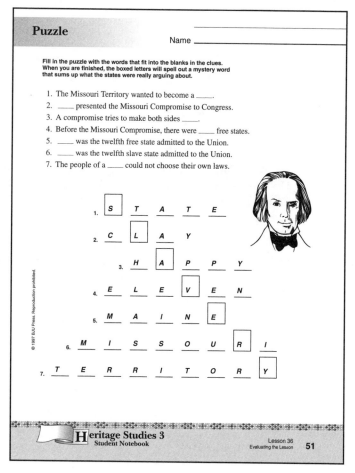

Puzzle

Name _____

Fill in the puzzle with the words that fit into the blanks in the clues.
When you are finished, the boxed letters will spell out a mystery word
that sums up what the states were really arguing about.

1. The Missouri Territory wanted to become a ____.
2. ____ presented the Missouri Compromise to Congress.
3. A compromise tries to make both sides ____.
4. Before the Missouri Compromise, there were ____ free states.
5. ____ was the twelfth free state admitted to the Union.
6. ____ was the twelfth slave state admitted to the Union.
7. The people of a ____ could not choose their own laws.

1. S T A T E
2. C L A Y
3. H A P P Y
4. E L E V E N
5. M A I N E
6. M I S S O U R I
7. T E R R I T O R Y

Heritage Studies 3
Student Notebook

Lesson 36
Evaluating the Lesson **51**

➤ **How did the Missouri Compromise make both the free states and the slave states happy?** *(It said that Missouri would be a slave state but that Maine would be a free state.)*

➤ **What bad thing did the compromise keep from happening?** *(It kept certain states from leaving the United States to start their own country.)*

The slavery question had been only partially answered. Thomas Jefferson showed his wisdom when he said that this was not the final sentence. The problem had been solved for the moment, but it would come up again later.

Evaluating the Lesson

Notebook Activity, page 51

➤ Read the instructions for the puzzle on Notebook page 51.
➤ Complete the page.

──── Going Beyond ────

Enrichment

Provide your child with paper and pencil. Instruct him to write about a time when he had to make a compromise with a family member or a playmate.

Additional Teacher Information

Territories had to meet certain requirements before they could become states. At least sixty thousand free people had to live in the territory. The territory had to apply to Congress for statehood, write a state constitution, and then wait until Congress voted on whether it could become a state.

Henry Clay was known as the Great Compromiser. At the time of the Missouri Compromise, Clay was the Speaker of the House. His compromise set a boundary line at the southern border of Missouri, 36°30' north latitude, in the Louisiana Purchase. In the future, slavery would be prohibited in all states north of this line, with the exception of Missouri. Although Henry Clay, a resident of Kentucky, owned slaves, he often protested proslavery legislation in Congress. He was first and foremost a man of the Union, and preserving the unity of the states was always his top priority. Later in his life he even recommended lowering tariffs, an action with which he disagreed, to keep South Carolina from seceding from the Union. Henry Clay was mercifully spared from seeing the Union dissolved. He died in 1852, eight years before the secession he had dreaded and fought against took place. On a carved tablet in his burial crypt are the words, "I know no South, no North, no East, no West."

LESSON 37
Remember the Alamo

Text, pages 134-36, 251-52
Notebook, page 52

━━━ Preview ━━━

Main Ideas

- When people are dissatisfied with their government, they respond in different ways.
- People will sometimes give their lives for the cause of freedom.

Objective

- Identify true and false statements about the Texan struggle for independence

Materials

- Appendix, page A38: map of the United States in 1820*
- Red and blue pencils or crayons
- The figure of the Alamo (1836) from the TimeLine Snapshots
- The presidential figures of William Henry Harrison (9) and John Tyler (10) from the TimeLine Snapshots
- Maps and More 14, page M9

Day 1

━━━ Lesson ━━━

Introducing the Lesson

Map Activity

➤ Locate on the map of the United States in 1820 the area which was the United States during the 1820s.
➤ Color the United States with the red pencil.
➤ Locate Mexico on the map. Color Mexico with the blue pencil. (*NOTE:* Your child should color Texas blue also because it was part of Mexico in the 1820s.)
➤ **Was the area known as Mexico larger or smaller than Mexico is today?** (*larger*) If you have ever been to Mexico, tell about your experiences.
➤ **What country did many of the first explorers to Mexico originally come from?** (*Spain*)

Texas

About the time Missouri became a state, people began moving to another new territory. But this territory did not belong to the United States. It belonged to Mexico. Can you find Mexico on the map? It is south of the United States.

When the Mexican ruler said it was all right, the Americans moved to the Texas territory. They built towns and plantations. The hard-working people became citizens of Mexico. They called themselves *Texans*.

Santa Anna

After about ten years, more Texans than Mexicans lived in the Texas territory. The leaders in Mexico did not like that. They made new laws to keep more Americans from coming to Texas. And the Mexican president, Antonio López de Santa Anna, sent his army to Texas to make sure the Texans obeyed his laws.

134

➤ **Do you remember any of the items from the Hispanic culture that we studied in Lesson 33?** (*sombreros, tacos, guitar music, etc.*)

Even when Mexico became an independent country, it kept much of its Spanish culture.

➤ Draw a circle around the territory of Texas.

This territory had once been ruled by Spain, but as soon as Mexico won its freedom from Spain, Texas became part of Mexican territory. In this lesson we will find out what happened to this territory.

Teaching the Lesson

Text Discussion, page 134

➤ **Read the first two paragraphs on page 134 to find out what new territory people were beginning to settle.** (*Texas*)

Many Americans moved to Texas because they could buy good land for much less money than they could in other parts of America.

➤ **Why did the settlers who moved to Texas need permission from the Mexican ruler to settle there?** (*The Texas Territory was owned by Mexico.*)

At first the Mexicans thought it was all right for the settlers to come to their land. They even let them become citizens of Mexico.

➤ **Read the last paragraph to find out what made the leaders of Mexico change their minds about the Americans.** *(After a while, the Mexicans did not like the fact that there were more Americans calling themselves Texans than there were Mexicans in Texas.)*

The Mexicans were probably concerned that the Texans would try to rebel against the Mexican government.

➤ **What laws did the Mexican leaders make?** *(laws that would keep Americans from coming into Texas)*

➤ **What did Santa Anna do to make sure that the Texans would obey the laws?** *(He sent his army to Texas.)*

Text Discussion, page 135

➤ **Read page 135 to find out how the Texans felt about having Santa Anna's army in Texas.** *(They did not want the army there; they wanted to fight the army.)*

A man named Sam Houston was sent to Texas by the president of the United States, Andrew Jackson, to lead a Texan army that would fight Santa Anna's army.

➤ **What happened the first time Santa Anna sent his army to Texas?** *(The Texans defeated the Mexican army and sent it hurrying home again.)*

➤ **What did the Texan army think when the Mexicans left?** *(They thought that they had won their freedom from Mexico.)*

Many of the men who fought were not soldiers. They were just volunteers who had left their jobs or farms behind to help the Texas army. Because they thought their duties were over, they returned to their other work.

➤ **What happened after the volunteer army left?** *(Santa Anna himself attacked Texas with his army.)*

This time the Texan army was under the command of Lieutenant Colonel William Travis.

➤ **What building did the Texans use as a fort?** *(a mission called the Alamo)*

Do you think the Texans wanted Santa Anna's army in Texas? "We are tired of obeying strict Mexican laws." they said. "We will be ready to fight." Quickly the men of Texas formed an army of their own.

The Texas army was ready for Santa Anna's men. After just a few battles, the army of Mexico hurried home. The Texans thought that they had won their freedom. But Santa Anna did not agree. He decided to lead his army to Texas. "I will destroy the Texans myself," he said.

The Texans were not ready this time. Most of the men had gone home to their farms and plantations. Only around 180 people stayed in the little town of San Antonio. They were surprised when Santa Anna and several thousand men poured into the town and stopped in front of a mission called the *Alamo*.

Diagram of the Alamo

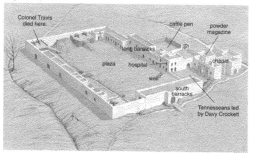

135

Discussion, Maps and More 14

➤ Study Maps and More 14. The Alamo looked something like this at the time of the Mexican siege.

➤ **Do you think the Texans felt safe behind the walls of the fort?**

The Texans were able to hold off Santa Anna's army for more than a week. They were just a small band of Texans trying to defend themselves against the Mexican army. By shooting at the Mexicans over the walls of the Alamo, the Texans were able to kill or wound many of Santa Anna's soldiers.

The Texas army gathered together again. But they were not fast enough to save the men in the Alamo. Santa Anna's army killed every man there. Then they burned the farms and houses around the town.

Texans wanted revenge for the deaths of the men in the Alamo. They waited for their chance. Then on April 21, 1836, the Texas army surprised Santa Anna and his men. After a twenty-minute battle, the Texans captured Santa Anna. They made Santa Anna agree to let Texas be a country by itself.

Now that Texas was free from Mexico, the Texans wanted to make their land part of the United States. But Texans had slaves on their big cotton plantations. Do you think the North wanted Texas to become a state? Some Americans also thought that making Texas a state might cause a war with Mexico. Do you think they were right?

136

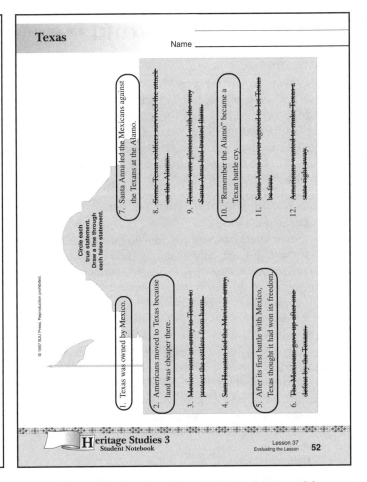

Texas

Name _____

Circle each true statement. Draw a line through each false statement.

1. Texas was owned by Mexico.

2. Americans moved to Texas because land was cheaper there.

3. Mexico sent an army to Texas to protect the settlers from harm.

4. Sam Houston led the Mexican army.

5. After its first battle with Mexico, Texas thought it had won its freedom.

6. The Mexican gave up after one defeat by the Texans.

7. Santa Anna led the Mexicans against the Texans at the Alamo.

8. Some Texan soldiers survived the attack on the Alamo.

9. Texans were pleased with the way Santa Anna had treated them.

10. "Remember the Alamo" became a Texan battle cry.

11. Santa Anna never agreed to let Texas be free.

12. _____

© 1997 BJU Press. Reproduction prohibited.

Heritage Studies 3
Student Notebook

Lesson 37
Evaluating the Lesson **52**

Text Discussion, page 136

➤ **Read page 136 to find out what happened to the Texans at the Alamo.** *(All the men were killed by Santa Anna's army.)*

➤ **How did the other people in Texas feel after this happened?** *(They were angry; they wanted revenge on the Mexicans.)*

During the siege of the Alamo, Texas had declared its independence from Mexico. Now the Texans elected Sam Houston as commander in chief of their army. These men used the phrase "Remember the Alamo!" as their battle cry.

➤ **What did Sam Houston and his men do?** *(They surprised Santa Anna's army and defeated it in a twenty-minute battle. They captured Santa Anna and made him agree to let Texas be independent.)*

➤ **How do you think that remembering the Alamo helped the Texans defeat Mexico?**

The Texans must have been inspired by the courage of the men who had given their lives so that Texas could be free from Mexico. (BAT: 8d Courage) They wanted to carry on the cause that these men had died for.

➤ **What did the Texans want to do after they were free from Mexico?** *(become an American state)*

➤ **What did the Americans think about making Texas a state?** *(Northerners did not want another slave state, and many thought that making Texas a state would cause a war with Mexico.)*

TimeLine Snapshots Activity, pages 251-52

➤ Place the figure of the Alamo on the TimeLine at the year 1836.

➤ Locate the figures of William Henry Harrison and John Tyler on the presidents' strip. Read the dates during which each man was president.

➤ **What year did both Harrison and Tyler become president?** *(1841)*

Tyler became president at the death of Harrison, who had served only a month in office.

➤ **Read the information about Presidents Harrison and Tyler on pages 251-52.**

Evaluating the Lesson

Notebook Activity, page 52

➤ Read the instructions on Notebook page 52.
➤ Complete the page.

Going Beyond

Enrichment

Provide red, white, and blue construction paper, a pencil, a ruler, scissors, a cardboard star pattern, and poster board or cardboard for backing. Display a picture or drawing of Texas's Lone Star flag and allow your child to make his own replica of the flag. Encourage him to use the encyclopedia to find out more about the flag's symbolism.

Additional Teacher Information

The name *Alamo* is Spanish for "cottonwood trees." Spanish soldiers gave the mission this name when they used it as a military outpost during their battle with the native Mexicans in the early 1800s. The cottonwood trees growing along the San Antonio River reminded them of their home village in El Alamo, Mexico.

Among the famous men who were killed at the Alamo were William Travis, Davy Crockett, and Jim Bowie. Popular legend tells us that Travis and Crockett died fighting at their guns and that Jim Bowie defended himself with pistols from his deathbed. But some historians believe that some of these men actually survived the battle and were then executed by Santa Anna. In any case, the only known survivors of the Alamo were women, children, and one African American slave.

Following Santa Anna's defeat at the Battle of San Jacinto, Sam Houston became the first president of the Republic of Texas. During the nine years that followed before it became a state, Texas adopted the Lone Star flag as its banner. Today, Texas is allowed to fly this flag as high as the American flag because it is the only state that was once a republic.

LESSON 38
New Land, Old Conflict

Text, pages 137-39, 252-53
Notebook, page 53

Preview

Main Ideas

- The territory gained after the Mexican War created new problems for the United States.
- The conflict over slavery became more bitter as a result of the Compromise of 1850.

Objective

- Match causes with their corresponding effects

Materials

- A Bible
- The presidential figures of James Knox Polk (11) and Zachary Taylor (12) from the TimeLine Snapshots

Day 1

Lesson

Introducing the Lesson

Cause and Effect Discussion

➤ **If you left a pair of in-line skates at the bottom of the stairs, what accident might occur?** *(Someone might trip and fall over them.)*
➤ **If I gave you a dish of ice cream and you left it on the table all afternoon, what would happen to the ice cream?** *(It would melt.)*
➤ **If you broke a friend's toy, what might the consequence be?** *(I might have to give him one of my toys or buy him a new toy.)*
➤ **If you take medicine when you are sick, what usually happens?** *(You get better.)*

Often our actions cause something else to happen. It may be good or it may be bad. Sometimes we refer to the sequence of events as a *cause and effect.* We have learned about many causes and effects in our study of heritage this year.

Remember that Lewis and Clark were brave enough to explore the West.

War with Mexico

It took almost nine years, but in March of 1845 Texas became a state. How do you think the Mexican leaders felt when they heard the news? They were angry. They still hoped to recapture Texas.

President James K. Polk did not want a war with Mexico. He sent an *ambassador* to talk with the rulers in Mexico. But they would not listen to the ambassador. One year after Texas became a state, the war with Mexico began.

The Mexican War lasted almost two years. Trained soldiers and volunteers fought to keep Texas part of the United States. In the end, the United States won a great deal of land from Mexico. Now the country stretched from one ocean in the East to another ocean in the West.

"Remember the Alamo!" became the battle cry of the Mexican War. This is the front of the Alamo as it looks today.

137

More Trouble

free states in 1850
slave states in 1850
territories open to slavery, 1850

The end of the Mexican War did not make everyone happy. Before long the North and the South were arguing over the new land. What do you think the arguments were about?

Do you remember what Thomas Jefferson had said? He had said slavery would cause more trouble later. He had been right. In 1850 the territory of California wanted to become a state. How many states were free and how many were slave now? What do you think the problem was?

Henry Clay made another compromise. This time he said that California should be free. But what about other new territories made from the land gained from Mexico? They should be able to decide about slavery for themselves. Mr. Clay also said that all runaway slaves had to be caught and sent back to their masters. What do you think of this compromise?

The compromise passed. But angry people on both sides said that the compromise was not fair. What do you think the people for slavery did not like? What do you think the people against slavery did not like?

138

➤ **What effect did the travels of Lewis and Clark have on many other people?** *(They were encouraged to travel to the West also.)*

Remember that Abraham Lincoln was a wise and honest citizen, congressman, and lawyer.

➤ **What important office did the people elect Lincoln to because of his wisdom and honesty?** *(president of the United States)*

After we study the events or causes from our lesson today, we are going to look again at the effects which many of them had on our country.

Teaching the Lesson

Text Discussion, page 137

➤ **Read page 137 to find out what happened after Texas became a state.** *(The United States went to war with Mexico.)*
➤ **Why did Mexico want a war?** *(It hoped to recapture Texas.)*
➤ **How did President Polk show that the United States did not want a war?** *(He sent an ambassador to Mexico.)*
➤ **What is an *ambassador*?** You may find the definition in the glossary. *("one chosen to represent his government to another government")*

If the Mexicans had listened to the ambassador President Polk had sent, they might have been able to make peace with the United States instead of going to war.

Read aloud II Corinthians 5:20. Christians have a job much like an ambassador's. Christ wants Christians to tell other people about Him so that they can be reconciled to God rather than going into eternal judgment for their sin. (BAT: 5c Evangelism and missions)

➤ **How long did the war with Mexico last?** *(almost two years)*
➤ **What did the United States gain after the war?** *(more land from Mexico)*
➤ **What two oceans bordered the United States after the Mexican War?** *(Atlantic Ocean and Pacific Ocean)*

Day²

Text Discussion, page 138

➤ Look at the map on page 138 and read the key.
➤ **Read the page to learn what new problem arose in the United States after the war.** *(The North and the South argued over whether California should be a slave state or a free state.)*

No one asked the slaves what they thought. Slaves were not thought of as people. They were called property, like horses. But they were people—with souls, with families, with hopes and fears. More and more slaves were trying to run away. Many were caught and punished. Some made it to freedom.

"Art thou called being a servant? care not for it: but if thou mayest be free, use it rather.

"For he that is called in the Lord, being a servant, is the Lord's freeman: likewise also he that is called, being free, is Christ's servant."

I Corinthians 7:21-22

This slave escaped from Virginia to Pennsylvania inside a wooden box.

Freedom for Slaves

Do you think all people in the North hated slavery? Not everyone did. Some Northerners were afraid that freed slaves would take their jobs. They were glad to help capture runaway slaves. Anyone who caught a runaway got a big reward.

But other people in the North thought they should not return a runaway slave to his master, even if it was the law. They said and believed that owning another human being broke a more important law—God's law. These people wanted to *abolish*, or get rid of, slavery at once. They became known as *abolitionists*.

139

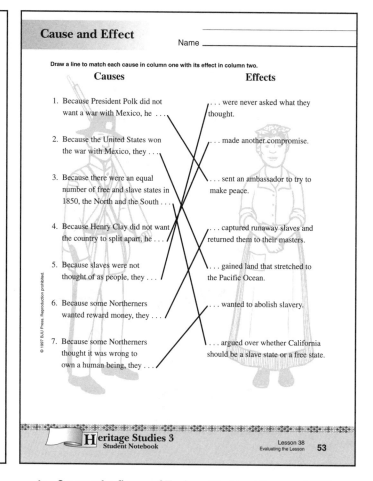

Cause and Effect

Name _____

Draw a line to match each cause in column one with its effect in column two.

Causes

1. Because President Polk did not want a war with Mexico, he . . .
2. Because the United States won the war with Mexico, they . . .
3. Because there were an equal number of free and slave states in 1850, the North and the South . . .
4. Because Henry Clay did not want the country to split apart, he . . .
5. Because slaves were not thought of as people, they . . .
6. Because some Northerners wanted reward money, they . . .
7. Because some Northerners thought it was wrong to own a human being, they . . .

Effects

. . . were never asked what they thought.

. . . made another compromise.

. . . sent an ambassador to try to make peace.

. . . captured runaway slaves and returned them to their masters.

. . . gained land that stretched to the Pacific Ocean.

. . . wanted to abolish slavery.

. . . argued over whether California should be a slave state or a free state.

Heritage Studies 3
Student Notebook

Lesson 38
Evaluating the Lesson **53**

➤ Use the map on page 138 to determine how many free and how many slave states there were in 1850. *(fifteen of each)*
➤ Describe the compromise Henry Clay made at this time. *(California would be a free state, but the other territories gained from Mexico could decide about slavery for themselves. All runaway slaves had to be returned to their masters.)*
➤ **How did this affect the balance of slave and free states?** *(There was one more free state than there were slave states.)*

Many people did not like the decision. The people who were for slavery did not like the fact that California would be a free state. The people who were against slavery did not like the fact that runaway slaves had to be returned to their masters. However, the fact that the North and the South were willing to compromise at all showed how hard everyone was working to preserve the United States. The republic was so important to them that they made sacrifices to keep it.

TimeLine Snapshots Activity, pages 252-53

➤ Locate the figure of James Knox Polk on the TimeLine at the year 1845. **What territory became a state in the first year of Polk's presidency?** *(Texas)*

➤ Locate the figure of Zachary Taylor at the year 1849. **What territory became a state the second year of Taylor's presidency?** *(California)*
➤ **Read the information about Presidents Polk and Taylor found on pages 252-53.**

Text Discussion, page 139

➤ **Read the first paragraph on page 139 to learn which group of people were left out of the decision making.** *(slaves)*
➤ **Did the compromise stop slaves from trying to run away from their masters?** *(no)*
➤ **Read the rest of the page to find out if all people in the North wanted to help the slaves.** *(no)*
➤ **Why did some Northerners want to capture runaway slaves?** *(They were afraid the freed slaves would take their jobs; they wanted the reward money.)*
➤ **What did the *abolitionists* believe about returning runaway slaves?** *(They could not do it because they believed God's law does not allow a human being to own another person.)*

Evaluating the Lesson

Notebook Activity, page 53

➤ Read the instructions on Notebook page 53.
➤ Complete the page.

Going Beyond

Additional Teacher Information

The slogan "manifest destiny" was popular in the United States around the time of the Mexican War. Many Americans believed that God had destined their country to stretch from the Atlantic to the Pacific and were willing to fight a war to make the expansion a reality.

The land that Mexico gave to the United States was called the Mexican Cession and included what is now California, Nevada, Utah, and parts of Arizona, New Mexico, Colorado, and Wyoming. John Slidell, the ambassador Polk sent to Mexico, was prepared to offer Mexico twenty-five million dollars for this territory before the war if Mexico would agree to let the Rio Grande be the southwestern border of Texas. War began when Mexican soldiers attacked General Zachary Taylor's troops north of the Rio Grande in 1846. The war ended shortly after American forces under General Winfield Scott marched into Mexico City in 1848. Zachary Taylor's victories distinguished him during the war, and he was elected president of the United States in 1848.

The law requiring runaway slaves to be returned to their masters was called the Fugitive Slave Act. The law also stated that anyone who helped a slave to escape to freedom could be fined one thousand dollars or imprisoned for six months.

LESSON 39
By Books and Bloodshed

Text, pages 140-43, 253-54
Notebook, page 54

Preview

Main Ideas

- Many individuals and groups have shaped the nation's heritage.
- When people are dissatisfied with their government, they respond in different ways.

Objective

- Supply missing words in sentences about the slavery controversy

Materials

- Maps and More 15, page M9
- The presidential figures of Millard Fillmore (13), Franklin Pierce (14), and James Buchanan (15) from the TimeLine Snapshots

Day 1

Lesson

Introducing the Lesson

Listening Activity, Maps and More 15

➤ **What was an abolitionist?** *(someone who wanted to do away with slavery)*

Abolitionists had different ways of showing the world what they believed.

➤ Look at the picture of the abolitionist Harriet Beecher Stowe shown on Maps and More 15.
➤ Listen as I read aloud the following story.

"I know what I will do," said Harriet Beecher Stowe. "I will write something!"

She placed her hat and her Bible on the table and picked up her pen. She began to write about the people she had seen in her mind as she had sat in the pew at church that morning. An old, kind slave named Uncle Tom. A beautiful maid named Eliza and her lively little boy, Harry. A cruel farmer named Simon Legree.

On and on she wrote. She wrote about things she had heard about. She wrote about slaves being beaten to death. She wrote about slave children being sold away from their mothers and about slave husbands being taken from their wives. She wrote about slaves making dangerous escapes over icy rivers and secret forest paths. She wrote about the slaves' yearning for freedom. She worked on her story for a year.

At last Harriet was finished. "Perhaps my book will make enough money for our family to celebrate with a special meal," she told her husband.

Twenty thousand copies of Harriet's book were sold during the first three weeks after it was printed. People all over the United States were talking about it. Many Northerners loved it. Most Southerners were angry about it. But everywhere in America people were buying the book and reading it. "I didn't know slaves were treated like this," some people said. "Maybe slavery really *is* wrong."

➤ In this lesson, you will learn the name of Harriet Beecher Stowe's book.

➤ Look at the picture of John Brown on Maps and More 15. Listen as I read aloud another story.

"It's time we gave these slave hounds a taste of their own medicine," said John Brown to his men. "Sharpen your swords. We leave tonight after dark."

Darkness surrounded John Brown and his little band of eight men as they approached the first house on their list. Armed with their long, flat broadswords, they called out the name of the proslavery man who lived there. When no one answered, Brown forced his way into the house. He dragged the man and his two oldest sons outside, and he and his band killed them with their swords.

Through the night, Brown and his men continued on their deadly mission. They killed two more men. They even killed some dogs that barked at them when they came near the houses.

By the next morning, news of the killings was already spreading throughout the Kansas Territory. People called it a massacre, a cruel and needless mass murder. Children were afraid to go to sleep at night. Men were afraid to leave their wives and families alone. Everyone wondered what would happen if John Brown and his men came back.

➤ **How were the beliefs of Harriet Beecher Stowe and John Brown alike?** *(They both hated slavery and believed it should be abolished.)*

➤ **How were their actions different?** *(They used different methods of getting their message across. Stowe used writing; Brown used violence and killing.)*

◆ FAMOUS PEOPLE ◆

Harriet Tubman
1820-1913

She had escaped to Pennsylvania. She was free at last. But she was not satisfied. She had to help others escape. And she did. Her people called her "Moses" because she led more than three hundred slaves to the freedom of the North. But not all at one time. She made nineteen daring trips back to slave country.

Harriet Tubman ran part of the escape route known as the *Underground Railroad.* The "railroad" was the back roads and the paths that slaves followed north. The "stations" were houses and barns of people who wanted to help the slaves get away. Harriet was a "conductor." She was fearless and determined.

Her last trip to the South was her most important. She went to get her parents. She dressed like an old woman, walked right into the plantation where she had once been a slave, and took a wagon. Then she got her parents in the wagon and drove them out of slavery forever.

140

Teaching the Lesson

Text Discussion, page 140

➤ **Have you ever heard of the *Underground Railroad?***

➤ **Read page 140 to find out what the Underground Railroad really was.** *(an escape route that runaway slaves followed to freedom in the North)*

➤ **Why was Harriet Tubman called "Moses"?** *(She led more than three hundred slaves to freedom, just as Moses led the children of Israel out of slavery in Egypt.)*

➤ Describe how the Underground Railroad worked. *(The slaves followed back roads and paths and stopped at "stations" where people gave them food and shelter.)*

➤ Describe Tubman's last trip to the South. *(She dressed as an old woman, went to the plantation where she had been a slave, took a wagon, and drove her parents away.)*

➤ **Why was this trip Tubman's most important one?** *(Answers will vary; Harriet loved her parents and wanted them to have a taste of freedom before they died.)* (BAT: 5a Love)

Some abolitionists helped run the Underground Railroad. They hid runaway slaves during the day. At night, they helped the slaves get farther north. What might have happened if they had been caught?

Some abolitionists wrote books and essays. Have you ever heard of *Uncle Tom's Cabin?* That book told about the horrible lives of slaves on a plantation in the South. People all over the country read this story. In the North, more people began to agree with the abolitionists.

Still other abolitionists believed that they could force slave owners to give up their slaves. These abolitionists killed and stole, burned and kidnapped. They thought that it was all right to do hurtful things to reach a good goal. What do you think of their idea? Because this group broke good laws, people in the next new territory lived in danger and fear.

141

The Right to Choose

What right did Henry Clay's last compromise give to new territories in the Southwest? They could decide for themselves about slavery. The South wanted all territories to be able to choose for themselves. In 1854, the Kansas-Nebraska Act gave two more new territories the right to choose.

Nebraska was too far north to become a slave state. But Kansas was not. People who were for slavery packed up and moved to Kansas. People who were against slavery packed up and moved there too. Why do you think so many people wanted to move to the new territory? Each group wanted to have the most people living in Kansas when it was time to vote.

The people who moved to Kansas were not always peaceful. Each side sent men who would fight to be sure its side won the most votes. The fighters were mean and sneaky. The fighting was so bad that people called the new territory *Bleeding Kansas.*

142

Day 2

Text Discussion, page 141

➤ **Read page 141 to find out what kinds of things abolitionists did to try to get rid of slavery.** *(hid runaway slaves in their homes and helped them to freedom, wrote books and articles, used violence and committed crimes against slave owners)*

The Fugitive Slave Act said that runaway slaves had to be returned to their masters. It also said that anyone who helped a runaway slave could be fined or put into prison.

➤ **What is the name of Harriet Beecher Stowe's book?** *(Uncle Tom's Cabin)*

This book was translated into other languages so that people all over the world could read it.

➤ **Did the book make a difference in the way people felt about slavery?** *(Yes, more people agreed with the abolitionists after reading the book.)*
➤ **Do you think writing books and articles was a good way to fight against slavery?**
➤ **How did abolitionists like John Brown fight against slavery in the new territory?** *(They killed, stole, burned, and kidnapped.)*
➤ **Why did some people think it was all right to do these hurtful things?** *(They thought it was okay if they were trying to reach a good goal.)*

➤ **What was the good goal they were trying to reach?** *(stopping slavery)*
➤ Pretend that a person sitting beside you in church falls asleep. **Would it be right to "help out" the preacher by punching that person in the nose and shouting for him to wake up?** *(no)*

Many abolitionists might have believed they were helping the slaves by killing people who were for slavery.

➤ **Is it ever right to break God's laws to accomplish something good?** *(no)* (BAT: 2a Authority)

Text Discussion, pages 142-43

➤ **Read page 142 to find out which two new territories were given the right to choose for themselves about slavery.** *(Kansas and Nebraska)*
➤ **Why was it easy for Nebraska to choose to be a free state?** *(It was too far north to become a slave state.)*
➤ **Why did so many people move to Kansas?** *(Both proslavery and antislavery groups wanted to have the most people living in Kansas when it was time to vote.)*
➤ **What was Kansas called and why?** *(Bleeding Kansas, because of all the fighting that took place there)*

The right of the people in a new territory to choose about slavery had seemed like a good thing. But with the terrible fighting in Kansas, people began to change their minds. One man was willing to stand up and speak out against the problem. His name was Abraham Lincoln.

A Man Named Lincoln

Abraham Lincoln was not famous. He did not come from a rich family. He was not educated in the finest schools. But his plain and simple way of talking was easy to understand. And many people agreed with what he said.

Abraham Lincoln was born in the woods of Kentucky in 1809. He lived with his family in a one-room log cabin with a dirt floor. In all, he spent about one year in a school. How much more time have you spent in school already? Even though his time in school was short, Abraham did learn to read and write. He taught himself many things by reading books over and over.

143

People, Places, and Things

Name _____

A person, a place, and a thing are missing from each sentence below. Use the following word lists to fill in the blanks. Each word is used only once.

People	Places	Things
slave	Kansas	*Uncle Tom's Cabin*
Harriet Tubman	South	slavery
John Brown	Pennsylvania	freedom
Moses	North	Underground Railroad
Harriet Beecher Stowe	Nebraska	raid

1. **Harriet Tubman** escaped out of **slavery**
   (person) (thing)
   to the free state of **Pennsylvania** .
   (place)

2. She was called **Moses** because she led over
   (person)
   three hundred slaves to the **North** on the
   (place)
   Underground Railroad
   (thing)

3. People in the **South** did not like
   (place)
   Harriet Beecher Stowe 's book, **Uncle Tom's Cabin**
   (person) (thing)

4. Settlers in **Nebraska** wanted
   (place)
   freedom for every **slave**
   (thing) (person)

5. **John Brown** was an abolitionist who led a
   (person)
   raid in **Kansas** .
   (thing) (place)

Heritage Studies 3
Student Notebook

Lesson 39
Evaluating the Lesson **54**

Settlers in both groups were involved in the killing and raiding that went on.

➤ **Read the first paragraph on page 143 to find out who spoke out against the problems being caused by slavery.** *(Abraham Lincoln)*

The rest of text page 143 will be read in the next lesson.

TimeLine Snapshots Activity, pages 253-54

➤ Locate the figure of Millard Fillmore on the TimeLine at the year 1850. **How long was he in office?** *(less than two years)*
➤ Locate the figure of Franklin Pierce at the year 1853.
➤ Add the next presidential strip containing the figure of James Buchanan. **In what year did he become president?** *(1857)*
➤ **Read the information about Presidents Fillmore, Pierce, and Buchanan found on pages 253-54.**

Evaluating the Lesson

Notebook Activity, page 54

➤ Read the instructions on Notebook page 54.
➤ Complete the page, using the text as needed.

Going Beyond

Enrichment

Provide your child with paper and a pencil. Encourage him to pretend he is a journalist in the 1850s and to write a newspaper article about "Bleeding Kansas." The article should not only describe events that happened there but also express the author's view on the slavery issue.

Additional Teacher Information

Harriet Tubman's real name was Araminta. Born into a family of slaves in Maryland, she learned early to work hard and was soon doing a man's work in the fields. Harriet heard of the Underground Railroad from other slaves who worked with her on the plantation. Once, when she was thirteen, her master ordered her to help him by holding another slave while he whipped him. Harriet refused, and she stretched out her arms to block her master when he tried to chase the fleeing slave. In his anger, the master threw a two-pound weight at Harriet, and it struck her in the forehead. From that day on, she suffered from sudden sleeping spells. But the slave had escaped, and Harriet vowed that she, too, would take the Underground Railroad someday. At age twenty-nine, she fled.

During the Civil War, Tubman served as a spy and a nurse for the Union army, and, occasionally, she even shouldered a gun along with the soldiers. Following the war, she spent the remainder of her life fighting for issues such as women's rights, temperance, and schools for blacks.

The name "Bleeding Kansas" was first applied to the Kansas Territory in 1856 in a speech by James Lane, a Northern party leader. By 1855 there were two legislatures in the territory: a proslavery one in Shawnee Mission and an antislavery one in Topeka. Many people believe that the Civil War unofficially began in Kansas with the guerrilla fighting between the two factions.

LESSON 40
A Man Called "Honest Abe"

Text, pages 143-45
Notebook, page 55

━━━ Preview ━━━

Main Ideas
- Many individuals have shaped our nation's heritage.
- Abraham Lincoln was known for his honest character and his concern for people.

Objectives
- Make a stovepipe hat
- Identify true and false statements about Abraham Lincoln

Materials
- Five $8\frac{1}{2}"\times11"$ sheets of black construction paper*

Day 1

━━━ Lesson ━━━

Introducing the Lesson

Stovepipe Hat Activity

➤ Tape two of the black sheets of construction paper together along one side, forming a long rectangle.
➤ Wrap the rectangle around your head so that I can mark where to tape the hat.
➤ Tape the hat closed, forming a cylinder.

➤ Place one flat sheet of black paper on top of another. Glue these two flat sheets of paper together, forming one thicker sheet.
➤ Center the cylinder on top of this double sheet and trace a dotted line around the bottom of the cylinder.

- Cut out a smaller circle inside this dotted line and cut several slits from the smaller circle to the dotted line, forming tabs.
- Insert the tabs into the bottom of the cylinder and tape the tabs to the inside edges of the cylinder. This will form the brim of the hat. You may then cut off the corners of the brim to make it more rounded.

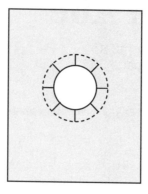 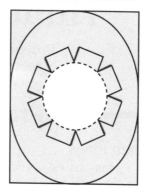

- To make the top of the hat, trace a circle around the top of the cylinder on the one remaining piece of construction paper.
- Cut out this circle and tape it onto the top of the cylinder to finish the hat.

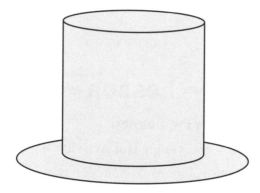

- **What man in America's history was known for wearing a hat like this one?** *(Abraham Lincoln)*

When Abraham Lincoln was young, he worked in a post office. Sometimes, when people were sick or unable to come to the post office, Lincoln would walk to their homes and carry their letters to them. He put the letters underneath his hat. People used to say that Abraham Lincoln carried his entire office around in his hat.

- **Do you think a postman today would wear a hat like this one?**

The right of the people in a new territory to choose about slavery had seemed like a good thing. But with the terrible fighting in Kansas, people began to change their minds. One man was willing to stand up and speak out against the problem. His name was Abraham Lincoln.

A Man Named Lincoln

Abraham Lincoln was not famous. He did not come from a rich family. He was not educated in the finest schools. But his plain and simple way of talking was easy to understand. And many people agreed with what he said.

Abraham Lincoln was born in the woods of Kentucky in 1809. He lived with his family in a one-room log cabin with a dirt floor. In all, he spent about one year in a school. How much more time have you spent in school already? Even though his time in school was short, Abraham did learn to read and write. He taught himself many things by reading books over and over.

143

Teaching the Lesson

Text Discussion, page 143

- **Read page 143 to learn what Abraham Lincoln was willing to do.** *(speak out against the problem of slavery)*
- **What kind of person was Abraham Lincoln?** *(plain, simple, hard-working, not rich or famous)*
- **How many years did Lincoln spend in school?** *(about one year)*
- **Do you think you could learn everything you needed to know in one year of school?**
- **What did Lincoln do while he was not in school to help himself keep learning?** *(He read the same books over and over again.)*

Often Abraham Lincoln borrowed books from neighbors because the only book the Lincolns had in their home was the Bible.

Abraham Lincoln was twenty-two when he left home to make a life for himself in Illinois. First he worked as a clerk in a general store. Later he owned his own store. But the store failed, and he found work as a surveyor. He also ran a post office. Would you want to have any of these jobs?

People who met Lincoln knew he was honest and dependable. He was always willing to help wherever he was needed. His friends asked him to run for public office. They wanted him to serve them in the Illinois state congress.

Lincoln's law office was on this street in Springfield. (See the X.)

Lincoln ran and won. He packed up his few belongings and moved to the state capital in Springfield. He worked hard in the congress to make good laws. He studied hard too. Lincoln wanted to become a lawyer. Before long he was one of the best and most trusted lawyers in Springfield.

144

Abraham Lincoln also wanted to keep slavery out of the new territories. He made speeches about Bleeding Kansas. In one speech he said, "He who would *be* no slave must consent to *have* no slave. Those who deny freedom to others deserve it not for themselves." What do you think about Lincoln's ideas?

Lincoln's ideas made him famous all over the country. About this time, the new Republican Party was formed by abolitionists and others who thought slavery was wrong. This new party picked Lincoln to run for president in 1860.

The South did not want Lincoln to be president. They knew he was against slavery. They thought that he would set all the slaves free. So the Southern states made a plan. If Lincoln won the race for president, they would leave the Union, another name for the United States. They would form a new country.

145

Day 2

Text Discussion, page 144

➤ **Read the first paragraph on page 144 to find out what jobs Abraham Lincoln had when he was a young man.** *(clerk in a general store, owner of a store, surveyor, person in charge of a post office)*

➤ **Read the rest of the page to find out what character qualities other people noticed in Abraham Lincoln.** *(He was honest, dependable, hard working, and helpful.)* (BATs: 2b Servanthood, 4c Honesty)

> Abraham Lincoln got the nickname "Honest Abe" while he was working in the general store. It is said that he once walked all the way to a customer's house after closing the store to give her the six cents he had overcharged her.

➤ **Do you think it would be good to have a man like Abraham Lincoln to help govern our state?**

➤ **What happened when Lincoln ran for Congress in the state of Illinois?** *(He won.)*

➤ **What new job did he begin doing after he moved to Springfield, Illinois?** *(He became a lawyer.)*

Text Discussion, page 145

➤ **Read the first paragraph on page 145 to find out what Abraham Lincoln wanted to do about slavery.** *(keep it out of new territories)*

➤ **What did Lincoln mean when he said, "He who would be *no* slave must consent to *have* no slave"?** *(A person who would not want to be a slave should not keep slaves.)*

➤ **Do you think Lincoln was right?**

➤ **Read the rest of the page to find out how most Southerners felt about Lincoln.** *(They did not like his ideas about slavery; they did not want him to be president because he would set their slaves free.)*

➤ **What new political party chose Lincoln to run for president?** *(Republican Party)*

➤ **What did the South plan to do if Lincoln won?** *(leave the Union or United States and form a new country)*

Abraham Lincoln

Name _____

Write *T* for true or *F* for false in the blank beside each statement.

___F___ 1. Abraham Lincoln grew up in Illinois.

___F___ 2. Lincoln was born into a wealthy family.

___T___ 3. Lincoln did not spend much time in school as a boy.

___F___ 4. Lincoln did not like to read.

___T___ 5. Lincoln was a hard worker.

___T___ 6. One job Lincoln had was working in a post office.

___F___ 7. Many people did not trust Abraham Lincoln.

___T___ 8. Lincoln's nickname had to do with his truthfulness.

___F___ 9. Lincoln ran for the Indiana state congress.

___T___10. After winning the election, Lincoln moved to Springfield.

___F___11. While in Springfield, Lincoln became a famous doctor.

___T___12. Abraham Lincoln hated slavery.

___F___13. Everyone in the nation liked Lincoln's ideas.

___F___14. Lincoln was a member of the Democratic party.

___T___15. Lincoln ran for president of the United States in 1860.

___T___16. The South wanted to start its own country if Lincoln became president.

Heritage Studies 3
Student Notebook

Lesson 40
Evaluating the Lesson **55**

Evaluating the Lesson

Notebook Activity, page 55

➤ Read the instructions on Notebook page 55.
➤ Complete the page.

▬▬ Going Beyond ▬▬

Enrichment

Have available magazines, old books, calendar pictures, scissors, and glue. Allow your child to make a collage of pictures that remind him of Abraham Lincoln, such as the kind of home in which he grew up, the type of clothing he wore, the different jobs he held, the kind of person he was, and things he said.

Additional Teacher Information

Abraham Lincoln's mother, Nancy, died when he was nine years old. His father married again, and Lincoln's stepmother, Sarah, encouraged him to learn to read and write. At age twenty-five, Lincoln joined a small troop of volunteers during the Black Hawk War. The other men in the troop elected him as their captain, and he later said that nothing else in his life had given him greater satisfaction.

Lincoln met his wife, Mary Todd, while he was practicing law in Springfield. They had four sons, one of whom died at age four. Lincoln got to know many people in central Illinois during this time by "riding the circuit." For six months of the year, he rode around to small outlying towns and got to know the people. His fairness earned him respect and trust, and later many of his political supporters came from these small towns.

Lincoln became a Republican in 1856 and ran against Stephen Douglas for a U.S. Senate seat. He lost this race but beat Douglas four years later in the presidential election.

LESSON 41
A House Divided

Text, pages 146-48, 255
Notebook, pages 56-57

━━━ Preview ━━━

Main Ideas
- People have needs, feelings, interests, and preferences.
- A nation divided against itself will not last.

Objectives
- Read a circle graph and answer questions about it
- Identify whether statements apply to either the North or the South

Materials
- A jump rope or some other sturdy rope, at least ten feet in length*
- A 12-inch strip of masking tape
- The presidential figure of Abraham Lincoln (16) from the TimeLine Snapshots
- Books, magazines, or newspapers that contain circle graphs*
- A sheet of paper

Notes
Place the masking tape on the floor in an area where there is ample room to safely play tug of war with your child. You will want to begin your lesson for the day by going to that spot.

━━━ Lesson ━━━

Introducing the Lesson

Demonstration

➤ Take one end of the rope and step behind the line of masking tape.

We are going to play a game of tug of war. I will hold the other end of the rope. We must begin with equal lengths of rope on each side of the line. When I say to begin, you should pull as hard as you can on your end of the rope. The goal is to pull the other player over to your side of the line.

➤ Begin!

Match your strength to that of your child's for a period of time, until it becomes apparent that neither one is going to win. Then tell him that you are going to stop pulling.

➤ **Could we have gone on forever pulling the rope against one another?** *(no)*
➤ **What would have happened eventually?** *(One person would get tired and quit, so the other would become the winner.)*

The arguing between the North and the South over slavery was like this game of tug of war. For a long time neither side could win, and neither one was willing to give up.

➤ Listen to the following statement by Abraham Lincoln.

" 'A house divided against itself cannot stand.' I believe this government cannot endure permanently half slave and half free."

➤ **What do you think Abraham Lincoln meant by this statement?**

Lincoln meant that the nation could not go on forever being divided over the issue of slavery. In this lesson, we will see how the South "dropped the rope" when it realized that neither side was going to give up its side of the disagreement.

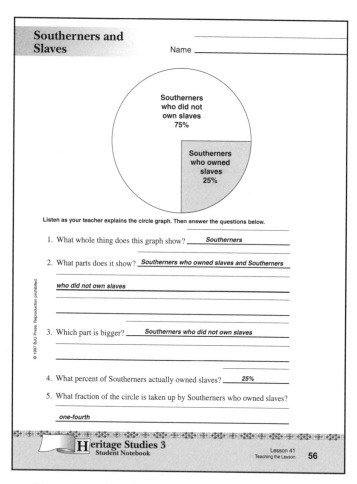

Southerners and Slaves

Name _____

Southerners who did not own slaves 75%

Southerners who owned slaves 25%

Listen as your teacher explains the circle graph. Then answer the questions below.

1. What whole thing does this graph show? _____Southerners_____

2. What parts does it show? _Southerners who owned slaves and Southerners_

who did not own slaves

3. Which part is bigger? _____Southerners who did not own slaves_____

4. What percent of Southerners actually owned slaves? ___25%___

5. What fraction of the circle is taken up by Southerners who owned slaves?

one-fourth

© 1997 BJU Press. Reproduction prohibited.

Heritage Studies 3
Student Notebook

Lesson 41
Teaching the Lesson **56**

To Read Circle Graphs

1. Get Notebook page 56, a pencil, and some books, newspapers, or magazines.

2. Circle graphs compare the parts of a whole thing. They show the differences in the sizes of the parts. Listen as your teacher explains the circle graph. Then answer the questions on the Notebook page.

3. Find a circle graph in a book, newspaper, or magazine. How does the graph compare things?

146

Teaching the Lesson

Learning How Activity, page 146 and Notebook page 56

➤ The graph shown on Notebook page 56 is named for its shape. **What is this type of graph called?** (*circle graph*)

A *circle graph* compares the parts of a whole. It looks something like a pie cut into different-sized slices, with each slice representing a part of the whole. Some people refer to circle graphs as *pie graphs.*

➤ **Read all the steps on page 146**.

➤ Look again at the circle graph on Notebook page 56.

This circle graph compares Southerners who owned slaves with Southerners who did not own slaves.

➤ Answer the questions on the Notebook page, using the circle graph.

It may be easier for your child to answer the last question on the Notebook page if you sketch in lines on the circle graph that divide it into fourths.

➤ **Which part of the graph did you expect to be bigger?**

Many people think that most Southerners in that time period owned slaves. Even though only one-fourth of all Southerners owned slaves, almost all Southerners were in favor of slavery. They thought that slaves were needed to help with the work in the fields. If they had no slaves to help them, they would not get work done as quickly and the South would lose money.

➤ **Read step three on page 146 again and follow the instructions.**

You will want to save Notebook page 56 so that your child can compare the circle graph with the line graph in Chapter 8.

Abraham Lincoln was elected president in 1860. Soon after, South Carolina did what the Southern states had said they would do. It left the Union. Not much later, six more Southern states left the Union. These states made themselves into a new country. They called their new country the Confederate States of America, or the Confederacy.

For more than fifty years, the North and South had argued about slavery. But slavery was not the only thing that made the North and the South different. Most people in the North lived in cities and worked in factories and shops. The Southern people lived and worked on farms or big plantations. Neither side understood the way of life on the other side.

The two sides disagreed, too, on the rights of the states. The South thought that each state could make laws for itself. They

Northern and Southern ways of life differed.

could choose whether to allow slavery or whether to leave the Union. But the North believed that the laws made by the United States were more important than laws made by one state.

By 1860 the problems between the North and the South were too big. A compromise would not work this time. There seemed to be only one way left to settle all the disagreements.

147

Day 2

Text Discussion, page 147

➤ We read in Lesson 40 that Abraham Lincoln was making many important speeches. **What important position was Abraham Lincoln running for?** *(president of the United States)*

➤ **What did the Southern states say they were going to do if he won?** *(leave the Union)*

➤ **Read page 147 to find out who won the election and what happened as a result.** *(Abraham Lincoln; South Carolina and six other Southern states left the Union and formed a new country.)*

➤ **What did the Southern states call their new country?** *(the Confederate States of America or the Confederacy)*

➤ **How do you think this made Abraham Lincoln feel?** He was sad and discouraged.

TimeLine Snapshots Activity, page 255

➤ Add the figure of Abraham Lincoln to the History TimeLine at the year 1861.

➤ **Read the information about President Lincoln on page 255.**

Review Activity

➤ **How long had the arguments between the North and the South been going on?** *(for more than fifty years)*

➤ *Fold the sheet of paper in half lengthwise. At the top of the left side write the word* North *and on the right side write the word* South.

➤ Name some differences between the North and the South, and I will list them in columns beneath the two headings. *(The North did not want slavery, and the South did; many Northerners lived in cities, and many Southerners lived on farms; many Northerners worked in factories and shops, and many Southerners worked on farms or big plantations; the North wanted the national government to be stronger than the state governments, and the South wanted the state governments to be stronger than the national government.)*

 You will need to save this list for review in Lesson 47.

It must have been very hard for the two sides to understand one another because they had such different ways of life.

➤ **Did either side really listen to the other side's ideas?** *(no)* (BAT: 2b Servanthood)

➤ **What do you suppose most people thought was the only way left to settle the disagreements?** *(war)*

Inside Fort Sumter
Charleston, South Carolina
April 12, 1861

Inside Fort Sumter as it is now

The soldiers in blue coats looked out at Charleston. The city was quiet. The water was quiet. Soon the sun would come up, and soon the soldiers would know what the South planned to do.

Suddenly, a red flash swept across the dark sky. It made an eerie whistle as it went, and sparks shot from it. Then an awful roar, like a thunderclap, shook the fort. A Confederate shell burst over the small group of Union soldiers.

Major Anderson put out his hand to steady himself for the blast. He knew what that shot meant. There was no hope for peace now. The war between North and South had begun.

Fort Sumter after the bombardment

148

North and South

Name _____

Draw an arrow pointing north (↑) beside each fact that was true of the North.
Draw an arrow pointing south (↓) beside each fact that was true of the South.

↑ 1. Most people here lived in cities.

↑ 2. Most people here hated slavery.

↓ 3. Many people here owned slaves.

↓ 4. Most people here believed state laws were more important than national laws.

↑ 5. Most people here worked in factories and shops.

↓ 6. Most people here lived on farms and plantations.

↑ 7. Most people here wanted a strong national government.

↓ 8. Most people here did not want Abraham Lincoln to be president.

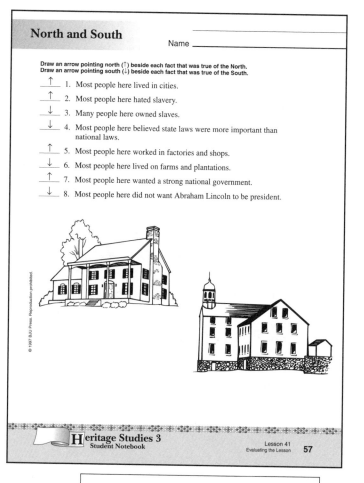

Heritage Studies 3
Student Notebook

Lesson 41
Evaluating the Lesson **57**

Text Discussion, page 148

Major Robert Anderson was the commander of a troop of Northern soldiers. These soldiers went to Fort Sumter, off the coast of Charleston, South Carolina, and raised the Union flag. This action was a warning to the South that the fort was national property, not Confederate property.

➤ **Read page 148 to find out what the South did.** *(They fired a shot at the soldiers in the fort.)*

➤ **What did this shot mean for the divided nation?** *(The war between the North and the South had begun.)*

➤ **How do you think Major Anderson and his men felt after the shot was fired?**

They probably felt sad that there was no more hope for peace.

➤ **Do you know the name of the war that began at Fort Sumter?**

This war is called the ***American Civil War.*** Although the North and the South had been arguing and fighting for many years before this, Fort Sumter is the place we recognize as the official beginning point of the American Civil War.

The War Between the States or just the Civil War are also correct names. Many different countries have had civil wars, or wars between citizens of the same state or country. The term *American Civil War* sets America's war apart from civil wars of other countries.

Evaluating the Lesson

Notebook Activity, page 57

➤ Read the instructions on Notebook page 57.
➤ Complete the page.

Going Beyond

Enrichment

Provide paper, pencils, rulers, a round object that may be traced, and felt-tip pens or crayons. Encourage your child to make his own circle graphs. The graphs might show the relationship between the number of adults and children in your home, the amount of time he spends doing various activities at home, the way he divides his allowance, and so on. Supply pictures of various circle graphs to give him ideas.

Additional Teacher Information

Abraham Lincoln's "house divided" quotation is taken from Christ's words in Matthew 12:25: "Every kingdom divided against itself is brought to desolation; and every city or house divided against itself shall not stand." Lincoln used this quotation in 1858 in his speech accepting the nomination to run for the U.S. Senate against Stephen Douglas.

The South and the North disagreed on how much authority the state governments should have. The South wanted states to have the rights to incorporate a bank, build national roads and canals, establish institutions of higher learning and research, and nullify protective tariffs. The North, however, believed that these rights should belong only to the national government.

The Confederate States of America elected Jefferson Davis as their first president. Before the secession, Davis had served as a congressman, senator, and secretary of war in the United States government. The commander of the Confederate forces at Charleston was General Pierre Gustave Toutant Beauregard. It was he who notified Major Anderson of the South's intention to fire on Fort Sumter in one hour. After the South began firing, Anderson waited nearly two hours before returning fire, still hoping to prevent war. Finally, he ordered his men to fire their cannons at the Southern battery, but the cannonballs only dented the iron armor surrounding the Confederate gun stations. When his Union soldiers began to run out of ammunition, Major Anderson was forced to surrender Fort Sumter to the Confederate troops.

Songs of War and Peace

This chapter focuses on the importance of songs and songwriters in America's history. Highlighted are the works of Stephen Foster, cowboy songs, spirituals, and the war songs "Dixie" and "The Battle Hymn of the Republic." Your child will discuss musical instruments in the Bible and will make some musical instruments. He will have several opportunities to listen to recordings and to sing some favorite songs of America.

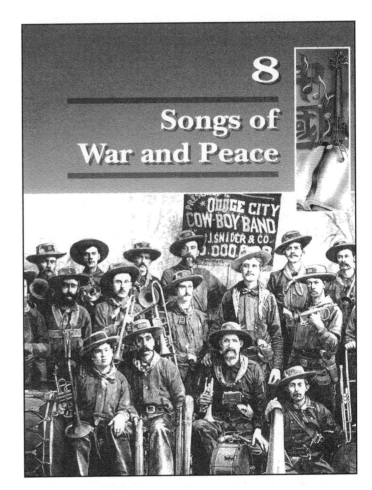

8

Songs of
War and Peace

Materials

The following materials must be obtained or prepared before the presentation of the lesson. These items are labeled with an asterisk (*) in each lesson and in the Materials List in the Supplement. For further information see the individual lessons.

- Recordings of Stephen Foster songs (optional) (Lesson 42)
- Chenille wire (Lesson 43)
- 30 to 40 small metal tabs from soft-drink cans, metal washers, or large safety pins (Lesson 43)
- Several decorative beads (optional) (Lesson 43)
- An empty soft-drink bottle or ketchup bottle (Lesson 44)
- 2 small blocks of wood (Lesson 44)
- 2 pieces of sandpaper (Lesson 44)
- 4 rubber bands (Lesson 44)
- A small box (Lesson 44)
- *Egermeier's Bible Story Book* (optional) (Lesson 45)
- Drum or bugle supplies (Lesson 46)
- "B" and "C" volumes of an encyclopedia (Lesson 46)

LESSON 42
Singing with Stephen Foster

Text, pages 150-53
Notebook, pages 58-59

━━━ Preview ━━━

Main Ideas
- Many different people and groups have contributed to American culture.
- Popular songs are songs that people love to hear and sing.
- Throughout history, cultures have borrowed from each other.

Objectives
- Sing "Oh, Susanna!"
- Read a line graph
- Answer questions about Stephen Foster

Materials
- *HERITAGE STUDIES Listening Cassette A*
- Recordings of the following Stephen Foster songs: "My Old Dog Tray," "My Old Kentucky Home," "Old Folks at Home," and "I Dream of Jeanie with the Light Brown Hair" (optional)*

> You may want to have your child begin preparing for a cowboy/cowgirl dress-up day for Lesson 43.

Day 1

━━━ Lesson ━━━

Introducing the Lesson

Favorite Songs Activity

➤ **What are some of your favorite songs?**
➤ Let's sing some of them. This lesson is about favorite songs and a famous songwriter of long ago.

Do you have a favorite song? Almost everyone does. We like songs with catchy tunes that are fun to sing. We might like one song because it makes us happy and another song because it makes us sad. Some of our favorite songs make us proud to be Americans.

As long as people have lived in America, songwriters here have thought up songs to sing. The songs tell about things that happened to the writers or to people they knew. The songs tell about things that were special to the whole country or to just a small part of it.

We can learn about some important things that happened in the past by learning the songs that were *popular* then. Popular songs are songs that the people loved to hear and sing. Some popular songs from long ago are still loved today. How many of these old-time songs do you already know?

150

Teaching the Lesson

Text Activity, page 150

➤ **What is happening in the picture on page 150?**
➤ **Read the page to find out what we call songs that we like to hear and sing.** *(popular songs)*

The favorite songs that we sang earlier would be called **popular songs.** Many songs become popular because they are about things that the songwriter and the listeners especially like.

Listening Activity (optional)

➤ Listen as I read the song titles and play recordings of the following songs: "My Old Kentucky Home," "Old Folks at Home," "My Old Dog Tray," and "I Dream of Jeanie with the Light Brown Hair."
➤ *After each song, pause and ask the question:* **What was the songwriter probably thinking about as he wrote this song?** *(home, family, a favorite pet, someone he loves)*

Singing in Times of Peace

Stephen Foster

Many popular songs told about everyday things. One of these songs might tell about home, family, or a favorite pet. It might remind you of someone you love. Stephen Foster wrote this kind of song. He was the first American to make his living by writing songs.

Foster liked music even when he was young. Do you like music? In those days, arts like music and painting were not important to most people. Foster's family hoped he would find something more important to do. But nothing else was important to Foster.

Stephen Foster wrote 189 songs. "Oh, Susanna!" was one of his first. He wrote "Oh, Susanna!" in 1848. The next year, men heading for the gold mines in California made new words for the song. They sang it this way:

Oh, California,
That's the land for me!
I'm bound for San Francisco
With my washbowl on my knee.

Foster's song "Oh, Susanna!" was a favorite of the forty-niners.

151

Oh, Susanna!

I come from Alabama with my banjo on my knee;
I'm going to Lou'siana, my true love for to see.
It rained all night the day I left,
The weather it was dry;
The sun so hot I froze to death—Susanna, don't you cry.

Chorus:
Oh, Susanna! Oh don't you cry for me;
For I've come from Alabama with my banjo on my knee.

I had a dream the other night when everything was still;
I thought I saw Susanna come a-walking down the hill.
A red, red rose was in her hand,
A tear was in her eye;
I said, "I come from Alabam'. Susanna, don't you cry."

152

Text Activity, page 151

➤ **Read page 151 to find out the name of the first American to make his living by writing songs.** *(Stephen Foster)*

➤ **Why did Stephen Foster's family hope that he would find something more important than songwriting as a job?** *(Answers will vary but should include that the family thought that songwriting could not support a family. They thought that songwriting was strictly for fun, not a job.)*

➤ **Do you think Stephen Foster's family liked music?**

Music was a very important, enjoyable part of the family fun times for the Fosters. The girls in the Foster family played the piano and guitar. Everyone in the family sang. When Stephen was six years old, his father gave him a drum so that he could join in the family musical times; soon after, Stephen carried a flute around with him everywhere he went. Everyone used to say of young Stephen Foster, "Stephie's head is full of tunes."

Discussion and Listening Activity

➤ **How many songs did Stephen Foster write?** *(189)*
➤ Look at the TimeLine on the wall. **In what year did many men go to California looking for gold?** *(1849)*

➤ Listen as I play "Oh, Susanna!" from the listening cassette.

Foster's idea for the song came from watching slaves sing as they worked, worshiped, or relaxed. He listened to their rhythms and saw how they made up new words as they went along. All his life Stephen Foster found music wherever he went. He heard rhythms and music in the wagon's wheels, horse's hooves, the babbling brook, and the whip-poorwill's song. Stephen Foster used to say repeatedly, "Everything sings!"

Point out that God created this marvelous world full of interesting sounds that Stephen Foster listened to so intently. Take a few minutes to sit quietly, listening to the sounds around you. Allow your child to mention the sounds that he hears. (Bible Promise: I. God as Master)

Day 2

Singing Activity, page 152

➤ **Read the words of "Oh, Susanna!" on page 152 to find examples of nonsense in the song.** *("It rained all night the day I left; the weather it was dry"; "The sun so hot I froze to death.")*
➤ Sing "Oh, Susanna!" with me.

◆ LEARNING HOW ◆

To Read a Line Graph

1. Get Notebook page 58 and a pencil.

2. Line graphs help you see how a thing has changed over time. Each dot on the graph stands for a number. What does the graph on your Notebook page show? What do the numbers across the bottom of the graph represent? What do the numbers on the left side of the graph mean? Answer the questions on the Notebook page.

3. Look back at the circle graph on Notebook page 56. How are a circle graph and a line graph different?

153

Stephen Foster's Songs

Name _____

Stephen Foster's First Songs

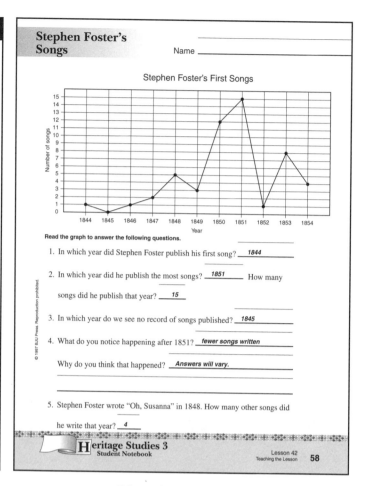

Read the graph to answer the following questions.

1. In which year did Stephen Foster publish his first song? __**1844**__

2. In which year did he publish the most songs? __**1851**__ How many songs did he publish that year? __**15**__

3. In which year do we see no record of songs published? __**1845**__

4. What do you notice happening after 1851? __**fewer songs written**__

   Why do you think that happened? __**Answers will vary.**__

5. Stephen Foster wrote "Oh, Susanna" in 1848. How many other songs did he write that year? __**4**__

© 1997 BJU Press. Reproduction prohibited.

Heritage Studies 3
Student Notebook

Lesson 42
Teaching the Lesson **58**

Learning How Activity, page 153 and Notebook page 58

➤ **Read Step 1 on page 153.**

➤ **Read Step 2 and answer the questions.** *(The graph shows the number of songs that Stephen Foster wrote in his early years. The years are at the bottom of the graph. The number of songs is at the left of the graph.)*

Stephen Foster wrote fewer songs after 1851 because of discouragement and sadness. Both of Foster's parents died in 1855.

➤ **Read Step 3.**

➤ **What is the circle graph showing?** *(percent of Southerners owning or not owning slaves)*

➤ **Which graph, the circle graph or the line graph, do you think is easier to read?**

Listening Activity

Some years Stephen Foster wrote a great many songs for just a little bit of money. These songs never became as popular as his earlier songs. He died sad, poor, and discouraged; but at his death, his brothers came across a handwritten song in one of Foster's notebooks. The brothers had never seen or heard this Stephen Foster song before. The song was called "Beautiful Dreamer."

➤ Listen as I play the recording of "Beautiful Dreamer" from the listening cassette.

➤ **Do you think that this song became popular and brought in money for Stephen Foster's family?** *(Answers will vary, but the correct answer is yes.)*

Though Foster wrote some fine songs, even some fine religious songs, he probably was not a Christian.

Songs

Name _____

Read the clues to help you fill in the puzzle below. Then read down the circled boxes to find the name of the state whose state song is "Old Folks at Home."

1. the first American to make his living writing songs
2. type of song that people love to hear and sing
3. a Foster song written in 1848
4. where men started searching for gold in 1849
5. what Susanna was "a-walking down"
6. the kind of rose Susanna had in her hand
7. the place I come from "with a banjo on my knee"

1. S T E P H E N F O S T E R
2. P O P U L A R
3. O H S U S A N N A
4. C A L I F O R N I A
5. H I L L
6. R E D
7. A L A B A M A

© 1997 BJU Press. Reproduction prohibited.

Heritage Studies 3
Student Notebook

Lesson 42
Evaluating the Lesson **59**

Evaluating the Lesson

Notebook Activity, page 59

➤ Read the directions on Notebook page 59.
➤ Complete the page.

Going Beyond

Enrichment

Allow your child to listen to other recordings of the songs of Stephen Foster.

If you live in one of the following areas, you may want to arrange a field trip to a Stephen Foster memorial.

The Stephen Foster State Folk Culture Center in White Springs, Florida

The Foster Museum where Stephen Foster was born in Pittsburgh, Pennsylvania

My Old Kentucky Home State Park ("Federal Hill") and Bardstown Historical Museum in Bardstown, Kentucky

Additional Teacher Information

Stephen Collins Foster was born July 4, 1826, the ninth child in a family who loved music. The house slave, Olivia Pise, who cared for young Stephie, influenced him greatly with her songs. The Fosters even allowed Stephie to attend Olivia's church, where he observed the African Americans clapping their hands, strumming their banjos, and making up new songs as they went along. He observed the slaves at work and at play as they sang their troubles, their prayers, and their hallelujahs too.

Stephen Foster made up tunes all the time. The first song he put on paper was "The Tioga Waltz," a melody for three flutes and a piano. Stephen was fifteen. While still a teenager, Stephen formed a singing club that met around his family's piano twice weekly, singing new songs that Stephen had written.

In 1848, Foster sold "Oh, Susanna!" to a publisher for one hundred dollars. His "Camptown Races" and fifteen other songs were sold outright for two hundred dollars. Foster's songs were popular in the minstrel shows, especially with the famous singer E. P. Christy. In fact, in 1851 Stephen Foster sold the copyright of two songs, "Old Folks at Home" and "Oh, Boys, Carry Me Along," for fifteen dollars each to Christy. Christy refused to return the copyrights and placed his name on these songs as the composer until the copyrights ran out in 1879.

In 1864, Stephen Foster at age thirty-seven was depressed and was smoking and drinking heavily. He was also probably suffering from tuberculosis. He lived in poverty, writing any kind of song he could, selling to anyone who would buy them. At his death he left little: a few worn clothes and his purse. In his purse were a few cents and a scrap of paper on which he had scribbled a new idea for a song, "Dear Friends and Gentle Hearts." He died before he could write the song. "Beautiful Dreamer" was published a few weeks after his death as were several other of his songs.

LESSON 43
Riding the Range

Text, pages 154-55, 282-83

══════ Preview ══════

Main Ideas

- Many different people and groups have contributed to American culture.
- Folksongs were made up by everyday people and were passed on by word of mouth, not written down.

Objectives

- Make a pair of spurs
- Sing "Git Along, Little Dogies"
- Identify true and false statements about cowboys and the song "Git Along, Little Dogies"

Materials

- Two 6-inch lengths of chenille wire*
- 30 to 40 small metal tabs from soft-drink cans, metal washers, or large safety pins*
- *HERITAGE STUDIES Listening Cassette A*
- Several decorative beads (optional)*
- Maps and More 16, page M10

══════ Lesson ══════ *Day 1*

Introducing the Lesson

Making Spurs Activity

➤ *Give your child two 6-inch lengths of chenille wire and the thirty to forty small metal tabs from soft-drink cans.*

➤ Put fifteen to twenty tabs on each length of chenille wire. You may place decorative beads on the chenille wire between groups of three to four metal tabs.

➤ Bend each end of the chenille wires into a knot and wrap tape around each knot.

You may need to add layers of tape to prevent the last tab from slipping off the wire. Help your child bend down the ends of his lengths of chenille wires to form small hooks that will easily hook onto his shoes.

People all over America sang "Oh, Susanna!" But sometimes songs were sung by a smaller group of people. The songs told about things only those people knew. These things were not important to everyone in the country. Can you guess what group of people sang "Git Along, Little Dogies"?

Cowboys sang songs like this one to calm their little dogies. "Little dogies" were the longhorn cattle; each one weighed about one thousand pounds. Do you think the cowboys' name for the cattle was a good one? The job of the cowboys began with the spring roundup. Then they spent most of the spring and summer *driving*, or guiding, the longhorn cattle from the pastureland to the markets. Do you think the cowboys' job sounds like fun?

Many of the songs sung by the cowboys in the West are *folksongs*. We do not know who wrote the words and the music to this kind of song. One person or a group of people might make up a folksong. If others liked the song, they sang it too. But they never wrote it down and tried to sell it as a songwriter would.

➤ Hook the spurs around the backs of your shoes. Try walking around the room like a cowboy or cowgirl.

The jingle-jangle of the cowboy's spurs announced the cowboy's approach, kept him company, and helped keep the cattle calm. This lesson will tell you more about cowboys through the songs they sang.

Teaching the Lesson

Text Activity, page 154 and Maps and More 16

➤ **Read the first paragraph on page 154 and answer the question.**

➤ **Read the rest of page 154 to find out what *little dogies* are in this song.** *(longhorn cattle)*

 Dogies (dō´gēs) are motherless or stray calves. At one time, *dogies* referred to any young steer. Young steers can weigh 500 to 1,000 pounds. Full-grown steers can weigh 1,500 pounds.

➤ Look at Maps and More 16. **Is *longhorn* a good name for this type of cattle?** *(yes, because they have long horns)*

➤ **How much does each longhorn weigh?** *(about one thousand pounds)*

➤ **What does *driving the cattle* mean?** *(guiding the cattle from pasturelands to the markets to be sold)*
➤ **What seasons of the year were the cowboys involved in the cattle drives?** *(spring and summer)*

During the fall and winter, the cowboys were expected to "check the lines," or ride around the ranches, checking to make sure that the animals were corralled within the correct boundaries. They also did repair work or odd jobs on ranches and took care of the cattle that did not go to market but were used in breeding.

➤ **Do you think that the cowboy's job sounds like fun?**

The job of the cowboy, no matter what the season, was always long and hard. Often it was dangerous work too.

> The example of the cowboys on the long cattle drives, doing such hard, demanding work, serves as a challenge for Christians to work hard and always to do their best. (BATs: 2d Goal setting, 2e Work, 3a Self-concept)

Day 2

Text Activity, pages 155 and 282-83

➤ **Read the first verse and chorus of the song on page 155 to find out where the cowboy was driving the cattle.** *(Montana)*
➤ Find the location of Montana on the map on pages 282-83.
➤ Name the states that surround Montana. *(Idaho, Utah, Wyoming, North Dakota, and South Dakota)*
➤ **How long do you think the cattle drives might have taken?** A trail drive could take three to four months, usually at a rate of ten to twelve miles each day.
➤ Find another name for a cowboy in the first verse of the song. *(cowpuncher)*

Singing Activity, page 155

➤ Follow along in your textbook as I play the recording of "Git Along, Little Dogies" from the listening cassette.
➤ Let's sing the first verse and chorus with the recording.
➤ **Read through verse two to find out what the cowboys do to the cattle before heading up the trail.** *("mark them, and brand them, and cut off their tails")*

Git Along, Little Dogies

As I was a-walkin' one mornin' for pleasure,
I spied a cowpuncher come ridin' along.
His hat was throwed back and his spurs was a-jinglin',
And as he approached he was singin' this song:

Chorus:
Whoopee ti yi yo, git along, little dogies;
It's your misfortune and none of my own.
Whoopee ti yi yo, git along, little dogies;
You know that Montana will be your new home.

Early in springtime we round up the dogies,
Mark 'em and brand 'em and cut off their tails.
Then we all load up the old chuck wagon,
An' hitch up our hosses and start up the trail.

It's whoopin' and yellin' and drivin' the dogies,
And oh how I wish you would only go on!
It's whoopin' and punchin', go on, little dogies;
You know that Montana will be your new home.

Some boys, they go up on the trail just for pleasure,
But that's where they get it most awfully wrong.
You haven't a notion the trouble they give us,
It takes all our time to keep movin' along.

➤ **What kind of things were loaded in the chuck wagon?** *(Answers will vary but should include food, ingredients for cooking, pots, and pans.)*

 > Additional information regarding cowboys, branding, and the chuck wagon will be provided in Lesson 64.

➤ **Read the fourth verse of the song to find out how the cowboys felt about the boys who came along for pleasure or fun.** *(They felt like the boys were along for pleasure and to cause trouble.)*

Evaluating the Lesson

Oral Evaluation

➤ I will read some statements.
➤ Move your feet to jingle your spurs for each true statement. Stay still for each false statement.

- "Little dogies" were the longhorn cattle. *(true)*
- We do not know who wrote the music or the words for most early folksongs. *(true)*
- When early folksongs were sung, they were immediately written down. *(false)*
- "Cowpuncher" is another name for a cowboy. *(true)*

- In the song "Git Along, Little Dogies," the cattle were being driven to Texas. *(false)*
- The cowboys who went on the trail just for pleasure gave the other cowboys a lot of trouble. *(true)*
- To keep the cows moving along was a hard job. *(true)*

Going Beyond

Enrichment

Prepare cards in the form of cowboy boots. (*NOTE:* See Appendix, page A39 for the pattern.) Write the following terms on cards of one color and the meanings on cards of a different color.

> *bronco*—a wild horse or pony of western North America
>
> *chuck*—food
>
> *maverick*—an unbranded cow whose owner is unknown
>
> *muley*—a hornless cow
>
> *mustang*—a small wild horse
>
> *paint*—a horse with irregular patches of white
>
> *quirt*—a cowboy's whip
>
> *rustler*—a cattle thief
>
> *Stetson*—a cowboy hat
>
> *tenderfoot*—a person who is new on the job

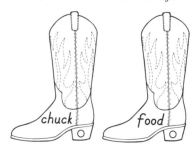

Additional Teacher Information

Most cowboy songs did not come from professional composers but rather from the folk tunes of pioneers and settlers. Songs were often made up to make the laborer's work seem easier or to calm the cattle or to make the cowboys less lonesome on the long trail. Cowboys were African American, Native American, Mexican, or white, and they brought to the songs their own musical traditions.

"Git Along, Little Dogies" tells the history of cattle raising. The first verse tells about the cowboy: He rides alone ("doesn't gallop, doesn't canter, doesn't trot"). He wears his hat a certain way—"throwed back." He allows himself one whim—his jingling spurs. "Git Along, Little Dogies" is also a lullaby to keep the cattle calm and moving along.

The great blizzard of 1886-87 wiped out 80 to 90 percent of the range cattle and brought to a close the great trail drives.

LESSON 44
Making Music

Text, page 156
Notebook, page 60

Preview

Main Ideas
- People communicate in many ways.
- Music is made with instruments that are blown into, tapped, hit, or plucked.
- Musical instruments are mentioned in the Bible.

Objectives
- Make simple musical instruments
- Make music with a simple instrument
- Identify musical instruments in a puzzle

Materials
- An empty soft-drink bottle or ketchup bottle*
- 2 pencils or rulers
- 2 small blocks of wood*
- 2 pieces of sandpaper*
- 4 rubber bands*
- A small box*
- A Bible
- Supplement, page S9: David playing his harp for King Saul

Day 1

Lesson

Introducing the Lesson

Making Instruments

➤ *Place the soft-drink or ketchup bottle and the two pencils on the table.*

➤ Today you will make and use some simple musical instruments. Lay the first block of wood on a piece of sandpaper.

➤ Trace the wood onto the sandpaper.

➤ Cut the sandpaper and glue it to one side of the block of wood.

➤ Follow the same procedure for the second block of wood. Place the blocks of wood beside the pencils and the soft-drink bottle.

➤ Stretch the four rubber bands around the small box. Place the box on the table.

◆ THINGS PEOPLE DO ◆

Playing Musical Instruments

Do you play a musical instrument? Would you like to learn to play one? It takes practice to play a musical instrument well. People who can play an instrument like the piano or the flute have practiced for a long time.

We can play some instruments by blowing into them. We can play other instruments by tapping or hitting them. A third kind of instrument is played by plucking strings. Which kind do you think would be easiest to play?

The Bible tells about many kinds of musical instruments. David played the harp. The priests in the temple played cymbals and trumpets and harps. Do you know what musical instrument Gideon and his army used? How did all these people use their musical instruments? They used them to bring glory to God.

"Praise him with the sound of the trumpet: praise him with the psaltery and harp.

Praise him with the timbrel and dance: praise him with stringed instruments and organs.

Praise him upon the loud cymbals: praise him upon the high sounding cymbals."

Psalm 150:3-5

156

Teaching the Lesson

Sound-Making Activity, page 156

➤ **Read the first two paragraphs on page 156 to find out three ways to make sounds with instruments.** *(blowing into them, tapping or hitting, and plucking strings)*

➤ **Do you know a fourth way to make sound?** *If your child does not know, rub your hands together as a clue. (rubbing)*

➤ Try each one of the "instruments" on the table.

➤ Decide which instrument shows making sound by blowing *(bottle)*, tapping or hitting *(pencils)*, plucking *(box with rubber bands)*, and rubbing *(sand blocks)*.

➤ Choose an instrument to "play." I will choose a different one. Let's "perform" "Mary Had a Little Lamb."

➤ **Which kind of instrument do you think is the easiest to play?**

Text Activity, page 156 (cont.)

➤ **Read the last paragraph of page 156 to find out what musical instrument David in the Bible played.** *(the harp)*

➤ *Show the picture of David playing his harp for King Saul.* **How is music made on a harp—by blowing air, hitting, plucking strings, or rubbing?** *(plucking strings)*

➤ **Read I Samuel 16:23 to find out what happened when David played his harp before King Saul.** *("Saul was refreshed, and was well, and the evil spirit departed from him.")*

God gave David the ability to play the harp well, and the beautiful music soothed the soul of Saul. (BATs: 3b Mind, 3c Emotional control) Remind your child that God has given each of us special abilities. Invite him to suggest ways that Christians can use their musical abilities in service for the Lord. *(Answers will vary.)* (BAT: 3a Self-concept)

➤ **Read Judges 7:16 to find out what kind of musical instrument Gideon and the men in his army used.** *(trumpets)*

Read together Psalm 150:3-5 on page 156. Remind your child that the Lord is pleased when our songs honor and praise Him. (BATs: 7b Exaltation of Christ, 7c Praise)

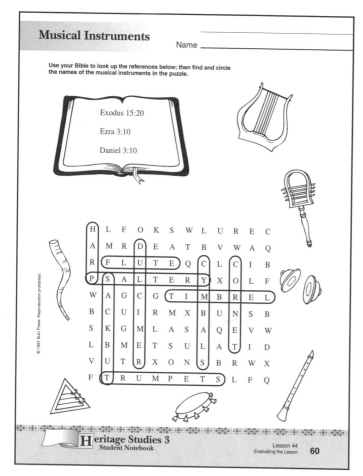

Musical Instruments

Name _____

Use your Bible to look up the references below; then find and circle the names of the musical instruments in the puzzle.

Exodus 15:20

Ezra 3:10

Daniel 3:10

```
H L F O K S W L U R E C
A M R D E A T B V W A Q
R F L U T E Q C L C I B
P S A L T E R Y X O L F
W A G C G T I M B R E L
B C U I R M X B U N S B
S K G M L A S A Q E V W
V B M E T S U L A T I D
F U T R X O N S B R W X
F T R U M P E T S L F Q
```

Heritage Studies 3
Student Notebook

Lesson 44
Evaluating the Lesson **60**

Evaluating the Lesson

Word-Search Activity, Notebook page 60

➤ Read the directions on Notebook page 60.

➤ Complete the page. *(Exodus 15:20—timbrel; Ezra 3:10—trumpets, cymbals; Daniel 3:10—cornet, flute, harp, sackbut, psaltery, dulcimer)*

━━ Going Beyond ━━

Enrichment

Encourage your child to listen to a recording of several musical instruments and try to identify each instrument by its sound.

Additional Teacher Information

Timbrel is sometimes translated in the Bible as *tabret* or *tambourine;* other times it is described as a drum.

The harp is sometimes translated in the Bible as *psaltery,* sometimes as *viol,* and sometimes as *lyre.*

The trumpet was usually made of the horn of a ram or goat. *Trumpet* and *cornet* in the Bible are synonymous. In Numbers 10:2, Moses is commanded to prepare two trumpets of silver.

The flute mentioned in Daniel 3 means *whistle* and could refer to any wooden instrument that was blown.

LESSON 45
Worshiping in Song

Text, pages 157-59
Notebook, page 61

━━ Preview ━━

Main Ideas

• People communicate in many ways.
• Singing is a part of worshiping God.
• Many different people and groups contributed to American culture.

Objectives

• Sing "Pick a Bale of Cotton"
• Sing "Go Down, Moses"
• Write about ways the Lord can be served

Materials

• *HERITAGE STUDIES Listening Cassette A*
• A Bible
• *Egermeier's Bible Story Book* (optional)*
• Supplement, page S8: a cotton boll
• Supplement, page S10: a bale of cotton
• Supplement, page S11: "Pick a Bale of Cotton"

Day 1

━━ Lesson ━━

Introducing the Lesson

Singing and Pantomiming Activity, page 157

➤ **Read the first paragraph of page 157 to find out from whom some of our favorite folksongs come.** *(slaves)*

➤ **Which slaves sang the song "Pick a Bale of Cotton"?** *(slaves that picked cotton in the fields)*

➤ *Show the picture of the cotton boll and then the picture of the bale of cotton.*

A bale is a large mound of cotton, banded together and weighing about five hundred pounds. One bale of cotton is about the size of a large home refrigerator. (*NOTE:* Cotton bales measure about 56"×28"×45". Six yards of jute or other strong bagging material covers each bale, which is then bound with six steel ties.)

Folksongs came from many different groups of people. Some of the folksongs we think of as favorites today came from the slaves. The black people in the South made up songs to help them bear their work and sorrow. "Pick a Bale of Cotton" was one of these songs. Can you guess which slaves sang this one?

Some of these work songs are still popular today. But we remember more a second kind of song the slaves made up. These songs told about people from the Bible. The slaves identified with the hard life of some of the people in these Bible stories. One of their favorite stories was about Moses. God used Moses to lead his people out of slavery. Why do you think slaves liked this story?

We call these slave songs *spirituals*. They tell about the slaves' faith in God to protect and deliver them. Perhaps you know some spirituals. Songs like "Swing Low, Sweet Chariot," "When the Saints Go Marching In," and "Nobody Knows the Trouble I've Seen" are well known. These songs were first sung by groups of slaves who gathered to worship God.

157

➤ *Show your child the words to "Pick a Bale of Cotton."*
➤ **Read the words.**
➤ **Do you think it would take a long time to pick enough cotton to make a bale?**
➤ Listen as I play "Pick a Bale of Cotton" from the listening cassette.
➤ Let's sing along as I play the recording again.
➤ **Why did the slaves like to sing as they worked?** *(Answers will vary but will probably include that singing helped to make the work seem easier and go faster.)* This lesson tells about another type of song that the slaves sang.

Teaching the Lesson

Text Activity, page 157 (cont.)

➤ **Read the second and third paragraphs on page 157 to find out the name given to another type of song that slaves sang.** *(spirituals)*
➤ **Why did the slaves especially like the story of Moses and his leading God's people out of slavery?** *(Answers will vary but will probably include that the story gave them hope about being free someday.)*

 A simplified version of this biblical account is given in *Egermeier's Bible Story Book*. You may prefer to use it.

➤ **Can you remember what plagues or trials the Lord used to try to persuade Pharaoh to let His people go?** *(Answers will vary. See Exodus 7-10.)*
➤ **Read Exodus 11:4-5 to find out the last thing the Lord was going to cause to happen to Pharaoh and all the people in the land.** *(death of the first-born child in each family)*
➤ **Read Exodus 11:10 to find out whether Pharaoh agreed to let God's people go when he heard of God's plan.** *(no)*
➤ **Read Exodus 12:28-31, 37 to find out what happened next to Pharaoh and the children of Israel.** *(God killed the first-born of every family who had not obeyed His commands. Even Pharaoh's first-born died. Then Pharaoh allowed God's people to leave.)*
➤ **Read Exodus 12:40 to find out how long the children of Israel were slaves in Egypt.** *(430 years)*

Ask your child whether he thinks the children of Israel ever got discouraged, wondering whether they would ever be freed. Remind him that God promises to take care of His children always. God grants courage and peace to those who faithfully trust Him, no matter what the circumstances. (BATs: 6b Prayer, 7c Praise, 7d Contentment, 8a Faith in God's promises)

Go Down, Moses

When Israel was in Egypt land,
"Let my people go."
Oppressed so hard they could not stand,
"Let my people go."

Chorus:
Go down, Moses,
Way down in Egypt land,
Tell ol' Pharaoh to let my people go!

"Thus saith the Lord," bold Moses said,
"Let my people go.
If not, I'll strike your first-born dead!
Let my people go."

The Lord told Moses what to do,
"Let my people go,"
To lead the children of Israel through.
"Let my people go."

158

Lowell Mason
1792-1872

Young Lowell tapped lightly on the door and then entered his friend's shop. George, a little older than Lowell, was bent over an organ. Lowell sat down at a dusty piano in the corner and picked out a tune that he had created. He loved to watch George fix these old organs and pianos, but more than that, he loved music and beautiful songs.

Along with his love of music, Lowell Mason loved the Lord. As he became older, he combined his interest in music with his love for the Lord. By the age of sixteen, Lowell was directing his church choir. A few years later, he wrote his first song. Lowell also directed a band, teaching himself to play different instruments.

As an adult, Mason was one of the first music teachers in the Boston school system. By the end of his life, Lowell Mason had written the music for over one thousand hymns. Some of his most famous hymns are "Nearer, My God, to Thee," "There Is a Fountain," and "My Faith Looks Up to Thee."

159

Day 2

Singing Activity, page 158

➤ Listen as I play "Go Down, Moses" from the listening cassette.
➤ **Read the words of the song on page 158.**
➤ **Do you remember where the children of Israel were going?** *(to Canaan, which was also called "the Promised Land")*
➤ **Read Exodus 5:1-2 to see what Pharaoh thought about God.**

> Remind your child that even though Pharaoh was the ruler of Egypt, he was not the ruler of the world and mankind. God is the highest ruler. Only God has all power. (BATs: 6a Bible study, 7b Exaltation of Christ; Bible Promise: I. God as Master)

➤ Let's sing the song together as I play the recording again.

Text Activity, page 159

➤ **Read the first paragraph on page 159 to find what Lowell Mason loved to watch his friend fix.** *(pianos and organs)*
➤ **Read the rest of the page to find out how Lowell Mason combined his interest in music with his love for the Lord**. *(He wrote hymns.)* Each one of us has special talents and gifts that we should use to serve the Lord. (BATs: 2b Servanthood, 3a Self-concept)
➤ **How many hymns did Lowell Mason write?** *(over one thousand)*
➤ Name some of the hymns Lowell Mason wrote. *("Nearer, My God, to Thee," "There Is a Fountain," and "My Faith Looks Up to Thee")*

> You may want to take time now or later to lead your child in singing one of these hymns.

Service

Name _____

Draw a picture of a job or activity that you do or like.

On the lines below, explain how you can serve the Lord through this activity.

_____
_____
_____
_____
_____
_____
_____
_____
_____
_____
_____
_____

Heritage Studies 3
Student Notebook

Lesson 45
Evaluating the Lesson

61

Evaluating the Lesson

Notebook Activity, page 61

➤ Remember that Lowell Mason used one of his favorite activities, playing music, to serve the Lord.
➤ Read the instructions on Notebook page 61.
➤ Complete the page.

Going Beyond

Enrichment

Give your child the words for the spiritual "Swing Low, Sweet Chariot." (*NOTE:* See Appendix, page A40.) If possible, also have available a recording of this song that your child may listen to as he tries to memorize the words of "Swing Low, Sweet Chariot."

Additional Teacher Information

In 1795, Bishop Francis Asbury worked closely with the African Americans, teaching and helping them in their need. He was well liked by those he helped. Eventually, Bishop Asbury became known as a type of Moses, providing deliverance for a troubled people. It was during this time that the song "Go Down, Moses" developed.

Like most spirituals, "Go Down, Moses" changed over the course of time. As the abolitionist movement progressed, many of those participants who helped fugitive slaves became associated with the song. Harriet Tubman was known by many African Americans as "Moses" for her part in the Underground Railroad. After the Civil War, many of the minstrels, particularly the Fisk Jubilee Singers, popularized the song, performing it for distinguished guests, such as President Grant and Queen Victoria.

LESSON 46
Marching Along

Text, pages 160-64
Notebook, page 62

Preview

Main Ideas

- People communicate in many ways.
- Histories of regions form a national heritage.
- Songs of war stir the citizens' national pride.

Objectives

- Make a drum or a bugle
- Sing "I Wish I Was in Dixie"
- Sing "The Battle Hymn of the Republic"
- Use encyclopedias to find information

Materials

- *HERITAGE STUDIES Listening Cassette A*

 You will need the materials to make either the bugle or the drum for this lesson.

- Drum supplies
  An empty coffee can or an oatmeal canister*
  A piece of vinyl or cloth large enough to cover the opening for the coffee can*
  A large rubber band or 12" length of string*
  Construction paper (optional)
- Bugle supplies
  Transparent packaging tape*
  A mouthpiece from a musical instrument (optional)*
  A 12"×12" piece of poster board*
  A stapler
- A "B" volume of an encyclopedia*
- A "C" volume of an encyclopedia, containing the entry for "Civil War"*

 You will need to select a page from the encyclopedia that gives information about the Civil War before beginning the lesson. See the Teaching the Lesson section for details.

◆ LEARNING HOW ◆

To Make a Musical Instrument

1. Gather one of the following sets of materials.
   a. an empty coffee can or an oatmeal canister, a piece of vinyl or cloth to cover the opening, and string or a rubber band
   b. tape, poster board, and a mouthpiece from a brass instrument, if possible

2. Use the first set of materials to make a drum. Stretch the vinyl tightly over the opening of the can. Fasten it in place by wrapping it with the rubber band or string. Tap the vinyl with your hand or the end of your pencil. How does it sound?

3. Make a bugle using the second set of materials. Shape the poster board into a cone and tape or staple the seam. If you have a mouthpiece from a brass instrument, place the mouthpiece into the smaller end of the cone. Blow into the mouthpiece or the small end of the cone. How does your instrument sound?

4. The Union and Confederate armies used the drum and the bugle. What do you think they used them for? How can you find out?

162

 The text pages will be taught out of order in this lesson.

Day 1

Lesson

Introducing the Lesson

Learning How Activity, page 162

➤ **Read Step 1 on page 162.**

➤ **If you will be making the drum, read Step 2.**

Have available construction paper, tape, and crayons if your child would like to decorate his drum before securing the cloth to the top.

➤ **If you will be making the bugle, read Step 3.**

If your child would like to decorate his bugle, encourage him to color designs while the poster board is flat. To ensure greater durability, staple the wide end of the cone before taping the seam with the packaging tape. If you have a mouthpiece from a brass instrument, tell your child to insert it in the small end of his cone.

➤ Try playing your instrument.

Use an encyclopedia to answer the following questions.

1. In which encyclopedia volume would you find an entry for *bugle*? __B__

2. Read the entry for *bugle*. Write a simple definition for *bugle*. *Answers will* *vary; a wind instrument consisting of a curved tube made of brass or copper.*

3. How is music made with a bugle? *by blowing into the mouthpiece*

4. Did the earliest bugles have keys to push? *no* How were different tones made? *by changing the tension in the lips*

5. How many valves do most modern bugles have? *three*

6. How did armies use bugles? *to give instructions to large groups*

7. List any bugle calls that are mentioned. *Possible answers include taps* *and reveille.*

8. Draw or trace a picture of a bugle.

© 1997 BJU Press. Reproduction prohibited.

Heritage Studies 3
Student Notebook

Lesson 46
Introducing the Lesson

62

Singing in Wartime

Many songs of America are not light and happy. Song-writers wrote more serious songs when the people wanted them. Patriotic songs told about liberty, freedom, and loyalty to the land. War songs were more serious yet. They called men to fight for their country and their cause. What two groups needed war songs in 1860?

The war song for the South was written in 1859, two years before the war began. Dan Emmett wrote the song on a cold winter weekend. He was a traveling entertainer, and he needed a new song. He remembered how his friends wished to be in the warm South, or Dixie's land, when it was cold outside. Emmett performed the new song on Monday. It was a hit.

Soon people all over the country were singing Emmett's song. The people of the South especially liked the song. It made them proud of their Southern land. When Confederate soldiers found that it was easy to march to, "Dixie" became their favorite song. Dan Emmett was a Northerner, loyal to the Union. How do you think he felt when his song became so important to the Confederacy?

160

Encyclopedia Activity, page 162 (cont.)

➤ **Read Step 4.** Try to answer the questions.

➤ Name the type of reference book that could help answer these questions. *(encyclopedia)*

➤ **Which words could you look up in order to find the answers to these questions?** *(Possible answers are* bugle, drum, Civil War, Union, Confederate, *and* soldiers.*)*

➤ *Give your child volume "C" of an encyclopedia.* Look up "Civil War."

Show the amount of information that the encyclopedia includes about the American Civil War or the War Between the States. Share the pre-selected portion with your child. Ask the following types of questions regarding the use of the information on the page.

- **What do the bold type words tell you?**
- **What names of important people are mentioned here?**
- **What names of important towns are mentioned here?**
- **What kinds of information do the pictures give you?**
- **Are any graphs or charts included? If so, what do they tell you?**

If you are using a computerized encyclopedia, you will need to vary some of the questions listed.

Encyclopedia Activity, Notebook page 62

➤ Read the directions on Notebook page 62.
➤ Complete the Notebook page.
➤ *Check Notebook page 62 together orally.* You will learn more about war songs in this lesson.

Day ²

Teaching the Lesson

Text Activity, page 160

➤ You may march around the room and play your instrument as I play "I Wish I Was in Dixie" from the listening cassette.

The name Dixie *refers to the states south of the Mason-Dixon Line or "Dixie's land."*

➤ **Read page 160 to find out who wrote "Dixie" and when it was written.** *(Dan Emmett wrote "Dixie" in 1859.)*

➤ **What war was being fought in 1861?** *(the American Civil War or the War Between the States)*

Dixie

I wish I was in the land of cotton,
Old times there are not forgotten,
Look away! Look away! Look away! Dixie Land.
In Dixie Land where I was born in,
Early on one frosty mornin',
Look away! Look away! Look away! Dixie Land.

Chorus:

Then I wish I was in Dixie,
Hooray! Hooray!
In Dixie Land, I'll take my stand to live and die in Dixie;
Away, away, away down south in Dixie,
Away, away, away down south in Dixie.

There's buckwheat cakes and cornbread batter,
Makes you fat or a little fatter;
Look away! Look away! Look away! Dixie Land.
Then hoe it down and scratch your gravel,
To Dixie's Land I'm bound to travel,
Look away! Look away! Look away! Dixie Land.

161

The song that most people think of as the war song of the North was not even written when the war began. That is, the words were not written. The tune had been around for a long time. At the beginning of the American Civil War, soldiers sang "John Brown's Body" to the tune. The song was about a man some people in the North thought was a hero. But the words of the song did not fit the tune.

Julia Ward Howe heard Union soldiers singing "John Brown's Body." A friend said, "That tune needs better words. Julia, you should write new words for it." She promised to try. That night as she listened to more soldiers tramp past her window, she thought of new words. And she quickly wrote them down on a scrap of paper. Soon Union soldiers everywhere were singing Howe's words to the old tune.

As the years went by, the things people sang about changed. But people sang some of the old favorites over and over again. The old favorite songs are national songs because they are part of America's heritage. Today people may not know the stories of the national songs. But they know when a song makes them happy or when a song moves them to love and serve God better. These are the songs America loves to sing.

163

You may want to allow your child to reread page 148 to familiarize himself with the beginning of the War Between the States.

➤ **What two groups needed war songs during that time?** *(the North, called the Union, and the South, called the Confederacy)*

➤ **Why were war songs important?** *(Answers will vary. They called men to fight and encouraged people to support the cause of the war.)*

➤ **Which side, the North or the South, adopted "Dixie" as its favorite song?** *(the South)*

➤ **Was Dan Emmett, the composer, on the side of the South, the Confederacy?** *(no)* (*NOTE:* Dan Emmett wrote a version of "Dixie" for the Union, but it never caught on.)

Song Activity, page 161

➤ Follow along with the words on page 161 as I play the song again from the listening cassette.

➤ Let's sing the song together.

Text Activity, page 163

➤ The war song for the North was written by a woman in the North. **Read page 163 to find out this woman's name.** *(Julia Ward Howe)*

➤ **Did Mrs. Howe write the tune of the song?** *(no)*

➤ **What other American Civil War song used the same tune?** *("John Brown's Body")*

(*NOTE:* This song was about a man who killed people and destroyed property in his opposition to slavery. He was convicted of treason.)

➤ Listen as I play "John Brown's Body" from the listening cassette.

➤ **Have you ever heard this tune before?**

➤ **What was the complaint often heard about "John Brown's Body"?** *(The tune needed better words.)*

➤ **What inspired Mrs. Howe to write new words to this tune?** *(A friend encouraged her. Mrs. Howe heard the soldiers marching by.)*

The Battle Hymn of the Republic

Mine eyes have seen the glory of the coming of the Lord;
He is trampling out the vintage where the grapes of wrath
    are stored;
He hath loosed the fateful lightning of his terrible swift sword;
His truth is marching on.

Chorus:

Glory, glory, hallelujah!
Glory, glory, hallelujah!
Glory, glory, hallelujah!
His truth is marching on.

I have seen Him in the watchfires of a hundred circling camps;
They have builded Him an altar in the evening dews and damps;
I can read His righteous sentence by the dim and flaring lamps;
His day is marching on.

He has sounded forth the trumpet that shall never sound retreat;
He is sifting out the hearts of men before His judgment seat.
O be swift, my soul, to answer Him! Be jubilant, my feet!
Our God is marching on.

In the beauty of the lilies Christ was born across the sea,
With a glory in His bosom that transfigures you and me;
As He died to make men holy, let us die to make men free,
While God is marching on.

164

Song Activity, page 164

➤ *Play "The Battle Hymn of the Republic" from the listening cassette.*

➤ **Do you know the title of this song?**

➤ Read page 164 to find the title of this song that **Julia Ward Howe wrote for the North.** *("The Battle Hymn of the Republic")*

➤ **What do the words "His truth is marching on" mean?** *(God's truth and power will endure forever.)*

➤ Look at the third verse of the song. **What do you think is meant by "He is sifting out the hearts of men before His judgment seat"?**

It refers to the final judgment day when Christ will open the Book of Life and send to eternal punishment anyone whose name is not written in the book. (BATs: 1a Understanding Jesus Christ, 1b Repentance and faith)

Julia Ward Howe wrote "The Battle Hymn of the Republic" in 1861. She wrote out the words to this song one night after hearing the soldiers march by outside her window. The next day she copied her new song and sent it to the *Atlantic Monthly,* who paid her ten dollars for the song. They entitled it "The Battle Hymn of the Republic" and printed it on the front page of their magazine. It is said that when President Lincoln first heard Mrs. Howe's song, he cried and said, "Sing that prayer again." "The Battle

Hymn of the Republic" has often been called the greatest song of the American Civil War. It gives glory to God and courage and hope to those who trust in Him. (BATs: 7b Exaltation of Christ, 7c Praise)

Evaluating the Lesson

Oral Evaluation

➤ **Which song was the Civil War song of the South?** *("Dixie")*

➤ **Which song was the war song for the North?** *("The Battle Hymn of the Republic")*

➤ I will read some items associated with either the South and "Dixie" or the North and "Battle Hymn." Play your instrument and sing (or toot) the line "I wish I was in Dixie" for each item related to the South and "Dixie."

➤ Play your instrument and sing (or toot) the line "Glory, glory, hallelujah" for each item related to the North and "Battle Hymn."

- Dan Emmett *("Dixie")*
- the Union *("Battle Hymn")*
- "John Brown's Body" *("Battle Hymn")*
- traveling entertainer *("Dixie")*
- written after the American Civil War began *("Battle Hymn")*
- Julia Ward Howe *("Battle Hymn")*
- the Confederacy *("Dixie")*
- written before the American Civil War began *("Dixie")*

▬ Going Beyond ▬

Enrichment

Show your child military pictures and memorabilia of his relatives and/or friends.

Make available for your child a recording of military songs for each of the main branches of the armed services.

"Off We Go into the Wild Blue Yonder"—Air Force

"The Caissons Go Rolling Along"—Army

"Anchors Aweigh"—Navy

"Marine's Hymn" or "From the Halls of
    Montezuma"—Marines

Additional Teacher Information

Dan Emmett started the first minstrel show in 1842, and "Jolly Dan" was one of the most famous minstrels. He knew the slave dialects well and used them in his singing and storytelling. "Dixie" was first heard in the South in New Orleans in the late 1850s where the performer was asked to sing the song eight times in one show.

Some say that the term *Dixie* came from a Mr. Dixie, a farmer in New York, who offered shelter and kind treatment to runaway slaves. Others say that "Dixie land" is a slave term for a region of peace and plenty, a place all slaves wished to go someday.

Julia Ward Howe was from a wealthy family. Her ancestors were greatly involved in the heritage of America. Grandfather Ward was a colonel under George Washington; her great-uncle was the famous "Swamp Fox," Francis Marion; her four great-grandfathers were all governors, and one of them signed the Declaration of Independence. Henry Wadsworth Longfellow introduced Julia to his friend "Chev," better known as Dr. Samuel Gridley Howe. Julia and Chev were married, reared six children, and were both actively involved in the causes of the day. Dr. Howe worked with the soldiers on the battlefields during the American Civil War and later founded what came to be known as the Perkins Institute for the Blind. Julia organized the first women's clubs to sew and cook for the soldiers. Together, the Howes edited *The Commonwealth,* a Free-Soil newspaper to advocate the abolishment of slavery. After the war, Mrs. Howe continued her work with women's clubs, especially working for women's suffrage.

In 1872 Julia Ward Howe made the first suggestion for the observance of Mother's Day in the United States. For many years, Mrs. Howe held an annual Mother's Day meeting in Boston on June 2.

North Against South

In this chapter, your child will study the events of the American Civil War, starting with the firing on Fort Sumter and ending with the surrender at Appomattox. As he learns about the leaders for the North and the South, he will also read about and talk about the soldiers and the civilians whose lives were forever changed by the war. Use of the TimeLine Snapshots and an emphasis on photographs, journals, letters, and historic documents of the era will help your child to think of the events as more than isolated facts and dates.

Materials

The following materials must be obtained or prepared before the presentation of the lesson. These items are labeled with an asterisk (*) in each lesson and in the Materials List in the Supplement. For further information see the individual lessons.

- Appendix, pages A41-A49 (Lesson 47)
- Appendix, page A50 (Lesson 48)
- A variety of dried fruit (Lesson 49)
- Appendix, page A51 (Lesson 49)
- A magazine with photographs (Lesson 50)
- A square of blue or gray construction paper or cloth (Lesson 51)
- An addressed envelope (Lesson 51)
- 36 beans or buttons (Lesson 52)
- Appendix, page A52 (Lesson 52)

9

North
Against South

LESSON 47
North Against South

Text, pages 166-69
Notebook, page 63

━━━━━ Lesson ━━━━━

Introducing the Lesson

> You may want to spend a few minutes reviewing the events from Chapter 7 that led up to the Civil War. Review the list of differences between the North and South that was made in Lesson 41. Another form of review would be for your child to re-read silently pages 142-48.

Discussion

➤ The Union army fought for the North. **What does the word *union* mean?** *(a group of things that are united or together)*

When the word is capitalized, it means the United States of America or those states that remained loyal to the United States government.

➤ Attach the *Union* nameplate to the top half of the door.

➤ Two other names for the Union are the *North* and the *Yankees*. Attach these nameplates to the top half of the door.

➤ Attach the Union flag to the top half of the door.

➤ **Which side did the Confederate army represent?** *(the South)*

➤ **What states made up the *Confederacy*?** *(The Confederate states are those that left the United States to form a new country.)* The word *Confederacy* is another name for the Confederate States of America.

➤ **Do you know what other names could be used for the *Confederacy*?** Two other names are the *South* and the *Rebels*.

➤ Attach the *Confederacy* nameplate to the bottom half of the door.

➤ Attach the *South* and the *Rebels* nameplates to the bottom half of the door.

➤ Attach the Confederate flag to the bottom half of the door.

━━━━━ Preview ━━━━━

Main Ideas
- The North and the South each had certain advantages.
- Journals provide much information about the American Civil War.

Objectives
- Draw conclusions based on charts
- Identify true and false statements about the American Civil War

Materials
- Appendix, page A41: the maps with the capitals*
- Appendix, pages A42-A43: Union and Confederate flags*
- Appendix, page A44: Lincoln/Davis nameplates*
- Yarn, string, or ribbon
- Appendix, page A45: Union/Confederacy nameplates*
- Appendix, page A46: North/Yankees nameplates*
- Appendix, page A47: South/Rebels nameplates*
- Appendix, page A48: A Nation Divided nameplate*
- Appendix, page A49: Fort Sumter*

> All of the Appendix pages may be colored if you desire. Cut apart the two maps with the capitals.

Notes

A space on a wall or the back of a door in the schoolroom should be set up as follows for this chapter. Divide the space or door in half horizontally with yarn, string, or ribbon. Place the title, *A Nation Divided,* on the upper half of the door. Your child will place the Confederate and Union flags, the nameplates, and the Fort Sumter page on the door during this lesson. The other parts will be added throughout the chapter, culminating in Lesson 52 with the Appomattox figure and the subtitle, *A Nation Reunited. (NOTE:* To simplify, this area, the wall space or the back of the door, will be referred to as *the door* in the lessons.)

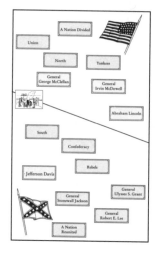

Inside Fort Sumter
Charleston, South Carolina
April 12, 1861

Inside Fort Sumter as it is now

The soldiers in blue coats looked out at Charleston. The city was quiet. The water was quiet. Soon the sun would come up, and soon the soldiers would know what the South planned to do.

Suddenly, a red flash swept across the dark sky. It made an eerie whistle as it went, and sparks shot from it. Then an awful roar, like a thunderclap, shook the fort. A Confederate shell burst over the small group of Union soldiers.

Major Anderson put out his hand to steady himself for the blast. He knew what that shot meant. There was no hope for peace now. The war between North and South had begun.

Fort Sumter after the bombardment

148

The firing at Fort Sumter did not kill one soldier on either side. The city of Charleston was not damaged at all. Most of the people in the United States thought the whole war would be over in three months.

It was more than three months, though, before the first big battle of the Civil War even began. President Abraham Lincoln had called for seventy-five thousand volunteers to help fight for the North. The men had come. They were training for war.

Look at the chart. Did the Confederacy or the Union have more free people? Who had more miles of railroad? Which side had more factories? Who produced more firearms? Why do you think the Union thought the Confederacy could be beaten quickly?

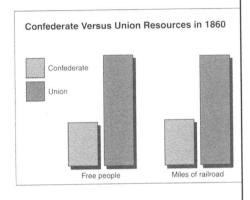

Confederate Versus Union Resources in 1860

Confederate
Union

Free people   Miles of railroad

166

Review, page 148

➤ Read silently page 148 to review what happened at Fort Sumter.

➤ Tell what you remember about Fort Sumter from Lesson 41. *(Answers will vary but should include that Northern soldiers, after raising the Union flag at Fort Sumter off the coast of Charleston, South Carolina, were fired upon by Southern soldiers, and the war between the North and the South was begun.)*

➤ **What was the war called?** *(the War Between the States or the American Civil War)*

➤ Attach the picture of Fort Sumter on the left side of the door on the dividing line.

➤ Name the president of the Union. *(Abraham Lincoln)*

➤ Attach the *Abraham Lincoln* nameplate to the Union side of the door.

➤ The Confederacy chose Jefferson Davis to be its president. Attach the *Jefferson Davis* nameplate to the Confederacy side of the door.

Day 2

Teaching the Lesson

Remember to discuss the questions in the textbook with your child as he reads the page.

Text Discussion, page 166

➤ **Read page 166 to find out whether the Union army thought it could beat the Confederate army.** *(yes)*

➤ **Why did the people in the United States think the whole war would be over quickly?** *(No one had been killed in the firing upon Fort Sumter, and the city of Charleston had not been damaged.)*

(NOTE: The defenders of Fort Sumter fought for thirty-four hours, but on April 13 they were forced to surrender. At noon, Sunday, April 14, 1861, the Union flag was lowered. The only casualty was a gunner who was killed when a charge of gunpowder exploded during the last salute to the flag. It was not raised over the fort again until April 14, 1865.)

The Union had many advantages. It had more men. It had more factories to make things an army would need. What things might these factories make? And the Union had more ways to move the soldiers and the supplies to the places that needed them. Why do you think this was important?

But the Confederate States had some advantages too. Some of the best military leaders were from the South. Do you think these men stayed in the United States Army when their states left the Union? They did not. They left the Union army to become leaders in the Confederate army.

These leaders knew that something else would help their side. To make the Confederate States part of the United States again, the Union army would have to *invade*. That means the Union would have to send its army onto Confederate land. It would need more men and more supplies to invade than the Confederate army would need to protect the Southern land.

Factories   Firearms produced

167

This is how a map of the country looked in May 1861. Eleven states had left the Union and joined the Confederate States of America. How many states were still part of the Union?

The leaders in the new Confederacy finally decided the city of Richmond would be their *capital*. The capital of a country is the home of the president and other leaders. It is where they work to make the laws. Can you find the Union capital?

168

Text Discussion, page 167

➤ **Read page 167 to find out what advantages the Union and Confederate States had.** *(Union—more men, more factories; Confederate—some of the best military leaders, being able to stay on their own land to fight)*

➤ **How could fighting on one's own land be both an advantage and a disadvantage?** *(Answers will vary.)*

The soldiers would fight harder for their own land, but the fighting would cause damage to their homes, farms, livestock, roads, and bridges. The Union's advantages of more men and more factories would be offset by their having to ***invade*** or go into Confederate land.

➤ **What might the Union factories have made?** *(weapons, uniforms, means of transportation, food)*

➤ **Why was it important to have more ways to move soldiers and supplies?** *(The soldiers could fight in one place and then be moved to another place to fight again. The supplies could be delivered from the factories to the soldiers.)*

Map-Reading Activity, page 168

➤ **Read page 168, looking at the map to find out how many states had joined the Confederacy and how many were still in the Union by May 1861.** *(Confederacy—11; Union—24)*

(*NOTE:* Missouri, Kentucky, Maryland, and Delaware were border states that did not secede. West Virginia became a border state when it was formed in 1863.)

➤ Put one finger on the Union capital and another finger on the Confederate capital. The two capitals were about one hundred miles apart.

➤ Attach the appropriate capital sign to each section of the door.

◆ THINGS PEOPLE DO ◆

Keeping Journals

Much of what modern people know about the American Civil War comes from journals. Journals of soldiers, journals of wives who waited at home, journals of freed slaves, and journals of preachers. From those pages we learn what life was like in Lincoln's day. One soldier wrote:

A Southern wife tells of different hardships: "In the street a barrel of flour sells for one hundred and fifty dollars. . . . Mrs. Davis says . . . they are going to dispense with their carriage and horses."

Do you keep a journal? What does it tell of your times? Why do you think fewer people keep journals now?

169

Day 3

Text Discussion, page 169

➤ **What is a *journal*?** *(a personal record or account of daily events)*
➤ **Read about keeping journals on page 169 to find at least one thing about life during the American Civil War.** *(Answers will vary.)*
➤ **Listen as I read the quotation from the soldier's journal.**
➤ **Have you ever been cold and wet like the soldier or stood near a smoky fire?**
➤ **Read aloud the last two paragraphs on page 169.**
➤ **Do you know what the Davises were going to have to do with their carriage and horses?** *(sell them)* **Why?** *(to get money for the more basic necessities of life like food, which was very expensive)*

➤ **Were those good times or bad times?** *(bad times)*

Some first-person records indicate that a "Great Revival" swept over the Confederate army in the opening months of 1863. One young soldier, Benjamin Jones, wrote the following:

> I hear that a great religious spirit and revival is spreading throughout Lee's army, and there are evidences of it here, and in other camps about Richmond. . . . Many of the openly sinful are growing more temperate and reverent in their conversation and regard for religious things. There is less cursing and profligacy [reckless wastefulness], and much less of card playing in our Company.

➤ **Why do people often turn to the Lord during hard times?** *(They realize that they need help.)*

Discuss with your child what a person needs to realize to be saved. *(that Christ died for him)* (BAT: 1b Repentance and faith; Bible Promise: A. Liberty from Sin)

➤ **Do you know why quotation marks are used in paragraph two on page 169?**

The quotation marks show that the words inside the marks are the exact words—quotations—from the journals.

➤ **Why do you think there are three periods in the middle of some of the sentences in the journal entries?**

Series of periods inside a quotation are called ***ellipses.*** The marks let the reader know that some words not necessary to a person's understanding of the quotation are left out. One of the best ways to study history is to read the words of the people who lived during the time.

➤ **When will journals written today be considered history?** *(Answers will vary.)* Help your child to understand that once an event is over, it becomes part of history.

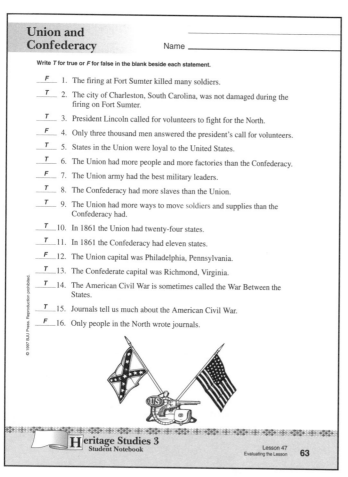

Union and Confederacy

Name _____

Write *T* for true or *F* for false in the blank beside each statement.

_F_ 1. The firing at Fort Sumter killed many soldiers.

_T_ 2. The city of Charleston, South Carolina, was not damaged during the firing on Fort Sumter.

_T_ 3. President Lincoln called for volunteers to fight for the North.

_F_ 4. Only three thousand men answered the president's call for volunteers.

_T_ 5. States in the Union were loyal to the United States.

_T_ 6. The Union had more people and more factories than the Confederacy.

_F_ 7. The Union army had the best military leaders.

_T_ 8. The Confederacy had more slaves than the Union.

_T_ 9. The Union had more ways to move soldiers and supplies than the Confederacy had.

_T_ 10. In 1861 the Union had twenty-four states.

_T_ 11. In 1861 the Confederacy had eleven states.

_F_ 12. The Union capital was Philadelphia, Pennsylvania.

_T_ 13. The Confederate capital was Richmond, Virginia.

_T_ 14. The American Civil War is sometimes called the War Between the States.

_T_ 15. Journals tell us much about the American Civil War.

_F_ 16. Only people in the North wrote journals.

© 1997 BJU Press. Reproduction prohibited.

Heritage Studies 3
Student Notebook

Lesson 47
Evaluating the Lesson **63**

Evaluating the Lesson

True/False Activity,
Notebook page 63

➤ Read the instructions on Notebook page 63.
➤ Complete the page.

━━━ Going Beyond ━━━

Enrichment

Provide handwriting paper, colored construction paper, a stapler, colored felt-tip pens, and crayons for your child to use in making his own journal. Encourage him to write journal entries as if he were living in the times of the American Civil War.

Additional Teacher Information

Historians credit the South's early military successes to superior organization and training. Although the North had the benefits of arms, factories, and a standing army, each benefit had its accompanying drawback. Many of the arms dated back to the Revolutionary War, and it took a year to retool the factories for supplying what the army needed. When the fighting began, the Northern army numbered only sixteen thousand, and many soldiers and officers eventually resigned to join the Confederate army.

What the South lacked in arms, factories, and soldiers, it gained in experienced officers. Seven of the eight military schools in the country in 1860 were located in the South, and officers generally were loyal to the regions in which they were trained. For example, of the nineteen hundred men trained at Virginia Military Academy, over seventeen hundred served with the South. In addition, the president of the Confederacy, Jefferson Davis, was a former soldier and secretary of war.

LESSON 48
The Battle at Bull Run

Text, pages 170-72, 288-89
Notebook, page 64

Preview

Main Ideas
- Individuals have unique attributes and skills.
- Man's view of God determines his philosophy and history.

Objective
- Write three reasons for naming General Thomas J. "Stonewall" Jackson to a Hall of Heroes

Materials
- Maps and More 17, page M11
- Appendix, page A50: McDowell/Jackson name-plates*

Day 1

Lesson

Introducing the Lesson

Clustering Activity

➤ *In the center of a sheet of paper, write the word* hero *and circle it.*
➤ Name words or phrases that describe a hero.

As each word is given, write it above, below, or beside the word hero *until you have made a word cluster. Discuss each description and erase any word that your child decides does not accurately describe a hero. Help him to focus on the positive aspects of true heroism: courage, nobility of purpose, special achievements, and so on.*

The First Big Battle

The soldiers in both armies listened and learned; then they *drilled*, or practiced, again and again. Most of the soldiers were *volunteers*, men who had offered to fight for their countries. The volunteers had never fought in a battle before.

The people at home became impatient. This drilling was taking too long. Do you think the soldiers needed much practice? They did, but the people wanted the fighting to begin soon. The sooner it began, the sooner it would be over, they thought.

The generals, or leaders, on both sides listened to the people. They told the soldiers to be ready for battle. Then Union General McDowell marched his men into Virginia. Was Virginia a Confederate state or a Union state?

170

➤ **Are all famous people heroes?** *(no)* As you read about a famous person in this lesson, you should try to decide whether he was a hero.

Teaching the Lesson

Text Discussion, page 170

➤ **Read page 170 to find out why the people wanted the fighting to begin soon.** *(They thought the sooner it began, the sooner it would be over.)*
➤ **Why was it taking so long for the fighting to begin?** *(Most of the soldiers had never fought before and had to be trained.)*

Before the first big battle of the American Civil War, the soldiers from the North and from the South drilled again and again for hours on end.

➤ **Do you think you would have gotten tired and impatient with drilling so much?**
➤ **Why did the soldiers on both sides need so much practice?** *(Most of them were* volunteers *who had never fought before.)*

During the Civil War, drums were used to pass orders to the soldiers. While the soldiers were in camp, certain drumbeats called the soldiers to line up for inspection or for meals. Drums also set the pace for marching drills. During battles, when smoke covered the battlefields and soldiers could

General McDowell and his army headed to the South. They wanted to capture Manassas Junction. It was a place in which two railroads met. One railroad led to Washington, D.C. What was important about that city? If McDowell could capture that spot, he could protect the Union capital.

People from Washington followed the Union army. They rode in fancy carriages wearing their Sunday best. They brought picnic lunches to eat while they watched the battle. Do you think that was a wise thing to do?

The Union army and the Confederate army met on the banks of a creek called Bull Run. The creek was near Manassas Junction. The fighting began early in the morning and went on for most of the day. In the end, the Union soldiers turned and ran. They ran past the people with the fancy carriages and picnic lunches. Some soldiers ran all the way back to Washington, D.C.

171

not see their commanders, drumbeats told the soldiers how and when to move. Many drummers were young boys. One named Johnny Clem was only eleven years old. The Civil War was the last time drummers were used in battle, though. Thereafter, bugles were used to pass the orders along.

➤ **Did the generals listen to the people and begin the fighting?** *(Yes, General McDowell marched his soldiers into Virginia, a Confederate state.)*
➤ Attach the *General Irvin McDowell* nameplate to the Union side of the door.

Day 2

Text Discussion, page 171 and Maps and More 17

➤ **Read page 171 to find out why General McDowell wanted to capture Manassas (mə năs´ əs) Junction.** *(If he could capture this junction, he could protect the Union capital.)*
➤ Point to the Union capital on Maps and More 17. *(Washington, D.C.)*
➤ Point to the Confederate capital. *(Richmond, Virginia)*
➤ Find Manassas.

➤ Point to Bull Run Creek.

The battle that was fought there is sometimes called the Battle of Bull Run and sometimes referred to as the Battle of Manassas. The reason that this American Civil War battle has two names is that Confederates named it after the nearest settlement (Manassas Junction) and the Northerners named it after the nearest body of water (Bull Run Creek).

➤ Notice how far the battle site is from the Union capital and from the Confederate capital. The site is approximately three times farther from Richmond than from Washington.
➤ **What advantages and disadvantages did these distances present for each side in the fight?** *(Answers will vary. Your child may mention that if the Confederates won the battle, they could move on to the Union capital and capture it or that the Union could send additional soldiers from Washington more quickly than the Confederate side could send soldiers from Richmond.)*
➤ **Who followed the Union army toward Manassas Junction?** *(people from Washington)*
➤ **Read aloud the sentences that make it sound as if the people from Washington had never seen a battle before.** *(sentences 2 and 3, paragraph 2, page 171)*
➤ **Why do you think it was not wise for people to gather to watch the battle?**
➤ **Which soldiers turned and ran at the end of the battle?** *(the Union soldiers)*

As the Union soldiers fled, they ran into the picnickers who had been watching from the hill. Soon everyone was running. On a bridge over a stream called Cub Run, a wagon fell over, blocked the road, and caused a huge traffic jam. Because President Lincoln's ninety-day enlistment period was over on the day of the Battle of Bull Run, some of the volunteer soldiers kept running and never went back to their armies.

Map Activity, pages 288-89

➤ Look at the map of major Civil War battle sites on pages 288-89.
➤ Find the location of the Battle of Manassas (Bull Run).

The battle you have just read about occurred on July 21, 1861. Another battle was fought there a year later.

➤ Look at the map and find the locations of the two other battles that were fought before this first Manassas battle. *(Harper's Ferry, Fort Sumter)*

Thomas J. "Stonewall" Jackson
1824-63

At one point during the Battle of Bull Run, the Union seemed to be winning. The Confederate generals were afraid their men would turn and run. One man saw brave and calm General Thomas Jackson leading his troops. The man called out, "Look! There stands Jackson like a stone wall. Rally behind the Virginians!" After the battle everyone called General Jackson by a new name—Stonewall Jackson.

Thomas Jackson's father and mother died when he was very young. Then Tom lived with his uncle. He liked to help with the work on the big plantation. Tom worked hard at everything he did. When he was older, he got the chance to go to a special school called West Point. Do you think he worked hard there too? He learned how to be a good soldier.

Jackson also worked hard for the Lord. He started a Sunday school for the slaves where he lived. During the war, he tried to keep from fighting on a Sunday. If he did have to do battle on the Lord's Day, he set aside another day in the week to worship God. Jackson praised God every time he won a battle.

Stonewall Jackson died before the war ended. His own men shot him accidentally. His soldiers and everyone in the South mourned. They had lost one of their best generals.

172

Text Discussion, page 172

➤ One of the Confederate generals during the Battle of Bull Run was Thomas J. Jackson, nicknamed "Stonewall." Attach the *General Stonewall Jackson* nameplate to the Confederate side of the door.

➤ **Read page 172 to find out how General Jackson got his nickname.** (*Someone said that he stood like a stone wall.*)

➤ **Do you think General Jackson was a hero?**

➤ **Read aloud the sections from page 172 that you think show General Jackson to be a hero.** (*Answers will vary.*)

His good qualities—bravery, calmness, and diligence—showed that his love for God was most important to him. (BATs: 5c Evangelism and missions, 7b Exaltation of Christ, 7c Praise)

Listening Activity

➤ Listen as I read a story.

Townspeople crowded around the door to the small post office in Lexington, Virginia. Many folks had already pushed their way into the building, where people stood elbow to elbow in the warm, stuffy room.

Young Jeffrey White had come this morning with his father, the Reverend White. They had decided to stand outside and back from the crowd. That way, more of the women and babies could get close to the postmaster. They could hear any news that might come in from the battle. Until now, the only word about what had happened at Bull Run was from a few soldiers who had dragged themselves into town with only their guns and the clothes on their backs. As one soldier had said, "It was terrible—bullets flyin', people cryin', men runnin'. I ran too, and I'm never goin' back!"

The red-faced postmaster appeared in the doorway. He called out, "Letter for Reverend White!" Jeffrey's father waved from the edge of the crowd. He reached for the letter that was being passed from hand to hand toward him. One look at the handwriting, and Reverend White knew who had written the letter. No one else but his beloved deacon-soldier, General Thomas Jackson, formed his letters like that. The pastor took a deep breath and announced to the crowd, "Now we shall know the facts."

The promise of details about the fighting—who had been injured, who was safe, how the battle had gone—brought everyone outside. The crowd grew quiet as Reverend White opened the letter. No one moved as the pastor read the words to himself. Everyone saw the pastor smile. The ones closest to him saw the tears in his eyes. After a moment, Reverend White stood up with the letter in his hand. He said to the crowd, "Our friend and neighbor Tom Jackson has written on a most important matter. The burden of this letter is as weighty to him as the burden he carries in battle." Then Reverend White read,

My dear pastor—In my tent last night, after a fatiguing day's service, I remembered that I had failed to send you my contribution for our colored Sunday-school. Enclosed you will find my check for that object, which please acknowledge at your earliest convenience, and oblige yours faithfully, T. J. Jackson.

Story Discussion

➤ **What do you think Reverend White meant by "the burden of this letter"?**

Jackson was burdened (concerned) because he had not sent the money that he had evidently promised.

➤ **What kind of a Sunday school did Stonewall Jackson start?** (*one for slaves*)

➤ Do you think this was the same Sunday school as the "colored Sunday-school" mentioned in the letter?

➤ **What does the story tell you about Stonewall Jackson as a hero?** (*Even on the battlefield, Jackson was concerned about his responsibility to contribute money for a Sunday school class. He was evidently responsible, faithful to a promise, and perhaps generous with his money.*) (BAT: 5b Giving)

Evaluating the Lesson

Notebook Activity, page 64

➤ Read the directions for Notebook page 64.
➤ Complete the page.

━━━ Going Beyond ━━━

Additional Teacher Information

Letters and journals written by soldiers during the Civil War contained many references to food. If soldiers were not complaining about long-overdue food supplies, they were commenting on the lack of quality and variety of the food they did have. To add to their meager meals, soldiers often went foraging—gathering food supplies from the land around them. Some hunted deer or bear, some picked nuts and berries, and some daring ones stole honey from beehives. Others, not willing to take the time or exert the effort required to forage, begged for food at farmhouses. As time went on, both the Northern and Southern armies issued strict rules against foraging.

LESSON 49
Lessons Learned

Text, pages 173-76
Notebook, page 65

━━━ Preview ━━━

Main Ideas
- The Union and the Confederacy learned important lessons at the Battle of Bull Run.
- Individuals have unique attributes and skills.

Objective
- Write a letter from a soldier to his family

Materials
- A variety of dried fruit*
- Appendix, page A51: McClellan/Lee nameplates*

Day 1

━━━ Lesson ━━━

Introducing the Lesson

Food-Tasting Activity

➤ I have a snack of the kinds of fruit eaten by soldiers during the American Civil War. **Can you identify any of the kinds of fruit?**
➤ As you eat a piece of fruit, give me a description of how the fruit looks, feels, smells, and tastes.
➤ **Why did the soldiers have dried rather than fresh fruit?** (*Fresh fruit would spoil quickly; it took up more space in the soldiers' knapsacks; it was messier than dried fruit to carry and to eat.*)

Although the soldiers missed their mothers' and wives' home cooking, they learned to like a number of different foods and were thankful for any food they could get. (BAT: 7d Contentment)

The Union and the Confederate soldiers learned important lessons at the Battle of Bull Run. Both sides knew now that the war would not be over in just a few months. Each knew the enemy would fight hard for its country. It would be a long, bloody war.

Both armies also learned something about needing uniforms. The Union soldiers, or *Yankees,* were supposed to wear blue. The Confederate soldiers were supposed to wear gray. But before this battle, neither army had a uniform. The soldiers wore whatever clothes they had. Why might this be a problem?

During the battle a group of soldiers dressed in blue came upon some Union soldiers. Who do you think the soldiers in blue were? The Union men thought they were more Union soldiers coming to help. But the soldiers in blue were Confederates. They did not plan to help the Union soldiers. The Confederates shot and captured almost four hundred Union men.

173

New Leaders for the Armies

President Lincoln learned something from the battle too. He saw that General McDowell was not a good leader for the Union army. He picked General George McClellan to be the army's new leader. The president had a good reason for picking General McClellan. He had won small battles in the West. Maybe he could win bigger battles too.

General McClellan was a planner. He planned what he should do with the Union army. He planned how the men would be trained. Then he made sure that their training went as he had planned. After many months the general had 150,000 men who were ready to fight.

But while General McClellan worked with the army, President Lincoln grew tired of waiting. He thought that McClellan might never do more than drill and practice with the men. Finally the president told McClellan that he must lead the men into a battle.

McClellan alone and with some of his men

174

Teaching the Lesson

Text Discussion, page 173

➤ **Read page 173 to find two important lessons that the Union and the Confederate soldiers learned.** *(that the battle would be long, that uniforms were important)*

➤ **Why would it be a problem for soldiers to wear whatever clothes they had?** *(No one could tell which side a soldier was on.)*

➤ Look at the pictures of the uniforms of each army on page 173.

At the beginning of the war, soldiers in both armies wore a variety of uniforms. Since this was confusing, each side soon decided upon a standard uniform as shown on the page. The uniforms varied slightly in each army, depending upon the rank or regiment of the soldiers. The soldiers shown are privates in rank.

➤ **Which soldier is dressed in blue?** *(Union)*

Text Discussion, page 174

➤ **Read page 174 to find out what President Lincoln learned from the battle.** *(that General McDowell was not a good leader)*

➤ **Why did President Lincoln choose General McClellan?** *(President Lincoln thought that General McClellan could win some battles.)*

➤ Attach the *General George McClellan* nameplate to the Union side of door.

➤ **Why was the president not satisfied with the new general?** *(He thought General McClellan would never do more than drill and practice.)*

➤ **Can you remember another time when people became impatient with drilling and practicing?** *(just before the Battle of Bull Run)*

The text pages will be taught out of order in this lesson.

General McClellan moved his huge army. He planned to attack the city of Richmond. Do you remember why Richmond was important? McClellan was a good planner, but he was not a good leader in battle. The men in blue lost many battles. The Confederates pushed them back to where they had started.

By now the Confederate army had a new leader too. General Robert E. Lee took charge of the Grays after the first leader was shot. Of all the good generals in the South, Robert E. Lee was one of the best. Lee had worked with many leaders of the Union army. He knew how they acted in battle. And he made good guesses when he did not know.

Now the new leader of the Confederate army decided to take the war into the North. Lee thought he might scare the people there into giving up on the war. He headed his men toward Pennsylvania.

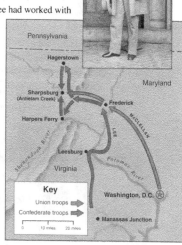
Robert E. Lee

176

Text Discussion, page 176

➤ **Read page 176 to find out what General McClellan did in response to President Lincoln's order.** *(He moved the army to attack Richmond, the capital of the Confederacy.)*

➤ **Why did the Union lose so many battles even though they had many soldiers?** *(General McClellan was a good planner but not a good leader in battle. Also, Robert E. Lee, one of the South's best generals, had taken leadership of the Confederate army.)*

➤ Attach the *General Robert E. Lee* nameplate to the Confederate side of the door.

➤ **Read aloud the sentences that tell why General Lee was such a good general.** *(Lee had worked with many leaders of the Union army. He knew how they acted in battle. And he made good guesses when he did not know.)*

General Lee realized that General McClellan was capable but very cautious. To try to make McClellan think that the Confederates had more soldiers than they really had, Lee ordered large groups of soldiers to stand around in the open, where the Union scouts could see them. Then, leaving a few soldiers behind, Lee would move the groups farther down the line, where they would stand around again. General Lee also ordered his troops

to set up large logs sticking out of mounds of earth. From a distance, the logs looked like cannons. Union scouts counted soldiers and cannons and came up with wildly exaggerated ideas of the Confederacy's strength. At one point General McClellan thought he was outnumbered two to one and pleaded for reinforcements. Cautious McClellan was finally forced to fall back from his attack on Richmond.

Map Activity, page 176

➤ **Why did General Lee decide to move his soldiers toward the North?** *(He thought he might scare the people there into giving up on the war.)*

➤ Look at the map of General Lee's route toward Pennsylvania on page 176.

➤ **Where did General Lee's route start?** *(at Manassas Junction)*

➤ **What battle was fought here?** *(the Battle of Bull Run)*

Remember that two railroads joined at Manassas Junction. The Union's General McDowell had wanted to capture that spot to protect Washington from Confederate attack.

➤ **What does the map show about the movement of General Lee's troops after Frederick?** *(The troops went two different directions.)*

One of the understood "rules" of warfare was that a smaller army would never divide itself when battling a larger army. However, Lee knew that he could surprise McClellan, the cautious general, by "breaking the rules" because McClellan would never expect Lee to do such a thing. One of Lee's greatest strengths as a general was his knowledge of the way McClellan thought.

➤ **What might be a benefit of General Lee's sending part of his soldiers one way and part another way, as illustrated on the map?** *(Answers will vary.)*

Lead your child to conclude that if McClellan, not knowing or even suspecting that Lee had divided his forces, were to send his soldiers to the North in pursuit, Lee's other branch could swing around and come up behind the Northern troops.

➤ **Do you think General Lee's plan was a good one?**

The Battle of Antietam will be discussed in the next lesson.

208

◆ THINGS PEOPLE DO ◆

Spying from Balloons

One day near the beginning of the war, the Southern soldiers saw an amazing sight: a colorful flying ball in the sky over their camp. In a basket under it was a Northern soldier, looking down on them. The Grays tried to shoot the thing down, but it landed safely on the ground.

Soon a dazzling silk balloon was spying over the Blues' tents. Up and up it flew, dragging ropes behind. The Blues tried to catch the ropes to pull the bright balloon down. They could not. But it came down on its own far away. And the best-trained balloonist of the South was glad to be on the ground again.

Another Southern general wanted a balloon to spy with too. Women from many Southern towns sent their best silk ball gowns to the army. What did the soldiers need with ball gowns? They needed the light material to make a balloon. But the South never used this balloon to spy on the Blues. The Union soldiers captured it before it ever left the ground.

175

Letter to Home

Name _____

Pretend that you are a Confederate or Union soldier writing a letter to your family back home. You may want to write about your uniform, a battle, or your leader.

Day 2

Text Discussion, page 175

➤ **Read page 175 to find out why the Southern army needed ladies' silk gowns.** *(to make a hot-air balloon for spying on the North)*

➤ **Was the special balloon successful?** *(No, it was captured before it left the ground.)*

➤ **What could a spy learn about enemy soldiers from a balloon?** *(Answers will vary.)*

Help your child to think about the advantages of looking down on an enemy who is used to being approached from the ground rather than from the air: soldiers would usually hide behind camouflage or barriers and not think of setting up protection above them; from above, a spy could see for great distances and determine where backup soldiers were positioned, and so on. Lead your child to conclude that from a balloon a Union soldier could probably have seen that Lee's "cannons" were really logs sticking out of mounds of earth.

➤ **What do you think would be the dangers of spying from a balloon?**

➤ **How do you think a hot-air balloon might be helpful in drawing maps?**

In France in 1851, photographs taken from hot-air balloons were used in mapmaking for the first time.

If your child is especially interested in ballooning, encourage him to find more information in an encyclopedia.

Evaluating the Lesson

Creative-Writing Activity, Notebook page 65

➤ Read the instructions on Notebook page 65.

➤ **What would be the approximate date for your letter?** *(sometime after July 21, 1861, if your child wants to write about the Battle of Bull Run)*

➤ Complete the page.

Going Beyond

Enrichment

Explain that a common food that the soldiers on both sides ate was a type of cornbread called *corn dodgers*. Allow your child to mix a batch of cornbread, spoon it into prepared muffin pans, and—under your supervision—bake the bread and eat it.

Additional Teacher Information

Most of the first recruits on both sides in the Civil War wore their own clothes, not the issued uniforms that we think of today. They also carried makeshift guns and swords, some fashioned from wood, as they trained.

Though some towns provided uniforms for their native sons, little consistency was evident on either side. One regiment called the Highlands wore kilts. Another group wore baggy red pants, bright purple shirts with flowing sleeves, and red hats called *fezzes*. Until consistency in uniforms could be established, confusion reigned.

Making uniforms for hundreds of thousands of soldiers took much time. Each soldier had to be measured. Then his uniform was cut and sewn by hand. Eventually, to speed up production, uniform manufacturers were given a series of graduated measurements for uniforms and shoes. Before long, the items were being produced by the thousands. Mass production had begun, and the concept of sizes would be used in civilian production from that time on.

LESSON 50
Free at Last

Text, pages 177-81, 288-89
Notebook, page 66

Preview

Main Ideas
- Photographs document history.
- Individuals have unique attributes and skills.
- Significant documents have influenced American history.
- The American Civil War changed American history.

Objectives
- Contrast photographs taken in the 1800s with current photographs
- Complete a crossword puzzle with names and terms relating to the American Civil War

Materials
- A magazine with photographs*

Day 1

Lesson

> The text pages will be taught out of order in this lesson.

Introducing the Lesson

Photography Study, page 178

➤ Open your textbook to page 178.
➤ Compare the photographs in the magazine with the photographs in your textbook. Think about these questions to help with your comparisons.

- **Did the people in the photographs know that their pictures were being taken?** Consider whether the person is looking directly at the camera, standing still, or appearing rather stiff.
- **Can you tell whether the pictures were taken during the day or during the night?**
- **Were the pictures taken with black-and-white or color film?**

Through the observations and the discussion, help your child understand that in the 1800s people usually knew when their pictures were being taken because they had to hold their poses for several minutes so that the photographs would not be blurry.

Heritage Studies 3 Home TE

Mathew Brady
1823-96

Mathew Brady

The smoke had not yet cleared from the battlefield. But Mr. Brady was out there, setting up his huge camera, calling for the glass plates to put into it. He had been the richest photographer in New York. Now he was quickly becoming poor.

Mathew Brady felt a duty to photograph the worst war his country—or the world—had ever seen. But the government told him he had to pay his own way. By the end of the war, Brady had taken thirty-five hundred photos and had spent all of his one hundred thousand dollars in savings.

Brady worked hard the rest of his life and paid off his debts. But he never had much money again. When he died, he left only a cane and a ring. But the United States had a priceless treasure: thousands of pictures of men and women who shaped history.

Two of the many photographs taken by Mathew Brady

178

Freedom at Last

Since the beginning of the war, some people had been asking the president to free the slaves in the South. Lincoln and the other Union leaders said, "We are fighting this war to keep the states together. The war is not about freeing the slaves. We will do something about them later." But the abolitionists kept asking Lincoln to do something soon.

Finally the president agreed. He understood that freeing the slaves would hurt the South. It might even help the North win the war. But Lincoln did not want to make his announcement about freeing the slaves right away. He decided to wait until the Union army won a battle.

The Blues did not have to wait long for another chance to win a battle. President Lincoln heard that General Lee was marching his army into the North. He sent General McClellan to catch him. This time the two armies met on the banks of Antietam Creek near the little village of Sharpsburg, Maryland.

The Antietam battlefield today

177

Day²

Teaching the Lesson

Text Discussion, page 177

➤ **Read the first paragraph on page 177 to find out what President Lincoln said about why the war was being fought.** (*"We are fighting this war to keep the states together. The war is not about freeing the slaves. We will do something about them later."*)

➤ Name the group that kept asking Lincoln to do something about the slaves soon. *(the abolitionists)*

➤ Can you define *abolitionist?*

If your child does not remember what the word means, write the word abolish. *Explain that abolish means "to do away with" and ask whether that word gives a clue to the definition of* abolitionist. *(someone who wants to do away with slavery)*

➤ **Read the rest of page 177 to find out what President Lincoln decided to do.**

➤ **Why would freeing the slaves have hurt the South but would have helped the North to win the war?** *(Answers will vary.)*

Plantations and farms would lose workers. The Southern economy would suffer. Freed slaves fleeing to the North would increase the Union army.

When the pictures on page 178 were taken (mid-1800s), the subjects had to stand or sit very still for a few minutes rather than for the few seconds required for taking photographs today. Although some pictures taken more recently are posed, many are *candids,* pictures taken when the subject is unaware that he is being photographed. Before the flashbulb and the electronic flash, photographs had to be taken in the daylight. Now pictures can be taken at any time, day or night. Although some photographers still choose to shoot pictures in black-and-white film, photographers in the 1800s did not have a choice. They had only black-and-white film.

Text Discussion, page 178

➤ **Read page 178 to find out who Mathew Brady was and what priceless treasure he gave the United States.** *(a photographer who took thousands of pictures of men and women who shaped America's history)*

➤ **What did Mathew Brady give up to provide these pictures?** *(He gave all of his savings and much hard work. He left only a cane and a ring when he died.)*

Along with journals, photographs like these let us know firsthand information about the American Civil War.

➤ **Why did the president not make his announcement about freeing the slaves right away?** *(He
decided to wait until the Union army won a battle.)*
➤ **Where did the two armies meet for the next
battle?** *(on the banks of Antietam [ăn tē´ təm] Creek
near Sharpsburg, Maryland)*
➤ Look back to page 176 to find Sharpsburg on the
map of General Lee's move into the North.

A copy of General Lee's plans to split his army,
sending part to Harper's Ferry and part toward the
North, was left behind and found by a Union soldier.
General McClellan wrote to President Lincoln, "I
have all the plans of the rebels, and will catch them
in their own trap. . . . [I] will send you trophies."

Text Discussion, pages 179
and 288-89

➤ **Read the first paragraph on page 179 to find out
what happened in the battle at Antietam Creek.**
*(Neither side really won, but after fierce fighting the
Confederates retreated, or went back to the South.)*

The battle is called the "worst single day in all
the war" because the 26,134 casualties (dead,
wounded, and missing) on that day (September 17,
1862) were more than all the casualties during the
Revolutionary War, the War of 1812, and the Mexican War combined.

➤ Look at the map on pages 288-89.
➤ Find the Battle of Antietam.
➤ *Read the heading under the picture to your child,
pointing to the words as you read.*
➤ **Read the rest of page 179 to find out what
emancipation means.** *(freeing)*
➤ **What did President Lincoln do after the South's
invasion failed?** *(He issued the Emancipation
Proclamation.)*

As you discuss the result of the proclamation—
making slaves outside the Union "forever free"
from slavery—discuss also the result of Christ's
death on the cross—making those who accept His
sacrifice forever free from the penalty of sin.
(Bible Promises: A. Liberty from Sin, B. Guiltless
by the Blood, E. Christ as Sacrifice)

The fighting was fierce. It was the worst single day in all
the war. When it was over, both armies knew that neither had
really won the battle. But the men in gray went back to the
South. Their invasion had failed.

President Lincoln's first reading of the Emancipation Proclamation before the cabinet

Now President Lincoln felt that it was time to make his
announcement. Just days after the battle, the president read the
Emancipation Proclamation. Can you guess what *emancipation*
means? It means "freeing." Lincoln's announcement said that
slaves in states outside the Union were "forever free."

The president gave the Confederate States a little time to
think about his announcement. If the states came back into the
Union before January 1, 1863, the people could keep their slaves.
Do you think any states came back? None did. The war went on.

179

➤ **What would the Confederate states have had to
do in order to keep their slaves?** *(go back into the
Union before January 1, 1863)*
➤ **Did any states go back into the Union?** *(no)*

When President Lincoln signed important papers, he usually signed "A. Lincoln." However,
when he signed the Emancipation Proclamation on
January 1, 1863, he wrote his full name, Abraham
Lincoln. Historians tell us that Lincoln thought that
if his name was ever to be remembered in history, it
would be for his signing of this document.

➤ **What happened on the first day of the year 1863?**
*(Slaves in the states outside the Union were declared
free because those states refused to go back into the
Union by the date set by the Emancipation Proclamation.)*

Heritage Studies 3 Home TE

Since the beginning of the war, slaves had come to the camps of the Union army. The Union soldiers called these slaves *contraband* of war. Contraband is property taken from the enemy. Why were the slaves called contraband?

The Emancipation Proclamation made a change in the way the Union leaders thought. The slaves were no longer contraband but free men and women. The Union army gave jobs to the freed slaves. Some washed clothes and cooked for the soldiers. Others helped to dig ditches and care for the horses that belonged to the army. Soon there were more freed slaves than there were jobs for them to do. What do you think the Union leaders did then?

The Union leaders formed *regiments*, or groups, of black soldiers. The men got uniforms and guns. They learned how to march and shoot. Many freed slaves signed up to fight. Free black men from the North volunteered too. Most of the officers of these regiments were white men. But Major Martin R. Delany was the first black officer in the Union army.

Martin R. Delany

181

◆ HOW IT WAS ◆

The Union Hotel Hospital
Washington, D.C.
Mid-December 1862

Before the American Civil War, almost all nurses were men. But with so many men needed in the armies, women volunteered to help. More than three thousand women became nurses during the war.

Army hospitals were often dirty and crowded. The Union Hotel Hospital was one of the worst. It was cold and damp and dark. Sickening smells filled the rooms and hallways.

Many of the patients had been wounded in battles. But other patients were sick with diseases like pneumonia and measles. A nurse's day was filled with washing faces, passing out medicine, and feeding the men. If the nurse had time, she would read to the men or help them to write letters to home. Sometimes she had to comfort the family of a dead soldier.

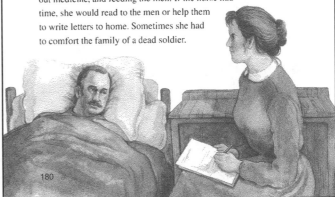

180

Day 3

Text Discussion, page 181

➤ **Read page 181 to find out how the freeing of slaves helped the Union army.** *(The army hired freed slaves and then accepted them as soldiers.)*

➤ *Contraband* is smuggled goods or property brought into a country illegally. **Why do you think the slaves who escaped to the Union army camps were called contraband?**

Before the Emancipation Proclamation, slaves were considered their masters' property. Slaves who escaped from Confederate masters and went to Union camps were, then, property taken from the enemy, or contraband.

➤ **How did the Emancipation Proclamation change the way Union leaders thought or acted?** *(No longer contraband, the slaves were given jobs in the Union army and then accepted as soldiers.)*

Black soldiers took part in more than four hundred Civil War battles.

➤ **What is a *regiment*?** *(a group of soldiers)*
➤ **Did freeing the slaves do what Lincoln thought it would do: help the North to win the war?** *(yes)*
➤ Look at the picture of Major Martin Delany on page 181.

Major Delany was not only a distinguished officer but also a writer and a surgeon who received his medical training at Harvard University. He wrote for an abolitionist newspaper, urging readers to support the freeing of slaves.

Text Discussion, page 180

➤ Read the title on page 180.
➤ **What does the name and the location of the hospital tell about the hospital?** *(Answers will vary. Your child may deduce that because of the location and the name* Union, *the hospital was established by the Union for its soldiers and, perhaps, its prisoners. Also, the hospital was probably set up in the Union Hotel.)*
➤ **Read page 180 to find out what duties the nurses had.** *(washing faces, passing out medicine, feeding the men, reading to the injured, writing letters home for them, and comforting families of dead soldiers)*
➤ **Read some of the words and phrases that describe the conditions of the hospital.** *(dirty, crowded, cold, damp, dark, filled with sickening smells and many diseases)*
➤ **Why would a hospital like that be such an unhealthy place?** *(Answers will vary; lack of cleanliness, medical supplies, adequate lighting, and heat.)*
➤ Tell the differences between the Union Hotel Hospital and hospitals of today.

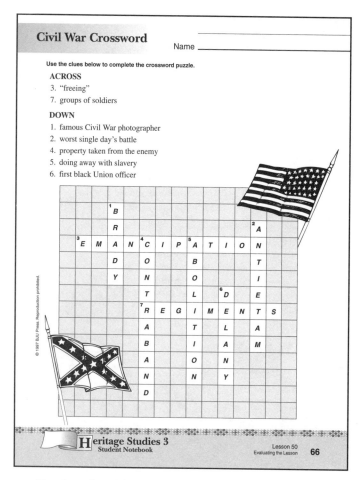

Civil War Crossword

Name _____

Use the clues below to complete the crossword puzzle.

ACROSS
3. "freeing"
7. groups of soldiers

DOWN
1. famous Civil War photographer
2. worst single day's battle
3. property taken from the enemy
4. doing away with slavery
5. first black Union officer

© 1997 BJU Press. Reproduction prohibited.

The crossword grid contains:

1B							
R						2A	
3E	M	A	N	4C	I	P	5A	T	I	O	N
D			O		B		T	
Y			N		O		I	
		T		L	6D	E	
	7R	E	G	I	M	E	N	T	S
	A		T		L		A	
	B		I		A		M	
	A		O		N		
	N		N		Y		
	D						

Heritage Studies 3
Student Notebook

Lesson 50
Evaluating the Lesson   **66**

Evaluating the Lesson

Notebook Activity, page 66

➤ Read the instructions on Notebook page 66.

The answers to the crossword puzzle are names of people and terms that you have read about in this lesson. The clues are descriptions of the people and definitions of the terms. (*NOTE:* You may choose to let your child refer to textbook pages 177–81 as he completes the puzzle.)

➤ Complete the puzzle.

━━ Going Beyond ━━

Additional Teacher Information

On September 22, 1862, five days after Union forces won at Antietam, Lincoln read the preliminary proclamation. The draft was printed in newspapers the next day. When the South rejected Lincoln's policy, he issued the proclamation on January 1, 1863.

The Emancipation Proclamation affected only areas under Confederate control, excluding slaves in border states and in Southern areas under Union control (Tennessee and parts of Louisiana and Virginia). It led eventually to the Thirteenth Amendment to the Constitution, which became law on December 18, 1865, and ended slavery in all parts of the United States.

By the war's end, more than five hundred thousand slaves had fled to freedom behind Northern lines. About two hundred thousand black soldiers and sailors, many of them former slaves, served in the armed forces and helped the North win the war. The proclamation also aided the North by making the war an open fight against slavery and thus discouraging England and France from siding with the South and entering the war on her behalf.

Heritage Studies 3 Home TE

LESSON 51
Gettysburg

Text, pages 182-85, 274-75, 288-89

──── Preview ────

Main Ideas
- Gettysburg was one of the most famous battles of the Civil War.
- Maps help one to understand the events of the Battle of Gettysburg.

Objectives
- Recognize important locations on a map
- Be able to give short answers to content questions about the Battle of Gettysburg

Materials
- Supplement, page S12: Definitions for Gettysburg Address
- *HERITAGE STUDIES Listening Cassette A*
- Maps and More 18, page M12
- The figure representing the Gettysburg Address (1863) from the TimeLine Snapshots
- A square of blue or gray construction paper or cloth*
- A straight pin
- An addressed envelope*
- A dictionary (optional)

Day 1

──── Lesson ────

Introducing the Lesson

Art Activity

➤ *Give your child the construction paper or cloth square.*
➤ Print your name and address on the square.
➤ Pin your identification tag to your clothing.
➤ **Do you know what soldiers call their identification tags?** *(dog tags)*

Today we will talk about the Battle of Gettysburg. It was the first battle in which dog tags were used.

➤ Define the word *casualties* or look up the word in the dictionary.

Because there were so many casualties in this battle, the soldiers pinned cloth tags to their uniforms so that their families could be informed in case of injuries.

The Battle of Gettysburg is one of the most famous battles of the American Civil War. Can you guess why? More men were hurt or killed at Gettysburg than during any other battle. The fighting lasted three days. Then the beaten Grays went south again. Their army was never quite so strong again.

When the fighting was over, the whole town of Gettysburg became a hospital. Wounded men were carried to homes and churches and barns. Many townspeople kept busy caring for the soldiers. But others helped in a different way. They buried the more than six thousand soldiers who died.

Gettysburg National Cemetery

The people of Gettysburg wanted a special place to bury these men.

They bought land on Cemetery Hill. Can you find Cemetery Hill on the picture map? They made the land into a National Soldiers Cemetery. When the cemetery was ready, many people came to see it. They listened to President Lincoln speak about the brave soldiers who had fought for their beliefs.

185

Teaching the Lesson

Text Discussion, page 182

➤ **Read page 182 to find out what state General Lee headed his armies toward.** *(Pennsylvania)*
➤ **How long had it been since the South had invaded the North?** *(almost a year)*
➤ **Why was it important for General Lee to try to win a battle in Northern territory?** *(He believed he could scare the North into ending the war.)*

Text Discussion, pages 185 and 288-89

➤ **Read page 185 to find out how many soldiers died at the Battle of Gettysburg.** *(more than six thousand)*

There were more than 48,000 casualties (dead, wounded, and missing) in the Battle of Gettysburg.

➤ Define the word *morale* or look up the word in the dictionary. *(the spirit or enthusiasm shown by a person or group working toward a goal)*
➤ **How did the loss of so many lives affect the morale of the men who were fighting?** *(Answers will vary.)* The men probably grew even more desperate and discouraged.
➤ Although the Union did win, many men on both sides lost their lives. **Do you think the Union was**

Gettysburg

It was almost a year before the Confederate army tried to invade the North again. General Lee's first try had not worked. But he still believed that he could scare the North into ending the war. He just needed to win a battle on Union land. So he headed his army toward Pennsylvania again.

The Union army followed Lee and his men. They marched north, neither army knowing exactly where the other army was. Men from the Union and Confederate armies ran into each other near the little town of Gettysburg. The meeting was not what either army had planned. But now the battle would be fought here.

Lee's army meets Northern troops north and west of Gettysburg, driving them through town. Union forces rally on Cemetery Ridge and Culp's Hill. In the meantime, Union reinforcements are arriving throughout the night.

The Confederates attack the left and right flanks, almost succeeding. Union troops hold Culp's Hill and Little Round Top.

After a two-hour artillery barrage by 140 guns, 15,000 Confederates march toward the Union center. "Pickett's Charge" fails. Lee's forces withdraw on July 4, returning to Virginia.

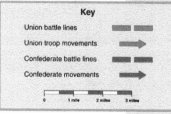

Key

Union battle lines	
Union troop movements	
Confederate battle lines	
Confederate movements	

0   1 mile   2 miles   3 miles

182

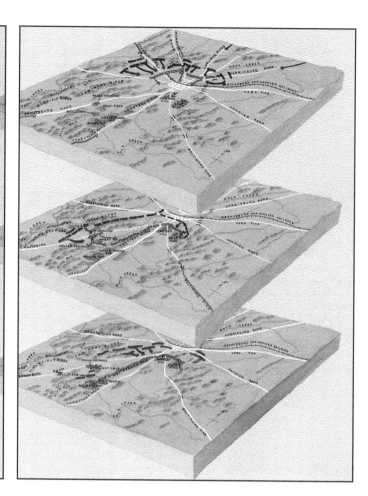

happy with this victory? Yes and no—yes, because they gained advantage in the war; no, because so many men were killed.

➤ **Why did the people of Gettysburg want to bury and honor these men?** *(They were brave and had sacrificed their lives.)*

➤ Find the place on the picture map on page 183 where they buried the soldiers who had died. *(Cemetery Hill)*

➤ Find the Battle of Gettysburg on the map on pages 288-89.

Day 2

Learning How Activity, pages 182-84 and Maps and More 18

➤ **Read the steps on page 184.**
➤ Look at pages 182-83 or Maps and More 18.

- **What does the picture map show?** *(the area of the Battle of Gettysburg; Union and Confederate battle lines)*
- **What things tell that the picture is a map?** *(the compass directions; the key; the names of rivers, mountains, roads, and specific locations, etc.)*
- **What place is north of Devil's Den?** *(the wheat field)*
- **Which army fought from the top of Cemetery Ridge?** *(the Union army)*

◆ LEARNING HOW ◆

To Read a Picture Map

1. You will need the map on pages 182-83 of your textbook.

2. Look at the picture map. What does the map show? What things tell us that the picture is a map?

3. Find the place called Devil's Den. What place is north of Devil's Den? Find Cemetery Ridge. What army fought from the top of the ridge? Answer other questions your teacher asks. Then study the map and make up questions of your own.

4. Compare the picture map with the map on page 176. How are the maps different? How are they the same?

184

Lincoln immediately after he gave his speech at Gettysburg

The Gettysburg Address

President Lincoln spoke these words at the dedication of the Gettysburg cemetery. Many people thought his speech was too short. But it told how he felt about the brave soldiers in both armies.

Four score and seven years ago our fathers brought forth on this continent, a new nation, conceived in Liberty, and dedicated to the proposition that all men are created equal.

Now we are engaged in a great civil war, testing whether that nation, or any nation so conceived and so dedicated, can long endure. We are met on a great battlefield of that war. We have come to dedicate a portion of that field as a final resting place for those who here gave their lives that that nation might live. It is altogether fitting and proper that we should do this.

But in a larger sense we can not dedicate— we can not consecrate—we can not hallow—this ground. The brave men, living and dead, who struggled here, have consecrated it, far above our

poor power to add or detract. The world will little note, nor long remember what we say here, but it can never forget what they did here. It is for us the living, rather to be dedicated here to the unfinished work which they who fought here have thus far so nobly advanced. It is rather for us to be here dedicated to the great task remaining before us—that from these honored dead we take increased devotion to that cause for which they gave the last full measure of devotion—that we here highly resolve that these dead shall not have died in vain—that this nation, under God, shall have a new birth of freedom—and that government of the people, by the people, for the people, shall not perish from the earth.

Lincoln's hand-written copy of the Gettysburg Address looked like this.

• **How might this position have helped the North to win?** *(The higher vantage point gave a better view of advancing Confederate troops.)*

➤ Compare the map on pages 182-83 with the map on page 176. **How are the two maps similar and different?** *(Answers will vary, but some similarities are that both maps have keys and names of rivers and mountains and both show Union and Confederate troop movements. Some differences are that the Gettysburg map shows railroads, roads, a field, and an orchard while the map on page 176 does not and that the Gettysburg map is in three levels while the map on page 176 is only one level.)*

Definitions Discussion

➤ *Show your child an addressed envelope.*

The envelope contains one kind of address, but there is also a different type of address. It is a speech. President Lincoln delivered this type of address after the Battle of Gettysburg.

➤ *Read and discuss the Definitions for Gettysburg Address on the Supplement page.*

Text Discussion, pages 274-75

➤ **Read the Gettysburg Address on pages 274-75.**

➤ **On what special occasion was this speech presented?** *(the dedication of the cemetery at Gettysburg)*

➤ **How many years earlier had America's forefathers established the new nation?** *(four score and seven years or eighty-seven years)* A *score* is twenty.

➤ Find the sentence that Lincoln used to explain why they were at Gettysburg. *("We have come to dedicate a portion of that field as a final resting place for those who here gave their lives that that nation might live.")* **Read the sentence in a bold speaking voice as Abraham Lincoln would have used to speak to the crowds.**

➤ **What did Lincoln say about the government?** *("that government of the people, by the people, for the people, shall not perish from the earth")* **Read the words as Abraham Lincoln would have read them.**

➤ I will play the reading of the Gettysburg Address from the listening cassette. Follow along in your textbook.

Discuss with your child that in the Gettysburg Address President Lincoln honored the brave soldiers who fought at Gettysburg. Many of them sacrificed their lives for their country. Remind him that Jesus Christ sacrificed His life for the whole world, not for just a few people or for only a country. (Bible Promise: E. Christ as Sacrifice) Invite your child to tell some ways Christians can sacrifice for the Lord and for others.

TimeLine Snapshots Activity

➤ Point to the year 1863 on the TimeLine.

The Battle of Gettysburg led to the famous speech called the Gettysburg Address.

➤ Place the figure representing the Gettysburg Address on the TimeLine at the year 1863.

Evaluating the Lesson

Interview

➤ Pretend you are General Lee after the Battle of Gettysburg. I am a newspaper reporter. Answer my questions about the battle from the perspective of the character you are playing.
  - **Why did you want to win a battle on Union land?** *(to scare the North into ending the war)*
  - **How long did the fighting last?** *(three days)*
  - **How many soldiers died?** *(more than six thousand)*
  - **How did the loss of lives at the Battle of Gettysburg affect your men?** *(My men were very discouraged.)*
  - **Why did the people of Gettysburg want to bury the soldiers?** *(They wanted to honor them for their bravery and for sacrificing their lives.)*

Going Beyond

Additional Teacher Information

General Lee decided that a victory in Northern territory would be an important means of breaking the North's will to fight. This decision led to the terrible battle at Gettysburg, where the main force of the Union army met General Lee's troops. The Union forces were strategically placed on Cemetery Ridge, giving them a distinct advantage over the lower Southern regiments. The Confederates tried to break through the line of cannon and musket fire but were soon beaten back. As a result, the South lost nearly one-third of its army. Lee took the entire blame for the defeat and submitted his resignation to Davis, who did not accept it. Long after the battle, he reportedly confided to a friend, "If I had had Stonewall Jackson with me, so far as man can see, I should have won the Battle of Gettysburg."

LESSON 52
The End, at Last

Text, pages 186-90, 255, 288-89
Notebook, page 67

Preview

Main Ideas
- The people were ready for the war to be over.
- Both Lee and Grant helped to end the war.
- The long process of reconstruction began after Appomattox.

Objectives
- Explain the circumstances surrounding the close of the Civil War
- Recognize the people who had a significant part in ending the war

Materials
- A man's white handkerchief
- 36 beans or buttons*
- The figure representing the Thirteenth Amendment (1865) from the TimeLine Snapshots
- The presidential figure of Andrew Johnson (17) from the TimeLine Snapshots
- Appendix, page A52: Grant nameplate*
- Appendix, page A52: A Nation Reunited nameplate*

Day 1

Lesson

Introducing the Lesson

Discussion

Later in the lesson you will read about how a change in the Constitution was made just after the end of the American Civil War. Changes to the Constitution are called *amendments.*

➤ **Do you know what *amend* means?** If you do not know what the word *amend* means, look it up in the dictionary. *(to change for the better, improve, correct)*

➤ *Place thirty-six beans on the table.*

In order for a constitutional amendment to pass or become law, three-fourths of the states have to vote for the change. Let's pretend that each of these beans represents a state. Each state receives one vote.

The End, at Last

When the soldiers fought at Gettysburg, the American Civil War was more than two years old. In the North and South, families were ready for the fighting to end. They wanted their sons and husbands and fathers to come home. But it would take almost two more years for the end of the war to come. And it would take another new leader for the Union army.

The Union army had many different leaders. President Lincoln had not yet found a leader as good as the South's General Lee. But he believed that his new choice would be the man to win the war.

Ulysses S. Grant was a strong leader. He had already won battles for the Union in the West. The army he led had taken Forts Donelson and Henry. Then his forces had won at Vicksburg and Chattanooga. General Grant knew how to fight. And he would not give up until the Union had won the war.

Ulysses S. Grant

186

General Grant pushed his army against General Lee's men. Sometimes fighting went on for days at a time. Even when it seemed that he had lost the battle, Grant would not turn back. General Lee had thought faster and moved quicker than the other Union leaders. But he could not outdo General Grant.

Finally the Confederate army and people could take no more. And General Robert E. Lee knew that his army could not win. His men were tired and hungry. Many were barefoot and dressed in rags. About half his men did not even have guns anymore. General Lee decided to surrender. Do you think he made a wise decision?

Both North and South were glad that the long and bloody war was over. The Union and the Confederacy were one country again. President Lincoln wanted to "bind up the wounds" of bitterness and pain felt by all Americans.

Richmond, Virginia, in 1865

187

➤ Count how many states or beans we have. *(thirty-six)* We will pretend that thirty-six states are voting for an amendment.

➤ To have a three-fourths majority of thirty-six states, at least twenty-seven states must vote *yes*. Count twenty-seven beans and put them in a separate pile so you can see how much three-fourths would be.

The purpose of this activity is to show your child what a three-fourths majority would be. The number thirty-six was chosen for ease in handling—not to correspond to the number of states.

Teaching the Lesson

Text Discussion, pages 186 and 288-89

➤ **Read page 186 to find out whom President Lincoln chose to lead the Union troops.** *(General Ulysses S. Grant)*

➤ Attach the *General Ulysses S. Grant* nameplate to the door.

➤ **How long did the Civil War last?** *(four years)*

➤ **How had General Grant proved himself to be a good fighter?** *(He took Forts Donelson and Henry and won the battles at Vicksburg and Chattanooga.)*

➤ Find Vicksburg, Mississippi, and Chattanooga, Tennessee, on the Sites of the Civil War Battles map on pages 288-89.

Day 2

Text Discussion, page 187

➤ **Read page 187, looking for some of the reasons General Lee probably surrendered.** *(His armies were tired and hungry, clothing and army supplies were low, the people were tired of war, morale was low, and Grant would not turn back.)*

➤ Put yourself in General Lee's place. **What do you think he probably had to consider before surrendering?**

General Lee probably thought about how the South would be affected by his surrender, what his men and the people would think of him, and what it would be like to admit defeat.

➤ Look at the picture on page 187. War can be very hard on a country and its people. **How did the Civil War affect the people and the country?** *(Answers will vary. Many homes were damaged, families torn apart, businesses hurt, the unity of the country broken, etc.)*

The rebuilding process after the war was long and tedious because of all the damage caused by the fighting. Homes were ruined, livelihoods destroyed, and families torn apart. Hatred and anger remained on both sides.

➤ **How do you think President Lincoln must have felt when he received the telegraph message that General Lee had surrendered?**
➤ **What new decisions did the president now face?** *(Answers will vary.)*

He would have to decide how to handle the needs and, perhaps, the anger of the South. He would have to try to unite the country after years of division and strife.

Text Discussion, pages 188 and 288-89

➤ **Read page 188 to learn more about the surrender of the South.**
➤ **Where did the surrender take place?** *(Appomattox Court House, Virginia)*
➤ Find Appomattox on the map on pages 288-89.
➤ *Discuss the characters of General Grant and General Lee.*
➤ Tell how General Grant and General Lee behaved at the surrender at Appomattox. *(Both men were serious and showed respect for one another.)*
➤ Name some actions of General Grant that show what kind of leader he was. *(He provided food for the Confederate army, let the soldiers keep their horses, and treated General Lee and his men with respect.)*

All of these actions showed his humility and servanthood. General Grant easily could have gloried in this victory and reacted in pride. Instead, he showed true humility by treating General Lee, his rival, with kindness and respect.

General Lee was faced with a tough decision, but he did what was best for his army and his people. He could have been stubborn and proud by refusing to surrender, but he showed both humility and an attitude of servanthood.

Christians should have the same attitude of humility and servanthood. Servanthood is accompanied by true humility. Encourage your child to think of ways that he can be humble and serving at home, at church, with friends, and even with "enemies." (BATs: 2b Servanthood, 7e Humility)

➤ **How do you think these men helped to reunite the United States?**
➤ Attach a white flag (man's handkerchief) to the door to represent the surrender at Appomattox.
➤ Attach the nameplate *A Nation Reunited* to the bottom of the door.

◆ HOW IT WAS ◆

Sunday, April 9, 1865
Afternoon
Appomattox Court House, Virginia

The horses of General Lee and General Grant stood quietly outside a farmhouse near the last battlefield of the war. Men also stood quietly around, hardly talking. Inside the house, the two generals were deciding how the war would finally end.

Grant and Lee sat at small tables. Their aides stood along the walls. Grant said, "I will write out the terms." Lee nodded. When Grant finished, Lee read the paper. He thanked Grant for letting his men keep their own horses. Then Colonel Parker, an Iroquois in the Northern army, copied the paper. Both generals signed it. Grant then told one of his men to see that food was sent to the whole Southern army.

Lee and Grant stood and shook hands. Then Lee swung into his saddle and rode away, his gray uniform straight, his hair shining white. Along the fences, his men cheered for him. One soldier called out, "We love you just as well as ever, General Lee."

McClean House at Appomattox Court House, Virginia, where the surrender took place

188

Day 3

Text Discussion, page 189

➤ **Read the title on page 189 to find out what amendment was passed.** *(the thirteenth)*
➤ Follow along as I read the box at the top of the page.
➤ **Read the rest of the page to find out what this means.**
➤ **What document was created to free the slaves in the Confederate states?** *(the Emancipation Proclamation)*
➤ **What does it mean to amend something?** *(to change for the better, improve, correct)*
➤ **How did the Thirteenth Amendment change or improve the Constitution?** *(It made slavery against the law.)*
➤ **How was this amendment different from the Emancipation Proclamation?** *(The Emancipation Proclamation applied only to the Confederate states. The Thirteenth Amendment applied to the entire country. It was more effective than the Emancipation Proclamation had been.)*
➤ **Why do you think Congress did not immediately pass the amendment?**

There was still great debate over the slave issue, and neither side was ready to resolve their differences so easily.

ECHOES IN HISTORY

The Thirteenth Amendment

> **Amendment XIII:** *Slavery*
> **Section 1.** *Neither slavery nor involuntary servitude, except as punishment for crime whereof the party shall have been duly convicted, shall exist within the United States, or any place subject to their jurisdiction.*
> **Section 2.** *Congress shall have power to enforce this article by appropriate legislation.*

The Emancipation Proclamation had freed the slaves in the Confederate States. But slavery still went on in territories and some other places. Some people wished that the writers of the Constitution had done away with slavery from the start. Others said that the Constitution needed an amendment. *Amendments* are additions to the Constitution. What do you think it means to amend something?

The amendment about slavery said that no slaves could be held anywhere in the United States or in any of its lands. How is this amendment different from the Emancipation Proclamation? The Congress did not pass the amendment at first.

President Lincoln said that it was "only a question of time" until the amendment would pass. "May we not agree," he asked the Congress, "that the sooner the better?" In 1865 the amendment passed and slavery ended, though the wrongs "echo" in our land to this day.

189

President Lincoln never got to see his nation restored. Just six days after the end of the fighting, a Southern man named John Wilkes Booth shot the president. He thought what he did would help the South. Instead he took away the South's best hope for peaceful reunion with the North.

Four years of war had left an ugly mark on the South. It took time and hard work to make new homes and farms and factories. Slowly the South rebuilt. But it was many, many years before the anger and bad feelings of the Civil War began to heal.

John Wilkes Booth

War Department, Washington, April 20, 1865.
$100,000 REWARD!
THE MURDERER
Of our late beloved President, Abraham Lincoln,
IS STILL AT LARGE.
$50,000 REWARD
$25,000 REWARD
$25,000 REWARD

Reward poster printed after the death of President Lincoln

> *"If my people, which are called by my name, shall humble themselves, and pray, and seek my face, and turn from their wicked ways; then will I hear from heaven, and will forgive their sin, and will heal their land."*
> **II Chronicles 7:14**

190

➤ **Why do you think President Lincoln said "the sooner, the better" for the passage of the amendment?** He probably wanted the differences resolved quickly so that the nation could become unified.

Text Discussion, page 190

➤ **Read page 190 to find out what John Wilkes Booth did.** *(He shot President Lincoln.)*

➤ **How do you think the death of Abraham Lincoln harmed the country's recovery from the war?** It probably caused more anger between the states and took away a caring and wise leader.

➤ **Read II Chronicles 7:14 on the text page.**

Ask your child what God promises to do for His people, according to II Chronicles 7:14. *(He promises to hear their prayers, forgive their sins, and heal their land.)* Ask your child to read aloud the part of the verse that tells what Christians must do in order to receive that promise. *("If my people, which are called by my name, shall humble themselves, and pray, and seek my face, and turn from their wicked ways")* Discuss the importance of asking forgiveness and of forgiving others. (BAT: 6e Forgiveness)

➤ An *epitaph* is brief lines of writing that honor a person who has died. Write an epitaph honoring President Lincoln.

TimeLine Snapshots Activity, page 255

➤ In 1865, a new addition to the Constitution was made. **What was this addition called?** *(the Thirteenth Amendment)*

➤ Place the figure representing the Thirteenth Amendment on the TimeLine at the year 1865.

➤ Point to the figure of Andrew Johnson on the TimeLine. He became president after Abraham Lincoln.

➤ **Read the information on page 255 about President Andrew Johnson.**

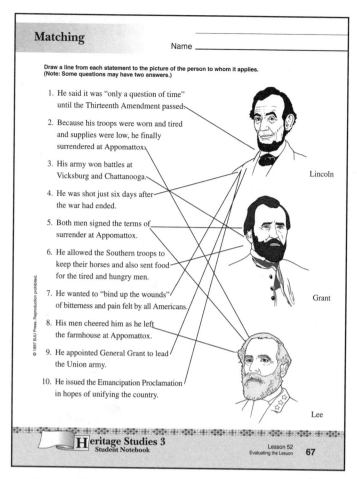

Matching

Name _____

Draw a line from each statement to the picture of the person to whom it applies.
(Note: Some questions may have two answers.)

1. He said it was "only a question of time" until the Thirteenth Amendment passed.

2. Because his troops were worn and tired and supplies were low, he finally surrendered at Appomattox.

3. His army won battles at Vicksburg and Chattanooga.

4. He was shot just six days after the war had ended.

5. Both men signed the terms of surrender at Appomattox.

6. He allowed the Southern troops to keep their horses and also sent food for the tired and hungry men.

7. He wanted to "bind up the wounds" of bitterness and pain felt by all Americans.

8. His men cheered him as he left the farmhouse at Appomattox.

9. He appointed General Grant to lead the Union army.

10. He issued the Emancipation Proclamation in hopes of unifying the country.

Lincoln

Grant

Lee

Heritage Studies 3
Student Notebook

Lesson 52
Evaluating the Lesson   **67**

Evaluating the Lesson

Notebook Activity, page 67

➤ Read the directions for Notebook page 67.
➤ Complete the page.

Going Beyond

Enrichment

Remind your child that the Civil War used many of the country's resources, making items such as clothing and paper scarce. During and after the war, many people used carpet and curtains to make clothes. Newspapers were often printed on the back of wallpaper.

Cut paper bags or scraps of wallpaper into smaller pieces approximately $8\frac{1}{2}$" $\times$ 12" so that their shapes resemble a miniature newspaper. Instruct your child to make a newspaper, using a felt-tip pen to write a short article about some aspect of the war that he has studied. He may cut out pictures from magazines and glue them onto his "newspaper" to illustrate his stories. Encourage him to write advertisements, draw pictures, and so forth.

Additional Teacher Information

On April 9, 1865, just eight months before the passage of the Thirteenth Amendment, a somber occasion took place at Appomattox Court House, a small town in Virginia. Two great men met to end four years of fighting. In many ways, Appomattox marked a beginning—the beginning of a new era of emancipation. Both General Grant and General Lee demonstrated humility and respect for one another. While Grant drew up the terms of peace, Colonel Babcock reportedly signaled with a twirl of his hat to one of the men on the porch. Seeing the signal, Henry Wing rode off to send a telegram to President Lincoln, announcing the end of the Civil War.

America Celebrates

This chapter takes your child through the months of the calendar year, focusing on eight of America's major holidays. Each lesson gives background information about a particular holiday, helps him to appreciate America's traditions, and gives him a greater understanding of the reasons for celebrating each of these special days.

Materials

The following materials must be obtained or prepared before the presentation of the lesson. These items are labeled with an asterisk (*) in each lesson and in the Materials List in the Supplement. For further information see the individual lessons.

- A hard-boiled egg for each participant (Lesson 54)
- Felt-tip pens or watercolor paints (Lesson 54)
- Parade items (Lesson 56)

10

America Celebrates

LESSON 53
Famous Birthdays

Text, pages 192-95, 247, 255
Notebook, page 68

━━━━ **Preview** ━━━━

Main Ideas
- We celebrate birthdays to honor people who are special to us.
- We build monuments to help us remember people who did great things.

Objective
- Identify true and false statements about two famous presidents

Materials
- A calendar showing the month of February
- A red pen
- Supplement, page S13: February Birthdays

Notes
Some people honor all former U.S. presidents on Presidents' Day; others honor just Lincoln and Washington on that day.

Day 1

━━━━ **Lesson** ━━━━

Introducing the Lesson

Calendar Activity

➤ *Show your child a calendar of the month of February. If your child's birthday is in February, mark the date.*
➤ *Turn to February Birthdays in the Supplement.* Many famous people were born in this month.
➤ **Read each name and the occupation for which that person achieved fame.**
➤ This lesson is about two famous people with February birthdays. *With the red pen, circle February 12 and 22 on the calendar.*
➤ **Do you know which two famous presidents were born on these days?**

Abraham Lincoln was born on February 12, and George Washington was born on February 22.

"Happy birthday to you. Happy birthday to you. Happy birthday, dear. . . . Happy birthday to you!"

Every person has a birthday, and most people like to have others help them *celebrate* their birthdays. To celebrate means to set apart a special time for remembering and for having fun. What kind of things do you do to celebrate your birthday?

Birthdays are not the only special days for celebrating. Can you think of other days that you celebrate? In America there are many days for celebrating. We call those days *holidays*. Your family and friends celebrate your birthday. But everyone, all across the country, celebrates holidays.

192

Teaching the Lesson

Text Discussion, page 192

➤ **Read page 192 to find a word that means a special day to celebrate.** *(holiday)*
➤ *Write the words* halig daeg *(hālig dæg). Our word* holiday *comes from this Old English expression.*
➤ Guess what the expression means. *(holy day)* Today the word **holiday** refers only to a day set apart to remember a special event or to honor a person.
➤ Tell about some of the things our family does for you on your birthday to make the day special.
➤ **Do schools and businesses close to honor your birthday?**
➤ **Why do you think schools and businesses do not close for every birthday?**

If places of business did this for every birthday, they would be closed every day of the year. Stores would never be open for us to buy things we need, and people would never get work done.

Famous Birthday Celebrations

Sometimes a birthday celebration can become a holiday. When George Washington was president, people celebrated his birthday, February 22, 1732. (When he was a general, the men in the American army also celebrated his birthday. They could not give him a big party. But they played songs for him and wished him a happy day.) In Philadelphia, men fired cannons and rang church bells. Everyone wanted to shake George Washington's hand and wish him a happy day.

Americans still celebrate George Washington's birthday. They remember him because of the things he did. He led the American army during the War for Independence. He helped to write the Constitution. He became the country's first president. On February 22, Americans think about the man they call the Father of Our Country.

George Washington

193

Abraham Lincoln

Americans celebrate a second birthday in February. Abraham Lincoln was born February 12, 1809. His family did not have much money. And there was little time for Abe to go to school. Life was hard in the back-woods where Abe lived.

Young Abe Lincoln did not seem to have much going for him. But he studied hard and worked hard. He kept his promises. And he became one of the best presidents America has ever had. He was a strong and brave and wise leader during the terrible Civil War. He helped to bring America back together.

Today in most places, Americans celebrate the birthdays of these two presidents on one day. Presidents' Day is the third Monday in February. On that day, they honor two men who helped to make their country free for everyone.

194

Text Discussion, pages 193 and 247

In 1800 the U.S. government decided that the whole country should celebrate a special person's birthday.

➤ **Read page 193 to find out whose birthday became a national holiday.** *(George Washington's)*

➤ **Why do the people of the United States want to honor George Washington in this way?** *(Everyone loves and admires him for his leadership as general of the army and as first president of the nation.)* (BAT: 2a Authority)

➤ **Turn to page 247 and read the information about George Washington.**

Text Discussion, pages 194 and 255

➤ The birthday of another important president became an American national holiday also. **Read the first two paragraphs of page 194 to find out who this person was.** *(Abraham Lincoln)*

➤ Name some accomplishments that made Lincoln such an important man in U.S. history. *(Answers will vary. He overcame a background of poverty and little education to become a lawyer, worked and studied hard, became the sixteenth president, abolished slavery, led the country wisely during the Civil War, and helped to reunify the states.)* (BAT: 2e Work)

➤ **Read the information on page 255 about our sixteenth president.**

➤ Find the birthdates of Abraham Lincoln and George Washington on the February calendar.

➤ **Read the last paragraph on page 194 to find out what day in February Americans celebrate these famous birthdays and what that day is called.** *(the third Monday; Presidents' Day)*

➤ **What day is Presidents' Day on your calendar?**

◆ THINGS PEOPLE DO ◆

Building Monuments

One way to help people remember an important person is to name a holiday for him. But it is not the only way. People sometimes build a *monument* to help people remember. Have you ever seen a monument?

A monument is a building or a statue. Usually, an artist or a builder makes the monument from stone. He puts the monument where people can see it. When people visit the monument, they remember the person it honors. Sometimes we call a monument a *memorial*. What smaller word can you hear in the word "memorial"?

Many cities have monuments. Two of America's best-known monuments were built to remind us of presidents. You can see the Washington Monument and the Lincoln Memorial in the same city. Do you know the name of that city? The city is Washington, D.C. It is America's capital.

Lincoln Memorial

Washington Monument

195

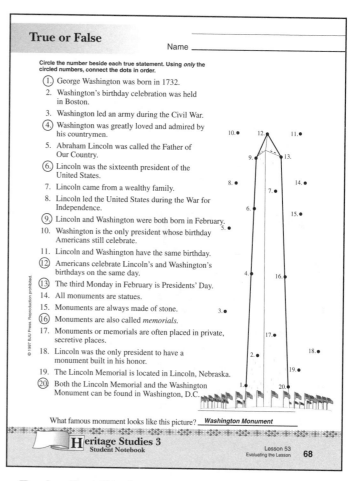

True or False

Name _____

Circle the number beside each true statement. Using *only* the circled numbers, connect the dots in order.

1. George Washington was born in 1732.
2. Washington's birthday celebration was held in Boston.
3. Washington led an army during the Civil War.
4. Washington was greatly loved and admired by his countrymen.
5. Abraham Lincoln was called the Father of Our Country.
6. Lincoln was the sixteenth president of the United States.
7. Lincoln came from a wealthy family.
8. Lincoln led the United States during the War for Independence.
9. Lincoln and Washington were both born in February.
10. Washington is the only president whose birthday Americans still celebrate.
11. Lincoln and Washington have the same birthday.
12. Americans celebrate Lincoln's and Washington's birthdays on the same day.
13. The third Monday in February is Presidents' Day.
14. All monuments are statues.
15. Monuments are always made of stone.
16. Monuments are also called *memorials*.
17. Monuments or memorials are often placed in private, secretive places.
18. Lincoln was the only president to have a monument built in his honor.
19. The Lincoln Memorial is located in Lincoln, Nebraska.
20. Both the Lincoln Memorial and the Washington Monument can be found in Washington, D.C.

What famous monument looks like this picture? __Washington Monument__

Heritage Studies 3
Student Notebook

Lesson 53
Evaluating the Lesson **68**

Text Discussion, page 195

Sometimes we honor people not only with a special day but also with a special landmark that everyone can see.

➤ **Read the first paragraph of page 195 to find out what this special marker is called.** *(a monument)*
➤ **Have you seen a monument?** Describe the monument you saw and tell what person or group it was meant to honor.
➤ **Read the next paragraph to find out what other word we often use for a monument.** *(memorial)*
➤ **What smaller word can you hear in "memorial"?** *(memory)*

One of the main purposes of a monument is to help us remember a person after he has died. The two monuments pictured on the page are made from stone, but monuments do not always need to be made of stone.

➤ **Read the final paragraph on the page to find the names of two monuments that remind us of U.S. presidents.** *(the Washington Monument, the Lincoln Memorial)*

Evaluating the Lesson

Notebook Activity, page 68

➤ Read the directions on Notebook page 68.
➤ Complete the page.

━━ Going Beyond ━━

Enrichment

Make available a piece of sturdy cardboard, a cutting board, construction paper, scissors, and a heavy-duty needle. Allow your child to choose and to cut out a patriotic picture from a magazine or an old calendar. To ensure that the design stays in place, tape the patriotic picture to the construction paper with masking tape. Your child should place the piece of cardboard on top of the cutting board. Then he should place the construction paper with his chosen picture on top of the cardboard. Let him prick holes with the needle around the lines of the picture to outline it and around any other object inside the outline that he would like to emphasize. Remind him to make sure his pinpricks are going through both the picture and the construction paper beneath it. When he is finished, hang the piece of construction paper against a windowpane to let the light shine through the holes. This type of art, called pinpricking, was popular in early America.

Additional Teacher Information

At the time of George Washington's birth in 1732, an older style of calendar was in use, making his actual birthdate February 11. But with the institution of the newer calendar, the date was moved to February 22. The year 1790, when Washington turned fifty-eight, was the first year his birthday was celebrated on the twenty-second. Washington's daughter Nellie Custis was married on February 22, 1799, which was also Washington's last birthday. He died in December of that year. In 1932, the U.S. government organized an enormous bicentennial celebration of this great leader's birthday. The festivities lasted from February 22 through Thanksgiving Day, with special emphasis on each patriotic holiday in between. Special activities included parades, programs and speeches, historical exhibits and flag displays, fourteen murals painted for the National Gallery, the publishing of Washington's complete writings, the planting of ten million trees in his honor, and a pageant at the base of the Washington Monument. The event was observed throughout the United States and in nine other countries.

Abraham Lincoln's birthday was made a holiday in 1892, twenty-six years after his death. On the hundredth anniversary of his birth, in 1909, Booker T. Washington gave an address in honor of Lincoln. Washington was a former slave who had been freed as a result of Lincoln's Emancipation Proclamation, which ended slavery in the South. Lincoln is honored today throughout the United States by statues, memorials, and paintings.

LESSON 54
Holidays of Springtime

Text, pages 196-97
Notebook, page 69

═══ Preview ═══

Main Ideas

- Easter is a holiday to remember Christ's death, burial, and resurrection.
- Memorial Day is a holiday to remember people who have died in wars.

Objective

- Compare and contrast two different holidays

Materials

- A hard-boiled egg for each participant*
- Felt-tip pens or watercolor paints*

> The Egg-Rolling Contest requires at least two participants. This can be a family activity or you may participate with your child.

Day 1

═══ Lesson ═══

Introducing the Lesson

Egg-Rolling Contest

The egg-rolling contest is an Easter game practiced in many parts of the world, including America. Every Easter a contest is held on the White House lawn, with prizes awarded by the president himself. The rolling of the egg traditionally symbolizes the rolling away of the stone from Christ's tomb after His Resurrection.

Remind your child that Christ's Resurrection after His death on the cross is what Christians celebrate at Easter. (BAT: 1a Understanding Jesus Christ)

➤ Decorate your egg with felt-tip pens or watercolor paints.

Take your child to the place where the contest is to be held. It is most authentic to have the contest outdoors on a grassy hill or on any sloping ground. If no suitable location is available, you may have the contest indoors on a carpeted floor. Set up your own "hill" by propping a long piece of cardboard up against a chair, leaving enough space for the egg to roll a long distance at the bottom.

➤ We will take turns rolling our eggs down the slope. The egg that rolls the farthest is the winner.

Teaching the Lesson

Discussion

➤ The lamb, the egg, and the chick are symbols of the true meaning of the Easter celebration. **What do you think the lamb, the egg, and the chick might symbolize or stand for?**

The lamb is a symbol of Christ, the Lamb of God who was sacrificed on the cross for the sins of mankind. (Bible Promise: E. Christ as Sacrifice) The egg is a symbol of birth, pointing to the spiritual rebirth a person experiences when he accepts Christ as his Savior. (Bible Promises: A. Liberty from Sin, B. Guiltless by the Blood) The chick is a symbol of new life, pointing to Christ's Resurrection from the dead and to the new life a Christian receives when he accepts Christ. (Bible Promise: D. Identified in Christ)

➤ **Do the symbols of Easter ever become more important to people than the true Easter story?** *(yes)*

➤ **Should the true story or the symbols of that story be the most important part of our Easter celebration?** *(The true story of Christ's death and His Resurrection should be most important.)* (BAT: 1a Understanding Jesus Christ)

Day 2

Text Discussion, page 196

Read Matthew 28:5-6 from page 196. Ask your child why Christ's Resurrection from the tomb is still important to Christians today. *(Answers will vary. Help your child to understand that Christ's Resurrection brought victory over death. When Christians die, they go to heaven to be with Christ forever.)*

➤ **Read the rest of page 196.**
➤ **What does a person have to do to be able to live in heaven with Christ?** *(Believe that Christ's death paid for his sins and ask Him to be his Savior.)* (BAT: 1b Repentance and faith)

Easter

Each spring we celebrate a special holiday. On this day, we honor a person who was not a president. He was someone far more important. We remember the most important thing He did. Do you know what we remember at *Easter*?

"And the angel answered and said unto the women, Fear not ye: for I know that ye seek Jesus, which was crucified. He is not here: for he is risen, as he said, Come, see the place where the Lord lay."

Matthew 28:5-6

We remember the Savior, Jesus Christ. We think about how He died on the cross to save all men from sin. We are joyful when we remember that He rose from the dead. Because He died for our sins and rose again, we can live forever with Him in heaven.

196

➤ **What kinds of activities do you do with our family to focus on the real meaning of Easter?**

Text Discussion, page 197

Easter is the holiday on which Christians remember the most important person who died, Jesus Christ. But there is also another holiday to honor people who have died.

➤ **Read page 197 to find out what this day is called and who is honored on this day.** *(Memorial Day; men and women who have died in wars)*

At first, Memorial Day was meant to honor only those who had died in the Civil War. But since the United States has fought many more wars since then, today Memorial Day is for honoring all people who have died in any of the wars that the United States has fought.

➤ **What did the holiday used to be called?** *(Decoration Day)*
➤ **Why do you think it was called this?** People decorate the graves of their friends and relatives with flowers and flags on this day.
➤ **Why do you think people put flowers and flags on graves of people who cannot see or appreciate them?** Decorating the grave of someone who died in a war is a way of showing respect and thankfulness for that person's sacrifice. (BAT: 5a Love)

228

Memorial Day

Memorial Day is another springtime holiday. Each year on May 30, Americans think about the men and women who died in wars. They think about how these soldiers fought to make America great. Many people put flowers and flags on the graves of those brave men and women. The flowers and flags remind us that people gave their lives to make America free.

Americans celebrated the first Memorial Day a few years after the Civil War ended. No one knows for sure who first thought of this holiday. But it was called "Decoration Day" then. Why do you think the people called it that?

197

Holidays

Name _____

Read each statement. If the statement is true only of Easter, draw a cross (†) in the blank. Write *M* if the statement is true only of Memorial Day. Write *B* if the statement is true of both holidays.

__B__ 1. On this day we remember someone who has died.

__†__ 2. On this day we think of someone who has risen from the dead.

__M__ 3. On this day we think of people who died in wars.

__B__ 4. On this day we put flowers on graves.

__†__ 5. On this day we sometimes attend sunrise services.

__B__ 6. On this day we will probably think of a tombstone.

__†__ 7. On this day we will think about an empty grave.

__B__ 8. On this day we can thank God for His power over death.

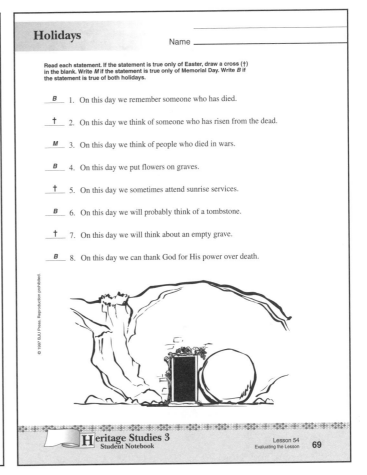

Heritage Studies 3
Student Notebook

Lesson 54
Evaluating the Lesson   69

Evaluating the Lesson

Comparison Activity, Notebook page 69

➤ Read the directions on Notebook page 69.
➤ Complete the page.

> Answers to numbers four and six may vary from those given. Keep in mind regional practices and family traditions.

——— Going Beyond ———

Enrichment

Provide a Bible, paper, and crayons. Instruct your child to read the Easter story found in Matthew 27 and 28 and to make a picture time line of at least four events in the story of Christ's Crucifixion and Resurrection. He should label each event on his time line.

Additional Teacher Information

The name *Easter* probably came from the Anglo-Saxon name for the goddess of spring, *Eostre*. Pagan festivals to this goddess celebrated an awakening of the earth from her long winter sleep. Since Christ's Resurrection is an awakening from death, it is appropriate that we should remember it in the spring of the year. The name *Easter* may also contain a reference to the east and to the rising of the sun.

Easter is always celebrated on the first Sunday after the first full moon following March 21. This date was established by Constantine at the Council of Nicea in A.D. 325. The use of the bunny as an Easter symbol probably originated from the Greek legends that used the hare as a symbol of the moon. The practice of egg giving also had its origins in ancient times, long before the first Easter. Records show that in Egypt the giving of an egg was a symbol of peace.

LESSON 55
Honoring Patriot Dreams

Text, pages 198-200, 269-71
Notebook, pages 70-71

━━━━ Preview ━━━━

Main Ideas

- On Flag Day Americans honor the flag by showing their respect for it.
- On the Fourth of July Americans celebrate their independence and remember the courage of their forefathers.

Objectives

- Fold a flag properly
- Answer questions about two patriotic holidays

Materials

- Maps and More 20 and 21, page M13
- A large towel
- The figure of the Stamp Act (1765) from the Time-Line Snapshots

Day 1

━━━━ Lesson ━━━━

Introducing the Lesson

Flag Activity, page 269 and
Maps and More 20 and 21

➤ *Show your child Maps and More 20.* Before the colonies all agreed on one design for their flag, they used many different types of flags.

➤ **Do you recognize anything on any of the flags?** *(Answers will vary. Two of these flags have alternating red and white stripes. One flag has stars. One flag has the symbol of the British flag in one corner.)*

➤ **Would you like having a snake as a symbol on your flag?**

➤ **Which flag do you like best? Why?**

➤ *Cover half of Maps and More 21 so that only the early American flag is showing.*

This is the design of the flag that the American people finally agreed upon to represent their nation. George Washington explained the meaning of the design.

Signs of Freedom

The Flags So Far

Many flags have flown over the United States. Here are the ones that flew before the American Civil War.

The Grand Union flag, or Cambridge flag

Two versions of the flag of 1777

The flag of 1795

Two versions of the flag of 1818

The flag of 1861

269

We take the stars from heaven, the red from our mother country, separating it by white stripes, thus showing that we have separated from her, and the white stripes shall go down to posterity, representing liberty.

➤ **Why did George Washington think it was important for people to know that the stars on the flag represent heaven?** *(Answers will vary, but help your child to see that Washington wanted to acknowledge God's help and protection over the country.)*

➤ **Which country did Washington mean by "our mother country"?** *(England)*

England's flag had a solid red background, and Washington wanted the American flag to show the flag of the country that they had been a part of. *Posterity* means "a person's descendants or future generations of families." Washington wanted the white stripes on the flag to be a symbol to Americans today that they live in a free country.

➤ *Uncover the bottom of the Maps and More 21.* This is the current American flag.

➤ **How is it different from the early flag?** *(It has more stars; the stars are arranged differently.)*

➤ **Why are these differences necessary?** *(because the United States now has fifty states instead of thirteen)*

➤ **Read page 269.**

Flag Day

You may see America's flag each day. You may even have one in your classroom. But on one day of the year you will see the flag in many other places too. The flag flies at homes and businesses on that day. Many Americans display the flag on June 14. That is the flag's "birthday."

What do you think of when you look at the flag? Each part of the flag means something. The thirteen stripes make us think of the thirteen colonies. Those colonies fought for their freedom. They became the United States of America. How many stars does the American flag have? There are fifty stars—one for each state in the United States today.

Even the colors have special meanings. Red stands for courage. It makes us think of the men who fought to make America great. It reminds us to have courage to do what is right. White in the stripes and the stars stands for liberty. Liberty means freedom from unwanted rulers. And blue stands for loyalty. It reminds us of the men and women who cared more for their country than they did for themselves.

198

To Fold the Flag

1. Get an American flag. (You may want a beach towel to practice with first.) Work with your Heritage Studies partner.

2. Open the flag out flat. You hold the striped end while your friend holds the end with the stars. Be sure that the flag does not touch the floor.

3. Fold the flag in half the long way; then fold it in half again. Fold your end up to the right side, making a triangle. Continue folding the triangle shape.

4. Tuck the end of the flag in as your teacher shows you. This will keep the flag folded. What does the folded flag look like? Do you know any rules for taking care of the flag?

199

Teaching the Lesson

Text Discussion, page 198

➤ **Read the first paragraph on page 198 to find out when Americans celebrate the birthday of their flag.** *(June 14)*

The Continental Congress officially chose the flag with the thirteen stars as the national flag on this date in 1777.

➤ **Read the second paragraph on the page.**

➤ **What was George Washington's explanation of why there are alternating red and white stripes on the U.S. flag?** *(The red was taken from the British flag and separated by white stripes to show that the United States had separated from England.)*

➤ **Read the third paragraph on page 198 to find out what each of the colors represents.** *(Red stands for courage; white stands for liberty; blue stands for loyalty.)*

➤ **Why do Americans put their hands over their hearts when pledging to the flag or singing the national anthem?** *(to show respect for the flag and loyalty to the country)*

➤ **What kinds of things can Americans do to honor the flag on June 14, Flag Day?** *(Answers will vary but should include displaying a flag at home.)*

Learning How Activity, page 199

One way of showing loyalty to a nation's flag is by treating it with respect. In this activity, you will learn how to fold the American flag properly and discuss some rules for taking care of a flag. *Give your child a large towel.*

➤ **Read the directions for folding the flag on page 199.**

➤ Let's practice how to fold the flag using the towel.

➤ **Do you know any other rules for taking care of a flag?** *The following rules may be discussed with your child.*

- Never let the flag touch the ground.
- Never let it fly outside during rain or bad weather.
- Never leave it out all night unless it is lighted.
- Never use it as a tablecloth, curtain, or item of clothing.

Independence Day

Independence Day is a holiday with two names. We know it as the Fourth of July too. It is America's birthday. On that day Americans remember how their country began.

Fifty-six men met in Philadelphia. They came from every colony in America. These men knew that the people of the colonies were tired of King George's rules. They had asked him before to make better laws. Do you remember what King George did instead?

The men voted. They decided to tell the world that the colonies did not belong to the king. The men said the people in America were part of a new country. Today the United States of America is a great country. Americans celebrate their freedom with parades, picnics, and fireworks.

Fireworks over Washington, D.C.

200

The Great Seal

This sign appears on all important papers of the United States government.

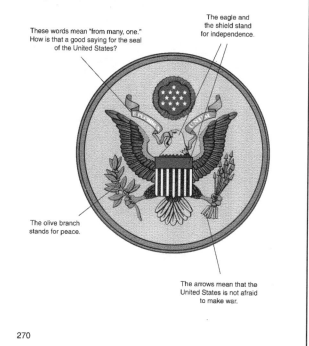

These words mean "from many, one." How is that a good saying for the seal of the United States?

The eagle and the shield stand for independence.

The olive branch stands for peace.

The arrows mean that the United States is not afraid to make war.

270

Day 2

Text Discussion, page 200

➤ **Read page 200 to find out whose birthday Americans celebrate on Independence Day.** *(the United States')*
➤ Tell the official name of the meeting of the fifty-six men. *(Continental Congress)*
➤ Name the document that was drawn up and signed at this meeting. *(the Declaration of Independence)*

Thomas Jefferson worked on writing the Declaration of Independence for many days before it was actually ready to be signed.

➤ **On what date did the men sign the Declaration of Independence?** *(July 4, 1776)*

TimeLine Snapshots Review

➤ Place the Stamp Act on the TimeLine at 1765.

The colonists had not been happy for many years with the way King George had treated them. They were unhappy with his rules.

➤ **Can you remember the things that King George had done to anger the colonists?** *(He made them pay taxes to him; he would not let them have a say in the government; he sent soldiers to the colonies to enforce his laws.)*

➤ **What did the Stamp Act make the colonists pay tax on?** *(everything that was made of paper)*

Discussion, pages 270-71

➤ **What did the Declaration of Independence mean to the colonies?** *(It meant that the colonies were no longer part of England but that they were free states that could govern themselves as they liked.)*

Remember that the colonists' independence did not come easily. Even though the Declaration of Independence was published, the colonists had to fight a war to get King George to agree to it too.

➤ **What was that war called?** *(the American War for Independence or the Revolutionary War)* The bravery of early Americans made the country free for Americans to live in today.
➤ **What should Americans remember on the Fourth of July?** *(They should remember the courage of these men and remember to thank God for a free country.)* (BATs: 5a Love, 7c Praise)
➤ **Read about the symbols of America's freedom on pages 270-71.**

The National Bird

Benjamin Franklin wanted the turkey to be the bird of the United States. He said that it would "attack . . . the British Guards, who should invade his farmyard with a red coat on,"

But other people thought the eagle was a better symbol for the United States. The eagle is mighty and beautiful.

In 1782, Congress voted for the eagle to be the national bird.

271

Evaluating the Lesson

Crossword Puzzle Activity, Notebook pages 70-71

➤ Read the instructions on Notebook page 70.
➤ Complete the puzzle.

Explain to your child that some puzzle entries are more than one word and that there are no spaces between the words. You may find it beneficial to put all the word selections in the white space at the bottom of the crossword puzzle.

Going Beyond

Enrichment

Provide 1"×6" construction-paper strips of red (about 213), white (about 213), and blue (about 100). Demonstrate looping the strips into a chain. (*NOTE:* Connecting the loops with a small stapler works best.) Some of the chains will be completely red; some will be completely white; and some will be half red or white and half blue. The completed flag needs three red chains of about thirty-five loops and three white chains of about thirty-five loops. The remaining chains should include four chains of eleven blue loops connected to twenty-four red loops

---

Clues

Name _____

Use the following clues to fill in the crossword puzzle on page 71.

ACROSS
3. wrote the Declaration of Independence
6. the colors of the flag
9. On the Fourth of July, we might watch a ____.
11. king of England in 1776
14. stands for courage
16. Blue stands for ____.
17. stars and ____
18. The colonists fought the ____ in the War for Independence.

DOWN
1. a famous song about America's flag; also America's national anthem
2. In 1776, the colonists declared their ____.
4. number of stars on the first flag
5. Americans celebrate Flag Day in this month.
7. a symbol on an early colonial flag
8. White stands for ____.
10. On Flag Day, Americans ____ the flag.
12. The colonists were unhappy with King George's ____.
13. Americans celebrate Independence Day in this month.
15. Washington said, "We take the ____ from heaven."

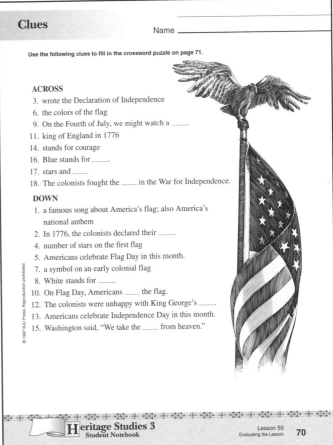

Crossword Puzzle

Name _____

and three chains of eleven blue loops connected to twenty-four white loops. The blue/red and blue/white chains should be the same length as the all-red and all-white chains.

When all the chains are made, arrange them in order. Refer to the illustration for the correct layout. Use additional red, white, and blue strips to connect all the rows together vertically at the blue field end of the flag. Provide a 32" thin cardboard tube or a dowel or a curtain rod to slide through the vertical row of loops. Affix fifty 1" gummed silver foil stars to the blue field.

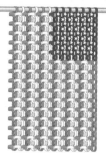

Additional Teacher Information

America's flag is called by many different names: Old Glory; the Stars and Stripes; the Red, White, and Blue; and the Star-Spangled Banner. According to popular legend, a Philadelphia seamstress named Betsy Ross made the first national flag of America. The legend says that George Washington, Robert Morris, and Colonel George Ross, Betsy's uncle, were assigned the task of designing a flag. They drew a pattern on paper and took it to Betsy Ross. She had some better ideas for the flag. She decided to use five-pointed stars rather than the six-pointed ones on the pattern, and she arranged them in a circle instead of in rows. The Continental Congress was pleased with Betsy's flag and approved it right away. Although the story of Betsy Ross's making the first flag has never been proved true, there really was a woman named Betsy Ross who made flags in Philadelphia.

LESSON 56
Celebrations of Home and Harvest

Text, pages 201-4, 277
Notebook, page 72

═══ Preview ═══

Main Ideas
- Columbus Day is a day for honoring the man who discovered America.
- Thanksgiving Day is a day for remembering God's blessings and for giving thanks.

Objectives
- Plan and conduct a parade
- Write a letter of thanks to a historical figure

Materials
- Construction paper
- Crepe paper*
- Paint*
- Paintbrushes*
- Old clothes for costumes*
- Wood blocks*
- Cardboard boxes*
- Tin cans*
- Wagons*

Day 1

═══ Lesson ═══

Introducing the Lesson

Learning How Activity, page 201

➤ **Have you seen a parade?**
➤ Describe the parade.
➤ **Read the instructions for planning a parade on page 201.**

Most parades celebrate a particular event. Parades are often part of holiday celebrations such as Thanksgiving, New Year's Day, and the Fourth of July.

➤ Follow the steps listed on page 201 to plan and have your parade.

◆ LEARNING HOW ◆

To Plan a Parade

1. Gather some construction paper, crepe paper, tape, paint, paintbrushes, and clothes for costumes. Also find some wood blocks, cardboard boxes, tin cans, and wagons.

2. First, make a list on the chalkboard of things you might see in a parade. Include as many things as you can think of. Then decide which ones you will want for your parade. Which one will come first in the parade? What will be last?

3. Choose a day and a time for your parade. What will you celebrate with the parade? Invite other people to watch.

4. Divide the work among the people who will be in the parade. Let each person make an instrument or put together a costume or decorate a "float." Plan your work so that everything will be finished by the day of the parade.

201

Columbus Day

Three little ships sailed west from the country of Spain. The men on the ships were afraid. Do you know why? They were sure the world was flat. They thought that their ships might sail off the edge of the world.

Their leader was not frightened. Christopher Columbus believed that the earth was like a ball. He thought he could find Asia by sailing west. His plan would give the people in Spain an easy way to get things like silk, pepper, and cinnamon from Asia.

Today we know that Columbus was both right and wrong. The world is like a ball, just as he said. But the land Columbus found was not Asia; it was a "new" part of the world. People in North America and South America celebrate Columbus Day on October 12. They remember the day that Columbus found a "new" land.

202

Some ideas for your parade are a family reunion parade, a neighborhood parade, or a birthday party parade.

Day 2

Teaching the Lesson

Text Discussion, page 202

➤ **Read the first two paragraphs of page 202 to find out why Columbus sailed from Spain.** *(He wanted to find a water route to Asia so that people in Spain could trade with the Asians for things like silk, pepper, and cinnamon.)*

Columbus had to wait eight years for Queen Isabella to give him money with which to sail. The reason it took the queen so long was not that she feared that the world was flat. Rather she feared that Columbus was wrong in his calculations about how far away Asia was. She thought that his food and water supply would run out before he reached his destination, as indeed it would have done if America had not stood in the way. Most educated people of that day believed that the world was like a ball. Only some uneducated people, such as many of Columbus's sailors, feared that the world was flat.

➤ **What do you think made Columbus keep asking for money when it seemed hopeless?**

He was convinced that his theory about the world was right. He believed that one day the queen would agree to give him the money, and he was willing to wait as long as it took. Columbus had endurance and perseverance. (BATs: 2c Faithfulness, 2d Goal setting)

➤ **Read the last paragraph on page 202 to find out what holiday people in North and South America celebrate on October 12.** *(Columbus Day)*

◆ HOW IT WAS ◆

Near San Salvador
October 12, 1492

Three ships waited close to an island. Christopher Columbus and some of his men sailed in smaller boats toward the shore.

The island people watched from the shore. They had seen the large boats with white sails far out to sea. They had thought the boats were three white birds.

At first the island people, or *Arawaks*, were afraid. Then they saw Columbus and his men. The Arawaks brought the white men gifts. They thought the white men were gods.

Christopher Columbus believed that he was on an island near India. He called the island people *Indians*.

203

Thanksgiving

Pilgrims, Indians, harvest, feast. What do these words make you think of? They remind us of Thanksgiving, of course. Almost four hundred years ago, the Separatists and other Pilgrims made a special feast. They asked their friends the Indians to join them. Did the Indians come? They did, and they brought even more food. The feast lasted for three days.

Why did the Pilgrims prepare such a big feast? They had lived through a cold winter without much to eat. They had worked hard in the spring to plant food. The Indians told them the things to grow. Now they had enough food to eat during the next cold winter. The Pilgrims wanted to thank God for His love and care for them. They wanted to thank Him, too, for bringing them to a new home in which they could worship Him.

Our Thanksgiving is a family holiday. Some people travel many miles to be with their parents, grandparents, and others they love. They gather to thank the Lord for the good things He has given them. And they remember the brave Pilgrims and their Indian friends.

204

Text Discussion, page 203

➤ **Read page 203 to learn what Columbus's landing was like.**
➤ **Was Columbus's voyage successful even though the land he found was not Asia?** *(Yes, the land Columbus found is part of what we now know as the Americas.)*

Many cities, such as New York, Boston, and Los Angeles, celebrate Columbus Day with parades. In South America people decorate statues of Columbus with flowers on October 12.

➤ **What special things could our family do to celebrate Columbus Day?**

Text Discussion, pages 204 and 277

➤ **What holiday do Americans celebrate to thank God for His blessings?** *(Thanksgiving)*
➤ **Read the first paragraph on page 204 to find out how long the first Thanksgiving feast in 1621 lasted.** *(three days)*

King Massasoit brought ninety braves with him to the feast, and there were only fifty-five people in the Plymouth settlement. There were more Native Americans than Pilgrims at the first Thanksgiving. The braves brought five deer to the feast, and the Pilgrims served turkey, quail, seafood, corn, squash, beans, and cranberries.

➤ **Read the next paragraph to find out why the Separatists wanted to thank the Lord.** *(He had provided a good harvest of food for them to eat during the next winter, and He had brought them to a new home where they could worship Him.)* (BAT: 7c Praise)
➤ **Why did the Pilgrims want to thank the people who had helped them?** *(because they had showed them how to plant crops and had given them food)*
➤ **Read page 277.**
➤ **What day did Abraham Lincoln set aside to celebrate Thanksgiving?** *(the last Thursday of November)*

In 1941 Congress ruled that the fourth Thursday of November would be observed as Thanksgiving Day.

➤ **Read the last paragraph on page 204.**
➤ Share what we do with our family on Thanksgiving Day.

Thanksgiving is not only a time to remember the Pilgrims and enjoy good food but also a time to thank the Lord for blessings He has given us. (BATs: 7b Exaltation of Christ, 7c Praise)

Thanksgiving

The Pilgrims and Native Americans celebrated a thanksgiving day in 1621. But Thanksgiving was not always celebrated at harvest time. And it was not celebrated every year until 1863.

The Thanksgiving celebrations begun in 1863 by Abraham Lincoln gave Americans the tradition of eating turkey on the last Thursday of November.

277

Letter of Thankfulness

Name _____

Write a letter to Columbus or to a Pilgrim and tell him why you are grateful to him.

© 1997 BJU Press. Reproduction prohibited.

Heritage Studies 3
Student Notebook

Lesson 56
Evaluating the Lesson   **72**

Day ³

Evaluating the Lesson

Letter-Writing Activity, Notebook page 72

➤ Imagine that Columbus and the Pilgrims are still alive today. Think about what kinds of things you would like to thank these historical people for if you could speak with them now.

➤ Read the instructions on Notebook page 72.

➤ Complete the page.

■ Going Beyond ■

Enrichment

Provide paper, pens or pencils, crayons, and a stapler. Allow your child to make a diary. The diary can be either a ship's log as written by Columbus or one of his men, or the diary of a Pilgrim child or a Native American at the first Thanksgiving. Encourage him to illustrate his diary.

Additional Teacher Information

Although Columbus is honored as the discoverer of America, it is possible that other ancient peoples, such as the Phoenicians, Irish monks, Polynesians, Africans, and Vikings, might have visited the American continents many centuries before him; and, of course, Native Americans had lived on the land for years. The Native American

group who met Columbus is generally known as the Arawak people; however, some historians believe it may have been the Taíno, a smaller group of the Arawak. Although others had lived on this land for many years, Columbus was the first man to plant a flag and claim the discovery of the land for Europe. October 12 was first honored as a holiday in New York in 1792, three hundred years after Columbus made his discovery. In 1892, a national celebration was held and a monument was erected in a cathedral in Havana, Spain, where a casket bearing Columbus's name had been found. People of Seville, Spain, later claimed their city as the actual burial place of Columbus, so now there are memorials in both cities.

The idea for a day of thanksgiving might have sprung from a number of different sources. In the Pilgrims' mother country of Britain, a holiday called Guy Fawkes Day was set aside to express gratitude to God for His deliverance from a plot to blow up Parliament in 1605. Holland, where the Pilgrims lived for several years before coming to America, also celebrated a Thanksgiving Day in remembrance of her victory over Spain in 1575. Thanksgiving could even have originated partly from a Native American custom since the people had many days of thanksgiving.

Thanksgiving was for many years the main holiday in the colonies because the celebration of Christmas was forbidden by law. Colonial leaders would announce when the holiday would be held each year. In the New England colonies, a fine of five shillings was required of anyone who did any form of work on Thanksgiving Day.

The celebration of Thanksgiving as a national holiday is due largely to the influence of Mrs. Sarah Hale, editor of *Godey's Lady's Book*. For many years Mrs. Hale worked for this day to become a recognized holiday, even writing to the governors of all the states and to President Lincoln himself. In 1864, Lincoln finally pronounced the last Thursday in November an annual holiday in America. Although Thanksgiving is traditionally celebrated only in the United States and Canada, many other countries have similar days of celebrating their harvests and of thanking God.

LESSON 57
Traditions of Christmas

Text, pages 205-6, 280-81
Notebook, pages 73-74

——— Preview ———

Main Ideas
- Christmas is a day for celebrating the birth of Christ.
- Holidays are a way of remembering the past.

Objective
- Identify significant national holidays and the reasons for those holidays

Materials
No additional materials are necessary.

Day 1

——— Lesson ———

Introducing the Lesson

**Describing Activity,
Notebook page 73**

➤ **Read the poem "December" by Aileen Fisher on Notebook page 73.**

Notice some of the comparisons in the poem. Snow is compared to a white collar, and the moon is said to look like a silver dollar.

➤ Name other comparisons in the poem. *(Hills are compared to an eiderdown [ī´ dər doun] blanket; breath is compared to steam from an engine; snowflakes are compared to feathers; snow under the eaves is compared to petticoats.)*

➤ Comparing a thing to something else often helps us to get a better picture of that thing in our minds. Make up a comparison about something you have observed during December.

> If your child has trouble thinking of something to describe, suggest things such as Christmas lights, a melting snowman, frost on the windows, fire in the fireplace, and the decorations in his house.

➤ **What do you think the speaker in the poem likes best about the month of December?**

DECEMBER
Aileen Fisher

I like days
with a snow-white collar,
and nights when the moon
is a silver dollar,
and hills are filled
with eiderdown stuffing
and your breath makes smoke
like an engine puffing.

I like days
when feathers are snowing,
and all the eaves
have petticoats showing,
and the air is cold,
and wires are humming,
but you feel all warm . . .
with Christmas coming!

Copyright ©1991 by Aileen Fisher. Used with
permission from HarperCollins Publishers.

© 1997 BJU Press. Reproduction prohibited.

Heritage Studies 3
Student Notebook

Lesson 57
Introducing the Lesson

73

Christmas

One of the last holidays of the year is a favorite one for many people. It reminds us of the birth of Jesus. Do you know the name of this holiday?

We celebrate Christmas at the end of December. Long ago, people decided to celebrate Jesus' birth on December 25. Do you think they knew when Jesus' birthday was? They did not. We do not know either. But we still celebrate His birth on the day they chose.

Many people decorate and give gifts at Christmas.

People today think of Christmas in many ways. Some people think of it as a time to give and get gifts. Others think of it as a time to do good things for those they love. And a few people think of it as a time for parties and pretty decorations. All of these happy things are part of our celebrations. But they are not the most important part. We know that remembering God's gift, Jesus, is what makes Christmas special.

205

Teaching the Lesson

Text Discussion, pages 205 and 280-81

➤ **Read the first two paragraphs on page 205 to find out why Christmas is celebrated on December 25.**
(People long ago chose that day to celebrate the birth of Christ.)

The custom of celebrating on this date was begun in A.D. 354 by a Roman bishop named Liberius. Some people in those days believed Christ was born earlier, around November 17. Others thought His birth actually happened later, on March 28.

➤ **How would the holiday be different if it came at one of these other times?**

➤ Look at the world map on pages 280-81.

In the Southern Hemisphere or the southern part of the world, the seasons are opposite those in the Northern Hemisphere. For the people living in that part of the world, December 25 comes in midsummer. Africans celebrate the day with outdoor games and picnics. Australians and South Americans use sprays of flowers in place of fir trees for their Christmas decorations.

Day ²

➤ **Read the last paragraph on page 205.**

Gift giving, parties, and pretty decorations at Christmastime have been traditions throughout the world for centuries. A problem occurs when these things become more important to us than the reason for the holiday. You can keep the right focus during the Christmas season by making the birth of Christ the central part of your celebrations.

➤ Name special things we could do with our family to keep our focus on the Lord's birth at Christmastime. (BAT: 7b Exaltation of Christ)

Why do we celebrate so many holidays? Holidays help us remember things that happened long ago. We like to think about brave things people did. Americans want to learn about what their country was like in the past. And most of all we need to be reminded of the things God has given His people—a good country, His Son, and a home in heaven.

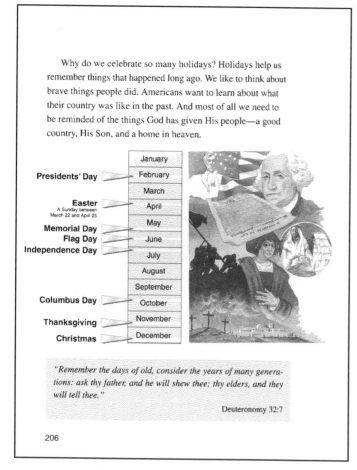

Presidents' Day	January
	February
	March
Easter A Sunday between March 22 and April 25	April
	May
Memorial Day	
Flag Day	June
Independence Day	July
	August
	September
Columbus Day	October
	November
Thanksgiving	
Christmas	December

"Remember the days of old, consider the years of many generations: ask thy father, and he will shew thee; thy elders, and they will tell thee."

Deuteronomy 32:7

206

Holiday Information   Name _____

Fill in the chart with information about the holidays you have studied.

	Holiday	Date Celebrated	What We Remember
1.			
2.			
3.			
4.			
5.			
6.			
7.			
8.			

© 1997 BJU Press. Reproduction prohibited.

Heritage Studies 3
Student Notebook

Lesson 57
Evaluating the Lesson **74**

Text Discussion, page 206

➤ **Read page 206 to learn why we celebrate holidays.** *(to help us remember things that happened long ago; to be reminded of the things God has given us)*

➤ Look at the time line of holidays for the year. Point to the place on the line where your birthday would fit in.

➤ **What holiday is your favorite? Why?**

Read Deuteronomy 32:7 from page 206. While not all holidays are religious, each one of the holidays on the time line can remind Christians to thank God for something He has given them. (BAT: 7c Praise)

Evaluating the Lesson

Chart Activity, Notebook page 74

➤ Look back over the chapter to find information to fill in the chart for the various holidays you have studied.

Going Beyond

Enrichment

Provide wallpaper or decorative wrapping paper cut into 5" × 12" rectangles, household glue, different styles of ribbon in colors that match the wrapping paper, lace, pearls or colored beads, and a stapler. (*NOTE:* If using wrapping paper, you might want to double it so that the fan will be sturdier. Patterned wrapping paper as well as gold or silver foil make beautiful fans.) Allow your child to make accordion-pleated fans out of the wrapping paper, stapling the folds together at the bottom of the fan to hold the pleats in place. He may tie ribbon into bows to glue over the stapled portion at the bottom of the fan. He may decorate the sides of his fan with beads as desired. If he would like a lace-edged fan, he should glue the lace to the edge of his paper and wait for the glue to dry before he begins folding. Victorians used decorative fans as a festive touch on Christmas trees, evergreen swags, wreaths, and packages. If your child's fan is to be used as a Christmas tree ornament, he may want to punch a hole in the bottom of the fan and loop ribbon through it so that the fan may be hung upside down.

Provide books, magazines, and encyclopedias that give information about how Christmas is celebrated in other lands. Encourage your child to research Christmas celebrations of a particular country and write a paragraph or draw a picture portraying the traditions of that land.

Additional Teacher Information

Christmases in medieval England were times of great feasting and celebrating. In the homes of English nobility, celebrations lasted for several weeks at a time. The song "The Twelve Days of Christmas" originated during this period as well as the traditions of burning a yule log and kissing beneath the mistletoe. The festivities were unruly and often reflected pagan tradition. A person was chosen to be crowned the Lord of Misrule for the days of the feast, and unrestrained eating, drinking, and dancing went on. Men called *mummers* performed plays about the Nativity, and people played games that were takeoffs on various pagan rituals. The holiday was abolished by Parliament in 1643 because of the lawless behavior it generated. The Puritans continued to frown upon the holiday for many years afterward, and in 1659 they made any sort of Christmas celebration a penal offense in the Massachusetts Bay Colony. Over one hundred years passed before Massachusetts again celebrated Christmas to any degree.

Some of America's Christmas traditions originated in countries other than England. The Christmas tree originated in Germany and came to the United States with Hessian Germans who fought for the British during the War for Independence. According to one legend, Martin Luther began the tradition. He brought a pine tree into his home one Christmas and decorated it with candles to show his family what a forest tree looked like under the light of the stars. The custom of giving gifts began with the wise men and is a universal tradition at Christmastime. Caroling is also practiced all over the world. In many countries, children go singing from house to house with large bags, and neighbors are expected to give them treats or small gifts. Another custom practiced in many countries is serving pudding or cake with gifts or coins baked inside.

Railroads

This chapter traces the development of some early modes of travel in the United States. Your child may participate in a choral reading about the first successful steamboat, the *Clermont,* in the Supplemental Lesson. The remaining lessons emphasize the development of steam locomotives, the building of the first transcontinental railroad, and the continual improvement of trains and railroad systems. Your child will have opportunity to work with a map scale of miles, a train timetable, and time zones. Railroad songs and signals as well as the board game Sidetracks add a spark of variety and enjoyment to the chapter.

Materials

The following materials must be obtained or prepared before the presentation of the lesson. These items are labeled with an asterisk (*) in each lesson and in the Materials List in the Supplement. For further information see the individual lessons.

- Items associated with a train (Lesson 58)
- Appendix, page A53 (Supplemental Lesson)
- Some model trains and tracks of different sizes and types (optional) (Lesson 59)
- A picture of Old Ironsides (optional) (Lesson 59)
- Appendix, page A54 (Lesson 59)
- A lump of coal (optional) (Lesson 60)
- A map of your state (Lesson 61)
- A railroad spike (optional) (Lesson 62)
- 6 analog clocks or watches (Lesson 63)

11

Railroads

LESSON 58
Early Travel

Text, pages 208-10
Notebook, page 75

Preview

Main Ideas

- People travel from place to place by different modes.
- People and goods travel in different ways.
- The earliest modes of travel included walking as well as riding on animals, wagons, and boats.

Objective

- Complete a crossword puzzle about early modes of travel

Materials

- Items associated with a train (e.g., parts from a model train, an engineer's cap, a red bandanna, a railroad spike, and so on)*

Day 1

Lesson

Introducing the Lesson

Guessing Activity, page 208

➤ *Read the portion of the poem given in the green box on page 208.*

➤ Guess what is being talked about in this poem.

➤ I have some more clues about the mystery item. *Show as many of the train-related items as you were able to obtain.* Tell me when you know for sure what the mystery item is. *(a train or a locomotive)*

Teaching the Lesson

Text Discussion, page 208

➤ **Read page 208 to find out what the huge, shiny monster puffing smoke was.** *(a locomotive)*

The train was a strange new way to travel. It was dirty, smoky, and extremely noisy. People did not think trains were safe.

I like to see it lap the Miles,
And lick the Valleys up,
And stop to feed itself at Tanks. . . .
Emily Dickinson

The huge black monster puffed and chugged across the prairie. It breathed out smoke—sometimes grayish white, other times thick black and full of sparks—as it rolled along. People and animals rushed to get out of the path of the giant beast. But other people followed close behind the monster in a long line. They calmly read, ate, talked, and even slept. What was this monster, and where was it leading those people?

The big black contraption was not really a monster, but for a time, some people thought of it as one. It was a *locomotive*, and it pulled a *train* of cars. Trains like this one were a new way of traveling from place to place.

208

➤ **What were the sections of the train called?** *(cars)*

➤ **Read the lines of the poem on page 208 aloud with me.**

➤ **How do you think a train could "lap the Miles" and "lick the Valleys up"?** This is a description of a train as it travels across the land.

➤ **What do you think the line "And stop to feed itself at Tanks" refers to?**

The early steam locomotives had to stop for more water and for more wood or coal. The wood or coal in the locomotive's firebox would heat up the water in the boiler in order to make the steam that would power the locomotive and move the train.

Heritage Studies 3 Home TE

Early Ways to Travel

Before the early 1800s, people traveled in one of three ways. Can you name these ways? The easiest way to travel was by boat. Boats traveled across oceans and down rivers, canals, and streams. But boat travel was not very handy. People could not always get to where they wanted to go when they traveled by boats. Rivers, canals, and oceans did not go everywhere. What other ways did people travel?

Many people walked wherever they wanted to go. Walking was a handy way of traveling. A person could leave when he wanted. He could go just where he wanted. Can you think of any problems that a walking traveler might have?

"We took sweet counsel together, and walked unto the house of God in company."
Psalm 55:14

209

Often a person wanted to take things with him when he traveled. Farmers wanted to take their crops to market. Fathers wanted to move their families to a new home. These people had to travel in the third way. They went by horse and wagon.

Canals in early America

People traveling by horse and wagon could not go as many places as people who walked. They followed roads and paths. The roads and paths in the early 1800s did not look like our paved roads. Most roads were dirt. What would happen to these dirt roads on a rainy day? People could not travel over the roads on days like that. They had to either find another way to travel or stay at home.

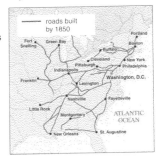

Roads in early America

210

Text Discussion, page 209

➤ **Read page 209 to find out two early ways of travel.** *(boats, walking)*
➤ Name some problems that a walking traveler might have. *(Possible answers include dealing with dangerous animals, enduring bad weather, getting tired, and not being able to carry much with him.)*
➤ **Read Psalm 55:14 from the page.**
➤ **Why do we like to walk with friends or family members?** *(Answers will vary but may include the following: It is relaxing; we can look at things as we walk along; we can talk with another person uninterrupted and usually unhurried; we feel safe.)*
➤ **Is walking with another person considered a pleasant experience?** *(yes)*

Read the verse again and tell where the people were walking. *(unto the house of God; to church)* God wants Christians to go to places that are pleasing to Him and that give glory to His name. Remind your child of the children's songs "O Be Careful" and "A Sermon in Shoes." Sing these songs if you wish, reminding him that Christians need to be good testimonies for the Lord as they live their lives before God and others. (BATs: 1c Separation from the world, 3b Mind, 4b Purity)

Day 2

Text Discussion, page 210

➤ **Read page 210 to find a third way that many farmers of long ago traveled.** *(horse and wagon)*
➤ Name some of the problems with traveling this way. *(People had to travel over rough dirt roads. The wagons could get stuck in holes or in the mud. The wagons could break down.)*

Map Activity, page 210

➤ **What does the map at the top of the page show?** *(canals built by 1850)*
➤ **Do you know what a *canal* is?** It is a waterway that men have designed to make boat travel easier.
➤ **In which part of the United States were most of the canals?** *(northeast)*
➤ **What does the map at the bottom of the page show?** *(roads built by 1850)*
➤ **In which part of the United States were most of the roads located?** *(northeast and southeast)*

Travel Crossword

Name _____

Use the following clues to fill in the crossword puzzle below.

ACROSS
3. Boats traveled on rivers, oceans, and _____.
6. "a huge, shiny, black monster, puffing smoke"
7. the kind of roads during early years of travel
8. Sometimes horses pulled these to carry goods.

DOWN
1. a section of a train
2. Only your feet are needed for this way of traveling.
4. a vehicle for traveling on water
5. an important farm animal to ride

Heritage Studies 3
Student Notebook

Lesson 58
Evaluating the Lesson   **75**

Evaluating the Lesson

Notebook Activity, page 75

➤ Read the instructions on Notebook page 75.
➤ Complete the page.

══ Going Beyond ══

Enrichment

If there is a steam locomotive or a train museum in your area, arrange to take your child on a field trip to learn more about trains.

Additional Teacher Information

From the earliest times, men have been trying to improve transportation to make travel easier and quicker and to move their goods from place to place. Among the first improvements was the taming of oxen, donkeys, camels, and horses to carry men's goods. Eventually, men built sleds and wagons to assist with travel and transportation.

SUPPLEMENTAL
LESSON
Steamboats

══ Preview ══

Main Ideas

• The use of steam engines made travel by steamboat possible.
• People are linked by transportation.

Objectives

• Participate in a choral reading
• Write a journal entry from the perspective of a person viewing the *Clermont* on August 17, 1807

Materials

• Appendix, page A53: choral reading*

══ Lesson ══

Introducing the Lesson

Poem Discussion

The idea of using steam power for locomotives resulted from the success of steamboats years before. This lesson gives a firsthand account of a person who saw the first successful run of the *Clermont*, a now-famous steamboat. This account is presented as a choral reading.

➤ **Do you know what a choral reading is?**

It is similar to a play, but it does not include costumes, props, acting, or very many speaking parts.

Teaching the Lesson

Choral Reading

➤ *Give your child a copy of the choral reading.*
➤ **Read the choral reading silently to find out what most people thought about steamboats at first.** *(They did not think that they would work. They did not trust them.)*
➤ **How did the attitudes change after the successful journey of the *Clermont*?** *(People realized that steamboats were a good, safe way to travel.)*
➤ **Are there any words you had trouble recognizing when you read the poem silently?**
➤ Let's read the choral reading together. I will read the part of the narrator.

You may want to perform the choral reading for family or friends. If you have other family members participating, adjust the parts accordingly.

Evaluating the Lesson

Journal-Writing Activity

➤ Write the date *August 17, 1807* on the top line of a sheet of notebook paper.
➤ Write *Dear Journal,* on the next line.
➤ Imagine that you were part of the crowd of people watching the *Clermont* on her first voyage.
➤ Write at least three sentences, telling about that eventful day. Include what you saw, what you thought, and how you felt about the steamboat—this new way of traveling.

Additional Teacher Information

Robert Fulton (1765-1815) showed his inventiveness even as a boy in Pennsylvania. His tinkering produced lead pencils, household utensils, fireworks, a paddle wheel for a rowboat, and even a rifle. At age seventeen, Fulton was apprenticed to a jeweler and there became interested in the business of art. He later went to England to study with the famous American artist Benjamin West. Though Fulton made his living as a painter of miniatures and portraits, his interest in science and engineering increased. Soon his whole attention was given to maritime engineering. First, he worked with canal construction, designing new types of canal boats and a system to replace canal locks. He also invented a machine for spinning flax and a machine for making rope. From these successes, Fulton then ventured into submarine warfare and built an experimental submarine called the *Nautilus*. A great influence in Fulton's life was Robert R. Livingston, the United States minister to Paris who was involved with steamboat engineering in the United States. Fulton returned to the United States in 1806. He and Robert Livingston formed a partnership, dominating all of the Hudson River's steamboat travel.

Robert Fulton's first steamboat was a failure. Its wooden hull broke in half and sank under the weight of the machinery. He built another steamboat in a shipyard on the East River, New York. His new steamboat, the *Clermont*, was 133 feet long and had a 20-horsepower engine to drive its 4.5-meter (15 feet) diameter paddle wheels. The *Clermont* made its trial voyage on the Hudson River in 1807 and was a great success. It was immediately put into service, steaming upriver from New York to Albany at 4.7 miles per hour.

LESSON 59
The First Railroads

Text, pages 211-13
Notebook, page 76

━━ Preview ━━

Main Ideas

• People depend on other people to help them meet their needs.
• Railroads and steamboats help people travel from place to place.
• People have unique attributes and skills.

Objective

• Identify true and false statements about early railroads

Materials

• Maps and More 22, 23, and 24, pages M14-M16
• The figure of Peter Cooper (1830) from the TimeLine Snapshots
• A dictionary
• Some model trains and tracks of different sizes and types (optional)*
• A picture of Old Ironsides (optional)*
• Appendix, page A54: Tom Thumb story*

Some hobby shops may have model trains set up. You may want to take your child to see such a display as part of this lesson.

Day 1

━━ Lesson ━━

Introducing the Lesson

Definition Discussion

➤ Look up the word *locomotive* in the dictionary.
➤ **Read the definition aloud.** *(Exact wording will vary, but the definition will probably include that a locomotive is the engine of a train.)*

The First Railroads

Do you think most people who lived in the early 1800s liked to travel? They did not. They wanted an easy *and* handy way to go from one place to another. What would you have done to make traveling better?

Some men thought of a plan. They would put wood or iron rails on the roads. The wagon wheels could roll along the rails. Then the wheels would not stick in the mud. It was a good plan. These rail roads made traveling handier and easier.

But the rail roads still were not perfect. The horses walked between the rails. Sometimes horses still got stuck in the mud. The travelers needed a better way to pull the wagons along the rail roads. Do you think they found a better way?

211

About the same time, men were making a new kind of boat. These boats had an engine that let them travel faster than other boats. This new engine even helped a boat travel up a river against the current. People called the boats *steamboats* because steam made the engine run. Could the same kind of engine pull a wagon?

Most people did not believe that steam-powered engines could pull wagons along the railroads. But some did. And one man built a small steam engine on wheels, a *locomotive*. Peter Cooper wanted to prove that a steam engine could pull wagons faster than horses could.

Cooper called his locomotive Tom Thumb. Why do you think he gave it that name? The men at the Baltimore and Ohio Railroad let Cooper test his little locomotive on their railroads. Tom Thumb raced a horse. Both Tom Thumb and the horse pulled wagons. Do you think Cooper's locomotive won the race?

Peter Cooper's locomotive, Tom Thumb

212

Teaching the Lesson

Text Discussion, page 211

➤ **Read page 211 to find out how the idea of rails began.** *(Wagons could roll on iron rails instead of getting stuck in the mud.)*
➤ **Why do you think people were searching for better ways to travel?**

Text Discussion, page 212

➤ **Read the first paragraph on page 212 to find out how steam engines were first used.** *(Steam engines were first used in steamboats.)*
➤ It is difficult for a boat to travel against the current. **How did the steam engine change that?** *(It was faster and allowed the boats to travel against the current.)*
➤ **Read the rest of page 212 to find out the name of the man who used a steam engine to travel over land.** *(Peter Cooper)*
➤ **What powered the locomotive of the Tom Thumb?** *(steam)*
➤ **Does the Tom Thumb pictured on page 212 look as large as modern train engines?** *(no)*

The Tom Thumb was small. It pushed or pulled one passenger car. A train is a line of connected railroad cars. The *locomotive* or *train engine* has the power to push or pull the cars.

➤ **Which railroad company allowed the Tom Thumb to run on its tracks?** *(the Baltimore and Ohio Railroad)*

Day 2

Story, Maps and More 22, 23, and 24

➤ *Read the Tom Thumb story from the Appendix page, showing Maps and More as indicated.*
➤ **Do you think that the race changed peoples' opinions about steam locomotives?**
➤ **What do you think might have happened if the belt had not broken on the steam engine during the race?**

After the race most people thought that steam locomotives were a good idea. Businessmen soon formed companies to build other steam locomotives and railroads for them to travel on.

TimeLine Snapshots Activity

➤ *Show your child the TimeLine figure of Peter Cooper.*
➤ **Did most of the people believe that a steam engine could be used to pull wagons along the railroads?** *(No, most people did not believe that this would work.)*

◆ THINGS PEOPLE DO ◆

Building Model Railroads

Tiny *replicas*, or copies, of trains have been around almost as long as the full-sized ones. In the 1830s Mathias Baldwin made a model of a train. He wanted to show people his new locomotive design. Later, he built a full-sized train just like the model. He called the big locomotive Old Ironsides.

Big trains like Old Ironsides thrilled people of all ages. Soon companies began making little pull toy trains for children. Some toy trains came with track to pull or push the train around on.

Toy shops sold the first *working* toy trains about sixty years ago. The trains ran on tiny tracks carefully laid out on the floor. These working trains were popular toys. Soon older boys and girls, and even some adults, began working with the tiny trains. But they did not think of the trains as toys. They called them "model trains" instead.

Today there are many different sizes and kinds of model trains. You can buy a whole train set complete with train and tracks. Or you can buy one piece at a time. You can even buy a kit and build the locomotive and cars yourself. Some people still lay the track out on the floor and put it away each day. Others build elaborate railroads with mountains, rivers, bridges, and towns. Models like this can fill a whole room. Have you ever seen a model railroad that big?

213

Travel True or False

Name _____

Read the following statements. Draw puffs of smoke around the statements that are true. Draw a line through the statements that are false.

People in the early 1800s liked to travel often.

Wagon wheels rolled along on wood and iron rails.

Steamboats could travel with the current and against the current.

Peter Cooper built the first successful steamboat.

Most people believed that steam engines could pull wagons along the railroads.

A locomotive was a small steam engine on wheels.

Peter Cooper built the Tom Thumb.

The Tom Thumb won the race against the horse.

The Tom Thumb ran on the Baltimore and Ohio Railroad.

The big locomotive built by Mathias Baldwin was called Old Ironsides.

After the race, steam locomotives were not used any more.

Working toy trains are called model trains.

A model of a train is a small replica or copy.

© 1997 BJU Press. Reproduction prohibited.

Heritage Studies 3
Student Notebook

Lesson 59
Evaluating the Lesson   **76**

➤ **What do you think most people thought about Peter Cooper and his ideas?** They thought he was crazy.

➤ Place the figure of Peter Cooper on the TimeLine at 1830.

Peter Cooper not only built the Tom Thumb but also successfully manufactured and sold the glue, gelatin, and iron beams used in building the locomotive. Peter Cooper was eager to learn new things and enjoyed working hard to accomplish his goals.

Remind your child that each person has talents and skills that God gave to him. Christians have a responsibility to do their best for His glory. (BATs: 2d Goal setting, 2e Work, 3a Self-concept)

Day 3

Text Discussion, page 213

➤ *Show your child some model trains and tracks of different sizes and types, if available.*

➤ **Read page 213 to find out the name of the locomotive that Mathias Baldwin built first as a model and then as a full-sized train.** *(Old Ironsides)*

➤ *Show a picture of Old Ironsides if you have one available.* Compare this locomotive with the Tom

Thumb. *(Answers will vary but will probably include that Old Ironsides was much bigger than Tom Thumb.)*

(*NOTE:* The Tom Thumb was a small engine of only one cylinder, traveling up to eighteen miles an hour. Old Ironsides was made of iron and wood, weighed six tons, and could travel up to twenty-eight miles an hour.)

➤ Tell how a working toy train is like a real train. *(Answers will vary but should include that the working toy train has many of the details of a real train and looks like a small version of a real train; also, the working toy train really moves along little tracks.)*

➤ **What name was given to the working toy trains?** *(model trains)*

Evaluating the Lesson

Notebook Activity, page 76

➤ Read the directions for Notebook page 76.

➤ Complete the page.

Chapter 11: Lesson 59

249

Going Beyond

Additional Teacher Information

As a teenager, Peter Cooper showed a talent for mechanics and invention. He helped his father with hat making, was apprenticed to a coach builder, and later served as a mechanic. Throughout his life, he was active in government and civic affairs, promoting telegraph and cable companies and working for better public education, improved water systems, and better police and fire protection. When Cooper was eighty-five years old, he ran for president of the United States on the Greenback Party ticket.

LESSON 60
Trains at Work

Text, pages 214-15
Notebook, page 77

━━━ Preview ━━━

Main Ideas
- Steam is an effective source of power.
- People work at different kinds of jobs.

Objective
- Distinguish the jobs of a train engineer from those of a train's fireman

Materials
- A lump of coal (optional)*
- A saucepan with a lid or a whistling teakettle

Day 1

━━━ Lesson ━━━

Introducing the Lesson

Demonstration

➤ Let's go to the kitchen to begin our lesson today.
➤ *Fill the saucepan or teakettle three-fourths full of hot water, cover it with the lid, and set it on the stove.*
➤ Watch the covered container until you see something happening. (*NOTE:* If you use a whistling teakettle, tell your child to close his eyes until he hears something happening.)
➤ Describe what is happening and what has been made. (***Steam*** *has been made and is escaping as the water boils or as the lid moves up and down.*)
➤ **Is the water in the pan hotter, cooler, or the same temperature as when I poured it in?** *(hotter)*
➤ **How do you know that steam has power?** *(It makes the lid jump up and down or makes a whistling sound.)*
➤ Describe the steam. *(Answers will vary but will probably include odorless, colorless or grayish, or like a cloud.)* You will learn more about steam and how it was used in locomotives long ago.

How Railroads Worked

Steam made locomotives like Tom Thumb and Old Ironsides work. Do you know what happens when water turns to steam? It takes up more room. The steam presses on pipes inside the locomotive. It moves a special part that turns the wheels. Then the steam escapes through the smokestack. How do you think that part got its name?

Look at the diagram below. Can you find the water in this locomotive? We call that part the boiler because the water there is boiling hot.

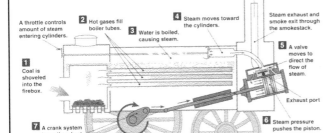

1 Coal is shoveled into the firebox.

2 Hot gases fill boiler tubes.

3 Water is boiled, causing steam.

A throttle controls amount of steam entering cylinders.

4 Steam moves toward the cylinders.

Steam exhaust and smoke exit through the smokestack.

5 A valve moves to direct the flow of steam.

Exhaust port

6 Steam pressure pushes the piston.

7 A crank system turns the wheel, moving the train.

214

How did the men running the locomotive make the water hot? What do you think they called the man who kept the fire burning?

The fireman had an important job. If he let the fire die down, the water would not be hot enough to keep the heavy train moving. If he shoveled too much coal into the firebox, the steam would build up too much. The train might travel too fast then. Or something even worse could happen. The boiler might blow up.

The fireman was not the only man who worked on the locomotive. The *engineer* was the boss on the train. He had to keep the train moving at a good speed. He had to watch the rails, or track, ahead. It was the engineer's job to bring the people and things on his train safely to the next town.

215

Teaching the Lesson

Text Discussion, page 214

➤ Read page 214 to find out which takes up more room—water or steam. *(steam)*

➤ Read the two sentences in the first paragraph that explain how steam works to move a locomotive. *("The steam presses on pipes inside the locomotive. It moves a special part that turns the wheels.")*

➤ What is a *smokestack?* *(the part of the locomotive where the steam escapes)*

➤ Why do you think that the steam needs to escape?

The used steam escapes to make room for new steam. Too much steam would cause great damage.

➤ Look at the diagram on page 214. *As you discuss the parts, point to them on the diagram in the text.*

➤ Locate the boiler. **What happens in the boiler?** *(The water gets boiling hot.)*

➤ What makes the water get hot and boil? *(fire)*

Text Discussion, page 215

➤ Read page 215 to find out what fuel is used to keep this locomotive going. *(coal)*

➤ *Show your child a lump of coal if you were able to acquire one.*

➤ Where do you think coal comes from? It comes from deep in the ground.

➤ Why is the fireman's job important? *(If the fire is not hot enough, the train cannot keep moving. If the fire is too hot, the train might move too fast or the boiler might blow up.)*

➤ What is the boss on the train called? *(the engineer)*

➤ What does the engineer do? *(He keeps the train moving at a good speed. He drives the train, looking ahead on the tracks for any danger that might be in the way of the train.)*

➤ What kinds of problems might the engineer see in front of the train? *(Possible answers are animals or other things on the tracks, or broken track.)*

➤ The engineer has to make many important decisions as he drives the train. **What characteristics would an engineer need to have?** *(Possible answers are knowledge, dependability, and good judgment.)*

These are traits of a good leader. (BATs: 2c Faithfulness, 2e Work, 3a Self-concept)

Chapter 11: Lesson 60

251

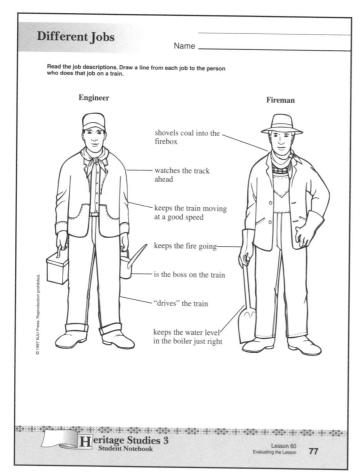

Different Jobs

Name _____

Read the job descriptions. Draw a line from each job to the person who does that job on a train.

Engineer   Fireman

shovels coal into the firebox

watches the track ahead

keeps the train moving at a good speed

keeps the fire going

is the boss on the train

"drives" the train

keeps the water level in the boiler just right

Heritage Studies 3
Student Notebook

Lesson 60
Evaluating the Lesson   **77**

Evaluating the Lesson

Notebook Activity, page 77

➤ Read the instructions on Notebook page 77.
➤ Complete the page.

━━━ Going Beyond ━━━

Enrichment

If you live in an area where coal is mined, talk to a coal miner about his job.

Additional Teacher Information

Early locomotives burned wood, not coal. Every twenty-five miles along the tracks were huge woodpiles of four-foot logs. The trains stopped there when more fuel was needed. To supply the necessary water for the locomotives, trainmen and passengers formed bucket brigades, hauling water from a stream. Later, track-side water tanks were built.

Coal is made from plant material that many scholars believe was deposited by the waters of the Noachian Flood. The plants were covered immediately by layers of mud, and the process of coal making began. (*NOTE:* A good reference is *Scientific Creationism* by Henry Morris.) Coal was formed relatively quickly, not over millions of years.

Coal is a soft black or brown sedimentary rock that burns easily, providing power and heat. Coal deposits are found between layers of rock and dirt. Coal can be near the surface or deep in the ground. Baked coal results in these byproducts: coke, coal tar, light oil, ammonia, and coal gas. *Coke* (coal residue) is an important part of steel production. The chemical, cement, paper, and metal industries also use coal to make thousands of products. Among the products that use coal in their production are fertilizers, cosmetics, detergents, medicines, perfumes, paints, plastics, and numerous fuels.

LESSON 61
For Miles and Miles

Text, pages 176, 216
Notebook, pages 78-81

━━━━━ Preview ━━━━━

Main Ideas
- Maps help people travel.
- Distances on maps can be calculated with the use of the scale of miles.

Objectives
- Measure distances on a map using a scale of miles
- Answer questions about two maps of the same region, each using a different scale of miles

Materials
- A ruler
- A map of your state*
- An atlas (optional)

Day 1

━━━━━ Lesson ━━━━━

Introducing the Lesson

Poem, Notebook page 78

➤ **Read the poem "Song of the Train" on Notebook page 78 silently as I read it aloud.**
➤ **Do you think the train in the poem is going fast?**
➤ I will read the first two stanzas of the poem aloud as you make the background sounds of the train, "Choo, choo, choo, choo."
➤ You read the last two stanzas of the poem, and I will provide the background sounds.

Teaching the Lesson

Learning How Activity, pages 216 and 176 and Notebook page 79

➤ **Read Steps 1 and 2 on text page 216.**
➤ Point to the scale of miles on Notebook page 79.
➤ **How many miles does one inch represent on this map?** *(1 mile)*
➤ **Do you think every map uses the same scale of miles?**

Song of the Train

Name _____

Song of the Train
David McCord

Clickety-clack,
Wheels on the track,
This is the way
They begin the attack:
Click-ety-clack,
Click-ety-clack,
Click-ety, *clack*-ety,
Click-ety
Clack.

Clickety-clack,
Over the crack,
Faster and faster
The song of the track:

Clickety-clack,
Clickety-clack,
Clickety, clackety,
Clackety.
Clack.

Riding in front,
Riding in back,
Everyone hears
The song of the track:
Clickety-clack,
Clickety-clack,
Clickety, *clickety,*
Clackety
Clack.

From *ONE AT A TIME* by David McCord. Copyright ©1952 by David McCord.
By permission of Little, Brown and Company.

Heritage Studies 3
Student Notebook

Lesson 61
Introducing the Lesson **78**

◆ LEARNING HOW ◆

To Use a Map Scale

1. Get a large map of your state, a ruler, and Notebook page 79.

2. Look at the map on your Notebook page. It shows the area around Center Station. Find the scale on the map. According to the scale, how many miles does one inch equal?

3. Use your ruler to measure the distance from Center Station to End-of-Track. How far apart are the two places on the map? How many miles apart are they? Measure the distance to other points on the map. How far are they from Center Station in real distance?

4. Look at the map of your state. Can you find the scale on it? How many miles are equal to one inch on this map? Find your town on the map. Then use the scale to find the distance to the nearest large town. How far is it to the border of your state?

216

General McClellan moved his huge army. He planned to attack the city of Richmond. Do you remember why Richmond was important? McClellan was a good planner, but he was not a good leader in battle. The men in blue lost many battles. The Confederates pushed them back to where they had started.

By now the Confederate army had a new leader too. General Robert E. Lee took charge of the Grays after the first leader was shot. Of all the good generals in the South, Robert E. Lee was one of the best. Lee had worked with many leaders of the Union army. He knew how they acted in battle. And he made good guesses when he did not know.

Now the new leader of the Confederate army decided to take the war into the North. Lee thought he might scare the people there into giving up on the war. He headed his men toward Pennsylvania.

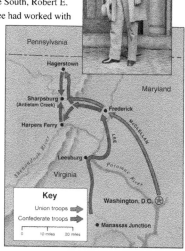

Robert E. Lee

176

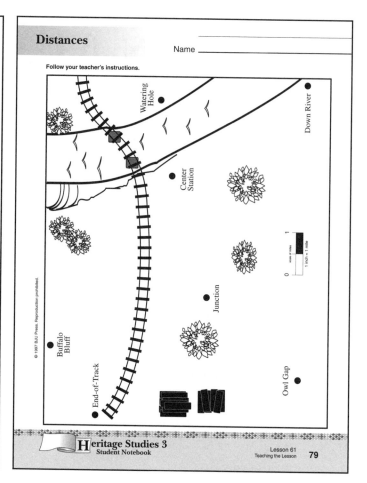

Follow your teacher's instructions.

Heritage Studies 3
Student Notebook

Lesson 61
Teaching the Lesson   **79**

➤ Turn to page 176 in your text. Find the scale of miles.

This scale of miles does not tell you how many miles are represented by an inch. You must measure the scale with your ruler.

➤ Place your ruler under the scale of miles on page 176.

➤ Line up the zero mark on the left end of the ruler with the end of the scale marked "0."

➤ **How many miles does an inch represent?** *(20 miles)*

You may want to show your child other maps that use different scales of miles. The scale of miles on many maps does not show a precise mileage for one inch. You will need to show your child how to round the distances.

➤ Look at the map on Notebook page 79 again. **How many miles does one inch represent here?** *(1 mile)*

➤ **How many miles would two inches represent?** *(2 miles)*

➤ **How many miles would ten inches represent?** *(10 miles)*

Measurement Activity, page 216 and Notebook page 79

➤ **Read Step 3 on text page 216.**
➤ Locate the inch marking on your ruler.

When measuring, you must place the zero mark of your ruler exactly at the beginning of the distance to be measured. You may place pencil marks on your map to help you keep track of the number of inches measured.

➤ Measure the distance from Center Station to End-of-Track on Notebook page 79. *Give your child help in measuring this first distance. (6 inches)*

➤ **Using the scale of miles, how many miles would this be?** *(6 miles)*

➤ Measure from Center Station to Down River and calculate the actual distance. *(4 inches; 4 miles)*

➤ Measure from Center Station to Junction and calculate the actual distance. *(3 inches; 3 miles)*

➤ Follow the same procedure from Owl Gap to Down River, calculating the actual distance. *(7 inches; 7 miles)*

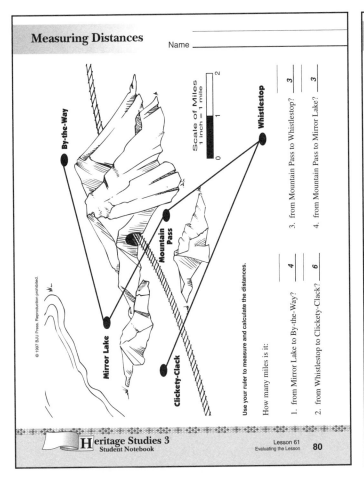

By-the-Way

Mountain Pass

Mirror Lake

Clickety-Clack

Whistlestop

Scale of Miles
1 inch = 1 mile

0   1   2

Use your ruler to measure and calculate the distances.

How many miles is it:

1. from Mirror Lake to By-the-Way?   _4_

2. from Whistlestop to Clickety-Clack?   _6_

3. from Mountain Pass to Whistlestop?   _3_

4. from Mountain Pass to Mirror Lake?   _3_

© 1997 BJU Press. Reproduction prohibited.

Heritage Studies 3
Student Notebook

Lesson 61
Evaluating the Lesson   **80**

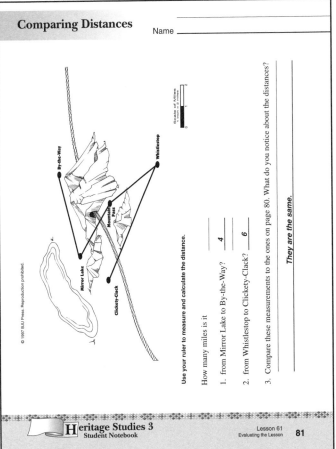

Comparing Distances   Name _____

By-the-Way

Mountain Pass

Mirror Lake

Clickety-Clack

Whistlestop

Scale of Miles
1 inch = 2 miles

0   1   2

Use your ruler to measure and calculate the distance.

How many miles is it

1. from Mirror Lake to By-the-Way?   _4_

2. from Whistlestop to Clickety-Clack?   _6_

3. Compare these measurements to the ones on page 80. What do you notice about the distances?

They are the same.

© 1997 BJU Press. Reproduction prohibited.

Heritage Studies 3
Student Notebook

Lesson 61
Evaluating the Lesson   **81**

This might be a good opportunity to remind your child that there is one distance that he cannot measure. God promises that when Christians repent, their sins are removed from them as far as the east is from the west. (BAT: 1b Repentance and faith)

Day 2

Map-Reading and Measurement Activity, page 216

The scale of miles on your state map may not show an exact representation for an inch. You will need to help your child round or estimate the mileage for an inch.

➤ **Read Step 4 on page 216.**

➤ *Give your child the state map.*

➤ Locate your city on the map and draw a star there.

➤ Find the scale of miles. **How many miles does each inch represent?** *(Answers will vary, depending on the map.)*

➤ Find a large town near where you live. Draw a circle there.

➤ **Which direction is our town from this large town?**

➤ Measure and calculate the distance in miles from our town to the large town.

➤ Measure the distance from our town to the nearest state border.

Day 3

Evaluating the Lesson

Notebook Activity, pages 80-81

➤ Look at the maps on Notebook pages 80-81. The maps are of the same area and have the same towns marked.

➤ **What is different about the maps?** *(the scale of miles)*

➤ Tell what each map uses for its scale of miles. *(page 80: 1 inch=1 mile; page 81: 1 inch=2 miles)*

➤ Use your ruler to measure and calculate the distances indicated and then compare the two maps to answer the questions.

Going Beyond

Enrichment

Encourage your child to memorize the poem "The Song of the Train." Provide an opportunity for him to recite the poem.

Additional Teacher Information

A mapmaker, one who plans a map, is called a *cartographer.* The original drawing for a map is put on paper by a cartographic artist or draftsman. It is the draftsman who adds various features to the map to make it more readable, accurate, and attractive.

Historians say that mapmaking in early America began with John Smith's map of Virginia, made after English settlers ventured to Jamestown. The map was published in England in 1612.

LESSON 62
East Meets West

Text, pages 217-19, 256
Notebook, page 82

━━━ Preview ━━━

Main Ideas
- The building of the first transcontinental railroad joined the United States from east to west.
- Places change over time.

Objectives
- Sing a spiritual
- Determine elevation by reading a map key
- Answer questions about the building of the transcontinental railroad

Materials
- *HERITAGE STUDIES Listening Cassette A*
- The figure of the first transcontinental railroad (1869) from the TimeLine Snapshots
- The presidential strip with Ulysses Simpson Grant (18) from the TimeLine Snapshots
- A railroad spike (optional)*
- A dictionary
- Supplement, page S14: "Get on Board"
- A sheet of paper (optional)

Day 1

━━━ Lesson ━━━

Introducing the Lesson

Sing a Spiritual

➤ *Turn to the spiritual "Get on Board" in the Supplement.*
➤ Follow along as I play the recording of the song from the listening cassette.
➤ **What do we call this kind of religious song?** (*a spiritual*) Remember that spirituals were often part of the African American worship service.
➤ **What kind of train is being described in the song?** (*a gospel train*)
➤ The word *gospel* means "good news." **What good news might this gospel train be carrying?** (*Answers will vary but should include the hope of salvation through Jesus Christ.*)
➤ **Read the words of the song again to determine where the train is going.** (*to heaven*)

From Coast to Coast

railroads built by 1860

Railroads soon were a popular way to travel. Men laid out tracks to connect cities and towns from state to state. In 1830, when the first steam locomotives began running, there were only seventy-three miles of iron railroads. Just thirty years later, more than thirty thousand miles of track were ready to use. Most of the railroads were built in one part of the country. Can you tell which part by looking at the map?

President Lincoln knew that railroads would help the United States grow. Trains made travel easier. Trains carried *goods*, or things people needed and wanted, all over the eastern part of the country. When people decided to build a railroad in the West, President Lincoln wanted to help. How could a president help to build a railroad?

President Lincoln signed the Railroad Act of 1862. This act gave two companies the right to build the first *transcontinental* railroad. *Trans-* means "across." What other word do you see? What do you think *transcontinental* means? The Railroad Act promised the companies money and free land to put the track on.

217

TimeLine Snapshots Activity

➤ Find the figure of Peter Cooper on the TimeLine.
➤ **What is the date of the first steam locomotive?** *(1830)*
➤ **What year was the Railroad Act passed?** *(1862)*
➤ Subtract to find out how many years had passed between the first steam locomotive and the Railroad Act. *(1862−1830=32 years)*
➤ **Had any railroads been built during those years?** *(yes)*

Map-Reading Activity, page 217

➤ The map on page 217 illustrates the railroad tracks in America as they were in 1860. **Which part of the United States is shown?** *(the East Coast and the Midwest)*
➤ **What ocean is next to the East Coast?** *(Atlantic Ocean)*
➤ Notice that most of the railroad tracks stopped when they reached the Mississippi River. **Why do you think this happened?**
➤ **Why was a transcontinental railroad a good idea?** *(to transport people and goods more quickly and easily from the East to the West)*

➤ Let's sing the spiritual as I play the listening cassette again.

In this lesson you will learn about a time in America's history when the people from the East and from the West were invited to "get on board" a railroad line that stretched from shore to shore.

Teaching the Lesson

Text Discussion, page 217

➤ **Read page 217 to find out how President Lincoln helped build a railroad.** *(He signed the Railroad Act, which allowed the building of the first transcontinental railroad.)*
➤ *Write the word* transcontinental. ***Transcontinental*** means "across the continent."
➤ **On which continent were the railroad companies building?** *(North America)*
➤ **What did the Railroad Act of 1862 promise the two companies who were building the railroad?** *(money and free land)*

The Central Pacific Railroad Company laid out tracks toward the east from Sacramento, California. These men began work even before the president signed the Railroad Act. Their work was slow and hard. A huge barrier stood in their path, less than one hundred miles from where they began. Can you find that barrier on the map?

How could the railroad tracks pass through a big mountain range? The path for the tracks wound back and forth, slowly climbing up the sides of the mountains. But in some places the sides were too steep. The men used dynamite and shovels to dig tunnels to the other side.

The Union Pacific Railroad Company's tracks began in Omaha, Nebraska. Can you find Omaha on the map? Their tracks headed west across the prairie. Do you think their work was as difficult as the work of the Central Pacific men? Because the land in Nebraska was flat, the Union Pacific men could work faster. They built more than one thousand miles of the railroad.

218

◆ HOW IT WAS ◆

Promontory Point, Utah
May 10, 1869

The two railroad companies worked for almost eight years to build a railroad that crossed the country. They had laid 1,776 miles of track. Now just one set of thirty-foot rails was left.

Trains carried people all the way from Omaha and Sacramento. The companies planned a big celebration.

The companies made a special spike for the ceremony. It was not iron like all the other spikes. This spike was gold. The gold spike was the last one pounded into the rails. Men from each company took turns hitting the spike into place.

The two locomotives inched forward until their cowcatchers—metal grills— touched. The engineers shook hands. The transcontinental railroad was done!

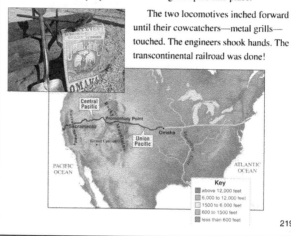

219

Day 2

Text Discussion, pages 218-19

➤ **Read page 218 to find out the names of the two companies who were building the transcontinental railroad.** *(the Central Pacific Railroad Company and the Union Pacific Railroad Company)*

➤ **Which company started laying track first?** *(the Central Pacific)*

The name *Central Pacific* sounds as though the railroad should have originated in the central part of the United States, but it did not. It was heading toward the central part.

➤ On the map on page 219, find the place where the work of the Central Pacific began. *(Sacramento, California)*

➤ **Is this town on the East Coast or the West Coast?** *(the West Coast)*

➤ **Do you know what the word *barrier* means?** If not, look up the word in the dictionary. *(The Christian Student Dictionary defines barrier as "something that holds back or stops movement or passage.")*

A mountain range known as the Sierra Nevada formed the barrier which slowed the progress of the Central Pacific railroad.

➤ **What did the workers have to do in order to get past the mountains?** *(They dug paths up the sides of the mountains. In some places they made tunnels through the mountains.)*

➤ Look at the cross section of the tunneling work on page 218. **Was this work hard or easy?** *(hard)*

Many men were wounded or lost their lives. Crews often were suspended at dangerous heights and angles to carve roads through the rugged mountains. The blasting of dynamite to make tunnels was extremely dangerous. The intense winter months brought frigid, windy working conditions, frequently with monstrous snowdrifts and destructive avalanches. Many men died of disease, of the cold or conditions caused by the cold, by accident, from bullets, or from Indian attacks.

Map Activity, page 219

➤ Find Sacramento, California, again on the map on page 219.

➤ **Is Sacramento close to the Sierra Nevada?** *(yes)*

➤ Look at the map key.

This key shows elevations. The height above sea level is called the *elevation.*

➤ **What do you think the root word of *elevation* is?**

The root word is *elevate*. Elevate means "to cause to go up."

➤ Look at the Sierra Nevada on the map. **What colors do you see where the mountains are located on the map?** *(yellow and orange-brown)*

➤ Look at the map key to find out how high the Sierra Nevada are. *(between 1,500 and 12,000 feet)*

➤ Find Omaha, Nebraska, on the map. **In which part of the United States is Omaha located?** *(the Midwest)*

➤ Use the map key to determine the elevation of the region around Omaha. *(between 600 and 1,500 feet)*

➤ **Which railroad company began its work in this city?** *(the Union Pacific Railroad Company)*

➤ **Why do you think the work here was not as dangerous as that of the Central Pacific?** The elevation was not as great, so the work was not as difficult and dangerous.

➤ Put your finger on Omaha and move west toward the coast. **How does the elevation of the land change as you move farther west?** *(The land gets higher.)*

An Account, page 219

➤ The two railroad companies worked for almost eight years to build the first transcontinental railroad.

➤ Listen as I read aloud page 219. *Read aloud the account with great expression and drama, giving your child "a feel" of* How It Was.

➤ **Where did the two railroad companies meet?** *(Promontory Point, Utah)*

➤ **What are *cowcatchers*?** *(metal grills on the front of the locomotives)*

➤ **What special kind of spike was used in the celebration marking the completion of the transcontinental railroad?** *(a golden spike)*

After the ceremony, the golden spike was removed and replaced with a regular spike. The golden spike is now on display in the Stanford Museum in Palo Alto, California. *Show a railroad spike if you obtained one.*

TimeLine Snapshots Activity, page 256

➤ **How do you think the workers felt at this occasion on May 10, 1869?**

➤ Place the figure representing the first transcontinental railroad on the TimeLine at 1869.

➤ Ulysses Simpson Grant was president of the United States at this time. Point to the figure of President Grant on the TimeLine.

➤ **Turn to page 256 and read the information about President Grant.**

Transcontinental Railroad   Name _____

Read each sentence. Fill in each blank with the correct letter.
Choose from the following answers.

A. barrier   E. continent   I. Central   M. Omaha
B. Mississippi   F. Irish   J. Lincoln   N. Ulysses S. Grant
C. Promontory   G. eight   K. Union   O. locomotive
D. three   H. cowcatcher   L. gold   P. Sacramento

__P__ 1. The Central Pacific Railroad Company began laying tracks in ____.

__J__ 2. ____ passed the Railroad Act of 1862.

__M__ 3. The Union Pacific Railroad Company's tracks began in ____.

__I__ 4. The ____ Pacific Railroad Company worked hard to dig tunnels and lay track through the mountains.

__K__ 5. The ____ Pacific Railroad Company worked faster on flat land.

__C__ 6. The tracks of the two railroad companies met at ____, Utah.

__O__ 7. The engine of a train is the ____.

__E__ 8. *Transcontinental* means "across the ____."

__A__ 9. The mountains became a ____, or something that stood in the way of building the railroad.

__G__ 10. The railroad workers worked for almost ____ years to complete the transcontinental railroad.

__L__ 11. During the ceremony, the last spike hammered into the rails was made of ____.

__B__ 12. In the 1860's, most railroad tracks stopped at the ____ River.

__N__ 13. ____ was president when the transcontinental railroad was completed.

__H__ 14. The front low part on a train is called the ____.

Heritage Studies 3
Student Notebook   Lesson 62
                                    Evaluating the Lesson   **82**

If you choose to do the Notebook activity on another day, you will want to take time to review the information from pages 218-19 before your child begins his work.

Day 3

Evaluating the Lesson

Notebook Activity, page 82

➤ Read the instructions on Notebook page 82.
➤ Complete the page.

If you are teaching Heritage 3 to more than one child, you may want to use the following activity.

Mock Railroad Building Relay (optional)

➤ *Divide the children into two teams—the Union Pacific Railroad Company and the Central Pacific Railroad Company.*

➤ *Write these railroad company names on a sheet of paper.*

➤ *Explain that each correct answer will earn a "railroad tie" for their company.*

➤ *Read aloud the first question from Notebook page 82, calling on a child to give the correct answer.*

➤ *Instruct all the children to raise their hands if they have the correct answer written on their Notebook pages.*

For each question, count and record vertical tally marks for the total number of correct answers from each railroad team. To make the tally marks resemble a section of railroad track, draw horizontal lines on the top and bottom of the tally marks to connect them. Continue this action, using each question on Notebook page 82. When all the questions have been answered, the railroad company with the longest section of track wins the relay.

Going Beyond

Enrichment

Provide your child with other recordings and/or music books of additional railroad songs. Instruct him to list the titles of the railroad songs that he finds. Encourage him to listen to the recordings and then sing some railroad songs or play them on a musical instrument.

Additional Teacher Information

Nearly eight years passed between the laying of the first rail at Sacramento by the Central Pacific and the ceremony held as the workers hammered in the last spike.

The greatest challenge for the Central Pacific Railroad Company was crossing the lofty, snow-covered peaks of the Sierra Nevada. Charles Crocker was in charge of construction. He brought thousands of Chinese coolies to work in the mountains, often in heavy snowfalls and avalanches. On a single day, the workers of the Central Pacific laid ten miles of track, winning ten thousand dollars in prize money. Someone has calculated that on that day 25,800 ties were laid and 3,520 rails were spiked to them. No one even tried to count the number of spikes.

The Union Pacific started their work about two years after the Central Pacific. Steamboats up the Missouri River serviced them well by hauling necessary track and locomotives.

Although the track ran unbroken from Omaha to California, for years both the Union Pacific and the Central Pacific had control of the line. Passengers from the East had to change from a Union Pacific train to a Central Pacific train at Ogden, Utah, the city closest to the companies' linkup at Promontory Point.

L E S S O N 6 3
Problems and Solutions

Text, pages 220-24
Notebook, pages 83-84

Preview

Main Ideas
- Inventions and ideas spread from one part of the world to another.
- People work at different kinds of jobs.
- The development of time zones came about as a solution to a problem with the railroad system.

Objectives
- Read a timetable
- Identify the time zones in the United States
- Identify the time zone in which the child lives
- Calculate the time in each time zone
- Use railroad signals to identify statements about railroad problems and solutions as either true or false

Materials
- A flashlight
- A globe
- Plasti-Tak
- Maps and More 24, page M16
- 6 analog clocks or watches*

 Analog clocks or watches will work best, but digital ones can be used. Your child will be able to see the differences in the time zones better if all the clocks are the same type.

Notes

The board game Sidetracks (Appendix, pages A55-A60) is introduced in the Enrichment section. If you choose to use the game, use the following instructions to prepare the game pieces.

 Laminating all the parts of the game or covering them with Con-Tact paper will give the game greater durability.

First, to assemble the *game board,* affix the copies of the game board sheet side-by-side inside a manila file folder to form the railroad scene. Color alternating spaces red, blue, or green to indicate the categories in the game.

Next, make one copy of the sheet of *game cards,* lining up the arrows front and back to align the questions with the answers. On the question side as well as the answer side of each card, color the top oval red, the middle oval blue, and the bottom oval green. Cut the cards apart.

Also, make one copy of the sheet of *Train Schedule Cards.* On each card, color the top oval red, the middle oval blue, and the bottom oval green. Cut the cards apart.

To make the *game markers,* use the pattern provided to construct several engines for the players. Make each engine a different color.

Finally, affix the *spinner* sheet to a stiff backing. Cut out the numbered square and the arrow. Place the end of the arrow over the center of the numbered square. Add an adhesive paper reinforcement to the arrow for extra durability around the hole. Then push the brad through to assemble the spinner. To let the arrow spin freely, bend the prongs of the brad approximately $\frac{1}{8}$" from the head. Tape the prongs to the back of the square to keep the brad from spinning with the arrow. For additional spinning ease, bend the square slightly away from the arrow, and the arrow will spin freely.

Put the spinner and the game cards in a resealable plastic bag or an envelope and attach the bag or envelope to the back of the game board folder.

Day 1

Lesson

Introducing the Lesson

Timetable-Reading Activity, Notebook page 83

➤ Look at the timetable for the two railroads on Notebook page 83.

➤ **What are the names of the trains?** *(Thundercloud, Swift Arrow)*

➤ **What are the trains' numbers?** *(Thundercloud—18, Swift Arrow—32)*

➤ Tell when each train runs. *(Thundercloud on Mondays and Fridays; Swift Arrow on Tuesdays and Thursdays)*

➤ Find the words *departure* and *arrival.*

➤ **What do the terms *departure* and *arrival* mean?** *(Departure refers to the time of leaving. Arrival is the time that the train gets where it is going.)*

Timetable

Name _____

Thundercloud	◀ Train Name ▶	Swift Arrow
18	◀ Train Number ▶	32
Monday and Friday	◀ Days of Operation ▶	Tuesday and Thursday
READ DOWN ▼	TOWNS	READ DOWN ▼

Departure	Arrival		Departure	Arrival
9:40 A.M.	11:40 A.M.	Eagle Point to Downing	8:10 A.M.	10:00 A.M.
12 noon	3:30 P.M.	Downing to White Plains	10:30 A.M.	2:30 P.M.
4:30 P.M.	8:30 P.M.	White Plains to Junction	4:00 P.M.	7:00 P.M.

Use the timetable to answer the questions.

1. ow long is the trip from Eagle Point to Downing on Thundercloud?

   __2 hours__ on Swift Arrow? __1 hour and 50 minutes__

   Which train is faster? __Swift Arrow__

2. What time does Swift Arrow arrive in Downing? __10:00 A.M.__

   What time does Swift Arrow leave Downing? __10:30 A.M.__ How

   long is the wait in Downing? __30 minutes__

3. Thundercloud leaves Eagle Point at __9:40 A.M.__ and arrives in

   Junction at __8:30 P.M.__ . How long does the whole trip take?

   __10 hours and 50 minutes__ Would you like to travel by train? _____

   Why or why not? __Answers will vary.__

_____

Lesson 63
Introducing the Lesson   **83**

© 1997 BJU Press. Reproduction prohibited.

➤ **What do A.M. and P.M. mean?** *(A.M. means in the morning, between midnight and noon. P.M. means the time between noon and midnight.)*

➤ Look at the center of the timetable. Notice that both trains travel to the same towns but on different days and at different times.

➤ Use the timetable to answer the questions. You will want to use scrap paper to complete the calculations.

Give help where needed. Give your child the correct answers, showing the calculations if necessary. Allow him to mark and correct any incorrect answers.

Trains did not always use timetables. In fact, most towns had their own times, different from the times of other towns. This problem of timekeeping was solved with the development of timetables. You will learn more about railroad problems and solutions in this lesson.

George Westinghouse
1846-1914

One man solved some of the railroad's worst problems. When he was a little boy, George Westinghouse worked in his father's machine shop. Before long he was trying to make new and different kinds of machines. He tested and rebuilt each new machine until it worked just the way he wanted it to. George Westinghouse made almost four hundred new machines, or *inventions*.

We remember George Westinghouse most for his invention called the *air brake*. Do you know what a brake is? A brake is a way to stop something. For many years, trains did not have good brakes. When an engineer saw that he must stop the train, he gave three toots on his whistle. When the brakeman heard the signal, he ran up and across the moving cars. He had to turn a wheel that set the brake on each car. The train would not stop until the brakeman turned every brake wheel. Sometimes the brakeman did not turn the brake wheels fast enough. What do you think happened then?

Westinghouse's air brake worked much faster. The engineer knew best when he needed to stop the train. He was the man who worked this new brake. The engineer turned one switch to set all the brakes. The train stopped!

220

Teaching the Lesson

Day 2

Text Discussion, page 220

➤ **Read page 220 to find out who solved one of the railroad's worst problems.** *(George Westinghouse)*
➤ **What was the problem?** *(Trains did not have good, safe brakes.)*
➤ **What was the old method of stopping a train?** *(The engineer gave three toots when he wanted to stop the train. When the brakeman heard this signal, he climbed up and ran across the moving cars, turning a wheel on each car that set each brake.)*
➤ **Why was this system not good?** *(Answers will vary.)*

This method was dangerous for the brakeman. The engineer did not have complete control over stopping the train. Sometimes one car would run into another car because it was not stopped quickly enough.

➤ **How did George Westinghouse solve this problem?** *(He developed air brakes.)*
➤ **In what way were the air brakes easier?** *(The engineer turned one switch to set all the brakes at once.)*

George Westinghouse was a young man, twenty-two years old, when he developed the air brake. This invention was not the first or the last for George Westinghouse. In all, he patented 361 different inventions. Obviously, George Westinghouse had special abilities that he developed and used effectively.

➤ **What are some characteristics of this inventor?** *(Possible answers include hard working, dependable, curious, and intelligent.)*

Challenge your child to try to solve everyday problems rather than to give up. Encourage him to seek the wisdom of God through daily Bible reading and prayer and to learn by following the examples of his parents, teachers, and pastor. (BATs: 2d Goal setting, 2e Work, 3a Self-concept, 6a Bible study, 6b Prayer)

Changes, for Better and Worse

Do you think travel by railroad was always safe? It was not. Sometimes the locomotives ran off the track. Sometimes the sparks from the smokestack set the wooden coaches on fire. Sometimes trains ran into animals, wagons, or even other trains stopped on the track. But it was still faster and more exciting than any other way of getting around.

As more and more trains used the new tracks, the railroads faced another problem. How could two trains travel in different directions on the same track? Unless someone thought of an answer, trains would always be in danger of running into each other.

Someone did find an answer. The railroads hired men to build *sidetracks* next to the main tracks. An engineer could pull his train onto the sidetrack to get out of the way of another train. The companies put a signal at each sidetrack. They put signals at other places too. The signals told the engineers when to stop on the sidetracks and when to keep going. Have you ever seen signals like these? What do they mean?

sidetrack

signal

all clear   caution   stop

221

This signal system worked well when trains ran on time. But no one could agree on what the right time was. Each town set its clocks by the sun. One town's clock showed a little earlier time than the clock in the next town to the east. Sometimes an engineer left the station too soon, and people missed the train. Sometimes a train stayed in the station too long, and another train ran into it from behind.

Important men from each railroad company met in one place. They wanted to find a way to solve the time problem. The men decided to divide the U.S. map into four parts, or zones. Each part would have its own time. The time zones helped keep trains running on schedule. Soon people everywhere, not just on the railroad, set their clocks by the time zones.

222

Text Discussion, page 221

➤ **Read page 221 to find out what** *sidetracks* **are and how they were used.** *(They are other tracks built next to the main track. A train could pull onto a sidetrack to make way for another train to travel in the opposite direction on the main track.)*

➤ **How would a train engineer know to pull his train onto a sidetrack?** *(by use of signals)*

➤ Look at the signals on the page. **Read the label for each signal.**

➤ **What does the word** *caution* **mean?** *("be careful")*

➤ **When do you think this signal might be used?**

The signal might alert the engineer to danger ahead, animals on the tracks, or a possible switch to another track.

➤ **What would the engineer probably do when he saw the caution signal?** *(slow the train)*

➤ **Do you think this signal system worked well?**

Text Discussion, page 222

➤ **Read page 222 to find out about another railroad problem and the solution that was found.** *(Trains did not run on time. The solution was to set up time zones.)*

➤ **Why did the trains not run on time?** *(Every town set its clocks by the sun; therefore, the times were different in each town.)*

➤ **What kind of problems were caused by trains not running on the same time?** *(People missed their trains. Sometimes a train stayed on the tracks too long and other trains ran into it.)*

➤ **Who finally decided to solve the problem?** *(important men from each railroad company)*

➤ **Into how many parts did these men divide the map of the United States?** *(four)*

➤ **What did they call these parts?** *(They were called zones.)*

➤ **How did** *time zones* **help to keep trains running on time?** *(Each zone would have its own time—a set time related to the time of the zones on either side of it.)*

➤ **Were railroad engineers the only ones to use this newly established time schedule?** *(no)*

➤ **Read the sentence in the text to prove your answer.** *("Soon people everywhere, not just on the railroad, set their clocks by the time zones.")*

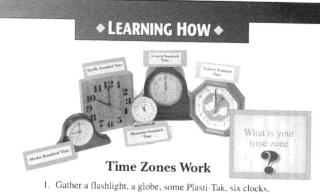

◆ LEARNING HOW ◆

Time Zones Work

1. Gather a flashlight, a globe, some Plasti-Tak, six clocks, and Notebook page 84.
2. Place the globe on a table. Put a bit of Plasti-Tak on the globe to show where you live. Darken the room. Pretend the flashlight is the sun and shine it on the globe right above the Plasti-Tak. What time is it at that spot on the globe? Slowly turn the globe to the east. Is the Plasti-Tak always right under the flashlight? In what part of the world is it noon now?
3. Set one of the clocks for the correct time where you are now. Then set the other clocks as your teacher tells you. Each clock represents the time it is now in a different part of the country, or time zone. Look at the map on your Notebook page. Can you find your state? Which time zone is it in?

223

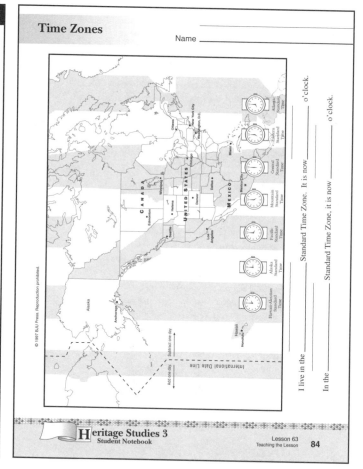

Time Zones

Name ______________________

I live in the ______________ Standard Time Zone. It is now ________ o'clock.

In the ______________ Standard Time Zone, it is now ________ o'clock.

Heritage Studies 3 Student Notebook — Lesson 63 Teaching the Lesson — 84

Day 3

Learning How Activity, page 223 and Notebook page 84

- ➤ **Read the steps on page 223.**
- ➤ Follow the procedures in the first two steps.
- ➤ Set one of the clocks you collected with the correct time for your location.
- ➤ Locate your state on the map on Notebook page 84.
- ➤ Draw a star there.
- ➤ **What is the name of your time zone?**
- ➤ Shade red the clock and the section of the map that corresponds with it.
- ➤ Write the name of your time zone and the time it is now in the spaces provided on the Notebook page.

The earth is divided into twenty-four time zones, but only six of them apply to the United States.

- ➤ *Help your child set each of the remaining clocks to represent one of the other time zones. For example, the clocks might be set at 8 A.M. (Hawaii-Aleutian), 9 A.M. (Alaska), 10 A.M. (Pacific), 11 A.M. (Mountain), 12 noon (Central), and 1 P.M. (Eastern).*
- ➤ As you set each clock, locate the new time zone on the map. Use the same color for shading the clock and the section of the map that makes up the corresponding time zone.
- ➤ **Read aloud the time zones, from West Coast to East Coast, noting the change of time from zone to zone.**
- ➤ **Which of the time zones were included in the path of the first transcontinental railroad?** *(Pacific, Mountain, Central, Eastern)*
- ➤ **Do you have a relative or a friend who lives in a different time zone?**
- ➤ Write the time and the time zone in the spaces provided on the Notebook page.

Little by little, people found ways to solve the railroad's problems. Men found safe ways to stop fast-moving trains. Others thought of a safe way to *couple*, or join, the cars and locomotives. Companies built comfortable, pretty cars for people to ride in. New and bigger locomotives pulled long trains faster.

Today the railroads have a new problem. Few passenger trains travel across the United States. Faster, easier types of travel have taken their place. Do you know some of these new ways to travel?

Freight trains, or those that carry goods, still criss-cross the country. You might see an old steam locomotive in a museum or at a railroad yard. Would you like to ride on one of these trains?

You could probably ride a train similar to this one at your local zoo or amusement park.

224

Text Discussion, page 224

➤ **Read page 224 to find some other solutions to the railroads' problems.**
➤ **What does it mean to *couple* the railroad cars?** *(to join them)*
➤ **What does a *freight* train carry?** *(goods)*

Evaluating the Lesson

Signaling Activity

You may find it more convenient to use text page 221 instead of Maps and More 24b.

➤ *Show Maps and More 24b, the chart of railroad signals.*
➤ **Read the meaning of each signal as I point to it.**
➤ *Demonstrate with your arm how to make the* All Clear *signal and the* Stop *signal.*
➤ Make the signals with your arm.
➤ I will read some statements to you. You will use these signals to indicate the answers. The *All Clear* signal will mean true and the *Stop* signal will mean false.

- George Westinghouse invented the air brake. *(true)*
- A brake is a good way to make something go. *(false)*
- Before the air brake was invented, three toots on a whistle would send the brakeman running up and across the moving train cars. *(true)*
- With the air brake, the engineer turned one switch to stop all the train cars at once. *(true)*
- Sidetracks were tracks built next to the main tracks. *(true)*
- An engineer could pull his train onto a sidetrack whenever he wanted. *(false)*
- The signal system worked well when the trains ran on time. *(true)*
- Each town used to set its clocks by the sun. *(true)*
- At first, the railroad men divided the United States map into eight time zones. *(false)*
- Each time zone has its own time. *(true)*
- As you move farther west, each time zone is one hour earlier than the time zone you just left. *(true)*
- To couple the railroad cars means to repair them. *(false)*
- Now thousands of trains travel across the United States. *(false)*
- Freight trains carry goods—food, building materials, and other things that people need. *(true)*

Going Beyond

Enrichment

Tell your child that the board game Sidetracks is a review game about railroads. (*NOTE:* See Appendix, pages A55-A60.) Explain the pieces of the game to him.

Game board—with the depot, train tracks, and many sidetracks; the object of the game is for each player to get his train back to the depot.

Game cards—each colored oval represents a different question category; the categories are *People* (red), *Places* (blue), and *Things* (green).

Train-schedule cards—place a crayon tally mark for each correctly answered question.

Spinner—the numbers on the spinner indicate the number of spaces to be moved on each turn.

Engine game markers—move around the tracks and then back into the depot.

Give directions for playing the game. Play begins with all the trains in the depot and the cards shuffled and placed facedown. Each player spins the spinner. The player spinning the highest number goes first. That player spins again and moves his train the number of spaces indicated on any section of track that leads out of the depot. The player must then answer a question from the category on which he has landed. Another player selects the top card and reads aloud the question from the category indicated. If the player answers correctly, he may draw a tally mark on his train schedule card next to the category answered. If he answers incorrectly, he keeps his game marker where it is until his next turn. The next player then spins, moves his train the number of spaces indicated, and tries to answer a question in the category on which he has landed. A player must answer two questions in each category before spinning to move his train back into the depot. The players may travel on any sidetrack that connects to a track that they are on. The first player to reach the depot wins the game.

Additional Teacher Information

George Westinghouse received his first patent when he was nineteen years old. The patent was for a rotary steam engine that he had designed. He received nine more patents before he reached the age of thirty. In all, George Westinghouse had 361 patents, which is an average of one every month and a half of his working life. Among Westinghouse's inventions were the automatic telephone-exchange system, electric signals to control railroad traffic, a method of transmitting natural gas through pipes, a natural gas meter, and a redesigned transformer through which electric current could pass into homes and factories. Westinghouse built companies to make and sell many of his inventions. He started sixty companies whose products used electricity to assist man in his labors. Some of his largest, most well-known companies include the Westinghouse Air Brake Company, the Union Switch and Signal Company, and the Westinghouse Electric Company.

The earth is divided into twenty-four time zones. Each zone is approximately 15 degrees wide. The 180-degree meridian is the international date line. If you cross the date line going east, you subtract a day. If you cross it going west, you add a day. (*NOTE:* Remember east is least [loses]; west is best [gains].) The prime meridian passes through Greenwich, England. Traveling west from the prime meridian, you gain one hour per meridian crossed until you reach the international date line.

The Wild West

This chapter tells about many things in the Old West—trail drives, outlaws such as Jesse James, and the way of life of many Plains peoples. It also tells of the conflicts and compromises that inevitably arise when many people want the same land. It ends with a look backward to improve the look forward.

Materials

The following materials must be obtained or prepared before the presentation of the lesson. These items are labeled with an asterisk (*) in each lesson and in the Materials List in the Supplement. For further information see the individual lessons.

- A picture of a locust (optional) (Lesson 64)
- Appendix, page A61 (Lesson 65)
- Appendix, page A62 (optional) (Lesson 66)
- Appendix, page A63 (Lesson 67)
- Appendix, pages A64-A65 (Supplemental Lesson)

LESSON 64
Homesteading

Text, pages 226-29

━━━━━━ **Preview** ━━━━━━

Main Ideas
- Many kinds of people made up the Old West.
- Homesteaders were people who acquired ownership of land by living on it for five years.

Objective
- Finish a story about homesteaders

Materials
- A picture of a locust (optional)*
- Supplement, page S15: covered wagon

━━━━━━ **Lesson** ━━━━━━ *Day 1*

Introducing the Lesson

Discussion, page 226

➤ **Read the first paragraph on page 226.**
➤ **What do you think the author means by "yes and no"?**

Many of our ideas about the Old West come from television programs, videos, and films. Although some of the events shown in these programs may have happened occasionally, they were not as common as we are led to believe.

➤ **As you read the rest of the page, decide whether the events and people mentioned were common in the Old West.**
➤ **What kind of transportation did the settlers use to travel west?** *(covered wagon)*

Show the covered wagon picture. Many people used this kind of wagon to carry their goods. Most people walked beside the wagons.

➤ **Why do you think the people did not ride?**

Walking gave the people more room for clothes and food and made the pulling easier for the animals.

➤ **Would you like to walk from the East to the West?**

What was so wild about the West anyway? Was it really a place of gunfighters and Indian raids and outlaws? Well, yes and no.

At the chuck wagon

The West did have some cattle thieves and a few shootouts and people who took the law into their own hands. But also in the West were honest ranchers and missionaries and Indians who wanted to live peaceably with the settlers.

There were good lawmen and a few bad lawmen. There were many farmers who plowed and reaped their fields year by year. There were soldiers and train robbers. There were schoolteachers and preachers, miners and mountain men. And there were lots of children.

A settler's daughter feeding the family's chickens

A roundup on a ranch in Kansas in 1902

A family in front of their sod house in Nebraska in 1886

226

Teaching the Lesson

Text Discussion, page 227

➤ **Have you camped out overnight?** If so, tell about sleeping outside.
➤ **Read the page to learn about Tom's home.**
➤ **Would you like to live that way all the time?**
➤ **Why did Tom's mother hold an umbrella while she was cooking?** *(to keep the water off her and out of the cooking)*
➤ **How do you think Tom liked his wake-up call?**
➤ **Do you know how a sod house was made?**

On the plains there are few trees. Settlers had to make houses out of whatever was available. The most readily available material was the sod, the tough grass with its tangled roots holding tightly to the soil. People cut blocks of sod out of the ground to use as building material.

➤ **Where did the beetle that Tom's mother had to kill come from?** *(Answers will vary. It probably lived in one of the sod blocks that made up the wall of the house.)*
➤ **What other problems would a sod house have?** *(Answers may include that it collected rainwater and was dark and damp inside.)*

This Nebraska homesteader also lived in a sod house.

Everyday Life

"Sod Busters" and Homesteaders

Tom woke up to a steady dripping on his face. He rolled over, and the water dropped on the floor beside his head. It had rained two days before. But the ceiling of the sod house was still "raining" inside. Another drop hit his ear. Tom got up.

His mother stood beside the low fire. She held an umbrella over the cooking. "Awake?" she said. "Papa wants you in the barn." A beetle ran out from the sod wall. Tom's mother smacked it with her hand.

In the barn, Tom's father was sharpening his scythe. "Morning," he said. "Soon as the sun dries things off, we'll get started." Tom nodded.

227

Tom drew water from the well for his mother. He glanced at the trees his father had planted three years before. Everyone had said that apple trees could not grow in the plains. But the thick leaves and the small round apples proved that they could.

If Tom's family could live here just two more years, the land would be theirs. Sometimes he thought that his mother would not make it. She cried when the cloth fell off the ceiling and dirt rolled all over. And she often was so tired that she would go to bed without even pulling back the covers.

Once he had seen his father cry. That was the day last summer when the locusts came. The huge insects had swarmed past. They made it dark in the middle of the day, there were so many. They made a roar, a horrible buzzing roar for hours. They ate every stalk and stem; they ruined everything that Tom's father had grown that whole summer.

228

Sometimes the settlers dug into the side of a hill, using the top of the hill for the roof and forming three walls from the sides of the cave. Then they had to cut only enough sod to make the front wall. Windows of glass were expensive and hard to get from back East. Many sod houses had oiled cloth over the windows and a cowhide covering the doorway.

➤ **Do you remember what a *scythe* was used for?** It was used to cut down grain.

A picture of a scythe can be found on page 21 of the student textbook of *Heritage Studies 2 for Christian Schools* (Second Edition).

Day 2

Text Discussion, page 228

➤ **Read the first paragraph on page 228.**
➤ **Have you pumped water from a pump or drawn water from a well?**
➤ **Do you think Tom had much time to play?** *(probably not)*

Remind your child that the Lord wants Christians to be good workers. (BATs: 2c Faithfulness, 2e Work)

➤ **Read the rest of page 228 to find out what things Tom's parents found hard to bear.** *(Tom's mother did not like the dirt falling on her and being so tired that she could hardly get into bed; Tom's father found it hard to accept the locusts' eating everything he had planted.)*
➤ **Do you know what a locust is?**

Show a picture of a locust, if you have one available. It is an insect that is similar to a grasshopper and that eats crops. Buzzing went on for hours or days when locusts were swarming. Sometimes the insects swarmed in hordes one hundred miles long and one hundred fifty miles wide. Such clouds of grasshoppers or locusts could devour a hundred acres of corn in just a few hours. There was no way to fight them.

But Tom's father had said, "If God wants us to have this land, He'll help us stay the five years." The *Homestead Act* promised settlers who lived on land five years that they could own that land. So Tom's parents did not give up. They were *homesteaders.*

But there was more trouble. Tom's father wanted to fence in some of the land. The ranchers to the south did not want the fence. They wanted to drive their cattle to market. They did not want to go around fences. They called his father a "sod buster." What do you think they meant?

Tom set the pail inside the door. "Here," said his mother. "Eat a biscuit before you go." Tom sat outside where it was dry and ate the biscuit. He prayed that there would be no locusts this year.

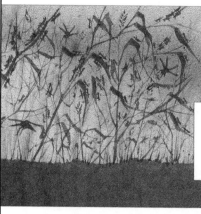

"The Lord redeemeth the soul of his servants: and none of them that trust in him shall be desolate."

Psalm 34:22

229

Text Discussion, page 229

➤ **Read page 229 to find what other problems the settlers faced.** *(lasting the five years in order to own the land; trouble from ranchers who did not like the fences that farmers built)*
➤ **What do you think *sod buster* means?**

Sod means "soil" or "ground," and *bust* means "break up." The name was used by nonfarmers to make fun of farmers. It meant "dirt breaker." The name referred to the plowing the farmers did.

Ask your child whether he should call people names to make fun of them. *(no)* Ask how he thinks the name made Tom feel when he heard it used about his father. *(sad)* Remind your child that the Lord expects Christians to be kind to others. (BATs: 5a Love, 5e Friendliness)

➤ **What law said settlers could keep their land if they lived on it for five years?** *(Homestead Act)*
➤ **Do you know what a *homestead* is?**

It is a place where a family makes a home. A home can be large or small, made of brick or sod or wood, near other houses or by itself. A home is not a certain kind of building. Rather, a home is a place where people love each other.

Evaluating the Lesson
Story-Sharing Time

➤ **Where do you think Tom was going after he ate the biscuits?** Finish the story about Tom and his family from the textbook, telling whether they stayed the five years, whether the locusts came, and what happened to the family after that.
➤ Think through your story and jot down the outline of events.
➤ Tell the ending you have given the story.

You may want to tape-record the story. As your child tells his story, listen to see that he accounts for the family's staying or not staying. If he fails to mention whether the family got the land, ask some questions to test his knowledge of the Homestead Act, the threat of locusts, and complaints from ranchers. You may want to let your child illustrate his story.

━━━ Going Beyond ━━━

Additional Teacher Information

Not everyone who went west traveled overland. Some chose to go by water. One route was an eighteen-thousand-mile, around-Cape-Horn adventure that required six to eight months. Others opted for the shorter but in some ways more harrowing voyage over the Isthmus of Panama. Going by way of the Chagres River and trekking through a jungle, the bold traveler could cut perhaps four months off the long route. The vast majority of pioneers and adventurers, however, preferred the cheaper and somewhat less risky overland trails.

LESSON 65
Ranchers and Cowboys

Text, pages 230-34
Notebook, pages 85-87

Preview

Main Ideas
- People make their livings in different ways.
- People use the land to meet their needs.

Objectives
- Devise a cattle brand and explain its meaning
- Trace a trail on a map

Materials
- *HERITAGE STUDIES Listening Cassette A*
- Maps and More 25, page M10
- Supplement, page S12: Cowboy Word List
- Supplement, page S16: the altered brand
- Appendix, page A61: Saddle Parts*

Day 1

Lesson

Introducing the Lesson

Matching Game

➤ *Show your child the Cowboy Word List in the Supplement.* These words relate to the subject of the day.
➤ Guess the topic for today. *(ranching, cowboys)*
➤ **Do you think you can define the words?**
➤ Choose a word to fit the definition I will read.

- a vehicle for carrying food and equipment *(chuck wagon)*
- to run wild suddenly *(stampede)*
- a long rope with a loop at one end *(lariat)*
- a group of a single kind of animal *(herd)*
- marked with a hot iron *(branded)*
- herding together of cattle *(roundup)*

The people who used to own and work on ranches would be surprised to learn that modern ranchers and cowhands use helicopters and trucks in their work.

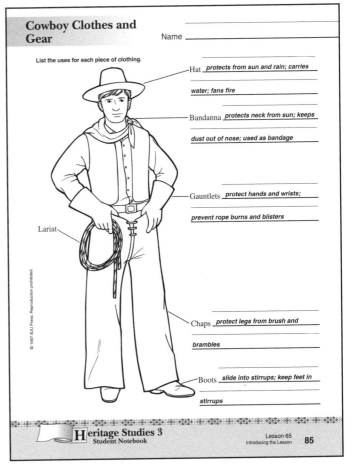

➤ **What do you think these modern machines are used for?** Helicopters are sometimes used for rounding up cattle and for keeping track of herds. Trucks carry feed and equipment.

The horses the cowboys rode and the cattle they herded came from horses and cattle that had been wild. *Mustangs* are wild horses, small but tough. They can run a long way without tiring, and they have a good sense of direction. Wild cattle in the West were often *longhorns.*

➤ **Where did the name *longhorn* come from?** *(the animals' long horns)*

Some horns reached seven feet from tip to tip. The men caught the horses and the cattle and tamed, or domesticated, them.

Identifying Activity, Notebook pages 85-85a

➤ **Have you ever wondered why a cowboy's clothes looked the way they did?** Each piece of a cowboy's clothing and gear served at least one purpose, usually more.
➤ Look at Notebook page 85. As I read aloud a paragraph, list the uses of the cowboy's clothing on the lines on the Notebook page.

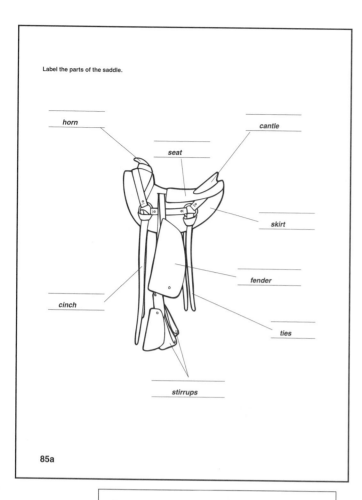

Label the parts of the saddle.

horn

cantle

seat

skirt

fender

cinch

ties

stirrups

85a

It wasn't really Will's horse. All the horses belonged to the owner of the Triple J Ranch. But this was the horse Will most liked to ride. He cinched up the saddle and swung into the seat. His **chaps** swished against the leather fender of the saddle. Will's legs would not feel the brush or the brambles under those leather coverings. The pointed toes of his **boots** slid easily into the stirrups, and the high heels kept his feet from sliding through. He adjusted the reins in his hand and pressed the heels of his boots into the horse's side. The horse sprang forward. Will rested his hand on the horn of the saddle and rode at a trot toward the other cowboys.

➤ Turn your Notebook page over to page 85a. *Place the Saddle Parts page in front of your child.*

➤ I will read part of the paragraph about Will again. This time label the saddle parts as I read about them.

Will <u>cinched</u> up the saddle and swung into the <u>seat</u>. His chaps swished against the leather <u>fender</u> of the saddle. Will's legs would not feel the brush or the brambles under those leather coverings. The pointed toes of his boots slid easily into the <u>stirrups</u>, and the high heels kept his feet from sliding through. He adjusted the reins in his hand and pressed the heels of his boots into the horse's side. The horse sprang forward. Will rested his hand on the <u>horn</u> of the saddle and rode at a trot toward the other cowboys.

➤ Label the last three parts that were not mentioned in the paragraph.

Encourage your child to write short phrases explaining each word. This will help him begin the note-taking process. You will need to pause, giving him time to write phrases in the blanks. You may prefer to read the entire paragraph aloud for his comprehension before your child begins writing.

Will went out to saddle his horse. On his head he wore a felt **hat** to keep off the sun and rain. He sometimes used it to fan a fire and to carry water. He looked at the sky. Today would be clear and hot, he thought. Around his neck he wore a **bandanna**, something like a large kerchief. If the dust blew, he could cover his nose and mouth with the bandanna. It also kept the sun from burning the back of his neck. Once he had used it as a bandage on his hand until he got back to the ranch. As Will walked toward the corral, he pulled on his **gauntlets**, their wide leather cuffs reaching halfway to his elbows. Many times those big gloves had saved him from a rope burn and blisters. As he twisted his lariat, he whistled for his horse. A big brown horse with a dark mane and tail came forward.

Ranchers

"Going up the Chisholm Trail?" The man threw a bedroll on the back of his saddle. "That's what I heard," said the other. He pulled the cinch on his saddle one more time. The two men got on their horses. They rode out to meet the *trail boss* and the other *cowboys*. They were setting out on a *cattle drive*.

The herd of cattle spread out before them like a sea. "Almost twenty-five hundred head," the trail boss told them. "We're heading up the old Chisholm Trail to Abilene. Head 'em up!" The cowboys swung out to the sides of the herd. The cattle drive was on.

Billy came behind with the extra horses. He was only fourteen, but he knew his job well. Horses liked him and he liked horses. Each of the nine cowboys had eight or nine extra horses. About how many horses did Billy look after?

A modern cattle drive

230

Late at night, the cowboys on watch sometimes sang to the cattle to keep them quiet. One song was about the very trail they were on. What do you think the song is called? One night a thunderstorm came up. Lightning shot through the sky, and a crack of thunder shook the ground. Suddenly the cattle bolted into a run. "Ho!" yelled a cowboy. "Stampede!"

Everyone, even the cook, flew to the horses and took off after the cattle. They rode all night. In the morning, most of the cattle had stopped running. But many were scattered far and wide. The trail boss wiped his face on his sleeve. He shook his head. "It'll take a week to get them all back," he said.

The cook made breakfast—beans and bacon and biscuits. He found some wild berries to throw in. But the food did not cheer the men up. The three-month trip had just gotten longer. Can you find the Chisholm Trail on the map?

This map shows the three major trails used when driving cattle to market.

231

Teaching the Lesson

Text Discussion, pages 230–31

Many people do not know about the real life that cowboys and ranchers led. Their impressions are influenced by the stories that were written and the films that were made about the cowboys.

➤ **Read pages 230-31, looking for the words we have discussed and any new words related to ranching.**

➤ Define each of the following words from what you have read:

- *trail boss* (the man in charge of the cattle drive)
- *cattle drive* (moving herds of cattle from one place to another)
- *cowboy* (a person who works with cattle)
- *head* (a cow or a way of referring to the number of cattle)
- *bedroll* (the bundle of blankets that a cowboy spread out to sleep on)

➤ Cowboys are sometimes called *cowpunchers*. **Did the cowboys actually punch the cows?** *(no)* The term means "to keep cattle moving."

One cowboy said, "My years on the trail were the happiest I ever lived. There were many hardships and dangers but . . . most of the time we were . . . adventurers in a great land."

➤ **In your reading where were the cowboys headed?** *(Abilene)*
➤ **What trail were they using?** *(Chisholm Trail)*
➤ **Whose job was it to take care of the extra horses?** *(Billy's)*
➤ **How old was Billy?** *(fourteen)*
➤ **How many horses did he watch?** *(between seventy-two and eighty-one)*

Billy was called a ***wrangler,*** and his horses were in a herd called a ***remuda.***

➤ **Do you think Billy was a responsible boy?**
➤ **What does "head 'em up" mean?** *(get the cattle moving)*
➤ **Do you think the men got tired of the same food every day?**
➤ **How long did the men expect the drive to take?** *(three months)*
➤ **What caused the stampede?** *(lightning and thunder)*
➤ **How much extra time would the drive take after the stampede?** *(at least a week)*

**Picture Reading Activity,
Maps and More 25**

➤ *Show your child Maps and More 25.*

The cowboys moved the cattle in a column about a mile long. The trail boss went ahead to find water and good grazing land. The cowboys were to keep the cattle safe from wild animals and thieves and to keep them from straying.

➤ **What position would you like to take on a drive?**
➤ **Do you think driving cattle was an easy job?**

Cowboys had to work all day and then take two-hour watches at night. Someone had to be guarding the cattle at all times. (BATs: 2c Faithfulness, 2e Work)

Cowboy Song,
Notebook page 86

➤ Follow the words on Notebook page 86 as we listen to the recording of "The Old Chisholm Trail" from the listening cassette.
➤ Let's sing the song together.
➤ Underline phrases in the song on Notebook page 86 that reflect or tell about information that you have read in your text. *(Chisholm Trail, Texas cattle, bacon and beans, punch cattle)*
➤ This song had at least 143 different verses. **Do you think one person made up all those verses?**

Map-Reading Activity, page 231

The song "The Old Chisholm Trail" is named for the trail some cowboys followed to drive cattle to Abilene. The Chisholm Trail was named for Jesse Chisholm, a storekeeper and trader who had used the trail when he traded with the Kansas Indian nation.

➤ Look at the map on page 231.
➤ **Read the three trail names from the key.**

The cattle drives went north to get to the railroads and to stay in good pastureland. The only way to get the cattle to eastern cities was by railroad. Where the cattle trails met the railroads, cities grew up.

➤ **Where did the Chisholm Trail begin?** *(San Antonio)* **Where did it end?** *(Ellsworth or Abilene)*
➤ **Where did the Goodnight-Loving Trail begin?** *(in Texas)* It began in San Angelo, Texas.

The Western Trail began in Fort Buford and San Antonio, Texas. The trail moved toward the middle and the railroads.

➤ Name some of the cities that began where the trails met the railroads. *(Abilene, Dodge City, Cheyenne, Ellsworth, Pueblo)*

How do you think the cowboys could tell their cattle from all the other herds in Abilene? Every ranch had its own *brand*, a mark the cowboys put on all the cattle. Ranchers branded their cattle so that thieves, called *rustlers*, could not take them and claim them. Look at the brands on this page. Can you tell how some of them got their names?

To brand the cattle, cowboys first had to catch them. Have you ever seen someone riding after a cow, swinging a loop of rope? That rope is the cowboy's *lariat*. The cowboy tried to get the loop around the cow's horns or neck. Once he got the cow stopped and down on the ground, he branded it.

A *branding iron* was a piece of metal bent into a shape. The cowboys heated the iron in a fire and then pressed it onto the hip of the cow. The hot metal singed away the hair. The print of the brand was left on the hide.

Walking 7

Bar Y's

Rocking chair

Lazy R

Bull head

Running W

Hat

Tumbling ladder

Sunrise

232

Calf roping

Bulldogging

Bronco riding

233

Text Discussion, page 232

➤ **Read page 232, watching for both new and familiar terms.**

➤ **What is a cattle thief called?** *(a rustler)*

➤ **What did the ranchers do to try to keep rustlers from getting the cattle?** *(branded their cattle)*

➤ Guess how each of the **brands** on page 232 got its name. *(Answers will vary.)*

➤ *Show the picture of the altered brand.*

Some rustlers rebranded the stolen cattle. For example, they might add lines to the Rocking Chair brand to make it into a Circle H. Ranchers tried to think of brands that were not easy to change. They also tried to make their brands easily recognizable and different from other ranchers' brands.

➤ Choose the brands on page 232 that you think would be the least likely to be stolen or confused with others.

◆ THINGS PEOPLE DO ◆

Holding Rodeos

When ranchers got together, they sometimes had contests. "I have a cowhand who can rope a calf quick as a wink," one might say. "I'd like to see that," another would say. The contests became yearly events. We call them *rodeos*.

Have you ever been to a rodeo? What did you like best—the calf roping, the bronco riding, or the bulldogging? The events at a rodeo are jobs that a cowboy had to do every day. Bronco riding came from breaking wild horses for riding. Bulldogging came from having to get a cow down to brand it.

Bulldogging, bringing down a steer by twisting its horns, was invented by Bill Pickett, the first black rodeo star. Bill was tall and strong. He could throw any steer. He became famous, traveling with rodeos all over the country. He even performed for Queen Victoria of England.

Text Discussion, page 233

➤ **Read page 233 to find out who invented the event called *bulldogging*. (Bill Pickett)**

➤ **What is bulldogging?** *(bringing down a steer by grabbing the horns to twist the neck, forcing the animal to fall)*

There was one trick that only Bill Pickett could do: he would grab the steer by its lip and flip it over.

About one-fourth of all the cowboys were African American and one-fourth were Mexican.

◆ LEARNING HOW ◆

To Make Up a Brand

1. Get Notebook page 87 and a pencil.

2. Make up a name for your ranch. Mark the place on the map where your ranch is. Write the name beside the mark and in the key.

3. Draw the brand that your ranch will use. Keep it simple. Check with your "neighbors" to be sure your brand is not too much like theirs.

Ready for branding

234

Evaluating the Lesson

Learning How Activity, page 234 and Notebook page 87

➤ **Read the steps on page 234.**

➤ Follow the steps to complete Notebook page 87. You may want to sketch a few brands on scrap paper before putting your final version on the map key.

➤ Mark on the Notebook page the route you will take to get the cattle to market. Look at text page 231 to find the available routes.

➤ Explain your route to me and your reason for choosing it.

My Ranch Name _____

Put your ranch on the map.

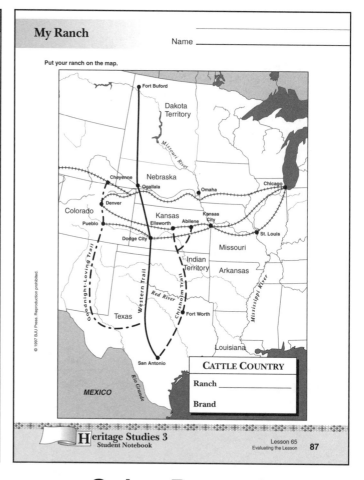

Heritage Studies 3
Student Notebook

Lesson 65
Evaluating the Lesson **87**

━━ Going Beyond ━━

Enrichment

Allow your child to make up his own verses for the song "The Old Chisholm Trail."

Additional Teacher Information

At first, most of the cattle grazed on *open range,* land owned by the government and available to anyone who wanted to use it for pasture. Little of this land was fenced, and cattle moved freely from place to place. Many cattlemen decided to buy land from the government so that they would have their own grazing land. They often fenced the land with barbed wire to keep their herds from roaming and from mixing with other herds. After the transcontinental railroad was finished in 1869, many more miles of railroad track were laid in the West. The cattlemen did not have to drive their herds so far to ship them to market. Thus, the days of the open range and the cattle drives ended, a glorious era that had lasted only twenty years.

LESSON 66
The Cavalry

Text, pages 235-37
Notebook, pages 88-92

━━━ Preview ━━━

Main Ideas

• The cavalry protected settlers.
• Native Americans settled in each region of what is now the United States.

Objectives

• Follow and use cavalry hand signals
• Relate events that may have occurred in a cavalry unit
• Recognize rank insignia
• Read a grid map and answer questions about it

Materials

• *HERITAGE STUDIES Listening Cassette A*
• Supplement, page S17: Cavalry Songs
• Supplement, page S18: the insignia
• Appendix, page A62: outpost (optional)*

Day 1

━━━ Lesson ━━━

Introducing the Lesson

Song Activity, Notebook page 88

➤ *Play or sing the tune from Notebook page 88 for your child.*
➤ Sing "To Horse" with me.
➤ **Who do you think sang that song?**

One part of the United States Army once sang and played it. The soldiers who sang it rode horses. They were in the *cavalry. Write the word, pointing out its different spelling, pronunciation, and meaning from* Calvary.

Inferring Activity

➤ *Show your child Cavalry Songs.* **Read the words to "Stable Call."**

The word *rue* in the fourth line means "to be sorry about."

To Horse

Name _____

Sing this song with your class.

To Horse
3

Go to the pic-ket line and get your horse; You are to get him where-e'er he may be of course.

Heritage Studies 3
Student Notebook

Lesson 66
Introducing the Lesson 88

➤ **What do you think the song was used for?** *(to get the horses fed and watered)*

The horses learned to recognize the bugle tunes to different songs. They responded quickly to this one.

➤ **Why would the horses respond to this tune?** *(It meant they would get food and water.)*
➤ **What does the song say about the captain?** *(He watches carefully; he makes the men obey the rules.)*

God knows everything we do and expects us to obey Him. (BATs: 2a Authority, 2b Servanthood)

➤ **Read the lyrics for "Mess Call."** A *mess* is a meal.
➤ **What did the soldiers think of their food?** *(They thought it was plain and that there was not enough of it.)*

Although the men made jokes about the food, most of them were thankful for what they had.

➤ Listen as I play "Mess Call" from the listening cassette.

Soldiers

Have you ever heard of the *cavalry?* The cavalry is the part of the United States Army that rode horses. The soldiers on this day had ridden fifteen miles. The dust rose from the dry ground. The saddles creaked, and horses snorted. Some men walked beside their horses to rest them.

The man with the bugle played a tune. Even the horses knew what the bugle tunes meant. This one told them that there was water to drink. The horses drank, and the men set up camp. After the horses were fed, supper was over, and the guns were cleaned, the bugle sang out "Taps." Have you ever heard that tune? It is played at funerals for soldiers. It signals that it is time to go to sleep.

Just as the sun came up the next morning, a band of Cheyenne rode down the ridge. They waved blankets and hollered at the horses. The horses started to jump and mill around. The soldier near the herd yelled, "They're after the horses!" The horses began to run. The bugler played "Stable Call" quickly. What do you think happened?

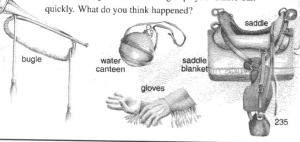

bugle

water canteen

gloves

saddle blanket U.S. CAVALRY

bridle

saddle

235

The horses heard the tune and came back toward the camp. By now the soldiers had caught a few and were riding around the herd. The Cheyenne got away with only three. "Just three, sir," a soldier said. "Very well," said the sergeant. "Sound 'Mess Call.' " To the soldiers, *mess* meant a meal.

The soldiers would not go after three horses. They were on their way to defend a town. Soon they were riding, their saddles creaking. Sergeant Madsen waved his right hand back and forth over his head. The soldiers looked up. Then Madsen held up two fingers. The soldiers formed two lines. Why do you think the sergeant used hand signals?

236

Teaching the Lesson

Day 2

Text Discussion, pages 235-36

➤ **Read pages 235-36, looking for the songs you have just studied.**
➤ Find the song you have not studied. *("Taps")*
➤ Listen as I play "Taps" from the listening cassette.
➤ **When was "Taps" played?** *(at funerals, when it was time to go to sleep)*
➤ **What tune was a signal to the horses that it was time to eat and drink?** *("Stable Call")*
➤ Tell how the soldiers used the tune later. *(to trick the horses out of running away)*
➤ **Why do you think the captain would not go after just three horses?** The need to protect the town outweighed his desire to catch three horses.

➤ **Did the captain make a good decision?** *(yes)*

> As Christians we should always ask the Lord's help in the decisions that we make. We want our decisions to be the right ones. (BAT: 3c Emotional control)

➤ **Why do you think the captain used hand signals when riding with the men?**

He used hand signals so that his directions could be understood by those too far away to hear him. His men could understand him even when the horses were running.

➤ **What hand signals do you use from time to time?** *(Answers will vary. Some may include putting a finger to the lips to signal quiet, wiggling the index finger to get someone to come over, etc.)*

To Follow Cavalry Signals

1. Get Notebook page 89.

2. Practice the hand signals on the page with your teacher.

3. As your teacher instructs, use the hand signals as though you were in the cavalry.

237

Cavalry Hand Signals

Name _____

Fill in the blanks.

1. Which picture shows Captain Madsen calling for attention? __1__

2. Which picture shows that the captain wants the riders to go to the right? __3__

3. Which shows the riders are to form two lines? __2__

4. Which signal do you think the captain uses most often? __Answers will vary.__

5. What do you think the captain does to get the riders to go to the left? __puts his left arm out straight; opposite of picture #3__

①
②
③

Heritage Studies 3
Student Notebook

Lesson 66
Teaching the Lesson 89

Learning How Activity, page 237 and Notebook page 89

➤ **Read the steps on page 237.**

➤ Look at the illustrations on Notebook page 89 and answer the questions about the hand signals.

➤ I will call out *attention, two columns,* and *ride right* at different times. You are to give the correct hand signal.

When your child has practiced the signals, you may want to lead him around the room or outdoors. You may also want to include other family members. Remind him that he represents a soldier in an honorable cavalry unit; therefore, he should respond quickly to the signals.

Insignia Discussion

➤ **How would you recognize the captain if you saw him?** *(Answers will vary. Some may mention his horse, his position at the front of the men, his uniform, his weapons, or his giving commands.)*

Soldiers wore signs called *insignia* on their uniform sleeves to show what position or **rank** they held. *Show the picture of the insignia.*

➤ **Do you think the insignia are in order of importance from top to bottom?** *(yes)*

➤ Describe each of the insignia.

➤ A corporal's insignia looks like the sergeant's but with only two stripes. **Which do you think is the higher rank, the corporal or the sergeant?** *(the sergeant)*

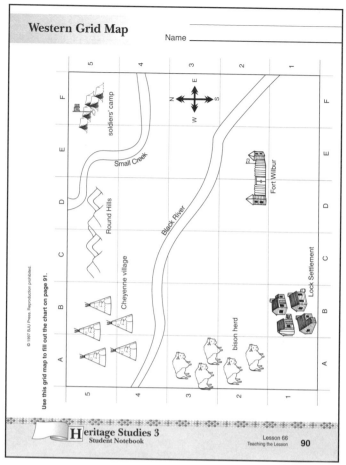

Use this grid map to fill out the chart on page 91.

Grid Map Information

Name _____

Fill out the chart and answer the questions according to your teacher's instructions.

Grid	Information
A4, A5, B4, B5	*Cheyenne village*
B1	*Lock Settlement*
D2, E2	*Fort Wilbur*
C5, D5	*Round Hills*
A2, A3	*bison herd*
E5, F5	*soldiers' camp*

1. If each grid is one mile long and one mile wide, how far is it from Fort
   Wilbur to the soldiers' camp? ____ *about 3 miles* ____

2. Where does the Black River end on the map? ____ *F1* ____

3. Where are the most bison (buffalo)? ____ *A3* ____

Day 3

Grid Map Activity, Notebook pages 90–91

➤ Study the grid map on Notebook page 90.

➤ Look at the first column of the chart on Notebook page 91. Look up the grids given in this column on Notebook page 90. Tell what you find in the grids in the second column.

➤ Answer the questions at the bottom of Notebook page 91.

Journal Reading

➤ I am going to read something that may have appeared in a cavalryman's journal. Listen for familiar cavalry terms.

"To Horse" sounded after breakfast. Sergeant, Ulysses, Bob, myself, and five others rode out with a week's rations. On the move before sunup. No coffee tonight.

Rained all day. Cold rain. Wet blankets and no good fire. "Taps" brought no sleep.

Morning was clear and cold. Sergeant waved us out just at sunup. Bob is coughing more, very sick. Mess was late today. Thunder scared horses. "Stable Call" got them back.

Rode fifteen miles. Weather improved.

➤ Name some of the familiar cavalry terms which you heard. *("To Horse," Sergeant, "Taps," mess, "Stable Call")*

➤ **How would you like the life of a cavalryman?**

Evaluating the Lesson

Narrative Activity, Notebook page 92

➤ Look at the picture on Notebook page 92.

➤ Write a journal entry as though you were in a cavalry unit in the West in the 1800s. Use information from the picture as well as information from the lesson. *You may give your child the outpost drawing to look at as well.*

Cavalry Account

Name _____

Imagine that you are a member of the cavalry. Write a paragraph about one day in your life.

Answers will vary.

_____
_____
_____
_____
_____
_____
_____
_____
_____

© 1997 BJU Press. Reproduction prohibited.

Heritage Studies 3
Student Notebook

Lesson 66
Evaluating the Lesson **92**

Going Beyond

Enrichment

Your child can pretend to be in a cavalry unit. Make a captain's insignia from paper or cloth that he can pin to his sleeve. As "captain" he should march around, using hand signals.

Give your child a copy of the outpost. (*NOTE:* See Appendix, page A62.) Also include materials such as toy building logs for constructing a model of the outpost.

Additional Teacher Information

Four regiments of the cavalry were known as "the Buffalo Soldiers." These regiments were composed of black soldiers. Since blacks were rare in the West, they caused much interest among the Cheyenne and other Native Americans at army posts. When several soldiers of the Tenth Regiment took off their caps, the surprised onlookers remarked that their hair was like a buffalo mane. They called the soldiers "Buffalo Soldiers," and the name spread.

The last living Buffalo Soldier received a belated campaign medal at the age of 103. He was Simpson Mann, born during the Civil War, and he served in action against the Sioux around Pine Ridge, South Dakota. (*NOTE:* See Lesson 68 for more information about these battles.)

LESSON 67
Lawmen and Outlaws

Text, pages 238-39
Notebook, page 93

Preview

Main Ideas
• Laws help people live together peaceably.
• Laws must be enforced to be useful.

Objective
• Identify right actions and wrong actions

Materials
• A safety pin
• Appendix, page A63: the Coffeyville map*

Day 1

Lesson

Introducing the Lesson

**Badge-Making Activity,
Notebook page 93**

➤ Color and cut out the badge.
➤ *Help your child secure the badge with a safety pin to his shirt or blouse.*
➤ **What people in the West do you think wore a badge?**

In the West one hundred years ago, people who wore badges were either marshals, sheriffs, or deputies.

➤ **Which one are you?**
➤ Name people who wear badges today. (*police officers, fire chiefs, security officers, etc.*)
➤ **Why do people wear badges?** (*to show that they are authorities to be obeyed*)
➤ **Why are laws and lawmen needed?** (*to keep people from hurting each other; to help people live together peaceably*) (BAT: 2a Authority)

Name _____

Color and cut out as your teacher instructs.

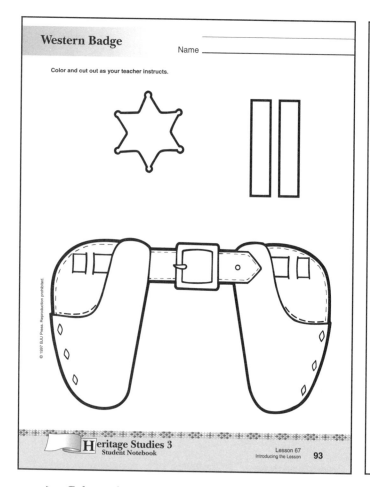

© 1997 BJU Press. Reproduction prohibited.

Heritage Studies 3
Student Notebook

Lesson 67
Introducing the Lesson **93**

Lawmen

Another group of people who were trying to keep the peace in towns were the United States *marshals.* Marshals were like policemen of today. They tried to stop trouble. Sometimes they had to go after bank robbers and cattle thieves. Lawmen who took care of huge territories were called *sheriffs.* Most of the lawmen were good men.

Sergeant Madsen became a marshal after he left the cavalry. He was quiet, but he was a man to be respected. Once he trailed some bank robbers to a hideout. The robbers shot at him and ducked back into hiding. Madsen hollered for them to come out. They shot again. This time the marshal shot back. Madsen won. He was an expert with a rifle. He became famous for keeping the law in the West.

United States Marshal Chris Madsen

238

➤ Color and cut out the holster.
➤ Cut slits on the bold dotted lines.
➤ Cut out the rectangles.
➤ Color one of the rectangles yellow on both sides and the other one green on both sides.
➤ Put the rectangles into the slits on the holsters. Put the holster aside until later.

Teaching the Lesson

Text Discussion, page 238

➤ **Read page 238 to find the name of one of the West's best marshals.** *(Chris Madsen)*
➤ **What was Madsen's background before he became a marshal?** *(cavalry)*
➤ **What was his cavalry rank?** *(sergeant)*
➤ **How do you think Madsen's cavalry experience helped him as a marshal?** He knew how to shoot, how to lead men, and how to keep order.
➤ Explain the difference between a sheriff and a marshal. *(Marshals worked in towns and cities. Sheriffs oversaw large territories.)*
➤ Decide whether you are a marshal or a sheriff today.

Most of the lawman's job was routine and even boring. The famous gunfights were rare and anything but glamorous. Television and films have often given outlaws and their deeds more excitement and acceptance than they had or deserved.

Robbery Account

➤ *Show your child the Coffeyville map.*
➤ You may look at the map as I read about a famous robbery by a group of outlaws called the Dalton Gang.

Do not be concerned about tracing all the actions of the story on the map as you read the story. You do not want your child to lose focus on the story. A few suggestions have been added to give him a general idea of the action. He will work with the map more after the story.

Nine-year-old Alexander Woodson Martin was on his way to school on a Wednesday morning in October 1892. The Coffeyville school was already in session, but he and his friend Bert Read had stopped to watch some men digging a foundation for a new building on Union Street. *(Point out Union Street and the Foundation for a new building on the map.)* The boys lost track of time; they were late, but they would not get scolded today.

On another street five riders came into town. The riders turned and went into an alley.

Mr. Brown, who owned a store on the street where the new building was going up, went down Union Street with a bundle. He saw Bert and Woodie, and he stopped a moment.

"You boys are a little late for school, aren't you?" Mr. Brown said. He winked at them. "But there's something to be said for learning about work too." He laughed a pleasant laugh and walked on. Up the street a young man came out on the sidewalk. It was Lucius, the clerk from Bert's father's store. Bert waved. Lucius waved back. He was whistling.

Bert said, "Lucius said he'd take us fishing Saturday. He doesn't have to work. Papa gave him the whole day off. Will your ma let you go, Woodie?"

"Not if I don't go to school," said Woodie. "Come on. We better go."

The five riders left their horses in an alley, not far from a barn. *(Point out the Alley and Barn.)* Then two of them went toward the First National Bank, just a few yards from where the boys still stood. Three others went toward the bank on the other side of the street. *(Point out the two banks.)* The boys did not think anything of men going into the bank. People went into banks all the time.

But Mr. McKenna thought something of it. He thought he recognized one of the men—a Dalton! He watched the men go into the bank and then ran into his dry-goods store. Soon he was back with a rifle, motioning for some men to join him.

Bert and Woodie suddenly realized that something was up. A wagon driver had joined Mr. McKenna and was waving to the men who were digging as though he wanted them to come over.

Another wagon driver slowed his wagon for a moment, looking into the First National Bank. Then he slapped the reins down, shouting "Robbing the bank! Robbing the bank!"

Men everywhere stopped what they were doing and ran for their guns. Bert and Woodie dropped to the ground and scrambled under a wagon. The man who owned the hardware store was passing out guns and bullets to men running up the street toward the bank. "Get ready, men," he was saying. *(Point out the hardware store.)*

Inside the banks, the robbers held the tellers and the other customers at gunpoint. In one bank, the men had taken $1,100; in the other, they were waiting for the safe to be opened. The three robbers with the money stepped out of the bank. The townspeople fired at them. One robber was hit, and the robbers went back inside.

"Go back," Bob Dalton yelled.

Lucius, gun in hand, walked down the alley toward the First National Bank. Bob Dalton shot him dead.

The boys under the wagon decided to run. They crawled around the corner of the building and ran to tell their fathers what was happening.

Bob and Emmett Dalton came out of the back of the First National Bank, ran up the alley, and turned toward the other bank. *(Point out this path on the map. Start at First National Bank. Go north up the Alley. Then turn west and go toward the other bank.)* A man was standing at the end of the street with a rifle. But he was looking the other way. Bob Dalton shot him four times, and the man fell dead in front of a store beside the bank. Mr. Brown ran out to help the man, and the Daltons shot him before he could even move the fallen man's rifle from his hands.

The three robbers across the street made a dash for their horses. The townspeople opened fire. All three robbers were wounded. One ran to a lumberyard and hid. One died as he tried to mount his horse. The other, Grat Dalton, waited by a barn for a chance to go for a horse.

Marshal Connelly and two other men went down to the alley where the horses were. Grat Dalton swung out of hiding and shot the marshal in the back. Then he ran for his horse. One of the men with the marshal leveled his gun and killed Grat Dalton.

The wounded robber who was hiding in the lumberyard jumped up and dashed to his horse. He rode away under heavy fire from the two men who had come with the marshal. He rode only a little way before he fell from his horse, dead.

Bob and Emmett Dalton now were running to the alley where they had left their horses. The man who had shot Grat Dalton shot Bob Dalton. Bob Dalton fell backward into the dust. Emmett Dalton had gotten onto a horse, but instead of riding off unwounded, he rode toward his brother Bob. The other man who had come with the marshal shot him in the shoulder as he reached down. He fell from his horse beside his brother.

For a moment there was a terrible silence. Then suddenly someone yelled, "They're all down!" A bank teller looked at the clock. Only fifteen minutes had passed since the Daltons had entered the First National Bank.

But in those fifteen minutes, four townspeople had died and three were badly hurt. Four of the robbers had been killed and one, Emmett Dalton, was arrested and taken to a doctor. All the money was found—$1,100 in Grat Dalton's pocket and $20,000 in a bag that Emmett had carried. The men who had died protecting the bank did not have any money in the bank. They were just trying to uphold the law.

Story Discussion

➤ **How do you think the families of the men who had died defending the town felt?**

➤ **Have you ever seen a film in which robbers were made to look daring and brave?**

Four honest men lost their lives because bad men wanted easy money. What the robbers did was not brave, but what the townspeople did was.

Map Activity

➤ *Direct attention to the Coffeyville map.*

➤ Help me fill in the key.

- **Where were the boys standing?** *(on Union Street in front of Foundation for a new building)*
- **According to the key, what symbol should you put on the map?** *(a circle)*
- Draw a circle on the map on Union Street in front of *Foundation for a new building.*
- **Where were the robbers' horses tied?** *(in the alley south of the barn)*
- Look at the key and draw the appropriate symbol.
- **Where did Lucius die?** *(in the alley behind the First National Bank)*
- Add the symbol to the map.

➤ **In which direction did Bob and Emmett Dalton run after they came out of the back of the bank?** *(north)*

➤ **In which direction were the horses from the banks?** *(west)*

➤ As I read the path the robbers took, use a colored pencil to trace the path on the map.

The gang rode in from the west and left their horses in the alley behind the barn. Then they went east to the banks. Bob and Emmett Dalton went out the back door of the First National and north to the end of the alley. There they turned west and then south, going down Union. All the robbers fled west toward the alley behind the barn again.

◆ FAMOUS PEOPLE ◆

Frank and Jesse James
1843-1915 and 1847-82

Young Jesse James

There is more than one way to become famous. The James brothers chose the wrong way. The two had been Confederate soldiers in the Civil War. When they went home to Missouri, Frank and Jesse were rousted out at night by men with guns. The men wanted to arrest the brothers for what they had done during the war.

Soon after, the James brothers and some other men began robbing trains and banks. During the robberies, many people were shot and killed. Thousands and thousands of dollars were stolen. Always the gang of robbers got away—until three from the gang were killed and three more were captured in Minnesota.

Frank James when he was older

Frank and Jesse were never caught. Years later, Jesse was shot in the head by a man pretending to be his friend. Frank turned himself in to the law. He stood trial for robbery and murder. Surprisingly, there was universal sympathy for him because of the way Jesse was killed, and he was acquitted. He returned home and worked in a small Wild West show. He later died peaceably at home.

239

Day 3

Text Discussion, page 239

➤ **Read page 239 to see what happened to another famous outlaw pair.** *(Jesse was killed; Frank was arrested and tried but was acquitted, or found not guilty.)*

➤ **Why do you think some people think the life of an outlaw is exciting and admirable?**

They do not understand the truth about how the outlaws really lived and what they were really like; perhaps they do not see right from wrong clearly.

> God tells us in His Word what is right and what is wrong and that we are to follow His Word. (BAT: 6d Clear conscience)

The stories about things that happened, both good and bad, make up the history of a people. Think about your personal history, the stories about yourself.

➤ **Is the history you are making showing forth Christ more and more?** (BAT: 7b Exaltation of Christ)

Evaluating the Lesson
"Fast-Draw" Game

➤ Take out the holster and rectangles you prepared earlier.

➤ The yellow rectangle stands for "wrong" and the green rectangle stands for "right."

➤ Put the rectangles in the slots on the holster and lay the holster in front of you.

➤ I will read several actions. You are to draw a rectangle out of your holster and hold it up as soon as you decide whether the action is a right action or a wrong one.

- Robbing a bank *(yellow)*
- Picking up litter *(green)*
- Lying to a parent *(yellow)*
- Getting angry because you lose a game *(yellow)*
- Cleaning up the kitchen after dinner *(green)*
- Hiding when you have broken something *(yellow)*
- Being friendly to a new neighbor *(green)*
- Warning someone of danger *(green)*
- Giving up free time to help someone *(green)*
- Obeying the law and your parents *(green)*

Going Beyond

Enrichment

Make an enlargement of the holster and rectangles from Notebook page 93. Write on the rectangles different actions, both right and wrong. Your child can color the rectangles: green for right actions, yellow for wrong actions. He should put all right actions into one holster and all wrong actions into the other.

Additional Teacher Information

The Dalton Gang was named for the three brothers in it—Gratton, Bob, and Emmett. These men had turned to horse thievery and then went on to train robbery and murder. They had begun as lawmen, wearing badges and searching for the men who had killed their deputy marshal brother, Frank. The raid on Coffeyville was meant to upstage the exploits of the Younger Gang, whose primary members, Bob and Cole Younger, were second cousins of the Daltons. The Daltons thought the simultaneous robbing of two banks in daylight would be unbeatable—especially since Coffeyville was their hometown.

LESSON 68
The Last of the Old West

Text, pages 240-44, 286-87
Notebook, pages 94-97

Preview

Main Ideas
- Nations gain land in many ways.
- Places change over time.

Objective
- Write a comparison of the Sioux life before and after the reservation system began

Materials
- The figure of the Battle of Little Bighorn (1876) from the TimeLine Snapshots
- A ruler

Day 1

Lesson

Introducing the Lesson
Naming Activity,
Notebook pages 94-94a

Many Native American nations counted time by full moons. The period between full moons they called a *moon.* The people often called the moons names that told what happened during that time of year. The names also told something about where the people lived and what was important to them.

➤ I will read several names of moons from the Tewa *(tā´ wə)* Indians of the Southwest. Listen to see what you can tell about where the people lived and what they grew. *(They lived where cedar trees grew; they grew crops of corn and other things.)*

Moon of the Cedar Dust Wind
Moon When the Leaves Are Dark Green
Moon When the Leaves Break Forth
Moon When the Corn Is Taken In
Moon When All Is Gathered In

Naming Activity

Make up new names for the months.

Sioux name	English name	Your name
Moon of Strong Cold	January	*Answers will vary.*
Raccoon Moon	February	
Moon When Buffalo Calves Are Born	March	
Moon of Greening Grass	April	
Moon When Ponies Shed	May	
Moon of Making Fat	June	
Moon When Wild Cherries Are Ripe	July	

© 1997 BJU Press. Reproduction prohibited.

Heritage Studies 3
Student Notebook

Lesson 68
Introducing the Lesson
94

Native Americans

Spotted Tail, the great Sioux chief, sat in the circle, smoking a peace pipe. He nodded to the soldiers and glanced at the other chiefs with him. Then he signed the treaty. Now part of the lands of South Dakota belonged to the white men. The soldiers told him, "White men will stay out of your part of the land. It will always be yours." Spotted Tail nodded again, but he did not smile.

Chief Spotted Tail

When white men wanted land, they told the Sioux and others, "We'll make a deal with you." The signed papers said, "As long as the grass grows and the water flows, this part of the land will belong to the Sioux." For a few years the white men would keep their word. Then someone would discover gold or need more ranch land. What do you think happened to the treaties then?

A settler found gold in the hills of the Dakotas. Soon the white men forgot about the treaty with Spotted Tail. They ran the Native Americans off the land. "Find somewhere else to live," they said. "We need this land to hunt for gold." Some Sioux just left. Others said, "No more giving in. We will fight!"

240

Moon When Geese Shed Their Feathers	August
Moon of Drying Grass	September
Moon of Falling Leaves	October
Moon When the Water Is Black with Leaves	November
Moon of Popping Trees *or* Moon When Deer Shed Their Horns	December

94a

➤ **Read the names of the moons on Notebook pages 94-94a and guess what was important to the Sioux.** *(wild animals: buffalo, deer, raccoons, geese; plants: cherries and grass; their ponies)*

➤ **Did the people live where it was cold or warm in winter?** *(cold)*

Most Native American nations who told time by moons had thirteen moons, rather than twelve like our months. The time between full moons is shorter than our average month, giving more sections to a year.

➤ On the Notebook pages, fill in names for months that will tell something about you and what you find important. An example might be "Moon of Vacation Bible School."

Map Activity, pages 286-87

➤ Find the Sioux land on the map on pages 286-87.

The people knew only the open life of the plains, as their parents and grandparents had known. The life of the Sioux was one of travel and hunting. They did not stay in one place all the time.

➤ **Why do you think that was?** They had to follow the wild game and the seasons.

Crazy Horse, Spotted Tail's nephew, wanted to fight. Sitting Bull, another Sioux chief, joined Crazy Horse. They gathered many warriors together. The United States government sent some cavalrymen to fight the Indians. The soldiers were led by General George Armstrong Custer.

Custer was supposed to wait for more soldiers to join his men. "No," he said, "I need no help." He went into battle against hundreds of angry warriors at Little Bighorn. The soldiers were outnumbered and outfought. When the battle was over, not one of Custer's soldiers was standing.

The government sent more soldiers after Sitting Bull. They chased him into Canada. When he tried to come back to his people, he was caught. He went to live on a reservation. But still some Sioux did not give up hope.

Chief Sitting Bull

241

Missouri   *River*

Yellowstone River

Missouri River

*Battle of Little Bighorn
June 25, 1876*

X

Little Bighorn River   *Rosebud River*   *Tongue River*   *Powder River*

Big Horn Mountains

Montana

Wyoming

Black Hills

South Dakota

© 1997 BJU Press. Reproduction prohibited.

Wyoming

Colorado

South Platte River

0 25 50 75

Heritage Studies 3
Student Notebook

Lesson 68
Teaching the Lesson   **96**

Teaching the Lesson

Text Discussion, pages 240–41

➤ **Read pages 240-41 to find out how the battles between the Sioux and the cavalry started.** *(Settlers broke treaties, and the Sioux and other nations fought the trespassers.)*

➤ **Have you heard the name *Custer* before?**

General Custer was an officer in the Civil War. Sitting Bull was a high chief, much respected by all the Sioux and some other nations as well.

➤ **Were the settlers right to break the treaty?** *(no)* **Why?** *(It is not acceptable to break your word just because keeping it has become inconvenient or unprofitable.)* (BAT: 4c Honesty)

➤ **What do you think of the decision to fight?**

The Notebook pages will be used out of order in this lesson.

Map-Reading Activity, Notebook page 96

➤ Follow on your Notebook page map as I recount the events.

When Sitting Bull refused to sell the Black Hills to the gold hunters, he made enemies. *(Let your child locate the Black Hills on the map.)* He said that his people had been promised these hills in a treaty many years earlier. But the white people, thinking of gold, had forgotten the treaty. Sitting Bull and other chiefs decided to move west into the valley of the Bighorn Mountains. *(Let your child find the Bighorn Mountains on the map.)* They and their people numbered in the thousands. The camp stretched along the Rosebud River for five miles. *(Let your child find the Rosebud River.)* Never before had so many Plains people gathered together.

Colonel Custer was supposed to wait for another cavalry unit, but he was too proud and impatient. He told his men to ride into the valley and to kill the warriors camped there. He didn't think that there were as many warriors as there were.

Custer's men rode in and attacked the camp. Several thousand warriors mounted their horses and gave a war cry. The soldiers suddenly realized that they were outnumbered. But it was too late. All of Custer's men died that day—and so did Colonel Custer.

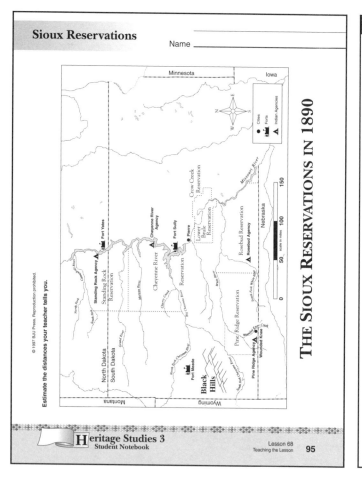

Estimate the distances your teacher tells you.

© 1997 BJU Press. Reproduction prohibited.

THE SIOUX RESERVATIONS IN 1890

Minnesota   Iowa

Cities
Forts
Indian Agencies

scale in miles

0   50   100   150

Missouri River

Crow Creek Reservation

Cheyenne River Agency

Fort Yates

Standing Rock Agency

Standing Rock Reservation

Cheyenne River Reservation

Fort Sully

Pierre

Lower Brule Reservation

Rosebud Reservation

Rosebud Agency

Nebraska

Pine Ridge Reservation

Pine Ridge Agency

Wounded Knee

Fort Meade

Black Hills

North Dakota
South Dakota

Montana   Wyoming

H eritage Studies 3
Student Notebook

Lesson 68
Teaching the Lesson   95

◆ HOW IT WAS ◆

Wounded Knee Creek in the Dakota Badlands
December 29, 1890

A Paiute medicine man had said he had a vision. The vision told him that if his people would do the "ghost dance," they would get their lands back. If warriors wore "ghost shirts," no bullets could harm them.

The battleground at Wounded Knee

Many believed the medicine man. Why do you think they did? Sitting Bull said, "The ghost dance will bring back our hunting lands." The government feared what the Indians might do. The soldiers came to arrest Sitting Bull. They hurried him out, and he was shot.

The Indians fled the reservation. Cavalry soldiers chased them. Believing their ghost shirts would keep them safe, the Indians shot at the soldiers. The soldiers fired back. More than two hundred Indian men, women, and children were killed. The Sioux never fought back again.

242

➤ Place an *X* on the map between the Rosebud and Little Bighorn Rivers, just north of the Bighorn Mountains.

This is where the Battle of Little Bighorn was fought. The battle has also been called "Custer's Last Stand."

➤ **What present-day state was the battle in?** *(Montana)*

➤ Write *Battle of Little Bighorn* beside the *X*. Add the date *June 25, 1876*.

➤ Look back at Notebook page 94. **What did the Sioux call this month?** *(Moon of Making Fat)*

For many years the only stories of this battle came from the warriors who survived. Many cavalry officers refused to believe what the warriors said. But archaeologists have found empty cartridges and arrowheads and skeletons which show that the warriors were correct.

Day 2

TimeLine Snapshots Activity

➤ Place the figure of the Battle of Little Bighorn on the TimeLine at 1876.

➤ **Where did the government chase Sitting Bull and his people?** *(into Canada)*

The Canadian government told Sitting Bull that since he was from the United States, he could not stay in Canada. When Sitting Bull tried to go home to the Black Hills, he was captured and sent to live on a reservation.

➤ **Do you know what a *reservation* is?**

It is a piece of land where the U.S. government says that Native Americans must live if they want to continue to live as their ancestors did.

Map Activity, Notebook page 95

➤ Find the scale of miles on the map on Notebook page 95.

➤ Lay your ruler under the scale.

➤ **How many miles does one inch represent?** *(50 miles)*

➤ **How many miles does two inches represent?** *(100 miles)*

➤ Find Pine Ridge Reservation on the map.

➤ Estimate the width of the Pine Ridge Reservation. *(about one hundred miles)*

➤ **In which direction would you go from Standing Rock Reservation to get to Pine Ridge Reservation?** *(south)*

➤ **What symbol represents a fort on the map?** *(a black rectangle with a flag)*

The West Today

The fights over land, the gold rushes, and the Indian wars are over. Where many bison grazed are now farms. Fruit trees grow over the places that once held camps of cavalry soldiers. Factories and roads have been built where before were the fires of Sioux and Cheyenne tribes.

A family crossing the prairie in 1886

Cheyenne, Wyoming, in 1876

The prairie that once was so hard to get over in covered wagons is crossed with wide highways full of cars and tractor-trailers. The wind that once swept only grass now whips around houses and sky-scrapers and airports. What would the pioneers think if they saw their West today?

Modern San Antonio, Texas

243

But not all of the Old West is gone. The sense of freedom is there. And the spirit of independence is still strong. In the West even now, the grandchildren and the great-grandchildren of the pioneers are changing the West again, inventing and building and exploring different frontiers. Native Americans are regaining their long heritage. State parks are keeping some of the land the way it was in earlier days.

Monument Valley Tribal Park, Arizona

The United States has taken many ways of many peoples and made new ways from them. We call that way the *American way.* But America also allows people to keep their own culture. This freedom is also part of the American way. Since the days before Jamestown and Plymouth until today, the people in America have been thinkers and doers. All Americans would do well to learn from those earlier comers, to correct what is wrong and to keep what is right and good.

Merced River, Yosemite National Park

244

➤ Locate the Black Hills on the map. Arguments over ownership of these hills caused a terrible series of events leading to the Battle of Little Bighorn.

➤ Find Fort Yates.

➤ **What reservation was it near?** *(Standing Rock)* Sitting Bull lived on Standing Rock Reservation and was killed there.

➤ Find Wounded Knee.

➤ **What reservation is it on?** *(Pine Ridge)* Later in this chapter, you will read about a battle that took place at Wounded Knee.

➤ Estimate the distance from Fort Yates to Wounded Knee. *(approximately 250 miles)*

Day 3

Text Discussion, page 242

The Battle of Little Bighorn was the last time the Sioux and other Native American nations ever won against the cavalry. It was also the last battle in history in which the winners used mostly bows and arrows to fight.

➤ Look at the second word in the text on page 242. This word is pronounced pī´ yo͞ot .

➤ **Read page 242 to find out about the last battle with the cavalry.**

➤ **Why do you think so many Paiute and Sioux believed in the "ghost shirts"?** They desperately

wanted to think that they could still win back their land.

➤ **Why do you think the people gave up fighting?**

They knew that they would never be able to get the land back and that they were outnumbered and overpowered. Many settlers at the time had fought back because they thought that the soldiers had been attacked. Today most people think that the soldiers were fearful of the Indians' belief in the ghost shirts and fired too soon, without clear orders.

Text Discussion, pages 243-44

➤ Look at the pictures of the Old West and the modern West on page 243.

➤ Describe how things have changed.

➤ **Read pages 243-44.**

➤ Find the sentence in the first paragraph on page 244 that sums up what the page is about. *("But not all of the Old West is gone.")*

➤ **What things about the character of America should be kept?** *(Answers will vary.)*

American citizens are responsible to speak up about things they think are wrong and to defend that which is right.

Poem Comparison

Name _____

Write about the Sioux way of life that each poem represents.

At Night May I Roam

At night may I roam
Against the winds may I roam
At night may I roam
When the owl is hooting
May I roam.

At dawn may I roam
Against the winds may I roam
At dawn may I roam
When the crow is calling
May I roam.

_____
_____
_____
_____

The Last Song of Sitting Bull

A warrior
I have been.
Now
It is all over.
A hard time
I have.

_____
_____
_____
_____
_____
_____
_____

The Last Song of Sitting Bull and At Night May I Roam in "Teton Sioux Music," by Frances Densmore in *Bureau of American Ethnology Bulletin Number 61, 1918* (Washington, D.C.: Smithsonian Institution). Reprinted courtesy Smithsonian Institution Press.

© 1997 BJU Press. Reproduction prohibited.

Heritage Studies 3
Student Notebook

Lesson 68
Evaluating the Lesson
97

Evaluating the Lesson

Comparison Activity, Notebook page 97

➤ Write about the kind of life that each poem describes. Use as many details from the lesson as you can.

> "At Night May I Roam" should inspire details about the free life on the plains, drawing upon the names of the moons. "The Last Song of Sitting Bull" should lead your child to discuss the battles and reservation life of the last part of the nineteenth century.

━━ Going Beyond━━

Additional Teacher Information

The name *Wounded Knee* comes from the Sioux. A Sioux chief had gashed his knee in a battle with the Crow by the creek. He jumped into the creek and swam to escape. The creek became known as Wounded Knee Creek, and the area took its name from the creek. Later, Crazy Horse, one of the chiefs at Little Bighorn, was buried secretly along the creek. Finally, the spot became the ground on which the Sioux nation lost all hope of regaining an old and cherished way of life.

Lesson
The West Before

Text, page 279

━━ Preview ━━

Main Ideas

- Many people lived in the West and all parts of the United States before Columbus came.
- People built cities in the West hundreds of years before the pioneers came.

Objective

- Write a news report about the discovery of the Anasazi ruins

Materials

- An atlas
- Red and green crayons
- Appendix, page A64: The West Before time line*
- Appendix, page A65: the Anasazi page*

━━ Lesson ━━

Introducing the Lesson

Time Line Study

➤ **Do you think people were living in the New World when Christ died?**
➤ *Give your child The West Before time line.*
➤ Find the line indicating Christ's Crucifixion. Color the line red.
➤ Look at the top portion of the time line. This shows events in the New World.
➤ Color the two dashed lines green. Shade the area between the lines green as well.
➤ **Were there people in the New World when Christ was on the earth?** *(yes)*
➤ **Have you ever heard of the Anasazi** *(ä nə sä´ zē)*?

Long before Columbus or even the Vikings came, people were living in what is now the United States. Some lived in the forests, some on the plains, some by the oceans. Some built large cities with many houses and public places. The Anasazi were a nation that lived in what is now the southwestern United States. You will be studying about one group of Anasazi that came to live in a special place.

Teaching the Lesson
Sequencing Activity

➤ Listen as I read a story.

It was near Christmas in 1888 when Richard Wetherall and Charles Mason rode out to look for stray cattle. The ranch they rode from was in Mancos, Colorado. As the men traveled, they came to the edge of a steep canyon. They dismounted and looked into the canyon. But they did not see cattle. Instead, they saw a most incredible sight.

There below them in the canyon was a city of stone buildings sitting under the overhanging rock on the opposite side of the canyon. They stared in amazement: some of the buildings were four stories high—not even big cities like Abilene had such structures. The sun blazed against the walls of the city, making it shine in splendor. The men went slowly down into the canyon to see what other wonders were there. They found baskets and pots and large round pits of smooth stone. They realized that more than two hundred people must have lived there at one time. But how long ago, they wondered.

Word got out about the beautiful stone city in the canyon. Many other people came to see the place. There were more stone buildings and cities nearby that other visitors soon found.

➤ *Point out Mesa Verde National Park on a map of the United States in an atlas, showing that it is near a place where four states meet: Colorado, New Mexico, Utah, and Arizona.*

In Mesa Verde National Park, you can see what Richard Wetherall and Charles Mason saw that December day. The park is in Colorado, in the southwest corner. This area is called the "Four Corners."

➤ **Why is this a good name for this place?** *(because the corners of four states touch there)*
➤ *Give your child the Anasazi page.* Look at the words at the bottom of the page. You will hear the definitions for the first two words as I read two paragraphs about the Anasazi.

You will need to pause while your child writes the definitions. The answers for the definitions are underlined.

The people who built the city in the canyon traveled throughout the Southwest, gathering wild plants and hunting animals. They made beautiful baskets. They lived in large family groups. The Navajo called them *Anasazi*, which means "the an-cient ones."

Mesa Verde means "green table" in Spanish. In the 1700s some Spanish explorers saw the area with its high plateaus and called it that—but they never went into the canyons. They thought the plateaus looked like green tables. They rode on, looking for

the cities of gold they had heard of, and missed seeing the amazing cities of stone.

➤ **Why do you think the Navajo called them "the ancient ones"?**

Possibly the Navajo had heard stories of the people who lived in Mesa Verde and knew they had lived there a long time ago. We do not know what name these ancient people had for themselves.

You may want to have your child number the illustrations as you read. You may want to read the paragraphs first and then number the illustrations. Choose the method that best suits your child.

➤ Look at the illustrations and the remaining word to define on your page. As I continue to read, number the Anasazi houses in order of their construction, with *1* next to the earliest dwelling or the one that was built first.

Around the year 550 or so (942 years before Columbus and 1,070 years before the *Mayflower*), the Anasazi began to build permanent houses and to grow their own crops, such as corn and beans. The houses had floors below the ground. The walls slanted over poles all around the floor pit. A hole in the roof served as window and chimney. There was a fireplace, a circle of clay, under the hole. The only light in such a house would come from the fire or the hole in the ceiling. *(1—bottom picture)*

After a while, the Anasazi made different houses. These were built on top of the ground and were almost square. Sometimes the houses were joined together in a row or on half a circle. We call this kind of community *pueblo*, from a Spanish word for "village."

At first, the new houses were made with wooden posts and walls plastered with mud. Later, the houses were built out of stone. The roofs were flat; the people often worked on the roofs and dried corn there. *(2—top picture)*

The last buildings the Anasazi made in Mesa Verde, the ones that Mason and Wetherall saw in 1888, were built right into the canyon wall. They are tucked under the rock ledge. Here the Anasazi lived for many years, until they left the city, never to return again. *(3—middle picture)*

➤ Look at the top picture. **Can you think of buildings in our cities that are somewhat like pueblos?** *(apartment buildings, row houses, townhouses, motels)*
➤ **Why would the Anasazi build homes under a rock ledge?** *(for extra protection from the weather; to keep the houses cool during the day)*

Text Discussion, page 279

➤ Look at page 279. Identify what you see in the pictures.

➤ Follow along as I read the page.

Inferring Activity

Much of what we know about the Anasazi comes from the places they built and the things they left behind. For instance, we know that they must have traded with people who lived south of them because they had some cotton clothes, and cotton will not grow in Mesa Verde. Cotton grows farther south.

➤ Listen as I read some other facts. Decide what you think the information tells us about the Anasazi people.

- Spears were found in the pueblo houses, but bows and arrows were more plentiful there. *(The pueblo dwellers must have hunted with bows more than with spears.)*

- Large fields were found around the city under the rock. Many rooms for storing grain were built into the city, and many pots were found with corn still in them. *(The people stored food for winter and for times of drought; they grew their own food, rather than gathering it from the wild.)*

- Growth rings on trees show that there was little water for the twenty-three years before all the Anasazi left the city. *(A drought may have caused the people to leave.)*

- Many decorations made with seashells were found in the houses. *(Anasazi must have traded with people who lived near the sea.)*

Because the climate is so dry in Mesa Verde, many things the people left are still in excellent condition. A jar with a bowl over it kept corn good for more than seven hundred years. A few of the walls still have paintings on them that were put there more than five hundred years ago. When people started visiting the place in the 1890s, taking things and climbing over the ancient walls, they destroyed more than centuries of weather had.

➤ Imagine that you had to leave for another place immediately. **What would the next people to come along think about you?**

> Christians should live so as to represent the Lord well, even by the patterns of their living. (BAT: 1c Separation)

Evaluating the Lesson

News Report Activity

➤ Write a news report about the finding of the Anasazi city.

➤ Tell as much as you can about the city and the people who lived there.

Going Beyond

Additional Teacher Information

When the Anasazi left Mesa Verde, they probably moved south. Some may have settled along the Rio Grande. Others may have joined the Hopi or Zuni in what is now Arizona and New Mexico. There is no record of what happened to these groups after the move between 1250 and 1300. The traditions and the customs of the Zuni and Hopi lead some to believe that they are descended from the Anasazi or from the people the Anasazi may have joined after the drought in the late 1200s.

The Anasazi were not the only ancient civilization on the plains of what is now the Southwest. The Mogollon people (of the Apache group) settled in the mountains of New Mexico and surrounding valleys and began to build communities as early as 100 B.C. Just shortly after, in the valleys of the Gila and Salt Rivers, the Hohokam began to irrigate their fields and build cities that would continue for twelve centuries. Both these groups, however, followed the Apaches, who had been living in the Southwest for centuries.

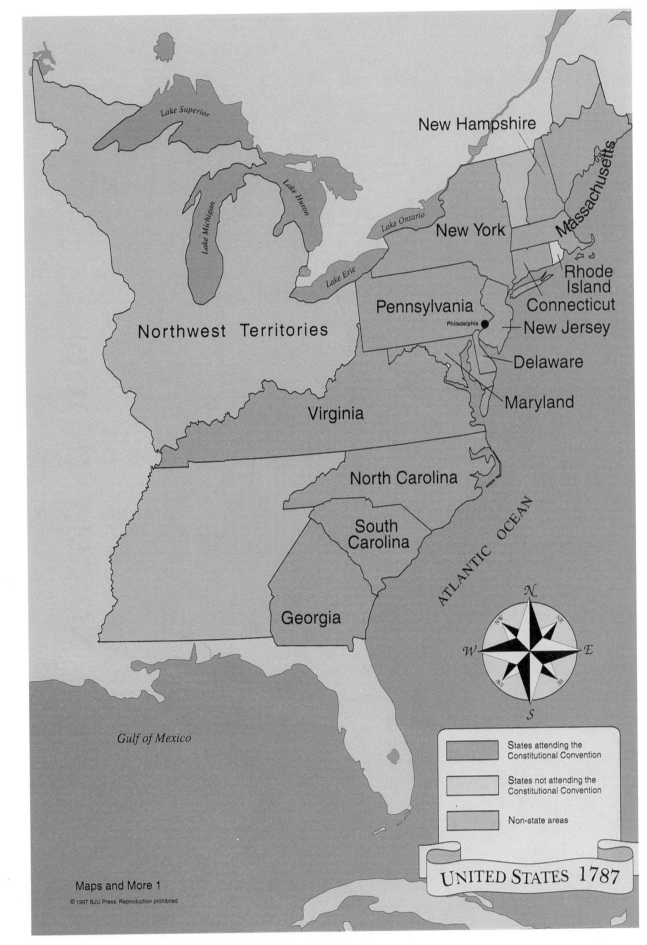

Lake Superior

Lake Michigan

Lake Huron

Lake Ontario

Lake Erie

New Hampshire

Massachusetts

New York

Rhode Island

Connecticut

Pennsylvania

Philadelphia

New Jersey

Delaware

Maryland

Northwest Territories

Virginia

North Carolina

South Carolina

ATLANTIC OCEAN

Georgia

Gulf of Mexico

States attending the
Constitutional Convention

States not attending the
Constitutional Convention

Non-state areas

UNITED STATES 1787

Maps and More 1

© 1997 BJU Press. Reproduction prohibited.

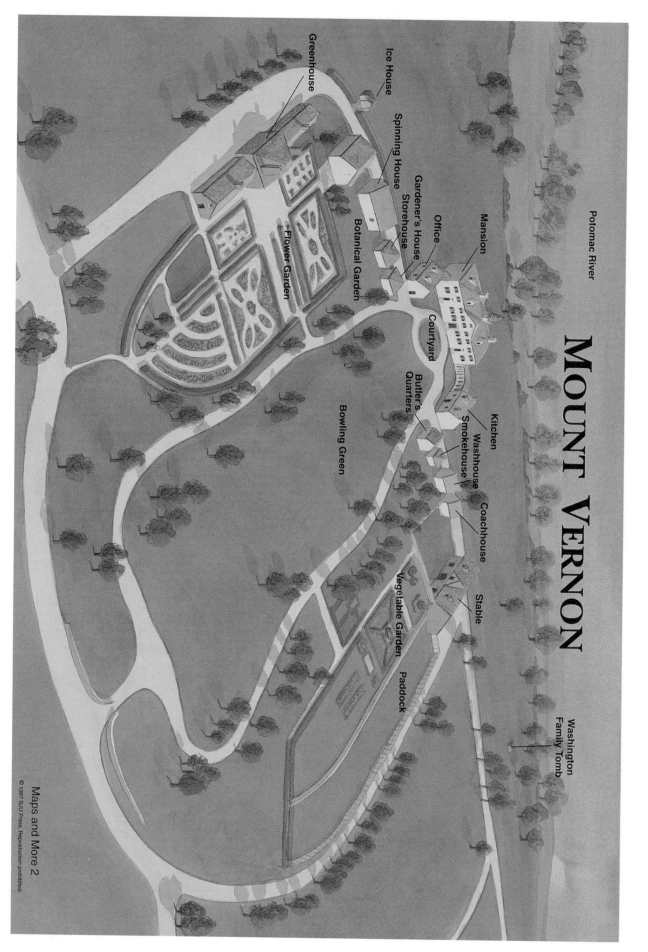

MOUNT VERNON

Potomac River

Mansion

Ice House

Greenhouse

Spinning House

Gardener's House
Storehouse

Office

Botanical Garden

Flower Garden

Courtyard

Butler's
Quarters

Kitchen

Washhouse
Smokehouse

Coachhouse

Stable

Bowling Green

Vegetable Garden

Paddock

Washington
Family Tomb

Maps and More 4

© 1997 BJU Press. Reproduction prohibited.

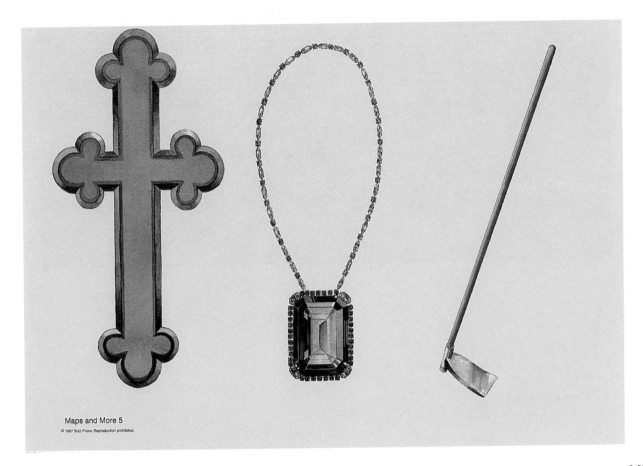

Maps and More 5

© 1997 BJU Press. Reproduction prohibited.

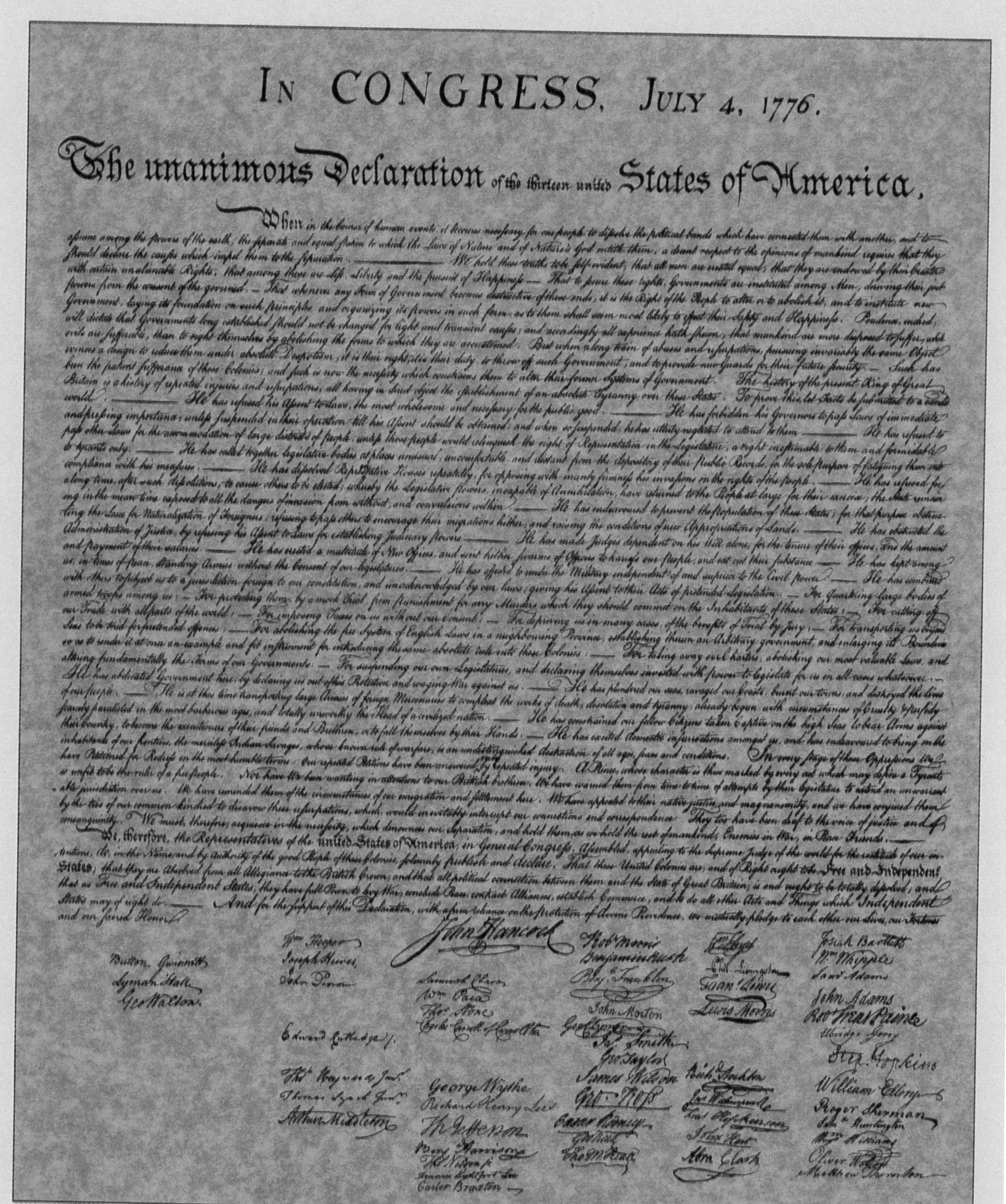

PROTECTION.

ᏣᎳᎩ ᏧᎴᎯᏌᏅᎯ.

CHEROKEE PHŒNIX.

VOL. I. **NEW ECHOTA, WEDNESDAY JUNE 4, 1828.** **NO. 15.**

EDITED BY ELIAS BOUDINOTT
PRINTED WEEKLY BY
ISAAC H. HARRIS,
FOR THE CHEROKEE NATION.

At $2 50 if paid in advance, $3 in six months, or $3 50 if paid at the end of the year.

To subscribers who can read only the Cherokee language the price will be $2,00 in advance, or $2,50 to be paid within the year.

Every subscription will be considered as continued unless subscribers give notice to the contrary before the commencement of a new year.

Any person procuring six subscribers, and becoming responsible for the payment, shall receive a seventh gratis.

Advertisements will be inserted at seventy-five cents per square for the first insertion, and thirty-seven and a half cents for each continuance; longer ones in proportion.

☞All letters addressed to the Editor, post paid, will receive due attention.

[illegible]

AGENTS FOR THE CHEROKEE PHŒNIX.

The following persons are authorized to receive subscriptions and payments for the Cherokee Phœnix.

Henry Hill, Esq. Treasurer of the A. B. C. F. M. Boston, Mass.
George M. Tracy, Agent of the A. B. C. F. M. New-York.
Rev. A. D. Eddy, Canandaigua, N. Y.
Thomas Hastings, Utica, N. Y.
Pollard & Converse, Richmond, Va.
Rev. James Campbell, Beaufort, S. C.
William Moultrie Reid, Charleston, S. C.
Col. George Smith, Statesville, W. T.
Rev. Bennet Roberts—Powal Me.
Mr. Thos. R. Gold, an itinerant Gentleman.

LAWS
OF THE CHEROKEE NATION.
[CONTINUED.]

New Town Nov. 14, 1825.

Resolved by the National Committee and Council, That a memorial be drawn up and presented, through the United States' Agent for this nation, to the Congress of the United States, claiming, & respectfully soliciting, the allowance of interest on the twenty years annual instalment of one thousand dollars per annum, arising from the treaty of Tillico, 24th October, 1804, which has recently been ratified on the part of the United States; and that the proper papers, showing, that this nation had heretofore demanded of the United States' government the fulfilment of the treaty, with interest, also to accompany the memorial.

Be it further resolved, That a communication be addressed to the United States' Agent, for this nation, touching the non-compliance, on the part of the Unicoy turnpike company, to make the annual payments, promised under the articles of agreement, granting the opening said road, and to request that measures may be taken to coerce the said Unicoy turnpike company to comply with the articles of agreement which have been ratified by the treaty of 1818.

By order of the N. Committee,
JNO. ROSS, Pres't. Nat. Com.
his
PATH ⋈ KILLER,
mark.
A. M'COY, Clerk N. Com.
E. BOUDINOTT, Clerk of N. Council.

Creek nation, at General William M'Intoshes, in council between the Creeks and Cherokees have this day made a Treaty about their boundary line; viz:

Article 1. A line we do hereby acknowledge, shall be run from the Buzzard Roost, on the Chattahoochee river, a direct line so as to strike the Coosa river, opposite the mouth of Will's creek, thence down the bank of said river opposite to Fort Strother, on said river; all north of said line is the Cherokee lands, all south of said line is the Creek lands.

Article 2. We the Commissioners, do further agree that all the Creeks that are north of the said line above mentioned shall become subjects to the Cherokee nation.

Article 3. All Cherokees that are south of the said line shall become subjects of the Creek nation.

Article 4. If any chief or chiefs of the Cherokees, should fall within the Creek nation, such chief shall be continued as chief of said nation.

Article 5. If any chief or chiefs of the Creeks, should fall within the Cherokees, that is, north of said line, they shall be continued as chiefs of said nation.

Article, 6. If any subject of the Cherokee nation, should commit murder and run into the Creek nation, the Cherokees will make application to the Creeks to have the murderer killed, and when done; the Cherokee nation will give the man who killed the murderer, $200.

Article 7. If any subject of the Creek nation, should commit murder and run to the Cherokees, the Creeks will make application to the Cherokees to have the murderer killed, and when done the Creek nation will give the man who killed the murderer $200.

Article 8. If any Cherokees should come over the line and commit murder or theft on the Creeks, the Creeks will make a demand of the Cherokees for satisfaction.

Article 9. If any Creeks should come over the line and commit murder or theft on the Cherokees, the Cherokees will make a demand of the Creeks for satisfaction.

Article 10. All claims of theft from the time of the meeting held at Hickory ground, Coosa river, near Fort Jackson, with the Four Nations, at the time Bools was taken, up to this date, it is agreed by the commissioners of both nations that they shall be foreclosed by this treaty.

Article 11. All individual debts, the creditors will look to their debtors.

Article 12. The Commissioners of both nations do agree the lines described in the foregoing treaty, shall be ratified, when the heads of both nations sign the treaty.

We, the Commissioners, do hereby set our hands and seals this eleventh day of December, 1822.

The above treaty of boundary run by Gen. Wm. M'Intosh and Samuel Hawkins, commissioners duly authorised by their nation, and Thomas Pettitt and John Beamer, authorised commissioners of the Cherokee nation, is forever hereafter acknowledged by both nations to be permanent.

CHEROKEE NAMES.

Chuliowah,	(Seal)
Old Turkey,	(Seal)
Ta,car.sut,tah,	(Seal)
Walking Stick,	(Seal)
Thos. Woodward,	(Seal)
Ta,car,sen,na,	(Seal)
Oo,ta,le,tah,	(Seal)
Will Interpreter,	(Seal)
The Boot,	(Seal)
Small Wood,	(Seal)

Approved.
his
PATH ⋈ KILLER,
mark.

CREEK NAMES.

Gen. Wm. M'Intosh,	(Seal)
Es,tun,e,tus,tun,e,gee,	(Seal)
Ts,us,he,hou,lock,	(Seal)
Cau,chau,tus,tun,e,gee,	(Seal)
Tuskinhou,	(Seal)
Tus,tin,e,gee,	(Seal)
Na,han,lockopy,	(Seal)
Chau,the.se,tus,tin,e,gee,	(Seal)
Is,po,go,mico,	(Seal)
Dick, Interpreter.	(Seal)
Ha.be,he,lus,tin,ne,gee,	(Seal)
Tus,ten,ne,cho,poy,	(Seal)
Ha,poy,e,hau,gee,	(Seal)
Tus.ke.he,now,	(Seal)
John Stodhouse,	(Seal)
William Hambly,	(Seal)
his Big ⋈ Warrior, mark.	(Seal)

Witnesses.
Major Ridge,
Dan'l. Griffin.
A. M'COY, Clerk N. Com.
JOS. VANN, Cl'k. to the Commissioners.

Be it remembered, This day, that I have approved of the treaty of boundary, concluded on by the Cherokees, east of the Mississippi, and the Creek nation of Indians, on the eleventh day of December, 1821, and with the modifications proposed by the committee and council, on the 28th day of March, in the current year. Given under my hand and seal at Fortville, this 16th day of May, 1822.

CHARLES R. HICKS, (Seal)
Witness,
LEONARD HICKS.

Whereas, The treaty concluded between the Cherokees and Creeks, by commissioners duly authorised by the chiefs of their respective nations, at General Wm. M'Intosh's on the eleventh day of December, (A. D.) one thousand eight hundred and twenty one, establishing the boundary line betwen the two nations, has this day been laid before the members of the national committee, by the head chiefs and members of council of the Cherokee nation, and Saml. Hawkins, Sah,naw,-wee, Ninne,ho,mot.tee and In.des.-le,af,kee, chiefs duly appointed and authorised by the head chiefs of the Creek nation, for a friendly exlpantion & full understanding of the constructions to be placed on the different articles contained in the aforesaid treaty, and to make such alterations as may be conceived necessary for the peace and harmony and friendship existing between the two nations; therefore, we the undersigned, in behalf of our respective nations, do hereby enter into the following agreement; viz:

The first Article of the aforesaid treaty, establishing the boundary between the two nations from Buzzard Roost, on the Chattahoochee river, in a direct line to Coosa river, opposite to the mouth of Wills creek, thence down said river opposite to Fort Strother, is hereby acknowledged and shall forever be permanent.

The 2d and 3d articles, making provision for the citizens of both nations, who may fall within the limits of the other, after running the line, to become subjects thereof shall not be construed so as to compel the individuals falling within the limits of the other to become subjects of that nation, but it shall be left entirely to their choice.

The 4th and 5th articles providing for the chiefs of both nations who may fall within the limits of the other, and choose to become subjects thereof, shall not be construed so as to compel either nation to keep such chief or chiefs in the authorities of their respective councils, but the two nations, shall exercise their own authorities in the selection and appointments of their own chiefs.

The 6th and 7th articles are hereby repealed and made void and the following agreement substituted; viz: In case a citizen of either nation, committing murder in their own nation, and escaping to the nation of the other party for refuge and the chiefs of the nation from whence the murderer or murderers so absconded, should, in their council, issue a p[roclamation] offering a reward for t[he] apprehension of such murderer [or] murderers, the chiefs of the contra[ct]ing nations agree to use every meas[ure] in their power to have the offende[r or] offenders apprehended and deliv[ered] over to the chiefs of the nation [from] whence such murder or murder[ers] have escaped.

The 8th and 9th articles, s[o far as it] relates to crossing the line a[nd com]mitting murder on the subjects of the other, is approved and adopted; but respecting thefts, it is hereby agreed that the following rule be substituted, and adopted; viz: Should the subjects of either nation go over the line and commit theft, and he, she or they be bpprehended, they shall be tried and dealt with as the laws of that nation direct, but should the person or persons so offending, make their escape and return to his, her or their nation, then, the person or persons so aggrieved, shall make application to the proper authorities of that nation for redress, and justice shall be rendered as far as practicable, agreeably to proof and law, but in no case shall either nation be accountable.

The 10th article is approved and adopted, and all claims for thefts considered closed by the treaty as stipulated in that article.

The 11th article is approved and adopted, and it is agreed further, the contracting nations will extend their respective laws with equal justice towards the citizens of the other in regard to collecting debts due by the individuals of their nation to those of the other.

The 12th article is fully approved and confirmed. We do hereby further agree to allow those individuals who have fell within the limits of the other, twelve months from the date hereof, to determine whether they will remove into their respective nations, or continue and become subjects of that nation; and it is also rgreed that in case the citizens of either nation, who may choose to remove into the nation of the other and become subjects, such person or persons shall be required to produce testimonials of their good character from the councils of their respective nations and present the same before the councils of the other nation; & should the chiefs thereof then think proper to receive and admit them, it may so be done.

In behalf of our respective nations, we do hereby adopt the above modifications and explanations of the of the several articles of the treaty establishing the boundary line between the two nations, and also, the additional agreement now made, shall hereafter be considered the basis on which our respective citizens shall be governed. In witness whereof we have hereunto set our hands and seals, this 30th day of October, 1823.

John Ross, President N. Com.
George Lowrey,
Richard Taylor,
Thomas Foreman,
Thomas Pettit,
Hair Conrad,
John Baldridge,
Sleeping Rabbit,
John Beamer,
John Downing,
Kelechulah,
Cabbin Smith,
Chu,wal,loo,kee,

Approved,
his
PATH ⋈ KILLER,
mark.
Going Snake,
Chickasawtechee,
MAJ'R. RIDGE, Speaker.

Creek Commissioners,
Sam'l. Hawkins,
In,de,le,af,kee,
Sah,now,wee,
Nin,ne,ho,mot,tee,

ELIJAH HICKS, Clerk N. Coun.
A. M'Coy, Clk. N. Com.

[illegible]

[illegible], 14 [illegible], 1825.

[illegible] 24 [illegible] 1804 [illegible]

[illegible] 1819.

[illegible]

[illegible], 14 [illegible], 1825.

[illegible]

[illegible], 14 [illegible], 1825.

[illegible]

[illegible], 14 [illegible], 1825.

[illegible]

Maps and More 8

NORTHEAST REGION

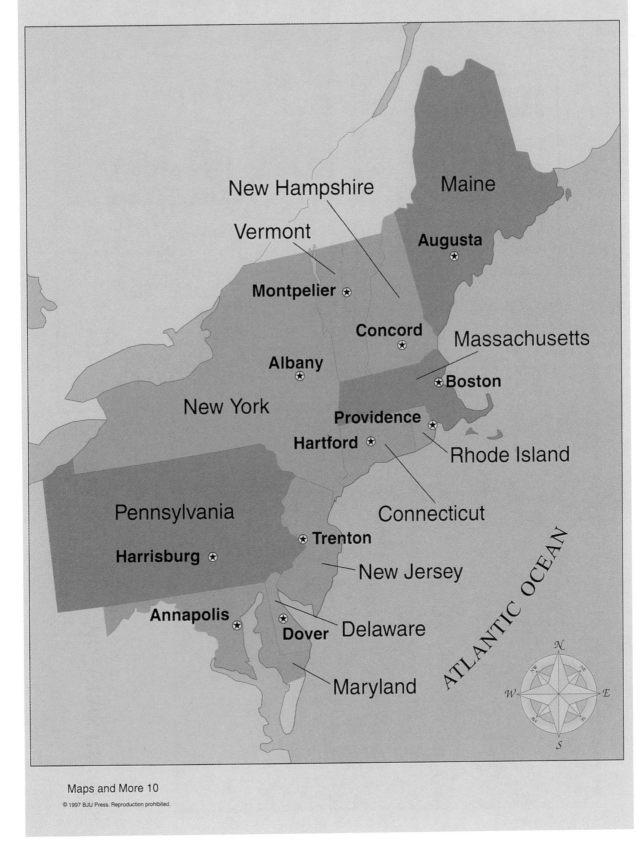

New Hampshire

Maine

Vermont

Augusta ✪

Montpelier ✪

Concord ✪

Massachusetts

Albany ✪

Boston ✪

New York

Providence ✪

Hartford ✪

Rhode Island

Connecticut

Pennsylvania

Trenton ✪

Harrisburg ✪

New Jersey

Annapolis ✪

Dover ✪ Delaware

Maryland

ATLANTIC OCEAN

Maps and More 10

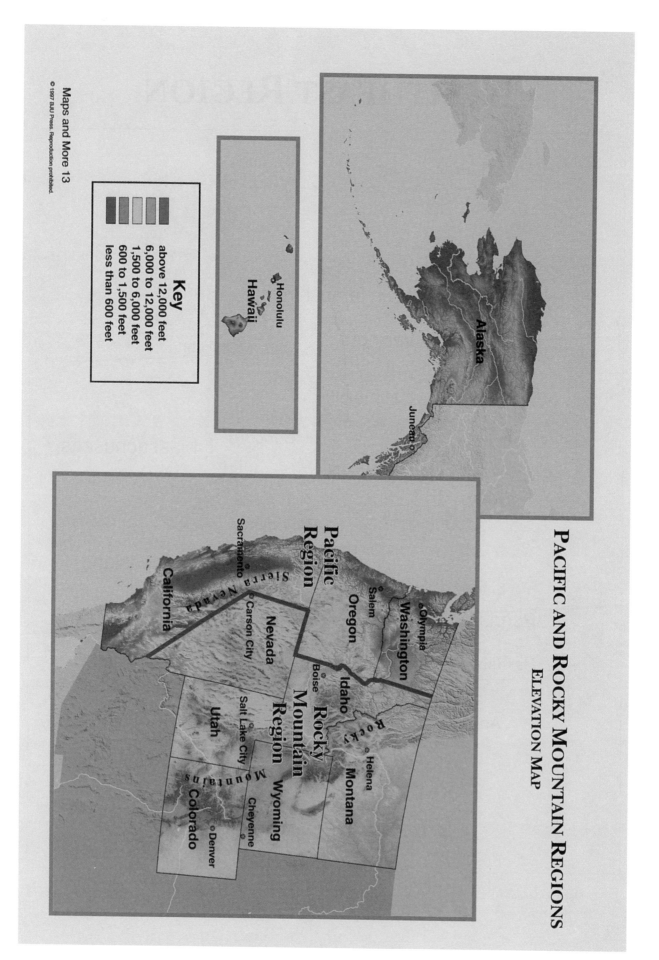

PACIFIC AND ROCKY MOUNTAIN REGIONS
ELEVATION MAP

Key

above 12,000 feet
6,000 to 12,000 feet
1,500 to 6,000 feet
600 to 1,500 feet
less than 600 feet

Alaska

Juneau

Honolulu
Hawaii

Pacific
Region

Sacramento

California

Sierra Nevada

Carson City

Nevada

Salem

Olympia

Washington

Oregon

Boise

Idaho

Rocky

Helena

Montana

Salt Lake City

Utah

Mountains

Colorado

Denver

Rocky
Mountain
Region

Wyoming

Cheyenne

Maps and More 13
© 1997 BJU Press. Reproduction prohibited.

THE ALAMO

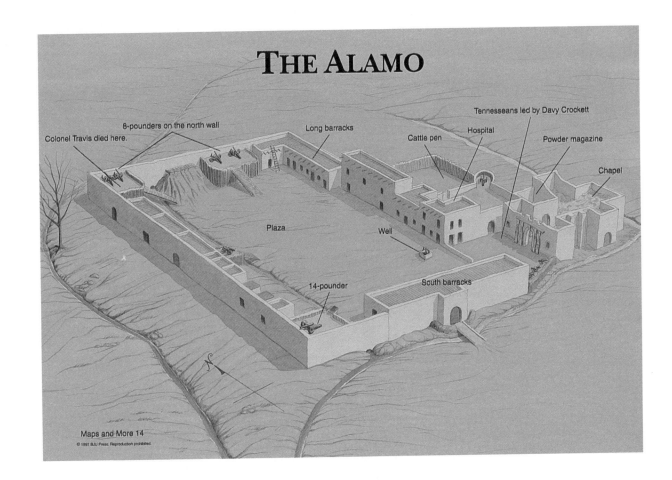

8-pounders on the north wall

Colonel Travis died here.

Long barracks

Cattle pen

Hospital

Tennesseans led by Davy Crockett

Powder magazine

Chapel

Plaza

Well

14-pounder

South barracks

Maps and More 14
© 1997 BJU Press. Reproduction prohibited.

Harriet Beecher Stowe

Library of Congress

John Brown

Boston Athenæum

Maps and More 15
© 1997 BJU Press. Reproduction prohibited.

A CATTLE DRIVE

Point

Swing

Flank

Chuck Wagon

Drag

Remuda

Trail Boss

Drag

Wrangler

Drag

Point

Swing

Flank

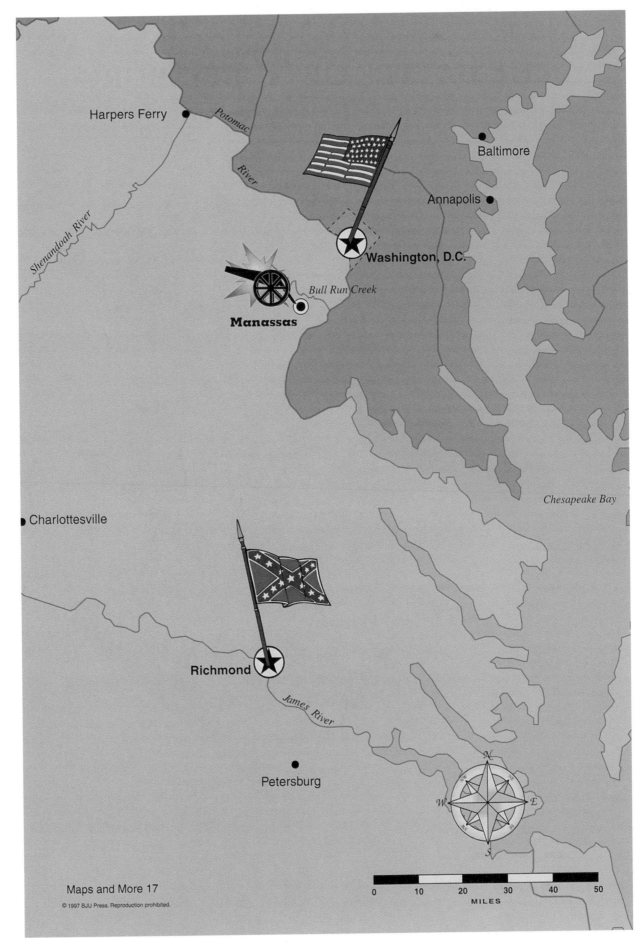

Harpers Ferry

Potomac River

Baltimore

Annapolis

Shenandoah River

Washington, D.C.

Bull Run Creek

Manassas

Chesapeake Bay

Charlottesville

Richmond

James River

Petersburg

N

W E

S

0 10 20 30 40 50
MILES

THE BATTLE OF GETTYSBURG

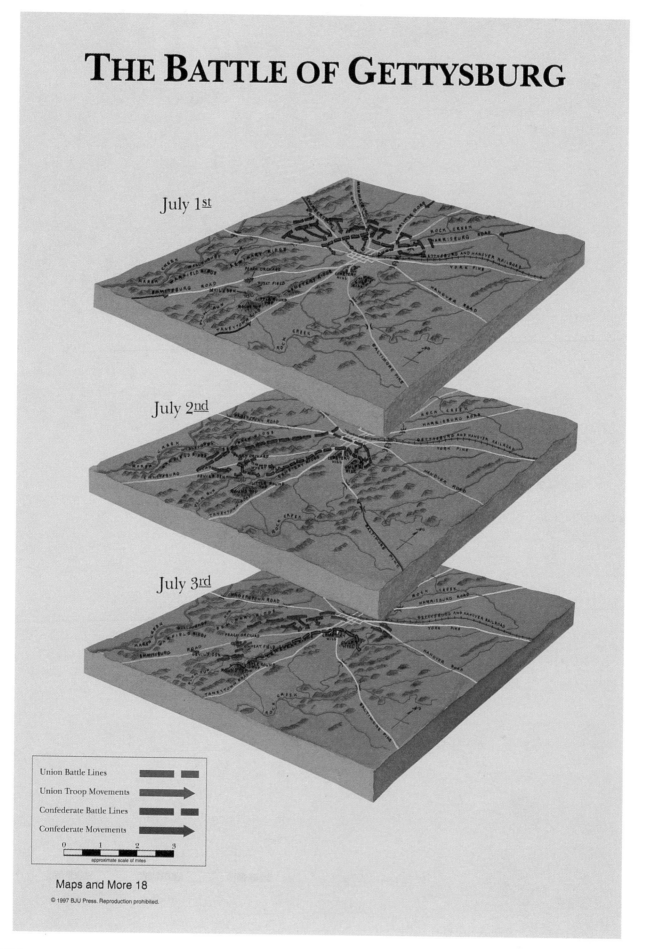

July 1st

July 2nd

July 3rd

Union Battle Lines

Union Troop Movements

Confederate Battle Lines

Confederate Movements

0   1   2   3
approximate scale of miles

Maps and More 18

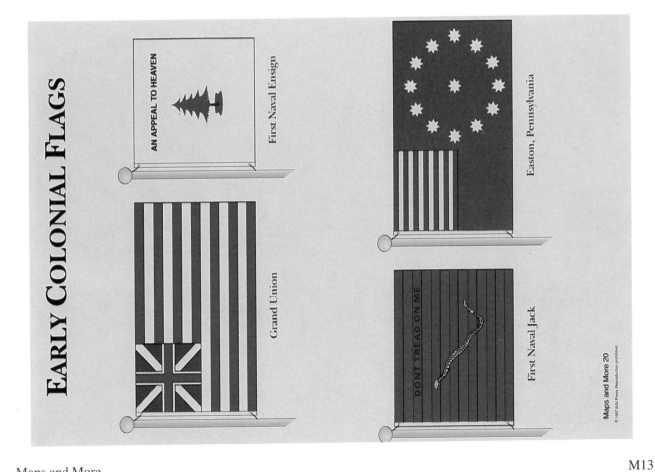

Maps and More 22a

Maps and More 22b

Maps and More 23a

© 1997 BJU Press. Reproduction prohibited.

Maps and More 23b

© 1997 BJU Press. Reproduction prohibited.

Maps and More 24a

© 1997 BJU Press. Reproduction prohibited.

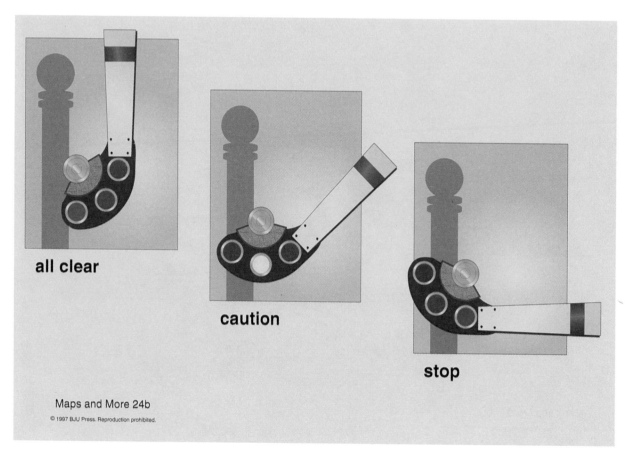

all clear

caution

stop

Maps and More 24b

© 1997 BJU Press. Reproduction prohibited.

Supplement

The Star-Spangled Banner

Francis Scott Key

John Smith

O__ say, can you see, by the dawn's ear - ly

light, What so proud - ly we hailed at the twi - light's last

gleam - ing? Whose broad stripes and bright stars, thro' the per - il - ous

fight, O'er the ram - parts we watched were so gal - lant - ly

stream - ing? And the rock - ets' red glare, the bombs burst - ing in

air, Gave proof thro' the night that our flag was still there. O

say, does that__ Star - Span - gled Ban - ner__ yet__ wave__ O'er the

land__ of the free and the home of the brave?

Home on the Range

American Tune

Oh, give me a home where the buf - fa - lo roam, Where the

deer and the an - te - lope play._____ Where sel - dom is

heard a dis - cour - ag - ing word, And the skies are not cloud - y all

day._____ Home, home on the range,_____ Where the

deer and the an - te - lope play._____ Where sel - dom is heard a dis -

cour - ag - ing word, And the skies are not cloud - y all day._____

©1989 BJU Press. "Home on the Range" arrangement.

THE STAR-SPANGLED BANNER

Oh! say, can you see, by the dawn's early light,
What so proudly we hailed at the twilight's last gleaming?
Whose broad stripes and bright stars, thro' the perilous fight,
O'er the ramparts we watched were so gallantly streaming?
And the rockets' red glare, the bombs bursting in air,
Gave proof thro' the night that our flag was still there.
Oh! say, does that star-spangled banner yet wave
O'er the land of the free and the home of the brave?

On the shore, dimly seen thro' the mists of the deep,
Where the foe's haughty host in dread silence reposes,
What is that which the breeze, o'er the towering steep,
As it fitfully blows, half conceals, half discloses?
Now it catches the gleam of the morning's first beam,
In full glory reflected, now shines on the stream.
'Tis the star-spangled banner. Oh! long may it wave
O'er the land of the free and the home of the brave!

And where is that band who so vauntingly swore
That the havoc of war and the battle's confusion
A home and a country should leave us no more?
Their blood has washed out their foul footsteps' pollution.
No refuge could save the hireling and slave
From the terror of flight or the gloom of the grave,
And the star-spangled banner in triumph doth wave
O'er the land of the free and the home of the brave.

Oh! thus be it ever when freemen shall stand
Between their loved home and the war's desolation,
Blest with vict'ry and peace, may the Heav'n-rescued land
Praise the Pow'r that hath made and preserved us a nation.
Then conquer we must, when our cause it is just,
And this be our motto, "In God is our trust."
And the star-spangled banner in triumph shall wave
O'er the land of the free and the home of the brave.

Use with Lesson 20.

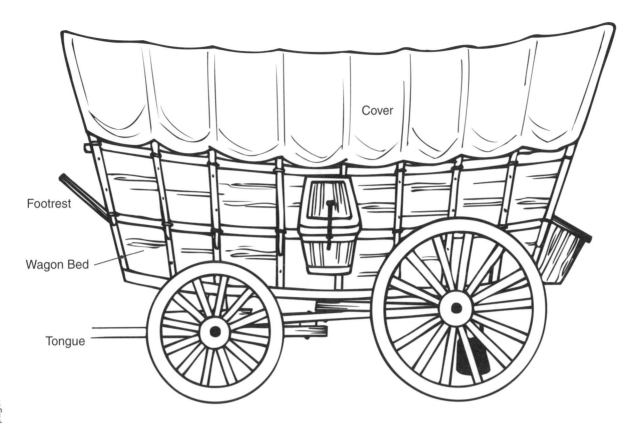

Cover

Footrest

Wagon Bed

Tongue

Conestoga Wagon

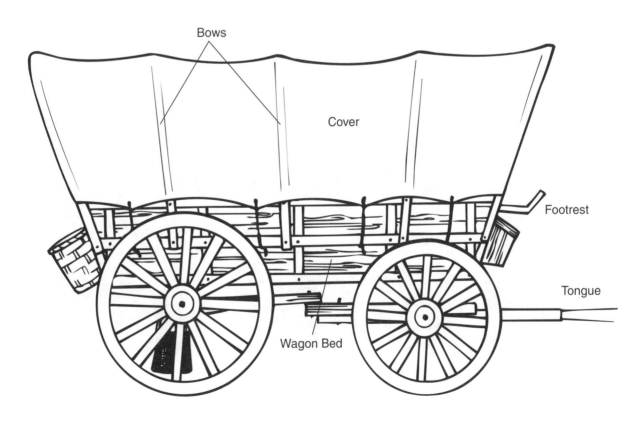

Bows

Cover

Footrest

Tongue

Wagon Bed

Covered Wagon

Brethren, We Have Met to Worship

George Atkins   William Moore

Breth-ren,__ we have   met to__ wor - ship__   And a - dore the   Lord our God;
Let us__love our   God su - preme - ly,__   Let us__love each   oth - er too;

Will you__ pray with   all your__ pow - er,__   While we__ try   to   preach the Word?
Let us__ love and   pray for__ sin - ners,__   Till our__ God makes   all things new.

All   is vain un - less the__ Spir - it   Of the Ho - ly   One comes__down;
Then He'll call us   home to__ heav-en,   At His ta - ble   we'll sit__down;

Breth-ren,__pray, and   ho - ly__ man - na__   Will be__ show-ered   all a-round.
Christ will__ gird Him - self, and__ serve__ us__   With sweet__ man - na   all a-round.

Story Starters

For paragraph 1:

Lizzie Famdanoodle has the biggest feet in all of Messer County.

Whenever Spittin' Spud touched a basketball, unbelievable things started to happen!

Old Ike can do most anything just by snappin' his fingers.

For paragraph 2:

She tromped all over the country making swimming pools for anybody who wanted them.

The crowd was always amazed at how high the ball would rocket and how accurate its mark would be.

There was always a long line of folks followin' Old Ike, askin' and askin' for things.

Introduced in Lesson 31

Supplement   Use with Lesson 44.   S9

Use with Lesson 45. Heritage Studies 3 Home TE

Pick a Bale of Cotton

Texas

Well, me___ and my part-ner Can pick a bale of cot-ton, Well,

me___ and my part-ner Can pick a bale a day. Oh,

pick a bale a - pick a bale A - pick a bale of cot-ton, Oh,

pick a bale a - pick a bale A - pick a bale a day.

Definitions for Gettysburg Address

Dedicate   to set apart for a special use or purpose

Consecrate   to set apart for a special or sacred purpose

Conceived   formed or developed

Use with Lesson 51.

Cowboy Word List

branded

lariat

chuck wagon

herd

roundup

stampede

Use with Lesson 65.

February Birthdays

Charles Dickens	novelist
Thomas Edison	inventor
Galileo Galilei	scientist
George Frederick Handel	composer
Charles Lindbergh	pilot
Henry Wadsworth Longfellow	poet
Pierre Auguste Renoir	artist
Babe Ruth	baseball player
Laura Ingalls Wilder	pioneer, author

Get on Board

Spiritual

Get on board, lit-tle chil-dren, Get on board, lit-tle chil-dren, Get on

board, lit-tle chil-dren. There's room for man-y a more. The

gos-pel train's a - com-ing; I hear it just at hand, I

hear the car wheels rum-bling And roll-ing through the land. Get on

board, lit-tle chil-dren, Get on board, lit-tle chil-dren, Get on

board, lit-tle chil-dren. There's room for man-y a more.

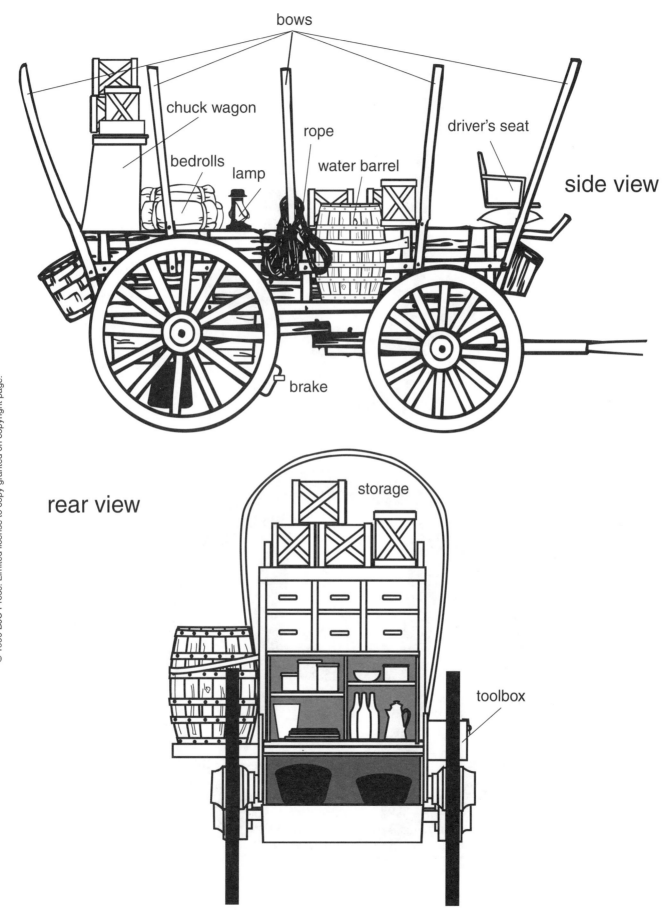

bows

chuck wagon

bedrolls

lamp

rope

water barrel

driver's seat

side view

brake

rear view

storage

toolbox

Rocking Chair

Circle H

Use with Lesson 65. Heritage Studies 3 Home TE

Cavalry Songs

Stable Call

Come all who are able and go to the stable,
To water your horses and give 'em some corn,
For if you don't do it, the Cap'n will know it,
And then you will rue it, as sure as you're born.
So come to the stable, all ye who are able and
Water your horses and give 'em some corn.

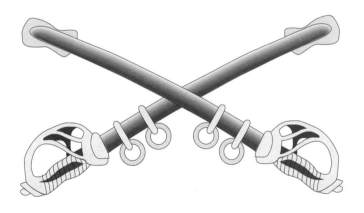

Mess Call

Soupy, soupy, soupy, without a single bean,
Coffee, coffee, coffee, without a bit of cream,
Porky, porky, porky, without a streak of lean.

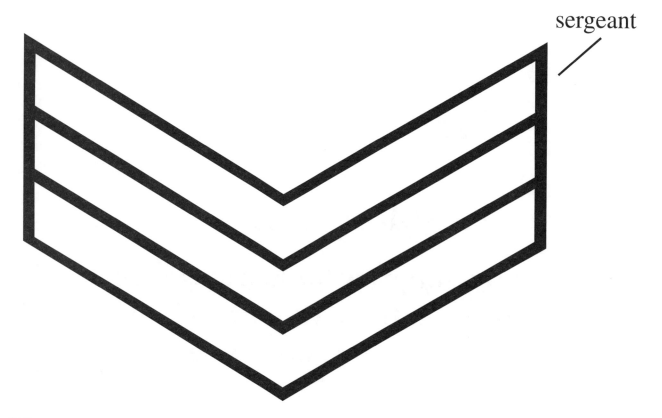

captain

sergeant

Use with Lesson 66.

Heritage Studies 3 Home TE

Materials List

Chapter 1

Lesson 1
- A box*
- Red, white, and blue paper or fabric (optional)*
- A length of red or blue ribbon (optional)*
- A few silver coins
- Appendix, page A2: We the People time line*
- Maps and More 1 and 2, pages M1-M2
- A *HERITAGE STUDIES 3 Student Textbook*
- A *HERITAGE STUDIES 3 Student Notebook*
- Pictures of Mount Vernon (optional)*

Lesson 2
- A copy of some of your rules*
- The mystery box used in Lesson 1
- Maps and More 1, page M1
- We the People time line from Lesson 1

Lesson 3
- A cassette player*
- *HERITAGE STUDIES Listening Cassette A*
- Maps and More 1, page M1
- We the People time line from Lesson 2
- The mystery box used in Lesson 2
- A fly swatter

Lesson 4
- A Bible
- 2 envelopes, one marked with a *1* and the other with a *2*
- We the People time line from Lesson 3
- Maps and More 1, page M1
- The mystery box used in Lesson 3
- Appendix, pages A3-A4: cards with state maps*

Lesson 5
- We the People time line from Lesson 4
- A Bible
- The mystery box used in Lesson 4
- The TimeLine Snapshots*
- The figure of the signing of the Constitution (1787) from the TimeLine Snapshots*
- Appendix, page A5: the viewer*
- Appendix, page A6: Property Tag*

Lesson 6
- A local newspaper in the mystery box used in Lesson 5
- The presidential strip which includes the figure of George Washington (1) from the TimeLine Snapshots
- Art paper
- We the People time line from Lesson 5
- The figure of the Bill of Rights (1791) from the TimeLine Snapshots

Chapter 2

Lesson 7
- Play money*
- A paper crown*
- A loaf of French bread*
- A Bible
- A globe
- Maps and More 4 and 5, page M3
- Appendix, page A7: map of France*
- Appendix, page A8: peasant*

Lesson 8
- A medium-sized cardboard box*
- 8 Pringles cans*
- Enough brown paper to cover the box and each can*
- Masking tape
- Maps and More 4, page M3

Lesson 9
- A dictionary (optional)
- Maps and More 6, page M4
- A wall map of the United States (optional)*
- The figure of the Declaration of Independence (1776) from the TimeLine Snapshots

Lesson 10
- A red hat or scarf*
- Two red ribbons approximately 18" long*
- A set of encyclopedias or an atlas*
- *HERITAGE STUDIES Listening Cassette A*
- Map of France from Lesson 7

Lesson 11
- The crown from Lesson 7
- The presidential strip with the figure of John Adams (2) from the TimeLine Snapshots
- A wall map of Europe or an atlas*

Chapter 3

Lesson 12
- An atlas with a physical map of North America*
- A globe*

Lesson 13
- *HERITAGE STUDIES Listening Cassette A*
- Pictures of animals and plants characteristic of eastern woodlands and the prairie *
- Supplement, page S3: Home on the Range
- Appendix, page A9: Areas of the United States map*
- An atlas*
- Appendix, page A10: Indian Nations of Long Ago
- Yarn or string (optional)*

Lesson 14
- An almanac (optional)*
- An atlas
- Pictures of animals and plants characteristic of North American deserts and mountains, particularly a saguaro cactus*
- Map display from Lesson 13

Lesson 15
- Pictures of ocean shorelines and plants and animals that live on the West Coast*
- Map display from Lesson 14
- A globe*
- Books about transportation (optional)*
- A sheet of drawing paper

Lesson 16
- The figure of Lewis and Clark (1804) from the TimeLine Snapshots
- The presidential figure of Thomas Jefferson (3) from the TimeLine Snapshots

Lesson 17
- 2 sheets of white or tan construction paper

Chapter 4
Lesson 18
- Appendix, page A12: The American Frontier map*
- Appendix, page A13: ovals*

Lesson 19
- A set of toy building logs or alternative materials listed in the Notes section*
- The American Frontier map and ovals from Lesson 18
- Maps and More 7, page M5
- An ear of corn still in the husk (optional)*

Lesson 20
- The figure of Francis Scott Key (1812) from the TimeLine Snapshots
- The presidential strip with the figure of James Madison (4) from the TimeLine Snapshots
- Play props such as flashlights, drums, rope, and toy rifles (optional)*
- *HERITAGE STUDIES Listening Cassette A*
- Supplement, page S4: words of "The Star-Spangled Banner"

Lesson 21
- The presidential strip with figures of James Monroe (5) and John Quincy Adams (6) from the TimeLine Snapshots
- Appendix, page A15: a copy of Notebook page 28*
- Appendix, page A16: a copy of Notebook page 29*
- Appendix, page A17: a copy of Notebook page 30*
- A Bible
- A sheet of paper with a simple star drawn on it and hung on a wall of the schoolroom

Supplemental Lesson
- A shoebox*
- Two $8\frac{1}{2}$" × 11" pieces of cardboard or poster board for the wagon wheels and tongue*
- 2 unsharpened pencils, at least $\frac{1}{4}$" longer than the shoebox is wide*
- Brown water-based paint*
- A sheet of white poster board, approximately 12" × 20" for the cover of the wagon*
- Gray water-based paint*
- Glue
- Enough newspapers to cover the painting area
- A small paintbrush*
- 4 pushpins*
- An old shirt to wear while painting
- Some paper towels, clean rags, or sponges
- The American Frontier map and ovals from Lesson 19
- Supplement, page S5: the covered wagon and the Conestoga wagon
- Appendix, page A18: the patterns for the wagon tongue and front wheels*
- Appendix, page A19: the patterns for the back wheels*

Lesson 22
- Maps and More 8, page M6
- The presidential strip with the figures of Andrew Jackson (7) and Martin Van Buren (8) from the TimeLine Snapshots
- Appendix, page A13: Trail of Tears*
- A Bible

Lesson 23
- *HERITAGE STUDIES Listening Cassette A*
- The American Frontier map and ovals from the Supplemental Lesson
- Supplement, page S6: "Brethren, We Have Met to Worship"
- Appendix, page A13: the picture of the Whitmans*

Lesson 24
- The figure of the prospector (1849) from the TimeLine Snapshots
- A globe
- Several small pebbles painted gold*
- A bucket of dirt
- A small foil plate*
- A large dishpan or tub*
- A large pitcher of water*
- The American Frontier map and ovals from Lesson 23
- Appendix, page A20: the Comparing Prices chart*

Chapter 5

Lesson 25
- Appendix, pages A21-A22: story papers (*NOTE:* Trim along the black-line border.)*
- *Egermeier's Bible Story Book* (optional)*

Lesson 26
- 4 moccasins, slippers, or shoes*
- A small, round stone
- A Bible

Lesson 27
- A Bible
- An apple, washed and cored*
- A 12-inch length of string*
- An atlas

Supplemental Lesson
- The date your state celebrates Arbor Day
- A large, round apple for each team*
- A box of round wooden toothpicks*
- Strips of masking tape
- Appendix, pages A23-A31: Seeds of Hope*
- Appendix, pages A32: labeled apples*
- Appendix, pages A33: apple tree outline*

Lesson 28
- Appendix, page A34: Evaluation Game*
- 8 pieces of construction paper
- Several different versions of the stories "Goldilocks and the Three Bears" or "Little Red Riding Hood" (optional)*

Lesson 29
- Maps and More 9, page M5
- Supplement, S7: Story Starters
- A sheet of $8\frac{1}{2}$"×11" notebook paper

Chapter 6

Lesson 30
- A road map or other large map of your state*
- *About Our States*, published by BJU Press (optional)*
- Maps and More 10, page M7
- A baby name book*
- Appendix, page A35: labeled map of the United States*
- Appendix, page A36: Travel Journal Passbook*
- A passbook folder*

Lesson 31
- An atlas
- Supplement, page S8: cotton boll
- A real cotton boll (optional)*

Lesson 32
- Post cards or brochures from the states of the Middle West region of the United States*
- Poster or picture with a border
- Labeled map of the United States from Lesson 30
- 12 small buttons or beans

Lesson 33
- A variety of items or pictures from the Southwest region of the United States, including five Hispanic-related items* (*NOTE:* See suggestions in the Introducing the Lesson section.)
- Labeled map of the United States from Lesson 32
- A recording of Spanish music*
- Spanish foods to sample (optional)*
- Spanish attire for yourself (optional)*
- An atlas

Lesson 34
- Maps and More 13, page M8
- Items or pictures from the Rocky Mountain and Pacific regions*
- A brochure from a local museum*

Chapter 7

Lesson 35
- A Bible
- Supplement, page S8: cotton boll
- A pint-sized basket (perhaps an empty strawberry carton)*
- Enough cotton balls to fill the basket*

Lesson 36
- Appendix, page A37: opinion cards*

Lesson 37
- Appendix, page A38: map of the United States in 1820*
- Red and blue pencils or crayons
- The figure of the Alamo (1836) from the TimeLine Snapshots
- The presidential figures of William Henry Harrison (9) and John Tyler (10) from the TimeLine Snapshots
- Maps and More 14, page M9

Lesson 38
- A Bible
- The presidential figures of James Knox Polk (11) and Zachary Taylor (12) from the TimeLine Snapshots

Lesson 39
- Maps and More 15, page M9
- The presidential figures of Millard Fillmore (13), Franklin Pierce (14), and James Buchanan (15) from the TimeLine Snapshots

Lesson 40
- Five $8\frac{1}{2}$"×11" sheets of black construction paper*

Lesson 41
- A jump rope or some other sturdy rope, at least ten feet in length*
- A 12-inch strip of masking tape
- The presidential figure of Abraham Lincoln (16) from the TimeLine Snapshots
- Books, magazines, or newspapers that contain circle graphs*
- A sheet of paper

Chapter 8

Lesson 42
- *HERITAGE STUDIES Listening Cassette A*
- Recordings of the following Stephen Foster songs: "My Old Dog Tray," "My Old Kentucky Home," "Old Folks at Home," and "I Dream of Jeanie with the Light Brown Hair" (optional)*

Lesson 43
- Two 6-inch lengths of chenille wire*
- 30 to 40 small metal tabs from soft-drink cans, metal washers, or large safety pins*
- *HERITAGE STUDIES Listening Cassette A*
- Several decorative beads (optional)*
- Maps and More 16, page M10

Lesson 44
- An empty, clean soft-drink bottle or ketchup bottle*
- 2 pencils or rulers
- 2 small blocks of wood*
- 2 pieces of sandpaper*
- 4 rubber bands*
- A small box*
- A Bible
- Supplement, page S9: David playing his harp for King Saul

Lesson 45
- *HERITAGE STUDIES Listening Cassette A*
- A Bible
- *Egermeier's Bible Story Book* (optional)*
- Supplement, page S8: a cotton boll
- Supplement, page S10: a bale of cotton
- Supplement, page S11: "Pick a Bale of Cotton"

Lesson 46
- *HERITAGE STUDIES Listening Cassette A*
- Drum supplies
  - An empty coffee can or an oatmeal canister*
  - A piece of vinyl or cloth large enough to cover the opening for the coffee can*
  - A large rubber band or 12" length of string*
  - Construction paper (optional)
- Bugle supplies
  - Transparent packaging tape*
  - A mouthpiece from a musical instrument (optional)*
  - A 12"×12" piece of poster board*
  - A stapler
- A "B" volume of an encyclopedia*
- A "C" volume of an encyclopedia, containing the entry for "Civil War"*

Chapter 9

Lesson 47
- Appendix, page A41: the maps with the capitals*
- Appendix, pages A42-A43: Union and Confederate flags*
- Appendix, page A44: Lincoln/Davis nameplates*
- Yarn, string, or ribbon
- Appendix, page A45: Union/Confederacy nameplates*
- Appendix, page A46: North/Yankees nameplates*
- Appendix, page A47: South/Rebels nameplates*
- Appendix, page A48: A Nation Divided nameplate*
- Appendix, page A49: Fort Sumter*

Lesson 48
- Maps and More 17, page M11
- Appendix, page A50: McDowell/Jackson nameplates*

Lesson 49
- A variety of dried fruit*
- Appendix, page A51: McClellan/Lee nameplates*

Lesson 50
- A magazine with photographs*

Lesson 51
- Supplement, page S12: Definitions for Gettysburg Address
- *HERITAGE STUDIES Listening Cassette A*
- Maps and More 18, page M12
- The figure representing the Gettysburg Address (1863) from the TimeLine Snapshots
- A square of blue or gray construction paper or cloth*
- A straight pin
- An addressed envelope*
- A dictionary (optional)

Lesson 52
- A man's white handkerchief
- 36 beans or buttons*
- The figure representing the Thirteenth Amendment (1865) from the TimeLine Snapshots
- The presidential figure of Andrew Johnson (17) from the TimeLine Snapshots
- Appendix, page A52: Grant nameplate*
- Appendix, page A52: A Nation Reunited nameplate*

Chapter 10

Lesson 53
- A calendar showing the month of February
- A red pen
- Supplement, page S13: February Birthdays

Lesson 54
- A hard-boiled egg for each participant*
- Felt-tip pens or watercolor paints*

Lesson 55
- Maps and More 20 and 21, page M13
- A large towel
- The figure of the Stamp Act (1765) from the Time-Line Snapshots

Lesson 56
- Construction paper
- Crepe paper*
- Paint*
- Paintbrushes*
- Old clothes for costumes*
- Wood blocks*
- Cardboard boxes*
- Tin cans*
- Wagons*

Lesson 57
No additional materials are necessary.

Chapter 11
Lesson 58
- Items associated with a train*

Supplemental Lesson
- Appendix, page A53: choral reading*

Lesson 59
- Maps and More 22, 23, and 24, pages M14-M16
- The figure of Peter Cooper (1830) from the TimeLine Snapshots
- A dictionary
- Some model trains and tracks of different sizes and types (optional)*
- A picture of Old Ironsides (optional)*
- Appendix, page A54: Tom Thumb story*

Lesson 60
- A lump of coal (optional)*
- A saucepan with a lid or a whistling teakettle

Lesson 61
- A ruler
- A map of your state*
- An atlas (optional)

Lesson 62
- *HERITAGE STUDIES Listening Cassette A*
- The figure of the first transcontinental railroad (1869) from the TimeLine Snapshots
- The presidential strip with Ulysses Simpson Grant (18) from the TimeLine Snapshots
- A railroad spike (optional)*
- A dictionary
- Supplement, page S14: "Get on Board"
- A sheet of paper (optional)

Lesson 63
- A flashlight
- A globe
- Plasti-Tak
- Maps and More 24, page M16
- 6 analog clocks or watches*

Chapter 12
Lesson 64
- A picture of a locust (optional)*
- Supplement, page S15: covered wagon

Lesson 65
- *HERITAGE STUDIES Listening Cassette A*
- Maps and More 25, page M10
- Supplement, page S12: Cowboy Word List
- Supplement, page S16: the altered brand
- Appendix, page A61: Saddle Parts*

Lesson 66
- *HERITAGE STUDIES Listening Cassette A*
- Supplement, page S17: Cavalry Songs
- Supplement, page S18: the insignia
- Appendix, page A62: outpost (optional)*

Lesson 67
- A safety pin
- Appendix, page A63: the Coffeyville map*

Lesson 68
- The figure of the Battle of Little Bighorn (1876) from the TimeLine Snapshots
- A ruler

Supplemental Lesson
- An atlas
- Red and green crayons
- Appendix, page A64: The West Before time line*
- Appendix, page A65: the Anasazi page*

Appendix

All the pages that need to be copied for use in the lessons can be found in the Appendix. At the bottom of each page, you will find the corresponding lesson number. Some pages include the word *Enrichment* beside the lesson number. You do not need to copy these pages if you will not be doing the Enrichment section of the lesson. If more than one copy of a page is necessary, it will be indicated at the top of the page. Some pages have gray shaded areas. If these areas do not copy, you may shade them an appropriate color. When teaching more than one child, you will need to refer to the individual lesson to determine whether the page needs to be copied additional times.

July 4, 1776

September 17, 1787

July 16, 1787

January 25, 1787

April 30, 1789

May 25, 1787

July 2, 1787

We the People . . .

Bill of Rights
December 15, 1791

Introduced in Lesson 1.

Cut apart; then put these cards together in Envelope 1.

South Carolina

Georgia

Virginia

Pennsylvania

Use with Lesson 4.

Cut apart; then put these cards together in Envelope 2.

North Carolina

Maryland

Delaware

New Jersey

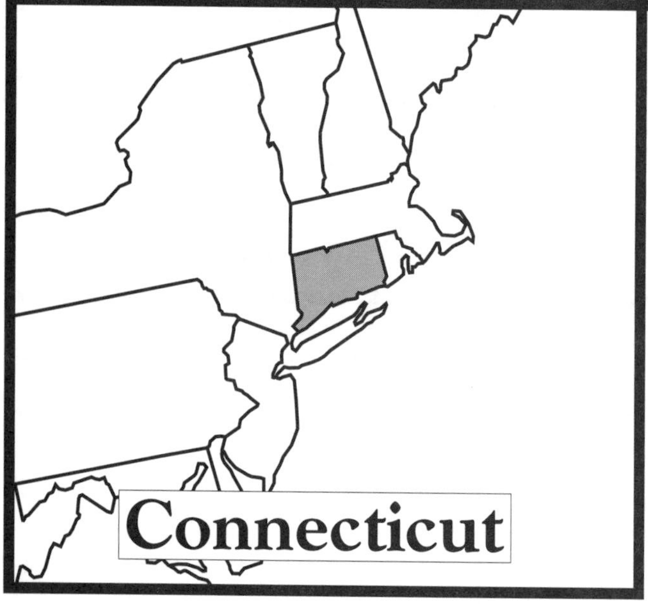

Connecticut

Use with Lesson 4. Heritage Studies 3 Home TE

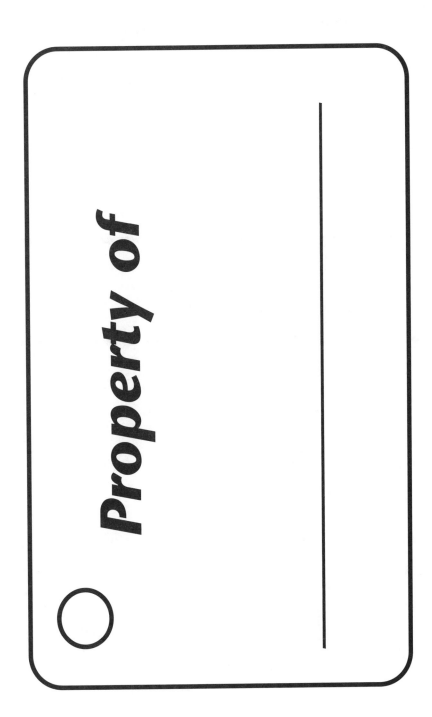

Property of

Use with Lesson 5.

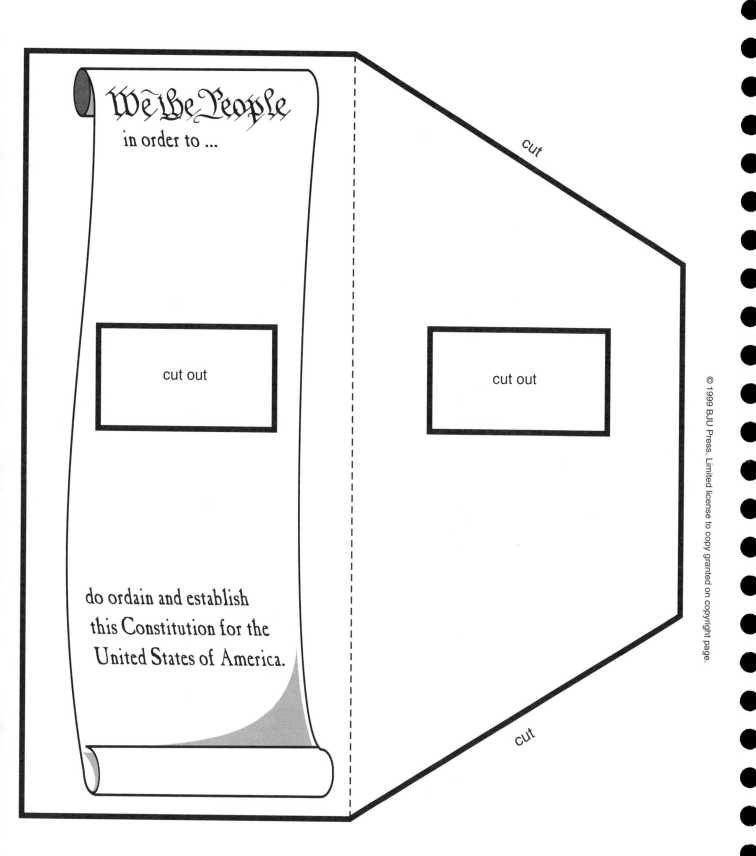

We the People
in order to ...

cut out

cut out

cut

cut

do ordain and establish
this Constitution for the
United States of America.

Use with Lesson 5.

Heritage Studies 3 Home TE

Vive la France!

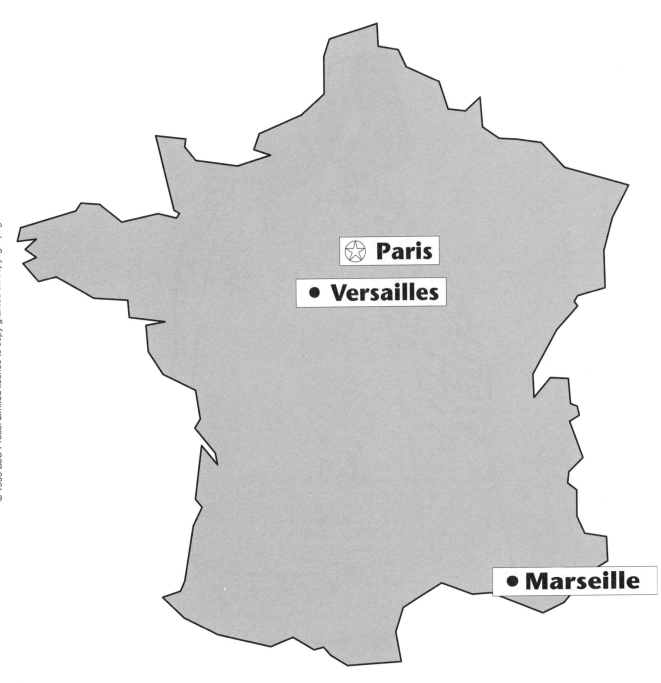

⊛ Paris

● Versailles

● Marseille

Use with Lesson 7.

Heritage Studies 3 Home TE

Areas of the United States

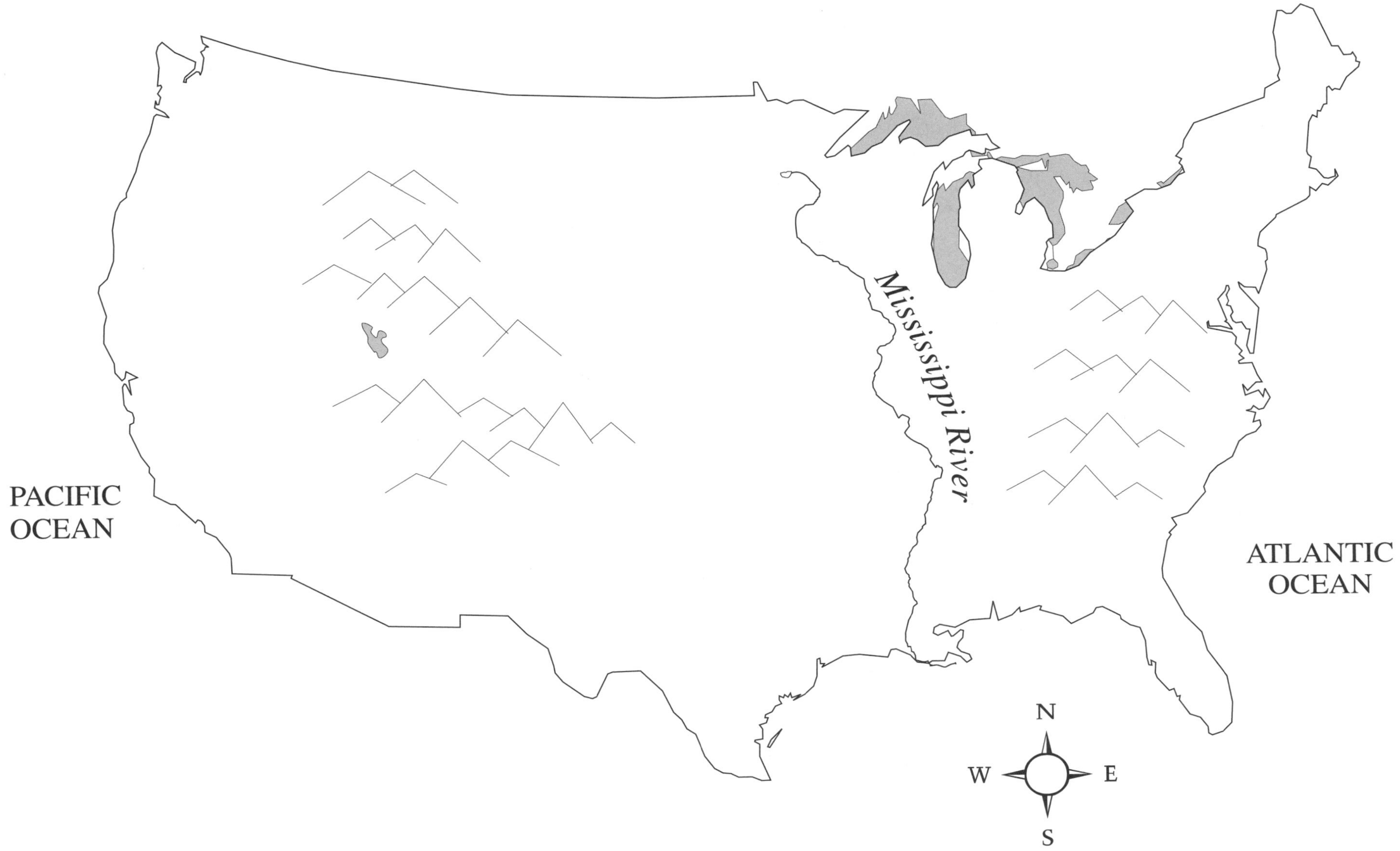

ATLANTIC OCEAN

N
E
S
W

Mississippi River

PACIFIC OCEAN

Introduced in Lesson 13.

Indian Nations of Long Ago

Introduced in Lesson 13.

Heritage Studies 3 Home TE

Use with Lesson 16 (Enrichment).

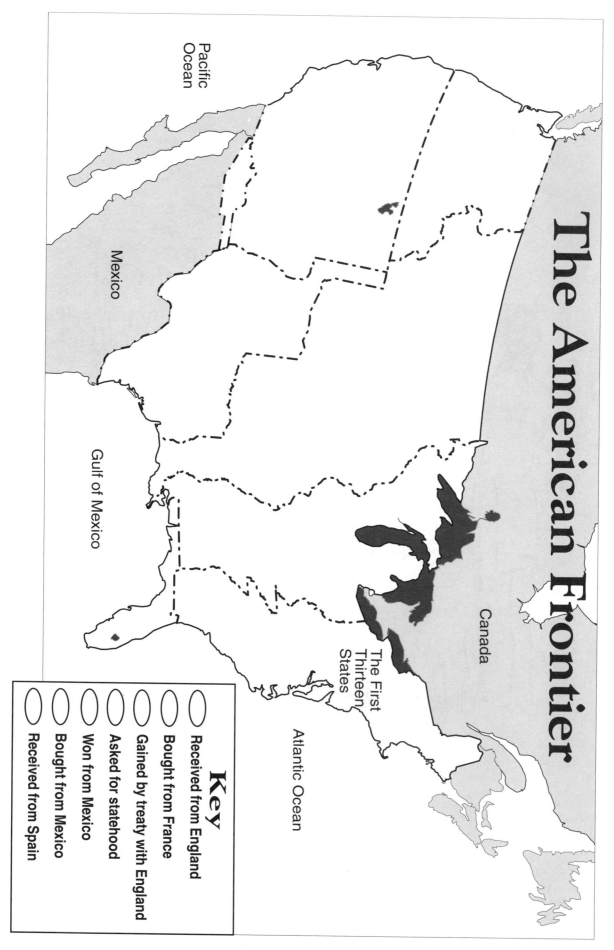

The American Frontier

Pacific Ocean

Mexico

Gulf of Mexico

Canada

Atlantic Ocean

The First Thirteen States

Key

○ Received from England
○ Bought from France
○ Gained by treaty with England
○ Asked for statehood
○ Won from Mexico
○ Bought from Mexico
○ Received from Spain

Introduced in Lesson 18.

Heritage Studies 3 Home TE

Ovals

(1791)

(1819)

(1783)

(1803)

(1845)

(1846)

(1848)

(1853)

Use with Lessons 18, 22, and 23.

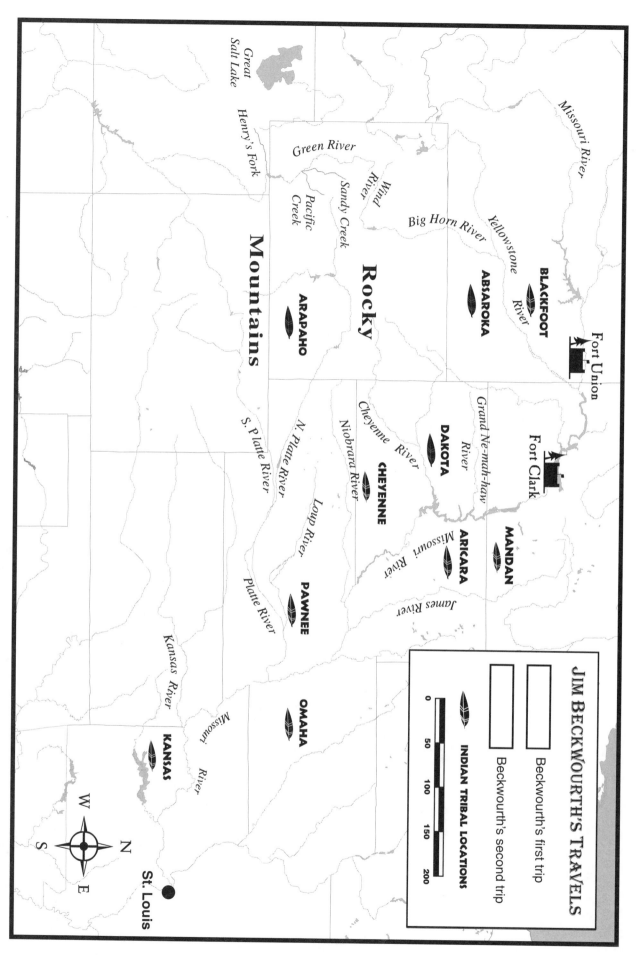

JIM BECKWOURTH'S TRAVELS

Beckwourth's first trip

Beckwourth's second trip

INDIAN TRIBAL LOCATIONS

0   50   100   150   200

Use with Lesson 18 (Enrichment).

Heritage Studies 3 Home TE

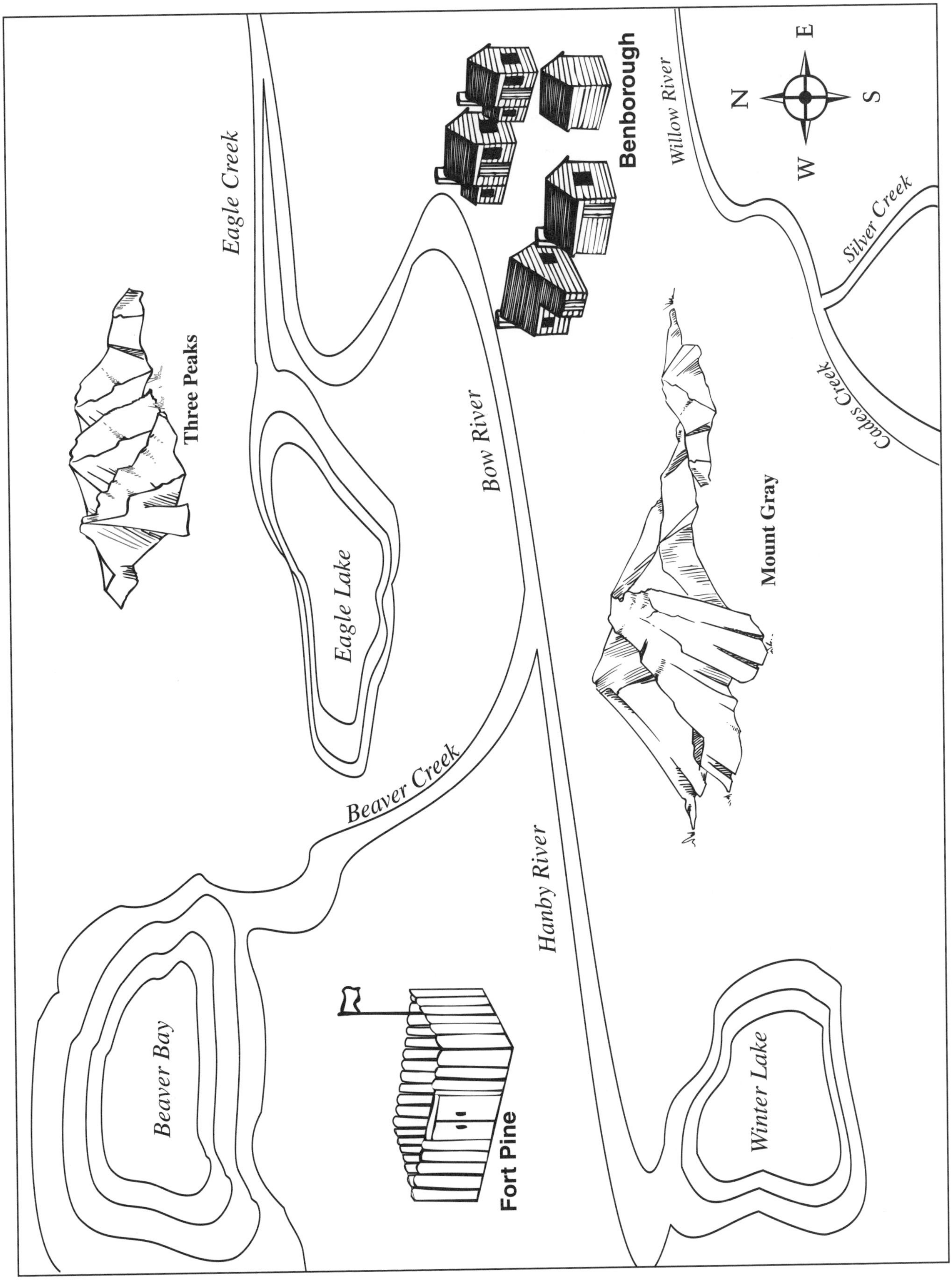
Eagle Creek
Three Peaks
Benborough
Willow River
N
E
S
W
Silver Creek
Cades Creek
Bow River
Eagle Lake
Mount Gray
Beaver Creek
Hanby River
Beaver Bay
Fort Pine
Winter Lake

Use with Lesson 21.

Write out directions for your route.

To go from Benborough to Fort Pine, you should _____

_____

_____

_____

_____

_____

_____

_____

_____

_____

_____

_____

_____

_____

Use with Lesson 21.

Heritage Studies 3 Home TE

Map labels:

- **Benborough**
- Willow River
- Silver Creek
- Cades Creek
- Eagle Creek
- **Three Peaks**
- Bow River
- Eagle Lake
- **Mount Gray**
- Beaver Creek
- Hanby River
- Beaver Bay
- **Fort Pine**
- Winter Lake

Compass: N, E, S, W

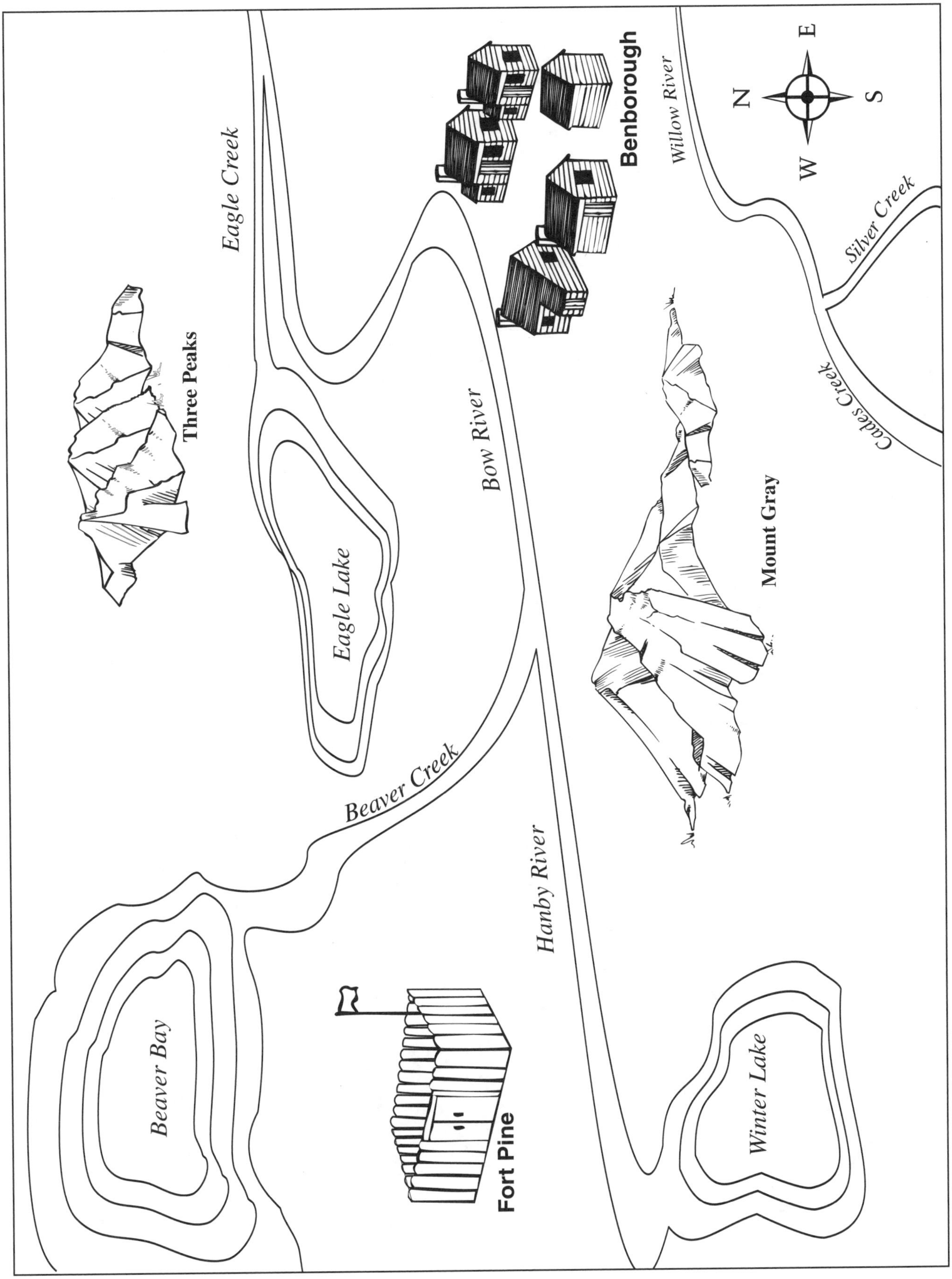

front wheels

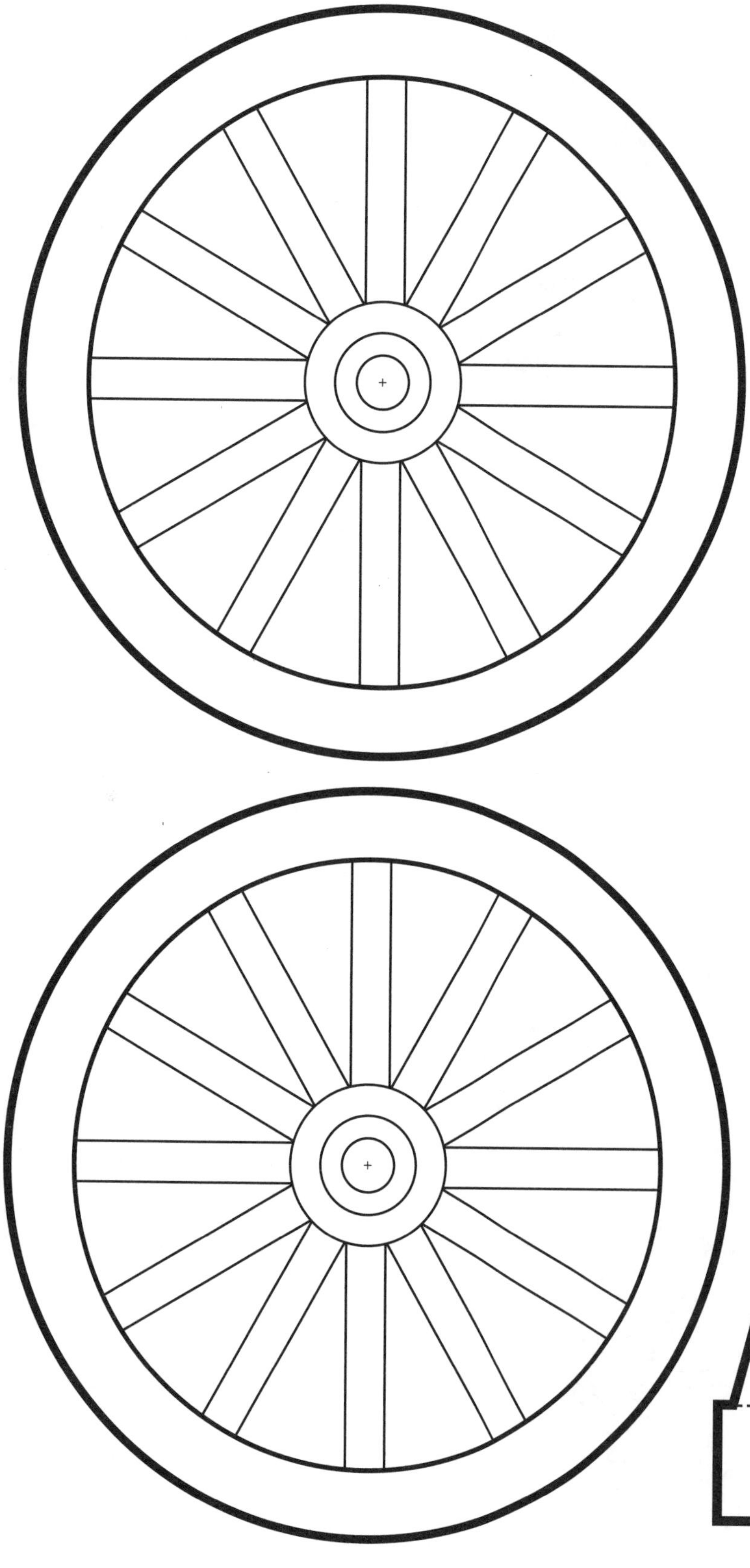

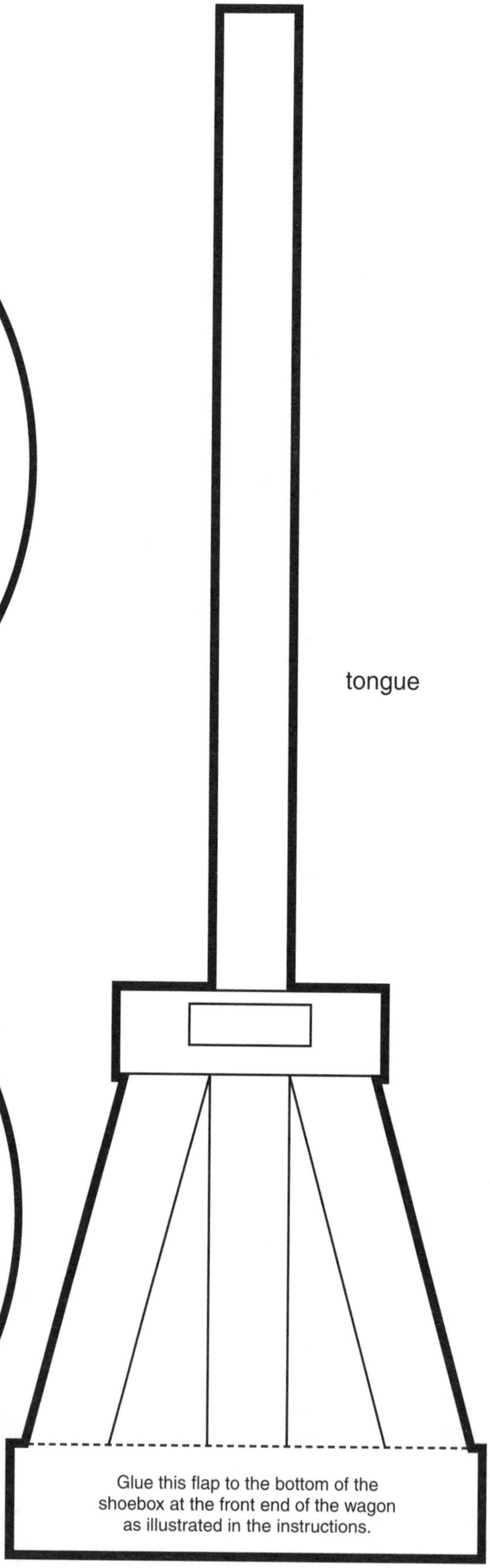

tongue

Glue this flap to the bottom of the
shoebox at the front end of the wagon
as illustrated in the instructions.

Use with Supplemental Lesson in Chapter 4.

Heritage Studies 3 Home TE

back wheels

Appendix   Use with Supplemental Lesson in Chapter 4.   A19

Comparing Prices

Item	Prices in 1849	Prices now
1 egg	$3.00	
loaf of bread	$2.00	
2 lb. of flour	$2.00	
1 potato	$1.00	
1 watermelon	$5.00	
1 pint of vinegar	$1.00	

Use with Lesson 24.

Heritage Studies 3 Home TE

Once upon a time there were two people traveling in a forest.

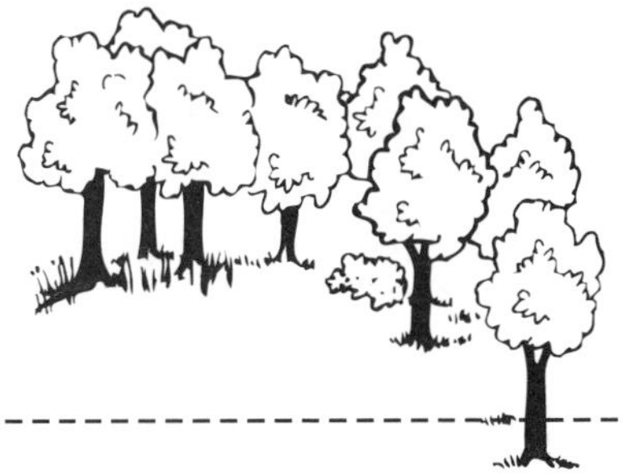

---

fold here

1. One was named _____ and was _____
_____.
(adjective describing character)

---

fold here

2. The other was named _____ and was
_____
_____.
(adjective describing character)

---

fold here

3. They were arguing about _____
_____
_____.

---

fold here

4. _____ came along and told them to
_____
_____.

_____ fold here

5. Later that day _____ came along.
                                           _____

    This was the advice that they were given: _____
_____
_____ .

_____ fold here

                         _____

6. Finally they decided to _____
_____
_____ .

_____ fold here

                         _____

7. And three months later they were both _____
_____
_____ .

_____ fold here

                         _____

8. Therefore, the lesson of the story is to _____
_____
_____
_____ .

Use with Lesson 25.

Heritage Studies 3 Home TE

Seeds of Hope

Cast of Characters

Narrator

John Chapman, young, adventurous man journeying to the West

Horace Stegall, the farmer

Martha Stegall, the farmer's wife

Johnny Appleseed, old, wise explorer and giver of apple seeds, apple trees, and great wisdom

Running Bear, an old Indian friend

William Marsh, a young settler heading west

Rebeccah Marsh, the young settler's wife

Several other settler families

Scene 1: Planting the Seed

(Narrator stands by the characters in Scene 1. A bale of hay is nearby. The farmer wears a straw hat and leans on a hoe.)

Narrator

Horace Stegall has been farming this land for only three years. The work is long and hard, but Horace is bound and determined to make a go of it. He pauses in his hoeing as he hears someone whistling. He turns, wiping his sweaty brow with his handkerchief. He sees a young man with a bright smile and flashing eyes.

John Chapman

Hi, neighbor! *(motioning)* Nice land you got here. *(spreading his hands out wide)* Wide open and peaceful.

Horace Stegall

Yes, we like it. Takes a lot of hard work, though.

Narrator

The stranger walks closer to the farmer in his field, picks up a handful of soil, and fingers it, thoughtfully.

John Chapman

Soil looks fine. Does it bear a good crop for you?

Horace Stegall

Yep, got some mighty fine corn and a mess of beans last year. Hope this year will be even better.

John Chapman

Many orchards around about these parts?

Horace Stegall

(rubbing his chin) Well . . .

Narrator

A door slams and Martha, the farmer's wife, approaches with a pitcher of water and a ladle. With her lips pursed tightly together and her eyes narrowed, she seems slightly annoyed about something.

Martha Stegall

(with irritation in her voice) Horace, what's gotten into you? Have you forgotten your manners? Didn't even offer this young man a drink!

Narrator

Horace's head droops and his eyes lower as his wife comes up to John and extends the ladle to him.

Martha Stegall

Here, young man, help yourself.

John Chapman

Thank you, ma'am. Name's John Chapman. Been askin' your husband about growing crops and whether there're any orchards in these parts.

Martha Stegall

Nice to meet you, John Chapman. Sorry to say, don't know of any orchards around here. Wish we had some, though. I miss those pies and fruit preserves that we used to have.

Horace Stegall

(rubbing his stomach) Mmm-m-m, me too. Sure would be great to have some orchards, but we don't have any place to get trees.

John Chapman

(thoughtfully, scratching his head slowly) Say . . . now . . . that gives me an idea. I used to be a Bible missionary down in Virginia. Took the gospel message all around those parts. Helped lots of folks.

Narrator

The farmer and his wife watch John intently and listen thoughtfully. They wait expectantly for him to go on. John's eyes sparkle with excitement.

John Chapman

(John's voice rises higher with excitement) I could do the same kind of work, going all around these parts and helping lots of folks. I could still share the gospel message while making orchards for folks around here. *(laughingly)* I could be an "apple missionary"!

Narrator

The farmer and his wife laugh with John but nod their heads in agreement.

Horace Stegall

Never heard tell of an "apple missionary" before. Sounds funny . . . but folks sure need to hear the gospel, and they would like the trees.

Martha Stegall

You're right, Horace. Just think what we could do with apple trees! Come on, John, join us for supper. You're the first "apple missionary" to come our way. Don't think we can let you get away without hearing more.

Narrator

The farmer nods his head in agreement and slaps John's back as he motions him toward the house. As they make their way toward the house, we hear talk of apple pies, apple jam, and applesauce. Even the breeze seems to stir with a sweetness slightly like that of ripe, crisp apples.

Scene 2: Doing the Work

(John Chapman now looks like the wilderness character Johnny Appleseed with no shoes, a coffee sack shirt, pouches of apple seeds, a backpack, and a cooking pot on his head. As the scene opens, Johnny is planting apple seeds.)

Narrator

John Chapman has changed since that time long ago with the farmer and his wife. He's been traveling a long time now, through the forests, across the plains, and over the streams. He looks a little strange. Some folks think he's crazy. Most folks, though, know he's kind and generous and good. This Johnny Appleseed is truly the settler's friend.

Johnny Appleseed

There . . . that's done. Ought to be a perfect spot for the beautiful, pink blossoms of apple trees. *(Johnny bows his head and closes his eyes to pray.)* Lord God of Heaven . . . Master of all creation . . . Father, thank You for strength to carry on Your work. Thank You for these seeds of hope . . . these tiny apple seeds that You make into a lovely tree with branches stretched heavenward. I praise You for Your great power to tend the earth and to make the fruit to grow for us, your humble servants. I pray Your blessing and care upon these new seeds. Make them to mature, take root, and grow strong for Your glory. May the fruit that they produce give nourishment and pleasure to all that pass this way. In Your most glorious name, Amen.

Narrator

This scene was to be repeated time and time again as Johnny Appleseed traveled hundreds of miles across the great land of America, clearing land and planting seeds of hope for settlers to come.

Johnny Appleseed

(with his head up high, ambling along the road, whistling a happy tune) My God is so good! His world is alive with color and life and joy!

Narrator

Johnny can contain his happiness no longer. He bursts into song. The birds seem to sing right along with him.

Johnny Appleseed

(singing to the tune of "Skip to My Lou")
With my pack on my back wherever I go,
With my seeds in my sack, I'll everywhere sow.
Then the Lord comes along with His sunshine and rain
Makes every apple seed blossom again.
Tra-la-la, pack on my back,
Tra-la-la, seeds in my sack,
Tra-la-la, sunshine and rain,
The Lord makes the apple seeds blossom again.

Narrator

As Johnny comes through the forest into the clearing, he continues whistling his song, wondering where he can plant his precious apple seeds next. His thoughts are interrupted by the sound of water, lapping on the banks of the rich land. The kind, strong voice of an old friend calls to him.

Running Bear

Ho, my friend . . . my own Appleseed John. What brings you here?

Johnny Appleseed

Apples, my friend . . . it's always apples that decide my journeyings. How is it with you, Running Bear? How are your apple trees doing?

Running Bear

Fine. Fine. The trees now spread their branches wide to the east and the west. Each season the pink clusters yield the red fruit of summer. My people rejoice. The land yields its measure. We thank you, Appleseed John.

Johnny Appleseed

The thanks goes to God. He alone does the work. I'm just a servant, doing His bidding. Take care, my friend. I must be on my way.

Narrator

Running Bear and Johnny Appleseed part with a hearty handshake. Each man goes his own way, doing his own work.

Scene 3: Giving Hope

(Johnny Appleseed in rustic garb as in Scene 2. Add a beard if you wish. Have available small "trees," apples, and pouches near him.)

Narrator

Johnny is now an old man, on his farm, with large, mature apple trees all around. Near the road are seedlings and seed pouches ready to be given to any passing settlers. Johnny waits at the end of the road as a wagon approaches. He greets a young couple with a newborn baby heading west.

Johnny Appleseed

Howdy, friends. Headin' west, are you? Want to stop and rest a spell?

William Marsh

Sure, guess we should get out to stretch our legs some. Got a long ways to go yet before we get to the West.

Narrator

The young settler tugs at the reins, and the two tired horses pull the loaded wagon to the side of the road. William Marsh hops down from his seat, takes the infant to his shoulder while extending his other hand to help his young wife down. Rebeccah Marsh looks relieved to change positions and have a chance to rest awhile. Her sweet, smooth face is tired but not complaining. Her glance goes to the face of Johnny Appleseed as she speaks softly.

Rebeccah Marsh

Thank you, kind sir. My family and I appreciate your kindness toward us. *(looking around)* What a beautiful place to rest . . . and dream. Is this your place, sir? My, my . . . it's like springtime itself!

Johnny Appleseed

Yes, ma'am, it's mine . . . mine and the great Lord's. Make yourself at home. I'll fetch you some cider and fresh apples.

Narrator

As Johnny Appleseed prepares to get the cider and apples, William Marsh gently hands the baby back to his wife. He studies his host carefully; then his face breaks into a wide grin.

William Marsh

Rebeccah, Rebeccah, do you realize who that is? It's Johnny Appleseed! We've heard so much about him . . . the thousands of trees that he's planted all around these parts . . . and how he's helped so many folks going west. Rebeccah, it's really Johnny Appleseed! And now he's helping us!

Rebeccah Marsh

You're right, William! No wonder this place looks and smells so perfect! Johnny Appleseed has made it a haven for folks like us!

Narrator

Johnny nears the couple just in time to hear the last statement. His pockets bulge with huge, red apples. In his hands he carries two mugs of sweet cider. He offers the refreshments to his visitors, smiling a sheepish grin.

Johnny Appleseed

Yep, it's folks like you, so brave and enthusiastic, that this Johnny Appleseed looks for every day. I used to go about rambling through the woods, across the streams, on and on for months at a time, planting my trees. Now my body is wearing out a mite, so I try to do my missionary work right from this spot. Kinda hard to stay put, but it's rewarding when folks like you come along.

Narrator

William Marsh sets his cup of cider and apple down on the plush green grass. He thrusts his hand out to shake Johnny's hand vigorously.

William Marsh

What a pleasure to meet you, Johnny Appleseed! William Marsh is the name. This is my wife Rebeccah and our little one, baby Joshua. Oh, Johnny, stories of you and your great work have spread far and wide. This land is the most beautiful that I've ever seen! Interested in selling it?

Narrator

Johnny shook his head slowly. He was used to that question. It was asked almost every day. He smiled at the eager William Marsh and his young wife and child. To a man by himself on horseback, Johnny usually thundered that there wasn't enough money in Uncle Sam's treasury to buy his beloved orchard. But to a young man with a family in a wagon, his heart stirred with a little more compassion.

Johnny Appleseed

Sorry, Mr. Marsh, I wish I could give you and your sweet family an orchard just like mine! But there is hope, sir. You can grow your own dear trees wherever you decide to settle. Just a little loving care for the tiny seeds and the good Lord does the rest.

Narrator

Johnny reaches down to cradle a leather pouch of his beloved apple seeds. He stretches them toward the young couple. It is Rebeccah who cups the treasure and presses it to her homespun gown.

Rebeccah Marsh

Oh, thank you, thank you, dear sir. We'll carry this precious package with us to tend and care for as lovingly as you tend yours. Maybe someday we'll have a beautiful resting place like this for weary travelers.

Narrator

William Marsh nods in agreement and once again shakes the hand of his new friend, Johnny Appleseed. With the thank-yous over, Johnny motions them to wait a moment. He rushes to the house and returns with a low, splint-bottomed rocker. The rustic benches and stools were suitable for most visitors, but not enough for this sweet, courageous lady with dreams of a bright future.

Johnny Appleseed

Here, Mrs. Marsh, rest yourself and your lad a bit in my orchard. A few moments here will make your long journey ahead easier to bear.

Narrator

Johnny steadies the chair as it rocks gently in the breeze. Rebeccah and baby Joshua seem right at home, peaceful and quiet. William and Johnny look on, careful not to disturb the scene before them. After a few minutes, Rebeccah speaks.

Rebeccah Marsh

How happy a woman could be with a brood of children playing all around her under trees like these. Maybe someday . . . maybe someday soon . . . with God's help . . .

Narrator

Rebeccah clasps the tiny pouch of seeds to her once more. Her eyes close in prayer; then she hums a lovely, sweet song to the babe in her arms. Her dreams would come true. They would plant the seeds. They would have their orchards. The children would play. And God would care for them all.

Scene 4: Continuing the Work

(As the Narrator reads his part, allow any students who have not already had parts to represent settler families that pass by Johnny Appleseed's farm. Encourage the students to pantomime the actions that the narrator describes.)

Narrator

For many more years to come, families would pass by the farm of Johnny Appleseed. They too would rest a while. They would eat apples and drink cider. The children would play. The grown-ups would exchange stories of adventures and dreams. Then Johnny would give them a pouch of apple seeds, pray with them, and speed them on their way. There would never be another man like Johnny Appleseed, but the apple trees that he loved would live on and multiply thousands of times over in this great land of America.

All Characters

Psalm 67:5-6—Let the people praise thee, O God; let all the people praise thee. Then shall the earth yield her increase; and God, even our own God, shall bless us.

Narrator

Johnny's song seemed to continue through the years.

All Characters

(singing to the tune of "Skip to My Lou")
With my pack on my back wherever I go,
With my seeds in my sack, I'll everywhere sow.
Then the Lord comes along with His sunshine and rain
Makes every apple seed blossom again.
Tra-la-la, pack on my back,
Tra-la-la, seeds in my sack,
Tra-la-la, sunshine and rain,
The Lord makes the apple seeds blossom again.

Color and cut out the apples that describe Johnny Appleseed.
Glue the apples onto the apple tree outline.

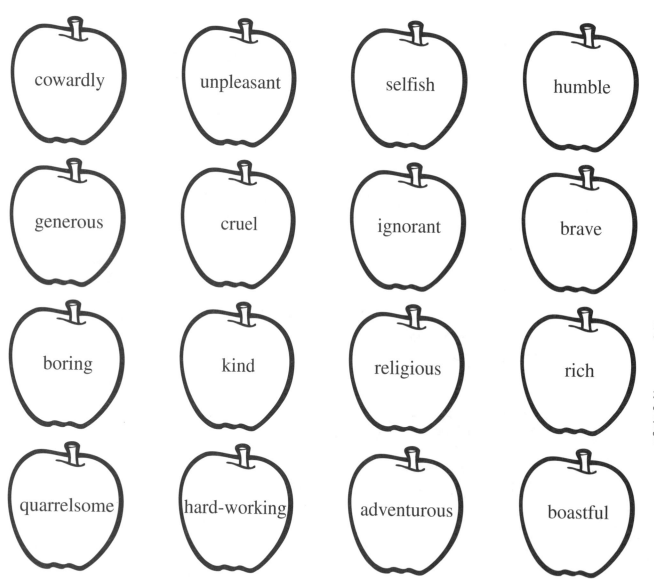

cowardly

unpleasant

selfish

humble

generous

cruel

ignorant

brave

boring

kind

religious

rich

quarrelsome

hard-working

adventurous

boastful

Use with Supplemental Lesson in Chapter 5.   Heritage Studies 3 Home TE

Use with Supplemental Lesson in Chapter 5.

Evaluation Game

Grimm Brothers	water	authors	Alligator
folktales	two	brother	African American
three	Indian	Deer	white man
agreement	Germany	rested	hounds

Map of the United States by Region

Northeast Region

Maine
New Hampshire
Vermont
Massachusetts
Rhode Island
Connecticut
New Jersey
New York
Pennsylvania
Delaware
Maryland

Middle West Region

Michigan
Ohio
Indiana
Illinois
Wisconsin
Minnesota
Iowa
Missouri

Southeast Region

West Virginia
Virginia
North Carolina
South Carolina
Georgia
Florida
Kentucky
Tennessee
Alabama
Mississippi
Louisiana
Arkansas

Rocky Mountain Region

North Dakota
South Dakota
Nebraska
Kansas
Montana
Wyoming
Colorado
Idaho
Utah

Southwest Region

Oklahoma
Texas
New Mexico
Arizona

Pacific Region

Washington
Oregon
Nevada
California
Alaska
Hawaii

Introduced in Lesson 30.

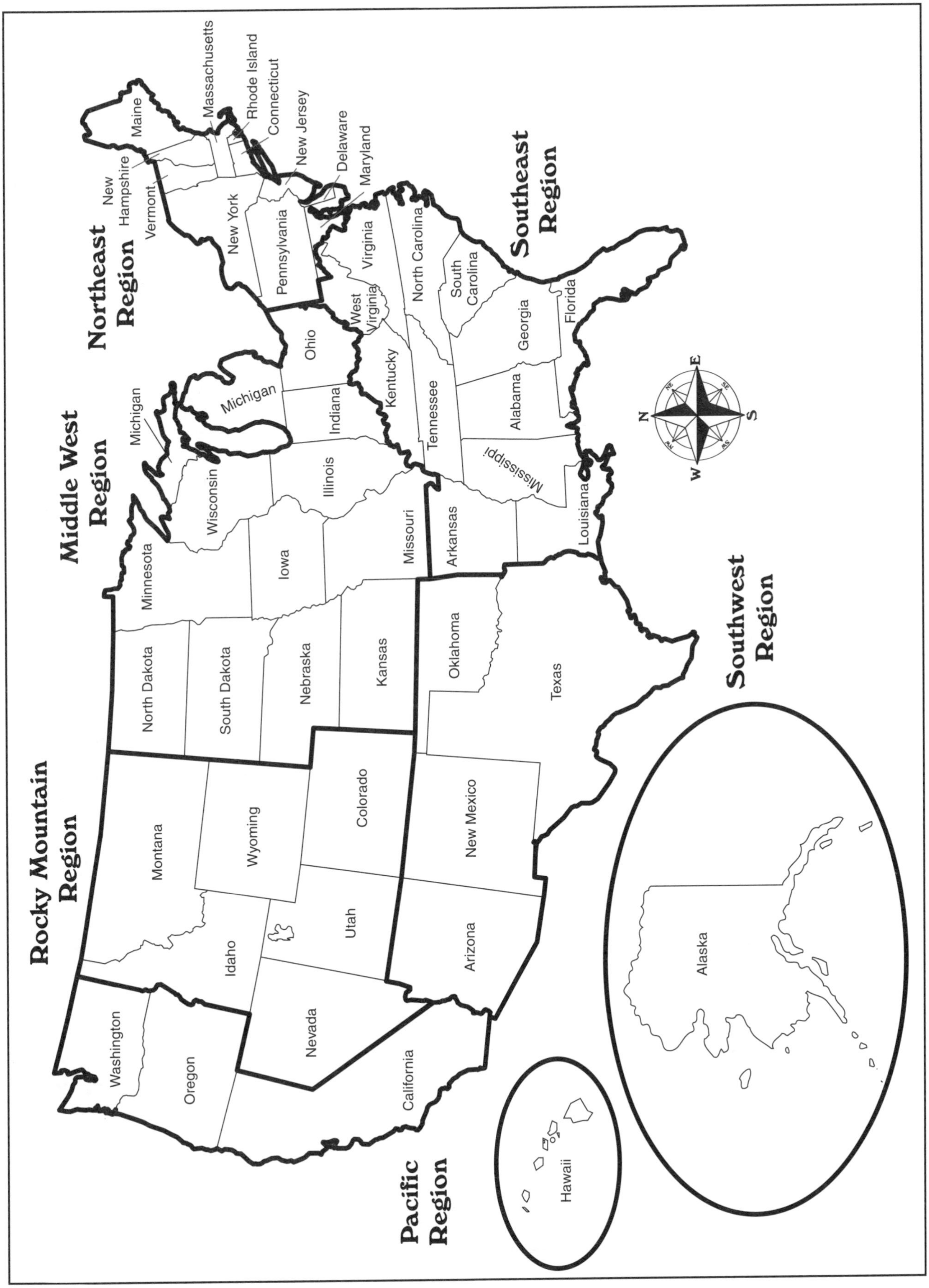

PACIFIC OCEAN

ATLANTIC OCEAN

TRAVEL JOURNAL
PASSBOOK

Introduced in Lesson 30. Heritage Studies 3 Home TE

Our schoolroom should not have gerbils because they might take our attention away from our schoolwork or cause allergy problems for someone.

Our schoolroom should have gerbils because they are entertaining and have many interesting habits to observe and study.

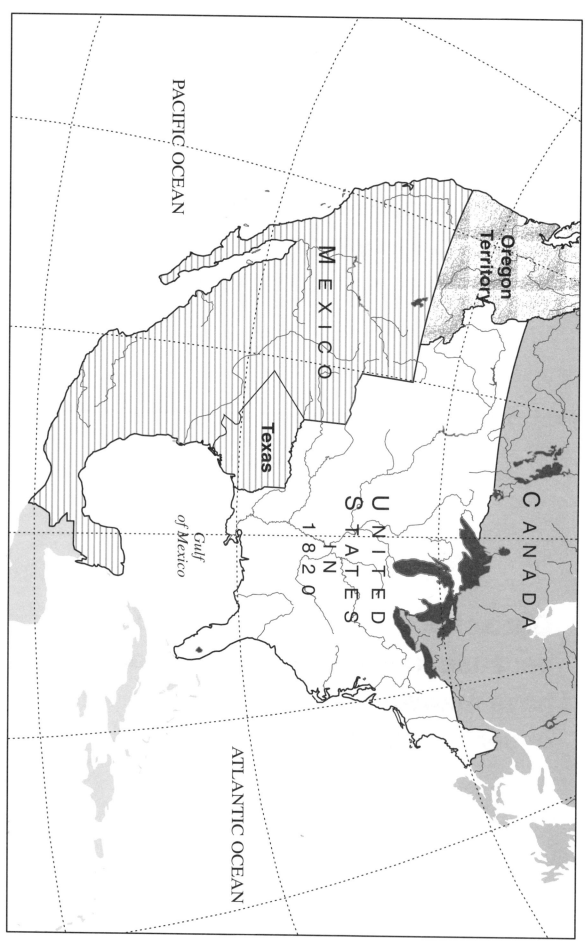

PACIFIC OCEAN

Oregon
Territory

M E X I C O

C A N A D A

Texas

Gulf
of Mexico

U N I T E D
S T A T E S
I N
1 8 2 0

ATLANTIC OCEAN

Use with Lesson 37.

Heritage Studies 3 Home TE

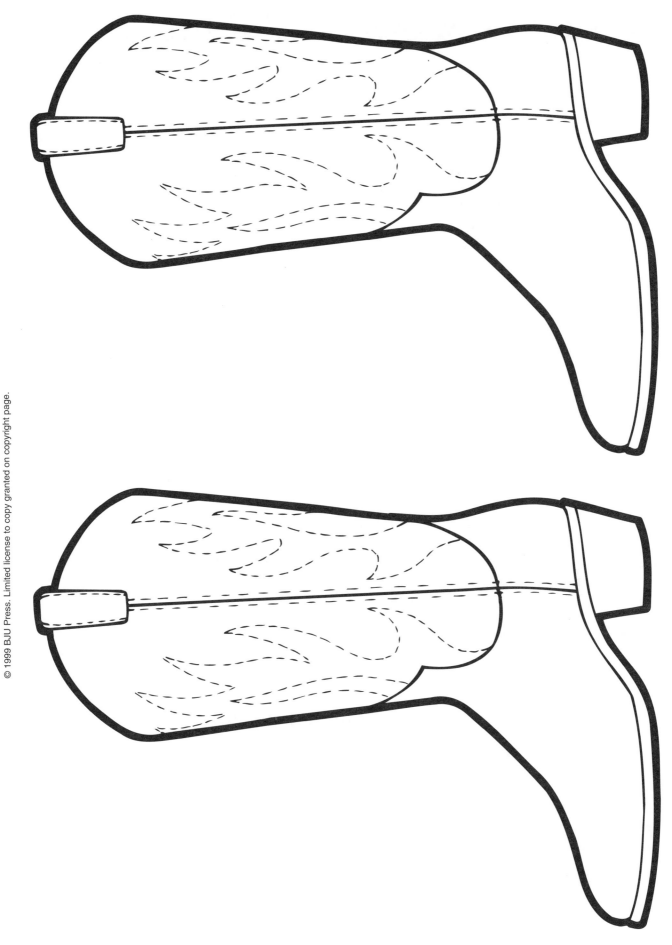

Use with Lesson 43 (Enrichment).

Swing Low, Sweet Chariot

Swing low, sweet chariot,
Comin' for to carry me home.
Swing low, sweet chariot,
Comin' for to carry me home.

1. I looked over Jordan and what did I see,
   Comin' for to carry me home?
   A band of angels comin' after me,
   Comin' for to carry me home.

2. And if you get there before I do,
   Comin' for to carry me home,
   Tell all my friends that I'm a-comin' too,
   Comin' for to carry me home.

3. The brightest of bright days that I ever saw,
   Comin' for to carry me home,
   When Jesus washed my mortal sins away,
   Comin' for to carry me home.

4. Now sometimes I'm up and sometimes I'm way down,
   Comin' for to carry me home,
   But still my soul feels heavenly bound,
   Comin' for to carry me home.

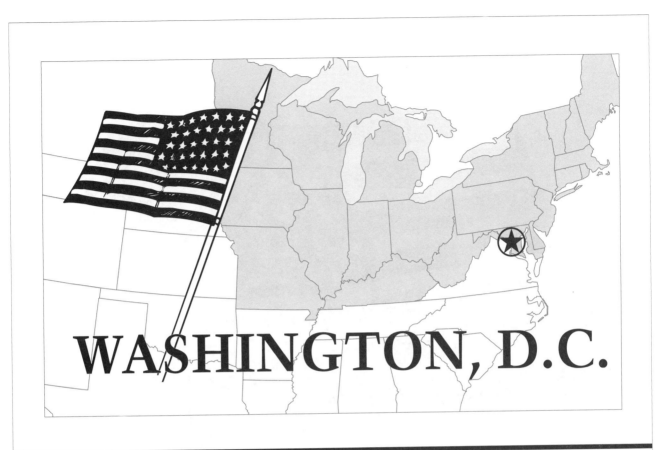

WASHINGTON, D.C.

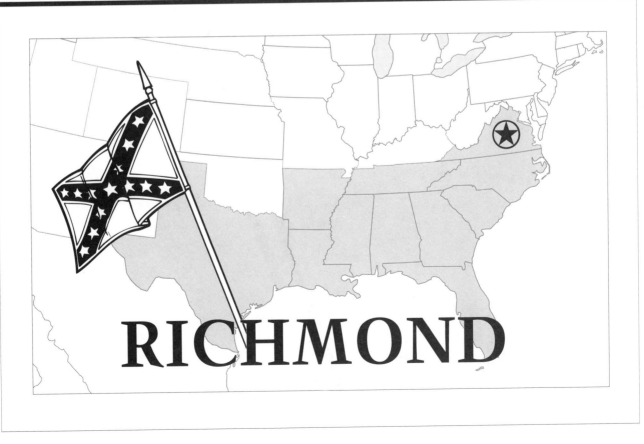

RICHMOND

Use with Lesson 47.

Heritage Studies 3 Home TE

Use with Lesson 47.

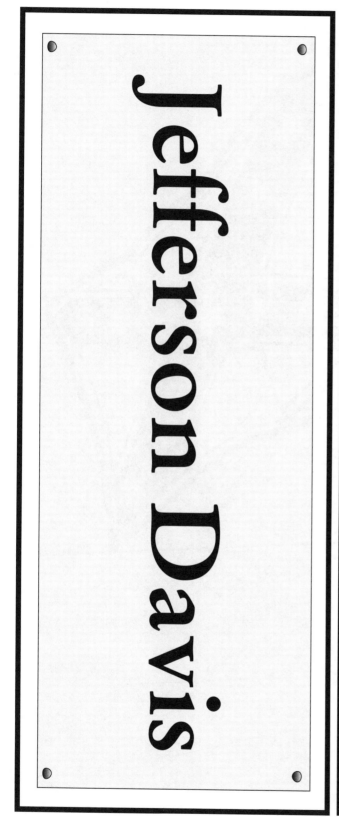

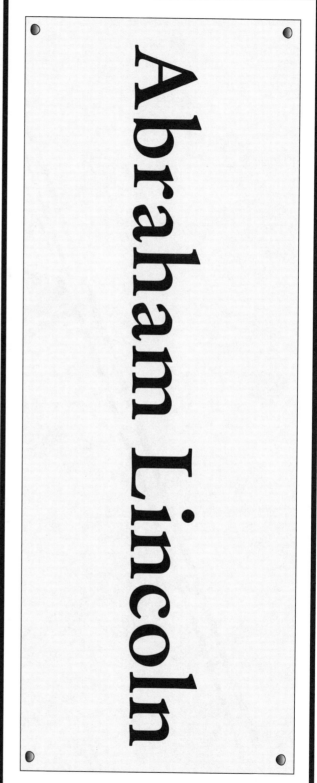

Use with Lesson 47.

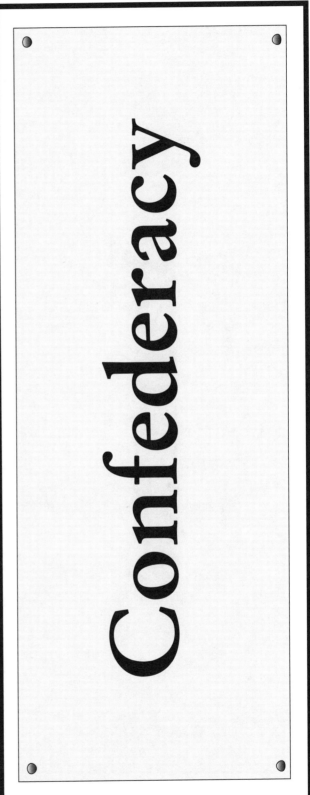

Use with Lesson 47.

Use with Lesson 47.

Heritage Studies 3 Home TE

Use with Lesson 47.

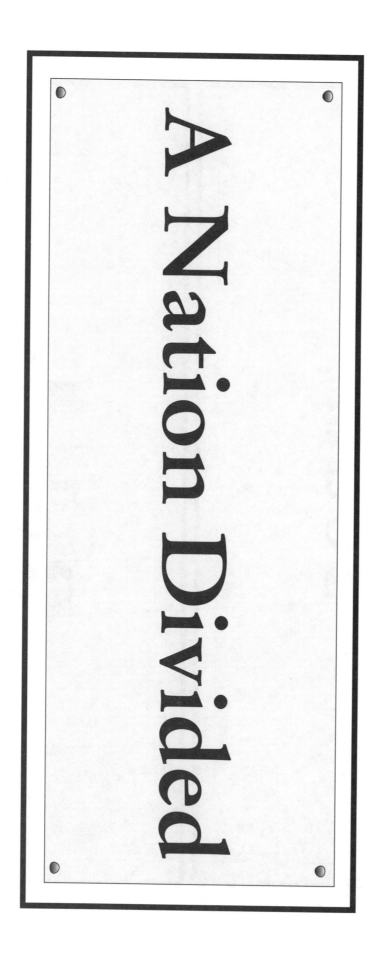

A Nation Divided

Use with Lesson 47.

Heritage Studies 3 Home TE

Use with Lesson 47.

General
Stonewall Jackson

General
Irvin McDowell

Use with Lesson 48.

Heritage Studies 3 Home TE

General
George McClellan

General
Robert E. Lee

A Nation Reunited

General Ulysses S. Grant

Use with Lesson 52.

Heritage Studies 3 Home TE

Steamboat's A-Coming!

Narrator: Grandpa gathers the children around him, settling them close by his side. He speaks with a thoughtful, far-off gaze. "You know, these new locomotives are certainly exciting things, but I'd much rather ride on a steamboat. They've been running steady routes for years now. Always can count on 'em. But I remember a time when people weren't sure about steamboats either. Yes, it seems like just yesterday. . . ."

Child: Everybody's gathered 'round;

Parent: Everybody's lining the shore;

Child: They're all down at the river.

Parent: 'Twon't be the same no more!

Both: The steamboat's a-coming!
  The steamboat's a-coming!
  Fulton's steamboat's coming today.

Parent: Her paddle wheel is churnin';

Child: The steam is mounting high.

Parent: Fulton's *Clermont* is a-smokin',
  Puffing black clouds to the sky.

Both: The steamboat's a-coming!
  The steamboat's a-coming!
  Fulton's steamboat's coming today.

Child: The folks are all a-jeering.

Parent: A strange sight they see!

Child: There will be no cause for cheering,
  No certain victory.

Both: The steamboat's a-coming!
  The steamboat's a-coming!
  Fulton's steamboat's coming today.

Child: She still keeps a-coming,
  Pushing her way through.

Parent: The engines are a-chugging,
  Puffing her smoke at you.

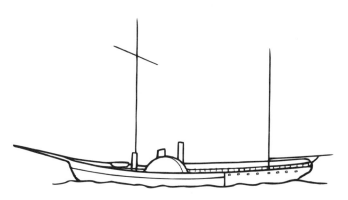

Both: The steamboat's a-coming!
  The steamboat's a-coming!
  Fulton's steamboat's coming today.

Parent: It looks like she will make it!

Child: The journey's almost done.

Parent: Yes, the *Clermont* keeps on coming
  'Til her victory is won.

Both: Now the steamboat's a-running!
  The steamboat's a-running!
  Fulton's steamboat's running every day.

Tom Thumb

(NOTE: Show Maps and More 22a with the bottom of the page covered.)

"Sure, I'll ride the train. But give me a horse-drawn car, not that iron bucket. It sputters and jerks. Covers everything with sparks and smoke. Won't catch me on that newfangled contraption!"

(NOTE: Show Maps and More 22b.)

Peter Cooper had heard this kind of talk for weeks now. His new little steam locomotive, the Tom Thumb, had stirred up the townspeople quite a bit. "Someday," he thought, "someday, we'll show them."

(NOTE: Show Maps and More 23a, covering the bottom of the page.)

It was a hot, sunny day in August 1830. A horse-drawn railroad car of the Baltimore & Ohio Railroad was running its regular route. On another track, the Tom Thumb was running. The two trains passed each other, their passengers hurling taunts and glares at each other. In a sudden outburst, someone challenged, "Let's race the horse against the steam locomotive. Then we'll see which is better."

The taunts continued from one railroad car to another. The crowds gathered, eager to see the spectacle. Both the horse and the engine edged up to place at the starting line. With a snort, the gray horse pawed the ground a little while his opponent, the Tom Thumb, let out a little puff of steam. The passengers braced themselves, wondering what they had gotten themselves into and wondering what would happen.

(NOTE: Ask your child who he thinks will win the race, the horse or Tom Thumb. Show Maps and More 23b.)

They were off! The crowd cheered while the rhythms of the racers kept time with each other. First a snort, then a puff, a snort, a puff, a snort, a puff—and on and on it went. The horse and the little engine started out side-by-side. The gray horse stretched his neck and pulled ahead. The little engine paused a little as all its parts were set in motion.

But soon it happened! Everyone saw it, but very few expected it. The horse was about a quarter of a mile ahead when the safety valve lifted and a thin, blue vapor streamed out of the Tom Thumb. His blower whistled as the steam became little clouds, pushing the engine along. Snort, snort, snort; puff, puff, puff; snort, snort, snort; puff, puff, puff. The horse and the little engine were neck and neck, nose and nose, running together. Then the Tom Thumb shot forward! The passengers jerked, shouting with excitement. The Tom Thumb passed the horse. The crowd stared in amazement! How could this be happening? A machine faster than a galloping horse?

(NOTE: Show Maps and More 24a with the bottom of the page covered.)

The horse's driver snapped the whip, urging the horse to try harder. Each muscle seemed to strain as the horse reached forward to outrun the Tom Thumb. It seemed that nothing would help. The Tom Thumb was chug-chugging along at a rate that nothing could catch until—

The people stared. What was happening? Snort, snort, snort; puff-a, puff, psst-st-st-st. . . . The little engine panted to a stop. A belt had broken! Peter Cooper worked furiously to fix it. Seconds became minutes. The crowd stared as the horse came galloping past the little engine. More determined than ever, Peter Cooper kept right on working. With the belt replaced, the Tom Thumb started up again. A-puff, a-puff, puff, puff, puff. Steam was once again doing its best for the little Tom Thumb. But the horse was too far ahead. The Tom Thumb just couldn't catch up. The people cheered as the horse crossed the finish line.

What a race! People crowded around the little Tom Thumb, admiring its parts and discussing what they had just witnessed. Maybe this contraption of Cooper's was not such a crazy idea after all. They had seen it work. In fact, they had seen it work well—very well! Maybe, just maybe, they would take a ride on a steam locomotive . . . someday.

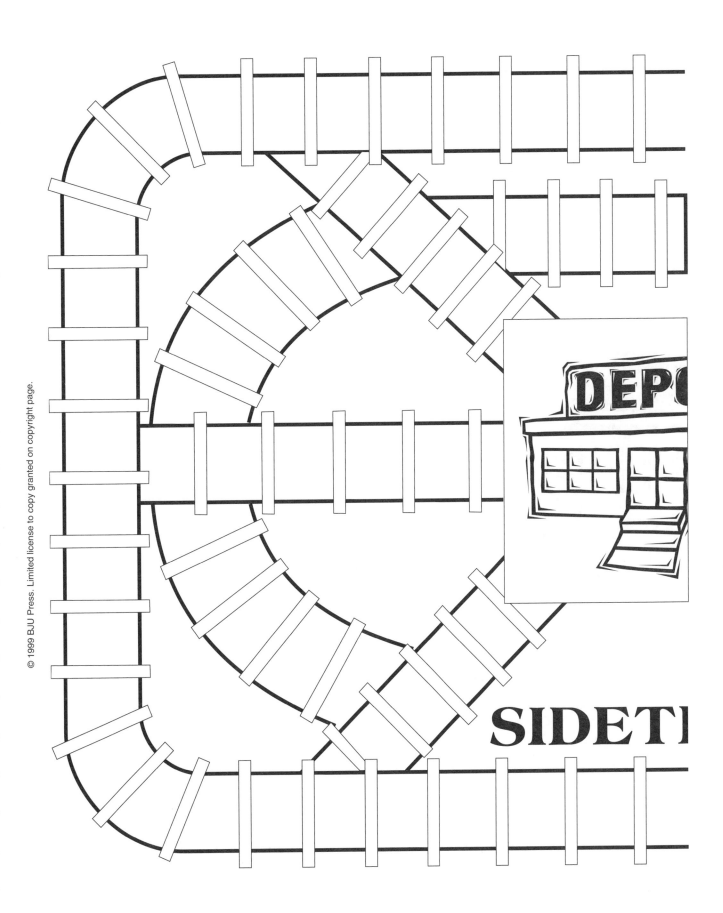

DEPO

SIDETI

Appendix   Use with Lesson 63 (Enrichment).   A55

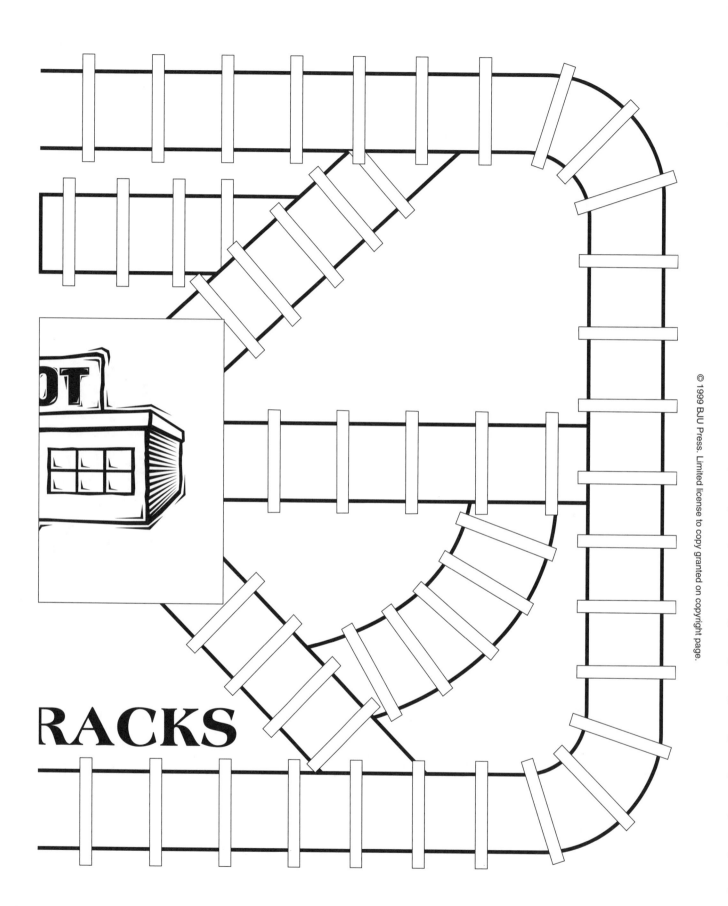

RACKS

Use with Lesson 63 (Enrichment).

Heritage Studies 3 Home TE

○ Who designed the Tom Thumb?	○ Who built the big locomotive Old Ironsides?	○ What railroad companies built the transcontinental railroad?
○ Where would you find a scale of miles?	○ What are the areas of time called?	○ Where are the Sierra Nevada?
○ What was the Native American name for a train?	○ How many time zones are there in the United States?	○ What were the boats powered by steam called?
○ Who reads the train signals to drive the train safely?	○ Who is the legendary African American railroader?	○ Who was in charge of the Central Pacific crew?
○ Where is the caboose on a train?	○ Where were most of the early railroads in the United States?	○ Where on a locomotive does the water become boiling hot?
○ What does *transcontinental* mean?	○ What are train tracks made of?	○ What did the Railroad Act give to railroad companies?
○ Who was the Tom Thumb named after?	○ How many inventions did George Westinghouse patent?	○ Who built the first successful steamboat?
○ What are tracks that are built next to the main tracks called?	○ What mountains were in the way of the Central Pacific?	○ On what river did the *Clermont* sail?
○ What did the Tom Thumb race against?	○ What powered early locomotives?	○ When did the first steam locomotives begin to run?
○ Who invented air brakes for trains?	○ Who shoveled coal into the firebox on a train?	○ Who was the president of the Central Pacific Railroad?
○ Where did the Central Pacific begin laying tracks?	○ What is a train station called?	○ Where did many workers of the Central Pacific come from?
○ What does it mean to "couple" cars of a train?	○ What time is it when the sun is directly overhead?	○ What is a tiny replica of a train called?
○ What special group of workers was a part of the Union Pacific?	○ Which president signed the Pacific Railroad Act in 1862?	○ How did the workmen make roads through the mountains?
○ Where can you find a train's schedule?	○ Where did the *Clermont* begin its trip?	○ Where did the Union Pacific begin laying tracks?
○ How long did it take to build the transcontinental railroad?	○ What does a brake do for a train?	○ What broke on the Tom Thumb, causing it to lose the race?
○ Who is the "boss" on a train?	○ What special group of workers was part of the Central Pacific?	○ Who built a model of his train Old Ironsides?
○ In the spiritual "Get on Board," where is the train going?	○ Where does coal come from?	○ Where did the tracks of the transcontinental railroad finally meet?
○ In what year did the *Clermont* make its first successful voyage?	○ Before trains, how did people travel?	○ What is the name of the part on the front of a train that can push things off the tracks?
○ Who won the race with the Tom Thumb?	○ Who hunted buffalo for food for the Union Pacific Railroad?	○ Who used to run on top of the train cars to set their brakes?
○ Where did the *Clermont* end its trip?	○ Where did the Tom Thumb race?	○ Where did steam locomotives stop to "feed" themselves?
○ What was the last spike of the transcontinental railroad made of?	○ Through what part of the train does the steam escape?	○ What is another word for *train engine?*

Use with Lesson 63 (Enrichment).

○ the Central Pacific and the Union Pacific	○ Mathias Baldwin	○ Peter Cooper
○ in the western United States	○ time zones	○ on a map
○ steamboats	○ six	○ iron horse
○ Charles Crocker	○ John Henry	○ the engineer
○ the boiler	○ in the East and Midwest	○ at the end
○ money and free land	○ wood and iron	○ across the continent
○ Robert Fulton	○ 361	○ a storybook character
○ Hudson River	○ the Sierra Nevada	○ sidetracks
○ 1830s	○ steam	○ a horse
○ Leland Stanford	○ the fireman	○ George Westinghouse
○ China	○ a depot	○ Sacramento, California
○ a model	○ noon	○ join them
○ They dug tunnels.	○ Abraham Lincoln	○ Irish workers
○ Omaha, Nebraska	○ New York City	○ timetable
○ a belt	○ It stops it.	○ eight years
○ Mathias Baldwin	○ Chinese workers	○ the engineer
○ in Promontory Point, Utah	○ deep in the ground	○ to heaven
○ a cowcatcher	○ boats, wagons, and walking	○ 1807
○ the brakeman	○ "Buffalo Bill" Cody	○ the horse-drawn train
○ "at Tanks"	○ Baltimore	○ Albany
○ locomotive	○ through the smokestack	○ gold

Use with Lesson 63 (Enrichment).

Heritage Studies 3 Home TE

TRAIN SCHEDULE CARD

People ⬭		
Places ⬭		
Things ⬭		

TRAIN SCHEDULE CARD

People ⬭		
Places ⬭		
Things ⬭		

TRAIN SCHEDULE CARD

People ⬭		
Places ⬭		
Things ⬭		

TRAIN SCHEDULE CARD

People ⬭		
Places ⬭		
Things ⬭		

Use with Lesson 63 (Enrichment).

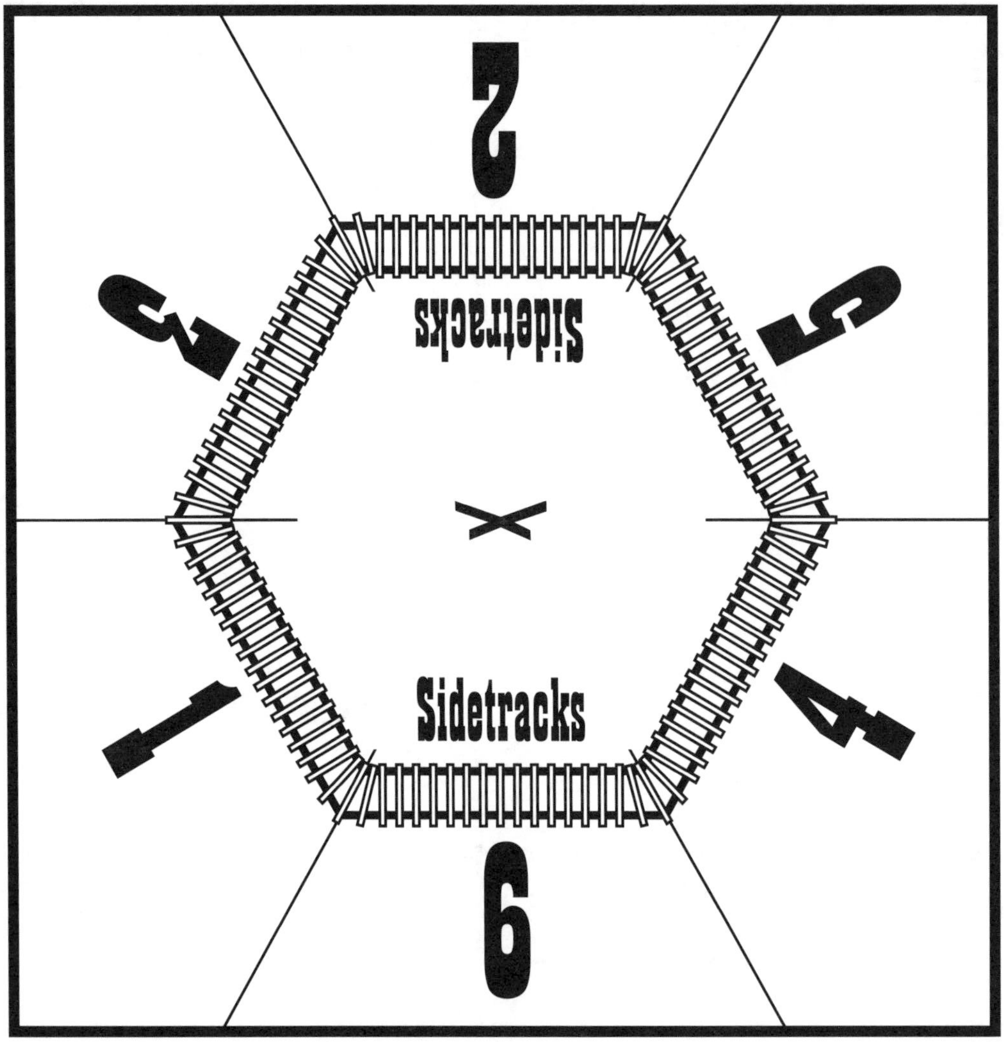

Sidetracks

Sidetracks

2

3

5

1

4

6

X

X

Use with Lesson 63 (Enrichment).

Heritage Studies 3 Home TE

Saddle Parts

horn

cantle

seat

skirt

fender

cinch

ties

stirrups

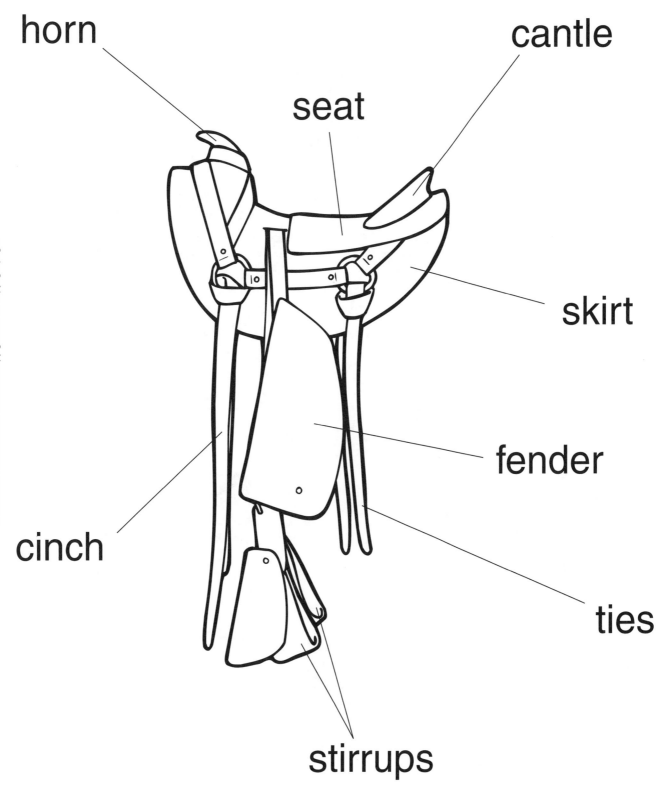

Typical Cavalry Outpost of the Late 1860s

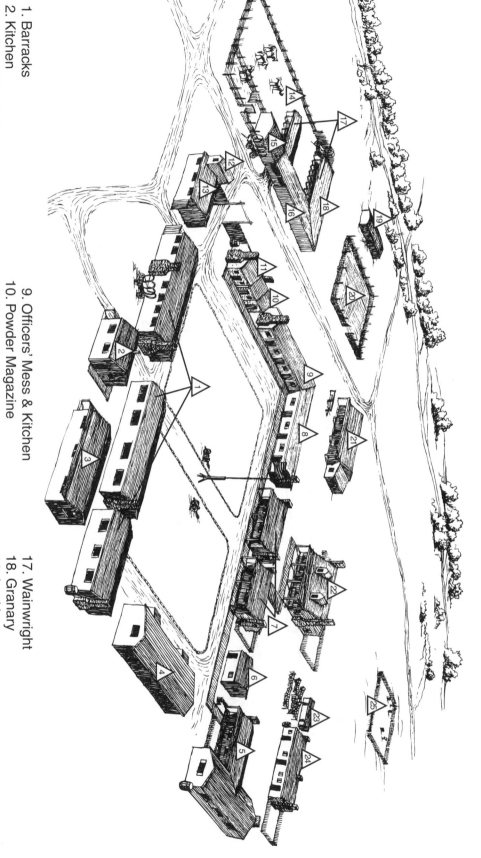

1. Barracks
2. Kitchen
3. Enlisted Men's Mess
4. Quartermaster Storehouse & Office
5. Infirmary
6. Guardhouse
7. Married Officers' Quarters
8. Bachelor Officers' Quarters
9. Officers' Mess & Kitchen
10. Powder Magazine
11. Bakery
12. Storeroom
13. Commissary
14. Corral
15. Harness Maker, Saddler, & Blacksmith
16. Stables
17. Wainwright
18. Granary
19. Ice House
20. Post Garden
21. Sutler's Store
22. Commandant's Quarters
23. "Suds Row"
24. Married Enlisted Men's Quarters
25. Cemetery

Use with Lesson 66 (Enrichment).   Heritage Studies 3 Home TE

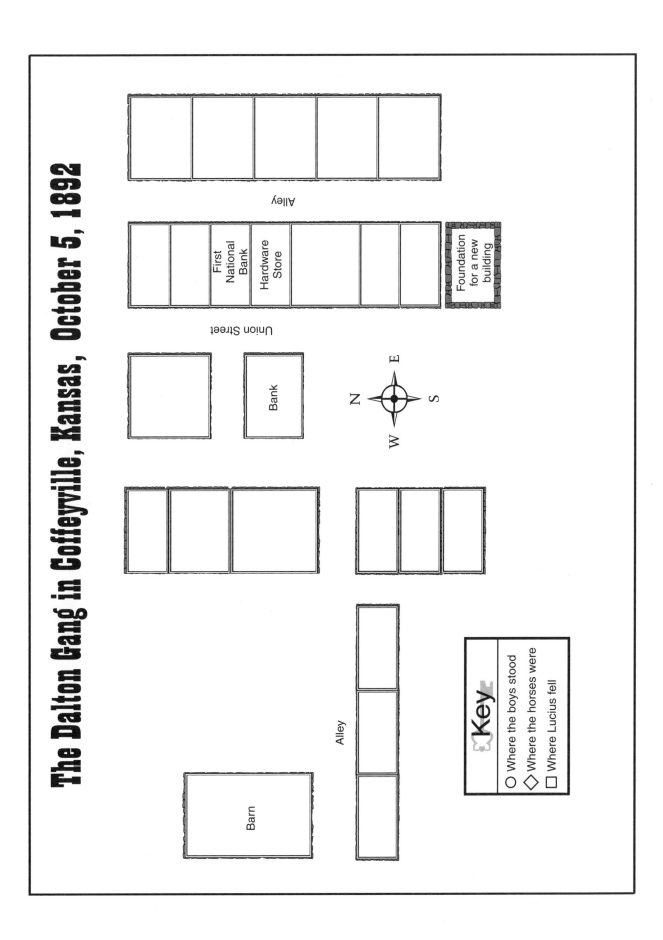

The Dalton Gang in Coffeyville, Kansas, October 5, 1892

Alley

First National Bank
Hardware Store

Foundation for a new building

Union Street

Bank

N
E
S
W

Alley

Barn

Key
- ○ Where the boys stood
- ◇ Where the horses were
- □ Where Lucius fell

THE WEST BEFORE

Old World

New World

Christ's Crucifixion

Paul in prison

Anasazi live in the Southwest

100 200 300 400 500 600 700 800 900 1000 1100 1200 1300 1400 1500 1600 1700 1800 1900 2000

Anasazi move into Mesa Verde

Viking ships sail into New World

Anasazi make cliff houses

Chinese invent gunpowder

First Gutenberg Bible printed

Columbus's voyage

Ute and Navajo in Mesa Verde

Spanish ships on West Coast

Mayflower sails to the New World

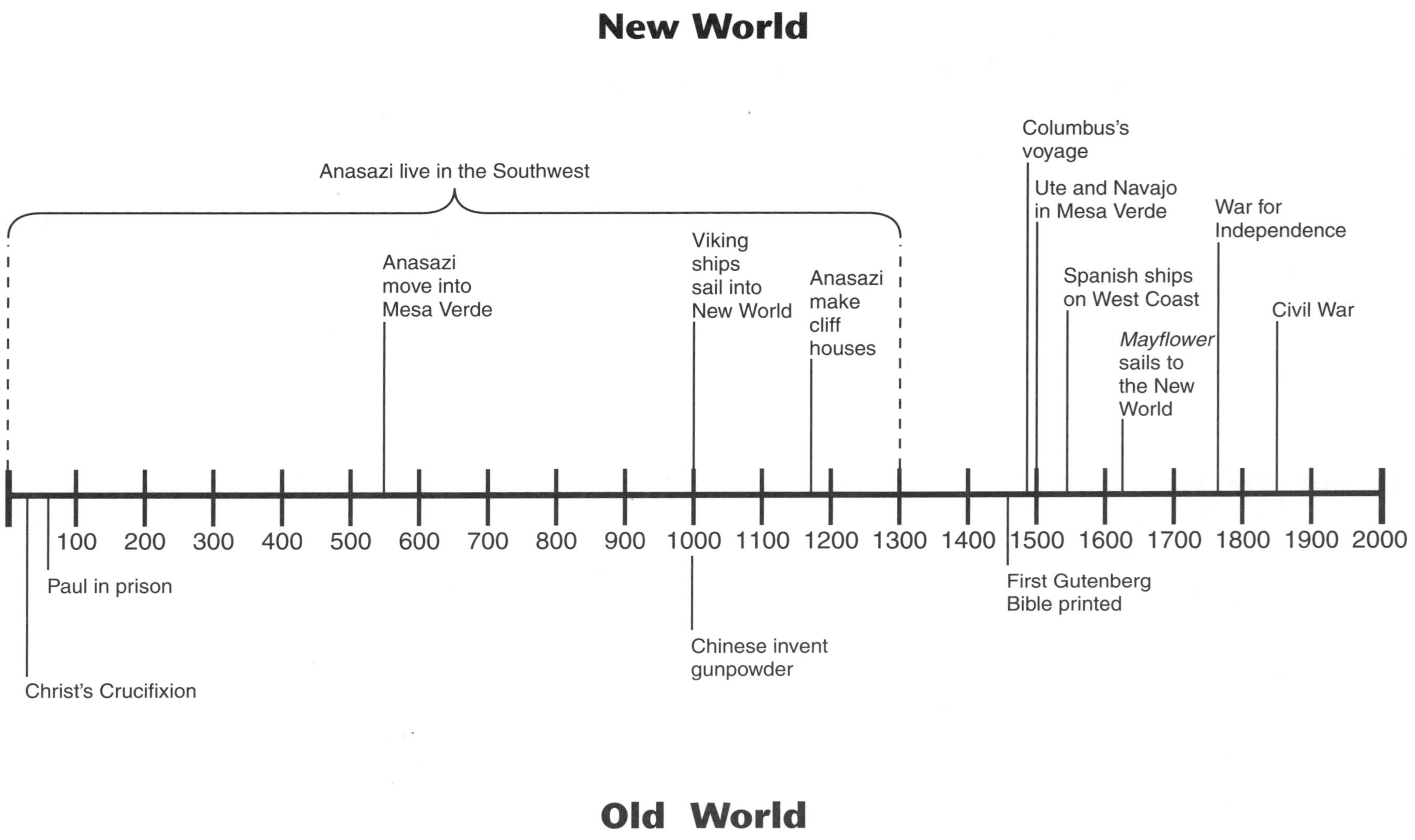

War for Independence

Civil War

Use with the Supplemental Lesson in Chapter 12. Heritage Studies 3 Home TE

Number the Anasazi houses in order of building, 1 being the earliest. Then fill in the blanks below.

☐ .

☐

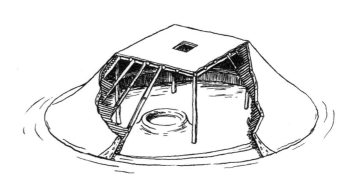

☐

1. *Anasazi* means _____.

2. *Mesa Verde* means _____.

3. *Pueblo* means _____.

Photograph Credits

The following agencies and individuals have furnished materials to meet the photographic needs of this textbook. We wish to express our gratitude to them for their important contribution.

Suzanne R. Altizer
George R. Buckley
Capitol Preservation Committee
Chessie System Railroads
George R. Collins
Corel Corporation
Terry M. Davenport
Dave Fisher
Illinois State Historical Library
Brian D. Johnson
Library of Congress
Ray Manley
R. J. McDaniel
Mt. Vernon Ladies Association
National Archives
National Gallery of Art

National Park Service
Nebraska Department of Economic Development
Nebraska State Historical Society
J. Norman Powell
Wade K. Ramsey
Reunion des Musees Nationaux
Karen Rowe
Salt Lake Convention and Visitors Bureau
South Dakota State Historical Society
Stock Montage, Inc.
Texas Tourist Development Agency
United States Air Force

United States Department of Agriculture (USDA)
United States Department of Transportation
United States Fish and Wildlife Service
Unusual Films
Brian Vogt
Ward's Natural Science Establishment
Dawn L. Watkins
The White House
Woolaroc Museum
Worldwide Slides
Yellowstone National Park
Zion National Park

Cover
Dawn L. Watkins (top, left); Texas Tourist Development Agency (bottom)

Title Page
Brian D. Johnson

Chapter 1
National Park Service 1; George R. Collins 2, 6, 12; National Archives 5; Capitol Preservation Committee and Brian Hunt of Hunt Commercial Photography 7, 17; Library of Congress 9; Unusual Films 13, 14, 18 (bottom), 19, 22; Official White House Photo 18 (top)

Chapter 2
Unusual Films 23, 40; Library of Congress 25, 42 (top); National Archives 26; Reunion des Musees Nationaux 32; Worldwide Slides 35; National Gallery of Art 42 (bottom)

Chapter 3
George R. Collins 43, 44 (center, right), 48–49, 54 (background), 62; U.S. Department of Transportation 44 (left); Unusual Films 47; National Park Service 48 (right), 50 (top), 53 (all); U.S. Fish and Wildlife Service 48 (center); Brian

Vogt 48 (left); Brian D. Johnson 50–51, 51; George R. Buckley 50 (center top, center bottom); Nebraska Department of Economic Development 50 (bottom); J. Norman Powell 52 (background); Zion National Park 52 (top); Corel Corporation 52 (bottom); Ward's Natural Science Establishment 53 (background)

Chapter 4
George R. Collins 63, 64 (top); Yellowstone National Park 64 (bottom); Unusual Films 69, 76, 84, 85; Library of Congress 80; Salt Lake Convention and Visitors Bureau 81; Woolaroc Museum, Bartlesville, OK 82; George R. Buckley 88 (bottom); South Dakota State Historical Society 88 (top)

Chapter 5
Unusual Films 89, 100, 108

Chapter 6
Brian D. Johnson 109; George R. Collins 111; National Park Service 113, 119; Wade K. Ramsey 114; Library of Congress 115; Unusual Films 118, 121, 123; Karen Rowe 124 (both); Terry M. Davenport 126

Chapter 7
Library of Congress 127, 129, 139, 140, 144 (both), 145 (right), 148 (center, bottom); R. J. McDaniel 137; Illinois State Historical Library 145 (left); Unusual Films 146; National Park Service 148 (top)

Chapter 8
Library of Congress 151 (both); Unusual Films 153, 156 (both), 162

Chapter 9
Unusual Films 165; Corel Corporation 170; National Archives 172, 178 (bottom left); Library of Congress 174 (both), 176, 178 (top, bottom right), 179, 186, 187, 188, 190 (both); National Park Service 177, 185; Stock Montage, Inc. 181

Chapter 10
Unusual Films 191, 192, 199 (both), 201, 205 (left, right); Mt. Vernon Ladies Association 193; Library of Congress 194; Wade k. Ramsey 195 (right); Dave Fisher 195 (left); Suzanne R. Altizer 197; United States Air Force 200; George R. Collins 205 (center)

Chapter 11
National Park Service 207, 219; Chessie System Railroads 212; Unusual Films 213, 216, 223, 224; Library of Congress 220

Chapter 12
George R. Collins 225; Nebraska State Historical Society 226 (bottom right); National Archives 226 (center, bottom left), 243 (top, center); Solomon D. Butcher Collection, Nebraska State Historical Society 227; Texas Tourist Development Agency 230 (both); Corel Corporation 233 (all); USDA 234; Unusual Films 237; Library of Congress 239 (both), 240, 241; South Dakota State Historical Society 242; Ray Manley 244 (top); National Park Service 244 (bottom)

Resource Treasury
National Park Service 271; Unusual Films 272–73, 276; Library of Congress 274; Corel Corporation 279 (bottom); Terry M. Davenport 279 (top)

Note: Page numbers correspond to the reduced copy of the student textbook pages that appear in this teacher's edition.

Index